The Importance of Being Black

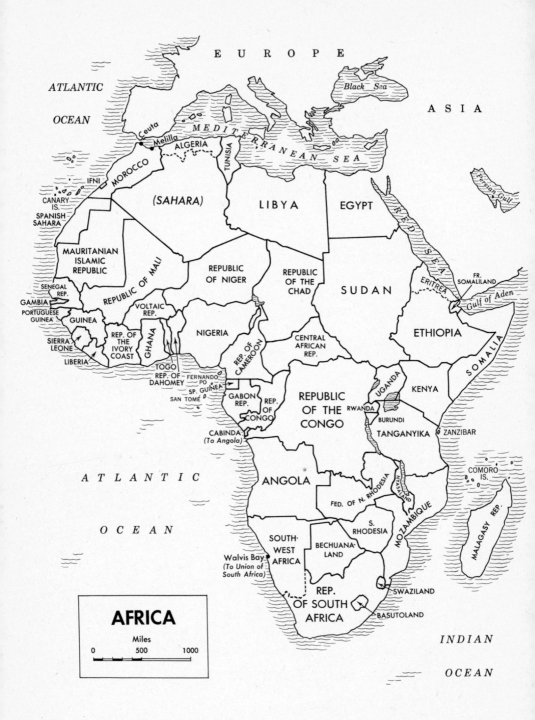

EUROPE

ATLANTIC

OCEAN

ASIA

Black Sea

Ceuta
Melilla
MEDITERRANEAN SEA

ALGERIA

TUNISIA

LIBYA

EGYPT

Persian Gulf

IFNI

MOROCCO

CANARY
IS.

SPANISH
SAHARA

(SAHARA)

MAURITANIAN
ISLAMIC
REPUBLIC

REPUBLIC OF MALI

REPUBLIC
OF NIGER

REPUBLIC
OF THE
CHAD

SUDAN

RED SEA

ERITREA

FR.
SOMALILAND

Gulf of Aden

SENEGAL
REP.

GAMBIA

PORTUGUESE
GUINEA

GUINEA

VOLTAIC
REP.

ETHIOPIA

SIERRA
LEONE

REP. OF
THE
IVORY
COAST

GHANA

NIGERIA

CENTRAL
AFRICAN
REP.

SOMALIA

LIBERIA

TOGO

REP. OF
DAHOMEY

FERNANDO
PO

REP. OF
CAMEROON

UGANDA

KENYA

SP. GUINEA

SAN TOMÉ

GABON
REP.

REP.
OF
CONGO

REPUBLIC
OF THE
CONGO

RWANDA

BURUNDI

TANGANYIKA

ZANZIBAR

CABINDA
(To Angola)

ATLANTIC

COMORO
IS.

OCEAN

ANGOLA

FED. OF N. RHODESIA

NYASALAND

MOZAMBIQUE

MALAGASY REP.

SOUTH-
WEST
AFRICA

S.
RHODESIA

Walvis Bay
(To Union of
South Africa)

BECHUANA-
LAND

SWAZILAND

REP.
OF SOUTH
AFRICA

BASUTOLAND

INDIAN

OCEAN

AFRICA

Miles

0   500   1000

The Importance of

BEING BLACK

AN ASIAN LOOKS AT AFRICA

FRANK MORAES

THE MACMILLAN COMPANY, NEW YORK
COLLIER-MACMILLAN LIMITED, LONDON

First Printing

Printed in the United States of America

The Macmillan Company, New York
Collier-Macmillan Canada Ltd., Toronto, Ontario

Library of Congress Catalog Card Number: 64-15453

FOR MARILYN

Who

Observed Far More

Than I Saw

FOREWORD

Africa is unpredictable. She changes almost from week to week. A book on Africa can only register the impressions of the author while he was there, and his observations and conclusions at the time of writing. This book claims to do no more.

It is the result of a four-month tour of the continent, almost entirely south of the Sahara, and of a study of various publications—books, reports, official memoranda, political handouts, and newspapers. It is also the result of discussions and conversations with many persons of widely varied views in Africa and elsewhere. I am sorry not to be able to acknowledge each source separately. But the conclusions are my own and so are the impressions.

This is probably the first detailed book to be written by an Asian recording the impact which the fast-developing and ever-changing Africa of today made on him. As such it might have a certain exotic interest for Europeans and Africans, representing as it does a betwixt-and-between view, for Africa poses a challenge not only to Europe but to Asia. Perhaps my fellow Asians might also be intrigued to examine my impressions and conclusions.

I am grateful to many friends and acquaintances—African, European, and Asian—who have given me the benefit of their knowledge and experience. My thanks are also due to B. Krishnaswamy and N. K. Narasimhan, who patiently typed my many drafts and made some useful suggestions.

FRANK MORAES

CONTENTS

The Importance of Being Black

1

THE "WIND OF CHANGE"

"I GRANT YOU that some African top leaders are capable men," remarked a white settler at Lusaka in Northern Rhodesia. "But what's below them? Nothing but scum and scoundrels."

I was to hear the same comment in different forms in various regions of Africa, more particularly in the Central African Federation and in East Africa. It came not only from Europeans but, oddly, from many Asians. Oddly, because much the same comment on Indian political leaders had been heard in British circles in preindependence India.

The Europeans, I noticed, were careful while talking to me to draw a distinction between the Africans and the Asians.

"Your people," said a Frenchman after dinner one night in Brazzaville, "have a civilization centuries old. These people have grown out of the jungle. Why, fifty years ago they were eating up one another. I was told that after the recent riots across the river at Léopoldville, human arms and limbs were on sale in the African meat market."

He was like many Europeans I had met in my journeyings through Africa—bitter, resentful and frustrated. But the Asian attitude, though not as aggressive, seemed to me almost equally frustrated. In Kenya, Uganda, and Tanganyika I had talked with several Asian businessmen, whose ties were either with India or Pakistan. Their general attitude,

1

though often differing in emphasis and detail, was with few exceptions curiously similar to that of the Europeans.

The common argument was: "We have contributed in many ways to the development of this continent. In some respects we were pioneers before the Europeans. Our labor opened up the jungles. Our *dukas* (small shops) served the needs of the African in the bush. Even Churchill, when he was colonial secretary many years ago, acknowledged it. We did all this at some personal and commercial risk. Yes, we did make our living out of it and some of us made considerable profits. But why should we have sweated and toiled in Africa, risked our resources and made our life here unless we had abundant and abounding faith in the country? Now the Africans do not seem to have faith in us."

It was in a way pathetic.

These people had made Africa their homeland—many of them had been born there—and the emergence of a new Africa, increasingly assertive and dominant, puzzled and exasperated them. They had not conditioned themselves to the traumatic speed of the wind of change. Africa, the Africa they thought they knew, had taken them by surprise.

The new Africa is as much a surprise to the Africans. Few, if any of them, could have imagined that their European masters would depart so speedily, leaving them almost overnight in unaccustomed seats of power and authority.

Listening to my African acquaintances, I found myself comparing their attitude and talk with that of the peoples of India and of the countries of Southeast Asia in the immediate postwar years which had seen them become independent. In those years I had roamed over many countries, from Indonesia to Indochina, through Malaya, Thailand, and Burma, to Ceylon and Pakistan. Because of our own intrinsic weaknesses we, too, had looked upon our departed rulers with some suspicion and possibly even with a degree of smoldering resentment. But these reactions had evaporated quickly, to be replaced in many spheres by a new relationship of understanding, friendship, and cooperation.

Freedom had taken us Asians also by surprise, though possibly its impact was not as sudden, sharp, and startling as it was on the Africans. Did this explain their strident, often virulent criticism not only of the European, but of the Asian, who in the eyes of many of them had conspired with their erstwhile masters to hold Africa in bondage? To some extent they were right in thinking so, and I could not altogether blame them. Yet the feeling of an adolescent Africa as against a comparatively adult Asia, with its own drawbacks and deficiencies, lingered and haunted me throughout my stay there. It seemed as if Africa bristled with very many angry young men. Like children they felt afraid to walk alone in the dark, but at the same time they were resentful and suspicious of anyone who might try to light their way.

In the world context the Afro-Asian relationship is as important, if not more vital, than the relationship between Africa and Europe, for together Asia and Africa represent nearly two-thirds of the world's population, the overwhelming majority of it on the bare borderline of existence and linked with each other emotionally by the memory of a common bondage over long years to the West. Yet the divisive elements which separate Asia and Africa are, I feel, far more acutely felt and perceived by the African, who is more sensitive to them today than he is to Europe's political and economic yoke, from which he is largely freed.

Because it implies equality in the fellowship of men, national independence has come to be equated with individual self-respect, one reason why the British Commonwealth, now predominantly Afro-Asian in composition, was led to edge South Africa out of that community. Dr. Verwoerd apart, color has largely ceased to count as a political factor. The possession or lack of independence is no longer a matter of epidermis. But Africa and Asia, while aware of this, are still conscious of the bond of color as the overworked term "Afro-Asian" implies. On the other hand one had the uneasy feeling as one traveled across that continent that, while political freedom has narrowed the psychological gulf which divided African from European, it has broadened it between Asian and African.

In African calculations, the rivalry now is between Asia and Africa to catch up economically with the West. Politically Africa has come up with a rush, outstripping in terms of time Asia's advance to freedom. Of this the African is aware, though perhaps not in all cases appreciative of some of the causes for it. Only in the realm of culture and civilization does Africa lag behind Asia, and that realization jars on not a few Africans. In fairness to them I must say that the assertively conscious feeling of superiority shown by some Asians explains, if it does not excuse, the African's aggressiveness.

"Of course," said an African at Accra challengingly, "you may claim that your civilization and culture are older than ours. So what? Let us assume that the Africans start from scratch. But that is an advantage, not a handicap. We're not cluttered with your inhibitions and complexes. We do not need to destroy in order to build. We can move quickly and in any direction we choose. The British advise us to go slow. Africa can't afford to take three hundred years to develop. We must do it in thirty years or less, and we are determined to do it. We'll do it the American, not the British way."

He was brash and unlike some other Africans I had met: the soft-voiced cab driver who drove me around Brazzaville; the friendly Congolese at Léopoldville who took me to his home for dinner, introducing me to his wife and three stocky children; and the guide in Cotonou, whose manners were as exquisite as his French. But all of them exuded the feeling of the importance of being black.

Both Asia and Africa look purposefully into the future, but Africa, unlike Asia, has in a sense no known past. We know what Europe and Asia were like in the centuries which preceded the Portuguese discovery of the Cape route in 1488. But of Africa south of the Sahara we know little or nothing before that. Around the beginning of the Christian era the Western world had contacts with the coastal belt of East Africa, but from then until Islam erupted on the world, Africa was a walled-in continent. No written records exist, for though a written alphabet is said to have been evolved by a Semitic people, probably the Phoenicians, between 1300 and 1200 B.C. and was in use at a very early period in North Africa, the Arabic script found its way to the western and eastern regions south of the Sahara only after the introduction of Islamic influence from North Africa into this area beginning about the tenth century. The Arab traveler, Ibn Batuta, writes of cities strung along the east coast, and also describes a number of well-established city-states south of the Sahara which he visited in the fourteenth century. Around these seaboard cities abutted the African bush, where the African lived his tribal life much as he does today.

When the modern period of exploration began in the late eighteenth century there were, apart from the Arabic script and Amharic in Ethiopia, only three other written scripts in the entire continent: one, employed by the Tuareg, known as Tamchek, which is a variety of Berber; a second, used by the Vai tribe, who are spread through parts of Sierra Leone and Liberia; and a third devised by the highly cultivated Bamum tribe, which inhabits the Foumban region of Cameroun, formerly the French Cameroons. Bamum art is believed to have been influenced by Egypt in the time of the Pharaohs, and the legends and history of this tribe are recorded in the Bamum script invented by Sultan Njoya. A local chieftain, Dualu Bukere, developed the Vai alphabet, which was perfected early in the nineteenth century. Both these African scripts have been in existence only for the past century or so and are not now in wide use. European domination brought European languages and the Roman script, which in Africa south of the Sahara predominates over the Arabic script.

This rootlessness explains the African's sense of insecurity and the exaggerated emphasis he places on his own dignity and importance. The French term, *négritude,* expresses the idea picturesquely, for it implies a pride in color, a belief in a distinctive cultural character, also projected by the phrase *Présence Africaine,* or African Personality, which denotes what Julius Nyerere, president of Tanganyika, defined as "a feeling of togetherness," a close kinship symbolized by a common history of slavery and suffering and the consciousness of the communal life represented by the tribe. While most French-speaking Africans attach a cultural connotation to the term *négritude* or African Personality, the English-speaking Africans, notably Nkrumah, present it as primarily a politico-economic concept, a sort of offensive-defensive weapon. There are other Africans, of whom Nigeria's Prime Minister, Sir Abubakar Tafawa Balewa, is the most conspicuous, who repudiate this idea.

I heard much about tribalism while I was in Africa from both European and Asian acquaintances, and the Congo as well as Kenya have highlighted this basic organization in the African way of life. Yet sometimes as an Indian I could not help thinking that our own caste-conscious society, riven by linguistic and local divisions, also represented a form of tribalism, though perhaps of a more sophisticated order. Another parallel obtruded. In India, as in Africa, tribalism or divisiveness has kept spilling over when the lid of foreign domination was lifted. Divisiveness was there during the period of political subjection, but only to be clamped down on or released when it suited the designs of the alien rulers.

Time and again I found myself comparing Africa and Asia. If Asia lives in its villages, Africa lives in its bush. But here again there is a difference deriving from the volcanic speed of the political and, to some extent, economic change which has swept the continent. Africa, as a known continent to the Western world, has existed for barely a century, if the Conference of Berlin of 1885 can be taken as signifying the first milestone in the European Scramble for that continent. In 1850, Kenya was an unknown wilderness and Nigeria wasn't there. The new look which many African cities and towns wear dates mainly from the last war, which intensified the drift from the bush to the urban centers, a process which had begun about fifty years earlier as industrial employment increased. In this process over 80 million rural Africans have migrated from their homesteads to the cities, towns, and villages, bursting their tribal boundaries and spilling over into the multiracial society of the urban world. The same process has taken place in India, China, and Japan, but over a longer period, because the Industrial Revolution in Europe, which began in the eighteenth century, had an almost immediate impact on these countries. As late as the seventeenth century the India of Akbar's days was economically not far behind the England of Elizabeth I. The English traveler, Ralph Fitch, who visited the country during Akbar's reign, describes the city of Agra as "much greater than London and very populous." Only with the free influx of cheap, foreign, machine-made goods which heralded the Industrial Revolution in Asia was the basic peasant economy of countries such as India and China undermined. Its impact on Africa was later and of a different character, for the Industrial Revolution did not touch Africa until the beginning of the twentieth century, when the European Scramble was completed, and it exploded on an economy divided between agricultural and pastoral living, with the vast majority of Africans eking out their existence as herdsmen or farmers, producing for subsistence and not for commerce.

In India the villager can take his caste from the rural to the urban centers, but the African, whose tribe is localized, cannot carry his tribe with him from his homestead to the town. Thus the large number of workers drifting to the urban centers find themselves cut off from their homesteads and implanted as the new uprooted urban proletariat away from their traditional moorings of family, clan, or tribe. The loss of these basic roots has intensified their sense of insecurity. The fears, frustrations, hopes, and ambitions of the urban, but as yet not completely de-tribalized, African are reflected in the new Africa which collectively shares his sense of insecurity. This is not altogether the case in India, where the vast number of urbanized Indians have their roots in the villages and where the transplanted Indian has no strong sense of being supplanted.

In a way Africa is not so much oppressed by the alleged nothingness of its past as it is irked by the consciousness that the intrusion of the West has disturbed where it has not displaced Africa's social moorings, distorting its pattern of living so that today this bears little relationship or resemblance to its immeasurably old tribal society. Recent historical and archaeological research has revealed the existence in parts of Africa of fairly complex social systems and cultural developments stretching over many eons, like the terra-cotta heads and figurines of the Nok culture of the Niger and Benue valleys, which date back nearly two thousand years. Later, between the eighth and the fourteenth centuries, came the stone antiquities of Ife, which in their turn inspired the Benin bronzes and ivories of the fifteenth to nineteenth centuries.

Among the Bini and Ife people of Nigeria, the tradition of metal sculpture goes back many hundreds of years, and was well developed at the beginning of the millennium. The Ife carvers belong to the thirteenth century. Most extant examples of African wood sculpture, because of the ravages of time and termites, are not more than a hundred years old, though the art of wood carving is among the oldest in the continent, and, far from being primitive in the sense of being primordial, is often sophisticated and reveals a technique of abstraction highlighted, among others, by the Bambarra carvers of Mali in their ingenious antelope concepts. The abstractionist motif in African art strongly influenced European painters and sculptors such as Picasso and Epstein in the early years of the twentieth century, as well as experimentalists and expressionists like Pechstein, Braque, Matisse, and Modigliani. The cubistic heads of the Basonge in the

Congo probably inspired Picasso's earliest efforts to cubism. African art has also a strong naturalistic base, as the Ife heads show. The range of its style is startlingly diverse.

In olden days the traditional centers of African sculpture were in the western and central parts of the continent, focused in areas like Mali, Guinea, the Ivory Coast, Ghana, Nigeria, and two Congos, Rwanda and Burundi, and south in Northern Rhodesia and Gabon, and east in Uganda and Tanganyika. To a large extent they are still localized there. To this day the Yoruba carvers in Nigeria produce some 30,000 traditional pieces of sculpture a year in the traditional religious style. Nor is African art, though tethered to ritualistic and tribal purposes, exclusively religious in its inspiration or confined only to sculpture. Much of it is secular and utilitarian like the "velvet of Kasai," an embroidered fabric of a wonderful texture, rarely produced. Some of it unfortunately, if inevitably, is degenerating into tourist or souvenir art. The African has a keen sense of the decorative, as displayed in his trinkets. Worked into the matted walls of Bakuba houses in the Congo are designs reminiscent in their delicacy of Japanese art, and in Rwanda baskets are so closely woven that they are used to carry liquids. Modeling clay is primarily a feminine occupation, and African pottery is notable for its graceful lines. In the southern areas of the Congo adjoining Angola live the Batshioko, who are famed for their ivory and wooden masks with drooping eyelids, which rate highly as collectors' pieces.

Research by scientific linguists and anthropologists reveals a fairly intricate and complicated structure of society* and language. African languages, far from being crude in form, are sometimes verbally so complicated as to hinder the spread of literacy and to make it difficult to reduce them to a written script. But, as in the case of Indo-European languages, conversion to writing has helped to simplify them. Equally complicated are the religious beliefs on which are founded the tribal and social structures. The African animist acknowledges God as a creator or a Supreme Being but does not worship Him and does not use His name lest he draw His awesome attention. Tribal kingdoms, even empires, have flourished in the medieval age to which belonged the empires of Ghana, Mali, Songhay, and Bornu, now reduced to a Moslem emirate in northern Nigeria. Zimbabwe, the Bantu palace in the kingdom of Monomotopa, whose ruins stand not far from Fort Victoria in Southern Rhodesia, is said to be over a thousand years old.

Therefore to assume, as do many Europeans and Asians, that Africa and the African people completely lack a cultural past is wrong. Such evi-

---

* Among the Keda tribe along the Niger there is a sliding scale of income tax according to the number of canoes a man owns.

dence as there is suggests that various civilizations and kingdoms once flourished in sub-Saharan Africa, as the seaboard cities of Kilwa and Malindi, going back to the eleventh century, testify. The ruins of the two buildings known as Husuni Kubwa and Husuni Ndogo, about a mile from the site of the ancient city of Kilwa, are, with the exception of Zimbabwe, probably the largest pre-European buildings in equatorial Africa.

Under the successive impact of Arabs, Moors, and Europeans, Africa's tribal way of life suffered heavy inroads. By the early sixteenth century Africa, for the larger part, had retreated into the bush, though the Arabs earlier and the Europeans from the fifteenth century had traded and until the nineteenth century continued to trade with various principalities and chieftains in slaves as well as in gold, ivory, and other products. The city-states of the East African seaboard were of Arab origin and bear the strong impress of that civilization and of Islam, though in time they assumed and developed an African character. Kilwa is described by the Portuguese as a town with "many fair houses of stone and mortar, and many windows after our fashion, very well arranged in streets."

Slavery branded the African with a social stigma from which he took centuries to recover, and the urbanization and industrialization which European infiltration brought completed the disruptive process. The growth of cities and industrial towns dislocated the tribal ties which had meant social security, though here and there a tribe attempted to carry its tribal gods into the new urbanized setting. As tribal life disintegrated, a sense of unrelatedness grew not only between the urban and bush African, but between the urban African and the strange new environment into which he found himself transplanted.

In many African cities and towns I was oppressed with this feeling of unrelatedness. Around one teemed the artificial superimposed life repre-sented by the luxury hotels, the Festival of Britain, and Italian architec-ture, the glittering lights and splashing fountains. Alongside were the squalid slums with tawdry tenements, shanties, and dilapidated old tin-roofed houses and huts. India presents the same contrasts and contradic-tions, but somehow in that country the squalor, the filth, the misery, the glory, and the grandeur seem to spring from the same soil. Here they appeared separate and apart, distinct layers disparate and divided. Even in Lagos, the picturesque, explosive capital of Nigeria, built on the low-lying mud swamps which overlook the Gulf of Guinea, a sense of something modern superimposed on a pattern of living to which it bore only an unreal, unnatural relation, remote and removed from the life of the people, seized one. I recall a barber's shop, unkempt and unclean, but resplendent with shining new equipment and chairs, and crowded with ragged customers. Here was modern Africa in microcosm. In India the urban or village barber, squatting usually under a tree, ministers to the wants of the worker or the villager, and it is unusual for a peasant or mill-hand to patronize a barbershop.

The same feeling of unrelatedness overcame one while looking at the Benin bronzes, the Nok terra-cotta heads, and the stone antiquities at the Ife Museum near Ibadan. The women of the Ajanta frescoes in India come to life at almost every street corner in cities, towns, or villages. But it was difficult to trace any affinity between the faces depicted in the Benin bronzes, which with their stern solemn profiles recalled medieval church art, and the faces of the Nigerians around one, though here and there one saw a living ebony Nefretiti with supple, elongated neck and high, delicately molded cheekbones.

The gap between the urban and rural areas is wider and more vividly evident in Africa than it is in India. Not twenty-five miles from the modern city of Accra, capital of Ghana, is a village called Aburi, where we went to witness a festival, or what in India is called a *durbar,* held by some tribal chiefs and subchiefs headed by the Adontenhene, who is the chief of one of the local Akan tribes. At Accra I had met many sophisticated officials and ministers, including the handsome, Oxford-educated Kojo Botsio, then minister of agriculture and minister of state for parliamentary affairs, and had shaken hands briefly with the spruce, very mannered, and more than slightly self-conscious "Osageyefo," as President Nkrumah is known in Ghana. At Aburi one saw Africa in the raw. Libations of what looked like schnapps or kirsch were poured on the ground by shrieking attendants, who also took swift swigs from the bottles, as the chiefs, grotesque and bizarre in gaudy raiment, with bloodshot eyes, clambered unsteadily into their palanquins along with their "souls," or tiny page boys, who are also their poison tasters. Crowds of half-naked, hysterical tribesmen screeched eerie war cries and the chiefs, brandishing their hatchets or swords, swayed as the drums beat and the horns blared. One had the feeling of being in the Africa of Rider Haggard.

Even within various tribal groups, Africa offers some startling contrasts. On the slopes of Mount Kilimanjaro, in the Moshi district of Tanganyika, reside the Chagga tribe, one of the most industrious and progressive of all African peoples, while less than seventy miles away, around the attractive safari town of Arusha, live the once warlike and still primitive Masai in rectangular, rounded mud hovels, not unlike railway wagons, fly-haunted and stricken with trachoma. Lack of communications has intensified the sense of separateness and isolation between town and country, but it does not entirely explain the phenomenon of an advanced community like the Chagga existing almost cheek by jowl with the backward Masai. The answer, I think, lies mainly in the strong instinct of tribalism which still pervades the African way of life and which enables each tribe to develop as it chooses—a lingering legacy of the primal urge for self-preservation. India's caste system is broadly horizontal in its structure, enabling four layers and more to live separately as part of a composite whole, but Africa's tribalism is vertical and multiple, each segment living its distinct life.

Urban industrialization, while making dents in the tribal system, has not destroyed it. Africa has grown up compartmentally in terms of tribes and to a large extent, particularly in Central and East Africa, continues to do so, for the tribes, not the boundaries of separate national states, divided and to a degree still divide Africans from Africans, and constitute the chief line of demarcation between them. Africa lived and lives not as a conglomeration of countries, but as a complicated congeries of artificially divided tribes. European colonialists, ignoring the natural tribal divisions, cut ruthlessly across the boundaries dividing tribe from tribe, arbitrarily creating states which with freedom can survive only through some form of association, either as a union, federation, or confederation. The imbalance of many present-day Africans owes not a little to the ignorance and insensitivity of the early European colonizers.

In his monumental *African Survey,** Lord Hailey makes the perceptive point that while in India the village, "the one political unit which has remained stable throughout the many changes of authority," represents a self-contained unit, even when composed of groups of different descent, there is little of this type of organization in Africa where, apart from certain regions in the west, as in the Yoruba areas of Nigeria, the community as such lives for the most part in homesteads on a kinship, clan, or tribe relationship. Until very recently the towns did not cater to the needs of the villages or vice versa. The link between the rural countryside and urban centers has been closer and longer in India, where the villager, even when transplanted to the town, retains his relationship with his village. One reason for this, as we have noted, is that the Hindu can carry his caste wherever he goes—whether to Cape Comorin or the foothills of the Himalayas. The African cannot transport his tribe with him. Nor is he, like the Hindu, a member of an amorphous but composite society which has a place for the Brahmin and the Untouchable, the Kshatriya and the Sudra, not only within the confines of India but outside it, as among the Hindu communities in various parts of Africa. Through the centuries, the one force which has preserved the unity in diversity which is India is Hinduism, for Hinduism is the incarnation of unity in diversity. But that leaven of religion Africa unfortunately does not possess.

Of Africa's 240 million people, roughly half are animists, about 40

* Oxford University Press, 1956.

million are Christians, and a growing number are Moslems, who now total around 90 million. Nearly 170 million continental Africans inhabit sub-Saharan Africa. Identified with foreign domination and racialism, Christianity, which might have been a cohesive force, has lost its propulsive drive, though such education as exists in Africa south of the Sahara owes much to the Christian schools and missions. Islam, on the other hand, is free of the taint of the color bar, and Moslem Nasser, seeking domination over the Arab world, gropes for a foothold in Black Africa. A manifestation of Christianity's declining influence, which to some extent is also noticeable in India, is the growing tendency to shed Christian names in favor of indigenous equivalents or substitutes.

Egypt belongs essentially to the Mediterranean world, but Nasser, as his book *Egyptian Liberation—The Philosophy of the Revolution** reveals, has for long cherished the vision of harnessing the untamed, prancing steeds of African nationalism to the Arab chariot. Hitler's *Mein Kampf* breathes the fierce passionate love of an Austrian-born German for the fatherland. Similarly, Nasser's *Philosophy of the Revolution* betrays the yearning of the Arab outsider for the Africa of which he insists he is part. "We Arabs," writes Nasser, "cannot stand aloof from the conflict between the 5 million whites of Africa and 200 million blacks. We are *in* Africa. We shall not stand idly by."

Nasser has not been idle. During the past ten years some 20 million Africans are said to have been converted to Islam, and they are grist to the U.A.R.'s increasingly productive and destructive mills. African students and political refugees are warmly welcomed in Cairo, from where also the "Voice of Islam" is transmitted over powerful short-wave radio. The two broadcasting centers in Cairo of the Voice of Africa and the Voice of Arabia are symbolic of this double objective. Assisted by former Nazi experts, Cairo has today the most powerful radio station in the Middle East and Africa, with regular broadcasts beamed to African territories in Arabic, English, French, Spanish, and Portuguese, and in a number of African languages, including Amharic, Tigre, Swahili, and various Sudanese dialects. Egypt is portrayed as the "liberator" of Africa. Cairo also plans to bring out translations of the Koran in all the major African dialects, and to have "religious attachés," or Islamic teachers and missionaries, at U.A.R. embassies throughout Africa and Asia. By progressively Islamizing Africa, Nasser calculates on drawing the pagan African peoples closer to the Arab world via Cairo.

Paganism in Africa takes various forms, differing with tribes and localities, but it is basically animistic and atavistic, manifesting itself in a reverence for the elements, for rain, lightning, thunder, and fire, and in the

* First published in 1955.

worship of ancestors and spirits. The tribal African lives simultaneously in the past, present, and future, for he belongs to a group or community which comprises the dead, the living, and those yet to come. Religious rituals are concerned mainly with rain and fire-making, and with inducing an increase in the supply of food for men and cattle. Ceremonial music and song are traditionally associated with these rites. Ancestor worship is not a distinctive atavistic attribute, for it exists in certain highly civilized Asian communities, notably in China and Japan. But the ancestor worship of an African animist seeks primitive expression through the medium of the witch doctor. Life for the animist is a continuous battle against the elemental forces of nature, and to wage it he needs the assistance of the witch doctor and the medicine man and of spirits who might assume the mundane shape of serpents and trees.

Just as certain distinctive Hindu attributes, such as caste and the joint family system, linger with many Christian and even Moslem converts in India, the superstitious aura of animism clings to many African Christians and is not easily shed. Christianity, though it came originally from the East, is identified today with the West, and so long as European domination lasted in Asia and Africa the indigenous Christian, with some exceptions, was more nearly the ruler than the ruled. Not as complex as Hinduism, Christianity as a doctrinal faith is nonetheless complex enough for the atavist and the animist, for whom the group is more important than the individual. The rivalries between competing Catholic and Protestant missionaries in Africa have puzzled the pagan, who cannot reconcile these antipathies and animosities with the Christian belief in one universal God. In the late 1880's this attitude of mind led to fierce rioting and looting between the African Catholics and Protestants in Uganda, who saw themselves as warring and hostile tribes.

In a way Christianity has proved as much a disruptive force in the life of the African as industrialization. The same is true of the Christian convert in Asia, but, being anchored to an older civilization and tradition, he is far less affected than his African counterpart even if the withdrawal of the West, with which Christianity is now identified, has taken some of the glitter off that creed. The African Christian, who again is a comparatively recent product compared with his Japanese or Indian equivalent, dangles uneasily between the old animistic world of Africa and the challenging new world which men like Nasser and Nyerere proffer.

So the spirit of the old primitive Africa survives in tribalism and animism, and how fast these will yield to the new erosive forces of national independence and enlightened thinking is incalculable. In certain areas, notably in the Congo, independence has intensified tribalism and given an edge to animistic practices. So also in India, independence, far from erasing linguistic, caste, and clan rivalries, threatens to sharpen and consolidate them. The backwardness of Asia and Africa, compared with the advance of Europe, cannot be explained away entirely by the scientific revolution of the seventeenth century and the Industrial Revolution in the last quarter of the eighteenth, for Europe's progress owes as much to a rejuvenation of the spirit and the mind as to material achievement. Left behind in the race for industrial and technological advance, Asia has tended to decry Europe's achievements as "materialistic" and to salve its own sense of injured pride by describing itself as "spiritualistic." What Asia and Africa lack is a mental spring cleaning.

Europe rediscovered itself in the Renaissance, which reached its culmination in a new flowering of the spirit and the mind in the last half of the fifteenth century, revitalizing in the process its neglected Greek and Judaeo-Christian heritage, and giving its civilization an impulse which in the regions of both mind and matter have propelled it ahead of Asia. In the sixteenth century came the Reformation, which in Germany was as much a revolt against papal theocracy as against the pagan practices of the Mediterranean races. The mental spring cleaning which this entailed has still to be undertaken purposefully by Asia, and even more so by Africa, though my Accra acquaintance might have been right when he argued that the African, starting from scratch, had an advantage over the Asian, who had many inhibitions to overcome and many complexes to shed. These, because the social structure has remained largely static, have fossilized into antediluvian habits and traditions. The comparative ease with which medieval social concepts are beginning to surface again in India, or for that matter in Japan (China is clamped down by communism) suggests that the influence of Western education on basic Eastern ways of thought and behavior has been relatively slight. Asia's mental structure remains largely unchanged, and, though the concepts of democracy and nationalism are older here than in Africa, they are still new. It is Asia, not Europe, whose intellectual attitudes and material postures need reshaping, for Asia, while in the throes of the Industrial Revolution, has still to experience the stimuli of the Renaissance, the Reformation, and the scientific revolution which preceded the Industrial Revolution in Europe and which changed profoundly the climate and structure of European thought. How much more so in Africa, where the pace of political change has far outstripped economic, intellectual, and social advance!

The speed of this wind of change in Africa has generated some whirlwinds in its wake. Africa's future will depend on how successfully its newly independent countries can control these whirlwinds and direct them to positive, progressive ends. The task of the African leaders is thus more onerous than that which earlier faced the Asian leaders, for to argue that

Africa begins from scratch is another way of saying that Africa emerges from a vacuum. The vicious circle of ignorance, insecurity, fear, disease, and want has generated this vacuum.

The continent's major priority is education. Roughly 90 percent of Africans are illiterate, and of the remainder very few have gone beyond the secondary stage for higher education. In certain areas, such as the Portuguese colonies of Angola and Mozambique, the literacy rate for the African is below 5 percent, and the average "educated" African there rarely receives more than three years of schooling. Although Britain, France, and to a certain extent even Belgium had provided facilities for the higher education of Africans, these were restricted in various ways by the subconscious feeling that the educational range for Africans must be appropriate to the subordinate position in the economy and society which they were meant to occupy. In the Union of South Africa it has taken the extreme form of separate educational compartments for European and Bantu culture, in which the African is largely shut off from a study of the humanities and of abstract or applied science. Even during the comparatively enlightened era of British rule in Nigeria, the University College at Ibadan had an honors course in classics for six years before it introduced a course in economics.

Education in Africa owes much to the missionaries, Catholic and Protestant, and to sects such as the Seventh-day Adventists, who have pioneered principally in the realm of primary learning, and whose missions and schools dot the countryside all over sub-Saharan Africa. At Kano in northern Nigeria I came across a school for Arabic studies run by some Sudanese of the Khatima sect. The school was about to be transformed into a college named after the Sardauna of Sokoto, who belongs to the Fulani clan and whose ancestor Othman Dan Fodio ousted the Hausa rulers in the first decade of the nineteenth century. For the most part, however, missionary effort has been restricted to the primary stage, providing at times limited facilities for secondary education. These facilities, supplemented by government effort at various levels, are still pitifully inadequate, and even in comparatively advanced regions such as Ghana and the eastern and western regions of Nigeria, where primary education is theoretically universal, it is of indifferent quality. The Ashby report on education in Nigeria, published in October, 1960, quoted some disquieting figures stressing the poor quality of primary teachers and pupils, the secondary-school-stage bottleneck, and the urgent need for rapidly expanding university and technical education. Nigeria is still saddled with an illiteracy rate of 85 percent, but then India's literacy figure is barely 25 percent.

Since the end of the last war higher education has been accelerated, not only in the British, but in the French areas, and to a more cautious degree in the Belgian Congo where, when independence was declared, there were only seventeen Congolese graduates in a population of about 14 million. The British and French records, though better, are not overly impressive. In the whole of former French West Africa there were approximately only fifty secondary schools among a population of about 30 million, and until recently the only university, which was founded in 1946, was at Dakar in Senegal. In 1961 the center of higher education at Tananarive, capital of the Malagasy Republic, which was then affiliated to a university in France, became a completely independent university. Other university centers are being organized at Abidjan, capital of the Ivory Coast, and at Brazzaville, capital of the Congo Republic. In addition, over 8,000 Africans are pursuing their higher studies in France.

In the English-speaking areas (outside South Africa, which has its tribal curricula) fewer than 8,000 African students attend the universities and higher technical institutes, but there are as many as another 20,000 studying abroad, mostly in Britain, with a few hundred in India and the United States, where scope for the education of African students from abroad is being enlarged.* In October, 1960, as the Democratic candidate for the presidency, John F. Kennedy outlined a six-point development plan for Africa which, among other things, advocated the setting up of a multi-nation African education development fund to plan the long-term development needs of that continent. Along with other schemes, Britain also has expansion plans for the African wing of the School of Asian and Oriental Studies in London, while the Russians have an Afro-Asian–Latin-American education center at Lumumba University in Moscow. The Czechs established the nucleus of a similar institution in Prague with the opening in 1961 of the "Seventeenth of November" University to commemorate Hitler's closing of all Czechoslovak universities in 1941.

"Mad with higher education," runs a Basuto proverb. The hunger for knowledge and learning is evident everywhere in Africa—most pathetically among the poor village children in the bush, more assertively among the younger men and women in the towns and cities. I visited many of the institutions for higher learning including the Legon University College, about ten miles outside Accra; the Ibadan University College in Nigeria; the School for Arts, Science, Agriculture and Technology near Zaria; the University College at Salisbury; and the Makerere University College† at

* There are also Africans studying in Russia, China, and Eastern Europe, but no reliable statistics are available.

† A University College is affiliated with a university outside Africa until an indigenous local university comes into being. The University Colleges of Legon, Ibadan, Salisbury, and Makerere were affiliated with London University. Legon and Ibadan now have the status of indigenous universities. Makerere is a constituent of the new East African University.

Kampala in Uganda. They are all magnificently housed and equipped, in these respects being superior to any equivalent institutions I have seen in India, but the output of graduates is not commensurate with the needs of emergent Africa, and, though provision for higher education is expanding and is bound to increase, certain overriding economic considerations obtrude. How many Africans can afford higher education, and how many of the economies of African countries can absorb the education contemplated?

At Legon and Ibadan, education at the university level is government subsidized, for few African parents can spare the money for the fees and other expenses incidental to higher learning. The official bounties are likely to diminish drastically and in time cease. Another disquieting deterrent is the bottleneck at the secondary stage, which for some time, until it relaxes, must restrict to a few thousand a year the number going up for higher education.

The need of more indigenous centers for technical, secondary, and university education is self-evident. In tropical West Africa, Fourah Bay College, founded in 1827 in former British Sierra Leone, was, until 1946 when Dakar University was opened in Senegal, the only institution for higher learning. Of the five Nigerian and three Ghanaian universities, only Ibadan and Legon rate around a decade in age. Lovanium at Léopoldville began only in 1954, while the University College at Salisbury is not even ten years old. The problem of African, as of Asian, universities is to relate more closely to their environment, background, and needs, and not to develop as mere faithful copies of their Western prototypes. They should lay more stress on scientific methods of preserving land, on biology and resource management than on technology and industrialization. But it is for the Africans to decide this.

The UNESCO report published in November, 1963, and entitled "The Development of Higher Education in Africa" points up the dimensions of potential expansion. In the countries of Middle Africa the present student population of about 31,000 is expected to rise to around 274,000 by 1980 —a ninefold increase compared with the two-and-a-half times increase in Britain during the same period as visualized by the Robbins Report. This expansion will need an additional teaching staff of 21,000 with an investment of about £535,000 (about $1.6 million). The report emerged from a conference held at Tananarive in Malagasy in September, 1962. Alongside the evolution of truly African institutions of higher learning, there is need to promote a bond of kinship with the larger human society. Britain has been particularly forward-looking here. The old concept of viewing Africa "through Hegelian spectacles as a continent without history until the nineteenth century" has largely disappeared. Besides the African

Studies Association of the United Kingdom under the presidency of Margery Perham in Oxford, there is the Research Institute of African Geology at Leeds, the School of African and Asian Studies in the University of Sussex, the Centre of African Studies at Edinburgh, and the Centre of West African Studies at Birmingham. London University has a degree course in African studies, and Edinburgh awards a diploma in the same subject, while Birmingham provides African options as special studies. At London there is also the celebrated School of Asian and Oriental Studies which has an African wing. According to British university teachers, interest in Africa is far wider today than interest in Asia.

Culturally, socially, and educationally the props which sustain Africa are slight. Time, with growing effort, achievement, and confidence, will overcome these drawbacks, but if Africa is to advance rapidly, its economic props require to be strengthened. Potentially it appears to be richer than Asia, and countries like Nigeria and Ghana have a higher standard of living than India. Ghana has a minimum national wage of about 95 American cents per day per laborer, while the Nigerian agricultural laborer, who daily earns around 67 cents, has an income over twice that of an Indian doing the same work. In India the per capita income is around 70 American dollars a year, compared with a little under 100 dollars for Africa. India's vast and rapidly growing population, now estimated at about 440 million, partly explains its low per capita income, for despite the five-year plans initiated in April, 1951, economic development has not kept pace with the growth of population.

One is apt to think of Africa as a rich and lush continent. Actually, hardly 10 percent of its land is arable, there are immense arid and empty tracts, and much of the continent is covered by swamp and savanna, desert and forest. According to Sir Julian Huxley,* at least half of the huge area from the Limpopo and the Kalahari to the southern Sudan and Ethiopia is "marginal in respect of 'productive' land use and ecologically brittle." Compared with its area of 11.5 million square miles—about 22 percent of the world's land surface and six times the size of India—Africa's population of 240 million does not seem excessively large. Some 80 percent of it lives within the tropics and is almost equally divided into northern and southern sectors by the equator. In Africa south of the Sahara the population density is seven to the square kilometer as against the world average of twenty and the Asian figure of more than a hundred. However, according to the United Nations *Demographic Yearbook* of 1961, Africa is the most prolific continent of the world, with an average birthrate of 47 per 1,000. Europe's average birthrate is only 19 per 1,000.

How will this rapidly growing population adjust itself to the economic

* *The Observer,* London, Sept. 24, 1961.

problems precipitated by political freedom and the withdrawal of European capital, managerial skills, technicians, trained personnel, engineers, doctors, lawyers, and various professional elements? The Congo provides the most starkly tragic example of the consequences of a sudden void. For instance, within two days, between July 11–12, 1960, some 3,000 Belgian doctors, technicians, farmers, and shopkeepers panicked and left Luluabourg, capital of Kasai, thereby virtually paralyzing the life of the province overnight. More stabilized regions like Nigeria and Ghana, which were fortunate in having comparatively enlightened colonizers, have been able to carry on. Nigeria for the time being has wisely not overaccelerated the pace of Africanization and, besides encouraging foreign investment, has retained or engaged foreign personnel wherever necessary despite extremist cries for speedier Africanization.

Africa's main impediments to rapid economic progress are its lack of top-grade organizers, skilled manpower, and technicians. Such investment capital as exists is overwhelmingly foreign-owned, and the problem facing capital-importing countries such as Kenya of attracting capital and simultaneously of staying the flight of capital, European and Asian, highlights a major deficiency.

The continent is fortunate in possessing considerable potential resources in minerals and raw materials. Excluding the U.S.S.R., it produces 98 percent of the world's diamonds, 65 percent of its gold, and nearly 60 percent of the global output of cobalt. Phosphates, copper, and asbestos are among its other products. It has also vast water resources such as the Kariba Dam on the borders of Northern and Southern Rhodesia, and the Volta project in Ghana, and if it lacks coal (except in Nigeria) its hydroelectric power, actual and potential, is immense in almost all areas. Unlike many Asian countries, most African countries, save in the bleak regions north of the equator, do not suffer from lack of resources but from lack of development. The power potential of the Congo basin is one-quarter that of the whole world.

A major weakness of Africa's economy lies in the undue dependence of certain countries, particularly the younger, newly independent states, on a single commodity or on a few. Ghana's economy is harnessed largely to cocoa and Tanganyika's mainly to sisal, which makes their local economy dependent on world raw material price fluctuations. Similarly, Uganda's economy is based on cotton and coffee. One answer is to diversify agriculture so as to include other cash crops. Another is for various countries, preferably adjacent, such as Kenya, Uganda, Tanganyika, and Zanzibar, to pool their economic resources and supplement one another's deficiencies, thus reinforcing the trend toward political federation. But the prospects here are fluid.

The deterrents to continental economic development are many and varied. They include a dearth of communications; erosion; lack of navigable rivers, harbors, and fertile regions; diseases such as bilharizia; and pests such as the tsetse fly. With the withdrawal of the White Presence, standards have deteriorated in some areas, notably in French Equatorial Africa where diseases like sleeping sickness and smallpox, which were once drastically curbed, are recurring. Similarly, economic and administrative standards show signs of sagging. But the African's greatest deterrent is his lack of education, which, while intensifying his sense of insecurity, makes him stubbornly impervious to ideas other than his own, and wafts him in a cloud-cuckoo-land of his own imagination and devising.

Again, economic progress can proceed only on a base of political stability, and this is not enjoyed by many of the newly independent states.

"The only discipline the African understands is the tribal system," said a white settler in Nairobi sententiously.

This may be true, but the emergence of purposeful, strong-minded detribalized leaders encourages the hope that tribalism will in time denote the gulf which separates the young from the old, the forward-looking from the traditional and archaic. Tribalism is still the basis on which Africa's social and political structure rests, though it is less assertive in the west than in the center and the east. I was interested to note that the more modern-minded African uses the term "tribalism" as a derogatory political epithet, much as his Indian counterpart uses the term "casteism." But tribalism and caste exist respectively in Africa and India, and will take time to eradicate.

The major problem for the African is to find a satisfactory modern political substitute for the tribal system of rule as exemplified, for instance, by the *indaba*, or conference, wherein Lobengula, the Matabele chief, thrashed out his tribal business in the days of Cecil Rhodes. Africa seems to be searching for a solution in the new ruins of European colonialism and the old debris of African tribalism. It is from the tribal community life that African nationalism derives its vitality and from which it must ultimately evolve, and a feature of the tribal life is the importance it attaches to decisions through unanimity or by consent. Even in olden days the chiefs, with rare exceptions (like some Zulu kings), had no military force at their disposal and in that sense enjoyed no executive power. They exercised their authority only in consultation with their councilors and with the support of the heads of kin groups and other units.

This was inevitably a long-drawn-out and laborious process, one reason why the more impatient of the detribalized leaders attempt to cut across these prolonged democratic procedures and to use parliamentary forms to cloak a one-man, one-party rule. Nkrumah, for instance, has a profound disbelief in the democratic tenet that there are always two sides to a question, and that both sides have a right to free expression. He prefers to rely on a system wherein as the "Osageyefo," or Redeemer, he embodies a sort of papal infallibility and an almost divine omniscience, though its glow seems to be rapidly waning. Here, oddly enough, he acts in line with tribal thought and tradition, for tribalism enjoins on the individual to think not as an individual, but as a member of a group, thereby upholding the democratic concept of rule by association and consent but decrying the equally democratic concept of the liberty of the individual. For the group, Nkrumah substitutes the party, which he proclaims is the state. Everything revolves around it, from the Trade Union Congress to the United Ghana Farmers' Council and the National Council of Ghana Women. Similarly the father figure or image embodied by the tribal chief is now symbolized by the Osageyefo, but, like the tribal chief again, the Osageyefo operates in association with leading members of his party. His rule enjoins conformity such as the tribal life demands, but it is rule by association, and there is no such thing as the right of the individual. This is not democracy as the West understands it, but it is a form of distinctive Afrocracy which, while ostensibly shedding tribalism, derives much of its inspiration and vitality from tribal traditions, and has a grass-roots basis in the tribe transmogrified into the ruling party or clan. In Africa it must be realized that a one-party government does not necessarily mean a dictatorship.

Unless Africa itself fills the vacuum from which it has emerged it must inevitably be the stamping ground of the two power blocs. For some time to come many of the independent countries of Africa will be in no position to fill that vacuum adequately. The Cold War will be projected into the continent as it already has been in the Congo. As a result, Africa is afflicted, as a continent, by a form of political schizophrenia, which expressed itself in the rival Brazzaville and Casablanca groups, the former led by the moderate M. Houphouet-Boigny, president of the Ivory Coast, and the latter dominated by Ghana, Guinea, and the U.A.R., though ostensibly these differences are now patched up as a result partly of divisions within the two rival groups. In between are countries committed to some sort of neutralism, such as Nigeria and Liberia, which incline to the Brazzaville group and which sponsored the Monrovia conference in May, 1961.

Even within the two groups, tensions, as we have noted, subsist. The older moderate leaders such as Léopold Senghor, president of Senegal, and Félix Houphouet-Boigny are bound to France by cultural and emotional ties, but the younger Paris-returned Africans are suspicious of too-close association with metropolitan France, and are resentful of and hostile to any move to bring their countries within the European orbit. In the Casablanca group, Ghana and the U.A.R., though pulling in the same direction, eye each other suspiciously and are rivals for the leadership. Thus Africa is split inside itself and out.

Not only Soviet Russia, but Communist China is reaching out for a foothold in the continent, and the Communist Presence, though by no means assertive, is evident everywhere. So is that of the West. The Cold War has entered Africa. Much as they might desire to edge out the old colonialism in order largely to fill the vacuum themselves, no African country or leader has any idea simultaneously of letting in the new colonialism represented by Russia and China. In helping Africa to keep communism out, the West must convince the Africans that it is concerned with the defense of Africa and not with the defense of Europe. Unhappily that is not the impression it makes on Africa. The Africans know what the West is against, but not as clearly what the West stands for. Paternalism must be replaced by partnership, for the peoples of Africa have now acquired a legal and political personality in the international world, and are able at the diplomatic level to deal directly with the world without the assistance of any intermediaries. Africa impinges as much on Europe as Europe does on Africa. This also applies to Afro-Asian relations.

No African country can do without non-African capital, and the newly independent states need the European and, to a lesser degree, the Asian as co-workers. Despite his superficial bitterness against the European and the Asian, the African, one hopes, is realistic enough to recognize that for some time at least he will need the assistance of both, and he will probably take it, provided it is realized on the other side that the African is the master of his house and that he will accept nothing less than to live and be treated as an equal.

"You can play a tune of sorts on the white keys of a piano," said the late Dr. J. E. K. Aggrey, the first African vice-principal of the celebrated Achimota Secondary School in Ghana, in an oft-quoted phrase, "and you can play a tune of sorts on the black keys; but for harmony you must use both the black and the white." This is the point of view of all reasonable, responsible Africans who recognize that, while the white man brought "legalized" prejudice, injustice, and inequity in his wake, he also provided Africans with a chance to participate in a world of greater freedom and opportunity. If, on the one hand, it is true that the areas with the largest number of white settlers, such as Algeria, Kenya, Southern Rhodesia, and the Union of South Africa presented or present the biggest political problems, it is equally true that these areas were the most economically developed, though the whites enjoyed the plums and the blacks were left only the pits.

In the preindependence stage, the Europeans provided the capital and know-how, the managerial talent, technicians, and administrators. To a much smaller degree this was also done by the Asians, particularly in East Africa. The Africans provided unskilled labor and natural resources, but too often the European and the Asian exploited the first and attempted to trick the African out of the second.

Will the world as represented by Africa, Asia, and Europe fall apart into three rigid groups, each assuming inflexible postures which will keep them more separate and divided from one another? Or will the world, European, Asian, and African, enter into a state of flux which might precipitate a mélange of closer racial, social, political, and economic cooperation than any yet known in history?

This is the problem which the new emergent Africa poses and faces.

2

THE LAST FRONTIER

AFRICA IS NO longer an extension of Europe, but in a way, allowing for the new exploration of space and the oceans, it still remains in the old sense the world's last great frontier. Some of the continent is still unexplored—its dense, often impenetrable forest areas comprising 21 percent of the world's total forest land. "You never see Africa whole until you're out of it." Only when the Arab slave traders traversed the continent south of the Sahara, to be followed by the early European explorers, were Africans to an appreciable extent brought into contact with Africans in other areas. Awareness of the fact that they inhabited a vast continental land mass probably first dawned on the slaves transported abroad. Significantly the idea of Pan-Africa was first expressed and espoused by American Negroes and by Africans in the West Indies.

Slavery has left an indelible mark on the African mind, for, though the institution of slavery has existed in various forms within Asian and Arab countries, the monstrous shape it took in Africa, which for centuries even before the Portuguese penetration of the continent in the fifteenth century was regarded as a reservoir of slave labor, branded the African as a sub-human apart from the rest of the human race. The Arabs, who were the pioneers in this trade, were also the most rapacious and cruel. But the Europeans who came later were only slightly less avaricious and insensi-

23

tive. Africans, too, participated in this traffic, chiefs such as the Obas of Lagos granting the foreign slave traders a monopoly for the purchase and shipment of slaves. Even today slavery subsists as between Africans, some of the emirs of northern Nigeria maintaining retinues of slaves.

This international traffic in human bodies and lives, operating at first as an overland trade confined almost exclusively to Islamic Africa, received a tremendous impetus overseas after the discovery of America in 1492. By the early nineteenth century, when slavery was declared illegal, first by Britain in 1807 and by all the other European powers by 1836, over 20 million Africans had been dehumanized into bondage. Today America has more people of African descent than any African country except Nigeria.

I was away from India when independence came,* and returned only two years later. These years were spent on the neighboring island of Ceylon, which achieved its freedom shortly after India. In both countries long years of political subjugation had bred an inferiority complex. But in both countries this complex, temporarily transformed by freedom into an assertive self-conscious feeling of superiority, soon disappeared, to be replaced by a better psychological balance. From being directed outward, criticism was turned inward. Self-awareness was always there, but with self-criticism the imbalance was largely righted. The Asian's specious sense of inferiority was to a degree induced by the European's equally specious sense of being socially different and superior. With independence this vanished to a wide extent on both sides.

Africa is passing through a similar phase, though its voice is more strident and shrill, for Africa labors under heavier layers of oppression—political, social, and psychological—and is burdened with the thought that its lack of sustained cultural traditions, the so-called "nothingness" in the past, combined with the degradation of slavery, has conspired to brand the African as a being whose place belongs on the outer periphery of mankind. Hence his insistence on Pan-Africanism and the African Personality, and on the importance of being black. More than with the Asian, color has intensified the African sense of apartness for, unlike the Asian, he cannot indulge in any assertion of cultural seniority and superiority, which the Asian, justifiably or not, can and does flourish before the European.

Does the concept of *négritude*, as the Martinique Negro poet, Aimé Césaire, saw it, spring from a hunger to recover one's roots, a longing to project the Negro as representative of a distinct culture and personality? This would seem to be the case with most French-assimilated Negroes, who regret their rootlessness and are eager to rediscover their roots. The same urge does not find a similar compulsive and aggressive outlet with English-

* August, 1947.

speaking Negroes, who seem more anxious to be integrated than assimilated, who seek political equality rather than tub-thumping their sense of social distinctiveness and superiority. Perhaps as the South African writer, Ezekiel Mphahlele, author of the book *The African Image,* points out, the white South African poet, Roy Campbell, in reasserting his African origin, was nearest the truth:

> My task demands a virgin muse to string,
> A lyre of savage thunder as I sing.

Césaire in stressing *négritude* was really overstressing the idea of the Noble Savage.

Africa is a giant with one foot in the primitive past and another in the twentieth century. India also has disparate layers of culture, from the highly sophisticated to the aboriginal, but the latter represents a microscopic minuscule. In India, too, there prevails a strong sense of diversiveness induced by its medley of castes and languages, and by the factionalism bred of provincial feelings. But Africa's divisiveness crisscrosses the entire continent and expresses itself in innumerable tribes, and in about a thousand languages and tribal dialects, a little under one-half of the world's total of 2,000 languages. This, for a population of 240 million, works out to one language or dialect per 240,000 of the population, though Kiswahili, a lingua franca developed by the Arab slave traders and merchants, a sort of Arabized Bantu, is widely spoken from the east coast to the Congo River near Stanleyville. It might be described as the Hindustani of Africa. India's constitution recognizes fourteen principal languages, including English, and India has a population nearly double that of Africa.

Broadly, Africa's peoples belong to three main racial groups—Bantu, Negro, and Hamite, of whom the Bantu, a mixture of Negroes and Hamites, are the largest. They number nearly 90 million and inhabit most of the continent below the Bulge and round the Horn of Africa south of the so-called "Bantu line," which runs along the frontier of Nigeria and the Cameroons, east across equatorial Africa and the former Belgian Congo, through Tanganyika and the hinterland of Mombasa, tapering in a thin strip to Mount Kenya. The term "Bantu" has a linguistic, not a racial connotation. The Bantu are less dark-skinned than the 70 million Negroes who inhabit West Africa from the mouth of the Senegal River to the eastern frontier of Nigeria. The latter are also found in parts of Central Africa. The Hamites exist in their purest form among the Somalis, the Ethiopians, and the inhabitants of Eritrea, but, penetrating down the Nile, they have mingled there with the original inhabitants and are represented today by the pastoral aristocracy of the Watusi in Rwanda and Burundi, and in the southwest kingdoms of Uganda and in the Bukoba district of Tanganyika.

All these tribes of Hamitic stock speak the Bantu languages and racially can probably trace some kinship with the Danakils and Gallas of Ethiopia, and with the Peuls of former French West Africa. Some say they are also related to the Chamites of ancient Egypt, whose silhouettes on the Pharaonic monuments they closely resemble.

Dr. C. G. Seligman* adds two more groups to the three principal African racial stocks. These are the Bushmen and the Hottentots, both of them numerically insignificant, who are to be found today mainly in the south, the former largely in the Kalahari wastes, the latter in southwest Africa north of the Orange River. The wall paintings of the Bushmen of South Africa, originally said to be as old as the cave paintings of Europe, are now reckoned to date from about 4500 B.C. Some are also to be found in Rhodesia and Tanganyika. About thirty miles south of Bulawayo in Matabeleland, ringed picturesquely by the Metapo hills, is the Nswatugi cave, which I visited. It contains a frieze of dim but delicate rock paintings depicting giraffes and antelopes in movement which date back to the Latter Stone Age, when Britain was inhabited by savages. But the Bushmen of today are far different from their culturally conscious prototypes and still live in the Stone Age. To a severely limited extent civilization has had an impact on them, but the march of culture has swept past them. The Hottentots, a pre-Bantu people, were, along with the Bushmen, the two local aboriginal types whom the Dutch first encountered on the fringe of the Cape. They are among the forebears of the Cape Coloreds.

There are also the Nilotes. Some African tribes, notably the Masai of eastern Tanganyika and the highlands of Kenya, who number around 1,300,000, are of mixed Hamitic and Nilotic stock. The Nilotes, totaling about 3 million, inhabit the upper Nile basin, and, like the Hamites, are often exceptionally tall. The Shilluks and Dinkas of the Sudan are of Nilotic stock.

There can thus be no clear-cut classification of tribes into racial groups, since the determining factor is language. As we saw, the Watusi, who are of Hamitic stock, speak some of the Bantu languages. Moreover, the European powers who partitioned Africa did so indiscriminately, oblivious of tribal divisions or boundaries—the Bakongo tribe, for instance, being bisected in the lower Congo basin on both sides of the river between what was formerly French Brazzaville and Belgian Léopoldville. In Central Africa the various racial stocks are intermingled in a maddening medley of peoples, tribes, languages, and dialects which it is impossible to sort out. This complicated racial, tribal, and linguistic pattern is repeated throughout Africa and recurs in every one of the thirty-four now-independent

* Races of Africa, 1930.

states. So do the multiple scourges of ignorance and illiteracy, poverty and disease.

"They are riddled with all sorts of disease," an Asian doctor remarked to me in East Africa. The list of major diseases is formidable. It includes malaria, leprosy, tuberculosis, and venereal afflictions, as well as sleeping sickness, smallpox, bilharzia, hookworm and filariasis. Guinea-worm infection and disorders of malnutrition are widespread. Sleeping sickness, along with smallpox, was once prolific, but vaccination and the war against the tsetse fly curbed these infections, though in certain newly independent areas in former French West and Equatorial Africa decreased vigilance threatens to see their return. Cholera, once widely prevalent in Asian countries, is comparatively rare in Africa, and so is sprue. The growing incidence of arteriosclerosis in Western lands is not conspicuously evident in Africa, nor is cancer, which appears to be less common among Africans than it is among Europeans, though primary carcinoma of the liver, induced by alcoholism, is relatively more widespread in Africa. One probable reason for the small incidence of cancer is that fewer Africans survive to the cancer age.

Census statistics being difficult to come by, and with conditions varying sharply in different areas, it is not possible to gauge accurately the relative health graph for the entire continent. In East Africa a census held in 1948 revealed that over two-fifths of those born in this region died before they were fourteen, compared at that time with India where one-quarter of the children born died before reaching adult life. In Africa, as in India, however, the chances of an individual surviving to be a sexagenarian or even a septuagenarian are good, once the critical age ceiling is surmounted. As a general rule the Africans are sturdier and bigger-boned than their Asian counterparts, and the children are stockier and chubbier. But their resistance to disease—resulting from their malnutritive habits (the African diet is heavily overloaded with starch), their crude sanitation or lack of it, and their primitive housing and personal hygiene—is lower than that of the average Asian, and makes the Africans more susceptible and prone to various diseases, many of which, like malaria, sleeping sickness, yellow fever, and blackwater fever, are insect-borne.

Blindness or partial loss of sight is common in Africa, and at Accra I saw street notices warning motorists, "Be careful of blind crossing the road." A local newspaper referred to 35,000 people as being afflicted by blindness in Ghana. An international survey held in 1950 noted that 10 percent of the adults in Kenya were blind in one eye. The rate of incidence varies within different localities in a territory, the same survey putting the number of blind Africans in the Union of South Africa at 1,351 to 2,000 per 100,000. In Nigeria the incidence in some parts was rated at

1,736 to 2,000 per 100,000, and in Sierra Leone from 1,470 to 1,890. In East Africa as a whole the figure for blindness was estimated at 0.5 percent of the entire African population, but in 1953 the British Empire Society for the Blind computed that in Kenya alone at least 50 percent of the Africans suffered from trachoma in an active or quiescent form. Trachoma also exists in large areas of North Africa. Another widespread form of blindness is onchocerciasis, carried by a fly which breeds for the most part in fast-flowing river water. It is common along the Nile.

Are venereal diseases a Western or Arab importation? There is no convincing medical or historical testimony, though syphilis by all accounts did not appear in Central Africa until after the middle of the nineteenth century. Gonorrhea existed there from the earliest known times. Following the foreign influx, venereal diseases spread as the slave trade expanded, and more recently, with the migration of rural Africans to industrial towns and cities, these diseases were carried back and forth from the urban centers to the bush. Even today prostitution and promiscuity are perhaps more uninhibited and rife in African industrial areas than they are in most Asian or Western cities and towns. In 1951, an article in the *British Journal of Venereal Diseases* put the incidence of gonorrhea among West African soldiers at 60 per 100, compared with 20 per 100 for British soldiers. The reluctance of many African women to undergo treatment is one explanation for this. Gonorrhea has brought about considerable sterility among the Masai of East Africa.

Mental disease and disorders among Africans, though induced largely by emotional, social, and religious disturbances and displacements, can also be traced to neurosyphilis, which in a hospital at Kampala in Uganda was at one time responsible for 30 percent of insanity cases. Though syphilis is found throughout Africa in various forms, congenital syphilis is rare. Besides syphilis, other contributory factors in inducing different forms of mental derangement are sleeping sickness, malaria, yaws, puerperal fever, and alcoholism. A survey of the African mind in health and disease made in 1953 reported that, though cases of mental disorder are frequent in the rural areas, its incidence is proportionately less than in similar areas in Europe and the United States. Whereas in the West the growing complications of social, domestic, and economic life induce a rise in the number of mentally afflicted, in Africa, particularly in the rural areas, it is often due to elemental, primitive fears and uncertainties. What the unsophisticated rural African most fears is the unknown and the invisible.

"The African," said a Belgian at Luluabourg, "is brave in the face of visible danger but is seized with an irrational fear at any invisible threat. His belief in occult powers and spells overwhelms him."

And yet the European and even Asian assessment of the African often seemed to me indicative of a frame of mind which has not jumped the same gap of decades as the modern African has. Most of these settlers or, rather, incipient ex-settlers referred to the African almost as a museum piece, as a being apart and out of the settlers' own civilized world. According to a number of them the African is capable of reasoning but has no words for abstract ideas such as love, faith, trust, and compassion in any of his languages. I do not know if this is correct, but it reminded me of an Englishman in Bangkok who many years ago told me the same thing of the Thais. Nearer home, I was reminded of many Englishmen in preindependence India who were accustomed to declare that the Indians had no indigenous equivalent for the phrase "thank you."

The African, one heard, has very quick observation, which is true and which is evident in his gift for mimicry. He particularly likes to mimic Europeans and often bestows on them an affectionate nickname, but oddly enough he has no sense of the ridiculous, and therefore in his apparel and behavior sometimes seems grotesque to non-Africans. He has a strong family feeling, much as has the Asian and, being an exuberant extrovert, he delights in oratory, singing, and dancing. They serve as emotional release valves. At my hotel in Luluabourg I was entranced by the waiters, who hummed, sang, and danced with their trays held high aloft as they threaded their way between the tables while serving the customers.

In a curious way the attitude of the Europeans to the Africans reflected the old attitude of the British to the Indians, and was succinctly summed up by a lively Ghanaian professor I met at Achimota. "The French," he said, "pampered the évolués, or indigenous intellectuals, but neglected the ignorant poor. On the other hand, the English treated the poorer elements fairly, but were suspicious of the educated." He was well situated to know, for, though a Ghanaian, he came from what was originally French Togoland.

I remember a not dissimilar incident when I was at Louisville, Kentucky, shortly after desegregation had been gently introduced into some schools. Visiting one such school I found myself talking with a schoolteacher who came from the Deep South and who frankly resented the desegregation policy. I liked her frankness and respected it, though it amused me to note a similarity between her attitude to the Negro and that of the old-time Briton to his Indian servant. It was feudal.

"We look after them when they're old," remarked the teacher with no trace of self-consciousness, much as if she were talking of an old dog or horse.

In the attitude of certain Europeans and Asians toward the Africans I sensed the same feudal approach. The irony lay in something they evidently did not realize—that they and not the Africans are out of date in Africa.

The wind of change has generated a whirlwind in the African mind, to which not only Europeans, but Asians as well, are not sensitive enough. Few things strike a visitor to the new Africa more forcefully than the tremendous will of the Africans, particularly of the young, to prove worthy of the unexpected heritage of freedom that has suddenly descended upon them like manna upon the Israelites. More than anyone else, the rising generation of young Africans want to attune their hearts and minds to the tempo of a free and developing Africa, and in many of the newly independent countries there are potential leaders worthy of the political advancement that has overtaken them and their people.

Like Asia, Africa has tremendous problems of disease, illiteracy, poverty, and gross superstition to overcome. But it would be a mistake to underrate the intellectual potentialities of Africa's peoples, which, though not as evident as the continent's undeveloped economic potentialities, could evolve in assertive challenge at the same tempo.

To talk today of the congenital, irremovable mental backwardness of the African is to talk in terms which have no reality, relevance, or meaning. Yet I heard this exploded dogma expounded more than once. Granted that in many respects the African does seem backward, compared with the European or Asian, will he still remain so tomorrow or the day after? The likelihood is that he will span the new dimension of development more quickly than the Asian or European who, exposed to the new Africa, will develop a new dimension of thought. The world outside Africa should condition itself to that continent's volcanic evolution.

I found small evidence of this adjustment to the new realities in either European or Asian. The old jargon they repeated seemed not only remote, but often ridiculous.

To a middle-aged Belgian in the Congo, who was arguing that the Africans would never in his lifetime be capable of exercising freedom with either efficiency or responsibility, I ventured to remark, "But you never trained them for that responsibility."

He answered, "We trained them according to their aptitudes."

The reply seemed to beg the question, for how could the Belgians determine the African's aptitudes unless they gave him a fair chance to demonstrate them at a level far higher than the African was arbitrarily allowed to attain?

Browsing through Belgian literature on the Congo, written and distributed before independence, was in many ways rewarding, for it unconsciously revealed much more than it was intended to convey. The Negro was described as of very quick intelligence in youth, with a capacity for learning easily, but his intelligence was prone to degenerate. This again suggested an Indian parallel, for it was the habit of the old-time Briton to pontificate that the Indian, while of quick intelligence, lacked initiative and drive, and could therefore never function effectively as an administrator at the highest levels. Also, it was believed that the Indian lacked scientific talent and aptitude. These superstitions were blown sky-high within a decade of independence.

Is the African worker lazy and shiftless? This view again was widely affirmed by Europeans and Asians. But one of the Belgian brochures had a more perceptive and charitable insight into the matter. According to it, "The Negro is not lazy or shiftless but is inclined to make little effort unless well trained and judiciously employed." The Bantu, it observed, "were capable of sustained effort but love change." It held that "the Negro readily adapts himself to new tasks." Instinct in this assessment, part of which is not unjustifiable, is the belief that the African, while capable of being trained into an efficient instrument of burden and toil, has not the mental mechanism or makeup to qualify him for the white man's responsibilities.

The average African today certainly lacks the education, training, and experience not only of the European, but of the Asian. If he is a hundred years behind Europe, he is at least fifty years behind Asia in the development of his aptitudes and abilities. Obviously I am not talking here of the new African leadership elite, of men like Nyerere, Nkrumah, Balewa, Kenyatta, Mboya, Sékou Touré, Léopold Senghor, or Houphouet-Boigny, who are capable of functioning effectively, even impressively, in any international forum, but of the African peasant and worker and, higher up in the scale, of tradesmen and commercial entrepreneurs compared with their opposite numbers in Europe and Asia. This seeming backwardness, however, is not the result of anything intrinsically inferior in the African's mental makeup, but of the deliberate denial to him of opportunity for development.

The myth of the African as an inferior species of the human race, induced subconsciously in the African's own mind by the stigma of slavery, and further incited by the ignorant assertions of many Europeans and Asians that scientific tests relegate the African to an almost subhuman status, is wickedly false and on its way out. If anything, science disproved it. There is no correlation between cranial capacity and mental intelligence, as recent experiments have demonstrated. Some of the Bantu have a higher average of cranial capacity than the French or the English. The old shape-of-the-skull theory has been proved equally fallacious. "There is," notes Lord Hailey, "no evidence that, as was at one time believed, the long-headed type have greater initiative; the Swede is long-headed and so is the Negro, but the Swiss who are certainly not less distinguished for initiative are of the round-headed type." A more popular fallacy is that frizzy hair goes with primitiveness. On the contrary, as the *Encyclopædia Britannica** points out, "In respect to hair . . . the white man stands in closer relation to the higher apes than does the Negro."

More recent researches suggest that diet and environment infl mental growth, which may partly explain the African's comparative wardness. But the long-continued isolation of Africa from the mainst of civilized progress and the branding of the African as subhuman proved stronger retarding forces, and their abrupt disappearance must portionately accelerate the pace of Africa's mental awakening and pro ress.

In Africa, as elsewhere, geography has conditioned history. Though there were Arab, Chinese, and Persian settlers in Madagascar and East Africa nearly two thousand years ago, they rarely penetrated the interior, which was unusually difficult of access. North of the Sahara there flourished for many eons a succession of Mediterranean cultures extending from the coastal plains of Algeria to ancient Troy in Asia Minor. Along the Mediterranean littoral, Egyptians, Minoans, Phoenicians, Greeks, and Romans traveled and traded, moving inland only down the waterway of the Nile. The Sahara stood as an impenetrable barrier, save along a few traditional trade routes. The continent's long coastline, with little safe anchorage for ships and few indentations, provided a challenging outer crust, while inland the rivers, with their rapids, sharp falls, and sandbars, were not easily navigable. Beyond lay disease and the unknown. As late as 1800 about 90 percent of Africa south of the Sahara was uncharted. Following the Portuguese, who arrived in the fifteenth century, came the Danes, the Dutch, the British, and the French. Livingstone began his explorations around the middle of the nineteenth century, and Speke solved the "riddle of the Nile" some ten years later. Stanley explored the Congo in 1875, and a decade later the European Scramble for Africa started.

The Africa which Europe stumbled upon was inhabited by innumerable tribes living a life, particularly in the center and the east, which was unbelievably primitive, haunted by taboos and totems, witchcraft, cannibalism, human sacrifices, fetishes, and all manner of crude ceremonial. Here was a world almost untouched by any of the progress mankind had made elsewhere. "They are a people," noted Sir Philip Mitchell, a former British governor of Kenya and Uganda, in an official report, "who in 1890 were in a more primitive condition than anything of which there is any record in pre-Roman Britain." In these areas the Africans had no wheeled or animal transport; no roads, no towns, no commerce or currency except

* Cf. article on Negroes.

for the occasional use of shells to assist the barter of produce; no alphabet, weights, or measures; no calendar or system of notating time; and no way of counting except by their fingers or by notches cut in a stick. Most of them were stark naked and the rest were clad in the bark of trees or the skins of animals.

Yet, less than three generations later, the peoples of both these territories achieved independence. This explains the influence and importance of environment and the receptiveness of the African mind to the stimuli of new ideas, habits, and ways of living. The interesting point is that Africa has benefited by its contact with the Western world not only to come up politically with a rush, but, despite the grave drawbacks and deficiencies which still afflict it, to advance in the social, educational, economic, and cultural spheres at a pace which, within some seventy years, has transported and transmuted a fair proportion of the people and of the continent from the Stone Age to the twentieth century.

Insofar as colonialism represents a system of ruthless exploitation of underdeveloped peoples and countries, it is rightly condemned and abhorred by Asia and Africa, in both of whose eyes it also carries the stigma of color, implying the domination by the white races of the black, brown, and yellow. For this reason, the concept of Soviet imperialism or colonialism makes little or no impact on the average Asian or African, who equates colonialism with color. Color, it was long thought, had no place in Soviet policies. More recent experiences by African students in Moscow and some eastern European countries belie this. In Asian and African eyes the Soviet-dominated countries of eastern Europe are not colonies in the old imperialist idiom they understand, and therefore they are inclined to regard the status, say of Albania or Rumania, as a result not of colonialism, but of something similar to the old wars and struggles of European countries for political or economic domination. Moreover, argue the Africans and the Asians, not all the so-called Iron Curtain countries are reservoirs of cheap manpower or sources of cheap raw materials, which in their eyes is Europe's yardstick for a colony. Indeed, at the time when Czechoslovakia came within the Soviet orbit, it enjoyed proportionately a higher industrial level than the U.S.S.R.

The importance of being black therefore signifies to the African the importance of self-respect. Even the highly cultivated Léopold Sédar Senghor, president of the Republic of Senegal, whom his critics deride as a "black Frenchman," has said of African writers, "The more they are inspired by African culture, the more they will raise themselves to international rank; the more they turn their back on Mother Africa, the more they will degenerate and weaken." The ebullient President Nkrumah of Ghana, who popularized the phrase "African Personality" at the Accra conference of April, 1958, has repeatedly stressed the same theme. "From now on," he declared at Accra, "nobody can look down on Africa. In the last century the Europeans discovered Africa; in the next century the Africans will discover Africa."

Nkrumah is right, but with one reservation. The Europeans did not merely discover Africa, but in the process of exploiting it they helped Africa to rediscover civilization and itself. Colonialism, intrinsically evil, fulfills itself ultimately by the serpentine gambit of sloughing its skin. While generating inertia within its own self, it injects vitality into its victims, as the history of most colonial powers since the Industrial Revolution demonstrates. Portugal and South Africa are the conspicuous exceptions today, but as a rule action generates counteraction till a stage is reached when aggressive colonialism shades into paternalism, to give way to self-government and finally to independence. Colonialism has spelled in most countries, African and Asian, economic and educational advance, increased social welfare, and better health conditions, but too often the opening of communications, harbors, and airfields, the expansion of agriculture, and the growth of commerce and industry are regarded by the colonized as evidence of an extractive economy designed primarily for the benefit of the colonizer, and only secondarily and incidentally for the welfare of the colonized. Even so, the benefits of colonialism, however incidental or accidental, cannot be denied.

In Africa, the immediate impact of the West was a diminution of tribal warfare and the establishment of some kind of order and security. In time slavery was abolished, and atavistic practices such as cannibalism and ritual murder were forbidden. Communications were opened, and, though these were generally established for the convenience of the European settlers, they were inevitably used also by the Africans. The colonizers opened up the continent, developing its natural resources, again primarily for their own benefit, but in the process also benefiting the Africans, introduced scientific agriculture, and fought such scourges as the tsetse fly— carrier of sleeping sickness to humans and of *nagana* to cattle—the malarial mosquito, waterborne bilharzia, tuberculosis, and trachoma. The resulting improvement in health standards led to an increase in population, particularly during the last two decades, though the figures are based on rough estimates rather than on scientifically compiled data. The devastation caused by floods, drought, locust invasions, and famines was checked. Educational facilities were established and, while these were pitifully inadequate and discriminatory, they opened a new world to the Africans, even as Western education did to the Asians, evolving a new class of educated Africans who, though numerically less than the so-called white "2 percent," have succeeded in displacing the latter over the greater part of the continent. The concepts of justice and the rule of law, of nationalism and self-respect symbolized by the African Personality gradually made headway. The introduction of Christianity and Islam freed many Africans from the grip of primitive fears and beliefs, and to an extent filled the social and spiritual vacuum which the breakdown of tribal frontiers, codes, and ethics induced by the Western encroachment had engendered.

Apart from the fact that, like the British in India, the British in Africa, as well as the French, unconsciously taught the Africans to revolt against them, the bug of political freedom bit Africans in the Belgian and even the Portuguese areas, as well as in the Union of South Africa, where it was possible to isolate them from modern spheres of knowledge and development but impossible to insulate them from the changes sweeping the continent. The impact of the Second World War, in which many thousands of African troops were engaged, was not negligible, for it brought with it the realization of certain concepts, such as self-determination, and the knowledge that Europe's colonial grip was weakening. The subsequent achievement of independence by India and other Asian countries stimulated the African fever for freedom, which Western-educated leaders such as Nkrumah, Nyerere, Banda, Awolowo, and Azikiwe were able to direct successfully to a positive climax. A remarkable feature, which is a tribute to both Africans and Europeans, is that freedom or self-government was achieved or is being achieved with very little bloodshed. Algeria was an exception explained by the aggressive presence of a million *colons*. In Kenya, the Mau Mau rebellion took an unnecessarily vindictive toll on both sides, and in the Congo there was more bloodshed after independence than before it. But generally the transfer of power has been effected peacefully. The partition of India precipitated a holocaust that consumed around 700,000 lives, excluding many thousands of freedom fighters who had died before that in the years of foreign rule and subjection.

Aside from the European, there was and is the Asian problem. The number of Asian settlers in the continent is difficult to compute, but their total is probably in the neighborhood of 900,000, with large concentrations in South Africa and in East Africa. In the Union of South Africa, Asians, including Indians and Pakistanis, are said to total nearly 500,000 while another 250,000 are to be found in East Africa. Over 50,000 Asians work and trade in Portuguese Mozambique and Angola,* and nearly 20,000 in Zanzibar. They are less numerous in Central Africa, where their total is below 25,000 in the two Rhodesias and only around 12,000 in Nyasaland. In West Africa their presence is negligible, but the Indian firm of Chella-

---

* Their number has been drastically reduced since India absorbed Goa in December, 1961.

ram, a major trading company, is conspicuous in the markets of Nigeria. Apart from the Asians, there are small colonies of Levantines, referred to generally as Syrians, but the majority are Lebanese. Their total is small and, in relation to the overall population, of no consequence. They are active in commerce, dealing mainly in textiles and the grocery-importing business.

In all likelihood the Asian, rather than the European, will be the first commercial casualty, because the Asian, engaged principally in retail trade, which brings him into daily contact with the African, differs from the European, whose economic presence is mainly impersonal, operating as it does institutionally through banks, insurance companies, and shipping firms. The Indian serving as a minor government employee, bank clerk, or shop assistant also naturally signifies in African eyes a competitor for employment. Among the Asians, I thought the Pakistanis had developed closer relations with the Africans than had the Indians, for, following the sagacious advice of the late Aga Khan, the Ismaili Khojas in particular have identified themselves with the African way of life, throwing their schools, hospitals, and various welfare and social centers open to the Africans, to whose development funds they also contribute generously. The Indians are more separate, self-centered, and aloof.

Competition by Asians in the retail trade, exploitation by slum landlords, petty profiteering, and the steep rise in the Asian population have been cited by the Africans as some of the causes for interracial animosity, which in the past has occasionally vented itself in interracial rioting. More recently, however, particularly in South Africa, Africans and Asians have been drawn closer by the common ignominy of apartheid. In this context Lord Hailey makes an interesting observation. "There can be little doubt," he writes, "that the movement which has associated Asians as protagonists in the cause of Africans has been encouraged from India itself, for there is among the leaders in Indian politics an almost missionary zeal for the 'liberation' of colored races. Had it been possible at an earlier date to foresee that a period might come when African advance might appear to Europeans in South Africa to constitute a menace to their own economic and social life, prudence might have suggested conferring on the Asian community a status which would have secured its support to the interest of Europeans rather than to that of Africans. Whether or not such a development would ever have been possible, it is certain that today it would be entirely impracticable."

How rapid has been the pace of Africa's race to independence! In postwar Africa there were only three independent countries: Ethiopia, Liberia, and Egypt. In December, 1951, Libya achieved freedom, being the first country to do so through the direct action of the United Nations.

She was followed by the Sudan (January, 1956), Morocco (March, 1956), and Tunisia (March, 1956). South of the Sahara, Ghana was the first country to receive its independence (March, 1957). After that came the avalanche.

The modern world's last frontier is vanishing rapidly as Africa enters the orbit of the twentieth century. Apart from the British High Commission territories of Bechuanaland, Basutoland, and Swaziland, and the Portuguese colonies of Angola, Mozambique, and Guinea, nearly all the remaining areas south of the Sahara are either free or self-governing. Technically, the Union of South Africa, which for all practical purposes has absorbed the mandated territory of Southwest Africa, is an independent country, but the Africans who are indigenous to it are further away from freedom, whether social, economic, or political. North of sub-Saharan Africa the only nonindependent areas are French Somaliland, the Spanish Sahara, and the Spanish-governed enclave of Ifni inside Morocco.

The patchwork quilt which is Africa has traditionally been divided into four basic segments. These are:

(1) *Black Africa*, which is south of the Sahara and excludes the Union of South Africa and the Rhodesias. Here live some 150 million people speaking diverse languages, divided into hundreds of tribes, and racially of mixed Negro, Bantu, and Hamite stock.

(2) *The Union of South Africa and the Rhodesias*, containing a little over 20 million people, including over 3 million whites. The remainder are predominantly Bantu. English and Afrikaans are the official languages in South Africa. The proportion of whites to Africans is one to four in the Union, one to thirteen in Southern Rhodesia, and one to forty-one in Northern Rhodesia. The two Rhodesias with Nyasaland, whose population is around 2,270,000, and is 99 percent African, formed the Central African Federation, now broken up into three separate entities.

(3) *Egypt and parts of neighboring Libya and the Sudan*, with a total population of about 40 million people who speak Arabic and follow Islam, Egypt having strong cultural, political, and economic ties with the Middle East.

(4) The Maghreb,* an area which includes Morocco, Algeria, and Tunisia, with a population of around 30 million. Its language is Arabic and its religion Islam. Algeria's 11 million people include around a million white settlers, who are of French, Italian, Spanish, and Maltese extraction, about 150,000 of them being Jews. But, with independence, some 800,000 Europeans have left.

In the whole of Africa there are only about 6 million Europeans, roughly 2 percent of the total population, but they once controlled most of

* *Maghreb* means "west" in Arabic.

the continent's wealth. Nearly 5 million of them are concentrated in the extreme north and south, in the Union of South Africa, the Rhodesias, and Algeria. Compared with its population of some 8 million, Kenya has a small number of white settlers, about 70,000, but they comprise an important minority who were once determined to protect their privileges and are now anxious to protect their property. The greater the proportion of whites, it is said, the greater the problem. Significantly, the most politically backward countries, such as the Union of South Africa, are economically the most advanced. So was the former Belgian Congo until political chaos and international intrigue engulfed it. But the Africans had little or no place—economic, political, or social—in any of them.

Not only is the face of Africa altering, but its lineaments are changing as economic urgencies and political necessities impel various moves toward different forms of federation. Even as they advanced toward independence, the former French Sudan and Senegal formed the Federation of Mali, whose independence the French recognized in June, 1960. This Federation existed only for two months when Senegal broke away and proclaimed itself the Republic of Senegal. The Sudanese Republic then set itself up as the Republic of Mali, and later, in December, 1960, entered into an association with the union already formed between Ghana and Guinea, the latter having voted itself out of the French Community in September, 1958. But there have been changes since then. The former British northern and southern Cameroons, in a plebiscite held in February, 1961, returned differing verdicts, the northern Cameroons voting for unification with Nigeria, the southern Cameroons for unification with the Republic of Cameroon, which had been set up on January 1, 1960. Four other former French African territories—the Ivory Coast, Dahomey, Niger, and Upper Volta—have formed themselves into the Council of the Entente, a cooperative association of sovereign states for mainly economic ends. The idea of federation is also being actively canvassed in East Africa, where an East African Federation embracing not only Kenya, Uganda, Tanganyika, and Zanzibar, but possibly also Nyasaland and Northern Rhodesia has been proposed but is still uncertain.

Thus within the last frontier of Africa, new alignments, and new and shifting frontiers are forming.

3

THE LION OF JUDAH

"BAD AND EVIL as the Italian occupation of our country was, it did one good thing," observed Dejazmatch Zawde Gabre Selassie, later minister of justice in the Ethiopian cabinet. "It ended Ethiopia's geographical and mental isolation. After that we no longer lived in a closed world of our own."

It was three months before the palace revolution of December, 1960. At that time Zawde, who had been one of Addis Ababa's most progressive mayors, was on the eve of being banished as envoy to Mogadishu, capital of the Somali Republic. He was stimulating to talk to, but unhappy, restive, and impatient. Still under thirty, he was among the more impressive of Ethiopia's many angry young men.

When I read the news of the revolution, one of the first persons I thought of was Zawde and I wondered what had happened to him. He had favored change, but evidently he took no direct part in the attempted coup, which occurred when he was away in Mogadishu. He was to be one of the twenty-five young men to whom the emperor later assigned ministerial or junior posts in the cabinet reshuffle of April, 1961, but today he holds no portfolio in the government.

Independence is not enough. This is the lesson which Ethiopia, along with the newly emergent nations of Asia and Africa, teaches. Ethiopia

39

emphasizes it more than most, for, with only a few brief interruptions, this ancient kingdom has known an isolated independence which for centuries has preserved it as a feudal backwater in a changing continent. As Gibbon wrote, "Encompassed on all sides by the enemies of their religion the Aethiopians slept near a thousand years, forgetful of the world by whom they were forgotten."

Tradition traces Ethiopia's royal house to Makeda, queen of Sheba, who, from her capital city of Axum in the northern province of Tigre, visited King Solomon in Jerusalem and is said to have borne him a son, who grew to be the great Emperor Menelik I. The story is told in Chapter 10, I Kings, in the Bible: "And when the Queen of Sheba heard of the fame of Solomon concerning the name of the Lord, she came to prove him with hard questions. And she came to Jerusalem with a very great train, with camels that bore spices, and very much gold, and precious stones."

The old kingdom of Axum, which first came to light in the first century A.D., was converted to Christianity around 340 A.D., when according to legend two Christian Phoenician boys who were wrecked in the Red Sea made their way to Axum and converted the king to Christianity. One of them, St. Frumentius, apparently traveled frequently between Ethiopia and Egypt, and he was reputedly the first *Abuna,* or archbishop, of Ethiopia's Coptic church, which belongs to the Monophysite branch of Christianity, preaching the doctrine of the single nature of God.

Historically, the second significant fact in Ethiopia's early history is the rise of Islam and the conquest of Palestine, Syria, Egypt, and the Red Sea coast by the Arab armies in the seventh century. These Moslem incursions put Ethiopia out of the orbit of the Christian civilization of Byzantium for nearly 800 years. As a result of these conquests Ethiopia retreated into itself, the center of political gravity moving from north to south until the core of the kingdom was contained in the four provinces of Amhara, Shoa, Tigre,* and Gojjam, where it has remained from the Middle Ages until today. During the Middle Ages these principalities grew up on the high Ethiopian plateau to the west of the Rift Valley, which separates it from the Somalia plateau to the east. The various chieftains of these regions fought with one another, but Axum remained the capital until 1538.

In the sixteenth century a Portuguese mission visited Ethiopia, drawn there by tales of the legendary Prester John, but by the mid-seventeenth century the Portuguese were no longer in evidence. The beginning of modern Ethiopia dates from 1855, when the Emperor Theodore, followed by his successor John IV, succeeded more or less in unifying the country and in rebuilding the central authority of the crown. Some thirty-four years

---

* In 1936 the Italians absorbed the northern half of Tigre into Eritrea.

later came the celebrated Menelik II, his reign coinciding with the European Scramble for Africa. When the Italians attempted to overrun Ethiopia in 1896, they were routed by Menelik at Adowa. By 1909, when the ailing Menelik made way for a regency, Ethiopia, except for Eritrea, which it absorbed on a federal basis in 1952,* covered the same area it occupied when Mussolini's Fascist armies invaded the country in 1935. Menelik II was the founder of modern Ethiopia.

Situated in the "Horn of Africa" in the northeast part of the continent alongside the Red Sea, Ethiopia lies between the valley of the Nile and the plains of Somaliland. Today its territory extends over nearly 400,000 square miles, an area more than four times the size of Great Britain, much of it comprising a vast plateau with an average elevation of 8,000 feet. Some of the mountains rise from 12,000 to 15,000 feet, dotting the plateau intermittently with truncated mountain cones known as *ambas*, flat on top with sheer sides, which give the countryside a series of natural forts. Until the Italian invasion the *ambas* served as ramparts against the foreign invader and, within the country, as rebel citadels or as isolation camps for political offenders of high degree. For nearly 3,000 years before the Fascists ravaged it, Ethiopia had known no invasion.

Flying from the Arabian peninsula across the Gulf of Aden to Djibouti in French Somaliland, where we changed into a gaudily painted Convair of the Ethiopian Airlines, the landscape was flat and arid. But over the plateau of Ethiopia the scenery grew more varied—green and untamed, with here and there a dry river bed and long, narrow trails snaking their way over the hillsides. Through the vapory clouds one saw little sign of habitation or life until suddenly below us, spread on a brilliantly verdant carpet, was Addis Ababa.

"In our country," said a lively young Ethiopian, "all things come from above."

Haile Selassie, though possessed of omnipotent power, has never been a tyrant in the traditional sense. Here he resembles two of his predecessors, the emperors Theodore and Menelik II, both of whom were contradictory bundles of liberalism and reaction, and both of whom felt that to attempt to convert a medieval African feudal state into a modern progressive country overnight was folly, if not madness. Theodore committed suicide in 1868 and, as we saw, Menelik was physically and, according to some, mentally incapacitated by 1909, four years before he died.

Haile Selassie walks grimly in these tragic footsteps. He was only fourteen when Menelik appointed him governor of Gara Huleta in his native province of Harar and, shortly after, he was summoned to the court at Addis Ababa, where his aptitude and poise, and his capacity for calcula-

* It was completely integrated in the Ethiopian Empire in 1962.

tion and decision attracted notice and uneasy respect. Even at that young age Haile Selassie had his ideas and plans. Menelik, who had nominated his grandson, Lij Yasu, as his heir, died in 1913, and by then the three leading personalities at the court were Menelik's daughter, Princess Zauditu; a prominent general, Fitaurari Habta Giorghis; and Haile Selassie, then known as Ras Tafari, son of Menelik's principal adviser, Ras Makonnen, who had died in 1906. Lij Yasu proved to be an eccentric playboy, with leanings toward Islam which outraged the Coptic court and church. He was dethroned in 1916, and Zauditu was crowned empress, with Ras Tafari as regent, heir apparent and *de facto* ruler. In 1928 Ras Tafari proclaimed himself king and in April, 1930, after the death of the empress, he was crowned emperor as His Imperial Majesty Haile Selassie the First, King of Kings, Conquering Lion of Judah, and Elect of God.

Like Menelik and Theodore, Haile Selassie also wanted to accelerate his country's progress, but simultaneously to hold it on a tight rein. As regent and heir apparent to Zauditu he had tried to reorganize the country, to build more schools and hospitals, and to send young Ethiopians overseas for higher study. In this period he had also traveled widely in Europe, and in 1923 succeeded in getting Ethiopia admitted to the League of Nations. The following year he formally abolished slavery in the kingdom. Most of all, Haile Selassie concentrated on the education of Ethiopia's youth.

One of the first questions I asked His Imperial Majesty when I interviewed him at the Guenet Leul* palace at Addis Ababa in September, 1960, shortly before the attempted revolt, was what he considered Ethiopia's major priority. He answered without hesitation, "Education." I inquired whether in time a new educated class would evolve to supplement and perhaps supplant the landed aristocracy which was the backbone of Ethiopia's administration. Haile Selassie's manner of speech is curiously like his method of government. He talks elliptically, giving an impression of forthrightness, though on analysis his statements are invariably qualified.

"I have great faith in my country's youth and great hopes in them," replied the emperor. "Yes, in time the new educated class should be the backbone of our administration. But remember this: wherever education expands, evolution takes place, and wherever evolutionary processes occur, things begin to happen. Progress needs to be orderly. Change can be beneficial only if it takes place in an atmosphere of law and order."

Almost 25 percent of Ethiopia's national budget was until recently expended on education, the students being spoonfed not only with the promise of good jobs on graduation, but with incredible inducements such as free education, supplemented by free board, lodging, books, pocket money, and even fares to enable the students in Addis Ababa and other

* "Princely Paradise."

urban centers to return home during the holidays, which they rarely did. Such prodigality could not continue indefinitely, and even before the revolt the number of day schools was stepped up while the disbursements were drastically reduced.

I found it difficult to ascertain the extent of literacy which official publications, based on generous guesswork, inflated unduly. A reliable foreign estimate placed it at around 5 percent, with about 600 college graduates, of whom about half have been educated abroad. A young Ethiopian who held an American Ph.D. degree in teaching, and his fiancée, who was also educated in America and had qualified for a B.Sc. degree in social welfare from a college in Ohio, estimated the figure of foreign-educated Ethiopians over the previous ten years at about 500, including some 60 women. In the previous four years they reckoned that around 180 students had graduated from the University College of Addis Ababa, which is run by the French Canadian Jesuits, and this number included 15 women. The University College is now known as the Haile Selassie University and is housed in the old Imperial Palace, where in 1960 the rebels shot some of Ethiopia's ablest young leaders. The emperor no longer lives there.

Facilities for college education in the arts, sciences, engineering, and technology are almost exclusively in Addis Ababa or in the larger urban centers. There is a college of agriculture as well as a military academy at Harar, and a medical faculty is being set up at the university. The naval academy is at Massawa in Eritrea. At Gondar is a health training center, and at Bahar Dar, at the southern tip of Lake Tana, a Soviet-built technical college.

An American Negro who claimed to have been a former resident of New York and Los Angeles (though a foreign embassy suggested that he was from the West Indies) had a variety of informative tidbits on Ethiopia, where he had lived for nearly twenty years. He agreed that the intelligentsia were overwhelmingly urban and were concentrated largely in Addis Ababa, but they could be dispersed only by drawing students from Addis Ababa to new towns created specifically around new industries. So long as the core of power and patronage was in the capital, neither the students nor the intelligentsia, he argued, could be expected to migrate elsewhere in any large numbers.

I asked him what his estimate was of the extent of literacy of Ethiopia. It was hard to say, he replied, but he computed that in terms of Western studies it was about 3 percent, though the number of those versed in liturgical learning, which is imparted by the Coptic priests attached to the churches and monasteries, could raise the grand total to about 8 percent. The education given at these ecclesiastical centers is uneven and often elementary, for the Ethiopian priesthood, regarded more as a profession than a vocation, is itself notoriously illiterate and corrupt. In Ethiopia, as in Tibet, one of every seven adult males is said to be a priest or monk, and driving from Addis Ababa to Debra Zeit, also known as Bishoftu, where the Swedish-trained air force has its main base some twenty miles from the capital, we came across droves of Coptic priests riding like weird, transplanted Sancho Panzas under straw umbrellas on donkeys. Some 60 percent of Ethiopia's farmers are tenants of the church; the remainder groan under the dead weight of absentee landlords.

Ethiopian students have come to expect free education as their right and, speaking to them, one had the impression that the majority of them felt no great obligation to return the benefit in the form of service to the less fortunate.

The ruling class of Ethiopians, with a few conspicuous exceptions, are not greatly interested in commercial enterprises, though some are beginning to be. They prefer to put their mony in land and houses, they are not drawn toward capital formation or private enterprise, and, indeed, they tend to look down on business and trade, much as did the country squires of England in the eighteenth century, when commerce was supposed to taint class and where only decades after the Industrial Revolution could the landed aristocracy be persuaded to send their younger sons into business.

"What have the Ethiopian youngsters of today to look up to?" a foreigner long resident in the country remarked. "All they can look up to are their feudal elders, whom they imitate. There is no other model. Ethiopia is slowly producing doctors, engineers, and technicians, but these are absorbed in government service. What chance is there for even medicine to grow up as an independent profession?"

He was right. Even journalists work under the aegis of the ministry of information, and in a population estimated to be about 20 million there are fewer than thirty qualified practitioners attached to government hospitals and welfare centers.

Most of the students appeared to hanker after government jobs, and their antipathy to trade and commerce reinforced this trend. As students, they had been reluctant to return to the countryside, and as bureaucrats the new urban intelligentsia found itself more and more divorced from rural life. Over the years their links with the countryside have progressively weakened. When the revolt came, it affected only Addis Ababa.

The bizarre contrasts that confront one in the Guenet Leul palace, a mixture of the archaic and the advanced, are intriguing and reflect the personality of its former chief occupant. As we drove in, the guards saluted stiffly, and the gardeners working in the park bowed low. A spruce military aide conducted us to an anteroom, where on a table were copies of *Country Life*, *The Spectator*, and *The Listener*. The room was quietly furnished, with nothing ornate or garish. Officials went tiptoeing through the corridors and rooms, and the atmosphere was suggestive of the hushed interior of a cathedral. As I left, a palace official, producing a rather battered, dog-eared notebook from his pocket, asked me to enter my name and address.

I was with the emperor for fifty minutes. He received us in his study, a long, narrow room with a writing desk to the left backed by a high bookshelf which contained, among other volumes, some books by Nehru. His Imperial Majesty sat at the far end of the room, wearing a marshal's uniform with rows of ribbons at least six inches deep across his chest.* On the table before him was a globe. Three tiny dogs, who invariably accompany him, gamboled around the room.

We had to bow three times as we walked up the room accompanied by the palace secretary—at the threshold, in the center of the room and before the emperor's table. Looking at him, as I shook hands, I thought for a moment that Haile Selassie was still seated and was a little taken aback to discover that he was standing. He is startlingly small in stature, but well proportioned, with tiny feet and hands, and there is an assured, imperious air about him. His smile is slow and sad. He carries himself with dignity and poise, but with an air of melancholy. His face, though slightly wizened, has an arresting profile, and his eyes are reflective and expressive. The emperor conversed in Amharic, though he understands English, choosing his words carefully and speaking with deliberation. French is his favorite foreign tongue.

The palace secretary, Ato Tafarra Worq Kidane Wold, who acted as the interpreter, was formerly a translator at the British embassy, and the British ambassador, Sir Denis Wright, told me later that Wold had been sentenced to death by the Italians and was saved only by Eden's personal intervention with Mussolini.

Talking of the Congo, the emperor affirmed his belief in collective security, and observed that the Congolese government at Léopoldville should accept the joint good offices of the Africans "who are concerned only with promoting unity and peace in the Congo." He was referring to his proposal for the creation of a Security Council Commission of African States to promote and effect conciliation among the Congolese leaders in order to avoid unnecessary bloodshed.

He evidently thinks in Pan-African terms and is anxious that Ethiopia should have a prominent place in the African picture. In June, 1960, the independent African states, at the emperor's invitation, had held their second conference at Addis Ababa, where in his opening address Haile

* He was to attend a ceremony later in the morning.

Selassie urged the need for closer collaboration among the African states. "Those who seek independence," he said, "must be prepared to struggle for it rather than accept it, and having won it to stand on their own feet without dependence and without favors." Some six months later, during his visit to Ghana, the emperor signed a communiqué with Dr. Nkrumah stressing the need for a joint African High Command.

Since the first African conference was held in Addis Ababa in May, 1963, Haile Selassie's prestige has soared impressively in the continent of Africa north and south of the Sahara. His dexterity and skill as a negotiator and his reputation as an experienced statesman and administrator have enabled him to guide his once insulated kingdom into the mainstream of African affairs.

I asked the emperor if his plans implied that Africa wished to settle its own problems without Asian collaboration.

"No," said His Imperial Majesty quickly, "my suggestion does not exclude Asian collaboration. We would welcome it."

But evidently the emperor's plan envisaged African initiative in the first instance, with Asian assistance, if necessary, in the secondary stage.

"The Congo situation," Haile Selassie went on to observe, "has been complicated because of foreign interference. If the Belgian troops and administrators had withdrawn quickly, other Belgians in the technical and industrial spheres would have been able to help, and could have remained if treated properly."

Mindful perhaps of my initial queries on Asian cooperation, the emperor frequently referred to the need for Afro-Asian collaboration.

"When I was in India," he remarked, "I discussed the Bandung Conference and other matters with Mr. Nehru. In my opinion it was a pity that the Bandung Conference was held only once. It has become a conference only in name, with no positive effect—rather the contrary. There is a great field for economic collaboration between Asia and Africa because there is economic interdependence between the two. We should establish an Afro-Asian bank among other institutions to help our economic growth. It does not matter in which continent it is situated."

While talking of the Congo the emperor frequently stressed the need for law and order, but he showed no awareness of the fact that he himself was sitting on the edge of a volcano.

Haile Selassie controls both the state and the church, for since 1948 the *Abuna* has ceased to be an Egyptian nominee of the Patriarch of Alexandria. He is now an Ethiopian nominated by the emperor, the nomination being formally confirmed by the patriarch. Ethiopia has been described as an island of Christianity in a sea of Islam. It claims to be Africa's oldest independent state, as well as the only Christian state on that continent. On the assumption that the royal line began with the legendary union of King Solomon and the Queen of Sheba, Haile Selassie is the 255th monarch of this line which, as we noted, was converted to Christianity in the fourth century A.D. But is Ethiopia, in fact, a Christian state with a majority of Christians?

No census has ever been taken, although a census commission was appointed some time ago, but the country's population is estimated to be about 20 million, of whom around 500,000 reside in Addis Ababa. Foreign diplomats who have traveled around the country describe the outlying districts as very crowded and some question whether, if a census were taken, the majority would be Christian. Though Moslems are not prominent in the administration, the emperor's own province of Harar contains a large element of Moslems, and so do the Somali and Danakil areas. The Gallas, who are racially akin to the Somalis and who immigrated into the central plateau in the sixteenth century, contain many Moslem tribes, particularly the warlike Wollos. In the extreme southwest reside many pagans, some of whom have a veneer of Christianity, and honor Jesus and Mary among their tribal gods. Knowledgeable foreign observers say a census might reveal a majority of Moslems and pagans.

The emperor is not unaware of this and, while allowing the Moslems full religious freedom, he has made it plain that they can enjoy it only so long as they remain loyal Ethiopians. He is also sensitive to pressure from outside, notably from Egypt and the Sudan, and from the now independent areas of former British Somaliland and Italian Somalia, which have joined to form the Somali Republic. On Ethiopia's eastern and southern flanks looms the threat of a free Greater Somalia which, in addition to the former British and Italian territories, aims at including French Somaliland and the Somali tracts of Kenya.

"Why should we not be suspicious of foreign designs?" asked Blatta Davit Ogbogzey, the then minister of state for foreign affairs. "We cannot forget that the Italian attack was launched on us from Mogadishu in Somalia in the south and from Asmara in Eritrea in the north. For years Ethiopia has been surrounded by French and British Somaliland, by Italian Somalia and Eritrea, and by Kenya, all of whom have helped themselves to bits of our territory. We have accepted the independence of British Somaliland and of Somalia, where the elections were fought on the issue of Greater Somalia. We ask nothing of them except that we be allowed to go our way."

But the face of Africa is changing rapidly. Christianity has lost much of its momentum. Islam is in the ascendant, and, as the countries of Africa emerge into freedom, the influence of Islam will spread on this continent, an eventuality to which even a small country like Israel seems acutely alive, judging from a conversation I had with the one-eyed Israeli, General Moshe Dayan, who was in Addis Ababa to offer Ethiopia technical know-how and the services of experts in many fields. Israel seems determined to break the Arab blockade with skilled technical and welfare assistance. "Israel has 5,000 doctors for a population of 2 million," remarked the general. "We are willing to spare them to countries which lack medical personnel and facilities." In Ethiopia, Israel has met with a friendly welcome.

To the west of Ethiopia lies the Sudan, and beyond, to the northwest of Asmara, lies Cairo. Though the relations of Addis Ababa with Khartoum and Cairo are correct, there are elements in both Egypt and the Sudan which make no secret of their dislike of the Coptic domination of Ethiopia. Until quite recently the Voice of Cairo radio was characterizing the Ethiopian government as a Christian administration hostile to Islam, and, though this propaganda has ceased, there are influential sections in Cairo and Addis Ababa which eye each other with distrust.

"Nasser," said a high Ethiopian official, "claims to represent the voice of the Arab world. Perhaps he does, though occasionally the Baghdad Caliphate and Saudi Arabia seem to dissent. It does not interest us who does, but it does interest us to maintain friendly relations with our neighbors."

In the Sudan, which is among the most genuinely friendly countries in the world, I sensed occasionally the same note of distrust toward Ethiopia. This was particularly noticeable in pro-Egyptian circles and among the religiously feudal elements which clustered around personages such as the late Mahdi, the Imam Sayed Siddik al-Mahdi of Ansar, whom I encountered at Omdurman.

Suspect in the eyes of Islamic Africa, Ethiopia is also regarded by the emergent independent territories south of the Sahara as a feudal and conservative backwater. The emperor, as the symbol of his anachronistic country and regime, is thus the target not only of external criticism, but of internal restiveness and resentment, the victim of an environment he sought in his own fashion to change, but which he could not control within his own country or influence outside it. There is additional irony in the fact that the Ethiopians, unlike their neighbors in sub-Saharan Africa, are acutely sensitive to the importance of *not* being black.

The original inhabitants of the Ethiopian highlands were of Hamitic stock, first cousins of the early Egyptians, racially and linguistically akin to the Danakil and Somali peoples to the east and southeast, and to the tribes of the Nubian desert to the northwest. The infiltration of Arab elements from the Yemen, who crossed the Red Sea around 500 B.C. and occupied the northern part of the highlands, injected a strain of Semitic blood, which is noticeable in the ruling clan of the Amharas who, like the Yemenis of Aden, are comparatively light-skinned, with aquiline profiles and an easy natural grace of manner and movement. But for their hair many Ethiopians could be taken for Indians.

The Amharas constitute about 35 percent of the population, roughly equivalent in numbers to the Gallas, who retain a stronger Hamitic strain. Next come the Tigreans, said to be the hardest working of all. The Ethiopians call themselves a Sabaean people, from their Semitic ancestors who came from the Levant and brought with them the Sabaean alphabet, which in a modified form is still in wide use in the country. The Ag'azi tribe from across the Red Sea has given its name to the liturgical language, Ge'ez.

Thus the nuclei of the Ethiopian people are Semitic in culture and predominantly Hamitic in blood. But in the southwest part of the highlands the Hamitic stock is strongly intermixed by the infiltration of Negro tribes from the Upper Nile, who in language and racial types differ markedly from the peoples of the central and northern plateau. Though the Ethiopians disdain to think of themselves as Negro or negroid, the Arabs regarded them as blacks, their name for Ethiopia being Habesh, meaning "black," from which the European name of Abyssinia is derived. Homer is not flattering to the Ethiopians, whom he describes as "Aethiopes" or "burnt-faced men," and catalogues as "the farthest from mankind." On the other hand Hesiod refers to them as "a high-souled folk," and Herodotus labels them "the most just of men."

Like other parts of Africa, Ethiopia abounds in many languages and dialects, totaling around forty and belonging to one of the three main linguistic groups: Hamitic, Hamitic-Semitic, and Nilotic Negro. Amharic is the leading language, with Galla and Tigre coming next. Tigre is also one of the official languages of Eritrea, now a province of Ethiopia. The national language, Amharic, is related to both Hebrew and Arabic, and is believed to be of Semitic origin, as is the liturgical language of Ge'ez. According to legend, the early Ethiopian scriptures were first translated from Greek into Ge'ez by the "Nine Saints" from Syria at the end of the fifth century. English is Ethiopia's second official language, but French and Italian are also spoken by some of the educated class and Arabic is well known in certain areas on the fringes of the country.

"In Ethiopia," said an Ethiopian student, "foreign people work for the country. The country doesn't work for foreign people."——> bullshit!

Foreigners number around 50,000 and, surprisingly, Ethiopian-Italian relations are by no means unfriendly,* even if the Martyrs' Memorial in Addis Ababa, presented by the Yugoslav government, is a persistent reminder of the massacre and atrocities which followed an attempt on

* The emperor recently accepted an invitation to visit Italy.

Marshal Graziani's life shortly after the Fascist conquest. Many of the building contractors are Italians, and business and trade are predominantly in foreign hands, with the Greeks as the most numerous and wealthy expatriates, the Armenians and Indians coming next. Most of the Indians have so far been engaged in the textile trade, but Japanese competition is forcing them out of this field into other lines.

The emperor is served by many foreign advisers, one of his principal advisers being a Yugoslav. The Yugoslavs are the chief consultants on economic planning and development. Swedish instructors are prominent in the air force, based on Bishoftu, which is commanded by General Asseffa, who was loyal to the emperor during the rebellion. The navy, with its main base at Massawa, is run largely by Norwegian advisers, and until recently there was an Indian military mission at Harar, of which the then defense minister of state, Major General Nega Haile Selassie, spoke in high terms when I met him at Addis Ababa. Nega explained that before the Italian occupation the imperial bodyguard constituted the core of the army, but they were now trying to build up a national army totaling around 50,000, of whom one-third would be conscripted, and they were also considering the introduction of compulsory military service. Though the Americans are more numerous than the British, the latter are said to constitute the bulk of advisers in the various ministries. The Russian presence is not obtrusive, but the U.S.S.R. has given Ethiopa the largest foreign grant, totaling 400 million rubles, part of which is earmarked for what Moscow euphemistically describes as a "geological survey."

How far does the emperor's writ and authority run? During the Italian occupation, communications inside the country were extended and improved, and Haile Selassie has wisely accelerated progress in this sphere. Though transport in most areas is primitive, serviced by oxcart, mule, donkey, or camel train plodding along the rough trails which run through the countryside, there are around 3,100 miles of improved roads operable by motor transport, the hub being the five American-maintained highways which radiate from Addis Ababa. Of these the best maintained is the 25-mile road to Debra Zeit, where the emperor has a country house named Villa Fairfield. Supplementing the improved highways, which taper into dust roads, are so-called "secondary" roads, for the most part graveled, dusty, and rock-strewn, which with the trails make a total of about 37,500 miles of road communication. But outide Addis Ababa, Asmara, and a few other towns, Ethiopia's communications are primitive and the countryside lives in the Middle Ages. In Addis Ababa itself the main highways are dotted with red-light districts where the gentry and *hoi polloi* congregate in dingy tenements crowded with their human ware and lit by bulbs which flicker feebly on tiny bars serving *tej* and *talla*. Air communications have also improved, the government-sponsored Ethiopian Airlines covering, besides their external services, some thirty domestic stations. This air service is run with the assistance of Trans World Airlines, and so far around twenty Ethiopians have qualified as captains, while others are being trained in management and control.

Only two railroads serve the whole of Ethiopia, the older of them being the single-track French railroad which traverses the nearly 500 miles from Djibouti to Addis Ababa. Since 1952, when Eritrea was attached on a federal basis to Ethiopia, the latter has gained an additional railroad running from the Red Sea port of Massawa up the 7,000-foot escarpment to Asmara, and from there to Keren and Agordat. Ethiopia has also secured the ports of Massawa and Assab, which give her an outlet to the Red Sea, and the emperor is keen on developing motor traffic on the Addis Ababa-Massawa route, one reason for this being that he does not want Ethiopia to lean too heavily on the Djibouti railroad. Apart from the road, rail, and air communications, airmail, radio, and telephone services are being developed inside the country, so that it is now possible for the government in Addis Ababa to maintain telecommunications with the principal cities and beyond them. This also helps to make for a more centralized and cohesive administration. Today the emperor's writs run to every corner of his spreading domain, but operate spasmodically in the more distant regions.

Yet, ironically, Haile Selassie had no inkling of the plot being hatched under his very eyes within the innermost ring of his confidants in Addis Ababa, for otherwise he would surely not have left his capital for Ghana and Brazil. Almost a year later, in September, 1961, he was able to go to the Belgrade neutrals' summit conference, which suggests that in the interval the emperor was able to reestablish and reassert his authority. Everyone recognizes that in the "Lion of Judah" is the one, most cohesive bond in the country.

The December, 1960, uprising in the emperor's absence abroad was not a popular, but a palace revolution, a revolt staged by his own praetorian guard and approved by the small intellectual class he had brought into being—the two groups on whom he had lavished his especial benefaction and care. In favoring them Haile Selassie might have calculated that he could play off his beneficiaries against the older feudal elements, whose power he wanted to curb for the advantage of himself and the country. In the rubbing-off process the emperor probably felt that he could dominate one or both. Haile Selassie ended in 1960 by being the astonished victim of his own subtlety and subterfuge, for, while his pampered imperial bodyguard, along with the equally pampered new intellectuals, lined up against him, the neglected sandal-shod imperial army with the feudal church, the rural peasants, and the urban populace stood by the emperor. As usual, the feudal lords were divided. In 1941, after his return from exile to Ethiopia, Haile Selassie had thought it wise to overlook the survival arrangement which Ras Seyoum, the last hereditary Duke of Tigre, had made with the Italians. Seyoum remained loyal to the emperor in 1960, and was butchered by the rebels. Similarly, after the 1960 revolt Haile Selassie deemed it politic to ignore the fact that his cousin, the liberal-minded, dignified Ras Imru Haile Selassie, who as commander of the western front during the Italian invasion had gallantly fought the Fascist armies and had continued doing so even after the emperor's departure, had inclined ideologically toward the rebel regime which had proclaimed him as prime minister, but without his consent. The Crown Prince, His Imperial Highness Asfaw Wosen Haile Selassie, whose sympathies were known to be with the young intellectuals, was probably the most frustrated and disgruntled of the emperor's immediate entourage.

I had an interview some weeks before the revolt with the forty-six-year-old crown prince, a plump, pleasant man with a heavy face and protuberant eyes, resembling closely his mother, the late Empress Menen. Perhaps his physical heaviness gives him an appearance of dullness, but, though much of our conversation was formal, he asked some perceptive questions on Communist China and Russia, in both of which he seemed to be especially interested. Of his visit to America he remarked that he thought the tempo of life there too fast. But something was obviously churning in his mind, suggesting a degree of mental incertitude and restiveness. He seemed incapable of initiative but susceptible to influence, and could, one felt, be a pliable instrument.

Palace intrigues and revolts recur in Ethiopia's Byzantine history and, as Ras Tafari, the emperor himself had led a revolt against the apostate Lij Yasu.* The palace revolt of December, 1960, was the second attempted coup in ten years, for in 1952, under the leadership of the then minister of the pen, who occupies a status roughly equivalent to that of Britain's Lord Privy Seal, some of the younger air force officers and civil servants had staged a forty-eight-hour revolt which failed. In accordance with customary practice on such occasions the rebels, apart from the more aggressive ringleaders, were leniently dealt with, most of them being banished to the more distant provinces. Even in the last revolt only two of the surviving ringleaders were publicly hanged, the emperor promising to be merciful to those who wrote personally to him confessing their crime and asking for forgiveness. Whether, in fact, there were no further executions, it is impossible to say.

The officers' revolt took both the palace and the people by surprise. Considering how quickly it collapsed, it is doubtful if much detailed plan-

* He is said to have been done to death in 1935.

ning preceded it. Ethiopians are naturally secretive and suspicious—of strangers and of one another. Though the revolt was led by General Menghistu Neway, commander of the bodyguard, whose chief accomplices were Brigadier Tsige Dibu, chief of police, and Colonel Workineh Gebayehu, chief of security, it was probably masterminded by Menghistu's younger brother, Girmane Neway, governor of the province of Jigjiga,* who was a man of drive and administrative ability. Also actively implicated in the plot was Lij Haile Mariam Kebede, former president of the Ethiopian House of Deputies.

The leaders of the revolt were in their twenties or early thirties. All of them were imperial favorites. Menghistu was a personal friend of the emperor, who had also paid for the university studies of Girmane, Kebede, and others. It was not the emperor's enemies, but his friends who turned against him. No wonder that Haile Selassie, when informed of the coup in faraway Brazil, was reluctant to believe that three of his most trusted confidants headed the uprising. "And now," he said ruefully, "our trust is betrayed."

The coup took place in the early hours before dawn on Wednesday, December 14, the rebels planning and hoping that the revolt would succeed at one blow. Superficially it did, for by early morning all the ministries had been taken over, the radio station was occupied, telephones and cables shut down, posses of the imperial bodyguard posted outside government offices, communication centers, and foreign embassies, and Addis Ababa sealed off. The civil airport was closed and for a time the capital's electricity was cut off. All the resident members of the imperial family, including the ailing Empress Menen, the grandchildren, and the crown prince, were placed under house arrest. Along with them the Patriarch Basilios and those of his bishops who were in Addis Ababa were held incommunicado.

The coup was a complete surprise to the ordinary population, though reports allege that the university students were alerted by a bodyguard officer on the night of December 13 that a revolt was imminent, and were told to support it the next morning by a demonstration with banners and placards, which some of them did. In the afternoon of December 14 the first public announcement of the coup was made in a broadcast by the crown prince, apparently acting under duress. His statement was repeated over the local radio station several times. "A few people," declared His Imperial Highness, "depending on their birth and material wealth, have been exploiting the people for their personal benefit. The Ethiopian people, in recent times, have shown their resentment at the prevailing conditions. Several attempts have been made to stifle this normal feeling of the people. Today

* Ethiopia is divided into thirteen general governorates, which are further subdivided into eighty-two governorates or provinces.

the will of the Ethiopian people has come to realization. I have made my decision to serve Ethiopia and the Ethiopian people, seeking no personal preference or advantage, only the legitimate salary determined by law."

In the same broadcast the crown prince announced the formation of a new government, which included himself, "the armed forces and the young educated Ethiopians." Later it was announced that the sixty-nine-year-old Ras Imru Haile Selassie had taken over the office of prime minister.

In fact he had not, for while agreeing on the need for reform, he had refused to conspire with the rebels behind the emperor's back. Along with the crown prince, Ras Imru was later rehabilitated in the imperial favor. "I will forgive you and forget you," the emperor is reported to have told his erring son on his return.

Ras Imru, a cousin of the emperor, ranks third in the official hierarchy, coming only after the emperor and the crown prince, though some rate the Coptic patriarch as officially, though not politically, above him. I spent a most agreeable hour while in Addis Ababa with this gallant soldier who, before going to Delhi as Ethiopian ambassador, served his country in the same capacity in Washington. Ras Imru was then due to leave as ambassador to Moscow, and many knowledgeable observers remarked on this, suggesting that it was proof that the emperor was suspicious of him and wanted to keep him out of the country as long as possible. Ras Imru is a progressive who might be described as a radical, and is extremely popular with the young intellectuals. He has voluntarily given away a considerable portion of his vast estates and, when I remarked on it, observed that he was planning to give away more. He was critical of the West, which he said never spoke its mind frankly, unlike Soviet Russia. He hoped for close Indian-Chinese friendship and recalled how, when he was Ethiopia's ambassador in Delhi, he had observed how cordial was the relationship between Chou En-lai and the Dalai and Panchen Lamas when they visited India in 1956. He expressed great admiration and regard for Nehru and Nasser.

Various declarations attributed to the crown prince were intermittently broadcast by an announcer over the radio condemning the emperor's rule and promising to end "three thousand years of injustice." "Ethiopia," he was quoted as saying, "will now try to catch up with the other states of Africa, and I am glad to tell you that this movement has created an authority that will work for the progress of this country and its people. . . . The laws and regulations of the country have been abused and deprive the common people of their rights and privileges in order to boost the riches of the favored few. The people of Ethiopa have waited for a long time with patience in the hope that they will be free some day of oppression, poverty, and ignorance. In doing this they have amply demonstrated their abundant patience. But empty promises can no longer satisfy the people, who now want concrete action aimed at improving their standard of living."

Rebel hopes that the majority of the armed forces, civil servants, and university students would join them failed to materialize. By the afternoon of the second day—Thursday, December 15—when fighting broke out, it was obvious that the regular army and the air force had remained loyal to the emperor. On the same day leaflets bearing the patriarch's signature were dropped from a light plane, urging the population to remain loyal, and stating that the air force and the army were against the revolt. General Merid Mengasha, chief of staff, whose divisional headquarters were based about a mile from the Addis Ababa railway station, led the loyalist forces which converged on the rebels. The presence of a few jet aircraft over Addis Ababa also demonstrated the loyalty of the air force commanded by General Asseffa.

For twenty-four hours, from the afternoon of December 15, there was brisk shooting by rifle, machine guns, and artillery between the loyalists and the rebels. Meanwhile, the emperor was hurrying home from Brazil, and a rumor of his return to the capital brought out cheering crowds and provoked shrill ululations of joy from the women, who were stilled only when darkness and the curfew descended. Actually the emperor's plane was delayed by engine trouble between Monrovia and Khartoum. It did not reach Asmara, in Eritrea, until the afternoon of December 16, when wildly cheering crowds greeted Haile Selassie, and the local garrison with the air force squadron pledged their loyalty to the emperor.

Shortly before the emperor landed at Asmara, General Merid Mengasha announced over the radio in Addis Ababa that he had the situation under control, and denounced by name the ringleaders of the revolt. By now the rebel leaders were cornered in a wing of the old imperial palace, where they had taken refuge along with the ministers of Haile Selassie whom they held in custody. On the afternoon of December 16, realizing that the revolt had failed, the rebels lined the ministers up against a wall and shot them before they themselves surrendered. Among those butchered in cold blood were the minister of commerce and industry, Ato Makonnen Haptewold, and the minister of defense, Ras Abebe Aregaye. In an atmosphere of official peculation Makonnen was reputed to be a man of high probity. Aregaye was a professional soldier.

The emperor landed at Addis Ababa airport at 4:30 P.M. on December 17. He was received by the crown prince, who had regained his liberty, and by a tumultuously cheering mob. Spasmodic shooting continued in the capital until December 17, and two more days elapsed before the army's mopping-up operations ceased. Of the three principal ringleaders only one, General Menghistu Neway, survived. He was wounded while resisting capture, and was subsequently tried and hanged in the public marketplace. Colonel Workineh Gebayehu committed suicide, but his dead body was nonetheless strung up in public. A fellow accused with Menghistu was a captain of the bodyguard, Kifle Wodaju, who was initially sentenced to ten years' imprisonment. He was imprudent enough to appeal, and the supreme court responded by sentencing him to death. He was later publicly executed. Menghistu's younger brother, Girmane, was killed in one of the many skirmishes in which most of the leaders of the revolt died.

The revolt, if it revealed deep-seated impatience with the old order of things, also showed that the intellectuals and, it may be, many others who sympathized with the rebels simultaneously respected the emperor. They felt, and probably were justified in their belief, that Ethiopia could progress only with and not without the emperor, for, despite his feudal background, Haile Selassie is in many ways an enlightened man, far more capable of holding Ethiopia together than any radical Ras or other more progressive elements.

Reading the broadcast communiqués from Addis Ababa during the revolt, I was intrigued by the Marxist idioms they employed, and for a while speculated if there were any Communist influences behind the uprising. The loyal armed forces, for instance, were described as "a group of bandits who opened fire on peaceful citizens." Despite the distinctive terminology, I do not think this signified more than the imitative patter of half-baked intellectuals.

The revolt was not an uprising by the people, but by the feudal lords, much like the revolt of the barons who forced King John to sign Magna Carta guaranteeing them "judgment by their peers," which meant judgment not by the common people, but by their fellow barons. Like another December rising, that of the Decembrists against Nicholas I at St. Petersburg in 1825, the Addis Ababa revolt was primarily a military affair. Had it succeeded, it is possible that certain overdue measures, particularly in the sphere of land reform and in the improvement of the present primitive farming methods, might have been accelerated, but the feudal overlordship of Haile Selassie would probably have given way not to a democratic setup, but to the rule of a centralized clique, more liberal perhaps than the emperor but only a little less authoritarian. The Marxist terminology of some of the rebels' communiqués suggested a crude familiarity with Communist phraseology and dogma, but more real was the spirit of Pan-Africanism, of a desire to move in line with the newly independent, more modern African states springing up around Ethiopia. The Italian occupation, the Second World War, the emergence of military revolutionary movements in Egypt, the Sudan, Turkey, Iraq, and Pakistan, and the student unrest in Japan, Korea, and Nigeria stimulated similar ideas in Ethiopia.

The emperor is not unaware of these trends, and in fact is attempting to hasten the pace of progress, but, temperamentally, decentralization is contrary to his outlook and inclination.

The tragedy of Haile Selassie is the tragedy of a well-meaning man of good intentions whose faith, hope, and charity have gone awry. He wanted desperately to modernize Ethiopia without unduly disturbing the feudal social structure, of which he was the center and the core. He wanted Ethiopia to keep in step with him as he marched toward the national progress of his conception, unmindful of the fact that the wind of change which was sweeping Africa would not leave him and his country unscathed. Though progressive, he was out of date and out of touch. He was also out of step.

The very colonialism from which the emperor sought to protect his country and people ironically propelled the country and stimulated the people in a direction and at a pace of which he disapproved. For if the Italian occupation ended Ethiopia's geographical and mental isolation, other developments, notably the inroads of modern colonialism in adjacent African countries and the resultant urge for freedom, left their impress and impact on this artificially insulated kingdom, and intensified the mood and drive for progress. Even the most carefully cloistered Ethiopians could not but sense the stir and wonder of achievement and advance within the continent around them, as former colonial African territories attained independence, many of them inspired by new ideas, however superficial and ill-digested, of politics, economics, social welfare, and administration. Because he wanted to centralize all power and authority in himself, while allowing his people to wear the habiliments of freedom and progress, Haile Selassie appeared to take away with the left hand what he gave with the right.

Thus, though the Ethiopians theoretically enjoy universal suffrage, their choice of representatives is restricted to individuals virtually screened by the emperor after approval and scrutiny by local officials. Ethiopia has a parliament of two houses, a nominated senate and an elected chamber of deputies, but it has no political parties. Theoretically either house may initiate legislation, but in practice the prior approval of the emperor is necessary, and differences between the two houses on any measure are referred to the emperor, who decides. The emperor also has the right of veto on all legislation. Though budgets are submitted to the legislature, no budgetary system as such exists, and I was told by a foreign adviser attached to a ministry that he had to buy shorthand pads at his own expense for his secretary because funds for this purpose in this particular ministry were either not available or not earmarked. The cabinet system exists, with a council of ministers, but its members, who change as the emperor desires, have neither collective nor individual authority.

Similarly, Ethiopia has a judiciary, ostensibly operating through original courts and courts of appeal with a supreme imperial court and an imperial high court at the highest level. But alongside these courts the emperor has his own court, where he exercises powers of life and death, and can overrule any other court. Access to the emperor's court, it was said, depends very largely on the bribes paid to the palace officials. In the sphere of social welfare bribery also abounds. Hospitals, though sparse and ill-equipped, do exist, the most notable among them being the Princess Tsahai Memorial Hospital at Addis Ababa, but in most of them the unfortunate families of patients seeking entry are dunned to an unconscionable degree before treatment is made available or the patient is allowed to leave.

Ethiopia must have the world's most top-heavy civil service, where the majority of educated Ethiopians, who also comprise the majority of Ethiopia's angry young men, occupy comparatively junior posts with no responsibility to exercise and often with no work to do. Deprived of responsibility and initiative, they resent, on the one hand, the emperor's highly paid foreign advisers and disapprove, on the other, of the royal relatives and friends, generally feudal and sometimes semiliterate, who, as senior civil servants, frustrate them in their forward-looking plans and policies. Not that either of these two categories exercises any power, for no civil servant, whether in the higher or lower echelons, will make a decision even on the most trivial issue without securing the emperor's sanction or approval. Haile Selassie is the lord and dispenser, the great provider and benefactor. To a large extent he has achieved Menelik's aim of unifying the kingdom by neutralizing the centrifugal forces of the regional *Rases*, or feudal lords, and by eliminating the dissident influence of the Moslem and pagan areas in the south.*

In the twenty-five years between the Italian invasion and the December Revolt Ethiopia had seen the flower of her talent and youth mown down in successive waves—first by the Italians, then in the resistance movement after occupation, again during World War II, and finally in the December coup, which cost the emperor some of his most experienced ministers and advisers. Haile Selassie could not afford to be ruthless when the revolt was quelled. He had been deprived of some of his most trusted counselors and was uncertain whom he could trust among the survivors.

The likelihood therefore is that the emperor, while he will defeudalize the administration in some respects and liberalize it in other directions, will not greatly relax his overall grip. After the revolt, Haile Selassie declared

---

* The title of *Ras,* roughly equivalent to "Field Marshal," is military in connotation, carrying with it a superlative social cachet which gives the holder an exalted status in the imperial hierarchy. The higher nobility consists of the *Rases* and *Dejazmatchs.* There were six *Rases* before the Italian occupation. Now their number is twelve.

that the rebel program was no different from his own, and that his policies would not change. But they will have to change in the outward form, inner spirit, and general pace. The major cabinet reshuffle which the emperor announced in April, 1961, was notable for the appointment of many young men to ministerial and junior posts, but, of all elements, the armed forces have emerged as the strongest factor, and the emperor has been quick to appease them by larger military expenditures and disbursements made at the cost of the now more heavily taxed and disgruntled civil servants. The old game of checks and balances continues in a new form.

Despite its veneer of modernization, Ethiopia remains pitifully poor, weighted down by the landed aristocracy, a fossilized state church owning a great deal of land and property, a top-heavy civil service, frustrated intellectuals, and the ambitious, increasingly assertive armed forces. To these elements the emperor, who appeared formerly as an archaic autocrat, no longer embodies the unchallenged fount of authority he was when he left Addis Ababa for Ghana and Brazil, for in their eyes, as in the eyes of those Ethiopians who encouraged and sympathized with the revolt, but survived, and of many who took no part in it, the emperor, now seventy, is no more a supremely wise despot, but a tired old man striving desperately to keep his empire together. Some 4,000 supporters of the 1960 revolution are said to be either in jail or in exile.

"After Nehru—what?" is a question often asked an Indian abroad.

I posed a parallel question to an Ethiopian intellectual, "After the Emperor—what?"

He smiled, and said, "After the emperor—Ethiopia."

Ever since he formally abolished slavery in Ethiopia, Haile Selassie has intermittently promised to put an end to feudalism. He has repeated this promise more than once since the palace revolt, but the manifestations are few and far between. Shortly after the attempted coup, the emperor appointed a committee to investigate the possibility of reforming the 1931 constitution which, as we have seen, provides a parliamentary apparatus but no political parties, with neither the council of ministers, the senate, or the chamber of deputies exercising any real authority. Power is concentrated in the emperor, from whom all privilege and patronage flow. The Committee in its report recommended that the prime minister should choose his own ministers instead of having them nominated by the emperor, and also suggested that the government should resign if it loses the confidence of parliament. But, simultaneously, the choice of a new prime minister and the approval of all legislation would continue to be vested in the emperor, leaving the chamber of deputies with little power and perhaps with even less inclination to assert its independence.

Although Haile Selassie's writ, due to improved communications, now runs throughout his kingdom, it is tenuous in many of the more distant provinces, such as Ogaden on the Somalia border and in Eritrea. The Gallas, particularly the Arusi Gallas, who have chafed at Amharic dominance since the days of Menelik, as well as the Tigreans, who inhabit much of northern Ethiopia and Eritrea, are continuously restive. Until now a sense of national unity has been imposed and to a large extent is maintained by the concept of loyalty to the person of a single ruler who has projected himself to his people as a father image. But after the revolt this concept, despite the emperor's efforts, is beginning to look very much like a fiction which is in the process of being replaced by the new concept of nationhood, with loyalty to the ruler transformed into loyalty to the state. There is much for Haile Selassie to do on the political and economic planes.

The Ethiopian farmers who form the bulk of the population are not as downtrodden as the Egyptian *fellahín* were before Nasser. They live by a subsistence agriculture, which is fairly thriving on the plateaus, but they have only an informal security of tenure, enjoying no legal title to their land, which is largely concentrated in the hands of rich, often absentee landowners, of whom the church is the biggest. The empress was believed to hold considerable business concessions, including all the eucalyptus trees within a twenty-five-mile radius of the capital. The average laborer earns about 42 U.S. cents a day. Coffee is the country's main export crop, totaling about 60,000 tons a year, but it is badly picked and inexpertly graded, and the trade is handled by avaricious middlemen. More recently an attempt has been made in conjunction with a British firm to start a cotton plantation scheme in the Awash Valley, which ultimately will enable the Ethiopian farmers as tenants to cultivate an area of 10,000 acres. The farmers will rent the land from the company, and the government will take 30 percent of the profits. The scheme is inspired by the Gezira project in the Sudan, but in Ethiopia plans unfortunately have a habit of rarely leaving paper. No real progress is possible unless the administrative structure, cluttered up with the emperor's ineffectual mandarins, is drastically overhauled, and such key departments as those of finance, the interior, justice, health, and commerce and industry are brought more into line with the twentieth century. Only then will the era of hieratic immobility end.

Ethiopia, suspect in the eyes of Islamic Africa as a Christian outpost on the continent, is also looked at askance by the newly emergent independent countries south of the Sahara. The emperor is aware that, unless he steers his course between these two forces, his country will be isolated from the main stream of African development and be submerged ultimately by one of these two expanding tides. Reform is overdue. But is the emperor temperamentally and physically capable of initiating it? He confronts a moment of agonizing reappraisal.

Some talk of the emperor having plans to bypass the crown prince to whom he is antipathetic and to name as his successor the son of the late Duke of Harar, who was Haile Selassie's favorite son; another grandson, Prince Alexander Desta, deputy chief of the Ethiopian navy, is also sometimes mentioned. But a change in the administrative spirit and structure must precede a change in the line of dynastic succession. Personalities have so far sustained Ethiopia, but principles cannot be ignored. In any case, the crown prince's supporters in parliament have so far successfully stalled the emperor's efforts.

A few of the younger educated Ethiopians with whom I spoke recognized the difficulties, but felt they were not insuperable. "No country," one of them observed, "depends on one man—whether Caesar, Napoleon, or Hitler. Today we talk as our forefathers did the day before yesterday. They talked like this in Menelik II's time. But look how far Ethiopia has traveled since then. We will travel further."

I should like to think that the young Ethiopian was right.

4

ISLAM IN AFRICA

GEOGRAPHICALLY AND RACIALLY the Sudan stands midway between the Arab and the African worlds. It is a bridgehead between the two, being both Arab and Negroid, Islamic and pagan.

Most of the Sudan's 15 million people are in the north and comprise a majority of Arabic-speaking Moslems, while in the south are about 4 million tribesmen predominantly pagan and negroid, from whence the north originally procured its slaves. The latter include some primitive nomads and the Zande tribesmen, who are not far removed from the cannibal era. Ethnologically the Sudanese of the north are believed to be of mixed African and Arab blood superimposed on an older Hamitic stock. They are generally lighter-skinned than the Sudanese from the south and are a vibrant, attractive people. Along the Red Sea littoral are the warlike Bejas, or "Fuzzy-Wuzzies," so christened by Victorian England because of their long unruly mops of hair.

The name "Sudan" is derived from the Arabic *Bilad-es-Sudan*, which means "Country of the Blacks." When I asked General Ferik Ibrahim Abboud, who headed the military *coup d'état* on November 17, 1958, and who is now president of the supreme council of the armed forces, prime minister of the republic, and minister of defense, whether he regarded his country as a bridge between the Arab lands and Africa proper, he replied simply: "We are all Africans. Why, even southern Egypt belongs to the African world."

This was assertively endorsed by the anti-Egyptian Sayed Abdalla Bey Khalil, a former prime minister and secretary-general of the UMMA (Independence) party, who was later placed in temporary detention. "I have not a drop of Arab blood in me," Khalil proclaimed proudly, thumping his chest. "I am a Nubian, an African."

But others one encountered stressed the betwixt-and-between role of the Sudan and its people.

A typical Sudanese reaction came from another ex-prime minister, also later held for a while in detention, Sayed Ismail El Azhari, former head of the National United Party, which won the 1953 elections, and who was then believed to be pro-Egyptian but who, to Nasser's discomfiture, plumped for independence despite or perhaps because of the antics of the "Dancing Major," the late Salah Salem.

Said Azhari: "We are neither Arabs nor Africans. We are just Sudanese."

The question of racial admixture is important insofar as it affects the Sudanese attitude internally and externally, within the country as between the north and the south, and outside it toward countries such as Egypt and Ethiopia. General Abboud stressed that the Sudan's relations with its neighbors were uniformly friendly, a view echoed by El Azhari, who, however, remarked that Ethiopia was feudal and conservative. "The Sudan's attitude to Ethiopia," he added, "has nothing to do with the religious outlook of the Ethiopian government."

The other ex-premier, Khalil, supported the good-neighbor policy with one important reservation: "Only Egypt," he remarked, "has designs on us, and Nasser is attempting to influence opinion in the Sudan by radio and newspaper propaganda. Some people are trying to help him." He did not specify who they were, but obviously it was an oblique thrust at the spiritual leader of the Khatima sect, El Sayed Sir Ali Mirghani Pasha, a wizened and wily octogenarian known widely as "The Fox," whom I also interviewed. Sir Ali was elaborately noncommittal, but his sympathies are reported to be strongly pro-Egyptian and, like his then rival, the late Imam of Ansar,* grandson of the Great Mahdi, Mohamed Ahmed, who freed most of the Sudan from Egyptian misrule and tyranny, he appeared to be very eager to Islamize the pagans of the south.† I heard it said in Khartoum that the military coup of November, 1958, was precipitated by the fear that certain Sudanese elements were working to sell out to Egypt.

* He died in October, 1961.
† In October, 1963, there were reports of unrest in southern Sudan, sparked by a rebel organization calling itself "Anyanya." Khartoum is suspicious of the activities of the Christian missionaries, some of whom have been expelled from the Sudan.

The late Mahdi, when I met him in his palace at Omdurman, remarked mildly that there were still some pro-Egyptian elements in the Sudan, but his entourage's ire was directed chiefly against Coptic Ethiopia.

The Sudan excels in human resources even if it lacks material wealth. The Sudanese are a virile, frank, friendly people who reminded me of the Pathans of the former North-West Frontier Province of India, now in Pakistan. The women also are intelligent and active. Two women teachers, one of them accompanied by her fiancé, drove us one morning to a village near Khartoum where I was surprised to see that the women wore no purdah and talked without a trace of self-consciousness to the strangers brought suddenly into their midst. The women even shook hands with us. It was an urbanized village. But there was no suggestion of slumming on the part of our educated hostess, who was greeted and treated by the villagers as an equal. We sat in their huts, where they offered us orangeade and soggy cakes, and talked freely of their own little world.

But this is not typical of the Sudan, where the question of women's emancipation can provoke sharp controversy, though as elsewhere in the world the younger generation is increasingly less orthodox and more assertively independent.

"My wife," remarked a Sudanese official, "is in purdah, but not my young sister."

If the north differs racially from the south, geographical propinquities are also diverse. Christian, Islamic, and pagan Africa are the Sudan's neighbors. To the east lie the high plateaus of Christian Ethiopia, with Egypt on the north, while on the west are Equatorial Africa and the wastes of the Sahara, which edge to the Sudan's northern frontier, where the soil is arid in an almost rainless zone. To the south are tropical forests, which extend over the frontier into the former Belgian Congo and Uganda. Here the rainfall is heavier and the land more lush and fertile. The rain follows the river, fading as the Nile moves northward to the Mediterranean. The Blue and the White Nile—rising, respectively, from Lake Tana in Ethiopia and Lake Victoria in Uganda—meet at Khartoum, where they mingle their waters and flow onward as the Nile proper for nearly another 2,000 miles through the Sudan and Egypt into the delta leading to the sea. The confluence of the two Niles at Khartoum presents an unusual sight with the two streams, blue and muddy brown, running alongside one another for some distance before they merge into one.

Nature links Egypt with the Sudan, for the Nile, which traverses the Sudan from south to north, is really Egypt's lifeline. With far scantier rainfall than her southern neighbor, Egypt is even more dependent on this waterway. One of the main reasons for the Anglo-Egyptian reconquest of the Sudan in 1898-1899 was the necessity of securing control of the Upper Nile, on whose waters Egypt's economy relied.

For about fifty-five years—from the Anglo-Egyptian condominium of January, 1899, which established the joint sovereignty of Britain and Egypt throughout the Sudan,* until the Anglo-Egyptian accord of February, 1953, which terminated the condominium, leaving the Sudan free to choose its own future within three years—the destinies of Egypt and the Sudan were linked. Because of the condominium, the Sudan, though under British authority, was never a member of the Commonwealth. In 1956, to the dismay of Egypt, which had hoped for a continuation of the association, the Sudan plumped for independence.

The Sudanese prize their independence. General Abboud, who is also the kaid or commander in chief, politely stressed this when I saw him in his room at army headquarters, Khartoum.

"We have friendly relations with Egypt and we want to maintain them," he explained. "We have good relations with both Arabs and Africans, but it must be realized by all that, so far as the Sudan is concerned, it is a completely independent country and intends to remain so."

This attitude is as typical of the Arab countries of North Africa as of the newly emergent nations south of the Sahara.

Neither economically nor politically does the Sudan believe in any ism. Unlike Egypt, she stands neither for socialism nor for Arab nationalism. The Egypto-Sudanese equation is interesting in that, while the Sudan desires peace and friendship with the African and Arab worlds, Nasser's objective is domination over both. Through the United Arab Republic, where he first jockeyed Syria into an artificial union with Egypt in February, 1958, Nasser planned to sit astride the Arab world on the Mediterranean littoral of North Africa, and across the Red Sea where Syria, Lebanon, Iraq, Jordan, Saudi Arabia, Yemen, and the sheikdoms of the Persian Gulf represent Arabia in Asia. Simultaneously, he planned to extend his influence over Africa south of the Sahara. To Nasser the Arab world stretches from the Atlantic coast to the Persian Gulf. The creation of the United Arab Republic was signalized by the issue of a new stamp, which showed an eye watching over both continents. In Nasser's own eyes, Syria's union with Egypt was a manifestation of Afro-Asian solidarity—a beginning, he hoped, of a unified Arab world extending across two continents under Egypt's hegemony and molded in the pattern of Nasserism.

Syria's abrupt secession in September, 1961, impaired Nasser's prestige immediately in the Arab sphere of influence and also consequently in the African world. Though a devout Moslem, Nasser is more interested in

* There is only one similar arrangement today—the island of New Caledonia in the South Pacific, which is administered jointly by France and Britain.

propagating Pan-Arabism than Pan-Islamism. Unfortunately for Cairo, Syria's secession showed that Arab alliances were as shifting as the sands on which they are built, and, following the collapse of the U.A.R., new alignments temporarily emerged, with Syria drawing closer to Iraq* through a trade agreement between the two countries, which signified a step toward making Arab economies complementary but not toward a full-blooded Arab economic union such as Nasser's U.A.R. had envisaged, with ultimate political absorption in and domination by Egypt. Syria simultaneously suggested an Arab confederation, or a Pan-Arab union, but this provoked no positive response anywhere. Since then Syria's internal politics have undergone several shifts and changes, as have Iraq's.

The pattern of the Middle East in which Nasser had hoped to plant one dominant foot, the other being in sub-Saharan Africa, grows increasingly fluid and confused. Iraq had previously embroiled itself with Kuwait by the late General Kassem's foolish claim to sovereignty over this oil kingdom, which, if absorbed in Iraq, would make the latter the richest of the Arab countries. Kuwait resisted and was supported generally by Arab opinion, which was symbolized in the Arab forces, including an Egyptian contingent, which went to her aid. One outcome of the Syrian countercoup in September, 1961, was Nasser's mysterious decision to withdraw the U.A.R. contingent from Kuwait, which provoked speculation on how loyal to its president the Egyptian army still was. Was Nasser nervous about exposing his younger officers to the blandishments and pressures of the Jordanians, Kuwaitis, and Saudis? Subsequently reports of military arrests in Cairo gave these rumors an edge, though they lacked confirmation.

Nasser's mystique that Cairo represents the cement which binds and holds together the Arab world was challenged inside Egypt by his candid friend, the newspaper editor Hassanein Heikal, who shortly after the Syrian debacle wrote that the "hero personality" could never become the foundation for an Arab union. The personality cult, he argued, was not enough, for, granting that Nasser's personality and popularity were the only links which bound Egypt and Syria, something more was obviously needed.

Nasser's answer was a massive program of nationalization and socialism, which was initially applied in July, 1961, to both Egypt and Syria, and was intensified in Egypt after Syria's breakaway. Here, perhaps, he commands the following of the Arab masses and of the younger Arab intellectuals to a greater degree than is generally supposed or admitted. For many years the Pan-Arab Socialist youth movement and the intellectuals have been the mainstay of the Baath party in Syria, and counted some clandestine supporters even in Nuri's Iraq. They are largely pro-Nasser and pro-U.A.R. After Nuri's assassination, the chief opponents of the Communists

* Then under Kassem.

in Iraq were the left-wing National Democrats and the Kurdish Democrats. This, however, brought Nasser and Kassem no nearer. Kassem's revolt in Iraq, like Nasser's in Egypt, signified a protest against outmoded feudalism. But each went his own separate way, with Iraq rejoicing jointly with Jordan over Nasser's reverses and discomfitures. Jordan and Iraq were among the first to recognize the Syrian countercoup against Nasser. Moreover, militant socialism has no attraction for the Trucial sheikdoms on the gulf, or for the backward kingdom of Saudi Arabia, or for Jordan. Its influence is slight in Lebanon, which is more Christian than Moslem, with the highest living standards in the Arab world and the highest literacy and highest health rating. Lebanon, in turn, split with Iraq by giving diplomatic recognition to Kuwait.

The concept of "Arab Socialist Union," though officially applying only to Egypt, has a wider relevance, and in Nasser's view represents a pattern applicable to the entire Arab world. This pattern is symbolized by the slogans of "unity," "socialism," and "freedom," but their acceptance by the Arab world obviously depends on how these slogans are put into practice. Syria's initial experience with Egypt represented a blow to Nasserism, which was revealed as something different from what it professed to be. To their consternation, the Syrians soon discovered that Nasser's concept of Arab unity demanded an organic fusion with Egypt as the nucleus of Afro-Asian solidarity. In another context, one reason why Nasser and Nkrumah are at loggerheads is that Ghana's now deflated dictator had a similar vision of Pan-Africanism, with Ghana as the hub round which the wheel of African unity would revolve.

The United Arab Republic was initially accepted in Syria by both the conservatives, represented by men such as President Shukry Kuwatly, and more reluctantly by the radicals, represented by the Socialist Baathists whose founder and secretary-general, Michael Aflak,* while a strong progressive, has no desire to keep Syria in the leading strings of Nasser. Both were quickly disillusioned, the former sooner than the latter, though both had plumped for unity with Egypt as an alternative to Syria being "Bolshevized" and drawn into the Soviet orbit. One of the conditions laid down by Nasser as the price of unity was the dissolution of all parties in Syria, which pleased neither the conservatives nor the radicals. The former were soon to discover that the union operated in favor of Egyptian businessmen, while the latter were disturbed by the rise of unemployment and the fall in the workers' living standards. Syria's natural market is Iraq, which was closed to it following the rupture of relations between Kassem and Nasser. Additionally, Nasser's agrarian reforms alienated the landowners.

* Aflak, like the former Syrian prime minister, Salah-el-Bitar, is a Sorbonne graduate. Aflak is a Christian; Bitar is a Moslem.

The imposed single-party system was equally a disappointment, having failed in Egypt itself, as the record of the Liberation Rally, the National Assembly, and the National Union showed. It left no room for the practice of political democracy within the state or union, where the reins were in the hands of Nasser and his junta of advisers. The Nasser regime has undoubtedly improved the social conditions of Egyptian workers and peasants, and, given the opportunity, might have done the same for the Syrian proletariat. But the condition of the Syrian workers and peasants was already vastly better than that of their counterparts in Egypt, and the Syrian standard of living at all levels was superior to that of the Egyptian. Egypt had surplus labor, which she was tempted to dump into Syria, depressing wages there. The first breakup of the union also caused fissures within the Baath party and, far from strengthening the advance of socialism in Syria, to some degree retarded it. Akram Hourani, former leader in Syria of the Baath party, pointedly protested, "Political democracy should not be crushed in the name of social justice."

The Arab world suddenly awoke to the fact that the Egyptian concept of Arab unity (*Wahida Awabiya*) was not theirs. Indeed it spelled a new imperialism, with Egypt not only as the chief pacemaker for social and economic advancement, but as an undisguised aspirant to political leadership. The sole basis on which Nasser was then willing to fashion Arab unity appeared to be socialism as he conceived it, and a political system where Egypt and he were dominant. To the highly individualistic Arab this seemed, as it still seems, more a challenge than a friendly invitation to cooperate in a common cause. Egypt seemed to be aspiring to domination, not cooperation, and the Arab world did not appear prepared to accept Egypt at its own estimation. Arab leaders praise Nasser as a "lion," but very few of them are inclined to enter his den. An archaic reaction to these developments was a conference of sheiks and *ulemas* sponsored by King Saud at Mecca to revive Islam as a political movement in opposition to Arab nationalism. This was followed by the fifth session of the World Islamic Conference at Baghdad which, however, concerned itself with largely secular subjects viewed in the Islamic context.

Between Islam and socialism, as Nasser realizes, is a link which makes it comparatively easy for radical economic doctrines to be propagated among the downtrodden masses of North Africa and simultaneously to embarrass the older feudal kingdoms across the Red Sea. Islam, with its stress on the equality and brotherhood of man, and its condemnation of usury, carries a superficial Socialist gloss, and Nasser, while concentrating on the achievement of Pan-Arabism, is not unaware of Islam as a potent instrument in achieving that objective.

From Nasser's own book, *The Philosophy of the Revolution*, it is clear

that this is his priority and pattern—the forging of a united Arab nationalism as an instrument to mold African unity under the banner of Cairo's
leadership and of Islam. Hitler, as later events proved, was baring his
mind in *Mein Kampf*. So is Nasser. To regard him as just another ranting
megalomaniac, as the democratic world did in its first assessment of Hitler,
could be facile and foolish. But the odds are more heavily weighted against
Nasser than they were against Hitler, and, though history has a habit of
repeating itself, men occasionally learn from their mistakes.

In *The Philosophy of the Revolution* Nasser visualizes Egypt as the
center, one might almost say the epicenter, of three concentric circles.
First and foremost is the Arab circle, with the unification of the Arabs as
the primary task. "If anybody," he writes, "tells me that the place for me
means this capital where we live, I differ with him. And if anyone tells me
that the place for us means the political boundaries of our country, I also
differ. Can we fail to see that there is an Arab circle surrounding us—that
this circle is a part of us, we are a part of it?" The original Egyptian constitution, which proclaimed Egypt to be "an Islamic Arab state under a
republican and democratic form of government," emphasizes the same
point. "We, the Egyptian people," it declares, "realize that we form an
organic part of a greater Arab entity, and are aware of our responsibilities
and obligations toward a common Arab struggle for the glory and honor of
the Arab nation." The new Egyptian constitution of January, 1956, drops
out the term "Islamic" and describes Egypt as "an Arab State." It no
longer proclaims Islam as the state religion.

The second circle is Africa. Here Nasser is no less explicit, for he sees
the Middle East as the crossroads of the world, forming a land bridge
between Europe, Africa, and Asia, an in-between world which belongs to
neither of the three continents, but carries on it the impress of the faith of
Islam and of the Arab civilization. It is a nodal point of air communications, and its wealth is oil. "We are in Africa," declares Nasser in his book.
"The peoples of Africa will look to us who guard their northern gate and
who constitute their link with the outside world. We will never in any circumstances be able to relinquish our responsibility to support with all our
might the spread of enlightenment and civilization to the remotest depths
of the jungle." Plainly Nasser sees the Arab world as the torchbearer of
enlightenment and civilization in darkest Africa.

The third circle represents world domination, projected through all
those who profess the Islamic faith in all corners of the earth. "When I
consider the eighty million Moslems in Indonesia," Nasser muses, "and the
fifty million in China, and the millions in Malaya, Siam and Burma, and
the nearly hundred million in Pakistan, and the more than a hundred million in the Middle East and the forty million in the Soviet Union, together

with other millions in far-flung parts of the world—when I consider these hundreds of millions united by a single creed, I emerge with a sense of the tremendous possibilities which we might realize through the cooperation of all these Moslems." Nasser's ecstatic imagination leads him into numerical hyperbole, but his meaning and objective are clear—the Crescent over the world, with Egypt in the self-ordained role of leading the Arabs, Moslems, and Africans to a new Promised Land.

The African stress on *négritude*, on the African Personality, which Nyerere once interpreted to me as "a feeling of togetherness," finds an echo in much of Nasser's reflections on the Arabs. Writing in an American magazine, Nasser ponders: "To me Arab nationalism means many things. Above all it is a spiritual drive, a voluntary solidarity of the Arab peoples everywhere based on a common heritage of language, culture and history. This is a feeling that comes from the heart; it cannot be imposed." Here, however, Nasser begs the question much as Nkrumah does when he talks of the African Personality, for while undoubtedly the emotional ties which bind the Arab peoples and the world of Islam are as strong as, if not stronger than, the sense of community and kinship based on long memories of common suffering which bind the Africans together, the divisive factors are assertive among both peoples, despite the mystique which infuses and inspires each.

Excluding the small sheikdoms around the Persian Gulf, and the Arabian and Red seas, some of which, however, are far richer as a result of oil than is Egypt, there are now ten Arab states in the Middle East and North Africa.* Only three things unite them—Arab nationalism, the common bond of Islam, and opposition to Israel—but differing traditions and historical developments, political rivalries, and religious sectarianism divide them at many points.

Traditionally, there has been the ancient clash of empires between the land of the Nile, which is Egypt, and the land of the Euphrates and the Tigris, which was Mesopotamia and is now Iraq. Over the centuries, one empire has intermittently lorded it over the other, the fabled Haroun-al-Rashid controlling the land of the Nile from Baghdad in the eighth century, while three centuries later the Fatimites of Egypt ruled over the river basins of Mesopotamia. A more modern equivalent was the rivalry between Nasser and Nuri, to whom Kassem succeeded.

There are again the political differences between the Wahabis of Saudi Arabia and the Hashemite rulers of Jordan, a dynasty which until recently also ruled in Iraq, added to which are the religious overtones which lead the puritanical Wahabis to look down on the less orthodox Moslems of

---

* Saudi Arabia, Syria, Lebanon, Jordan, and Iraq across the Red Sea, and Egypt, Tunisia, Morocco, Algeria, and Libya on the Mediterranean littoral of North Africa.

Egypt, Jordan, and Syria. Egypt's efforts to draw Syria, Jordan, and Lebanon into its political orbit met initially with temporary success in Syria's case, but have generally failed. Cairo's relations with Saudi Arabia are frigid, and that oil-rich kingdom, now surpassed in petroleum production by Kuwait, regards Nasser's expansionist plans with uneasy distrust and disquiet. So does Kuwait, to which Kassem staked a claim, and the smaller oil center of Qatar. Egypt's population of 26 million, the largest among the Arab countries,* lives precariously off some 7 million acres of intensively cultivated land. If Nasser could only get access to the oil-rich territories, his dream of an Egyptian hegemony over the Arab and African world would be nearer realization, though publicly he deprecates any such ambition on the ground that Egypt's economy depends greatly on the Suez Canal shipping dues, and it is in the country's interests to keep the oil moving through. The unfettered control of the Nile waters would also help Egypt's productivity. But here the Sudan politely bars the way. Tunisia's relations with Egypt, though temporarily repaired by the Bizerta crisis of July, 1961, have never been equable or happy, and Bourguiba's earlier denunciation of Egypt's "Pharaonic megalomania" is not forgotten in Cairo. Relations between Egypt and Algeria also show signs of chilling, and Nasser realizes, as does Ben Bella, that the latter, for all Cairo's braggadocio, has more seasoned troops, blooded in war, behind him. Thus neither the Arab nor the African world south of the Sahara is willing to accept Nasser's hegemony. "Getting Arabs to agree to anything is like nailing Jell-O to a wall" is a gibe common among Western diplomats in the Middle East. If anything, the Africans are beginning to display even more individualism, which is why Nkrumah's dream of Ghana's overlordship in Africa has even less chance of succeeding than Nasser's vision of an Arab world dominated by Cairo.

Apart from these schisms and divisions is the cleft in the Islamic world between the Sunnis and the Shias. Though the overwhelming majority of Moslems—quite 90 percent—are of the Sunni or orthodox faith, the Iranians, though not Arabs, are Shias, as are also the inhabitants of the Yemen. Most of the Iraqi Moslems are also Shias, but the overall majority, if one includes the Kurds, is Sunni. There are considerable Shia minorities in Turkey, Lebanon, and Syria, where the Aga Khan has many followers. Politically, however, this sectarian cleft is of no great significance, though here and there it might temporarily tilt the scales.

In a sense the Middle East, and to a degree North Africa, is not exclusively Islamic or Arab. Turkey, Iran, and Israel are non-Arab states, and even among the Egyptians, who represent one of the oldest civilizations,

---

* The population increase is over 500,000 a year. By 1980 the total would be nearly 40 million.

there is a tendency, which surfaces in unguarded moments, to speak of the Egyptians as distinct from the Arabs. Again, Islam, Christianity, and Judaism have each a place in the so-called Arab world, which is a crucible of races, religions, and sects. Can Egypt hope to superimpose an Islamic pattern on the Arab and African worlds when neither will accept the unchallenged authority of any one supranational state?

Even the former trusteeship of Somaliland, like the Sudan before independence, viewed Egyptian activities in its region with suspicion. In one of their petitions to the U.N., the representatives of Somaliland complained of Egypt's officious intrusions: "They [the Egyptians] say 'we brought you religion' but at the same time they mix religion with politics. We do not need their talk about religion. We were Moslems before they came. We ask the United Nations to stop these men from what they are doing." Nasser realizes that, just as the Sudan offers Egypt a convenient channel for penetration into sub-Saharan Africa, control of the Somali areas would enable him to overlook the approaches to the Red Sea and the Gulf of Aden, thereby enabling Egypt to spread its tentacles into East Africa. But neither Somalia nor the Sudan is willing to serve as a springboard for Cairo.

Again, some of the territories below the Sahara, such as northern Nigeria and the former French Sudan, are Moslem but non-Arab. The Arab bond is not as overwhelming and pervasive as Nasser seems to imagine. South of the Sahara, African reactions to Egyptian chauvinism have been equally sharp and, apart from the Nigerian press, Nigerian leaders have expressed their resentment forcefully. Thus Chief Obafemi Awolowo, former leader of the opposition Action Group in Nigeria's federal parliament and ex-premier of western Nigeria, was brutally frank in a statement of policy he issued as far back as September, 1958, on the eve of the London conference on Nigeria. "There is no community of interest whatever," he declared, "between Egypt and the Arab states on the one hand, and the other states of Africa, particularly those inhabiting the area south of the Sahara. We believe, in particular, that the activities of President Nasser in Egypt should be closely watched, as his attitude to non-Arab Africans does not appear to be conducive to mutual cooperation. It is clear that President Nasser will tolerate only an Arab leader for the continent of Africa. He is apparently convinced that the black peoples of Africa are backward and that Egypt has a mission of leadership to fulfill on the continent of Africa."

Nasser's line of reasoning is obvious. If Egypt does not dominate Africa, Africa will dominate Egypt. To his way of thinking, Africa is merely a projection of Greater Arabia, of which Egypt is the hub. But this view is fiercely resented and actively opposed in Africa north and south of the Sahara, in the Islamic Mediterranean belt no less than in the Bantu world below the straggling desert wastes. All in all there is no such thing as Arab unity, though there is Arab nationalism.

As an Indian I was intrigued by the fact that the Arab League, like the Indian National Congress, was partly a British creation and motivated by the same aim, to develop a form of nationalism or integration beneficial to Britain. Previous British attempts to form a Greater Syria, uniting Iraq, Jordan, Syria, Lebanon, and Palestine under Hashemite rule, failed. The Arab League was also born of a genuine Arab desire to reforge Arab unity, which the breakup of the old Ottoman Empire had destroyed. The ties which held the Arab League together weakened with the spread of independence in Arab lands, just as divisiveness has surfaced inside the Indian National Congress following India's independence. If Israel were to disintegrate and disappear, which is unlikely, one of the major focal points of Arab "togetherness" would vanish, leaving only the tenuous lifelines of Islamic brotherhood and Arab unity. Ironically, the Arabs and the Jews are racially akin, both being Semitic. Arabic is a Semitic language, its script deriving from the Aramaic, which Jesus spoke. The roots of Islam, Judaism, and Christianity are thus closely related.

Socialism is no new exotic growth in Africa, north or south of the Sahara. It existed long before Nasser achieved power. Trade unionism had fairly firm roots even before independence in the Sudan, Tunisia, Algeria, and Morocco, though its affiliations here were principally Communist, and a similar alignment governed the trade unions in French West Africa, where the Communist-controlled Confédération Générale du Travail made considerable inroads into the movement. It was strong also in Nigeria and on the Gold Coast, now known as Ghana. Indeed, with the growth of towns and the spread of industrialization between the two world wars and after, trade unionism was bound to expand in Africa. Mixed unions with white, Negro, and colored members worked effectively in South Africa before enforcement of apartheid.

Since the advance of independence, the political alignments which divide Africa are reflected in the economic sphere, where initially the two principal world trade union organizations—the Communist World Federation of Trade Unions (WFTU) and the International Confederation of Free Trade Unions (ICFTU)—contended for a foothold. ICFTU was by far the more successful of the two, particularly in the regions outside the Casablanca constellation, which consisted of the U.A.R., Ghana, Guinea, Mali, and Morocco.* In May, 1961, the Casablanca Powers sponsored the creation of the All-African Trade Union Federation (AATUF), which immediately called on all African unions to leave ICFTU within ten

* The prime minister of the then Algerian Provisional Government (GPRA) and the foreign minister of Libya, as well as an observer from Ceylon, were present at the first Casablanca conference in January, 1961.

months. This order of virtual ostracism was also extended to the International Federation of Christian Trade Unions (IFCTU).

Moscow was quick to welcome the creation of AATUF, and WFTU followed suit, urging Africans to support this organization, which consists of government-dominated trade unions who take their cue from their respective governments, more especially in Ghana and the U.A.R. The unions reflect the government's will, and carry out their behests and policies. The socialism of Nkrumah and Nasser is in essence the National Socialism of Hitler. Arab nationalism, like the African Personality, is the antithesis of communism, and neither Nasser nor Nkrumah recognizes the dictatorship of the proletariat. Both lay stress on nationalism and socialism, but whereas Nkrumah visualizes nationalism in terms of Africa, Nasser sees it in the image of Arab nationalism, a natural link between Asia and Africa. Like Nkrumah, who projects the African Personality, Nasser propagates the Arab Personality. The focal target of the two men also differs. The main enemies of Hitler were communism and so-called "World Jewry." Nasser's enemies are the Western colonialists and Israel. It is typical of Africa's veering alignments that, while Nkrumah agrees with Nasser in attacking the Western colonialists as enemy number one, he is friendly to Israel, whose economic and technical assistance he has gladly absorbed. So is Nyerere in Tanganyika and Haile Selassie of Ethiopia. At the Accra conference of African states in April, 1958, an anti-Israel "Palestine" resolution was opposed by Ghana, Liberia, and Ethiopia.

To the creation of AATUF the countries outside the Casablanca bloc countered with the establishment of a new African Trade Union Confederation (ATUC) at a conference held at Dakar, Senegal, in January, 1962. ATUC claims to represent forty-one labor organizations from thirty countries. Thus AATUF and ATUC symbolize, respectively, the two economic faces of two rival political blocs, the Casablanca group and the Monrovia group,* which includes the Brazzaville group of twelve former members of the French African community,† and which has the sympathy of Liberia, Nigeria, Sierra Leone, Tunisia, Somalia, Libya, Ethiopia, and the Sudan. The Sudan did not attend the Monrovia conference held in May, 1961, because of differences with Ethiopia, but Libya, which had attended the Casablanca conference, was also present at Monrovia. This Senussi kingdom is acutely conscious of its position as the

* Now ostensibly united.
† These are the Republic of Congo, the Ivory Coast, Upper Volta, Niger, Dahomey, Mauritania, Senegal, Gabon, the Central African Republic, Chad, Cameroun, and Togo. Malagasy (formerly Madagascar) is associated with the Brazzaville group in what is known as the "African States Union and Malagasy."

first postwar independent state created among North Africa's former colonial territories.

Thus loyalties are divided sharply by territorial rivalries within both groups and between members of the two. Within the Monrovia group, Ethiopia has differences with Somalia and the Sudan; Libya is suspicious of Tunisia; while Morocco has annexationist ambitions vis-à-vis Mauritania. Inside the Casablanca group, Mali, two years after leaving the French Community of Nations, entered into an economic, cultural, and technical assistance pact with France, and is a member state along with the Brazzaville group of the French franc zone. Mali, with Guinea, is also an enthusiastic participant in the social and economic programs of the Commission for Technical Cooperation south of the Sahara, known by its French initials as CCTA. Ghana, though it has joined the commission, is not overly cooperative, but vis-à-vis neighboring Togo it appears to cherish the same annexationist ambitions as Morocco vis-à-vis Mauritania. The irredentist spirit is rife among the bigger African states.

"Africa is always giving birth to miracles," declared President Léopold Senghor of Senegal at the concluding session of the Lagos conference in February, 1962. Africa is also perpetually giving birth to surprises. The murky blueprint for Pan-African unity which emerged from Lagos, and later from Addis Ababa in May, 1963, was more an affirmation of hope than a charter of positive achievement and accord, designed for consultation rather than for action, and highlighting the fact, as Dr. Azikiwe, president of Nigeria, stressed in his opening address, that unless the ideological differences which separate the Casablanca group from the majority of African states were bridged and the larger territorial units agreed to live in peaceful coexistence with the smaller, the dream of Pan-African unity would remain a mirage. One result of this was the charter of unity devised at Addis Ababa which set up a thirty-one-state African assembly, representing both the former Casablanca and Monrovia groups.

Nigeria, which is Africa's largest state in terms of population,* is Ghana's bitter rival. Again, though Ghana and the U.A.R. spearhead the Casablanca group, Accra eyes Cairo suspiciously, as does Lagos, where the Nigerian press, commenting on the absence of the Casablanca group at the Lagos conference, accused Nasser of putting the question of Arab unity above that of African unity. Nasser in turn is accused by his own Arab kinsmen of aspiring to the hegemony of the Arab world. "The hard truth," noted a writer in the Nigerian *Daily Times* of February 2, 1962, commenting on the abstention of the Casablanca group because of Algeria's omission from the list of invitees, "is that one group cannot pursue their own aims with such aggressive insistence that they attract

* Fifty million.

antagonism to themselves. The Afro-Arabs must scrupulously avoid behaving in any manner that would be suspected among Afro-Negroes, thus leading to a dangerous feeling among the latter that Arab nationalism takes preference over African unity."

The dream of Pan-African unity floats alongside the dream of Arab unity, with few points where the two converge or meet. There are sharp differences, as we have seen, on the political and economic planes within both camps and between the two. Territorially, Pan-African unity subsists as a concept largely south of the Sahara, while the ideal of Arab unity is confined mainly to the north. The developing link between north and south is Islam, which spills over the Saharan frontier into Senegal, Guinea, Mali, northern Nigeria, the southern areas of Niger and Chad, and, looping round the northern region of the Sudan through Eritrea, reaches Somalia on the east coast, from where it filters through northeastern Kenya to Zanzibar, the Coastal Strip of Tanganyika and down to Mozambique, tapering to a thin trickle in Durban.

Islam seeped into North Africa in the seventh century, a few years after Mohammed's death, and by the eleventh century had infiltrated south of the Sahara via the Saharan trade routes and the Nile to the so-called "Sudan Belt" stretching from the Atlantic Ocean to the Red Sea. In this belt, which includes the northern areas of former French and British West Africa, we touch Negro Africa, and it is here that Moslem Negroes cluster thickest. Islam penetrated East Africa from the sea, which explains the presence of Moslem coastal communities in this area, some of whom infiltrated inland into places like Uganda.

During the past few decades Islam's progress in Africa has been spectacular, and the religious appeal of Islam to the animist African has grown progressively stronger vis-à-vis Christianity, as has also its political appeal to the more sophisticated. The average sophisticated African, however, has no fanatical religious attachment, and in Nigeria I came across families where a father, mother, sons, and wives sometimes represented a miscellany of religious beliefs and lived under the same roof in apparent concord. In Nigeria one also encountered all manner of exotic sects like the Christian Church of Cherubim and Seraphim, whose ritual and beliefs are a mixture of Moslem and Christian.

Because the teachings of Islam are enshrined in a book, the Koran, and because of its civilization and system of law, the early Christian conquerors of Africa found it more convenient to deal with the Moslem Arabs than with the primitive pagan millions who then peopled the continent. In African eyes, however, Islam, which is associated with the Arab slave traders, carried with it the taint of that vicious traffic in human beings, to which the Europeans were also later drawn and which many Africans, as we have seen, actively aided and abetted. But Islam, unlike Christianity, was not identified by the Africans with colonial oppression, it had no color bias, and it preached the equality and brotherhood of man. Islam fitted more easily into the African's way of social life, which, for instance, recognizes polygamy, and into his political pattern, which accepts theocracy as symbolized by the tribal chief. It came also as a distinct civilization, offering a challenge to the West, but in some of its manifestations, particularly in its socioreligious system, it tended to be rigidly conservative and, while giving the Africans a new sense of equality, it created feudal backwaters and socially anachronistic societies, as in northern Nigeria. The younger generation of Moslem converts, as for example the Yoruba of western Nigeria, are noticeably more liberal and advanced than the older school of converts.

Islam's political influence, despite Nasser's efforts, is relatively slight in Africa south of the Sahara, and even in North Africa political alignments by no means coincide with religious beliefs. Where Moslems form a majority in the newly emergent states, as in northern Nigeria, Somalia, Senegal, and the Sudan Belt, Islam's political influence is perceptible, but elsewhere it is negligible. Even in most of the Moslem-majority states south of the Sahara, the Africans' innate secularism often asserts itself against any temptation to put religion above local loyalties.

Islam in Africa suggests some uneasy parallels to an Indian familiar with the days of the British raj and of newly won independence. I was particularly struck by them in northern Nigeria, where I had the opportunity of an interview with the premier, the egocentric and autocratic Sardauna of Sokoto, and by talks with many of his ministers, along with a number of the emirs, or local chieftains, who still adorn the political landscape.

"We in the north," said the Sardauna's information minister, Ibrahim Biu, "made the mistake of boycotting the secular schools of the British. It was only much later that we realized our error, but by then the south had established a lead."

By the "south" he meant eastern and western Nigeria. Lagos, the federal capital of Nigeria in the west, was ceded to the British in 1861, and only some forty years later, on January 1, 1900, was the Protectorate of Northern Nigeria created, with Colonel (later Lord) Lugard as the first high commissioner.

Listening to Ibrahim Biu, I thought how very much like India it was, where the orthodox Moslems after the Great Rebellion of 1857 boycotted English education until some thirty years later, when Sir Syed Ahmed Khan founded Aligarh College, now Aligarh University. It was the Indian parallel in reverse, for where in India the Moslem-majority regions ultimately broke away to form Pakistan, the Moslem-majority region of northern Nigeria has remained to dominate the entire country. Again, like many Moslems in India, the Moslems in northern Nigeria opposed independence and tried to delay it, the Sardauna of Sokoto insisting until 1953 on northern Nigeria being made a protectorate separate from the eastern and western regions. The north has a contempt for the south. Ibrahim Biu talked of Nigeria leading West Africa.

The reaction of the south was equally revealing.

"Those who contributed least to independence are now at the top," I heard Awolowo remark bitterly at Lagos during the independence celebrations.

An incalculable but intriguing factor in the changing Arab world is newly independent Algeria, which has had its teething troubles with the Arab countries fringing the Sahara, notably with Morocco and Tunisia, where Bourguiba accused Algeria of complicity in the December, 1962, plot to assassinate him. Bourguiba's support of Algerian independence was in the past tempered at times by support of De Gaulle's policies and criticism of some of the attitudes adopted by the Algerian nationalist leaders. But Tunisia had sheltered some 200,000 Algerian refugees, and also allowed the training and equipment of several thousand Algerian soldiers on its soil. In his pro-French leanings Bourguiba is close to President Houphouet-Boigny of the Ivory Coast and far away from Nasser, though the Bizerta fighting in July, 1961, led to a resumption of diplomatic relations between Egypt and Tunisia, which had been broken off in October, 1958. Both Morocco and Tunisia, however, made it clear that, while not resigning their claims to the Sahara, they are prepared to await a settlement of the problem with independent Algeria. This has yet to come. Other border states, such as Mauritania, Mali, Niger, and Chad, have also interests in the Sahara, which consists of Spanish Sahara and Algerian (formerly French) Sahara, the latter comprising the two districts or departments of Oases and Saoura, and covering an area of over 772,000 square miles, nearly four times that of France.

This "immense sea of sand" contains considerable oil and natural gas deposits, as well as iron, tungsten, and other mineral resources. Morocco's claims extend to all of Spanish Sahara and to a substantial slice of Algerian Sahara as far east as In Salah, which would include the French atomic testing ground of Reggane. Publicly, Bourguiba has claimed for Tunisia only a small strip of the Sahara in Algeria between Romani and Marker 233, but his idea of Tunisia's "Saharan window" is probably more ambitious. According to one report, the Tunisian claim extends to a corridor south of Fort Saint, all the way to the frontier of Niger, or about 400 miles farther south. This would account for a fair wedge of Saharan soil. Mali had earlier charged France with designs to create a Tuareg Republic consisting of portions of the Sahara now within Algeria, Chad, Niger, and Mali. The

Tuareg, of Berber blood, are nomadic tribesmen who inhabit mainly the western Sahara. Niger and Chad had also signed agreements with the French-run Common Organization of the Saharan Regions (OCRS), and thereby claimed a share in the Saharan oil royalties. Additionally, Algeria's threats to nationalize the Saharan oilfields and to revise the Evian agreements, which allowed the French for five years to stage atomic tests in the Sahara, have provoked vigorous protests from Paris, as have also Ben Bella's move to take over the large estates of French landlords.

For some years to come, the Algerian leaders will be too preoccupied with the task of rebuilding their ravaged country to concern themselves unduly with Africa south of the Sahara. After nearly eight years of violent warfare, Algeria gained her independence in July, 1962, only to be plunged in an internal feud for power which ended in favor of Ben Bella.* Algeria was the springboard for French expansionism in Africa in the nineteenth century, but, though reorientated toward Paris by economic necessity and by virtue of its long ties with France, it is part of the Arab world of North Africa, even if, as with Morocco and Tunisia, the gravitational pull of Paris is strong. France provides about 400 million dollars a year to the Algerian budget, and to the recovery and development programs. For all his outward aggressiveness, Ben Bella has been forced by the realities of the situation to lean more and more toward France. In January, 1963, Algeria signed agreements with France for French financial and economic credits through 1963 to the value of 1,700 million francs (over 336 million dollars).

The task of rebuilding ravaged Algeria must take some years, but nonetheless the emergence of Algeria as an independent country has had its immediate repercussions not only in Arab North Africa, but in sub-Saharan Africa, where it induced a *rapprochement* among the French Algerian leaders. It brought together the radical President Sékou Touré of Guinea and the reputedly moderate President Houphouet-Boigny of the Ivory Coast. Some months later Senegal and Mali agreed to forget past differences, and signalized this by an exchange of ambassadors and by the reopening of the railway which was closed when President Senghor and Modibo Keita parted company in 1960. Tenuous as interstate relations are

* Ben Bella has made Algeria a presidential republic and a one-party state. A constitution was approved and "elections" were held in August, 1963. The old guard, the so-called "uncles" of the revolution—Ferhat Abbas, Belkasem Krim, who negotiated the Evian agreement, Bomi Boumendjel, and Mohamed Boudiaf—were sent into exile or detention. Ben Bella rules as president, with Colonel Houari Boumedienne as first vice-president. The leader of the clandestine, largely Berber SFF (Socialist Forces Front), Hocine Ait Ahmed, revolted and was supported by the Berber forces of Colonel Mohammed Ou El Hadj in the mountains of the Kabylie. Algeria faced a threat of civil war which the frontier dispute with Morocco removed. El Hadj called off the Berber revolt. Boudiaf was released.

in Africa, these developments are indicative of a more mellow political climate, for which newly independent Algeria could claim some credit, though she herself now teeters on the brink of civil war.

Algeria's political resurgence has naturally had an even stronger impact on the Arab world of North Africa, where it initially precipitated differences with Tunisia, whom the new Algerian leaders pointedly ignored while paying court to Cairo. Bourguiba's accusation of Algerian complicity in the attempt to assassinate him further alienated the two countries. However, within two months of Bourguiba's violent denunciation, the foreign ministers of the Maghreb countries—Tunisia, Morocco, and Algeria —met around a conference table in Rabat.

An expression of Arab togetherness is the dream of a federation of North African nations which would bind Algeria, Tunisia, and Morocco in the union of the Maghreb. Bourguiba would like to add Libya and build Greater Maghreb as a counterpoise to Nasser's ambitions in North Africa. But here again divisiveness erupts. Morocco resents Tunisia's recognition of Mauritania, while both Tunisia and Morocco have claims on Algerian Sahara.

In October, 1963, Algeria was embroiled in a border fight with Morocco around two small oases, Tinjoab and Hassi Beida, in the Sahara desert area. These two oases straddle the caravan route leading from Tindouf, with its iron ore deposits, and the passageway to Mauritania, which Morocco claims, to Colomb Bechar. Hence their strategic importance. Intervention by seven African countries who formed themselves into an arbitration commission at the initiative of the Organization of African Unity set up by the Addis Ababa conference of May, 1963, halted hostilities. The seven countries are Ethiopia, Mali, Senegal, the Ivory Coast, Sudan, Tanganyika, and Nigeria. The commission is both small and neutral.

The Maghreb's relations with France, if Libya is included, would be complicated. Libya's colonial associations after a period of Turkish rule were with Italy from 1912 until the Second World War. She will find some difficulty in fitting into an association whose economic and political ties are primarily with France.

Ben Bella is no doubt aware that Algeria, with its growing material aid and rich mineral resources, along with its battle-tried army of some 120,000 veterans, can speak from a position of strength not only in the Maghreb, but to some extent in North Africa. He could in time aspire to the headship of the Arab League. Militarily, he poses the biggest Arab threat to Israel, and around Algeria now revive Arab hopes of regaining Palestine. Not that Israel has anything to learn from Algeria in the art of political terrorism or guerrilla warfare. Moreover, Israel is a compact state capable of compact defense and Ben Bella, heavily dependent on economic aid from France, is likely to move warily, even if he makes the appropriate anti-Israeli noises offstage.

With the exception of the French base at Mers el Kebir, the Evian accords gave Algeria full sovereignty over the Sahara, which in area is large enough to allow for border readjustments with neighboring Arab states without unduly constricting the Algerians. Moreover, the three Maghreb countries, which with Libya run westward along the Mediterranean, are conscious of the need for joint economic cooperation in developing and utilizing the power resources of the Sahara. The agreement signed at Rabat in September, 1963, between the foreign ministers of Algeria, Tunisia, and Morocco acknowledged the need for a closer *rapprochement* between them, even if it signified nothing else. True, such arrangements are generally short-lived in the Arab world, and the Rabat agreement was no exception. It proved as nebulous as the military and economic entente entered into between Jordan and Saudi Arabia in September, 1962. Politically the Maghreb countries appear to be poles apart, for Tunisia is pro-west, Morocco leans toward Nasser, and Algeria is neutralist.

In the Morocco-Algeria dispute, Nasser favored Algeria, a socialist republic like Egypt. Following the dispute, King Hassan of Morocco appointed Ahmed Bahnini as Prime Minister, heading a cabinet of the royalist Front for the Defense of Constitutional Institutions (FDCI). The FDCI has sixty-nine seats in the Lower House. The opposition consists of the conservative Istiqal party with forty-one seats and the Socialist National Union of Popular Forces with twenty-eight seats. While Morocco had earlier supported Ben Bella, Tunisia seemed inclined to back his rival, Ben Khedda. Whatever their political differences, the Maghreb countries are aware that economically they could work with greater mutual profit if they worked together. All three have preponderating trade ties with France. Being of common Arab and Berber stock, their cultural approach is largely similar. Ben Bella may have no Sahara policy, but the Maghreb countries realize that through mutual-benefit planning their economic and political differences have a chance of being ironed out more smoothly.

This also applies to sub-Saharan Africa. The general trend throughout the continent is now more toward closer economic association and increasingly against any type of political absorption or domination. Even undeveloped Mauritania, peopled by about 650,000 tribesmen, has argued that if Chad and Gabon can be viable and independent, so can Mauritania. Nasser's initial contretemps with Syria demonstrated that his policies ran counter to this trend. The overthrow of Kassem in Iraq has drawn Cairo and Baghdad closer. But this does not automatically imply that the new Iraqi regime is prepared to tie itself to Nasser's apron strings. The inclusion of seven Baathist ministers in the cabinet headed by Brigadier Ahmad Hasan al-Bakr was again no indication that the Baathists favored close links with Egypt, for the Baathists themselves are divided into two groups—those who want to work closely with Nasser and those who, while favoring union with Egypt, insist that this is conditional on the reestablishment of a real democratic government.

Nasser, however, believes that the present dictatorship in Egypt cannot be replaced by a parliamentary system for another ten years.* And as Syria showed, Nasser's conception of Arab unity consists in clamping down Egypt's political pattern, which has no room for parties, on every country which enters the United Arab Republic. Yemen's short and uneasy association with the U.A.R. was an artificial marriage of convenience which was abruptly terminated by the then medieval-minded Imam. When the Imam's son and successor was overthrown by a rebel regime, Cairo promptly supported the rebels and backed its support with arms and men. It is interesting to speculate whether, if a strongly pro-Nasser regime emerged from the confusion in Iraq and was embroiled again with Kuwait, Nasser would rush, as he did when Kassem ruled Iraq, to Kuwait's aid.†

In March, 1963, Nasser attempted to resurrect the U.A.R.—checkmated by the Syrian countercoup of 1961—to include not only Syria, but post-Kassem Iraq. Again, for a time it looked as if he were successful. In April it was announced that Egypt, Syria, and Iraq had agreed to merge into a new federal state to be called the "United Arab Republic," with its capital in Cairo and with a total population of about 37 million. The new state would have authority for foreign affairs, finance, economy, and defense. It would have one flag—the black, white and red flag of the previous U.A.R., with three stars to represent the Egyptian, Iraqi, and Syrian "districts." It would also have a common citizenship and aspired to become a basis for linking up with other Arab states such as Algeria and Yemen. Ben Bella, however, despite his own internal problems, was not receptive to the idea of political domination by Egypt, and in Yemen the royalist elements whom Cairo had actively suborned and had assisted the rebels in dislodging proved to be less yielding than Nasser had envisaged. The Baathist parties in Syria and Iraq, under the overall inspiration of Aflak, were difficult to woo or wean. They wanted real unity, real democracy, and real socialism. Nasser's emphasis is on socialism, but his ideas on nationalism and unity are far different from those of the Baath. The U.A.R., as he conceives it, would be a one-party state consisting of 26 million Egyptians, 7 million Iraqis, and 5 million Syrians. Aflak, a Syrian,

* Interview, *The Sunday Times,* London, Feb. 10, 1963.
† Iraq recognized the sovereignty of Kuwait in September, 1963. This was preceded by a generous loan to Iraq by Kuwait.

while willing that the Baathists should cooperate with Nasser in a national union, is unwilling to be dominated. He wants the Baath to be Syrian in Syria and Iraqi in Iraq.

In October, 1963, Syria and Iraq signed an agreement establishing a military union between the two countries, and it looked as if Aflak had succeeded in checkmating Nasser. But the Baathist triumph was short-lived. In November the Iraqi Baathist extremists led by the Deputy Prime Minister Ali Salah al-Saadi, who favored a tough line with Nasser, supported radical Baathism, and stood for closer union with Syria, clashed with the moderates headed by the Prime Minister, Hasan al-Bakr. The Syrian armed forces who were irked by the activities of the National Guard, a civilian militia organized by Saadi, intervened in the conflict, disbanded the National Guard and at gunpoint bundled Saadi and some of his associates into an aircraft bound for Spain. Aflak's intervention proved abortive, provoking a bloodless coup by the pro-Nasser President Marshal Abdul Salam Aref, who seized power. In Syria the Prime Minister, Salah Bitar, was replaced by General Amin Hafez with Bitar as Vice-President. Baathist prestige in both countries suffered a bad dent and undermined the party's ambitions for Arab unity on Baathist lines, the internal rifts exposing an open clash inside the top ranks.

But this does not spell Nasser's immediate triumph, for quite apart from Iraq's legacy of blood and violence, the unity negotiations between Egypt, Syria, and Iraq have trailed an uncertain, often incalculable course. The politics of the Middle East are almost as volatile as those of Africa. Intrigue and subversion are endemic to both. The Arab world, like its African counterpart, is crisscrossed by vertical and horizontal divisions. But as the Arab summit meeting in January, 1964, of thirteen states under the presidency of Cairo proved, Egypt dominates the Arab scene and with Algeria holds the key to the future of North Africa and the Middle East.* Whether geographical proximity and political stability will enable it in time to straddle the Arab scene while its influence infiltrates further into Africa south of the Sahara is a major imponderable depending on many minor incalculables. For the time being, Arab unity can be preserved only by the closer association of equal sovereign states, whether these be kingdoms or republics, Socialist, conservative or feudal. Egypt stands for its own brand of progressive politics but as the Cairo daily *Al Ahram* stressed at the conclusion of the Arab summit meeting, Egypt did not believe it had a duty to export revolution to other Arab states though it had an obligation to protect revolutions when and where they took place. If Egypt wishes to serve as the base and apex of a unified Arab pyramid, Nasser must mellow in his attitude to his neighbors.

* In July, 1964, the second African summit meeting of over 300 Heads of State was held in Cairo.

The urge for Arab unity is strong and is likely to grow stronger. But the urge expresses itself in a concept far different from Nasser's, for while accepting the necessity for closer political and economic cooperation, it rejects the notion of a supranational state imposed over the rest. This idea of closer cooperation between independent countries is being increasingly canvassed, even if rivalries and vendettas persist north and south of the Sahara. One manifestation of it was the plea of progressive leaders like President Sékou Touré of Guinea that the Casablanca and Monrovia groups should draw closer and bridge at least some of their differences. This was achieved, at least in principle and on paper, at the Addis Ababa summit conference in May, 1963. The Casablanca group had abstained from attending a similar conference held in 1962 at Lagos. It was strengthened by the Arab summit meeting in Cairo in January, 1964.

The emergence of an independent Algeria, the rebuilding of the U.A.R., the overthrow of Kassem, and the end of Katanga's secession in the Congo presage new modes of development and thought in both the African and Arab worlds. Islam, despite its spectacular progress on the continent, is unlikely to provide a springboard for political ambitions, though it might prove to be a more cohesive social cement than either animism or Christianity. Basically, the African tends to be more superstitious than spiritual and more attached to ritual than religion. Excepting the older converts, religion sits on most like a coat. The bond of Islam to some extent binds the Arab world, but its political significance seems slight in sub-Saharan Africa.

Even here a stable, developing Algeria has an advantage over a country like Egypt, whose links with the ex-French colonies south of the Sahara are slight, whereas the former French-dominated territories in North Africa have more natural associations with such Moslem states in sub-Saharan Africa as Guinea, Senegal, Mali, Niger, and Chad, all of whom once shared the same colonial master. Nkrumah, who has isolated himself in his own state and in the continent by his self-induced dreams of grandeur, though he is (so far unsuccessfully) attempting a comeback, offers no serious challenge to either Africa or the Arab world. His suggestion, made after the discovery of a plot to assassinate President Tubman of Monrovia, to set up a continental union government composed of all African states as a bulwark against "the imperialists and neo-colonialists" attracted no notice, and in any case was wildly impracticable. He revived the idea at Addis Ababa, but met with lukewarm response.

Personalities still dominate in Africa, but policies are slowly taking shape, and ideologies, while differing, incline to coexist in relative peace rather than to clash sharply. Thus the trend toward one-party states is gathering momentum, alongside a determination by each state to preserve its independence within the broad framework of Arab unity on the one hand and African unity on the other. Whether the two main streams of Pan-Africanism and Pan-Arabism will ever mingle their waters, it is too hazardous and too early to say.

Egypt, it would seem, is in a position to beat the big drum of Arab nationalism, but is finding it difficult to persuade or coerce others into climbing onto her bandwagon. The Arab world is beginning to question Nasser's easy assumption that he is its leader, and his subversive tactics in hostile Arab countries, his crude propaganda machinery to revile his opponents, and his habit of appealing to the Arab peoples over the heads of their governments are especially resented. But if Nasser is prepared to respect the political independence of other states while continuing to preach social justice and Arab unity, he might yet succeed in his dream of giving Arab nationalism a positive content without investing it with a negatively aggressive front.

"GIANT IN THE SUN"

AS WE SAT in the throne room awaiting the entry of the Emir of Kano, Alhaji Sir Muhammadu Sanusi,* a series of loud cries and bellows from the interior of the palace heralded his imminent arrival. Bird, the pleasant-mannered acting British Resident at Kano, turned to me. "Here he comes," he said.

We rose as the attendants, still shouting, entered the room, followed by the emir, a tall, bespectacled man wearing a billowing blue robe with fantastically outsized ostrich-feather shoes shrouding his feet. Bird, who had been some sixteen years in Nigeria, and spoke Hausa fluently, introduced me. The emir greeted me in English. He had a limp handshake.

He was carrying a two-pronged green staff, which an attendant placed on the ground before his feet as he took his seat on his throne, a gaudy settee with a colorful curtain as a backcloth. He spoke with Bird for a few minutes in Hausa, then looked inquiringly at me.

Two years previously the emir had provoked an uproar by stating in an interview to an American journalist that even after independence the Maliki or orthodox Islamic law prevailing in northern Nigeria would con-

* He resigned in March, 1963, following an inquiry into the financial affairs of the Kano Native Authority, and was succeeded in April by his uncle, Alhaji Muhammadu Inuwa, as the twelfth emir, who died in October, 1963.

tinue to apply. Under this law no Moslem could be executed for killing a non-Moslem, and in certain cases non-Moslems were precluded from giving evidence in court. Since then the emir has been averse to meeting journalists, and I learned later that he was persuaded to see me only with some difficulty. It was, however, stipulated that our conversation should be purely formal.

I began by asking the emir if he had been abroad. Yes, he had gone to England for the first time in 1934 with his father, the late Emir Alhaji Abdullah Bayero.* He had also visited the United States and Canada in 1959 with the Sardauna of Sokoto. How was he impressed by the United States? The emir's reaction was very like that of the crown prince of Ethiopia. He thought the tempo of American daily life far too fast.

"I couldn't guess what they were hurrying about," he observed, adding solemnly as an afterthought: "Some of them seemed to be mad."

A few more verbal pleasantries, and the interview ended. The emir rose, shook hands, and surrounded by his babel of attendants was bellowed out of the room with cries of what sounded like "Hutto!," which curiously is also the Hindi imperative for "Make way!"

The emir of Kano ranks third in the traditional hierarchy of northern Nigerian rulers, being preceded only by the sultan of Sokoto, who rates first, and the emir of Gwandu. But at political gatherings the Shehu of Bornu, whose religious sway extends from Bornu to Darfur in the Sudan, comes next in precedence to the sultan of Sokoto, who is the spiritual head of all Moslems in the western Sudan and is a direct descendant of the great Fulani leader, Othman Dan Fodio, who early in the nineteenth century led a *jihad* against the Hausa kingdoms,† overrunning most of them. Bornu, the homeland of the Kanuri, the third leading clan in the north, was never part of the Fulani empire of Dan Fodio. It is an ancient kingdom which dates back to the Middle Ages, and at one time controlled an empire from the Nile to the Niger.

I found myself comparing these feudal emirs with the princes as they existed in preindependence India, when in the old days as a newspaper correspondent at Delhi I used to watch their gaudy Rolls-Royces, ranging in color from vivid scarlet to bright heliotrope, sweeping by with their burden of bejeweled, turbaned, and ornately robed rulers on their way to the annual meeting of the Princes' Chamber. At Kaduna, capital of northern Nigeria, I attended a meeting of the House of Chiefs, which has fifty members and was presided over by the emir of Gwandu. Not as colorful as India's old Princes' Chamber, it had its meretricious parallels, though, unlike the Princes' Chamber, which always seemed like something out of

* He died in 1953.
† There were seven of them dating from the thirteenth century. Northern Nigeria was converted to Islam in the fourteenth century.

this world, the House of Chiefs seemed to fit more snugly into the background of northern Nigeria.

Here too the chiefs drove past in a gaudy cavalcade of cars, some of them equipped with electric horns which gave distinctive hoots identifying their occupants. "There," said a British acquaintance, "goes Sokoto, and here is Katsina."

Nigeria, described as "a giant in the sun," is Africa's most populous state, containing some 50 million people. Its territory stretches over some 373,000 square miles, with mountains, desert scrub, and arid plains in the north, and miles of mangrove swamps, rain forests, and savanna or grassland in the south. The northern, eastern, and western regions, which formed the federation when independence came, are each sharply distinct in their political attitude, their social composition, and economic structure. The north, territorially larger than the other two put together, is socially and educationally backward, but politically dominant. Here the main tribes are the Hausa-Fulani and Kanuri. The west, where two-thirds of the population is Yoruba, is the most urbanized, and the most commercially and politically conscious and advanced. No less go-ahead and purposeful are the Ibo, who constitute 66 percent of the population in the eastern region, which, however, is comparatively poor and overcrowded. Land hunger is a major affliction here, and this, coupled with economic pressures and an innate sense of individualism, accounts for the Ibo migration throughout Nigeria. The Ibo are to be found in the north as clerks in government offices and commercial houses, and in the larger cities and towns they serve in various capacities on hotel staffs and as artisans. I thought them less brash than the Yorubas and more likable. A good few work as small traders, and though they live primarily in tiny farming villages they have adapted themselves quickly to urbanization. Indeed, the Ibo's chief characteristic is his ability for adaptation.

Almost half of Nigeria's population, it is claimed, lives in the north, which contains 70 people to the square mile as compared with the eastern region's 270. According to the last census of 1952, which was held under British auspices,* the north has a larger population than the south, which comprises the eastern and western regions. This is contested in the south, particularly in the eastern region, the allegation being that the figures were unduly inflated for the north because the British wished to give it political preponderance. However, the 1920 census, when neither independence nor federation was being discussed, also showed a majority for the north.†

* There was a census held in 1962 but it was nullified as it proved unacceptable to the regional and federal leaders.

† The 1962 census figures were: North, 30,200,000; east, 12,500,000; and west, 10,500,000. Northerners and easterners accused each other of inflating their numbers. The latest Nigerian census, published in February, 1964, shows a rise in population

The Fulani-Hausa, Ibo, and Yoruba are the three main nations within the country, but there are in all some 250 tribes and languages in Nigeria and an incalculable number of dialects. The Ibo are split into hundreds of small tribes, clans, and groups, and though Nigeria claims to have twelve main languages besides English, there are as many as thirteen principal dialects in the eastern province of Ogoja alone. Literacy varies sharply. In the north the literacy rate in Roman script is barely 3 percent, compared with 16 percent in the east and 18 percent in the west. On an overall basis less than 10 percent of Nigerians know English and hardly 15 percent are literate. Among the major priorities is a rapid expansion of education. The Ashby Report, a joint Anglo-American-Nigerian effort, whose conclusions were published as Nigeria entered independence, stressed the urgency of educational standards, particularly in the primary stage and in the training of teachers. In the five years between 1955 and 1960 the federal government spent 20 percent of its total revenues on schools—the north 16 percent, the west 33 percent, and the east 43 percent. Since independence these outlays have been maintained, but at the cost of developments in other productive fields. Over 8,000 Nigerian students are now in universities, most of them in England. In itself education is no solvent of divisive trends. On the contrary, wider education seems to intensify the scramble for jobs and for places of power, as happened between the Hindus and the Moslems in India during the British period. Lowering over the south is the Moslem north, educationally backward but politically very much to the fore, underlining the disquieting moral that power is not necessarily associated with learning.

Many tribes also people the bleak north. Besides the Hausa and the ruling clan of the Fulani are the Kanuri with their strong admixture of Arab blood, but there are also the Shuwa Arabs, who have links with North Africa, and the Nupe, Tiv, Idoma, Igbira, Gwari, Ango, Tangale, Jukon, and Birom. The Tiv, who inhabit the province of Benue, are mostly animists, with a leaven of Christian converts, and are a warlike race numbering a million who once humbled the Fulani. The Tiv, with other tribes such as the Idoma and Igbira, form pagan pockets with Christian admixtures, but the north is predominantly Islamic, with Hausa as the lingua franca, and Islam and the Maliki law as the foundations of local administration and government.

The white-walled city of Kano fascinated me. Its ancient market, once as fabulous in Africa as London was in Europe, is bewildering in its con-

---

from 31,500,000 in 1952 to 55,653,821. The figures are: Northern Region (29,777,-986), Eastern Region (12,388,646), Western Region (10,278,500), Midwest (2,533,-337), Lagos (Federal Capital) 675,352. The Northern Region has more people than all the other regions combined. The figures have been challenged by Dr. Okpara, Premier of the Eastern Region.

trasts and startling in its contents. Here at the height of the season some 50,000 persons assemble to buy, barter, and trade. The open drains stink high to a blue heaven and permeate an odoriferous earth. Flies are everywhere. Ragged children abound, holding out grubby hands with cries of "dash," the Hausa equivalent for "baksheesh." Kano is noted for its weaving and embroidery, tanned red goatskin, and ornamented leather ware, its straw mats and bags, but the stalls are crowded with a jumble of imported wares, including watches from Switzerland and blankets from Czechoslovakia. There are trinkets from Birmingham and potash from Lake Chad, charms consisting of dried-up elephant pouches and snakes, birds' feathers, bones, and old shriveled roots, and kola nuts and calabash bowls, and medicine men and moneychangers. It is fantastic and incredible.

Just outside the old city, within which the mud houses stand, their walls decorated with abstract drawings and designs and with texts from the Koran, and their roofs adorned with phallic symbols, is the emir of Kano's palace, encircled also by high mud walls but with an impressive front studded with brilliant green-and-red doors. The guards' uniforms are of the same colors, the traditional colors of Kano which were first adopted by the celebrated Emir Mohammadu Rumfa, who built the present palace. Inside the palace, the walls of the throne room are plastered with shining mica, and the high-domed roofs carry ornate decorations in many colors and patterns, some of which look surrealistic, with swords, coffeepots, and airplanes as their dominating motifs. The atmosphere was redolent of Saladin and his Saracens, with a touch of Dali and Picasso, an impression heightened as we emerged into the hard noonday glare to be greeted by the grinning guards, their teeth a bright scarlet from the kola nuts they chew. A herd of long-horned Fulani cattle wended their way to the sales ring. Through a haze of dust, a posse of picturesquely clad Fulani horsemen rode by, their flowing multicolored robes swirling and swishing as they galloped past.

The western and eastern regions, collectively known as "the South," lie a little beneath the two upstretched arms of the Y formed by the Niger and the Benue as these rivers join to cascade south in a single mighty stream which spills into the Gulf of Guinea. Under the Y's left arm is the Yoruba-dominated western region inhabited by over 9 million people, and under the right arm the heavily populated, Ibo-dominated eastern region, with close to 11 million people.* Both regions bustle with activity, but in the south the tribal systems are more multicellular, complicated, and amorphous than they are in the north, where, because of the overall Islamic imprint, the social structure is more stratified and consolidated.

* The 1962 census, which was rejected, gave higher figures.

A considerable Moslem element exists in the western region—Lagos is 50 percent Moslem—and its population roughly trisects itself almost equally among animists, Christians, and Moslems, a fact which makes this area peculiarly susceptible to political controversy based on religious differences. Western Nigeria, however, is highly urbanized, and around 50 percent of the Yoruba live in towns, compared with 9 percent of northerners and 15 percent of easterners. The Yoruba's comparative freedom from religious prejudice is reflected in his household, where members of a family professing different faiths often live together under one roof. This would be difficult, if not impracticable, in India. Urbanization has also intensified a sense of local loyalty among the Yoruba, and, as in most parts of Africa, political alignments follow tribal, not religious affiliations.

Preponderant as the Yoruba are in the western region, there are districts where they do not form a majority. Edo-speaking tribes predominate in Benin and Delta provinces, which also contain a considerable minority of Ibos, Ijwas, and Itsekiri. This situation precipitated a proposal to carve a midwestern region out of the western region, which resulted in the creation of a fourth region formed of the two provinces, with Benin as the capital. The proposal, which was referred to a plebiscite in July, 1963, received overwhelming approval and fructified before October 1, when Nigeria was proclaimed a republic within the Commonwealth. The movement for the formation of a midwest region was sponsored by the midwest state movement, instigated, so it was widely alleged, by the Ibo-dominated National Convention of Nigerian Citizens (NCNC), one of the two parties forming the coalition federal government. Its moving spirit is the president, who was the first Nigerian governor-general, Dr. Nnamdi Azikiwe. The other party is the Sardauna of Sokoto's Northern People's Congress (NPC), which controls about 50 percent of the total Nigerian votes.

The motivations behind this move are complex, and to explain them as being designed to undermine the economic strength of the western region and to reduce the power of the opposition Action Group (AG), led at the time by Chief Obafemi Awolowo, is an exercise in oversimplification. Demands for a midwest state date back to about 1947, and ten years later were vociferous enough to be examined by a commission under Sir Henry Willink, which also examined non-Moslem demands for a middle-belt region in the Islamic north. Both demands were rejected. While the federal government supported the formation of the new region in the west, the NCNC was undoubtedly more interested in its creation. Ultimately, even the AG did not oppose it,* for one result of its formation was to tilt the precarious balance of stability in Nigeria's triregional, tripod form of government and to enable the south to have a majority in the upper house or

* It had supported the idea in theory as far back as 1956.

senate, holding at least thirty-six seats to the north's twelve. The major political parties eventually supported the idea, as did the midwest chiefs, including the Olu of Warri, who was initially opposed to it. Simultaneously, the demand for a middle belt region in the north is likely to grow more clamorous. There are minorities in all regions, including the eastern. The Ibo, though constituting 66 percent of the population, are in a minority in Calabar, where the Ibibios and Efiks, a great many of whom are Christians,* predominate. Here again a separate region, comprising the provinces of Calabar, Ogoja, and the Cross River, has been mooted. In the northern region the middle-belt movement, spearheaded by the Tiv, Idoma, and Igbira, favors the creation of a separate region covering broadly the Bauchi plateau. The northeastern kingdom of Bornu, homeland of the Kanuri, has always tended to hold itself conspicuously aloof from the Fulani.

Divisiveness is endemic in each of the three regions and among one another. Nigeria is a classic case of the confusion and conflict created by the artificial, compulsive clamping down of disparate regions in one colonial mold. Despite arguments that there exists a measure of ethnographic and cultural homogeneity among the people of Nigeria, there is no evidence historically of Nigeria existing as a unified entity before January 1, 1900, when the colony of Lagos and the two protectorates of northern and southern Nigeria were formally declared to be under British jurisdiction. The name "Nigeria," was suggested by Lady Lugard, who as Flora Shaw before her marriage to Lord Lugard, the founder of Nigeria, first proposed this name for the new territory in a letter to *The Times*, London, toward the end of the nineteenth century.

Lugard, who died in 1945 at the age of eighty-five, was a man of extraordinary character, prescience, and imagination. He is still recalled vividly in Nigeria by a generation that never knew him. Stories concerning him are almost a ritual at British breakfast and dinner tables, and I heard some amusing tales recounted by Sir Gavain Bell, governor of northern Nigeria, and by my old friend, Harry Twist, deputy British high commissioner at Kaduna, with whom I stayed.

Way back in those days Lugard foresaw the inevitability of freedom for Africa, and wrote with remarkable foresight: "For two or three generations we can show the Negro what we are; then we shall be asked to go away. Then we shall leave the land to those it belongs to, with the feeling that they have better business friends in us than in other white men." Characteristically, he set out to ensure this. In Nigeria and the old Gold Coast, which is now Ghana, Europeans were not allowed to own land, though they could lease it for commercial purposes. Inevitably there were

* There are over 4 million Christians but very few Moslems in the eastern region.

some exceptions, but these were few. "The land," declared Lugard, "is the property of the people, held in trust for them by their chiefs, and not purchasable by foreigners. No European may buy, sell, or speculate with land." For the European the choice was administration or trade. Perhaps the fact that the coastline abutting on the Gulf of Guinea was traditionally regarded as the White Man's Grave assisted this policy and process. But it does not dim or diminish Lugard's farsightedness or accomplishments.

To an Indian, Africa offers a study in parallels. The system of British Residents attached to the northern emirs was reminiscent of princely India in the days of the raj. Today the Sardauna has a resident commissioner attached to each emir. In India the administration was transferred from the East India Company to the British Crown in 1858, following the Great Rebellion. So also the charter of the Royal Niger Company, which operated along the rivers, was revoked on January 1, 1900, and formal responsibility for the territory was assumed by the British government. Some fourteen years elapsed before Lugard took over as governor-general of the north and the south. Nigeria was then born. Nigeria is younger than its fifty-one-year-old prime minister, Alhaji Sir Abubakar Tafawa Balewa.

Nearly four years have passed since the country achieved independence on October 1, 1960,* and the divisive forces have already begun to surface. Nigeria is a federation, but the fact that each of the three regions with which it started was self-governing and increasingly competitive with the other two tended to put the stress on the three regions separately, rather than on the country as a whole. Now there is a fourth region. Again, not only did the three regions differ in traditions, customs, language, and outlook, but each of them harbored suspicious, even resentful minorities.

Party and political loyalties are fluid and fluctuating, as the postindependence fissures in Chief Obafemi Awolowo's Action Group in western Nigeria demonstrated. The Action Group formed the government in this region until it was suspended in May, 1962. Opposing the Action Group at the center in Lagos, as also in eastern and western Nigeria, is the NCNC,† which constitutes the government of eastern Nigeria and at the federal level cooperates with the Northern People's Congress (NPC), whose leader is the fifty-three-year-old Alhaji Sir Ahmadu Bello, the Sardauna of Sokoto, who is also premier of the northern region, and whose nominee, Sir Abubakar Tafawa Balewa, is federal prime minister. Many consider the Sardauna to be the real ruler of Nigeria.

"Balewa may rule at Lagos," a European resident in the northern region observed, "but at Kaduna, the Sardauna rules. And the north rules the country."

* It was declared a republic within the Commonwealth on Oct. 1, 1963.
† Formerly known as the National Council of Nigeria and the Cameroons.

Another northern party, to which Azikiwe's NCNC is allied, is NEPU (Northern Elements Progressive Union), which at the federal level cooperates with Balewa and the NPC, but in the northern region opposes the Sardauna's government. NEPU's chief supporters are the urbanized youth of the north, but its influence seems to be on the wane. It has no appeal to the minorities. Similarly, the Action Group is allied to the United Middle Belt Congress (UMBC), which sponsors the idea of a separate region comprising the middle-belt areas in the north. Thus, the three main parties have each a regional and tribal mooring, along with affiliations with various minority groups.

Nigeria poses the problem of nationalism as envisaged by the regionalism of the south versus the feudalism of the north. But pervading all the present four units is the dominant rivalry of regionalism. Nigeria is really three countries in one, a reality projected by its three leading personalities, the Sardauna, Azikiwe, and Awolowo, who now, with various leading members of his Action Group, is in jail for treasonable felony. Both Azikiwe and Awolowo initially worked for a strong central cohesive government, so as to neutralize the political dominance of the north, but Awolowo, more tribal-minded than Azikiwe, toyed with the idea of a Yoruba-ruled Nigeria with its base in the western region. The gravitational pull of the north proved too strong. Unity was bought at a price whereby the Sardauna was enabled to hit the jackpot with the south's nickel.

The Sultan and Sardauna of Sokoto are described as cousins. A man of arrogant mien and of overweening ambition, the Sardaua is said to be more eager to succeed the Sultan than to rule as the federal prime minister.* He is a great-great-grandson of Othman Dan Fodio, founder of the Sokoto empire and has much of that personage's purposefulness, determination, and drive. He is a dominating and demanding individual.

I saw the Sardauna at the premier's office at Kaduna, where under the porch a huge, gaudy green Rolls-Royce indicated his presence. He has an impressive appearance and, sitting behind his desk in a black robe trimmed with gold, wearing a huge turban and a veil which concealed his chin, he looked regal but also sinister. He is evidently conscious of the power he wields. Northern Nigeria's two priorities, according to him, were more light industries and education. "We are doing all we can to develop them," he said.

Earlier I had talked with his education minister, Alhaji Isa Kaita, who is high in the councils of the Emir of Katsina. Kaita, like the Sardauna and Balewa, is a product of the well-known Katsina college and speaks excel-

---

* Some say he was persuaded to step aside in favor of Balewa, whom the Sardauna described as "my lieutenant at Lagos," by Sir James Robertson, the last British governor-general.

lent English. He too described the northern region's plans for developing university education, which he felt should be dispersed on the Welsh model —with law and teachers' training in Kano, courses for agricultural assistants in Katsina, technology and science elsewhere. "As our light industries develop, we shall need more technicians," he remarked.

The Sardauna's talk ranged over much the same sphere. Like his ministers, a number of whom I had met, he stressed the Islamic culture and learning of the north and did not conceal his contempt for the south. He observed that the reason why the missionaries were able to make converts in the south was because both the eastern and western regions had no cultural roots. I ventured to suggest mildly that educationally the north seemed to be less advanced than the south.

"Ho!" snorted the Sardauna. "That is because the northern Nigerians were always discriminated against when it came to sending our students for education abroad."

He was stiff and formal to begin with, but mellowed as we talked and was even gracious at the end. His basic loyalty is to Islam. "There is a close association and affinity," he remarked, "between northern Nigeria and western Sudan." He spoke of Pakistan, but only casually mentioned India. Since 1955 he has visited Mecca every year. Educationally and socially, the north is advancing slowly. The first qualified pharmacist among northern girls, Elizabeth Inusa, graduated recently from Zaria, and in other villages girls are taking more eagerly to education before marriage.

While in Kano, before coming to Kaduna, I was taken by a Sudanese, Sheik Bashir—who in Khartoum had acted as interpreter at my interview with the leader of the powerful Khatima religious sect, Sir Ali Mirghani— to a school for Arabic studies run by a staff of five Englishmen, five Sudanese, and eight Nigerians. This school is to be the nucleus of a college named after the Sardauna, from which will emerge the University of Northern Nigeria. The Sardauna realizes that Nigeria's political stability hinges on more widespread education and quicker economic development but very definitely he has his own ideas on how both should be shaped. Neither will be allowed to encroach on entrenched interests. "It is better to repair than to build afresh," runs an old Hausa saying.

The Sardauna can probably hold the north together. But can he preserve Nigeria as a compact, cohesive entity and prevent a damaging north-south confrontation? He is an explosive, extrovert personality calculated to arouse the most violent antagonisms. In his autobiography entitled *My Life* the Sardauna frankly admits he would have kept northern Nigeria out of the federation if only it had access to the sea and he could "complete the work of Othman Dan Fodio" by "dipping the Holy Koran in the ocean."

The one man who, given the time and opportunity, might hold Nigeria together is the federal prime minister. Sir Tafawa Balewa is a man of great dignity and poise, a devout Moslem, but politically a moderate who has no use for such exotic concepts as the African Personality and is genuinely concerned in building up a strong, unified Nigeria. Balewa does not belong to the local nobility of the north, but is a full-blooded Hausa commoner of the Habwe group. Like most African politicians he started life as a teacher. He was educated at the Katsina Higher College and holds a teacher's degree from London University. Balewa speaks perfect English in a deep resonant voice. He does not command the support of the emirs, as the Sardauna does, but his personality, unlike the Sardauna's, is more calculated to placate than to provoke. Balewa mirrors the basic lesson of modern Africa, which is that moderation has little place in the continent's politics, thereby reinforcing the old adage that moderate men fail not because they are moderate, but because they are few.

More reserved and distant than Nyerere, he has many personal and political affinities with the Tanganyikan leader and, like him, might ultimately be a victim of the extremists. The arc of tranquility he visualizes as the symbol and foundation of Nigerian unity, much as Nyerere envisages it for Tanganyika, is not conspicuously present today in either country, but Balewa, like Nyerere again, remains, at least ostensibly, an optimist. Whether, like Nyerere, Balewa will be pushed into the extremist camp depends on how long and how firmly the tenuous link which associates the NCNC with the NPC lasts. This in turn hinges on the personalities, politics, and policies of the Sardauna and Azikiwe, both of whom are astute and calculating, intrinsically selfish and egocentric men. Neither can do without the other so long as their respective parties together hold the balance of power at the federal level. Until recently Azikiwe operated from a position of comparative weakness, having linked the forward-minded east with the feudal-minded north against the progressive west, thereby enabling the north to rule Nigeria by dividing the south. Regionalism infects Nigeria in each of its main segments, but feudalism belongs distinctively to the north. Neither Azikiwe nor Awolowo is feudal in his outlook. But the Sardauna very definitely is.

"The poor are God's creatures," he observed sententiously.

He also attributed all diseases to the Almighty, though he did not specify whether in the case of the poor he regarded such diseases as afflictions or blessings.

As in India, the British attempted to extend their rule in Nigeria, and to a lesser degree in Ghana, by a policy of divide and rule. Admittedly, the divisive ingredients, as in India, were present in both these countries, Ghana, like Nigeria, being divided in Gold Coast days into three districts with a complicated mosaic of tribes and a mixed bag of chiefs headed by the Asantehena of Ashanti. Nkrumah, in his role of Osageyefo, has steam-rollered these elements into a consolidated pattern, redrawing the map and relegating the chiefs to the innocuous ceremonial status they enjoyed before the British tried to use them as political pawns. But in Nigeria, which is an artificial geographical creation, the divisive tendencies remain and are highlighted by the backward north, with its galaxy of feudal emirs dominated by the Sardauna.

The British attitude to the emirs is not unlike that of the old raj in India to the princes. "We like the emirs," said a high British official at Kaduna. "They're gentlemen, though, of course, they belong to a feudal order." But the process of conditioning them to the inevitability of inde-pendence was started only four years before it came, and though the Sar-dauna, with his passion for cricket and fives, might rate technically as a gentleman, he is no blazing visionary or idealist.

"Awolowo," said a veteran European resident, "is serious-minded and dull. Zik is flashy and has mass appeal." Azikiwe is popularly known as "Zik" and in the streets crowds cheer him with long-drawn wolf whistles of "Z-e-e-k." Privately, the word most commonly used in Nigeria to describe Azikiwe is "opportunist," and his career certainly betrays a serpentine subtlety of method and maneuver. He was involved in an unsavory bank case some years ago,* was held partly to blame by a commission but, undeterred, stood again for election and was returned by a bigger majority.

Zik is a dynamic demagogue and his oratory, combined with his chain of newspapers, of which the *West African Pilot* is the most prominent, has won him a large following in the south, particularly among the youths, artisans, and workers. His tall, loose-jointed figure and relaxed manner have helped to build up the image of an arresting public personality with a considerable emotional appeal. "Only the intellectuals have quarreled with Zik," said Chief H. O. Davies, who was once closely associated with him. "The masses never have. Zik has always been shrewd enough to exploit every issue to represent himself as the champion of the masses."

Azikiwe, who is fifty-nine, started in politics along with Awolowo, who is five years his junior, and both men were once associated with the Nige-rian Youth Movement (NYM), one of the earliest nationalist organiza-tions, which was active in the 1930's. In those days, Nigerian politics were traditionally centered in western Nigeria, but the temperamental antithesis between Awolowo and Zik, the former a Yoruba and the latter an Ibo, erupted on tribal lines, culminating with Zik and his Ibo followers leaving the NYM in 1941. At that time Awolowo was secretary of the Ibadan branch of the NYM, and Zik a member of the NYM executive at Lagos.

* In 1956, he was charged with improperly investing government money in the African Continental Bank, in which he held considerable interests. He was then premier of eastern Nigeria.

The breach came when Awolowo insisted on the regionalization of the movement and attacked the Lagos leadership. In Nigeria I heard both leaders separately blamed for the breach, depending on whether the person I spoke to was an Ibo or a Yoruba, but, judging by later developments, Awolowo seems the more tribe-conscious of the two. Zik is by far the shrewder.

The two men are dissimilar in almost every way. Personally, Zik, who is bespectacled and benign, is the more attractive, and one can understand the compulsion of his mass magnetism. Awolowo, when I saw him, looked slightly absurd, wearing a bright blue cap and an organdy gown over his suit. He is shorter than Zik and larger, with eyes that keep swiveling behind gleaming glasses. He is a barrister of the Inner Temple, London, but speaks English with a strange intonation, the vowel sounds being unexpectedly jumbled.* Zik is one of very few African leaders who is American-educated, and studied at Howard University, where one of his teachers was Dr. Ralph Bunche. In his variegated career, Zik has turned his hand to many things. He was once a banker. I was told that Awolowo was at one time a moneylender, "but honest." Zik is essentially a politician. Awolowo has no mass appeal, but prides himself on his learning. He struck me as smug, self-centered, and vain, with a fondness for high-sounding words and phrases like "democratic socialism." He seemed devoid of a sense of humor, though he attempted to exhibit his wit with a few shopworn stories.

As a nationalist leader, Zik tried in his earlier days to build up the concept of a Nigerian nationalism fused in a federation wherein the Ibo, Yoruba, and Hausa could live in peace among themselves and with the other tribes. He advocated this as far back as 1943, when, in a political blueprint, he suggested a federation of eight states. In 1944 he founded the Nigerian National Council, from which the NCNC was later to emerge. His popularity even then far exceeded that of Awolowo, who organized the Action Group only in 1950, three years after his return from London. The NCNC is predominantly Ibo, but is not as tribal in its aspect and aspirations as the Action Group, which evolved from a Yoruba tribal society, the Egbe Omo Odudawa, which Awolowo had founded in London while studying law. Zik's popularity was demonstrated by Zikism, or the Zikist movement, which at one time was identified with militant Nigerian nationalism. Indeed, in the late 1940's and early 1950's Azikiwe plumped for a unitary government, dropping this demand in 1953, when he returned to the earlier proposal for a federation.

During this period the Action Group had been demanding greater powers for the three regional governments and speedy self-government for Nigeria. Awolowo also favored the federal idea, but, whereas the NCNC

---

* "Sonday" for Sunday, "hoart" for heart.

has always stood for a tightly united, close-knit Nigeria, the Action Group stands for a loose federation with a readjustment of territories within the three regions by the creation of a midwestern region out of the west, a middle belt in the north, and a non-Ibo region in the east. By this system of checks and balances Awolowo obviously banked on neutralizing the political dominance of the north. "No state should be so large as to dominate the others," he declared.

Ironically he has been hoist with his own petard, for, pretending to take him at his word, the coalition federal government at Lagos, in April, 1961, proposed the creation of a midwestern region, knowing that this would weaken the west vis-à-vis the north and east, and would precipitate a crisis within the Action Group. To Azikiwe the carving of a non-Yoruba state out of the western region had an obvious attraction, but in fairness to Awolowo it should be recalled that his original plan, which was shared by Zik, visualized the breakup extending to all the three regions. The north could not complain so long as the east and the west were similarly carved out, and the same applied to the south vis-à-vis the north. In the resultant situation no single region, according to Awolowo, would exercise a political preponderance which would hinge on alignments between various states in each of the three regions, and lead to a series of permutations and combinations which might ensure stability but could precipitate further division and conflict. The plan offered a way out of the north's perpetual dominance, which to the other two regions signified a perpetual brake on the progress of Nigeria as a whole.

This was the rationale behind the Action Group's proposal which, until the NCNC decided to join forces with the NPC, had Azikiwe's oblique sympathy.

"I have no objection in principle to a coalition government," Awolowo explained. "But there should be no territorial party share-out, with the NPC controlling the north and the NCNC controlling the east. We must cut across territorial divisions."

Following the federal general election of December, 1959, Awolowo, whose Action Group captured seventy-five seats, was eager to cooperate with Azikiwe's NCNC, which had eighty-nine seats, and together form a coalition federal government. The NPC, with 148 seats, would then have functioned as the opposition.* According to Chief Ayo Rosiji, who at that time was federal secretary of the Action Group and a key man in the party,† Azikiwe was willing, but his party was divided, and the threat

---

* It won only 28 percent of the popular vote in the federal elections, but now commands a majority of seats in the Nigerian parliament.

† In May, 1962, Rosiji, with Chief Akintola, former premier of western Nigeria, was expelled from the Action Group for supporting the federal government's motion declaring a state of emergency in western Nigeria until December, 1962.

of Chief Festus Okotie-Eboh, now Nigeria's finance minister, to walk over to the NPC, finally deterred Zik. Chief Festus, a flamboyant character who on ceremonial occasions decks himself with a long, flowing silk train, some twenty yards in length, and sports a straw boater with a feather, comes from the western region but belongs to the minority Itsekiri clan. He is bitterly opposed to the Yoruba-dominated Action Group. His home is in Benin, now the capital of the midwestern region.

The Action Group's proposal in 1954 for the creation of new states was opposed by the British government, which warned that it would lead to the postponement of independence since it would take Whitehall some time to assess how the new units were working. This pushed the issue into the background, though it remained a plank in the Action Group's platform during the 1959 election and received official recognition in the western region, which set up a special advisory body for the midwest. The Nigerian constitution also provides for this eventuality by stipulating that a resolution to establish a new state must be passed by a two-thirds majority of the federal legislature and must also be approved by a simple majority in two of the three regions, one of which must be the region out of which the new state is to be carved. Alternatively, such legislation can be passed by a simple majority in the federal legislature, then submitted to a referendum in the area subject to the change. The proposal for a new midwestern region was approved by the required majority in the federal legislature, and by the legislatures of the eastern and northern regions. But the legislative assembly of the western region rejected it. This however did not deter the federal government from holding a referendum in the west.

An intensification of tribal and political animosities was inevitable. Awolowo's attempt to control, from Lagos, the western region's government at Ibadan was resented by the regional premier, Chief Akintola, who, though a prominent member of the Action Group, was temperamentally and politically at variance with Awolowo. The rift between Awolowo and Akintola was precipitated by the latter's eagerness to have the Action Group participate in the governing federal coalition, while Awolowo, stubbornly opposed to this move, insisted on remaining in radical opposition. The Action Group split on this. Akintola, a personal friend of Balewa, was summarily dismissed on a party vote of no confidence by the regional governor, the Oni of Ife, who was supported by the Awolowo faction. The Nigerian supreme court later held that the governor had acted in excess of his powers, but the Privy Council* upheld the governor. Akintola was replaced by Alhaji Adegbenro, who in turn was suspended by the federal government, which in May, 1962, declared a state of emergency and

---

* Final judicial court of appeal in London before Nigeria became a republic.

appointed a nonparty Yoruba, Chief Majekodunami, federal minister of health, as administrator of western Nigeria. The declaration of a state of emergency until December, 1962, followed rioting for a fortnight by various factions within the Action Group, culminating in fisticuffs and broken heads in a battle inside the regional assembly during which the ceremonial mace was shattered.

Awolowo, Akintola, and Adegbenro were placed under restriction, along with some other members and supporters of the Action Group, including two journalists. Following his dismissal, Akintola had set up a new party, the United People's Party (UPP), to oppose the Action Group. The chief beneficiaries from the breakup of the Action Group were the NCNC, which constituted the chief opposition in the western region house of assembly, and Azikiwe, who as governor-general and now as president continues to guide the party. By the creation of a midwest region, composed of the Benin and Delta provinces, and with the arrangement he reached with Akintola on his release to set up a coalition UPP and NCNC government in the western region, Zik planned to control both the eastern and western regions, thereby shifting the center of political control from the north to the south.

The federal government's swift offensive against the Action Group in the western region was impelled by a variety of motives. Chief among these was to denigrate the Action Group, and to bring Awolowo and his followers into public discredit. Some twenty-five mainly Action Group local councils were dissolved under the emergency regulations, and a government inquiry was initiated into six statutory corporations in the western region to investigate allegations of bribery and corruption against the Action Group government. The inquiry commission, headed by Dr. G. B. A. Coker, a judge of the high court of Lagos, accused Awolowo of planning a "financial empire" and of failure "to adhere to standards of conduct which are required of a person holding such a post." Akintola was absolved on all grounds. Additionally, Awolowo, with some of his colleagues, was convicted of treasonable felony and sentenced to ten years' imprisonment.

The lifting of the emergency on January 1, 1963, saw Akintola reinstalled as premier of the western region, heading a coalition government of twenty-five ministers. Three of these are traditional rulers. Of the fourteen cabinet ministers and the eight ministers of state, the portfolios were divided equally between the UPP and the NCNC. The Oni of Ife was replaced as governor by Chief Fadahunsi, a national vice-president of the NCNC, another demonstration of Azikiwe's key role in precipitating the emergency. Supporting the governor-general for their own reasons were the premier of the northern region, the Sardauna of Sokoto, the federal finance minister, Chief Festus Okotie-Eboh, who is an enthusiastic protagonist for the creation of a midwestern region, and Dr. Okpara, premier of the eastern region and president of the NCNC. The federal prime minister, Sir Abubakar Tafawa Balewa, does not seem to have shared Azikiwe's zest for the emergency, but was probably pushed into declaring it by the Sardauna.

Though Awolowo and the Action Group are temporarily immobilized, they are by no means politically extinct. Awolowo has won much sympathy by his restrained behavior against what many in the western region regard as naked political persecution by the NPC and the NCNC to deprive the opposition of leadership, power, and funds. Alhaji Adegbenro, who carries the mantle of leadership in Awolowo's enforced absence, is briskly active and no sign of defeatism is as yet evident in the Action Group, which is mustering its forces to meet the combined NCNC and NPC's challenge. But Awolowo's conviction could lead to the virtual dissolution of the Action Group and the creation of a new group comprising the younger radical elements of the Action Group and the NCNC. Even before his arrest and conviction, Awolowo appeared to be moving toward the conversion of his Action Group party into a radical pan-Africanist organization with an all-Nigerian appeal. After his conviction this trend toward a populist movement has been strengthened by some trade union elements joining hands with a new pressure group called the Nigerian Youth Congress to form the Socialist Workers and Farmers Party which is slowly proliferating into the towns.

Nor is Akintola with his new group, the UPP, at ease as a political bedfellow of the NCNC. In the old days, Akintola was fiercely opposed to the creation of a midwest region, which Awolowo then espoused. The Yoruba still seem to be largely behind the Action Group, their basic loyalty being regional. In the federal government's attempt to hive off a midwest state* from the western region they see an attempt to hamstring the Action Group by dividing the country's richest region and thereby impairing it politically and economically. Nor would the NPC and the Sardauna relish the prospect of the NCNC and Azikiwe gaining too strong a foothold in the western region and in the process tilting the political balance against the north.

Until independence elevated him to the governor-generalship, Azikiwe was a mercurial character, and he still remains incalculable. The British, it was said, hoped to clip his erratic wings by placing him on this exalted perch, tethering him there by a golden chain controlled by the NPC, which in turn the British thought they could influence. So far Balewa has played true to form, but the Sardauna has proved more elusive and intractable.

---

* This came into being in January, 1964, when elections were held. In the interim it was run by an administrative council.

At one time Azikiwe had hoped to be prime minister, but as head of the minority party in the coalition government after independence he had to be content with the governor-generalship, which he has now successfully inflated into the presidency, thereby probably hoping to outflank both the north and the Sardauna.

In November, 1961, Azikiwe, speaking at a special convocation at the University of Nigeria in Lagos, suggested the election of a president by a federal parliament comprising a house of representatives and a senate, and the appointment of a prime minister acceptable to a majority of members of the house of representatives. The governor-general made this proposal almost coincidentally with the return of the NCNC to power in eastern Nigeria's quinquennial general election, where his party obtained a clear majority. While the western region is normally scheduled to hold its next general election in 1965, the northern region is not due to go to the polls until 1966. The federal general election is scheduled for 1964.

Azikiwe's proposal was clearly for his own benefit. He wanted to be the first president, and the chances of this personage coming from the south are greater if his election is not by a popular vote, where the north might have the advantage, but through the system Azikiwe proposes of electing the president by the two federal houses of parliament sitting as an electoral college. Whether the president should exercise authority on the American model or enjoy only limited powers, as does the Indian president, was not elucidated by Azikiwe, though the governor-general appeared to favor a president possessing limited but quite substantial powers. The federal government's request for an Indian constitutional adviser suggests that Lagos favors a ceremonial head on the model of the Indian president. Awolowo was agreeable to the republican principle, though he would probably have preferred the issue to be delayed, because of the disarray of his Action Group. The Sardauna remained sphinxlike. In a republican setup the emirs would obviously be at a discount.

So Nigeria remains balanced precariously among its four regions and distracted by the contending rivalries of their leaders. The man at the center, ruling from Lagos, is the federal prime minister, Balewa. Will the keys of power ultimately rest in his hands? Balewa has grown greatly in stature despite or perhaps because of the hitherto aggressive rivalries of the three dominant leaders. Though he has no use for the concept of the African Personality, he is genuinely concerned in promoting African unity and, more urgently and immediately, in ensuring the unity of Nigeria. So far he has not fallen prey to the pendulum passions which seem to obsess the other regional leaders. On the contrary, he has been scrupulously correct in the moderate policies he pursues at home and abroad, and, though conciliatory, has shown himself capable of tenacity in principle and action.

The Sardauna might refer to Balewa as his lieutenant, but the latter is no docile camp follower. While conceding the need for a republic, he differed from Azikiwe in insisting that the president must either have limited powers or be elected by popular vote. Balewa would not like the federal prime minister to be bypassed or outflanked by the president.

His "weakness" is his moderation, the cardinal sin in most African eyes, and one on which his less scrupulous political opponents can be expected to capitalize. Some of his friends feel he is not sufficiently assertive, but, with a domineering party chief in the north and a Machiavellian governor-general, now president, in State House, it is hard to blame Balewa. His strength is his transparent integrity and his freedom from dictatorial ambitions. None of the three chief political parties can claim to be national, and more than once Balewa has reiterated the desirability of having a national government, and stressed the need for not concentrating power in the hands of a single individual or party. In this he is way ahead of the Sardauna, Azikiwe, and Awolowo.

Nigeria's malady is more than mere political schizophrenia. Its personality is riven into three, and from the main territorial trisection proceeds the curse of three main tribes and three main parties, each of which is permeated and poisoned with this built-in triple complex. Nigeria, unlike most democracies, has a coalition government of two parties opposed by a third. Had Awolowo emerged as a strong federal opposition leader at Lagos, the chances of Nigeria developing democracy on healthy lines were good. But Awolowo not only failed to measure up as an opposition leader in the house of representatives, but was unable to hold his Action Group together either at Lagos or at Ibadan.

Following the disintegration of the federal opposition and the confusion created by the rift in the Action Group, an intensification of regional polarization seems likely. One effective solvent could be the creation of new regions within each of the present three regions, on the model of the midwestern region carved out of the western region, but the manner in which the latter has been initiated can only further aggravate party and regional animosities. The Action Group's initial support of this proposal was consistent with its own party program but was conditional on the principle being simultaneously applied to the other two regions. For the north and the east to combine in parceling out the west, while keeping their own two regions intact, suggests an obvious conspiracy to undermine the influence of the west and to increase their own. The eastern region stands to gain directly by this move, since the new midwest region is a non-Yoruba area. But in the result the balance between the eastern and northern wings of the federal government would also be disturbed, with a stronger tilt toward the east. Azikiwe's hand would be strengthened.

The more ethical and logical course would be to apply the principle of subdivision to all three regions, thereby detracting from the preponderance of each and bringing into play a new pattern of checks and balances, which might help evolve a more cohesive, consolidated Nigeria. Here again an Indian parallel obtrudes, for the division of India into new states following independence was largely on a linguistic basis. In Nigeria, the creation of new regions would be roughly on a tribal basis, which for the first time would go beyond the artificial trisection of Fulani-Hausa, Yoruba, and Ibo, and in the process perhaps make for more stability in the administrative and governmental structure. In India, the introduction of the linguistic principle of division has unfortunately tended to give an edge to linguistic rivalries, and only the presence of a strong central government at New Delhi has stayed the drift to distintegration. Additionally, the Indian constitution, like the Nigerian, does not provide for secession.* But there will, similarly, have to be a strong united government at Lagos to see that no region makes a runaway break from the country, and in Nigeria's peculiar situation this postulates a national government representative of the three major parties, which is what Balewa appears to have in mind. With the creation of new states in each of the three regions, party alignments might cease to coincide with tribal divisions. And that again would be to Nigeria's good.

The urge for a national government appears to be gathering strength, though the declaration of emergency in the western region, the likely breakup of the Action Group, the formation of the United People's Party and the emergence of a coalition government comprising the UPP and the NCNC have complicated plans and upset calculations. It is doubtful whether the leaders of the Action Group, with their narrow tribal loyalties, would agree to participate in a national government. An added complication is the census, now challenged. In the event of another census being held, the east and the west might outnumber the north in population, in which case the political balance could change. For one thing the north would lose its present majority representation in the federal parliament and, with it, its claim to the federal prime ministership. For another, it would mean a reallocation of federal revenues.

This could alter not only the balance of parties, but the balance of power. If Akintola consolidates the UPP in the west, he might, in conjunction with the NCNC, tilt the scales against the NPC. But in that case the north-south cleavage would grow sharper and make for an uneasy federation, which would either preclude the formation of a national government or make it more difficult. As conceived at present, a national government implies a perpetuation of the present trisection based on the

* It now specifically provides *against* it.

assumption that the NPC would always control the north, the NCNC the east, and either the Action Group or the UPP the west. But, with the creation of a midwestern region, the Yoruba influence in the west will appreciably diminish.* Paradoxically, therefore, the Nigerian federation has a better chance of surviving and growing stronger by applying the principle of subdivision to all the present three regions, thus cutting across territorial and tribal loyalties, and, in the process of dividing, making for a more cohesive country than the present artificial trisection into Fulani-Hausa, Yoruba, and Ibo promises to ensure. A strong federation is preferable to a national government.

On the basis of territory and population, Nigeria should be the leader of West Africa, but Ghana, about the size of the United Kingdom, with a population nearly one-seventh that of Nigeria, is a keen contender for the primacy. Nigeria's annual income per head of about $75, while higher than India's, is lower than Ghana's. Ghana has also a larger proportion of literacy, and, though divided originally like Nigeria into three regions, Ghana is more compact and homogeneous, with a comparatively thin veneer of Islam in the north. It is also less feudal and less tribal. Politically, Ghana's internal one-man eruptions are balanced by Nigeria's growing party feuds and rivalries. Nor does either country look kindly upon the other.† Was it merely coincidental that the release of the Ghanaian opposition United Party veteran, Dr. J. B. Danquah, was announced by Accra twenty-four hours after Awolowo's removal from house detention to a remote isolated fishing village linked by neither road nor telephone with the rest of Nigeria? Awolowo, who has nothing in common with Nkrumah, had latterly cultivated the friendship of Ghana's president, who with equal cynicism had reciprocated the gesture. When the emergency was first declared in the western region, three Action Group leaders, including Chief Enahoro, opposition front-bench spokesman on foreign affairs, fled to Ghana. The charge against Awolowo and his followers of treasonable felony was based partly on the alleged discovery by the federal government of arms caches said to have been found at their residences and coming from "a foreign country, not far away." The Ghanaian press has often attacked the governing coalition in Nigeria, accusing it of keeping neo-colonialism in the saddle. Not surprisingly, Lagos has retorted by accusing

* The Action Group, the UPP, and the Midwest Congress jointly formed a new political party called the "Midwest Democratic Front," which opposed the NCNC in the elections held in January, 1964. These resulted in a decisive victory for the NCNC, which is in control in eastern Nigeria and a majority member of the western Nigeria government coalition with the UPP. The midwestern region's first Premier is Chief Dennis Osadeboy, who was interim administrator of the region. The NCNC is thus in an advantageous position politically in the republic.

† Since the Addis Ababa conference of May, 1963, relations have ostensibly improved.

Accra of attempted subversion. This has added to instability within both countries and in West Africa.

Nigeria's economy rests mainly on raw materials, agriculture being the basis of the country's wealth. Around 60 percent of its national income is derived from agriculture, including forestry and animal husbandry, and its export surpluses range from palm produce to cocoa, and from peanuts and oil to rubber and cotton. Nigeria is fortunate among West African countries in the diversity of its crops, but even more in their distribution over the country. The grain-growing areas in the north can exchange their surplus for palm produce, kola nuts, and fruits from the south. Similarly, while cotton is cultivated in the north, rubber production is a feature of the south, where it is located largely in the western region, though a beginning has been made in opening plantations in the east. Most of these, however, are owned by farmers from the west. Northern Nigeria holds a virtual monopoly in peanuts, and their oil, like that extracted from palm kernels, is used for margarine and also in smaller quantities in the manufacture of soap by local factories. Among the sights of Kano are the massive pyramids draped in green, each of which contains about 700 tons of nuts. Western Nigeria's tropical rain forests yield valuable hardwoods, which are exported in the form of logs and sawed timber.

By and large the standard of living in Nigeria is higher than that of India, and, unlike India, Nigeria is almost self-supporting in food. The children are stockier than Indian children, and most Nigerians enjoy an adequate diet, except in the crowded southeast, where the principal food consists of low-protein root crops. About 80 percent of the country's agricultural output comprises local foodstuffs, like yams, cassava, corn, rice, millet, beans, sugar cane, oranges, and other citrus fruit. The remaining 20 percent accounts for about 90 percent of Nigerian exports. Food appears to be keeping pace with the growth of population, whose annual rate of increase is around 2 percent. The national income is also increasing, in real terms, at a yearly pace of 2.5 percent. On the other hand, corruption is unfortunately widespread.

Satisfactory as the economic picture seems to be, Nigeria will find it increasingly difficult to meet her growing private consumption unless she accelerates the growth of light or secondary industries in order to reduce imports and increase employment. The need for developing communications is another top priority of which the federal government and regional administrations are aware, for quite 36 percent of development expenditure by the governments and statutory corporations is devoted to communications.*

Linked with these priorities is the problem of stepping up the exploita-

* Nigeria has a six-year development plan estimated to cost about $2 billion.

tion and extension of power and mineral resources. Ghana has her Volta project. Nigeria has her Niger hydroelectric schemes, toward which the British government has contributed substantially under the Colonial Development and Welfare Funds, but more foreign aid and investment will be needed to hasten the pace of industrialization. Over the last decade government investment has concentrated largely on developing communications, electricity, and water supplies. To accelerate industrial and economic growth, the governments at federal and regional levels are offering attractive terms to foreign investors, which include tax holidays for pioneer industries, duty-free importation of industrial machinery, refund of import duty on raw materials, and other incentives. Nigeria is one of the most compact markets on the African continent, and the presence of overseas capital is welcome in a country where indigenous capital, managerial skill, and technical talent are conspicuously restricted. The fantastic cost of building in Nigeria, compared with India, amazed me, but is not surprising, since almost everything from bolts and nuts to air conditioners, from cement to roofing materials has to be imported from abroad. According to the federal finance minister, Chief Festus, Nigeria plans to reduce her dependence upon imported goods, particularly consumer goods, and reduce the drain of invisible transactions. "Trade comes before aid," he has frequently declared.

But so does internal production. Industrialization, though progressing, is on a modest scale, being confined largely to processing local products or assembling imported goods. Latex is processed into sheet and crepe for export, and improved qualities are emerging from the two processing factories in the Benin area of western Nigeria. At Kaduna I saw a textile mill and was told of a plywood factory at Sepele in western Nigeria which, it was claimed, was the largest factory of its kind in the world. There is another plywood factory at Ewekoro, also in western Nigeria. Cement is now being produced in both the western and eastern regions, and in recent years a number of secondary industries have been established, which turn out a variety of products including tiles, soap, beer, cigarettes, margarine, plastics, steel drums, metal containers, wrought iron goods, furniture, and window frames. But statistics show that an overwhelmingly larger number of people are employed in trade or transport than in factories or mines.

Nigeria possesses a variety of minerals, which unfortunately are not sufficiently concentrated or accessible to justify extensive exploitation. Tin, coal, and columbite are notable exceptions, but the coal mined in a range of hills near Enugu, capital of eastern Nigeria, is of poor quality, and the country's railways are turning increasingly to diesel oil. Nigeria, however, is the only state in West Africa producing coal, which it exports to Ghana, though in declining quantities because the Ghanaian railways have also turned to diesel oil. For a time it sent coal to South Africa. In the peak period of 1958, the Nigerian Coal Corporation produced over 800,000 tons, but demand is falling, though the eventual creation of a chemical industry based on coal might help to revive it. Nigeria's annual coal output is around 680,000 tons today, and its coal reserves are estimated at 240 million tons. Tin is located in the province of Plateau in the north, and the output is about 11,000 tons today, but since the Korean War, when tin commanded abnormally high prices, production has slumped. So also with columbite, a rare ore used for hardening steel and in demand as an ingredient in the manufacture of alloys for modern jet engines. The output is about 1,500 tons a year. The cessation of American stockpiling and the increasing use of alternative minerals such as titanium has hit the columbite market. Oil, located in the Afana, Oloibiri, and Bomu areas of eastern Nigeria, offers more exciting possibilities, and in 1960 over a million tons valued at over $14 million were exported from the Niger delta worked by Shell B.P. Other petroleum companies, including Standard Oil, are prospecting in various parts of the federation. Oil finds are reported in Benin.

Nigeria, which many had hoped would shine as a symbol of stability, now glowers as Africa's latest "crisis country." Starting under relatively propitious auspices, she has begun to falter and kick over the traces within less than three years of independence. With her extensive territory and large population, she could be a focal point of unrest whose restiveness could infect large areas of West Africa.

"The differences are not among the masses, but among the politicians at the top," observed a senior British official. He was right. But in a nascent, restive democracy such as Nigeria, example is infectious and percolates from above. The politicians, not the people of Nigeria, are failing her.

CHAPTER

6

DEFLATED DICTATOR

CONFRONTED WITH RECENT developments in Nigeria, Ghana poses the problem of whether one-party rule is not the most suitable form of government for Africa's emergent countries. Alone of all African states, Nigeria had a comparatively strong three-party system poised on a delicate base of checks and balances, which if disturbed could create serious stresses within the structure, as events have proved. The move for a national or a united front government favored by Balewa and by Dr. Obeonukara Okpara, premier of the eastern region and president of the NCNC, has led many to feel that parties are a luxury Nigeria cannot afford for the moment. Ghana has a seemingly more solid base, but, insofar as its stability rests on one man, his withdrawal or removal from the scene could precipitate conflict which might end in chaos. In Africa, as in many Asian countries, stability hangs by a thin-spun thread.

Kwame Nkrumah has woven for himself an intricate web of power, and his claim that by giving Ghana a distinctively African look he is helping to project the African Personality is not as extravagant or exotic as it seems. Moreover it has an African appeal. As the Osageyefo, Nkrumah, though himself a detribalized leader, has created a father figure or image which accords with tribal tradition and thought, and is identified with the old tribal chief who exercised his authority only in consultation with his

110

counselors. This facade of rule by association, consultation, and consent, Nkrumah has maintained with varying success and setbacks. The elimination from the government* in September, 1961, of the old guard, represented by Komla Agbeli Gbedemah and Kojo Botsio,† who with Nkrumah constituted the triumvirs of the Ghana revolution, marked a break with the past, but not a break in the pattern. In fact the pattern is now set in a more rigid mold. The state remains identified with the party, which demands conformity from the people much as the tribal group does from its members. The party replaces the tribal group and each individual is required to think not as an individual, but as a member of the party. It is rule by association, such as prevails in the tribe, and on the tribal pattern the will of the party is paramount over the right of the individual. Ghanaian custom, interestingly enough, decrees that the chiefs do not normally make their intentions known except through their spokesmen, but in modern Ghana the Osageyefo speaks for all, including his counselors.

For four years after independence, Nkrumah was able to exert supreme authority over his colleagues by skillfully maintaining a balance between the rightist elements, led by Gbedemah, and the ultraleftists, comprising Tawia Adamafio, later minister of information and broadcasting, who was arrested after the first bomb attack on Nkrumah in August, 1962, tried and acquitted, but is still in detention; Martin Appah-Danquah, secretary-general of the United Ghana Farmers' Council; and John Tettegah, secretary-general of the Trade Union Council, who was also to fall from grace. Tettegah was arrested following the second attempt on Nkrumah's life in September, 1962, held for questioning, but released. Nkrumah's position might be described as revolutionary center leaning to the left, and his strength as a leader initially lay in his ability to balance and play off the various elements within the party and the government, who, while agreed on a Ghanaian way of socialism, differed on its range and pace. Nkrumah's definition of African socialism‡ is that it equals Marxism-Leninism minus Russian imperialism.

The breach came with the austerity budget of July, 1961, which Nkrumah personally introduced before leaving on a tour of Russia and China. Public opinion was not prepared psychologically for the sharp break with the happy-go-lucky economic past which the budget, with its scheme for a wage freeze and compulsory savings, represented. Neither the party nor the government was united in its support, and the proposal for compulsory savings combined with a wage freeze precipitated a strike by dock and railway workers which for some time paralyzed the ports of

* Ghana has been governed by the Convention People's Party (CPP) since 1951.
† Botsio was politically ostracized along with Gbedemah, but has now been restored to favor as foreign minister.
‡ From his book *Africa Must Unite,* Heinemann, 1963.

Sekondi and Takoradi, and immobilized the railway system. In Nkrumah's absence the cabinet was divided, and it is possible that certain ministers like Gbedemah and Botsio—though Botsio was normally associated with the left—were imprudent or indiscreet enough to identify the budget too closely with Nkrumah and to express unguarded criticism of both. The summary removal, following the president's return, of Major-General H. T. Alexander, British chief of Ghana's defense staff, along with some seventy other British officers, was probably influenced by Alexander's distaste for using the army to quell the strikers. But the president must also have sensed that the army and the rightist elements headed by Gbedemah were obvious rallying points for the opposition in and outside the government. The decision might also have been influenced by Ghana's wish to have Accra as the headquarters of the Africa Joint Command, to which some other states might have been averse if non-African officers continued in Ghana's armed services. Arrests under the Preventive Detention Act of not only Nkrumah's political opponents, but of individuals who until recently were keen supporters of the government, revealed the extent of popular discontent and the fissures within the party.

Nkrumah, who returned to Ghana in September, reacted characteristically to the crisis. In a democratic setup a government with its ranks divided and confronted by widespread public discontent, with dwindling foreign reserves, a growing balance of payments deficit, and a steep rise in the urban cost of living would have resigned and held new elections. Nkrumah was faced with a dilemma. He could either move toward more freedom or resort to more repression. He chose the latter course, preferring to rely on sterner authoritarian methods, which entailed a major reshuffle of the cabinet, a tightening of party discipline, and the adoption of a bill for setting up a special division of the high court comprising three judges to deal with crimes against the state, from whose decision there is no appeal. Attempts to overthrow the government by unlawful means or to procure any alteration in the policies of the government by force are punishable by death. It was announced that the Preventive Detention Act, which was promulgated in 1958 and which permits detention without trial, would be amended to empower the government to decide whether, at the end of the prescribed five-year term,* a detainee should be released or not. In a speech in March, 1962, at Kumasi, the nerve center of the opposition, Nkrumah threatened that if a detainee on release showed no change in conduct he would be detained again, "but this time for twenty

* In November, 1963, the Ghana National Assembly approved an amendment to the Preventive Detention Bill allowing the Government to hold in custody a convicted person for a further term of five years, a process that could go on indefinitely.

years." Later the additional term of detention was scaled down to five years.

In Nkrumah's absence a state of emergency had been proclaimed following the spate of strikes. One of the president's first acts on his return was to lift the state of emergency and to call upon the strikers to resume work. When this produced no response, the mortified Osageyefo realized that popular discontent was more widespread and deep-seated than he had thought, and that disaffection had infiltrated into the party and the government. Six members of the government, including Gbedemah and Botsio, were called upon to resign because of "their varied business connections," but Gbedemah's rejoinder that Nkrumah had another undisclosed reason suggested a political motivation. According to the deposed minister, his dismissal stemmed from the president's suspicion that Gbedemah had been disloyal to him and was plotting against the government. The shake-up also involved six other members of the government, four of them ministers who, however, were not relieved of office but were called upon to surrender to the state private properties in excess of more than two houses of a combined value of $5,600, more than two cars, and plots of land of total value exceeding $1,400. Among the four ministers was Krobo Edusei, of "Golden Bed" fame, who even then was known to be rearing a $224,000 marble mansion for himself on the outskirts of Accra. His retention in office until April, 1962, when he was dismissed following a public outcry against the "Golden Bed" and marble mansion scandals, reinforces Gbedemah's charge that the real reason for his own dismissal was political. Edusei was later restored to favor.

Nkrumah decided to identify himself more openly with the left, and in the process to neutralize and liquidate the right. Even then his intention seemed to be to give up the pretense of a multiparty state, which formally permitted an opposition, and to consolidate Ghana as a one-party state wedded to the ideal of "democratic centralism," which the Osageyefo has preached off and on. Later attempts on his life enabled him to proclaim Ghana a one-party state with the formal approval of parliament. Since September, 1961, his actions pointed in that direction, though occasionally he appeared to zigzag to his target, rounding up indiscriminately his political opponents and party dissidents, only to release them individually or in groups with a show of clemency and as "a gesture of reconciliation."

When I first landed at the airport at Accra I saw a placard with Nkrumah's portrait calling on all Ghanaians "to join me in this crusade against the introduction of gangsterism." Later, on reading the newspapers which off and on announced the arrest of people as "gangsters" under the Preventive Detention Act, it dawned on me that the term "gangster" signified "political opponent," an impression confirmed by the then minister of the interior, A. E. Inkumsah, when I saw him. Of him I mildly inquired why it was necessary to use the Preventive Detention Act* against "gangsters," who were presumably criminals and could surely be tried under the ordinary criminal law of the land. Inkumsah, in an unguarded moment, said they were political opponents and stormily asked: "What else do you expect? Anywhere else men who opposed the government, who planned to upset it, would be shot or hanged. Here we only put them away for five years."

In October, 1961, the government ordered the arrest of fifty people, including leaders of the opposition United Party and others known to have opposed Nkrumah's policies. Among those arrested were the veteran Dr. J. B. Danquah, once Nkrumah's close political associate, who opposed him in the presidential election of 1960; Joe Appiah, deputy leader of the parliamentary United Party and son-in-law of the late Sir Stafford Cripps; Patric Quaidoo, formerly social welfare minister, who was thrown out of the cabinet in May, 1961; and Kesse Edu, a journalist on the independent newspaper *Ashanti Pioneer*.† Three other M.P.'s were arrested along with Appiah, and the detainees also included senior members of the Ghanaian railway union and market "mammies" who had figured prominently in the eighteen-day railway and harbor strike at Takoradi and Sekondi during the preceding month. Those arrested were accused of subversive activities and of being implicated in a conspiracy to assassinate the president and some of his ministers. It was the second alleged conspiracy in two years, the first having occurred in 1958, when a similar plot to assassinate the president was said to have been discovered by the government. The open bomb attacks on the Osageyefo were to come later.

The four arrested M.P.'s were struck off the parliamentary rolls on the ground that they were in preventive detention, a procedure which, under the amended Preventive Detention Act, also automatically deprives a released detainee who shows no change of conduct or is rearrested of his right to vote, or to be a candidate in parliamentary or local government elections. Later, in January, 1962, the central committee of the Convention People's Party called upon Gbedemah and Botsio to vacate their parliamentary seats. The reshuffled cabinet announced on September 30, 1961, was notable for the replacement of the British attorney-general,

---

* In fairness it must be noted that India also has a Preventive Detention Act, though the government of that country does not use it so drastically. The detainee is informed of the evidence on which he has been detained, and he has the right to represent his case to a tribunal whose verdict is binding on the government. Since the Chinese attack in October, 1962, a state of emergency has been proclaimed in India which invests the government with overriding authority.

† Danquah was released in July, 1962, but rearrested in January, 1964, after another attempt on Nkrumah's life. Appiah was released in December, 1962.

Geoffrey Bing,* by a Ghanaian and by the transfer of Tawia Adamafio from the ministry of presidential affairs, which was abolished, to the ministry of information and broadcasting, while another up-and-coming leftist, Kwaku Boateng, was given the key ministry of interior and local government. The portfolio of defense was assigned to Kofi Baako, one of Nkrumah's oldest political associates and a founder of the CPP. Baako, reputedly a moderate, is trusted by the president. Though not militantly leftist in composition, the cabinet contained no one who could be described as a rightist, as was Gbedemah. Nkrumah's praetorian guard in the government was then believed to consist of Adamafio, Boateng, and Tettegah, who had an elevated niche by virtue of being secretary-general of the Trade Union Council.

Thus the government slid definitely to the left. Any effective opposition from outside the single, all-pervasive party was intolerable, and indeed, the United Party, though then vigorous within the limitations which oppressed it, was ineffective and was rendered even more ineffectual by the successive detention of its members. I had a long talk with Dr. J. B. Danquah, the symbol in Ghanaian and foreign eyes of opposition to the Osageyefo. Danquah, who was born in 1895, is the founder of the United Gold Coast Convention (UGCC), of which Nkrumah was once secretary and from which he later broke away. With his kindly face and grizzled white head, he recalled the image of Uncle Tom. Danquah is a capable lawyer, but no politician. "Perhaps," he said, wistfully recalling his ups and downs, "I was not made to be a politician."

The virtual persecution of the only opposition newspaper, the *Ashanti Pioneer*, whose editor along with four members of his staff was held in detention in January, 1962, further immobilized the opposition. By that date around a thousand persons were reckoned to be in preventive detention. With more coercion came more centralization. The party's control over the local government administration was tightened by transforming the 106 electoral constituencies into districts for the purpose of local government, each with a local council and administration headed by a district commissioner, who was a functionary of the ruling Convention People's Party. Lower down the line, the administration at village level was placed in the hands of new village communities composed of the chairman of the local branch of the ruling party and a number of other party members. Nkrumah now sought to carry out his ideas of strong government through greater reliance on his young functionaries and ideologists.

On the economic as on the political plane an authoritarian swing to

* Formerly a left-wing Labour M.P. at Westminster. As attorney-general he drew up the Preventive Detention Act.

the left was discernible, though here again the president zigzagged to his targets. However, the list toward the Eastern bloc grew more pronounced, though only a myopic mind would conceive of Nkrumah as a Communist or a Communist stooge. Nkrumah plays nobody's hand but his own. He is basically pro-Nkrumah.

The austerity budget was forced upon the country and the government by Ghana's steadily deteriorating economic situation, which by mid-1961 had reached proportions alarming enough to stir Nkrumah to drastic action. Despite the economy's growth rate of 8 percent, it was clear that the country was spending more than it was earning. The gaps in Ghana's internal and external budgets grew and showed no signs of contracting. Hard saving had to replace a heady spurt of easy spending. Two-thirds of Ghana's foreign earnings come from the sale of cocoa, but in the three years, 1959-1962, the world price of cocoa slumped steeply. It dropped from $1,400 a ton to $448 in 1962. Alongside this, Ghana's internal and external expenditure in order to keep the country in the forefront of the African picture, as the apotheosis of the African Personality, increased. Over a period of four years its foreign reserves dropped from over $560 million to $252 million while its balance of payments deficit kept edging precariously upward. The shrinkage in value of British gilt-edged securities, in which Ghana's balances are mainly invested, has reduced the value of the holdings. At the time of independence Ghana's sterling balances were £200 million. In 1963 they were down to £80 million. Within two months of 1961 the urban cost of living rose by 20 percent. The only answer was austerity, but a people pampered by easy living and free spending recoiled at this abrupt drastic reversal in their way of life.

Nkrumah's Pan-Africanism has proved a costly business. The union with Guinea and Mali was reinforced in 1961 by loans totaling over $28 million and, to sustain the image of Ghanaian leadership of the continent, has called for lavish subsidies to organizations such as Accra's Bureau of African Affairs,* the All-African Trade Union Federation, the All-Africa People's Conference, the maintenance of a Pan-African news agency along with a powerful radio station, and various other movements and organizations of a revolutionary or subversive character. Among the former are those designed to aid the Angola rebels and, previously, the Lumumba faction in the Congo. Underground attempts inspired and subsidized by Ghana to subvert the governments of "unfriendly" African countries like Nigeria, Liberia, Togo, and Sierra Leone are also alleged.

Nkrumahism at home has proved equally expensive. The projection of the personality cult takes many exuberant and costly forms, from prestige projects like Accra's vast Black Star Square and the uneconomic expan-

* A new ministry of African affairs was created in April, 1961.

sion of Ghana Airways to statues, highways, stamps, coins, and posters, all hailing the Osageyefo, who is also known modestly as "His Messianic Dedication" and as the "Nation's Fount of Honor, the Dynamic Leader, the Immortal." Nkrumah has done nothing to discourage the sycophants. Crowds greet him with cries of "Show Boy," a term used not in derision, but in admiration as signifying the nation's and Africa's most treasured showpiece.

Everywhere in Accra and elsewhere in Ghana one sees Nkrumah's face staring out from scores of placards displayed prominently at airports, at railway stations, in offices, commercial houses, and along the avenues and streets. Roads bear the Osageyefo's name and his profile appears on stamps and coins, one Accra newspaper carrying his silhouette every day on its front page. His statue, now damaged slightly by an explosion, stands before Parliament House, showing him in a Christlike pose with his right hand uplifted and his left holding a staff. On the pedestal runs a text in Biblical style: "Seek ye first the political kingdom and all other things shall be added unto it."

As an American journalist remarked, "The only thing now left is a statue of Nkrumah with his hand on Christ's head."

Until the dismissal of Gbedemah and Botsio,* who, with Ghana's chief justice, Sir Arku Korsah, had functioned as a presidential commission during Nkrumah's nine-week absence abroad, the differences between the right and ultraleft wings within the government, though known, were muted and never surfaced publicly. For some time before that the right wing had grown increasingly critical of certain aspects of the president's policies, particularly the inflated growth of the personality cult and the extravagantly wasteful expenditure on prestige projects. Gbedemah, who was sympathetic to Britain and the West, was opposed to overrapid Ghanaization on the plea that it would lower efficiency, and was also averse to too-speedy socialization, which, he felt, would deter foreign investment and hamper development. He was opposed to the austerity budget as politically unwise and economically unsound. Gbedemah's exit meant the end of the right wing within the CPP and a considerable accretion of strength to the ultraleft, with which the president's own pragmatic socialism now seems to be identified. But Nkrumah, as the maestro, knows he can still wield the baton as he chooses, and the orchestra must play to his direction.

* Botsio has been restored to favor. He was appointed chairman of the national council for higher education in May, 1962, and in November was named as the CPP candidate in a national assembly by-election. He is now the foreign minister. Gbedemah has left Ghana and has settled abroad. In November, 1963, restrictions on foreign travel were tightened both for members of the general public and of the government.

The reshuffling of the cabinet was followed by the acceleration of radical Socialist policies at home, a ruthless drive against political opponents and critics, more stringent restrictive measures, and attempts to curb the private sector to a minimum. Nkrumah also flattered the ultraleftists by looking more to the East, and his austerity budget seemed to accord with their advice to finance development by forced savings at home, helped by foreign aid or loans, preferably from Socialist or Communist countries. "Forward with the people" was the government's slogan, but the people, confronted with forced savings and a threatened wage freeze, showed no great enthusiasm for either austerity or the budget, the more so with ministers like Krobo Edusei vulgarly flaunting their ill-gained wealth before the country.

Discontent kept mounting. I did not meet the burly Komla Agbeli Gbedemah, who was still in office when I was in Ghana but was out of the country at the time. Gbedemah is said to have some German blood, which probably accounts for his Teutonic efficiency. I met Kojo Botsio, who was then minister for agriculture, and the volatile Krobo Edusei, at the time minister of transport and communications, and minister of state for ceremonies, who was also acting as secretary of the CPP in the absence of Adamafio. He was also principal national organizer for his party, and at the height of his influence.

No two men could have been so dissimilar as the grave, handsome Botsio, who looked like an ebony Roman senator in his *kente* robes, and the bouncing, ebullient Edusei, whose appearance is unprepossessing. He is short, squat, crude, and pugnacious. Edusei was known to foreign correspondents as "Crowbar," but in Ghana his nickname is "Moke," which on his downfall provoked the legend, "Moke has gone up in smoke."

Both men, echoing the Osageyefo, stressed the need for projecting the African Personality in all spheres and for popularizing the Ghanaian way of socialism as part of Ghana's Pan-African movement.

"We want agriculture to be Pan-African," said Botsio, and spoke of an African farmers' conference held recently in Ghana "to encourage a Pan-African bias in agriculture," to which Nigeria had been invited. Botsio seemed especially keen in interesting the Nigerian farmers, which was illuminating, since Nigeria is almost self-sufficient in food while Ghana annually imports $56 million worth of foodstuffs. He explained that Ghana was also trying to diversify its agriculture so as to include coffee, rubber, corn, rice, and peanuts, and to encourage this the government was subsidizing the farmers heavily. Cocoa, of course, was their main foreign exchange earner. It also accounted for some 45 percent of Ghana's total revenue and provided employment for around 1½ million people, roughly 20 percent of Ghana's 7 million population. The united Ghana farmers' cooperatives are now the sole buyers on behalf of the government of the country's cocoa produce. Because of the grip of the government on every department of national activity, it has been able through the Farmers Council to "persuade" the cooperatives to contribute "voluntarily" about $1.50 per ton of cocoa per year to the development plan, which would give the government about $70 million over five years. But since then the cocoa market has slumped sharply.

I asked Botsio if the African countries were economically so complementary as to supplement one another's deficiencies. He hesitated a moment before replying, and a smile crinkled his face. "For the moment," he remarked, "we are exploring it as an exercise."

Edusei, who began as a bill collector, contrasted strongly with the suave, Oxford-educated Botsio. He seems to have extended to politics the bulldozing methods he doubtless exercised in his earlier profession, and authoritarianism sits easily on his squat shoulders. He too aimed at making communications Pan-African. "We are determined," he said, "to give both flying and shipping an African look." Besides Ghana Airways, an expensive prestige project whose expansion has been motivated more by political than economic considerations, Ghana operates the Black Star Line, a shipping venture which until recently it ran in cooperation with the Zim Naviagation Company of Israel. The line, which has a tonnage of 245,000 tons, has been given parity with the Nigerian National Line, Ltd.

Edusei in his capacity of principal national organizer to the Convention People's Party gave me a revealing insight into the party and government setup, which is interlaced at various levels. The CPP, Edusei claimed, had a membership of 2.5 million, in addition to members of allied organizations such as youth leagues and bicycle leagues, which are spread out all over the country. Anyone aged eighteen can join the party, and there is a party ideological group which trains members in what Edusei termed "positive action." Enlarging on this, he observed, "We stand for a Ghanaian way of socialism."

Nkrumah is at the apex of the party in his dual capacity of chairman and secretary-general. He is also head of the state. Within the party, the Osageyefo heads the central committee, whose members he nominates and who include some associate members. Their names are never published.* As head of the state, the president draws his ministers from the single-chamber legislature consisting of 114 members, but he himself is not a member of the legislature. Under the 1960 constitution, president and parliament are linked, and neither can exist without the other, for, while the president, in case of dissension with his ministers, can dissolve parlia-

* "A legacy of British days," Botsio explained, "when we had to keep the names secret."

ment, by the same act he dismisses himself. A new election is then held in which each of the candidates has to nominate a person for the presidency, and the nominee of a majority of the successful candidates becomes head of state. Article 15 of the constitution empowers the president to appoint, enlarge, or diminish the cabinet as he chooses. Nkrumah is thus supreme in both the party and the state. From Caesar one can appeal only to Caesar. His pathological distrust of those around him makes him a moody dictator.

Under the same constitution the term "opposition" was abolished, which in effect signifies a single-party legislature, though in fact there were then eight opposition members. Today Ghana is a single-party state, following a parliamentary decision after the two attempts on the Osageyefo's life, the first on August 1, 1962, at the village of Lulungugu near the northern border of Ghana and Upper Volta, and the second at Accra on September 9, when some 2,000 people had assembled outside the president's residence to celebrate his previous escape. There followed other bomb explosions, also in Accra—three in the center of the capital on September 20 during a mass torchlight rally on the eve of Nkrumah's fifty-third birthday, and another early in January, 1963. The total casualties in these attempts were 21 deaths and injuries to 385 people. On September 22, 1962, Nkrumah declared a state of emergency and clamped a dawn-to-dusk curfew on Accra.

Following the first attempt in August at Lulungugu, the Osageyefo had ordered two of his ministers—Ako Adjei, the foreign minister, and Tawia Adamafio, minister for information and broadcasting—along with the secretary of the Convention People's Party, Horatio Cofie Crabbe, to be held in preventive detention.* Significantly, all three were members of the Ga tribe, who inhabit the Accra district, and the government party organ, the *Ghanaian Times*, labeling Adamafio a "master adventurer," denounced the arrested men as a "tribalist gang." It also demanded their execution. The three men, particularly Adamafio, were believed to be close to Nkrumah and their arrest surprised many Ghanaians. Clearly the crisis centered around the control of the party machine, and, in reacting, as he did, the Osageyefo probably recalled the old Akan adage: "The ant that is most likely to bite you is the one inside your toga."

Nathaniel Welbeck, who was once Nkrumah's ambassador extraordinary in the Congo and was ordered out of that country in November, 1960, after the fall of Lumumba, was appointed to succeed Coffie Crabbe as acting executive secretary of the CPP. Krobo Edusei later bounced back

---

* They were later tried on a charge of conspiracy to commit treason and actual treason.

into office as minister for agriculture, and the president personally assumed control of the country's civil service.

On September 6, shortly before the second bomb explosion, parliament opened with a debate on a private member's motion to declare Ghana a one-party state. Another private member's motion suggested that Nkrumah should be president for life. The motion to keep the Osageyefo as president for life was passed unanimously on September 7, and four days later the motion to make Ghana a one-party state was adopted by an overwhelming majority.*

In between occurred the second attempt on Nkrumah's life, to be followed within less than two weeks by more bomb explosions. Nkrumah was thrust into a position where he could trust nobody. On October 2, in his address to the opening session of parliament, he approved of the motion to make Ghana a one-party state but wisely rejected the suggestion that he should become president for life. "Ours, by the people's wish," he declared, "shall be a one-party state, a people's parliamentary democracy." Instead of making him president for life the Osageyefo suggested that the way for people to demonstrate their support was to return him and his party to power at the regular five-year elections.† Actually it amounted to the same thing. From one party to one press seemed a logical step. Shortly after, the government announced. that it had taken over the opposition newspaper, the *Ashanti Pioneer*.

The process of identifying the state with Nkrumah's Convention People's party was accelerated by yet another unsuccessful attempt on the Osageyefo's life in January, 1964. Prior to the attempt the acquittal by a special court of Adamafio, Adjei, and Cofie Crabbie, three of the five defendants‡ charged with conspiracy to commit treason and actual treason, led to Nkrumah's summary dismissal of the presiding judge, Sir Arku Korsah, who was also chief justice of Ghana. Simultaneously Nkrumah declared the judgment of the special court (presumably only insofar as it affected the three acquitted men) null and void. Sir Arku's dismissal was widely condemned abroad as a brazen assault on the independence of the judiciary, though inside Ghana the President's apologists derided Sir

* In January, 1964, Nkrumah announced that a referendum would be held to seek approval for constitutional amendments, making Ghana a one-party state and giving the president the right to dismiss judges. A new national flag would replace the old one, the colors of the new flag being those of the Convention Peoples Party. As expected, the referendum resulted in overwhelming approval of the amendments, 2,773,920 voting "yes" and 2,452 "no."

† Ghana held its last general election in 1956, and in 1960 parliament decided to extend its own life, so that the next election will be held in 1965.

‡ The other two defendants, Robert Benjamin Otchere, a former M.P. representing the opposition United Party, and Joseph Yaw Manu, a former civil servant, were found guilty and sentenced to death.

Arku as "a lounge boy" belonging to a class which was hostile to the social revolution as opposed to the "veranda boys" who made it. In fairness to Nkrumah it must be said that his action, though contrary to democratic practice, was technically within the Ghanaian constitution, which stipulates that while the appointments of judges of the High Court and of the Supreme Court could be terminated only by a two-thirds majority in parliament, the specific appointment of a chief justice may at any time be revoked by the president by instrument under the presidential seal. The Osageyefo proceeded to repair other lacunae in his powers. A bill was rushed through parliament and passed by it which empowered the president to quash any decision of the special criminal court which appeared to him to be against the interests of the state's security.

Nkrumah's one-party plan provoked no great reaction on the continent but his subordination of the judiciary to himself, as symbolizing the executive, offended and embarrassed many thinking Africans who realized that it would now be difficult to protest against repressive legislation by Verwoerd's government in South Africa or Winston Field's government in Salisbury. Some Commonwealth African countries and others outside it (like Togo), Nigeria, Sierra Leone, Kenya, and Tanganyika, irked by the Osageyefo's attempts to interfere in their affairs, resented his condescending attitude. Nigeria particularly was critical of Nkrumah's barnstorming politics, and Ghana's obstructive attitude to the East African Federation has made him increasingly suspect in the eyes of the leaders of Kenya, Uganda, and Tanganyika. In Ghana itself opposition to the Osageyefo, though submerged, is widespread and on the increase, particularly among the younger elements and the students. Apart from Kofi Baako and a shrinking number of his immediate entourage, Nkrumah (who reputedly wears a bulletproof vest day and night) trusts nobody.

Among his trusted associates I met Kawaku Boateng, then minister of information, now high in the president's inner circle. Boateng is a young man in his early thirties, suave and, on the surface, in no hurry, capable of being a good lieutenant, but who has still to attain the caliber of a leader. He is efficient, but more showy than profound. Less impressive was Dowuona-Hammond, who was minister of education, a subject which, with communications and a more diversified economy, ranks among Ghana's major priorities. Ghana's educational record is ahead of Nigeria's, and far ahead of most African countries. She is closer to the attainment of universal primary education than Nigeria is and though, as in all African countries, the number tapers off disturbingly in the realm of university education, Ghana does not appear to suffer quite so distressingly as does Nigeria with her secondary-education bottleneck. Both the Ibadan University College in Nigeria and the Legon University College some ten miles from Accra are impressively laid out. The Ibadan institution is more imposing, but I thought Legon more pleasing, set in a lovely countryside against gentle hills. Its buildings are white, with red-tiled roofs which contrast pleasantly with the green landscape.

Since the process of the Ghanaization of the administrative services and the professions cannot be accelerated without a speedier flow of graduates, steps are being taken to expand facilities for higher education and simultaneously to lower the prevailing standards. The report of a commission on university education was released in July, 1961, along with a government white paper substantially agreeing with its recommendations, and one of the commission's main suggestions—that the University College of Accra and the Kumasai Technical College, both of which were parts of the University of Ghana, should be given independent university status—has been implemented. A new university college is planned to open at Cape Coast which will specialize in part-time courses, and senior high school education in secondary schools is drastically revised so as to lower the requirements for university entrance. Senior high school work previously entailed a two-year, post-secondary-school course preparatory to university study. This is abolished, as is also the special entrance examination for university entrants. Instead, the secondary school diploma is now sufficient for university entry. All this implies a lowering of educational standards.

A significant recommendation of the commission urged the more rapid displacement of Europeans by Ghanaians on the staff of the various universities. This, in turn, means lower norms for the teaching staff. Entry standards for the civil service have already been revised and are far below the high qualifications previously demanded by the British government. Here Ghana's action is analogous to that of India, where the tests for the Indian administrative service are not as exacting as those imposed for the old British-controlled Indian civil service. The same is true of learning and teaching in India, whose need for indigenous personnel in the various professions and services has, like Ghana's, grown greatly since independence. The structure of higher education in Ghana is now supervised by a national council of higher education and research. Steps are being taken to enable more women to complete higher education. All in all, the new scheme reduces to sixteen years the twenty years it previously took a Ghanaian child to go through primary, secondary, and university education.

The process of creating, consolidating, and projecting the African Personality calls for state supervision of the individual from the cradle to the grave. Nkrumah is well aware of the importance of "catching 'em young," though some of the methods he employs to do so are crudely ludicrous.

One of the first things I noticed at my hotel in Accra was an array of colored postcards designed to prove that Africa was the world's pioneer in various realms of knowledge, the arts, and sciences. Aesop was depicted relating his tales and thus passing on the wisdom of Africa to the Greeks. According to one of the postcards it was Tyro the African who, while Cicero's amanuensis, invented shorthand, while another asserted that the science of medicine originated with Africans in the ancient empire of Ghana. Yet another claimed that the Africans had taught the alphabet to the Greeks. Mathematics, chemistry, agriculture, and paper were also shown as African benefactions.

Like Hitler, who propagated the supremacy of the Nordic race and culture, Nkrumah preaches a contrary chauvinism based on the importance of being black. In all Ghanaian schools, teachers are required to impress on their pupils the basic beliefs of the Pan-African cult. Yet, ironically, the university students both in Ghana and abroad have come out as the principal critics of Nkrumah's totalitarian tactics. At home the move to replace some twenty lecturers who had resigned from the staff of Legon University College—which in October, 1961, became the University of Accra—with teachers from Russia, East Germany, Poland, and Yugoslavia provoked a storm of angry protest. About 450 students of Legon, with placards proclaiming: "We want an independent university. No Russians—No Poles," were dispersed only by the appearance of four platoons of police accompanied by three armored cars. Even so, they booed the amiable Kofi Baako, reputedly the most popular cabinet minister, when he tried to address them. Abroad in Britain, where some 3,000 young Ghanaians reside as students, anti-Nkrumah demonstrations were staged in London by nearly 400 students who had broken away from NASSO (the National Association of Socialist Students' Organizations), whose founder is the Osageyefo, to form a New Ghana Students' Association. Their manifesto denounced "totalitarian practices" in Ghana and demanded the repeal of the Preventive Detention Act. In a television interview, their president challengingly declared, "One of Dr. Nkrumah's great weapons in crushing criticism is fear." Allowing for the exuberance of youth, these defiant gestures testified to a degree of conviction and courage, since most of the students involved were wholly or partly maintained by government funds and, moreover, ran the risk of having their passports withdrawn.

Nkrumah countered the mutterings of these angry young men by intensified courses of brainwashing, calling on his party members, particularly members of parliament, to go out into the country and to work closely with the principals of colleges and schools, talking to students on citizenship, African independence and unity, and the activities of the government.

This was part of the "go-back-to-the-people" movement which followed the September, 1962, upheaval. Since then, on the educational as on the other fronts, the Osageyefo has pursued his zigzag tactics. Much publicity was given in Ghana to the dispatch of Ghanaian students and trainees to Russia and Eastern Europe, but everyone knew that they represented a tiny trickle compared with the growing flow of students to the West. Simultaneously, the newspapers published the activities of young American students in Ghana and the arrival of American Negro dentists in Accra, as also donations from the Canadian government and the signing of a Peace Corps agreement. Nkrumah has publicly and warmly acknowledged American and British aid for the Volta project. He has also welcomed Russian geologists and Israeli state farm managers.

His new seven-year development plan* is masterminded by a Hungarian economic expert, Dr. Bognar, who is reported to have advised the president frankly that party objectives must be reconciled with economic realities. This can be done by leaving the door open to both the East and the West, which Nkrumah is fitfully doing. The bulk of Ghana's external trade, about 75 percent, is absorbed by the West despite the fact that Accra has entered into nearly twenty trade agreements with the Communist countries. Out of some 400,000 tons of cocoa produced in 1961, the Soviet Union bought barely 11,000 tons, though Russia has since undertaken to boost its purchases to 60,000 tons a year over a five-year period. When Washington decided to "take another look" at the Volta River project, for which reliance on American planning is almost total, Accra hinted that in that event it might seek Soviet aid for the undertaking. In September, 1961, Ghana actually signed a contract for Soviet technical aid in carrying out survey work and the building of a power station on the Black Volta which would supply electricity to Ghana's northern regions. It is also establishing a nuclear research station with Soviet aid. But Nkrumah, as well as the Americans and the Russians, knows that Accra could not go it alone with Moscow.

The seven-year plan† puts the emphasis on agriculture and industry, with the objective of raising the living standards of the people and of freeing Ghana from its dependence on cocoa and imported food. The country needs investment from the West, and the World Bank is said to be interested in the National Investment Bank. Britain is also taking a greater share of the industrial investment called for in the new plan, which toward the end of the plan period foresees 38 percent of expenditure being devoted to industry and mining. In 1962 the Ghana government was willing to use credit to a far larger extent than before, and the fact that credit

* Estimated to cost $1.5 million.
† A five-year plan was suspended in 1961.

financing is now acceptable points to a change in the official attitude to the capitalist system. All government expenditure has been brought under stringent control by a central state control commission, with wide powers deriving directly from the president. Meanwhile, steps are being taken to increase the number of secondary industries and to extend the program of agricultural diversification. The basis of the industrialization program is the Volta River scheme.

To Ghana, a small and poor country, the Volta project spells the difference between progress at a snail's pace and a more rapid advance to at least a southern European standard of living. The project visualizes the damming of the Volta River—a plan conceived by the former British government nearly fifty years ago and revived in 1952—to produce more electric power than New York City uses, and to link this with an aluminum smelting plant, which will thereby turn to productive use Ghana's rich reserves of bauxite. In turn this must stimulate secondary industries and public services, irrigate a large area of the country, and double the supply of Ghana's staple food, fish. Three steps are involved in the project—the building of the dam, the construction of the hydroelectric station, and the erection of the aluminum smelter. The project, originally conceived on somewhat spectacular lines, was revised in 1958, and preliminary works were carried out in the area of the new dam at Akosombo, where the contract for the 370-foot-high dam has been given to an Italian consortium, which is now on the job. The power plant will initially generate 512 milliwatts and subsequently 768 milliwatts, the power being fed to an aluminum smelter at Tema, twenty-six miles from Accra, where a new port designed to handle an annual traffic of 1 million tons has been completed. The hydroelectric scheme has been mounted, and work is said to be proceeding ahead of schedule. Production of electricity is expected to begin late in 1965. I visited Tema when the port was nearing completion. It represents one of the most extensive civil engineering works Ghana has seen, and will help greatly to relieve the congestion at the old harbor of Takoradi, farther down the coast. The bauxite deposits are at Kibi, not far from Tema.

Some $196 million will be needed for the hydroelectric project, half of which will come from the Ghana government, the remainder consisting of loans from the World Bank (about $45 million), the United States government (about $37 million), and the British government (around $14 million). This aid is conditional on an agreement being signed between the Ghana government and an American consortium to build the aluminum smelter, the United States having agreed to lend nearly $93 million to the consortium. Nkrumah, despite his threats, knows that Ghana will find it difficult to mobilize such massive assistance from the East. At the same time, both he and the Americans realize that a repetition of the Aswan High Dam muddle will not help either Ghana or the West. Nkrumah can for some time afford to sit pretty. But only for so long as he is able to maintain his authority at home and not alienate the West to the point of having them refuse to underwrite any more of his development projects. His naked emphasis on dictatorship tends to frighten away foreign investment.

Europeans in West Africa are fond of comparing the Nigerians with the Ghanaians, more often than not to the detriment of the latter, who are often described as frothy, emotional, unrealistic, and impractical. Personally, I was more impressed by the purposefulness and nimble minds of the Ghanaians than of the Nigerians, who are prone to be garrulous and intellectually are less inquiring. This broad generalization, based only on talks with Ghanaians and Nigerians of various age groups and maturity, is obviously subject to some qualifications. But I noticed that even among the Europeans there was an interesting division of opinion, depending upon whether the speaker was an official or a businessman. Most officials rated the Nigerians higher, as being more stable and reliable, while the majority of the businessmen plumped for the Ghanaian as being of quicker aptitude and intelligence. The Ghanaians themselves regard the Nigerians somewhat superciliously as "dull dogs." In commercial keenness and shrewdness there is little to choose between the Yoruba market mammies and their counterparts in Accra, but, as a rule, the Ghanaian takes less kindly to business than the Nigerian, and, in an economy where nearly every sector is government-controlled and where the sphere of private enterprise is shrinking, the scope for entrepreneurs and business executives is naturally restricted.

In both Nigeria and Ghana, however, increased prices for tropical produce, and enlarged professional and political opportunities, had created an African middle class even before independence. Paradoxically, the presence of this growing middle class in both countries has intensified rivalry and given a sharp edge to competition between the two. Each tends to look down on the other, and their mutual suspicion expresses itself in charges of subversion against the other. Awolowo, once critical of Nkrumah, latterly drew closer to him, and when the Nigerian federal government suspended the western region government, a number of Action Group members took refuge in Ghana. Lagos has charged Accra with planting its political and trade union agents in Nigeria. Exchanges between the two countries at governmental and press levels are often noted for their acerbity. But even with Nigeria, Nkrumah now seems inclined to more friendly relations, as his decision to have Ghana represented at the Monrovia-sponsored conference at Lagos, which the Casablanca group boycotted in 1962, suggests. Perhaps Nkrumah now realizes that his dream of Pan-African unity is possible only if the two African groups draw closer, and live in amity and cooperation with each other. His chastening experiences at home might be inducing a more mellow outlook abroad. The trouble is that he is unpredictable.

The Osageyefo's oft-proclaimed dream of a united Africa, for which Ghana's constitution provides, allows for a surrender of sovereignty by Ghana in favor of a union of African states, should such a union be possible. But Nkrumah's own pressure tactics vis-à-vis his neighbors seems to belie his declared intention of surrendering Ghana's sovereignty in favor of such a union. While his neighbors are prepared to acknowledge the Osageyefo as their brother, they refuse to accept him as their keeper. "I see before my mind's eye," declared the Osageyefo shortly before the July crisis of 1961, "a great monolithic party, united and strong, spreading its protective wings over the whole of Africa from Algiers in the north to Cape Town in the south, and from Cape Guardafui in the east to Dakar in the west." This messianic vision of an Africa dominated by Ghana amuses and alarms the rest of Africa, which, while agreeing that the independent African states must be united among themselves, does not want to be united under one man or country.

Nkrumah's lyrical calls for African unity seem ironical in the context of his rapidly shrinking prestige at home. His megalomania, like that of other dictators, has induced a situation where subversion and attempts at assassination have become a substitute for political criticism. Yet it would be a mistake to underestimate him as a romantic, for the realist is also present in the complex compound of Nkrumah's character. He is no exotic showman or absurd clown, though the more extrovert theatrical elements in his character tempt him to be both. Behind the airy lightheadedness is an unusual hardheadedness. The grandiose dreams which encumber his thought and cloud it go with a shrewd practicability which expresses itself in the precarious balance he maintained until recently between the exuberant activists and the staid conservatives inside the Convention People's party and in his encouragement of foreign private investors by assurances in the Capital Investment Act of April, 1963, and the Budget of October alongside diatribes against the neocolonialism of the West.

Extravagant expenditure on prestige projects accompanies his exhortations for austerity in private living. For himself he casts cake on the waters in the hope that some day it may return as bread. His "scientific socialism" demands heavy sacrifices from citizens who are normally carefree and resent the growing dead weight of new taxes and increased stringency. "At the rate we're being asked to tighten our belts we'll soon cut ourselves into two," is the general lament. The political explosiveness, ignited largely by economic resentment, was nourished by the popular belief that independence when it came would lighten the weight on the individual's back. On the contrary, freedom has increased both the economic and political burdens. Dissatisfaction, hitherto largely submerged, began to surface, expressing itself in open criticism in parliament of measures such as the Foreign Travel (Exit Permit) Act, the Security Services Act and the Preventive Detention Amendment Act. Nkrumah has sought to stifle criticism by clamping a lid on it, but this has only led to eruptions in other and more violent forms.

Yet a country saddled with heavy loan commitments, with an estimated deficit on recurrent account and a steady depletion of its reserves (though Ghana has still some $168 million in its reserves) has no alternative but to embark on austerity measures. Ghana needs an extra $62 million from her population of 7 million, and this spells stern taxation. Economically, however, Ghana is progressing faster than most of her neighbors and has started ahead of them in industrialization and modern agricultural methods. The Volta hydroelectric dam is halfway to completion and the $76 million Tema harbor with its constellation of new industries, including a refinery and aluminum smelter, is in operation. The seven-year development plan will shortly be launched. The marketing of Ghana's $188 million cocoa crop through the farmers council is making headway, and apart from copper mining it constitutes the biggest single business unit in middle Africa. Ghana generally is economically stable, but the most unstable factor within the state is Nkrumah.

As an ideal, Nkrumah's call for continental unity and for the liberation of all Africa rings a bell in most African minds. Ghana is also in many ways well positioned to symbolize the urge—Trotskyite in some respects— that independence, like revolution, is a commodity not merely to be enjoyed at home, but to be exported abroad. On the day of Ghana's independence on March 6, 1957, Nkrumah declared: "Our independence is meaningless unless it is linked up with the total liberation of the African continent."

He was right in his aim but wrong in his assessment of the sensitivities of his African brethren, who, while welcoming continental unity and freedom, do not relish them as a gift descending from Ghana. Nkrumah's monolithic conception of the state and the party has led him not only to ignore, but to steamroller the rights of the individual in his own country. His impatience with countries and leaders outside Ghana who do not share his doctrines and dogmas is not calculated to enhance his popularity or induce his acceptance as a continental leader, though, like Nasser in the Arab world, his ideas are attractive to many young radicals in sub-Saharan Africa. Moreover, Ghana is socially and economically more forward-looking than Nigeria, richer than the Ivory Coast, and educationally more advanced than most African countries. But Nkrumah's package deal is suspect as retaining the aces in Ghana's hand. Like Nasser, Nkrumah feels cramped within the confines of his country and would like to burst its boundaries. Ironically many of his countrymen in turn would like to burst the Nkrumah bubble within Ghana.

Between the Osageyefo's dream of a united Africa where the last vestiges of colonialism will be eradicated is the looming nightmare of "Eurafrica" which eighteen African States* are prepared to join as associate members. Ghana, Nigeria, Tanganyika, and former French Guinea have declined to enter the European Common Market as associate states.† If "Eurafrica" comes into being, as seems inevitable, it must undermine Nkrumah's central theme of continental unity, and will shake its political and economic foundations. Hence Ghana's fierce attacks on the Common Market at the U.N. and elsewhere.

The differences are largely a legacy of the differences between the French and British colonial systems in Africa in their political and economic manifestations. Whereas the French saw in their African territories a political extension of the mother country, which according to the parental concept had physically and economically to sustain its dependents, the British held before their African colonies the political ideal of self-government, but also insisted that economically they should as far as possible be self-supporting. Compared with the French subsidies, the British grants were modest, and while Britain conceded some imperial preference on tropical products, she had no analogous system to the French, who guaranteed that their colonies' internal overdrafts and external imbalances would be covered by Paris. Thus, while France drew its African colonies into a centralized economic system controlled by Paris, the British required their African dependencies to maintain themselves with little aid from London, and encouraged them to trade with the world. In effect the French system created a closed shop, with its colonies as part of a close-threaded economic web controlled from Paris and were members of a single monetary system, the franc zone, which did not lean heavily on world markets. The economic dependence of the former French colonies on the mother country is, therefore, far greater than that of the former British colonies on London. Politically, the Belgians in the Congo followed the

---

* The eighteen Associated States are: Cameroun, the Central African Republic, Ivory Coast, Dahomey, Gabon, Upper Volta, Malagasy, Mali, Mauritania, Niger, Senegal, Somalia, Chad, Togo, Rwanda and Burundi, and the two Republics of the Congo (Congo-Brazzaville and Congo-Léopoldville, respectively, the former French and Belgian Congo).

† More recently, Kenya, Uganda, and Tanganyika have asked the European Economic Community to open negotiations on a link between the European and East African Common Markets.

French model closely, but economically the system they adopted was nearer the British. The Congo as a wealthy colony financed its own development and was nondiscriminatory in trade.

Nkrumah sees in the bid to unite Europe a menace to the unity of Africa, which could be further Balkanized along the French-English linguistic frontiers in West Africa. Mali, despite the union with Ghana and Guinea, has identified herself with the European Common Market, and from 1959 to 1962 has collected $15 million from the aid fund of the European Economic Community. She is unlikely to sacrifice these bounties to placate Nkrumah, who insisted that only by the political elimination of colonialism and by economic planning on a continental scale, without dependence on foreign capital assistance, would Africa be able to redeem her economic and political soul. But the action of the eighteen African states willing to join the European Common Market as associate members demonstrates how heavily mortgaged the former French colonies still are to Paris. This economic mortgage spells renewed political dependence on Europe, which Nkrumah accuses of neocolonialism, of attempting to reenter Africa by the economic back door. It re-creates the old relationship between the colonial masters and their dependents, especially between France and its former African territories, who are reduced to the status of French "clients" and "valets of the imperialists." "Eurafrica," with its suggestion of the subordination of Africa to Europe, could be an inflammatory focal point capable of igniting both Europe and Africa.

At the Casablanca group meeting in Cairo in June, 1962, where Nkrumah was represented by his foreign minister, it was decided to form an African Common Market in 1963, but this would be limited largely to the six members* of the group whose economies are more competitive than complementary, and whose collective resources and potential represent a small proportion of all Africa's. The Cairo conference denounced Israeli "imperialism," but Ghana maintains economic ties with Israel, and neither Guinea nor Mali is likely to look askance at technical assistance from that quarter. Mali, moreover, is a member of the closed ring of the European Common Market, while Morocco has special ties with Europe, and Algeria will need massive French aid and assistance for some years. At the U.N. Economic Commission for Africa conference in mid-1962, the necessity for African states to keep out of agreements liable to impede inter-African trade was urged by Ghana, Nigeria, and Liberia, but was vigorously opposed by the French bloc and the former Belgian Congo, which favored association with Europe. Yet at Lagos and Monrovia these same ex-French African states had earlier agreed with Liberia and Nigeria on the African Common Market, an African Development Fund, and the

* Egypt, Ghana, Guinea, Mali, Morocco, and Algeria.

necessity for close intercontinental economic cooperation, even though in Brussels and Paris some of them had opposed extending the aid fund of the EEC to African states outside the French Community. Africa appears to suffer from a multisplit personality, which poses a serious if concealed challenge to Nkrumah's call for African unity. Ultimately, whether a state is a member of the Casablanca, Brazzaville, or Monrovia groups,* each country is likely to put its own individual interests before those of the group to which it belongs. And the interests conflict and compete.

The Osageyefo's efforts to make Accra the epicenter of the African world have ranged over a wide field. A decision to set up an All-African High Command at Accra was approved by the Cairo conference of the Casablanca powers in June, 1962, with an Egyptian general working in Accra under the civil authority of a Moroccan secretary operating in Cairo. Such an organization might conceivably provide weapons and training to U.N. African troops in trouble spots other than the Congo, though in that case the Monrovia group might resent the U.N.'s exclusive dependence on the African High Command. Early in 1962 the Osageyefo planned to double his 8,000-man army, and expand his navy and air force, so as to give Ghana a more powerful voice in West Africa and also, according to him, to stave off any projected attack on Ghana until help came. The Ghana-sponsored "World Without the Bomb" conference, held a few months later in Accra, announced the election of a ten-member council to work out a plan for the demilitarization of Africa and the mobilization of public opinion in favor of nuclear disarmament. The conference also called for an inter-African disarmament and nonaggression pact underwritten by the member states of the United Nations. The council elected at Accra consisted of members from nonaligned countries such as Morocco, Brazil, Switzerland, Afghanistan, the United Arab Republic, India, Ireland, Yugoslavia, Ghana, and Kenya.

What sort of man is Nkrumah? He has considerable charm, dignity, and poise, and on the only occasion I met him, at Accra for a brief moment when Krobo Edusei introduced two Indian newspaper colleagues and myself, he was gracious enough to shake hands and murmur a few polite pleasantries.† Nkrumah, whose language is a dialect of Twi, one of the Akan tongues,‡ is a personable man with a high-domed forehead, a sensitive mouth, and melancholy brooding eyes which occasionally light up, as Nehru's did, when something interests or amuses him. He is said to have a sense of humor. He speaks excellent English, which is not surprising, for he went abroad in 1935 when he was twenty-six, first to the United

---

* Which are now ostensibly one.
† Since he was allegedly misquoted some years ago the Osageyefo rarely gives interviews to foreign correspondents in Ghana.
‡ Attempts are being made to Akanize languages like Fanti, Ga, Ewi, and Twi.

States, where he studied at Lincoln and Pennsylvania universities, and also visited Canada, staying in North America for ten years. In 1945 he left the United States for England, where he studied for two years at the London School of Economics, though his main preoccupation in England appears to have been politics. He became organizing secretary, with George Padmore, for the Sixth Pan-African Conference at Manchester in 1945, and was later secretary of the West African National Secretariat. At Manchester the gospel of Pan-Africanism first burned itself into his mind. Nkrumah has a natural aptitude for organization and, unlike some African leaders, exults in hard work. His most severe critic could not challenge his absolute dedication to Ghana and to the cause of Pan-Africanism as he sees it.

Nkrumah also differs from some other African leaders in that, while afflicted with an inflated ego, he is far more purposeful, resolute, and dynamic than any of them. He is vain to the point of megalomania and conscious of the overwhelming authority he exercises. I have a feeling that Nkrumah really regards himself as the symbol of the African Personality and that, in wanting to project that personality throughout the continent, he wants to stamp his personal image and impress on the face of Africa. For a man of his political exuberance he can, when the occasion demands it, be resilient, cautious, and calculating, which is why, unlike other African extremists, he does not leap toward but zigzags to his targets.

Thus, while his objective remains a Socialist welfare state and a Pan-African socialism for the entire continent on the Ghana pattern, his tactics shift with the exigencies of the situation.

From the African stage the Osageyefo struts intermittently on the global stage, holding aloft the banner of world peace and Pan-Africanism, neither of which can be conjured into being by showmanship or sleight of hand, and both of which remain elusive ideals on a murky and distant horizon. But the African Personality looms larger every day, even if its image is divided and distorted. In the personalities of Nkrumah of Ghana and Sékou Touré of Guinea, Africa increasingly sees the promise of an entire continent united in rejecting imperialism and "neocolonialism"— united, too, in working for African independence and cohesion, and for the economic integration of the continent.

Despite his extravagances, his exuberance and theatricality, Nkrumah, like Nasser, cannot easily be written off. He is more of a deflated dictator than Nasser, but both men are in deadly earnest.

7

FRENCH SPECTRUM

HOW VARIED IS the impact of different European civilizations, cultures, and political systems on the peoples of Africa! Coming from Nigeria to Dahomey, once part of former French West Africa, was like stepping from one world into another. Nigeria with its 50 million people is Africa's most populous state. With an area of a little over 44,000 square miles and a population of 2 million, Dahomey is among the smallest of the former ten French West African territories.

But the contrast isn't only in size. Cotonou, the main port, where we flew in from Lagos, looks out on the Bay of Benin, along a coastline once notorious for slave-hunting. At the airport were bearded French priests in white cassocks, wearing sun helmets, while around them were vivacious family groups, many of them racially mixed. The Dahomeyans, though poor, have an exceptionally large educated elite, and carry themselves with an air of courtliness and assurance. Outside the airport, the sunlit landscape erupted with casurianas and bougainvillaea, with temple flowers and green cascading palms. It was humid, and an atmosphere of languor, lassitude, and lotus-eating permeated the place. It was like something out of a Somerset Maugham story.

French-reared Africans seem more lively than their British-bred equivalents, and one marveled how the impact of two different European civilizations could create two completely different types among the Yoruba who inhabit western Nigeria and the Yoruba who live in a part of Dahomey. The commercial zest which characterizes Nigeria's Yoruba women is not noticeable among the Yoruba of Dahomey, whose kings once ruled the country, and in Dahomey trade takes a placid pattern, unemployment is widespread, and the country's economy is poised precariously on palm kernels, palm oil, and coffee. Without generous French aid, Dahomey would not be viable.*

Although at one time a self-governing member of the French Community, Dahomey, like many of the other member states used the Communauté as a steppingstone to independence, but her links with France are sustained by treaties for economic, technical, and military cooperation. The Balkanization of former French Africa, which resulted in the creation of ten independent states in French West Africa† and of four—Gabon, the Republic of Chad, the Central African Republic, and Congo (Brazzaville)—in French Equatorial Africa, has induced a movement toward union or federation among some of them, alongside the recognition of the need for a close economic tie-up with France. Guinea with Mali preferred a union with Ghana, but this has not prevented Mali from belonging to the franc zone and from being an associate member of the European Economic Community.

At one time Dahomey was inclined to join the proposed federation of Senegal and Sudan,‡ which collapsed in August, 1960, after lasting a little over two months. Upper Volta tended the same way, but President Houphouet-Boigny of the Ivory Coast and the French were able to dissuade the two countries from taking this step. Later Dahomey and Upper Volta formed a Council of Understanding (Conseil d'Entente) with Niger and the Ivory Coast, chiefly at the latter's initiative. These four countries, which are independent and opted out of the French Community, coordinate their economic and foreign policies, and consult one another regularly. Along with Senegal and Mauritania, they also maintain a customs

* In October, 1963, the Dahomeyan army seized power, suspended the 1960 constitution, and dissolved the provisional three-man government headed by President Hubert Maga, and the national assembly. The trouble was sparked by the trade unionists who demanded Maga's resignation. Colonel Chrostoph Soglo headed the new provisional government. In January, 1964, a referendum endorsed the Dahomey Democratic party, the only organization to present a national list of candidates. M. Soupon Migan Apithy was elected president and M. Justin Ahomadegbe vice-president.

† The Ivory Coast, the Republic of Togoland, the Republic of Mali, Guinea, Cameroun, Dahomey, Upper Volta, Mauritania, Niger, and Senegal.

‡ Now known as Mali. The short-lived federation was known as the Federation of Mali.

union.* All look to France for economic aid and financial help. Dahomey also has a customs union with the Togo Republic.

To an Asian whose country is a member of the Commonwealth, the development of the French idea of Communauté and its virtual dissolution offers many interesting points of comparison and contrast with the Commonwealth. Despite De Gaulle, whose courage and imagination laid the foundations of a Free France in Africa, the French emerge as politically less resilient than the British and constitutionally less adaptable. The British, while converting the British Commonwealth, initially composed of white countries (devoted to the Crown and regarding it as the fount, symbol, and link which bound them together), into a Commonwealth to include the newly independent Asian and African countries, some of which were assertively republican, were confronted with a more complicated and delicate task. Through various stages, starting with the Brazzaville conference late in 1944, when De Gaulle recognized the inevitability of self-government in Africa but insisted on the indivisibility of France and her overseas territories, De Gaulle moved in 1959 to a position analogous to that of the British. He agreed then that the character and the composition of the Communauté could be changed to admit independent African states as members, but he rejected firmly the idea of an Afro-French federation in which France would be an equal partner, an idea zealously canvassed by Africans such as Houphouet-Boigny, who could not be suspected of any anti-French bias and indeed is derided by many of his countrymen as "a black Frenchman."

The result of this fiat was that by the end of 1960 all the former French colonies and trust territories† in Africa, including the island of Madagascar, now known as Malagasy, were independent, but of the fifteen only six opted to stay within the Community. They were the four former states of French Equatorial Africa, Senegal, and Malagasy. The remainder, plumping for complete independence outside the Community, retained their ties with France through bilateral agreements. While Houphouet-Boigny had advocated an Afro-French federation, the militant President Sékou Touré of Guinea, who was rightly apprehensive of the Balkanization of Africa, and desperately anxious to preserve its strength and unity, had urged the establishment of two independent federations, one of West, the other of Equatorial Africa. Both Sékou Touré and Houphouet-Boigny favored the federal idea, though their approach and plan differed. But the very idea of federalism was anathema to De Gaulle, a perplexing personality compounded of idealism and imperiousness. As

---

* Upper Volta left the customs union in 1961 and signed a customs union with Ghana.

† The trust territories were Togo and Cameroun.

a result of De Gaulle's strange imperviousness, France's African colonies, instead of comprising one or two federations, were split into fifteen independent units, six of them within the Communauté. On the rebound, Houphouet-Boigny, otherwise ardently pro-French, preferred to keep the Ivory Coast out of the Community.

What motivated De Gaulle in his stubborn rejection of the federal idea? Federalism was instinct in the French system of rule, for the territories of West Africa were formerly under a governor-general stationed at Dakar, while the territories of Equatorial Africa were under a governor-general at Brazzaville, both of whom were responsible to the French minister of colonies in Paris. The African suspicion that France thereby calculated on keeping her former colonies in her economic leading strings, while setting them politically adrift and independent, is not unjustified, and is confirmed by more recent developments within the European Economic Community. On the other hand, it might with some justification be argued that De Gaulle has subsequently veered round to a concept of association looser than that of the Commonwealth and that, though the term *Communauté* is largely out of date, a definite community of interests exists between Paris and the independent African states, even if it does not rest on the recognition of the French president as its head and no longer acknowledges the centralized authority of Paris. The link between France and its former African territories still continues, with the possible exception of Guinea,* through varying relationships, sometimes close and definite, as in the case of Senegal and the four states of former French Equatorial Africa, or imprecise, as in the case of Mali and Upper Volta, both of which have demanded the evacuation of French bases in their territory and spurn military alliances. Upper Volta left the entente customs union and has an association with Ghana, which gives her an alternative outlet to the sea through Accra instead of Abidjan, the Ivory Coast capital. Upper Volta has also three times the volume of trade with Mali and Ghana that it has with its entente associates.

It was the old centralization in Paris which accelerated the process of liberation. Here again the French system of colonial liberation differs from that of the British, who staggered the process of constitutional advance, at least in the case of their African territories. In Asia, the independence of India, Pakistan, Burma, and Ceylon was telescoped within a few months, India and Pakistan achieving their independence simultaneously with partition. But in Africa the British have moved more slowly.

* Guinea returned to the Western fold in May, 1963, France agreeing to pay $24 million in back pay to Guineans who had served in the French army, thereby wiping out Guinea's debt to France and leaving her with $6 million credit. Guinea is expected back in the franc zone.

France, in contrast, has pursued a common policy and worked to a time-table, fourteen separate territories in different stages of development being liberated within four years, while eight of them proclaimed their independence in 1960 within two days of each other. Except in Guinea, where Sékou Touré's initial decision to opt out of the Community enraged the French, who for so mature a people reacted adolescently, and Cameroun, where a large-scale revolt was staged by the leftist UPC (Union des Populations Camerounaises) led by Ruben um Nyobe and Felix Moumie, both of whom were killed, the transition to independence was generally smooth. The short-lived federation between Senegal and Soudan, now known as Mali, saw a brief flash of dislocation and unrest.

Politically, too, the British and the French areas initially differed in their constitutional setup, for, while the two-party rule prevailed in many former British colonies, the one-man, one-party system of government prevails in almost all the ex-French territories. Even in former British-ruled areas the trend today is toward one-party rule, with a few threateningly transient exceptions. In ex-French Africa the tendency is increasingly in the same direction. In Upper Volta, where there were at one time numerous opposition parties, President Maurice Yameogo adopted the summary expedient of either banning them or merging them in his party, the Union Démocratique Voltaïque. The more persistent and vocal of his opponents he exiled. Similarly in the Central African Republic, thirty-three-year-old President David Dacko silenced the opposition party in February, 1961, by banning it. There are, however, two or more parties in territories such as Gabon, Cameroun, and Malagasy.

In August, 1963, President Youlou's attempt to impose a one-party state in the Congo (Brazzaville) was checkmated by the workers, who freed their imprisoned comrades and forced the resignation of the forty-six-year-old Abbé Fulbert Youlou, a defrocked member of the Roman Catholic clergy. Youlou's attempt to use the French troops in Brazzaville against the demonstrators was vetoed by De Gaulle, who thereby exposed the falsehood of the Communist contention that an overt colonialism had been replaced by a covert one.* The successful overthrow of the Youlou regime also showed that at least some African workers do not subscribe to the view that democracy is a Machiavellian European invention, and that

---

* De Gaulle, however, permitted French troops under General Kergaravot to intervene in Gabon in February, 1964, to quell an army mutiny and to restore President Léon Mba to office. Help had been requested by the vice-president, and De Gaulle's action was strictly legal. But earlier he had refused to intervene not only in Brazzaville but in Dahomey. One reason might have been the precedent set by the intervention of British troops, also on request by the governments concerned, to quell the army mutinies in Tanganyika, Uganda, and Kenya in January, 1964. Gabon also has rich mineral deposits, produces yearly a million tons of petroleum, and has considerable forest wealth.

a one-party system is best suited to Africa and African conditions. There were three parties functioning in Brazzaville when Youlou sought to clamp down his one-party rule. The provisional government which replaced him consists chiefly of "nonpolitical" technicians headed by forty-two-year-old Alphonse Massamba-Debat, a moderate who belonged to Youlou's party and is also pro-French. The rebel leaders thereby proved that they bore no ill-will to France or to Europeans as a whole, and that the rights of the workers could not easily be tramped upon by a would-be dictator.

While British colonial policy in Africa aimed at making the Africans self-governing, French colonial policy aimed at making them Frenchmen. During the last war a story was told in India of the then French governor-general of Pondicherry, who had opted for the Free French. At a British dinner party held at Government House, Bombay, the wife of the British governor conversationally inquired of her French guest how many French-men there were in Pondicherry.

"Madam," he explained politely, "we are all Frenchmen."

Neither in Nigeria nor Ghana has the withdrawal of the British created a perceptible vacuum, but in the French territories the withdrawal of the French has done so in varying degrees. This is indicative of the difference between the British and French colonial methods, for, while the British concentrated on bringing up each territory separately and spacing its independence according to its rate of development, the French, with authority centralized in Paris, worked to no ordained timetable, but to a formula which did not take political maturity or constitutional progress very much into account. Algeria's belated independence was due to the aggressive presence of a million *colons*. Elsewhere, a rule of thumb was applied, which in effect made no real distinction between a comparatively advanced state like Senegal, the oldest French colony in Africa, which had a second generation of Africans in the professions, in the cadre of civil servants, and among its politicians, and, say, the poor and backward Central African Republic.

The French have succeeded in Gallicizing the Africans far more strongly than the British have in Anglicizing them, but, even as in Asia, so also in Africa the crust of foreign-educated individuals is thin, and even the French-trained Africans constitute a slim layer and are more removed from the masses than their Asian British-educated equivalents. This may be because of the deeper impregnation of French education and culture, which have infiltrated further into the African mind and being than British education and culture have in the Asian. Even so, the younger generation of radical Africans look upon such symbols of French upbringing as Houphouet-Boigny and Léopold Senghor as slightly old-fashioned and out of date. Among the younger generation, even among those who are

French-educated, the mystic tie with France is wearing thin. Perhaps one reason why the Asian* and African countries of the Commonwealth agreed to continue as members after independence, while most of the African states chose to opt out of the Community, was because the personality of Paris predominated in this relationship, and typified a subservience expressed in the earlier insistence on the indivisibility of France and her overseas territories, which many Africans found mortifying to their sensitivity and pride. Some French Africans still find it hard to understand how Nigeria and Ghana can remain in the Commonwealth without having their independence affected by Britain.

Economically, however, the new independent states of former French West and Equatorial Africa remain for all practical purposes mortgaged to France,† and in a sense this economic hegemony is far more insidious than direct rule, for the former French territories remain as firmly tied to the financial chariot wheels of France as they were before independence, and are subservient to her economic directives. Realization of this and consciousness of the dilemma in which they find themselves have led even pro-French Africans such as Houphouet-Boigny and Léopold Senghor to find alternative or complementary economic props elsewhere, though, during a tour of Western capitals in 1962, Houphouet-Boigny went out of his way in Washington to stress that the aid he was asking from the United States "would complement, not diminish French economic aid." As the London *Economist* commented at the time, the tour might have been intended "to reduce his dependence on France." On the other hand, the British in Africa refrained from drawing their colonies into a well-knit, centralized system controlled by London, but preferred to hold them on a loose economic rein, allowing them to trade with other parts of the world, to be self-supporting, and to keep the greater part of what they earned. This difference in economic approach has been reflected in developments since independence.

Virtually all the new independent countries of West Africa, whether of the former French or British bloc, rely, though in varying degrees, on foreign money, markets, and know-how. None of them likes it, but none of them can afford to do otherwise. Even the rebel states of Guinea and Mali are gravitating slowly toward France, and shortly after the Evian agreement, which removed the roadblock of Algeria, President Sékou Touré of Guinea, regarded as the most radical of them all, spoke of a *rapprochement* between his country and France. Earlier, in December,

---

* With the exception of Burma.

† A temporary exception was Guinea, whose brusque treatment by the French after it had chosen complete independence outside the Community forced it initially to seek other alignments.

1961, Sékou Touré had expelled the Soviet Ambassador, Mr. Daniel Solod, from Conakry for his connection with the left-wing antigovernment disturbances in Guinea. After the Evian agreement in March, 1962, Nasser, probably anxious to woo France away from her understanding with Israel, declared that the Algerian cease-fire could pave the way for new relations between France and Africa.

Compared with France's economic tie-up with her former territories, British aid to and investment in her ex-colonies is small. France spends several times more than Britain in Africa, hoping thereby to project and preserve her power and influence in the continent. In addition to continuing her preindependence aid on the pattern of Britain's Colonial Development and Welfare, and Colonial Development Corporation funds, France has succeeded in attracting thirteen of her fourteen former African colonies in west and equatorial Africa,* along with Malagasy and the Congo (Léopoldville), as associate members of the European Common Market. Britain has failed to persuade Ghana, Nigeria, or Tanganyika to step in. To Ghana and Guinea associate membership of the ECM spells a derogation of their political sovereignty and constitutes a neocolonialism, which they see as a threat to their Pan-African dream.

Within the last decade France has poured into Africa, south of the Sahara, public capital comprising subsidies, budgetary subventions, price supports, capital aid, and technical assistance which is conservatively estimated at $300 million a year. The real figure is believed to be far higher. Additionally the joint Common Market Fund for Development (FIDOM) makes available another $100 million a year to Africa. As against this tremendous outlay, Britain's contribution to Ghana's Volta project, rated to cost some $196 million, was about $4 million, and Britain gave a similar sum to Nigeria's $1.8 billion six-year plan, for which America provided $224 million. In Africa, as also in Asia, the countries of the Commonwealth, such as Ghana, Nigeria, Tanganyika, India, and Ceylon, who decline to be associate members of the ECM, will lose the former preferences they enjoyed in the British market and will be confronted by a rising tariff barrier which might exclude them eventually from Europe and Britain. If, for instance, Britain takes no step to safeguard the interests of her former African territories, the ECM could levy a tariff on cocoa from Ghana, but not from the Ivory Coast, and on peanut oil from Nigeria, but not from Senegal.†

Thus "Eurafrica," while uniting Europe, threatens to divide Africa. In turn this has accelerated a move for federation or closer union among the

* The exception is Guinea.
† France's opposition to British entry into the ECM has temporarily rendered the issue academic.

West African states which is supported not only by the militants like Guinea and Ghana, but by the moderates like Senegal and the Ivory Coast, all of whom increasingly realize that, while foreign economic aid has its temporary uses, it can be wielded as a political blunderbuss, and that a constant and consistent flow of trade between the African countries and with markets abroad is a sounder guarantee of political independence and long-term economic progress. The militants would like international trade to extend to both Europe and Asia, but the moderates seem to prefer keeping it to a restricted area. Houphouet-Boigny is often quoted as saying, "Africa must be an extension of Europe and not of Asia." In Paris, in August, 1961, he expanded on this theme in a reference to cooperation with the "so-called Afro-Asian group." Said the president of the Ivory Coast: "I do not see why we should be united with Asians any more than with formerly colonized Frenchmen or Americans. . . . I think it is in our interest that the problems of Africa should have an African solution."

Between themselves within Africa, the militants and the moderates also tend to draw closer. For different reasons both sides are anxious to create, consolidate, and cement greater continental unity. Nkrumah's dream of Pan-Africanism has led him to entertain President Mocktar Ould Daddah of Mauritania, a Monrovian nation which is not recognized by Morocco, Ghana's ally in the Casablanca group. He opposed Guinea's move to withdraw African troops from the Congo, and reached an agreement with President Maurice Yameogo of Upper Volta, another Monrovian state, to liberalize their common frontiers. Nkrumah would like the Monrovia and Casablanca groups to get together.* So would Prime Minister Sir Abubakar Balewa of Nigeria, a patron of the Monrovia group, who sees no aberration in visiting the president of Guinea. Similarly, Houphouet-Boigny spent a cordial week with President Modibo Keita of Mali, and while in Washington referred to "my brother Sékou Touré" and to other revolutionary leaders as "loyal and reliable partners who should be brought to adopt saner views by persuasion, not by threats or boycott." Houphouet-Boigny, however, does not share Nkrumah's dream of Pan-Africanism, with the whole African continent brought together under one man or country. He is for African unity, but "a unity of aspiration toward a constructive cooperation, in mutual respect, and in the affirmation of the personality of each state."

The spectrum of West African states reveals a variegated pattern. With the exception of the two tiny slivers of Portuguese Guinea and Gambia, which is self-governing but not independent, the great bulge of Africa from Port Étienne in Mauritania to the frontiers of Cameroun contains a hive of independent states, varying greatly in size, population, progress,

* This was effected on paper at the Addis Ababa conference of May, 1963.

potentialities, and wealth, all of which increase as one moves from north to south. In the wastes of the great northern deserts are infertile, indigent countries such as Niger and Chad. Central and northern Mauritania also cover arid tracts peopled largely by nomads who subsist on a pastoral economy, but along the alluvial valley of the Senegal River, which forms the southern boundary, the soil favors subsistence farming. Mauritania looks out on the west to the Atlantic Ocean, but the coastline is uninviting, with sandbanks and a battering surf. Only the existence of iron deposits in the northwest and of copper deposits lower down around Akjoujit saves the country from extreme poverty.

Below the bleak inhospitable north are the grassland plains of the savanna belt, where Senegal, Mali, and Upper Volta are largely confined. Mali, which takes its name from the empire which flourished over parts of the territory in the thirteenth and fourteenth centuries, is more than self-sufficient in food, watered as it is by the Niger, which flows from the mountains of Guinea, arching in a great loop southward as it bisects Nigeria to descend into the sea. Mali contains no large mineral resources, though there are indications of bauxite and diamonds. Its capital is Bamako. As in the Islamic north, Mali's people are mainly Moslem. The landlocked Republic of Upper Volta is poor in economic resources, its main wealth consisting of livestock, but, sharing as it does the same underlying geological formations as the neighboring areas of the Ivory Coast and Ghana, it is believed to have some mining resources, with known deposits of manganese and iron ore which, however, have small commercial value. Gold is also mined, but in negligible quantities. Senegal's economy is based on agriculture, with peanuts as the main cash crop, but it had the advantage for many years that its capital, Dakar, was also the capital of the former French West African colonies. Senegal's prosperity stems from Dakar, which is situated at the crossroads of three continents: Africa, Europe, and America. Like Mali, another principal source of Senegal's income is stock-raising and, as in other adjacent regions, there are mining potentialities which include phosphates and oil. An oil refinery at Dakar is in the offing.

The wealth of West Africa, however, is concentrated on the coastline, fronted by the mangrove swamps, with the screen of the rain forest behind. With the exception of Gambia, Togo, and Dahomey, which are too microscopic for independent commercial development, and Sierra Leone, starkly endowed by nature and one of the smallest and poorest of the West African territories, most of the other coastal states are economically progressive. Even Sierra Leone is thought to have iron ore and diamond deposits, but these have yet to be fully explored or exploited. Liberia, the oldest independent state in this area, was for long virtually underwritten by the Firestone Company, but more recently she has developed her iron ore resources to a point where they compete with the Firestone monopoly, which has also been eroded by the output of private Liberian-owned plantations, now accounting for 60 percent of the country's rubber output. Self-governing Gambia is poor and isolated, and, like Sierra Leone, can only remain viable with U.K. subsidies. The alternative is absorption by Senegal, which engulfs her.

At the top of the scale is Ghana, with an annual per capita income of nearly $200, with Senegal close behind, and tapering down to countries like Upper Volta, with less than $50 per head, and the microstates of Niger, Chad, Dahomey, and Togo, whose per capita income it is not possible even to compute. Geological surveys suggest that a good proportion of West Africa's mineral wealth, including Guinea's bauxite and iron ore, and Ghana's gold and manganese, lie within 300 miles of the coast. Nigeria's oilfields are in the mangrove swamps edging the sea. Even tiny Togo is hopeful of developing her phosphate resources and of exploiting the geographical situation of her capital, Lomé, to serve as an entrepôt not only for the hinterland, but for neighboring Dahomey and Ghana, and for Nigeria. The coastal states are rich in tropical agriculture, in cocoa, coffee, palm products, timber, and bananas.

These economic disparities and contrasts proliferate in other spheres— in population, where Nigeria's 50 million contrast with Mauritania's 700,000, and in the differing development of cities such as Accra and Lomé. Consciousness of these disparities has, again, stimulated the urge for some form of union or unity, expressed in such associations as the Union of Ghana, Guinea, and Mali; the Conseil d'Entente comprising the Ivory Coast, Dahomey, Niger, and Upper Volta; the African States Union and Malagasy, representative of the Monrovia group; the Equatorial Union of French Central Africa; and the miscellaneous elements of East, Central, and South Africa which are banded together in the Pan-African Freedom Movement.

Yet the divisive trends and influences, impelled largely by competitive forces and self-interest, are strong, if momentarily submerged, and it is doubtful if all or any of the more affluent African states are prepared to water down their wealth to share it with their needy neighbors. On the contrary, as we have seen, some of the associated African states within the charmed circle of the ECM and FIDOM, notably the Ivory Coast, are reluctant to extend it or throw it open to other African countries. They would like to enjoy even more exclusive advantages and exercise stronger trade discrimination. Nor is it correct to assume that the basic differences are polarized between the Casablanca constellation of Egypt, Ghana, Guinea, Mali, and Morocco, and the Monrovia group which comprises almost all the others. There are fissures within each group. What Barbara Ward describes as "a kind of second, submerged Africa just below the level of the present leadership"* has become increasingly strident within both groups and is likely to grow more assertive.†

In its issue of June 4–10, the Tunis weekly, *Jeune Afrique*, published the results of an inquiry it conducted among 300 African university students in France. The figures are intriguing. Of the students from the Casablanca countries quite 41 percent expressed disagreement with their leaders, while among students from former French Equatorial Africa, whose four state governments are right-wing, some 81 percent disagreed with their leaders. With the exception of Guinea and Mali, the other eight territorial governments in ex-French West Africa are middle-of-the-road administrations, but even so, 63 percent of the African students from these regions were critical of their governments. As priorities go, 28 percent of the students on an overall basis were of the opinion that the primary responsibility of Africans was to fight for African unity, but the majority of them, contrary to the views of the Casablanca bloc, favored the continuance of economic and cultural links with France and, by implication, with Europe. Only a third of them pressed for political links with Paris. It would therefore seem that a considerable element of the younger generation in both groups, while more radical than their leaders in domestic policies, are more realistic than many of them in their foreign attitudes. They do not want political subservience to France, but at the same time they would like to continue their economic and cultural associations with Paris. While they are not unduly enamored of the vision of Pan-Africanism, they favor more liberal and progressive governments at home. However, to assume from this restricted—and it may be selective—poll that the figures reflect the views of young Africa could be misleading and even glib.

Both groups are miscellaneous in their membership. The Casablanca group, though smaller, is less well knit, for it contains English-speaking and French-speaking members who are also conscious of the dividing line between Arab and African. With the sole exception of Mauritania, the Monrovians come from south of the Sahara, and the twelve countries of the African and Malagasy Union which form the core of the Monrovia group are all French-speaking and belong to the franc zone. They number some 30 million. Then there are the English-speaking countries such

---

* *Foreign Affairs*, April, 1962.

† The Addis Ababa conference decided to integrate the Commission for Technical Cooperation in Africa (set up in 1950 by European countries with African responsibilities including France and Britain) into the Organization of African Unity. France then decided to oppose unilaterally the convention, setting up the Commission which now consists predominantly of African members. Its secretary general since 1962 has been M. Mamadon Touré of Mauritania.

as Nigeria, Liberia, and Sierra Leone, which are guest members, as well as itinerant visitors such as Ethiopia, which belongs to neither language category. On the whole, the gravitational pull of "Eurafrica" appears to be overwhelming so far as the African French-speaking members of either group are concerned.

Political cleavage is likely to develop on the economic dividing line between the French-speaking and English-speaking African countries, and between Arab and African, for, with the exception of Tunisia, the other former French colonies in North Africa belong or incline to the Casablanca group, though even among them economic necessity impels countries like Algeria and Morocco toward Eurafrica. Egypt, with Ghana, spearheads the Casablanca group. Libya has its feet in both camps while ex-British Sudan, like Ethiopia, with whom it has differences, hovers on the rim of the Monrovia group, but would like to live at peace with both sides. Though each group may differ in its order of priorities within its member states, both Casablanca and Monrovia are united in denouncing colonialism, in supporting African independence and unity, and in paying lip service to some form of continental economic integration. But are the unities of Africa any greater than the unities of Asia? Geographically, Africa might claim to be less diffused than Asia, but its economic, racial, and cultural fissures are more complicated and contradictory, divided though Asia also is by economic and political rivalries, and by religious and cultural cleavages.

The continuing economic dependence on France, which is a feature common to almost all the former French African territories, distinguishes the French colonial system from the British, even if today its strength derives largely from De Gaulle's vision and stubborn policies, and might vanish abruptly with the departure of the "Man of Brazzaville." In Equatorial Africa, particularly in Brazzaville, one senses the deep, if inchoate emotional attachment of many Africans for the father image of le général. Our cab driver at Brazzaville, a pleasant-mannered, gentle-voiced African belonging to the Bakongo tribe, referred almost reverentially to De Gaulle as he pointed to the bronze effigy of the general in the compound of the Lycée and at the house which, he said, was once occupied by the great man. We drove around both the European and African towns, into which Brazzaville is divided, along broad avenues lined with the African equivalent of the Indian gold mohur tree, known in French as flamboyante. Climbing a knoll overlooking the Congo River we came across a young French couple, oddly old-fashioned in their attire, and sitting on a bench. It was like a drawing by Renoir.

The ex-French African differs strikingly from his ex-British counterpart, and, as an Indian reared for many years in British-dominated India, the contrast struck me forcibly. True, the Indian from former French Pondicherry or from former Portuguese Goa differs in may ways from the Indian in the rest of the country, but the contrast is not so forceful or compelling. In Africa the division is more distinctive and sharp. Perhaps it arises from the fact that the African was more susceptible to the impress and impregnation of a foreign culture and civilization than was the Indian. This observation, however, applies only at a sophisticated level, where the British-educated product differs noticeably from the French-educated. The mass of Africans, whether English-speaking or French-speaking, are moved by the same indigenous influences and inhibitions. After all, the borderline between the cultured and the primitive can be very thin not only in Africa or Asia, but in Europe, where the march of science and threatening nuclear wars also threaten a return to the caveman life, when men will be forced to burrow deep into the earth to preserve themselves from the self-created instruments of their own destruction and extinction.

In Africa one has the feeling that the borderline between the civilized and the primitive is even thinner and more precarious, and this applies equally to the ex-British as to the ex-French territories. I have described in Chapter 1 my impressions of a tribal festival at Aburi, a village less than 25 miles from Accra. It was the same in the ex-French areas I traversed. About ninety miles from Cotonou is Abomey, the old capital of the kings of Dahomey, who ruled from around 1620 to 1900. Dahomey was organized by France as a territory in 1893. If to land at Cotonou airport was to step into a story by Somerset Maugham, to visit the city of the kings of Abomey was like dipping into a novel by Rider Haggard. Here were the kraals one had read of, the red mud walls, the thatched huts, the House of Thrones with crude colorful symbols of bulls, ducks, elephants, and fish painted on its walls, and the ceremonial square where the king's victims were decapitated or disemboweled. One painting depicted a king pounding the head of his decapitated enemy with the victim's severed leg.

Dahomey's royal dynasty had eleven kings, and the throne of the second of them, who introduced the practice of human sacrifice, is poised gruesomely on four gleaming human skulls. In the ceremonial square of sacrifice are two circular, straw-thatched huts, one commemorating the eighth king, who secured independence for his Fon subjects from the Yoruba, and the other in honor of the queen mother. Both huts had their interior walls made of red mud mixed with human blood, wine, oil, and coral. Another hut marks the burial site of forty-one queens, wives of King Glele, who died in 1889. These unfortunate women died alongside their royal spouse's corpse, being lowered through a tunnel into an area surrounding the king's grave, where they had sat in a circle and drank a poison brew. King Glele's son, Lagbadjou Glele, the only living witness of this grisly ceremony, was presented to us. At the time of his father's death he was nearly twenty but is now a tall, sprightly nonagenarian who greeted us clad in a green robe and standing under an umbrella held by one of his grandsons, who was accompanied by his sister. When invited to pose for a picture, the granddaughter removed the sash tied under her arms and nonchalantly exposed her breasts.

Dahomey is even today infested with tribal chiefs, with whose ancestors the French entered into treaties before establishing Dahomey as one of their colonies. A lively relic of one of them is Allohinto Gbeffa Toffa VII, so-called King of Porto Novo, which is now the capital of Dahomey. Less sinister than the old kings of Abomey, he is nonetheless a tyrant in his own small way, and received us in his tin-roofed hut seated on a gaudy wooden throne flanked by two wooden lions festooned with what looked like charms. Some dilapidated chairs and a few decrepit side tables completed the furniture in the room.

The king was dressed in a white robe and wore a four-cornered white cap. On his feet were the most incredibly vivid yellow and red slippers. He carried a walking stick and seemed slightly inebriated. He was stocky and amiable, with a glinting twinkle in his eyes which reminded me of the eyes of a rogue elephant. He looked a most engaging rascal. Where did I come from, he inquired, and on being told registered a look of astonishment and pleasure, his eyes almost popping out of his head while at the same time he emitted what sounded to my untutored ears like a strangled scream, a cross between a squeal and a squeak. It was evident that the king knew little or nothing about India, for later, on being informed where an American colleague came from, he went through a similar pantomime.

He was entertaining, though quite obviously uninformed and probably illiterate. He spoke no French, but conversed in his tribal language. At one stage he shouted an order to his attendants, who rapidly fetched brandy and a bottle of Perrier. The king's hospitality was generous and informal. He invited us to charge our glasses and, when it came to opening the Perrier, he thrust his hand into one of his capacious pockets and, extracting a bottle opener, tossed it casually to an attendant. The king claimed that his ancestors had once enjoyed the powers of life and death over their subjects, and complained that the French had taken away these powers. As the afternoon wore on the room was filled with some of his subjects, a motley, ragged lot who squatted around him on the floor while naked children ran in and out, chasing turkeys, ducks, and hens, which darted intermittently among us. Flies buzzed around the room. The king looked sadly at his subjects. "The most I can fine these people," he said, "is a fowl or a bottle of liquor."

The new Africa, however, is no more represented by these relics of the past than is the new India by its old feudal order of princes and chiefs. Most prominent among the conservative leaders of former French Africa are Senegal's poet president, Léopold Sédar Senghor, and the president of the Ivory Coast Republic, Félix Houphouet-Boigny, whom the West regards as among the most enlightened and moderating influences in the new Africa, though the younger Africans incline to be increasingly impatient and critical of them. Old by African leadership rating—Senghor is fifty-seven, a year younger than Houphouet-Boigny—both men are among the finest *évolué* products of the French policy of assimilation.

Senghor is typical of Senegal, a country governed by intellectuals, which in its University of Dakar has one of the best-known seats of higher learning in French in the sub-Saharan region. Though he did not sponsor the concept of *négritude*, Senghor did much to popularize the idea in West Africa. Over the years he has moved away from the original exclusive definition and interpretation of the African Personality, which the sponsor of *négritude* initially posed as a challenge to the French policy of assimilation. Today he sees the concept as capable of being woven into a universal culture which would bind together modern Europe and modern Africa. But in consonance with the assertive Africanism which animates the younger radicals among his three million people, Senghor still speaks of *négritude* and of "African socialism." Senghor has in time evolved from Aimé Césaire's romantic concept of *négritude* a philosophical basis for African nationalism.

In his country's national anthem, which he composed, Senghor's main theme is expressed in the line, "The Bantu is a brother, and the Arab, and the white man." In a recent magazine article, Senghor describes Senegal as "a country of contrast," and explains: "Among French-speaking Negro territories Senegal was in the forefront of the struggle for autonomy and independence, yet it has remained in the Community. It has one of the more numerous and most bourgeois *élites*, yet it advances resolutely along the African road to socialism. It is one of the most literary countries, yet its prime minister is an economist,* and it has more engineers than lawyers. Its friendly people are reportedly 'frivolous,' yet in ten years they have more than doubled production. This nation is one of the most Arabized, undoubtedly the most Gallicized, and yet the most fervent militant for *négritude*." Senghor, a Roman Catholic, rules a 70 percent Moslem country.

Some might cynically suggest that Senghor would like to make the best

---

* He was the fifty-three-year-old Mamadou Dia, a devout Moslem, who attempted an unsuccessful coup in December, 1962, and was placed under house arrest. Dia, just back from a visit to Moscow, was moving left. He is now on trial. Senghor has since scrapped Senegal's two-man, president-premier system in favor of a single, strong presidency for himself.

of all possible worlds, and indeed his critics see in him a mixture of idealism and opportunism which can express itself equally in verbal rapture
or executive highhandedness. Senghor, though a poet, is no dreamer. He
has tried to implement his "African socialism" through a twenty-year development plan, and has set up an office of agricultural commercialization,
besides creating a development bank. "In six years our budgetary receipts
have doubled," Senghor claims. "In five years enrollment has doubled in
primary, secondary, and industrial schools; it has tripled at the University
of Dakar." Senghor's "African socialism," which was stoutly supported by
the ex-prime minister, Mamadou Dia, is flexible enough to have room for
private capital from abroad, free enterprise, and external aid. "As human-
izing socialists, as consistent socialists, we refuse to deny history," Senghor
proclaims. "We refuse to refuse European, French, and Arab-Berber
contributions."

Similarly, in the foreign sphere, while Senegal has a close tieup with
the West, particularly France, Senghor seems to share with Houphouet-
Boigny a realization of the need for closer inter-African cooperation and
collaboration, thus suggesting a move to loosen the economic and political
links with France. Both men insist on the independence of their foreign
and economic policies, and, while undoubtedly pro-West, they have
warned that this type of cooperation should not be used as a pretext or
cover to drag either of their countries into the orbit of either bloc.
Houphouet-Boigny once declared that the Ivory Coast was firmly committed to the Western world and would not have diplomatic, cultural, or
trade relations with Soviet and Communist countries, but alongside this
declaration he was careful to affirm that every African country has a right
to choose its friends. More recently he affirmed that the Ivory Coast would
willingly accept aid from the East provided it involved no interference in
African internal affairs. Both countries have also attempted to lessen their
economic dependence on France by forging economic links elsewhere, and
have sought closer collaboration with other African countries. Here
Houphouet-Boigny appears to have been more successful and assertive,
having sponsored the Conseil d'Entente with Niger, Dahomey, and Upper
Volta.

Senegal's short-lived experiment to build with Sudan the Federation of
Mali ended disastrously and precipitously, but Senghor, with Houphouet-
Boigny, is one of the principal architects of the Brazzaville group, and
both were associated with the Monrovia-Lagos grouping of African
powers. Shortly before Senegal's Independence Day celebrations in April,
1961, the Brazzaville group, meeting at Yaounde, capital of Cameroun,
formed the Union of African States and Malagasy, which other African
states "desirous of cooperating" were invited to join. The members of this

union have a joint airline and plan to harmonize their development programs. Broadly, the members have decided to coordinate their economic and external policies, but without renouncing their internal sovereignty. In March, 1962, at a meeting of the twelve members of the Brazzaville group at Bangui, capital of the Central African Republic, Senghor proposed refashioning the French Community into a kind of French Commonwealth which, like the British Commonwealth, would hold an annual meeting of the twelve presidents with General De Gaulle. His proposal was supported by Houphouet-Boigny, but was not enthusiastically received by the rest. It was decided to set up a common market and devise a flag for the Afro-Malagasy Union.

It is this ambivalence in their attitude to France which makes it difficult to dogmatize in which direction the Brazzaville group, on the one hand, and Guinea and Mali, on the other, are going. Are Guinea and Mali, the latter particularly, gravitating toward more interdependence with France? Or are men like Senghor and Houphouet-Boigny moving toward closer association with African radical leaders like Sékou Touré and Modibo Keita? The answer is that, while all the West African states, both English-speaking and French-speaking, are eager to achieve greater economic independence, realism forces them to recognize the likelihood of a fairly long continuance of their present condition of dependence on the West, and, while they do not relish the reality, they are compelled to recognize it. Hence the ambivalence.

During his tour of Western capitals in May–June, 1962, Houphouet-Boigny made it plain that he would welcome more foreign investment in the Ivory Coast, whose economic and political stability he emphasized. He went out of his way during his Washington visit to point out that the aid he was asking from the United States "would complement, not diminish French economic aid." Yet clearly the net result of his visit, which was generally successful, was to reduce, though only to a small degree, his country's dependence on France. Some months before this, Senghor went on a similar tour with broadly the same objective—the dilution of economic assistance from France.

The Ivory Coast, as one of the most prosperous of the French-speaking countries in West Africa, has also in Houphouet-Boigny one of the most outstanding of French-speaking African leaders. Houphouet-Boigny comes from a family of Baoule chieftains, and, though some regard him as even more rightist than Senghor, Houphouet-Boigny started political life to the left of Senghor. In 1945 he formed the Rassemblement Démocratique Africain (RDA) with Communist help, and at one time this interterritorial party was the biggest and most important to develop in French Africa, with branches in most of the countries in French West and Equatorial Africa.

Under pressure from the French Socialists, Senghor kept away from this party and in 1948 formed his own party, the Bloc Démocratique Sénégalais (BDS). For many years there was a rift between the two men and it was only recently that they came together again. The Balkanization of French Africa following independence destroyed the federal character of the RDA, which, however, still exists as an interterritorial party on paper.* But since 1951, when the RDA broke away from the French Communists, the political prestige of Houphouet-Boigny has been in the ascendant. It is interesting to recall that the breakup of the RDA as a federal party began in 1958, with the exit of Sékou Touré and Keita, who stood for independence, as opposed to Houphouet-Boigny who favored a federal type of Afro-French Community, with each territory having separate links with France rather than a united link between France and a federated French West Africa. In the same year Houphouet-Boigny became a cabinet minister in the French government. Senghor had entered the French cabinet the previous year.

In those comparatively early days Houphouet-Boigny denounced "the myth of African unity" and "nominal independence" to which he felt the French-speaking African countries would be condemned unless they maintained a federal link with France on a basis of equality. He has moved considerably from these attitudes. Like Senghor, he now seems anxious to extend and consolidate the unity of Africa under its Balkan patchwork. Houphouet-Boigny is a doctor—he qualified at Dakar—and is also a practical farmer. He brings to politics the healing and realistic qualities induced by these two professions. Among his first political acts was the formation of an African peasants' union as far back as 1944, and he was primarily responsible for the abolition of forced labor under French rule.

Politicians have their favorite words. Nehru's favorite word was "dynamic," but Houphouet-Boigny puts the stress on "fraternity." This expressed itself at one time in the "fraternal journey" with successive French governments, but today he seems to be renewing his ties, broken in 1956, with Sékou Touré and Keita. At the same time Houphouet-Boigny welcomes French private capital and investment (his finance minister is a Frenchman), retains French-paid French technicians and advisers in the administration, and French officers in the army, and has some 12,000 well-contented French settlers in the capital, Abidjan. In the Ivory Coast he has permitted a near-monopoly of franc-zone trade. Alongside this, he has more recently nationalized uncultivated land, taxed higher salaries, and imposed a special impost on foreign concerns who send too much of their profits out of the country. Houphouet-Boigny's great preoccupation is

* It has autonomous territorial branches in the Ivory Coast, Upper Volta, Dahomey, Niger, Chad, Gabon, and Congo (Brazzaville).

welding national unity from the mosaic of tribes, which include the Krus, one of Africa's few maritime tribes, and in improving the lot of the peasantry.

As a realist, he insists that the essential steps to African unity must start from below on such practical matters as transport and tariff. He sees in African associate membership in the ECM the benefits of an assured market, and of quicker and more extensive capital development. While he feels that no foreign power should expect to occupy African soil indefinitely, he thinks, mindful of the former Belgian Congo, that African colonies must be adequately prepared for independence, and he is opposed to rigid timetables. But over and above all, his key word remains "fraternity." "We black Africans," he observed while appearing before a committee of the United Nations in 1957, "are just becoming acquainted with political life at a time when the very notion of absolute independence of nations is undergoing remarkable development. The nations, even the largest, the most powerful, can no longer enjoy the deceptive luxury of isolation. Africa can be a meeting place among peoples—a land of reconciliation. We cannot accept isolation."

But from the Western world and the French, Houphouet-Boigny's concept of "fraternity" now stretches more responsively to his own fellow Africans and to the newly independent countries, including Mali and Guinea, who still regard him with reserve and suspicion. Since the breakup of the Mali Federation, the Ivory Coast's economic links with Mali have developed. Increasingly the West is concerned as to whether Houphouet-Boigny will be able to persuade Guinea's Sékou Touré and Mali's Modibo Keita to a more moderate line, or whether the Ivory Coast will move further toward the radicals. The likelihood is that in their eagerness to achieve unity both sides will make concessions and adjustments to suit each other.

What sort of men are Sékou Touré and Modibo Keita? Both are personalities imbued with vigor, determination, and purposefulness. Both are radicals, though neither is a Communist. Sékou Touré, the younger of the two—he is forty-one—is the son of poor Moslem peasants, but he claims direct descent from Guinea's legendary hero, Almamy Samoury, who fought the French in the 1880's long after the rest of Guinea had been subdued. Like Lumumba, he was at one time a postal clerk. He has little formal education, since he was a rebel even as a youth and was successively expelled from one school after another, but he is an unusually gifted organizer with an eye for detail and was interested in trade unionism at a very early state in his career.

Sékou Touré's radicalism has its roots in a burning indignation at the poverty and backwardness of the African people—a poverty of which, as he has said, "humanity should be ashamed." As a postal clerk, he became secretary-general of the Postal and Telecommunications Workers' Union, and was one of the founders of the Federation of Workers' Unions of Guinea, which was closely associated with the French Communist trade union movement, the Confédération Général des Travailleurs (CGT). For a while he served as secretary-general of the Guinea branch of the CGT, and in this capacity visited France and toured Eastern Europe, including Warsaw and Prague in his itinerary. In 1948, in Paris, he met Houphouet-Boigny and other leaders of the newly formed RDA, which had a territorial section in Guinea known as the Partie Démocratique de Guinea (PDG). In 1952 Sékou Touré became secretary-general of the PDG and built it up, against considerable French opposition, into a massive mass movement. After two unsuccessful attempts* to enter the National Assembly, he was returned in January, 1956. The year before he had been elected mayor of Conakry, and by the end of 1957 he was vice-president of the governmental council of Guinea, which under the French *loi-cadre*† meant that he was operating head of state.

Sékou Touré's espousal of what he calls "African Marxism" has misled many observers into dubbing him a Communist. He is a radical insofar as he is convinced that the capitalist system has no place in Guinea, but he has made it abundantly and repeatedly plain that Guinea needs and would welcome foreign capital whether from the West or the East. Like many African leaders, Sékou Touré's cry is: "We want capital but not capitalism." Nor did he conceal the fact that Guinea proposed to opt for complete independence in the French referendum of September, 1958. Indeed, De Gaulle, during his visit to Conakry at the end of August, had publicly declared: "I say here, even louder than elsewhere, that independence is available to Guinea. She can have it. She can have it on September 28 by saying 'No' to the proposition which is put to her, and in saying this I guarantee that Paris will raise no obstacles to it." Yet when Guinea said "no" by an overwhelming majority of 95 percent, De Gaulle pulled out the French administrators and technicians, removed capital equipment down to electrical fittings and telephones, and stopped the nearly $80 million investment program. By the end of November fewer than 20 French administrators remained of the 4,000 technicians, teachers, lawyers, judges, and doctors.

"We prefer poverty in liberty to riches in slavery," Sékou Touré had declared in the presence of De Gaulle. He now set out to seek cooperation and assistance from elsewhere, but he did not eschew the West. Soviet

* The French have been accused of rigging both these elections.
† The *loi-cadre,* introduced in 1956, retained control of the French overseas territories in the French governors, but allowed the Africans greater local autonomy.

Russia and her satellites were quick to offer aid and technical know-how. Guinea concluded trade agreements with the U.S.S.R., East Germany, Bulgaria, Poland, Hungary, and Czechoslovakia. But she also entered into trade agreements with Britain and the United States, and in 1958 signed a declaration of union with Ghana which gave Guinea a loan of $28 million, thereby helping it to tide over its immediate economic difficulties. Two years later Mali joined the union, and the three countries are among the founding members of the Casablanca group. In 1960 Guinea left the franc zone and established its own nonnegotiable currency, though it is expected to return shortly to the old fold. In the same year Sékou Touré visited China and received from Peking an interest-free loan of $25 million repayable by 1979.

"We value our personal dignity more than the lining of our pockets," Sékou Touré declared in a speech while visiting the United States and Britain in 1959. He is an ardent advocate of Pan-Africanism and keenly conscious of the importance of being black. He believes that in independence and unity lies the salvation of Africa. "It is evident," he has said, "that certain Marxist concepts suit African conditions, but it is no less evident that Africa will have to find its own revolutionary principles. As for the class problems, you will note that there exists in Africa one and the same class—that of the dispossessed." Hence his constant stress on what he terms "decolonization." "We mean to destroy the habits, the concepts, the ways of action of the colonizers. We mean to replace them with the formulas that are Guinea formulas, thought out by the people of Guinea, adapted to the conditions of Guinea, the means and aspirations of the people of Guinea."

Sékou Touré is sensitively aware of the backwardness of Guinea, which is one of the least developed territories in West Africa, of its social and economic degradation and misery, and, though his solutions often proffer what appear to be Marxist remedies like "democratic centralism" or a one-party system of government, he sees them as essentially African remedies for African ailments. Like Nkrumah, who is no Communist, one of Sékou Touré's first acts on becoming vice-president of the governmental council was to end the political domination of the chiefs, and to substitute elected district and village councils numbering over 4,000 and chosen by universal suffrage. In a country predominantly Moslem, he has encouraged women to take a more active part in political and economic life. Unlike many other leaders in former French West Africa, Sékou Touré, who had no university education either in Africa or France, is very little influenced by French traditions or culture, his approach being pragmatic and practical, and conditioned to the circumstances of Africa and its own people.

Since Africa's needs are vast and developing, he is prepared to take aid and know-how from wherever he can get it, from the East and the West, provided there are no political strings attached. He seems to realize that in the long run technicians are likely to play a more important role than politicians in bringing about African unity. While in the United States in 1959, Sékou Touré, in a talk at the National Press Club at Washington, chided both the American and the Russian scientists for "concentrating on the moon . . . Africa would ask that you think of development on this planet—Africa is still on this planet."

Similarly, as far back as April, 1956, he founded the Union des Travailleurs d'Afrique Noire (UGTAN), a Pan-African trade union, which was completely independent of non-African trade union organizations like the International Confederation of Free Trade Unions (ICFTU) or the Communist-dominated World Federation of Trade Unions (WFTU). Sékou Touré wanted, as he said, "to affirm the personality of African trade unionism."

His interpretation of "democratic centralism," which expresses itself in a one-party government, is shared by most other African leaders, including Nkrumah, radical President Modibo Keita of Mali, and even, it would now seem, by Senghor.* Here again the stress is on Africanism, not communism. Sékou Touré's party, the Partie Démocratique de Guinea (PDG), is the only party in the country, the other opposition parties having merged with it soon after independence, but this has not prevented the more extreme left-wing groups from occasionally demonstrating against the government, as they did in 1961, a move which culminated in the expulsion of the Soviet ambassador from Guinea for his alleged connection with the disturbances. In Sékou Touré's opinion, Guinea is not ready for the multiparty systems of Western Europe, and a one-party government is best suited to Africa's political needs, which are basically three—strong leadership, defined objectives, and precise ideas on how to achieve them. Sékou Touré claims that his system of democratic centralism, or one-party government, represents complete democracy because it is planned and organized from the base to the summit. "In Africa," he explains, "there is neither a socialist, a radical, nor a popular republican. There are simply men and groups of men with different labels who envisage the same objectives in the distant future, and who use different methods at present, according to their education in the economic, political, and social context that conditions them." Conservative countries like Senegal and the

---

* Senegal held its first legislative and presidential elections since independence (1960) in December, 1963. Senghor's ruling Senegalese Progressive Union (UPS) won an overwhelming victory though the opposition coalition did fairly well in the coastal towns where a number of violent incidents took place.

Ivory Coast have also one-party rule, though they do not call it "demo-cratic centralism."

So has Mali, where the government is in the hands of Modibo Keita's radical Union Soudanaise (US), which was founded as far back as 1946 by Mamadou Konate. Like Sékou Touré, Keita holds that "we have not the same reasons as France, Italy, or Belgium for having several parties and indulging in the luxury of a ministerial crisis every six months." One rea-son for the French-speaking Africans' antipathy to a multiparty system might conceivably be the pathetic example of successive governments in postwar France fluttering in and out of power. Like Guinea, Mali has extensive trade connections with the Soviet group, but, unlike Guinea, it belongs to the franc zone, is an associate member of the European Com-mon Market, and in 1960 signed a trade agreement with France. Simi-larly, while Mali's economy has been socialized, the major mineral and industrial concerns have been left undisturbed in private hands. Compared with Guinea, Mali is economically better developed and has a food sur-plus. A development program has been devised with the help of a French left-wing economist, M. Bettelheim.

Keita is, like Sékou Touré, a Moslem by birth and in many respects the careers of the two men have run a parallel course, both Guinea's PDG and Mali's US having started as territorial branches of the RDA. With Guinea, Mali is one of the founder members of the Casablanca group.

Like Sékou Touré, Keita's relations with the French Community had been fitful and, though he was at one time associated with Senghor in the short-lived Mali Federation, his Africanness and socialism have always been more assertive than that of the French-oriented Senghor. Keita studied in Dakar, and his affinities with Senegal probably derive from this period. In his early days he worked with the French Socialist party from which he broke away to join the RDA, of which, until 1958, when he left it, he was a prominent figure. Since then, Keita has headed successive governments in Mali. Less extremist than Sékou Touré, he has kept his radicalism within realistic bounds, and his continued insistence on social-ism and African unity has gone hand in hand with a comparatively mellow attitude toward France. Keita, who belongs to the Bambara tribe, comes of fairly affluent parentage, his family having held a high place in the Moslem community of former French Sudan.

West African unity will not be simple of achievement, but the urge for unity is common to African countries as a whole, whether they are members of the Casablanca constellation or the Monrovia group, whether they are French-speaking or English-speaking. There is some truth in the contention that personalities, more than principles, divide them. But even assuming that the issue of "neocolonialism" is one of the chief points of division between the two groups, the differences tend to blur when they enter certain basic fields such as greater economic cooperation, independence, and unity. No one can deny the political force of the desire for African unity, however chimerical it may seem today. The tendency the world over is increasingly to move toward massive federal structures, typified by the United States, by the U.S.S.R., and by the dream of a United Europe which, as Léopold Senghor points out, has been discussed as a concept since the seventeenth century.

In the greater part of Africa, as of Asia, colonialism is as dead as the dodo. Any attempt to take "Eurafrica," beyond economic cooperation, could exacerbate belligerent nationalism in Africa, where Pan-Africanism and positive neutralism still rate high as symbolic of the new African Personality. Realization of the importance of being black is spreading throughout Africa.

WITH
ALBERT SCHWEITZER

ON OUR WAY to Lambaréné in Gabon to see Dr. Albert
Schweitzer, we stopped briefly at Douala in Cameroun, then in a state of
considerable tension and turmoil. At the airport the officials seemed suspicious of journalists, and scrutinized my passport closely, with some reluctance granting me permission for a week's stay. The underground rebels of
the proscribed wing of the Union des Populations Camerounaises (UPC)
were then active in the vicinity, and the only open door to the post and
cable office was heavily guarded by armed soldiers who frisked all entrants,
examining even the women's handbags. There were soldiers with sub-
machine guns outside some of the more popular stores, and on asking the
local prefect why that was so, we learned that the terrorists had recently
launched an attack on a store, shooting indiscriminately, and throwing
incendiary bottles, as a result of which several persons were killed.

This was shortly before the referendum of February, 1961, when, in a
U.N.-organized plebiscite, the adjacent British Southern Cameroons voted
for unification with the Cameroun Republic while the British Northern
Cameroons voted for integration with the northern region of Nigeria.
The two sectors are separated by a forty-five-mile-wide strip of Nigerian
territory.

The Cameroun Republic, formerly known as the French Cameroons,

159

lies at the crook of Africa's western bulge and, with the addition of the former British Southern Cameroons, is now a neighbor of Nigeria. Before independence the British Cameroons were run from Nigeria and the French Cameroons from Paris. Until the end of the First World War the two Cameroons were ruled by the Germans, who colonized this territory in 1884, and, oddly enough, at the outbreak of the Second World War there were more Germans than Britons in the British Cameroons, where an exotic form of pidgin English lingers from German days.

Even before achieving independence, the French-ruled Cameroons were in a state of advanced political fermentation, and unlike the British sector, violence was a traditional part of political life in the French area. There are some six political parties functioning in Cameroun today including the two wings—one legal, one proscribed—of the UPC, one of whose rebel leaders, Dr. Felix Moumoie, was mysteriously poisoned in Geneva in 1961. The governmental party, the Union Camerounaise, is led by the forty-one-year-old Ahmadou Ahidjo, who is president of the republic and draws his support from the backward Moslem north, which is largely under the dominance of feudal chiefs.

The north ranges over dry arid country reaching up to Lake Chad, and is inhabited by a mainly Sudanese-speaking people. The south, humid and wet, with tropical rain forests, offers a fertile field for economic development, and the French have poured considerable capital into it. The south is Bantu-speaking, and from its volatile, comparatively educated population come the intellectuals who spearhead the opposition to Ahidjo's government, which they accuse of being too close to Paris. They are particularly critical of the presence of French troops under the special arrangements reached in the autumn of 1960. Cameroun, though not a member of the Community, is staunchly pro-West and belongs to the Brazzaville group. It was the first African territory during the war to rally to De Gaulle. In its ambivalence and contrasting loyalties, Cameroun is typical of the former French colonies which have emerged into independence.

Douala, the principal southern city and port, which is larger than the capital, Yaounde (also in the south), is picturesquely poised on the Wouri River, with Bonaberi, the chief banana port, on the other bank. From our hotel window overlooking the river we could sometimes see of a morning the misty silhouette of Mount Cameroun against a hazy sky. The sunsets were enchanting, with the sky a radiant quilt of orange, gold, blue, and near crimson.

Sitting almost in the middle of Africa, Cameroun stretches from the Gulf of Guinea to Lake Chad, and the contrast between the north and the south is reflected in its landscape and population, in the gray rivers, the green-clad hills and mountains, the cascades and craters, and the bleak stretches of savanna in the north. Its culture is centralized largely in the south, and from Foumbam emerged the Bamoun civilization, whose art is said to have been influenced by the Egypt of the Pharaohs, and from where also came an African script invented by Sultan Nijoya. The masked dances of Bamoun and Bamileke are celebrated. Missionaries have been active in the south, where a considerable proportion of the population is Christian, and not far from our hotel stood a Protestant church and a Catholic cathedral.

At a Sunday service in the cathedral we listened to the resonant voices of a choir of African deacons conducted by a French priest. In no other African town I visited were so many Western clothes evident. The towns-folk wore a raffish look, and in the pavement cafés the younger elements were Teddy-boyish in their behavior and attire. Perhaps the cloak-and-dagger atmosphere in which Douala then lived accounted for it.

The French were apprehensive and edgy. French investment, capital, and know-how provided the backbone of Cameroun's economy. Yet the French realized and appeared to resent the fact that their days as the ruling race were over.

"Each billion injected into an African country which produces nothing only creates more needs. It's the law of geometric progression," said a Frenchman in Douala. "Some of the money we spend here could be better spent in our own underdeveloped areas in France."

It set one wondering whether De Gaulle's policy of keeping France's former African territories within the French orbit by keeping them in the economic leading strings of Paris would some day be repudiated by his countrymen.

At the airport when we left Douala for Lambaréné was a young American surgeon from Boston on his way to work for two months with Schweitzer. The sky was aglow with another gorgeous, opalescent sunset, and across the Bay of Guinea on the other side of Douala one caught a glimpse of the Spanish isle of Fernando Po. We stopped the night at Libreville, capital of Gabon, at a hotel on the bank of a lagoon. The air was humid and clammy. Libreville takes its name from its first settlers, who were freed slaves. It is one of Gabon's two major population centers—the other is Port Gentil—and has some pleasant colonial architecture, many of the newer buildings being decked with multicolored slates brightly painted in red, green, blue, or lemon. We stopped at Port Gentil, which lies at the tip of Cape Lopez, where the sea raced in long ridges of white surf over the reefs. Petroleum deposits have been discovered at Port Gentil and, seen from the air, the oil installations rise like the antennae of some monster insect. At the airport were pale-faced French children and fat, lively

Yoruba women carrying incredible bundles and bags on their heads, with infants slung in hammocks over their backs, some of them with the large, lovely, liquid eyes which many African children have.

The jungle landscape grew thicker as the plane approached Lambaréné. From the air the clustering treetops looked like closely packed heads of broccoli. Almost the entire area of Gabon lies within the basin of the Ogowe River, and consists for the most part of dense tropical rain forests with savanna along the lower course of the river. The Ogowe is the largest river between the Congo and the Niger, threading its 750-mile-long way from the Congo (Brazzaville) through Gabon in a broad arc which divides the country into two roughly equal parts, emptying itself into the Atlantic at Cape Lopez.

We drove in a jeep with Bob Goldwyn, the American surgeon, and the other passengers to a ferry, where Goldwyn was met by one of Schweitzer's aides, a slim Dutch woman in an old-fashioned white nurse's uniform, wearing a white sun helmet, who escorted her charge to a pirogue, the local variant of a dugout canoe, in which they were paddled away. The riverbanks were thickly wooded, with trees drooping their green-gold branches into the water. It was like a scene from a movie on Africa in the early years of this century, which is the period Schweitzer's jungle hospital at Lambaréné recalls.

Actually the hospital isn't situated at Lambaréné, which is on an island, but at a place called Adolinanongo, which is on the mainland, a few miles up the river.

Schweitzer first came to Lambaréné in April, 1913. He was then thirty-eight. During the First World War he was interned as an enemy alien—he was born in Alsace, which at that time was German—and later was taken to France, where he spent nearly a year in captivity. He returned to Africa shortly after the end of the war, and a few years later moved from Lambaréné to his present habitation. Adolinanongo is said to have been the adventurous Trader Horn's first trading post in Africa.

Schweitzer's hospital is really an African village of tin-roofed wooden huts, with open drains, no electric lights—the only generator in the place services the operating room—no running water, and sanitary arrangements verging on the primitive. Frankly, I was a little taken aback on first seeing the place. Although the huts are well constructed—Schweitzer personally supervises the construction of most of them—the patients live in a state of untidy disorder tended by their relatives, who are allowed to stay with them and who do the routine nursing. Goldwyn later observed that he was at first frustrated by not being able to follow his patients' progress after they had left the operating theater, since no hospital wards such as he was accustomed to existed, but he came round to realizing that this was no modern hospital but a jungle village with a clinic. On reflection, I feel Schweitzer is right, for what good is electricity to a patient or mother who has no such amenity at home? Schweitzer is said to have dismantled some electrical fittings put up by a well-meaning donor during the doctor's absence abroad. The important thing is to make the patients feel at home.

It is an environment to which the Africans are accustomed and where they feel at home. The woods around serve for their toilet, the wells provide water, the river, fish, and many of the trees are laden with fruit to which they can help themselves. The hospital, which has room for 350 patients, provides them with diagnosis, treatment, and medicines, and also supplements their diet with bananas and rice. Patients pay what they can afford, which is generally around 20 cents a day. Schweitzer believes—I think again rightly—that Africans, like other people the world over, value medical advice more when they pay for it, and it also infuses a sense of self-respect in the patient and of corresponding obligation in the hospital staff. The inmates cook their own food.

Each hut has a kitchen, but occasionally one comes across a group of Africans cooking outside the huts, surrounded by all sorts of domesticated animals and birds, which wander freely around the place. Goats abound, but there are also pet monkeys and cats, antelopes and dogs, turkeys, ducks, hens, and a pelican with a bandaged leg named Parsifal after the hero of Wagner's longest opera. Here and there are tin cans with water for the birds and animals. Schweitzer's favorite goat, which wears a collar, is called Anita, and one of the chimpanzees answers to the name of Cosima, the name of Liszt's daughter, who became Wagner's second wife.

"I knew her," said Schweitzer with a twinkle in his eyes.

We met Schweitzer for the first time as he sat on a wooden stool working at his desk in the clinic, which that afternoon, as every afternoon, was crowded with patients who line "Hospital Alley," a long lane running outside the clinic and leading to the huts which serve as wards, and to the shacks which house the patients and their relatives.

He greeted us cordially. In the presence of few really great men does one feel the impact of greatness. Schweitzer is among the very few. I found myself comparing him with Gandhi as he lived in his ashram, or community center, though neither physically nor temperamentally does Schweitzer resemble the Mahatma, nor for that matter does his sprawling jungle hospital even remotely recall Gandhi's spruce, tidy, almost antiseptically clean ashram. But both men share certain traits, inherent in true greatness. Both are notable for their natural dignity, their innate humanity, and their strong sense of service, which in both is a fulfillment of their philosophy and personality. Both, while sensitive to the feelings of others, have a pronounced dictatorial streak, which expressed itself invertedly in the Mahatma through his well-known self-imposed fasts, and in Schweitzer extrovertly in bursts of explosive temper which subside quickly. In some respects the eyes of both men are similar—generally contemplative, but apt to flash when roused, and, as with Gandhi, Schweitzer's eyes, when displeased, can be stony. Another trait which Schweitzer shares with Gandhi is the earnestness which creeps simultaneously into his voice and eyes when he expounds on something that moves or concerns him. In their individual way both men will be remembered as perfectionists who sought to run their own lives, and to a degree the lives of others, as they felt they should be run.

Schweitzer has the most wonderful face I have seen—lined and weatherbeaten, but mobile and expressive—a fine head with deep-set eyes, and a leonine mane of shaggy, thinning hair through which while talking he often runs his fingers. In his crumpled clothes and wearing a frayed black bow tie, I thought he looked more majestic than a king in his coronation robes. His face and figure suggest a curious combination of ruggedness and frailty. His shoulders are stooped, but he walks briskly with his head thrust purposefully forward and with his hands often clasped behind his back. The face has sensitivity and strength.

On that occasion he spoke to us briefly, but asked us to lunch the next day when he said we could have a serious, more extended conversation or conversations if we were sufficiently interested. He was genial, and the deep-set, reflective eyes could twinkle and be even merry. Before we left he insisted that we should wear sun helmets, and called on one of his staff to produce two.

"But I'm from India," I protested, "and used to the sun."

Schweitzer's eyes grew suddenly steely.

"But you are now in Equatorial Africa," he insisted, "and you will wear a hat. If you don't and fall ill, I won't look after you."

We returned the next morning to visit the leper colony, which is supported partly by the Nobel Prize money which Schweitzer received when he won the award for peace in 1952. The colony, which housed about 170 lepers with their families, was in charge of a Japanese, Dr. Isao Takahashi, who was helped by four African assistants, all of them lepers. Takahashi, gentle, talkative, and ruminative, was a great favorite with his patients, particularly with the children, one of whom, a tiny tot nicknamed "General de Gaulle," was the child of leprous parents. He was carrying him in his arms. A woman about fifty was a victim of leonine leprosy, which is among the worst forms of that disease, while another, an asthmatic leper, was pathetic in her double affliction.

Takahashi, whose wife was with him and worked as a member of the household staff, was interested in Indian philosophy, and hoped to visit

India on his way back to Japan. He spoke with unusual frankness about Schweitzer and himself. He had corresponded with the doctor for fifteen years before coming out. Though a Buddhist, he would like, he said, to be baptized a Christian. He obviously admired Schweitzer, but was alive to his idiosyncrasies. "The doctor likes to do things his own way," he observed. So, I recalled, did Gandhi. Takahashi smiled. "Yes," he agreed, "like Gandhi he reveres all forms of life—human, animal, and plant. He frowns on plant pulling, won't allow weeding, will not hurt a flower or animal, and even insists on leaving animal droppings where they are. Probably they serve as manure."

Takahashi spoke of his marriage, and of the happiness which he and his wife experienced at Lambaréné. They had had only one child, but it had died when it was six months old. He had never regretted coming out. Here they found contentment, fulfillment, and peace. He was dedicated to his work and genuinely fond of the leper children, with whom he played and whom he fed from little bowls of rice and with sweets. The leftovers he distributed among the animals and birds who swarmed around.

Schweitzer met us near the bungalow where he and the more senior members of his staff live. The building is propped some six feet high on concrete piles. He took us to a nearby wired enclosure housing two tiny antelopes, one of them barely two months old, whom he stroked and fondled tenderly. A curious quirk, which I noticed later, was his generosity and tenderness to animals and birds, which accompanied a seeming indifference to the African children on whom I never once saw him bestow a lollipop or a pat. Yet a wistful smile lit his face when, in the midst of a conversation with us, an assistant rushed in with a newborn African baby, gray-pink in hue, nestling in her arms.

At lunch we had an opportunity of seeing his staff and of meeting some of them. Schweitzer's band of qualified workers consits of about twenty doctors and nurses comprising, when we were there, eight nationalities—Alsatian, German, Swiss, Dutch, Czech, American, Canadian, and Japanese. So far there has been no Indian, though Schweitzer said that at least one Indian doctor from Bombay had asked if he could come, and he had welcomed him. But the doctor did not eventually turn up. Ali Silver, Schweitzer's Dutch assistant whom we had met with Bob Goldwyn, introduced us to Mathilde Kottmann, like the doctor an Alsatian, and the first to join him and his wife at Lambaréné. She had come out in 1924 and worked, so far as one could gather, as a household supervisor and secretary. Besides Miss Silver and Miss Kottmann, the doctor is served by another factotum, Emmy Martin, who when we were there was away at Gunsbach, which is Schweitzer's birthplace.

In the dining room Miss Silver and Miss Kottmann sat on either side of the doctor, Miss Kottmann piling tidbits on Schweitzer's plate. It reminded me again of Gandhi's ashram, where the Mahatma's women disciples often vied with one another to show him special attention and solicitude. There were no Africans at lunch, and the only African in the room was a waiter with the word "boy" inscribed in red on his white apron, as quaint and anachronistic in its way as the sun helmets around. Beauty in the jungle is not as rare as one imagines, and a dazzling example was a young Dutch woman surgeon, Dr. Margaret van der Kreek, whose air of rapture and dedication enhanced her classic loveliness. Another interesting worker was Dr. Richard Friedmann, a Czech who, being a Jew, had been held by the Nazis in various concentration camps during the war and carried as a memento a tattooed number on the inside of his forearm. He had a heavy black mustache, which made him look like a youthful Schweitzer and, indeed, he bore a strong resemblance to a sketch of the doctor in his forties, which hung on a wall of the clinic.

Schweitzer took us to his living quarters shortly after lunch. We sat on small stools in his bedroom, which was full of books and newspapers, and had a picture of Charles Darwin on the wall. The books on his writing desk were mostly in German, which is the doctor's first language. His second is French. There were two fluffy woolen bluebirds on his desk.

I began by remarking that Schweitzer, like Gandhi, seemed to be a practical idealist.

"Yes, perhaps I am," he agreed. "Gandhi was predestined to be a great educator of the Indian people. What difference did it make if at that time the Indians were politically dominated by the British or not?"

He paused. "Frankly," he continued, "I found his politics incomprehensible. But then, Gandhi was more a humanitarian than a politician."

Schweitzer recalled that the late Charlie Andrews, a British missionary who had dedicated his life to India, and who was a friend of both Gandhi and Tagore, was his link with the Mahatma: "Andrews brought us together. In Gandhi I discovered a companion in arms. I consulted Andrews when I wrote my book *Indian Thought and Its Development*, and his advice was valuable."

The doctor went on to say that he had met Nehru at Lausanne in 1936, shortly after the Indian leader had emerged from a term of imprisonment. "I admire Nehru as a man of action and thought," he said, and asked, "How is he?"

Somewhat tactlessly I replied that, like all human beings, Nehru was aging.

"Aging!" exclaimed Schweitzer. "But he's only seventy."

In this and my subsequent conversation on the following day the doctor spoke at great length on his philosophy of "reverence for life," and on the importance of banning all nuclear tests, a course which he ardently advocates and which follows logically from his own philosophy of life. He related how, as a student of philosophy at Strasbourg, he had read Nietzsche, and been repelled by his doctrine of dangerous living and his cult of brute force. He had turned in vain to Plato and Kant to discover what the concept of good meant.

"Neitzsche's approach was inhuman," said Schweitzer, "but neither religion nor philosophy was opposed strongly enough to him. Neither had an answer to what 'good' meant. The true definition of 'good,' as I finally discovered here, should include all the virtues, like diffused rays in white light. Compassion needs no definition. Civilization and ethics do not depend solely on the relations between man and man, but between man the whole of creation. We must respect every living creature. That is what I mean by reverence for life."

The doctor described how, while brooding over this problem at Lambaréné, he had taken a trip in a pirogue up the Ogowe for nearly 200 miles. "Suddenly I saw the light."

"Reverence for life," explained Schweitzer, "is the one propelling force which drives people to do good. You do something for another creature because you respect him. The English philosopher, David Hume, has expressed the truth of the matter. Hume said what even Kant dared not say. Hume was a revolutionary. He was the first to point out that philosophy, supposedly scientific, had to take account of natural feelings like sentiment and emotion. Hume was right when he said that all ethics is a matter of sympathy."

I asked the doctor what the difference was between sentiment and emotion. "Sentiment leads to emotion," he replied, using the French term *sentiment* for the English word "feeling."

Schweitzer spoke passionately against nuclear tests and atomic warfare.

"I have never mixed in politics until now," he observed, "but I have been forced to out of a sense of duty, because an atomic war will mean not only the destruction of nations, but of life itself. India speaks, but she speaks too softly. People who create these arms do not seem to realize what the developing weapons or instruments of destruction ultimately mean. It was so in the First World War. It was emphasized in the Second, and yet people do not realize or learn that the Third World War, now imminent, means the destruction of life itself, of all life."

Schweitzer started to explain some of the effects of a nuclear bomb attack. The so-called "clean hydrogen bomb," he said, was only relatively clean, for its trigger was a uranium bomb made of the fissionable uranium 235. When detonated, this bomb produced radioactivity or radioactive fallout, which was also produced by the neutrons released in great numbers with the explosion. As is well known, one of the elements released is strontium 90, which induces diseases such as leukemia and bone cancer, and also affects the cells of the reproductive organs, leading to the birth of physically and mentally deformed children. Rice infected with strontium is particularly dangerous to children. Schweitzer reckoned that the deadly radioactive infection following the explosion of an H-bomb would have a range of around 45,000 square miles.

Our conversation took place a few months before Russia resumed her nuclear tests, to be followed by America.

"Some of these facts," said Schweitzer handing me a brochure, which he carefully inscribed, "are in this book." It contained his three broadcast appeals entitled "Peace or Atomic War?" and along with this he gave me another pamphlet, which he also inscribed, containing a speech he had delivered in 1952 before the French Academy on "Reverence for Life."

"You realize," he said, "that peace between the Russians and the Americans can be maintained only on the basis of mutual respect for the other's bomb. What a terrible prospect!"

He spoke affectionately of America and the Americans, mentioning Linus Pauling and Norman Cousins, who had visited him some time before I did, and who shared his views on nuclear tests and atomic warfare. "They both sat where you are now sitting," he said, pointing to the stool I was perched on. But Schweitzer was deeply critical of the late John Foster Dulles.

"I am not a Russian," he emphasized, "but truth compels me to recognize that the Russians were the first to suggest the banning of nuclear tests, and they keep on doing it. Dulles thought that the solution was the extermination of Russia by a quick war. He was said to be a great Christian. But where was his reverence for life? Even Gandhi helped to recruit soldiers in the First World War. I wept when I heard of it. India must speak more loudly and firmly. We must all speak out loudly against these criminal acts."

I told Schweitzer of my visit to Hiroshima some years before, and of my encounter with some of the survivors, who still bore the ghastly scars and disfigurements of that horrifying holocaust.

He listened intently.

"Do you know," he asked, "how the Americans during the war secured the secret of the atom bomb? The formula was worked out by Einstein and some other scientists. They were afraid that the formula was known to other scientists inside Germany who might reveal it to Hitler, who would then use it to destroy and dominate the world. So Einstein wrote to President Roosevelt offering the services of himself and the other scientists to create the atom bomb, provided it was used only in the event of Hitler using it. You know what happened. The Allies, including Russia, wanted a quick finish to the war. Truman ignored the promise to the scientists, and used it against the Japanese. Governments, whether Russian or American, behave like criminals when it suits them. A similar thing happened even before the war. By the Hague Agreement, the signatories, who were the leading nations of the world, solemnly pledged themselves, under Red Cross pressure, that none of their planes would carry explosive weapons. All of them went back on their word."

It was a long conversation, during which Miss Silver more than once came in and whispered into the doctor's ear. He rose finally. "I've got to see a patient," he said, "but don't go. I'll be back soon." He was back within fifteen minutes, but there was something obviously on his mind, for after a few desultory remarks he rose again in a gesture of dismissal.

"Read the books I gave you," he said, "and come to lunch tomorrow. We'll continue our talk."

We walked around the grounds of the hospital, accompanied for some time by a brisk Dutch nurse, Maria Langendyk, who introduced us to Joseph, Schweitzer's first African medical attendant, who has been with him almost since he came to Lambaréné. Joseph, a thin, mild-looking melancholy man, claimed to be the same age as the doctor. He is probably some ten years younger. Miss Langendyk is one of Schweitzer's veteran nurses. In our rounds we passed two crosses in a patch near the doctor's residence, which commemorate Schweitzer's wife, Helen Schweitzer Bresslau, who died at Zurich in June, 1957, and Emma Haussknecht, the second person to join the Schweitzers at Lambaréné, who had died at Strasbourg in June, 1956. The crosses are reared above their ashes. Schweitzer's wife was of Jewish origin.

In the densely wooded jungle towered huge mahogany trees whose wood, planed into planks, Schweitzer uses as floorboards. Mahogany is one of the hardest of woods and does not yield easily to termites. There were giant kapok trees with clustering tops which serve, I was told, as lightning conductors, and also clumps of papyrus. The forest was dank, sodden, and humid. Oil palms studded the water around. At Lambaréné it rains every evening around five. There were cemeteries, African and European, in the woods, the site of the African cemetery covering the grounds which once housed the palace of the Galoa kings, whose village stretched to the river bank. Some thirty years ago there were six villages between Schweitzer's hospital and the nearby mission, but now there are only two. The ruins of the other villages are still visible. The hospital also provides for European patients who come mainly from the nearby logging camps and have separate quarters.

Friedmann, who had been in Lambaréné for some years, was knowledgeable on the habits and customs of the local tribes. There were, he said, about forty distinct ethnic groups in Gabon, but the main tribes around Lambaréné were the Galoa, the Bakele, and the Fang, who have long, straight hair and aquiline features and are highly individualistic. Deep in the forests lived the Babingas, or Pygmies, who number barely 3,000 and are dying out rapidly. There was a Pygmy woman among the inmates, a mental case, who had been deposited surreptitiously one night in the hospital grounds, probably by her relatives, whose identity was not known. She gabbled cheerfully in a language no one understood and was christened *Maman sans nom*. Schweitzer runs a crude mental asylum consisting of two padlocked cells, which contained two inmates when I saw it.

Friedmann observed that the African had a greater capacity for bearing physical affliction and pain than the European, to whom it was far more fatiguing to attend. The African in pain was wonderfully patient. At the clinic one afternoon I saw an African lying on a litter with a monstrously swollen leg swathed in bloodstained bandages. He did not wince or whimper while he waited his turn. "A bad case of elephantiasis," said Miss Silver. "He will have to be operated."

Never in Africa did I feel so near the primitive as I did at Lambaréné. In the impenetrable blackness of the night we could hear the drums throbbing through the jungle. The conjunction of clouds, river, rain, mist, and forest was eerie but entrancing. From the lobby of the hotel overlooking the river we had a grandstand view almost every evening of twilight descending on the Ogowe. Once, as we paddled in a pirogue up the river, the rain came pattering through the sunlight, creating a frieze of gleaming, iridescent bubbles on the surface of the water.

My second extended talk with Schweitzer took place at the desk where I had first met him in the clinic. It was after lunch, when he generally speaks very little, confining himself to a few polite pleasantries, or to an observation or two. He was in great good humor and relaxed. I had read his two brochures, and we first discussed Christianity, on which his views as I understood them seemed somewhat unorthodox. He confirmed this in his talk. Christ, he said, never claimed to be a messiah but when He entered Jerusalem His followers proclaimed Him the prophet from Galilee. What Christ preached was the imminence of the Kingdom of God, but before that was achieved the people of the world would undergo much suffering. Christ did not die on the cross for the salvation of the world. He sacrificed himself to save the people from these tribulations and trials. In prophesying the imminent end of the world Jesus proved to be a false prophet. But that did not detract from His intrinsic greatness.

Schweitzer proceeded to speak of the Gospels and of the teachings of Christ. "The essence of Christ's teachings," he said, "is in the Sermon on the Mount, for there He teaches men how to act and do. The Gospel according to Matthew and Mark, His contemporaries, is real, for they wrote of the Jesus they knew. They lived the events they narrated. In my opinion the Revelations of John and the Gospel of Luke are embroideries on the accounts of Matthew and Mark. He mentioned several books on Christ, including Papini's biography, of which he did not appear to think much.

"Jesus," affirmed Schweitzer, "preached the perfection of the individual self. In the sixteenth and seventeenth centuries the secular spirit of the Renaissance joined with the philosophy of Christianity to make man's first duty a responsibility toward his fellow men. Christianity preached love, which means obligation toward others. I believe that reverence for life means not only obligation toward others, but also duty toward ourselves. This duty extends toward all life, human and animal."

I remarked that in that case, Christianity, according to Schweitzer, had traveled beyond Christ's conception of the perfection of the individual. The doctor nodded his head.

"It means," I continued, "that your concept of reverence for life, which embraces all creation, goes beyond Christianity!"

Schweitzer was delighted with the remark. Like all great men, he has a streak of vanity which occasionally surfaces. He chuckled and, shrugging his shoulders, said, "*J'en peux rien*" (I can't help it).

While emphasizing a point, the doctor often shuts his right eye in what looks like a long-drawn wink.

"Of course," he went on, "it isn't always possible to practice meticulously reverence for all life. You see this small window. It's an escape shaft I've had specially built for flies running away from spiders. But, then, I kill mosquitoes. I also have six fish killed daily to feed my pelican. I am guilty. But in life one has to make arbitrary decisions."

Nor is Schweitzer a strict vegetarian, though the food he serves at his table, which is deliciously cooked and nourishing, is largely vegetarian. There were leeks with bacon at one lunch and a meat pie at the other.

I tried to make him talk on Hindu philosophy, on which he has evidently read a great deal and written frequently, but he skirted the subject. From the little he said, I had the feeling that he thought it was not sufficiently assertive and positive. To him thinking is doing, and to him the Hindu metaphysical notion of existence, which holds that all true existence is nonmaterial, unchangeable, and eternal, appears negative and an attitude that can only lead to inactivity. In one of his books Schweitzer writes that *ahimsa*, as preached by Hinduism, Jainism, and Buddhism, opens the way for human egotism insofar as it makes a man entirely preoccupied with his own salvation, appealing to him not in the name of sympathy and compassion, but on purely metaphysical grounds. It is not activity inspired by the notion of doing positive good, but is an inactivity impelled by the negative notion of abstaining from evil. While the European is more interested in changing and improving his environment, which to him means progress, the Hindu is more concerned with changing and improving his inner self, which to him spells salvation.

Schweitzer reverted to the subject of nuclear tests and atomic warfare. "Did you read my brochure on it?" he asked.

I replied that I had and that I wanted to ask him a few questions. It seemed to me that whereas the United States, which relied upon nuclear armaments and widespread foreign bases, favored the more gradual elimination of nuclear weapons and a more cautious reduction of conventional forces, the Soviet Union, which has larger and less diffused conventional troops, would like to see a more rapid elimination of nuclear weapons, an earlier closing of foreign bases, and more radical cuts in conventional forces. What did Schweitzer think of these opposing stands?

"I do not specifically blame either side," said the doctor. "Both sides are to blame. I think that if Eisenhower had been left to himself he would have reached a working arrangement with Russia. But Dulles prevented him. Similarly, Truman wanted an international commission to control nuclear weapons, but Stalin prevented this. Now the Russians have the advantage. I am opposed to organizations like NATO because I believe that by ringing in your opponents with bases you do not ensure, but endanger peace."

Schweitzer rummaged among his papers and produced a cutting of a *Time* magazine map depicting American bases ringing Russia. He has an album with all sorts of cuttings, some of them with marginal comments in his meticulous handwriting.

"The new way of doing things," he observed dryly, "is to set off a rocket as far away from yourself as possible. Why, even off the Atlantic coast of Africa there are little islands being built up into bases. It's criminal. I said five years ago," he continued, "that Russia would never like the Chinese to have nuclear weapons at their disposal. They still would not, but America gives rockets to the NATO countries. All of us, including the press, must speak out boldly against these things. The greatest danger today is that anybody, even an obscure officer on a submarine manned with atomic weapons, can press a button and set the whole world on fire."

I remarked that with his own philosophy of reverence for life he must logically be opposed to nuclear tests and to all forms of atomic warfare.

"I am opposed to war," said Schweitzer simply, "to all forms of war. Yes, civilization means reverence for life."

We were to leave Lambaréné early the next morning. He asked us when we were leaving and suggested that we make a last round of the hospital with him. He talked about India and was specially interested in Vinoba Bhave, whose work he knew and admired, and he asked me to send him some literature on him. "I want to understand his philosophy." He had heard about Vinoba's land distribution crusade, and was impressed when I told him that Vinoba tramped on foot throughout the length and breadth of India preaching his mission.

Had Vinoba any influence, he inquired. Not among the politicians, I replied, but among a few intellectuals like Jayaprakash Narayan.

"Bah!" exclaimed Schweitzer. "Who wants the respect of politicians?"

It was threatening to rain, and the doctor carried an umbrella.

"Please not with an umbrella," he said, posing for a picture. "They'll mistake me for Chamberlain."

He accompanied us to the waterfront, where our pirogue was waiting. He was graciousness personified.

"You must stay with us the next time you come," he said. "I cannot offer you the luxuries of a hotel. But you will be comfortable. When will you come?"

He waved and doffed his white sun helmet as our canoe pulled away. My last memory of Lambaréné is Schweitzer's ruggedly frail figure standing with slightly bowed shoulders on the waterfront, with Friedmann and Miss Silver in her white uniform beside him, silhouetted against the vast, dense jungle and the setting sun.

What sort of a man is Schweitzer? Like all great men, he is a compound of many qualities, some of them contradictory. "The great man," wrote Goethe, "is just like everyone else, except that he has greater virtues and greater defects."

I was particularly interested in Schweitzer's attitude toward the Africans, among whom he has now worked for nearly fifty years. One afternoon we watched Schweitzer supervising a group of Africans moving some timber planks and placing them in neat symmetrical piles to be used later for a building in the leper colony. Lepers work on the soil, tending and digging the ground. Relatives of the patients also help at various chores servicing the community. Schweitzer directed the workers in a gruff voice, often lending a hand to see that the timber was placed just so. His manner was brusque, and at times he grew impatient and irascible. But when the job was done he thanked the workers courteously. Like Gandhi, Schweitzer is an exacting taskmaster and, like the Mahatma, he does not demand of others anything he himself is not prepared to do.

Some have described his attitude to the Africans as that of a paternal autocrat. He does not appear to regard them as equals, but rather as children or younger brothers who need a strong guiding hand. Politically, though I never discussed this aspect with him, I should imagine that his views on Africa and the Africans are old-fashioned, even colonial, not in the sense that he would approve of the Africans being dominated and exploited, but he evidently does not believe that they are grown-up. In his opinion they should be led. He treats the African as a fair-minded guardian would a wayward, rather backward ward. Schweitzer, it must be realized, has seen very little of Africa outside his small bailiwick, he speaks no African language, and the Africans to whom he is daily exposed in the jungle at Lambaréné are far behind the many developed and developing Africans in other areas of the continent. But obviously Schweitzer equates his Africans with Africans as a whole. Their lack of enterprise, initiative, and imagination alternately amuses and exasperates him, which is why, while he is prepared to work for the Africans, he does not seem willing to work with them as equals. At the same time the doctor realizes that environment influences character and temperament, and he knows that the African, if he can live off the fruit of the trees and the fish in the river, sees no reason why he should exert himself in putting up buildings and houses when he is quite comfortable in his mud hut or shanty.

But Schweitzer's attitude to others is also akin to that of a paternal autocrat, a patriarch whose word in his small community is law. If he is gruff with an African, he can be equally gruff and abrupt with a European, and impatient, even intolerant, of those whose views are opposed to his. Gandhi, too, had that streak of intolerance. In one remarkable respect, however, the doctor differs from the Mahatma, for, unlike Gandhi, Schweitzer is not interested in individuals as such, but in humanity as a whole—in all created life, as he likes to put it. This constitutes a curious contradiction in his character, for, like Gandhi, his philosophy is rooted in a strong sense of service, in giving himself to others. Gandhi was known to hold up important meetings with his political colleagues who had come from considerable distances to see him while he gravely listened to the woes of a widow from a neighboring village or to some problems which irked an inmate of his ashram. In Schweitzer there is an aloofness which was absent in Gandhi, and behind his kindliness and charm is an innate reserve. Of one of his close colleagues he is said to have exclaimed, "She came straight from Heaven to Lambaréné." Yet I noticed that he treated her no differently from other long-time colleagues and workers. The doctor's great quality is his ability to inspire others and to communicate his sense of service to them. In this, again, he resembles Gandhi.

I have heard him criticized for turning his back on civilization and burying himself in the jungles of Africa, when he might have enriched civilized life as a philosopher, scientist, theologian, and artist. This, say his critics, was an escapist exercise to enable him to work for a people he could patronize. I do not for a moment think so, though simultaneously I find it difficult to accept the view of his more ardent admirers that the doctor's decision to work in Africa was a gesture of renunciation. It was not renunciation which Schweitzer sought in Africa, but fulfillment. In renouncing Europe, he found fulfillment in Africa. In doing this he might have satisfied the ego which lurks in every man and which, with Schweitzer, expresses itself in a profound conviction in his own beliefs which, transplanted from Europe to Africa, found easier acceptance in both. Distance does lend enchantment to the view. But in the process of finding fulfillment Schweitzer has over the years served countless Africans whom he has tended, whose sufferings he has tried to alleviate, and many thousands of whom owe their lives to him. Moreover, his example has inspired men and women from different countries, of different religions and views, to work with him with the same dedicated fervor.

With all his foibles and quirks, Schweitzer represents the image of the truly civilized man who gives of himself to others regardless of color, creed, or country.

9

THE CONGO TRAGEDY

"I'M NOT A COMMUNIST. I'm an African. I am against both communism and imperialism."

The speaker was Patrice Lumumba, whom I saw at Léopoldville a few weeks before he escaped from detention on the tragic flight which ended with his death in Katanga. Lumumba spoke with great passion and fervor, but there was nothing of the paranoiac I was told he was either in his appearance, manner, or conversation. He was articulate and acutely intelligent. He looked far less sinister than his pictures had led me to imagine. His appearance, though slightly saturnine, an impression heightened by his rakish goatee and gleaming glasses, was in no way diabolical. His eyes were slightly shifty, but that is no phenomenon with politicians.

"This," he explained, "is not a Kasavubu-Lumumba problem. The real problem is the problem of the great powers, who do not want a united and neutral Congo. The West does not want leaders like me, who want to be neutral. The West only wants a chief of state 100 percent under their guidance."

Lumumba proceeded to amplify his assertion.

"They now pretend," he declared, his eyes flashing behind his glasses, "that I am against the U.N. I have never been against the U.N. I am against the methods they employ. What I begged for was the implementa-

176

tion of the Security Council resolution.* This resolution clearly authorized Mr. Hammarskjöld to provide the government of the Republic of the Congo with such military assistance as might be necessary. The text of the resolution states that the U.N. secretary-general was to do so in consultation with my government. What did Hammarskjöld do? He ignored me and went to consult Tshombe, a rebel. That was how my differences with Hammarskjöld arose."

Lumumba spoke in sharp, pithy sentences. I had heard him described as inexperienced, incalculable, and unreliable, and while I am prepared to concede the latter two failings, which were conspicuous in him, he struck me as the most able of the many Congolese leaders I met. Lumumba was blessed with great natural ability, but cursed with an erratically wayward temperament. Talking to him I could well understand the hypnotic charm he was said to exercise over most Congolese—"a charmer in a snake pit," as one obituary was later to describe him.

"Katanga," declared Lumumba, "is a part of the Congo. When I asked Hammarskjöld to use U.N. troops against Katanga, he refused, explaining it was an internal matter. I had no planes to transport my own troops. Parliament then authorized me to address any government to get the planes. I asked the United States government. They refused, saying that such assistance could come only through the U.N. I then turned back to Hammarskjöld. He again refused. What was I to do? I had to go to the Russians. It is like Nasser and the Aswan Dam. I went to the Russians not because I am a Communist, not because I am hostile to the U.N. or the United States, but because I wanted to defend and unify the Congo. I wanted desperately to solve our problems. I did not create the difficulties. They created them, and now they call me a Communist."

Listening to Lumumba, I could glimpse something of the tragedy which haunted the Congo and which has caused more heartbreak to Africa and the world than any other newly independent country of that continent.

In area the Congo, which covers some 900,000 square miles, is roughly the size of Western Europe and only a little smaller than India. Its boundaries, like those of most other African countries, were arbitrarily drawn by the European scramblers for territory, and have little or no relation to ethnic or tribal considerations. In this vast territory, potentially one of the richest in Africa, live some 15 million people divided into several ethnic groups, of which the Bantu are the most numerous, and subdivided into innumerable tribes and clans. Over 450 dialects exist side by side. Here, as in other parts of Africa, tribalism is the most divisive force. For administrative purposes the Belgians split the Congo into six provinces—Léo-

* Of July 14, 1960.

poldville, Katanga, Kasai, Kivu, the Equateur, and Orientale, again on an artificial basis, oblivious of tribal susceptibilities.

When independence came tribalism erupted in various forms. A basic cause of conflict in copper-rich Katanga is the presence of the enterprising Baluba in the north, who are hostile to the Lunda who predominate in the south. The moon-faced ex-President Moise Tshombe of Katanga is a Lunda. In the other mining province of Kasai, the Lulua in the north are bitter foes of the Baluba in the south, but, oddly enough, while the Baluba of south Kasai were anti-Lumumba, the Baluba of north Katanga were pro-Lumumba and anti-Tshombe.

"The Baluba," remarked a British officer of the Ghanaian contingent, "are the Irish of the Congo. They are against every government."

Lumumba was a Batatele and one of the very few high-ranking Congolese politicians who stood for a strong unitary government in his country, but even he remarked that he supported the idea of a Balubakat state in north Katanga as a counterpoise to Tshombe's Conakat party in the south. Lumumba's lieutenant, Jason Sendwe, led the Balubakat.

President Joseph Kasavubu, whom Lumumba described derisively as "a tribalist," is a staunch member of the Bakongo tribe, and his party, the Abako (Alliance des Bakongo), is a purely tribal political organization. The Bakongo, who inhabit the Lower Congo basin, are spread out on both sides of the river around Léopoldville and Brazzaville.

Tribalism will ultimately mold the Congo's political pattern. That the tribal call is the strongest of all compulsive forces was betrayed by the proclamation which the former prime minister, Joseph Ileo, addressed to his fellow countrymen in January, 1961: "I appeal to you Bangala, Ngwaka, Mbuza, Mongo, Nkundo of the Equateur, to you Bakongo of the plain, Mayindobe, Basakata of the Lake, Bayanzi, Bambala, Bampende of the Kwilu, Bayaka, Basuku of the Kwango. I appeal to you Atetela, Basonge, Lulua of the Kasai, Baluba of south Kasai, to you Tshokwe, Baluba of Katanga, Balemba, Lunda of Katanga. I appeal to Bashi, Warega, Wabebe, Bahunde, Banynaga of northern Kivu and southern Kivu, Bango-Bango, Wakeusu, Warumba of Maniema. I appeal to Lokele Topoke, Libinza of Stan, Azande of the Ulele, Bahuka of Ituri."

Incredible as it seems, there was not a single qualified Congolese doctor, lawyer, engineer, or scientist in the entire country after some fifty-two years of Belgian administration.* When freedom dawned on June 30, 1960, there were only seventeen African college graduates, but there existed a fairly substantial body of artisans and skilled workers to serve the needs of the Belgian plants and factories. Until 1956 the only Africans permitted to study abroad were the Catholic seminarists who went to

* The Congo was the personal property of King Leopold II from 1885 to 1908, when he bequeathed it to the Belgian nation.

Rome. The Catholic Church had the monopoly of education subsidies from 1925 to 1946, but later the Protestants also received subsidies. In 1954 the Catholic-run Lovanium University was set up seven miles outside Léopoldville, and two years later a secular university was opened at Elisabethville.

I visited Lovanium University, which is housed in magnificent buildings and has the only atomic reactor in the whole of Africa. In spaciousness and equipment it rivals any university I have seen in India. Yet, until two years before independence its curricula did not include courses in law, engineering, political science, or civics. When independence came, Lovanium could take only five medical students a year, and not more than fifteen doctors were expected to qualify by 1965. Since then the U.N., through the WHO (World Health Organization) and other agencies, has succeeded in getting the university to extend its facilities for training doctors and nurses, and is accelerating the dispatch of more students abroad for higher studies.

The bottleneck in the Congo, as in almost every part of Africa, is at the middle and higher school stage, the rate of increase at the university level hinging on the expansion of secondary education. In the year of independence the entire Congo produced about 450 high school seniors, the majority of whom came from mission schools. As the rector of Lovanium University remarked, "Had we graduated 200 persons before independence, it might have made a difference." About a million African children were receiving primary education in 1960, but there was a considerably smaller number in the secondary schools and only about 6,000 in the vocational training schools. Yet here again some of the primary schools in their buildings and amenities rate far higher than the overwhelming majority of similar institutions in India. For all practical purposes education in the Congo stopped virtually at the primary school level. The Congolese rate of literacy was the highest in Africa, but the quantum of educated Africans was among the lowest.

Lord Hailey rightly describes the Belgian system of rule as "paternalism in isolation." Of Belgian goodwill for the Congolese, so far as their social welfare and to a degree their economic well-being went, there was no dearth, but it was accompanied by a policy which for a long while denied the Africans higher education and suppressed them politically.

"They gave us everything except dignity," remarked a Congolese bitterly.

The Belgians built good hospitals for the Africans, with a high standard of equipment and welfare care. Before July, 1960, the level of wages paid to the Congolese was the highest in Africa south of the Sahara, and the Congolese worker also enjoyed in law the right to strike, which was bestowed on him as far back as 1908. In 1952 family allowances comprising subsidies to the wives and children of wage earners were introduced. The Belgians did some notable work in demography, and their agronomical studies have contributed much to the progress of agricultural and forest research in Central Africa. As the country's economy developed, there came into being a small African middle class, a few of whom in Léopoldville and Elisabethville commanded an income of nearly $20,000 a year. Léopoldville's African city is reputed to be the best of its kind on the continent, and would compare favorably with most Indian middle-class suburban settlements; in certain matters, such as running water and electricity, it outstrips many of them.

In short, the Belgians set out to make the Congo an ideal welfare state for the Africans, with the political reins held firmly by Brussels through the governor-general and with the overwhelming proportion of the economic pickings for themselves. If the Africans were denied all political rights, so were the Europeans in the Congo, though such denial naturally did not weigh on the latter, who regarded it more as a relief than a deprivation. Similarly, before independence neither the African nor the European was allowed after a certain hour at night to enter the other's civic sector except with a special pass. In theory there was no racial discrimination, though in practice it was rife. Like the French and the Portuguese, the Belgians attempted to build up a small African elite consisting of those who had achieved some distinction in business, education, or the religious sphere, and who were thereby deemed worthy to be absorbed into the "civilized" society of Europeans, but their number did not range beyond a few thousand. No African could be an architect or an attorney, but he could be a bishop. He could be a medical assistant, but not a doctor, a mechanic, but not an engineer. On the eve of independence, the highest military rank achieved by a Congolese in the army, known as the Force Publique, was that of a junior NCO.

The result was that when power was transferred it could not be effectually grasped. Why, then, did the Belgians suddenly decide to relinquish their political authority in the Congo? It has been argued that Belgium never set out to be a colonial power in Africa and that the Congo came to be a Belgian possession by the accident of Leopold II's personal acquisitiveness. To most Asians this sounds curiously like the plea that the British acquired their Indian empire "in a fit of absent-mindedness." Until 1954, when a liberal-socialist government came into power in Brussels, Belgium had no intention whatever of retreating from Africa. Even then it thought in terms of mild reform rather than of political autonomy. To most Belgians, certainly to the overwhelming majority in the Congo, the idea of Congolese self-government, let alone independence, was political lunacy. When in 1954 Governor H. J. J. van Bilsen published *A Thirty-Year Plan*

Photographs by
Marilyn Silverstone.

Tribal flare-up in a Léopoldville street near U.N. headquarters between
Bakongo and Bayaka supporters. In the fighting one man of the
Bakongo tribe was beaten to death by his opponents with sticks, bottles,
and bicycle chains.

Congolese Army parades past General Mobutu (at that time Colonel
Mobutu) in Léopoldville in a demonstration designed to impress U.N.
observers with the army's discipline.

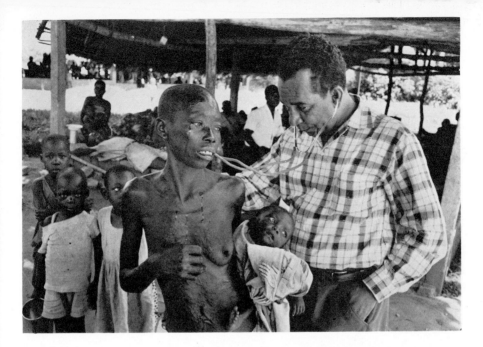

A Haitian doctor, a WHO public health expert, examining a tubercular patient at Matamba Sanatorium near Luluabourg in Kasai province, Congo. The sanatorium, like many other hospitals, had been left suddenly without a doctor when the Belgians fled. The hospitals were in the hands of partially trained Congolese medical assistants.

Emperor Haile Selassie, with the Crown Prince on his right (seated), presiding over the "Finding of the True Cross" ceremony at Guenet Leul Palace. Christianity came to Ethiopia in the fourth century, and the religion of the Emperor and the ruling caste is that of the Coptic sect of Christianity.

In West Africa shirts and women's dresses and wrappers often carry colorful portraits of national leaders and visiting celebrities. A Ghanaian patriot flaunts a picture of the Osagyefo on the back of his decorative sports shirt.

Lumumba and his two-year-old son Roland at the Congolese leader's residence in Léopoldville. "Déjà un petit nationaliste," said Lumumba of his son. Two weeks after this picture, Lumumba was taken prisoner and killed.

Starving Lulua refugees, victims of tribal warfare between Luluas and Balubas, in Kasai Province, Congo. Vegetable staple on table is manioc, containing carbohydrate but not the protein which used to be supplied by dried fish traded from Portuguese Africa. With disturbed conditions trade had stopped. Thousands starved, and children, Baluba and Lulua, suffered from kwashiorkor brought about by protein deficiency.

Landing freight in small boats over the surf at Sekondi, port near Accra, capital of Ghana. The freight is landed from ships anchored beyond the surf in deep water. A more modern port now functions at Takoradi where ships can dock.

...ulani "coming of age" ceremony. At Jogana vil-
..., near Kano, Nigeria, a Fulani boy is about to
...hrough the "beating" ceremony when he has to
...d up to a beating by boys of his age group. A
...lidate preens in a mirror, steeling himself for
...s he must bear without blinking or flinching.

After a blow that he took smiling, the candidate passes his hand over
his face. His eyes, unblinking, reveal the pain which he must not show.

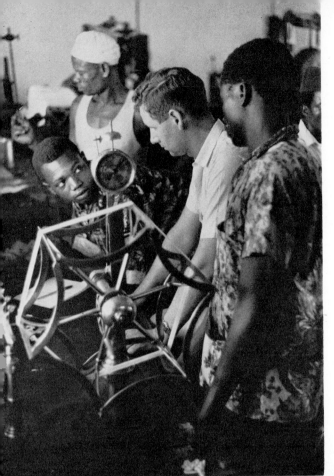

At a training school in a textile mill near Kaduna, capital of Northern Nigeria, promising millworkers receive training for technical jobs.

A copper refinery near Ndola in Northern Rhodesia's Copperbelt. Northern Rhodesia, whose wealth comes largely from this source, was known in the Central African Federation as "the goose that lays the copper egg."

for the Political Emancipation of the Belgian Congo, it was ostentatiously ignored by the government and denounced unofficially as an essay in utopian irresponsibility. But with the Congolese nationalists it rang a bell, which soon clanged like a tocsin.

Shortly after the end of the Second World War the Congolese *évolués* had begun to show the first faint stirrings of unrest and ambition, but, as Lumumba's posthumously published book, *Congo, My Country*,* reveals, there was a characteristic ambivalence in their attitude and approach. In this book, written in 1956–1957, Lumumba supports the idea of integration in a Belgo-Congolese Community and praises the civilizing mission that the Belgians had accomplished. At that time he urged a fusion of the best qualities of both peoples, and, while critical of the assimilation system, asked only for political rights for the Congolese elite. Indeed, he declared that there could be "no question" of adult suffrage until a "very distant" date, and even went so far as to declare that to enfranchise "dull-witted illiterates—that would be to put dangerous weapons in the hands of children." At most the book expresses the discontent of the black intellectual suffering under a growing sense of grievance and resentful of his inferior status.

Less than four years later Lumumba's attitude was bitterly anti-Belgian, leading him at the independence celebrations to taunt King Baudouin on the perfidy of the Belgian record, and to fling into the monarch's face the challenging gibe, "We are no longer your monkeys."† What had brought about this sudden change? By nature Lumumba was unpredictable, and, though more mentally gifted than most of his countrymen, he shared with them a strong streak of instability and immaturity. There was, however, more in it than that. In the belief that by treating the Congolese like children, mollycoddling them with welfare services, larger economic opportunities, and higher standards of living, they could deaden the Congolese urge for social and political equality and emancipation, the Belgians erred disastrously. All that their policy deadened was the Congolese sense of responsibility. When freedom came, the Congo almost overnight became a political bedlam, with no single person, party, or institution capable of exercising effective authority or control. No elements of real power existed, whether in the government, the army, the administrative service, or the economic structure. Everything disintegrated.

The Belgians tragically failed the Congolese both before and after independence. It is not that they lacked good intentions. They lacked understanding. At the end they understood the Congolese no better than

* Barrie & Rockliff, London, 1962.

† *Macac*, which means "monkey," was the white man's favorite abusive epithet for the Congolese.

at the beginning. They were as bewildered as anyone else, probably more so, by the situation they had precipitated, and an air of pained, often outraged bewilderment characterized almost every Belgian I met during my stay in the Congo. "To think that this should happen to us!" was the burden of their theme song. Yet they could not claim that they were not forewarned. The miscalculations were on their side.

In 1954 the formation of the Abako party, identified with Kasavubu and purely tribal in character, signified the first vague groping toward some form of political association. The Abako was the first recognizable party to be established in the Congo. It was confined to the Bakongo tribe in the Lower Congo and had local autonomy for its masthead, though later Kasavubu was to favor federalism. The party was formed originally in 1950 as the "association of the Bakongo for unification, expansion, and defense of the Kikongo language." In 1957 the Belgian liberal-socialist government introduced local government elections in the main Congolese towns, and in the Léopoldville councils the Abako won 130 of the 170 seats, and elected eight of the ten mayors, including Kasavubu, who was elected mayor of the Dendale council in Léopoldville. The Congolese were becoming politically conscious.

The year 1958 marks a milestone in the history of modern Africa. The Accra conference, where Nkrumah raised the slogan of Pan-Africanism, and which Lumumba attended, took place that year. In August, 1958, at Brazzaville, opposite Léopoldville on the other side of the Congo River, De Gaulle proclaimed the new concept of Communauté with local autonomy for each of the former French colonies. These two events accelerated developments in the Congo. Two months later, in October, Lumumba at Stanleyville, capital of his home province of Orientale, formed his Mouvement National Congolaise (MNC), which was also entrenched at Léopoldville. The new party functioned on a Congo-wide basis, opposed all forms of regional and tribal separatism, and stood for Congolese nationalism. As a counterpoise Belgian big business elements encouraged Moise Tshombe in Katanga to form his Conakat (federation of tribes of Katanga) party, which first stood for federalism but veered rapidly to the concept of confederation. Thus the Congolese power struggle was polarized between the two contending forces of federalism and unitary government.

A rash of other parties and breakaway groups erupted throughout the Congo. Favoring federalism, apart from the Abako and the Conakat, were the PUNA (Partie l'Unité Nationale Africaine), a conglomeration of moderate groups brought together by Jean Bolikango, who as an assistant departmental head in the information service was the only Congolese in the higher administrative ranks at the time of independence, and the PNP

(Partie Nationale de Progrés), another group inspired by the Belgians which stood for right-wing federalism. There was the Kalonji branch of the MNC, a breakaway federal wing formed by Albert Kalonji and Joseph Ileo after differences with Lumumba over the original MNC's highly centralized policy. Also for federation was the PSA (Partie Solidaire Africaine), headed by Cléophas Kamitatu, minister of the interior in the Adoula government at Léopoldville and one-time head of the Léopoldville provincial government. Kamitatu originally founded the PSA with Lumumba's chief lieutenant, Antoine Gizenga, a leftist who favored a strong unitary government and who, while Lumumba was held in custody, set up a rival central government at Stanleyville. The PSA under Kamitatu's leadership controls the Kwango-Kwilo region of Léopoldville province. Favoring unitary government are the Cerea (Centre de Regroupement Africain) party founded by Ancet Kashamuru, another of Lumumba's lieutenants, who was minister of information in his government and whose home province is Kivu, and Jason Sendwe's Balubakat party, which is fiercly opposed to Tshombe's Conakat and, as a provincial minority party based in north Katanga, supports unitary government as a safeguard against suppression by the local majority. The Balubakat stands for Baluba unity.

On his return from the Accra conference, Lumumba, fired with Nkrumah's dream of Pan-Africanism and his slogan of "Independence Now," launched on a series of inflammatory nationalist speeches which attracted countrywide attention. To some extent these speeches were responsible for the violence sparked by the unemployment riots in Léopoldville early in 1959, in which about forty Africans were killed. The explosiveness of these demonstrations shook the Belgian regime in the Congo and in Brussels. However, it was not Lumumba, but Kasavubu and his Abako party who capitalized politically on the demoralization of their rulers. With his chief lieutenants, Kasavubu, who was earlier arrested, was later flown to Brussels, where he had talks with the government.

In March, 1959, King Baudouin broadcast to the nation his government's new Congolese policy "to lead, without fatal evasion and without imprudent haste, the Congolese people to independence in prosperity and peace." Evidently neither the king nor his government even then envisaged a transfer of power to the Congolese within a year. In fact, Brussels felt that independence was feasible only in another four or five years.

Following King Baudouin's broadcast, preparations were made for nationwide elections for local and provincial authorities. The elections ended with the Abako party virtually controlling the lower Congo region in the province of Léopoldville, where Kasavubu and his men had their own militia, their tax officers, and their courts. Belgian authority was at a discount in this area. In Stanleyville, where Lumumba was arrested after rioting broke out as a result of his incendiary speeches, the MNC won fifty-five of seventy-seven seats in the municipal elections, while in Elisabethville Tshombe's Conakat staged an equally impressive triumph. Congolese opinion dramatically registered its anti-Belgian verdict.

In January, 1960, the Belgian government convened a round-table conference at Brussels, where twenty Congolese parties and groups were represented by sixty-two delegates, while another nineteen represented the so-called "traditional" authorities. By watering down the radical representation with a large moderate element, notably the PNP, the Belgians planned and hoped to secure Congolese support for a graduated timetable for independence. To their surprise the traditional authorities and moderate elements joined with the spokesmen of the radical parties in making a unanimous demand for independence by June 30, 1960. The Belgians yielded, reportedly against the advice of their civil servants in the Congo, but both parliament and the government in Brussels were apparently impressed by the Congolese united front, and perhaps influenced by the growing U.N. support for African nationalism. It is possible also that reluctance to embark on a policy of naked force, which might have led to a long-drawn colonial war in the heart of awakening Africa, impelled the Belgian decision, which to some extent was influenced by the big business lobby, which argued that, with over twenty African countries enjoying self-government, independence was inevitable in the Congo, and that to give freedom to a people incapable of running the administration or economy would be not to relinquish, but to consolidate their own political and economic interests.

The key figures at the conference were Lumumba, Kasavubu, and Tshombe. Finding Lumumba more flexible and conciliatory than Kasavubu, the Belgians at first inclined more to him than to the Abako leader. Moreover Lumumba's MNC party appeared to command the broadest national support. To the Belgians, Kasavubu then seemed a rigid tribalist who was also articulately anti-Belgian. They suspected Tshombe as a separatist supported by the gold of the conservative Belgian settlers. Brussels had always favored a unified Congo.

The first national elections before independence were fought mainly on the opposing planks of federalism or a strong unitary government. For the most part the federalists, led by Kasavubu and the Abako party, fought the elections, but Tshombe, with his Conakat, kept conspicuously apart. Even then Tshombe played the lone wolf. Lumumba spearheaded the pro-unitary-government groups.

Of the 137 seats in parliament,* Lumumba's MNC and its allies won

* The Fundamental Law governing the structure of the Congo emerged from the round-table conference discussions and was officially released in May, 1960. It pro-

forty-one. Lumumba's main gains were in Orientale and in part of Kivu, but he was the only Congolese leader to return representatives from all of the six provinces. Also in the unitary camp were Cerea, which captured ten seats, and the PSA, which gained thirteen. Of the federalist parties the Abako, although it won only twelve seats, controlled the Lower Congo region, with its predominantly Bakongo population and commanding the Congo's sole outlet to the sea through the Atlantic port of Matadi. Tshombe's Conakat secured seven seats, but it remained the leading power in Katanga. Of the other federalist groups Kalonji's MNC won eight seats, the PNP fifteen, and Puna seven. Thus, the unitarians, with sixty-four seats, and the federalists, with forty-nine, accounted for 113 members in parliament. The remaining twenty-four were made up of four independents and twenty representatives of the smaller parties and local interests.

When parliament assembled two weeks before independence, the rival contenders for power were the federalist Kasavubu and the unitarian Lumumba. Neither, however, was able to canvass sufficient support from the political fragments in and outside their respective camps to form a workable government. As a result, they were forced into an uneasy partnership, with Kasavubu as president and Lumumba as prime minister. The only link between the two men was their common antipathy to Tshombe, who in turn had no use for either of them. Unlike Lumumba, who could not rule in Léopoldville without the cooperation of Kasavubu and his Bakongo henchmen, Tshombe could function effectively in Katanga without dependence on the Abako in Léopoldville. Tshombe was also well aware that, while Katanga could exist without Léopoldville, the latter would find it difficult to sustain itself as a commercial metropolis without Katanga.

Tribalism overwhelmed independent Congo from its birth. On July 1 rioting broke out between the Bakongo and the Bayaka tribes in some suburbs of Léopoldville, to be followed by a flare-up in Kasai between the Lulua and the Baluba. More serious was the threat posed by the mutiny of the Congolese soldiers of the Force Publique, the Belgian-trained, Belgian-equipped, and Belgian-officered Congolese army on whom depended the maintenance of law and order. At the time of independence the force consisted of around 23,000 Congolese troops with a little over 1,000 Belgian officers and NCO's. On July 4 the Congolese soldiers, dissatisfied with their unchanged status in matters of promotion and pay, compared with the politicians and civil servants, who had cashed in on independence, mutinied against their Belgian officers at Thysville, about a

---

vided, among other things, for a house of representatives elected by universal suffrage and a senate composed of members elected by the provincial assemblies on the basis of 14 per province, including at least three custom-appointed chiefs or notables.

hundred miles downriver from Léopoldville. Almost coincidentally, disturbances broke out at Camp Léopold in the capital. The mutineers ran
amok, arresting and assaulting their officers, attacking European civilians,
including women, and indulging in an orgy of violence, looting, and rape.
Lumumba attempted to quell the outburst by promising every one of the
mutineers promotion and more pay. This absurd promise, if implemented,
would have meant that there would be no Congolese private in the ranks.
But the mutineers were uncontrollable. Violence and anarchy descended
on the other provinces, with centers like Luluabourg, Coquilhatville (capital of the Equateur), and Stanleyville as focal points. Arms were seized
by the mutineers, who established a reign of terror at Léopoldville, from
where the Belgian commander of the force, General Émile Janssens, was
rescued by helicopter. Kasavubu was proclaimed commander-in-chief.
The Belgians panicked and ran, crossing the nearest frontier they could.
In all, some 35,000 Belgians fled, thereby paralyzing the entire administrative machinery of the Congo. There was, in fact, no great reason for
panic. In all, about twenty deaths took place, though some cases of rape,
mostly by soldiers, were also reported. At the copper belt town of Ndola
in Northern Rhodesia, which borders on the Congo, I later heard accounts
of how the terror-stricken Belgians had fled in all manner of vehicles,
including armored cars, and of the hordes of frightened refugees who
poured across the border. With the loss of their empire, the Belgians lost
their nerve.

As van Bilsen, whose thirty-year plan was ignored by the Belgian government, is said to have ruefully remarked, "Liberation did not come too
early; its preparation was slow." How slow was shown in the last two years
of Belgian rule, when the Belgians tried to stampede the Congolese into
independence for which the latter were plainly not prepared. Within those
crucial two years the Belgians could not telescope what they could have
spread imaginatively over the previous fifty years.

On July 11 Brussels decided to fly Belgian paratroopers into Léopoldville and to other parts of the Congo in order to protect and evacuate the
Europeans, who, besides 80,000 Belgians, included another 20,000 Portuguese, Greeks, and Italians. On the same day, Tshombe, with the connivance of the big Belgian financial interests, who had rich investments in
Katanga, proclaimed the independence of that province. To the government in Léopoldville and to many outside the Congo it looked as if the
Belgian army was returning as a prelude to the reestablishment of Belgian
rule. Some of the Belgian government's actions gave credence to that
belief, for Brussels ordered its civil servants and the Belgian mining personnel who had fled to return to Katanga. Belgian troops were placed at

Tshombe's disposal, and Belgian officers were retained in the Katanga army. Tshombe was given arms.

On July 12 Lumumba appealed to the United States for aid against "Belgian aggression," but was advised by President Eisenhower to appeal to the U.N., which, along with Kasavubu, he did, also asking for the urgent dispatch of U.N. military assistance. This led to a Security Council resolution on July 14 calling upon Belgium to withdraw her troops and authorizing Secretary-General Hammarskjöld "to take all necessary steps in consultation with the Congolese government to provide it with such military assistance as may be necessary." The following day the first Tunisian troops, reinforced soon after by the Ghanaians, landed in the Congo. Hammarskjöld had decided that the U.N. troops would be drawn from African and Asian countries and—probably to reassure the Belgians—from certain neutral European countries. The latter were principally Swedes and Irish. In accepting the Security Council's mandate, Hammarskjöld declared that the U.N. force would not take any action making it a party to internal conflicts nor would it take the initiative in the use of armed force.

The point is important in view of subsequent developments. Lumumba in his appeal to the U.N. had accused the Belgian government of provoking the secession of Katanga, and in this context, as in the general context of Belgian aggression, had insisted "strongly on the extreme urgency of the need to send U.N. troops to the Congo." If, according to Hammarskjöld's interpretation of the Security Council mandate, the U.N. would not take any action making it a party to internal conflicts, how could the Security Council resolution requiring him "to take all necessary steps in consultation with the Congolese government to provide it with such military assistance as may be necessary" be implemented?

The U.N. stepped into the vast eruptive and disruptive vacuum created by the collapse of Congolese rule. Its mandate was confused and contradictory, and soon proved unworkable. Hammarskjöld chose Dr. Ralph Bunche, who had come to Léopoldville as the U.N. representative at the independence celebration, to be his representative in the Congo. "You are here," said Dr. Bunche in a directive to his staff shortly after the U.N. intervention, "to pacify and then to administer the Congo." There he was wrong. Administration was the affair of the Congolese government, and how was pacification possible if the initiative in the use of military force was precluded? The U.N. personnel were hamstrung by the Security Council resolution of July 14 and its interpretation by Hammarskjöld. Clarification was necessary.

On July 22 the Security Council met again and called on Belgium "to implement speedily the previous resolution," which meant the prompt withdrawal of all Belgian forces from the Congo and their replacement by U.N. troops for the purposes of maintaining law and order until such time as the Congolese security forces were in a position to do so. On July 23 the Belgian troops withdrew, except in Katanga, where the Belgian forces supporting Tshombe were reinforced by miscellaneous European military adventurers, including Belgian army personnel. Meanwhile the Force Publique, rechristened by the Congolese government the Arme Nationale Congolaise (ANC), assumed responsibility for maintaining law and order. The role of the U.N. forces was again rendered anomalous and invidious. The July 22 resolution had authorized the secretary-general to "take all necessary action to this end," supporting Hammarskjöld's interpretation that the earlier July 14 resolution applied to the Congo in its entirety, which meant the occupation of Katanga on behalf of the central government. Tshombe, secure behind the guns of his Belgian supporters, defied the United Nations, warning them that, if their troops were sent into Katanga, "they will be opposed, if necessary, by force."

Here Hammarskjöld made his first cardinal error. He hesitated. Worse, he decided to parley with Tshombe in the hope of making him see reason. Bunche proceeded to Elisabethville to discuss the situation with Tshombe, but, as the U.N. was to discover later, Tshombe could no more be pinned down to any commitments than an eel could be skewered by a dart. Bunche recommended that the proposed U.N. military operations in Katanga should be stayed, but by then irreparable damage was done to the relations between Léopoldville and the U.N., while Tshombe's secessionist ambitions were bolstered by his meeting with Bunche. Not surprisingly, Lumumba was outraged that the U.N. should bypass the central government and tacitly recognize the independence of Katanga by opening negotiations with Tshombe. He suspected the U.N. of plotting to keep the Belgians in Katanga.

"The U.N.," Lumumba complained when I saw him, "is complicating the situation and allowing the Congo to rot. The Belgians are behind it all. If it were not for the determination of the Afro-Asian people the Congo would by now be dead."

He was wrong in his suspicion, but one could not blame him for it in the invidious circumstances in which he and the central government found themselves. The U.N. was also in an anomalous position, for it did not know its mind. Hammarskjöld again sought clarification and instructions from the Security Council, which at a meeting on August 8-9 called on "the government of Belgium to withdraw its troops from Katanga" and declared "that the entry of the U.N. force into the province of Katanga is necessary for the full implementation of the resolution." This brought Tshombe immediately, though only temporarily, to heel—one of the many postures in the varied pantomime he was to enact in the months ahead. Tshombe promised not to use force provided the U.N. did not interfere with Katanga's police or try to disarm its army. On August 12 Hammarskjöld himself proceeded to Katanga with a token force and was correctly received. He succeeded in ridding Katanga of the 8,600 Belgian troops ensconced there, but he was unable to dislodge the many Belgian "military technicians" whom the wily Tshombe had wheedled into the Katanga army.

Meanwhile, the Congo had been reduced to a state of near-chaos. Even at the outset of independence three power centers existed in the country: Léopoldville in the far west, controlled by Kasavubu; Stanleyville in the center, which was Lumumba's stronghold; and Elisabethville in the southeast, dominated by Tshombe. In August Albert Kalonji, leader of the dissident MNC, declared the independence of the Baluba area of south Kasai, christening it the "Diamond State," with its headquarters at Bakwanga. From this region come 90 percent of the Congo's diamonds. Lumumba sought to suppress Kalonji's Baluba, killing 1,000 of them in the process, for which he was accused by Hammarskjöld of genocide. In north Katanga the pro-Lumumba Baluba, led by Jason Sendwe, opposed Tshombe, who was later to loose his South African mercenaries on them. In north Kasai, the indigenous Lulua, who favored Lumumba, fell upon their mortal enemies, the Baluba, whom they regard as invaders, resulting in a large-scale massacre of the latter. Luluabourg, the former provincial capital, became the headquarters of the Lulua after the expulsion of the Baluba and the exodus of the Europeans. In backward Equateur, the anti-Lumumba Jean Bolikango had a precarious foothold. The Lumumbists were soon to infiltrate into Kivu.

With the breakdown of law and order and the social and administrative services following the flight of the Belgians, the Congo was reduced to a shambles. The ANC, the one factor on which depended the countrywide maintenance of law and order, was in the words of Rajeshwar Dayal, who replaced Bunche as U.N. representative in the Congo, "a disorderly rabble." Kasai had practically ceased to exist as an administrative unit. With the secession of Katanga, "the Ruhr of the Congo," which before independence had contributed over 40 percent of the country's revenue and earned 60 percent of its foreign exchange, the central treasury was virtually empty. By the end of the first year of independence the Léopoldville authorities had a budget deficit of nearly $140 million on a total expenditure of less than $210 million, and were spending at a rate which threatened to bring about an excess of expenditure over revenue in the proportion of three to one. This was not due solely to the independence of

Katanga, for, even without the minerals of that province, the Congo is a potentially rich country.

Katanga's economic mainstay is the mammoth $297 million Union Minière, which has interlocking interests with Tanganyika Concessions, and whose ramifications extend to the Anglo-American Corporation representing part of the Oppenheimer empire, the British South African Company, and the Beneguela Railway, in which the Portuguese government is an important shareholder. But Britain and Belgium have greater financial stakes outside Katanga in the other five provinces, where the powerful Unilever interests and the influential Fédération des Enterprises du Congo operate.

What brought about the administrative collapse was the sudden vacuum created by the headlong flight of the Belgians, and the initial inability of the U.N. to fill it adequately and competently. Instead of contracting, the vacuum enlarged as a result of U.N. inexperience and Congolese inefficiency and irresponsibility. To the Congolese, individually catapulted into power and enjoying places of unaccustomed authority and patronage, the lure of the three Cs—cash, cars, and concubines—proved irresistible. The majority succumbed. Because of wildly extravagant concessions, around a third of the national income was absorbed by the wages of the government and the army, the latter costing nearly 500 percent more at the end of the first year of independence. Everybody demanded and generally got his cut, political appointees raising their emoluments by 400 percent, parliamentary deputies enhancing their salaries with government posts, and government servants extracting a 100 percent rise in pay. In turn the ordinary man, particularly the worker, demanded and usually got a wage increase.

At Luluabourg in north Kasai, which was among the most disorganized regions of the Congo, one heard grim tales of disorder, hunger, disease, cruelty, and death. On our way from Léopoldville to Luluabourg our Sabena plane was compelled to make a detour from Luluabourg to Bakwanga, capital of Kalonji's Diamond State in south Kasai, where the passengers, who had no intention of alighting there, were forced by armed militiamen at the point of their guns to descend and register their names. I noticed that the Congolese functionary who demanded my visa held it upside down while pretending to read it. With equal solemnity he then stamped it.

"If we had shown him our Memling menu cards,* he'd have been no wiser," remarked a Belgian standing behind me in the queue.

At the diamond center of Tshikapa, the airport was guarded by Ghanaian troops entrenched in dugouts. Fronting the airport ran a tree-lined

---

* The Memling Hotel is in Léopoldville.

road which a U.N. Haitian doctor remarked had been strewn with dead and dying Lulua only a month before. This was Baluba country, where the Lulua had paid dearly for the massacre they had perpetrated in north Kasai. The plaster on the walls of my hotel room at Luluabourg was pockmarked with rifle shots—a memento of the July shootings—and in a local restaurant the Belgian proprietor showed me some grisly photographs of the sliced and mutilated bodies of two Belgian cattle raisers who had been done to death on their ranch near Luputa in south Kasai by a Baluba clan which had reverted to ritual cannibalism. One heard some hair-raising tales not only about the Baluba and their allies, the Bampende and the Batshioko, but of their traditional enemies, the Lulua, all of whom had sporadically lapsed into near-cannibalism, hacking off the arms and legs of their victims, and flourishing them in orgies of ghastly ritual horrors. A Tunisian described how a U.N. patrol had come across a huge black cooking pot containing some human remains.

At Luluabourg I was permitted to interview a twenty-three-year-old British soldier of fortune, Captain John Roberts, who was then held in U.N. custody, but was later released and repatriated to Britain. Roberts had led some Baluba tribesmen against the Lulua, "for money and adventure," as he frankly confessed. The equipment of some of his Baluba warriors, he said, as also of the Lulua, consisted of bows and metal-tipped arrows, supplemented by spears, and before going into battle a witch doctor hung charms around their necks, which were supposed to render them immune to death. Roberts claimed that the Lulua were led by some Czechs, but I found no one to substantiate his story.

Apart from the breakdown in the administrative machinery, the flight of the Belgians paralyzed the social and welfare services, of which they were justly proud, but where again they had trained no Congolese to replace them. In the whole of Kasai, a province larger than France, there were only twenty-six doctors left, including state, company, missionary, Red Cross, and U.N. doctors, of whom not a single one was Congolese. Formerly there were seventy-eight. According to a U.N. specialist, the province needed a minimum of seventy. The Lulua hospital at Tshikapa was run by a Lulua, trained to be only a nurse's aide, who ignored the instructions of the qualified foreign doctors and insisted on prescribing for the patients! In the whole of Kasai there were only three Congolese medical assistants capable of working in country dispensaries or hospitals under a doctor's direction, but none of the three was willing to serve in a subordinate capacity. One was secretary-general of public health in Kasai, another director of the hospital at Port Franqui, and the third director of the hospital at Sendery. Many of the hospitals and dispensaries were in the charge of Congolese nurses' aides who had only one year's medical training. These nightmare conditions, aggravated by lack of communications and transport, the holding up of food supplies, and the inadequacy of medical aid, led to a sharp slump in public health, accelerated by grave protein deficiences and manifested by the rapidly rising graph of malaria, tuberculosis, and filaria. Combined with lack of medicine and preventive measures, deficient sanitation threatened a spread of endemic and contagious diseases, such as sleeping sickness, smallpox, leprosy, and yellow fever. A tragic postscript to the breakdown of law and order was the presence of four pregnant nuns in the leper colony at Kamonia, about sixty miles from Tshikapa.

Refugees, precipitated by the tribal flare-up, complicated the deteriorating health and economic situation. Famine broke out in Kasai, with some 300,000 Baluba refugees fleeing from the north. When I was there over 100,000 people were literally starving to death in south Kasai according to an FAO alimentation expert. Outbreaks of famine were reported in various parts of the Congo, the affected areas in south Kasai being Bakwanga and Miabi. A distressing feature was the spectacle of thousands of children suffering from kwashiorkor, which is advanced malnutrition.

I had a talk with the U.N. representative in Kasai, M. Veillet-Lavallier, who combined the dual functions of political adviser to the local government and coordinator of U.N. affairs in the province, where he headed the civilian operations. He spoke frankly. "One needs infinite patience and persistence with the Congolese," he remarked. "One also needs a core of good U.N. men."

Had he got the latter? He shrugged his shoulders. "Our work is hampered by political difficulties and differences," he explained. "Here in Kasai, the major obstacle is Kalonji's Diamond State. It must be got out of the way. Secondly," he went on, "how can we coordinate unless other agencies like WHO and UNESCO do what they promise?"

A general sense of frustration bedeviled the work of the U.N., whose personnel was uneven. Veillet-Lavallier was a dedicated man with considerable understanding and initiative, but not all his assistants shared his imagination and drive. "I find Léo depressing," he confessed. "The Royale* is a dreamland. I prefer to be here. If I leave, something always happens."

Like its personnel, the U.N.'s record of work varied in different fields. Within twelve months it was able to arrange or supervise short-term professional and technical courses for nearly 500 Congolese in twelve foreign countries. Another 600 were sent to Belgium, largely at the expense of the Belgian government but under the aegis of the U.N. Since then scholarships have been established at Lovanium University financed jointly by the

* U.N. headquarters at Léopoldville.

Congolese government, the U.N., and the Ford Foundation, and a further 500 Congolese have been absorbed by French and American universities. Since the Congo can be really independent only when its administration and government are run by a cadre of trained Congolese, the U.N. effort in nation-building is admirable and praiseworthy. The U.N. has also shown considerable ingenuity in improvisation. Indeed, its personnel appear to be more suited to improvise in an emergency than to carry on sustained day-to-day administration. Perhaps because of the U.N. desire to preserve a maximum nationalities pattern, its personnel has not always measured up to the needs and demands of the Congo.

When everything is said and done, it must be admitted that, of all the foreigners, the Belgians are best acquainted with Congolese conditions and needs, but like the Congolese, the Belgians are oppressed by a colonial holdover. The Belgians I met in the Congo and later in Ruanda-Urundi were uniformly courteous, considerate, and hospitable. But as an Indian, knowing as I do the difference between colonial rule and independence, I sensed in the Belgians a rigidity of outlook which distinguishes them from other ex-colonialists, such as the more resilient and flexible Britons and Frenchmen. They seemed peculiarly graceless in dealing with the Congolese as individuals, betraying at times an obtuseness to other people's feelings which bordered on the insensitive. And yet, without Belgian skills and experience, the task of rehabilitating the Congo would be more long-drawn and arduous. Not only as technicians, but as teachers in the schools and colleges of independent Congo, the Belgians could render real service. Moreover, the Belgians are as a rule paid less than equivalent U.N. officials or recruits. Antipathy is mutual between the Belgians and the greater part of the U.N. personnel in the Congo, each being allergic to the other and each accusing the other of hamstringing his efforts. As a result, the work of both is retarded.

It was in this confused, bewildering context that Lumumba's ramshackle government attempted to function from Léopoldville. Disunity and disorder were everywhere—within the country, where the administrative machinery had collapsed, and where tribal rivalries and hates had burst their artificial bounds and found vent in massacres and bloodshed; within the government, where the showdown between Lumumba and Kasavubu was mounting to a crisis; and within the U.N., where the East-West clash brought the Cold War not only into the Congo, but into Africa, with the countries of the Casablanca constellation and the Brazzaville group assuming different postures toward the Congo. With independence the Congo had not only split within itself, but had intensified the fissures and divisions in the continent. Internally, the Congo's first need was political agreement among its leaders. Externally, the prime necessity was unity within the United Nations. Neither of these prerequisites was forthcoming.

At this period Hammarskjöld's attitude toward Lumumba was one of distrust and suspicion. It was to alter later as a result of Rajeshwar Dayal's advice, which is reflected in the controversial progress report submitted by this adroit and highly skillful diplomat to the U.N. secretary-general in November, 1960. Dayal was critical of the role of the Belgians, who had been returning in steadily growing numbers following Lumumba's dismissal by Kasavubu on September 5 and his subsequent detention under house arrest in the state governor's residence at Léopoldville, where I met him. The U.N. special representative openly accused the Belgians of indulging in activities at variance with U.N. aims. Dayal was largely justified in his strictures, for, with few exceptions, the returning Belgians made no attempt to conceal their opposition to the U.N. role in the Congo, and their maneuvers, open or devious, were calculated to denigrate the international organization in the eyes of the Congolese. Dayal's report, which was released on November 2, on the eve of the United States Presidential elections which saw Kennedy win, was officially declared unacceptable by Washington. This further intensified the Cold War in the Congo, which the earlier Soviet onslaught on Hammarskjöld for his handling of the crisis and his attitude to Lumumba had precipitated.

Lumumba's stock had begun to slump some time before his dismissal. He was unable to redeem the two major pledges on which, had he succeeded, his prestige would have soared. He failed to undermine or dislodge the Belgians' civil and military influence. Without U.N. support and aid he could not bring Tshombe to book and compel Katanga to recognize the sovereignty of the central government. Kalonji was equally defiant. Before turning to the Russians, Lumumba made a desperate effort to cajole some African countries, which included Ghana, Guinea, and the U.A.R., to bypass the U.N. and support him directly. They were sympathetic, but politely refused. Thereupon he opened negotiations with the Russians, who offered him some planes and trucks. Without consulting Kasavubu, Lumumba decided to accept. On September 5 the U.N. closed all major airports in the Congo to traffic other than that of the U.N., and on the same day, Kasavubu, in his capacity as chief of state, dismissed Lumumba. Lumumba's riposte was to dismiss Kasavubu, a gesture typically Congolese in its airy absurdity and futility. For Lumumba it was the beginning of the end.

Not to be outdone, the chamber of deputies, on September 7, voted sixty to nineteen to invalidate both dismissals. During the Security Council session from September 7 to September 17, the Russians launched a frontal attack on Hammarskjöld and went so far as to veto an agreed Afro-

Asian resolution insisting, among other things, that no military assistance should be given to the Congo except by the U.N. Strictly, this resolution ran counter to the right of the Congo as a sovereign state to seek aid from whatever quarter it chose, but presumably if the U.N. was paying the piper by virtually sustaining the Congo, it had a right to call the tune. At a special meeting of the General Assembly summoned on the "uniting for peace" proviso, the resolution which the Russians had vetoed was confirmed by seventy votes to none. The Soviet bloc, France, and South Africa abstained.

At this stage there enters into the picture Colonel Joseph Mobutu, the Congo's alleged strong man, who was one of Lumumba's protégés and whom he had promoted chief of staff to General Victor Lundula, the commander-in-chief. Mobutu shortly after succeeded Lundula. Mobutu, with Kasavubu's connivance, was later to hand over Lumumba to his mortal enemy, Tshombe—and to death—in one of the most sordid episodes in a treacherous, bloodstained drama.

Mobutu, who comes from Equateur, belongs to the Bangala tribe, which in Léopoldville was traditionally opposed to the Bakongo. In the struggle for power between Lumumba and Kasavubu, Mobutu at first appeared to favor the latter, but when the breach between the two men became public he decided to act on his own, though some allege he acted throughout with Kasavubu's consent and connivance. On Lumumba's dismissal, Kasavubu had appointed Joseph Ileo, who belonged to Kalonji's MNC, as prime minister, and the Congo was thus saddled with two rival governments. On September 14 Mobutu, who had exploited the Lumumba-Kasavubu differences to entrench himself more strongly with the army, announced that he had dismissed both the governments, suspended Kasavubu and Lumumba from their functions, though he recognized Kasavubu as president, and closed parliament. He also announced that the army would take over the reins of government until January 1, 1961. Simultaneously, he ordered all officials at the Communist embassies to leave the Congo within forty-eight hours, which they did. This greatly reinforced Mobutu's reputation as a strong man.

It was obvious, however, that Mobutu's strength derived from the support of the West, which wanted Lumumba ousted and replaced by a pro-West administration which would keep the Congo free of all Communist influences. At that time the American, British, and French ambassadors at Léopoldville were openly working for this end. The legend of Strong Man Mobutu emanated from these sources. Ostensibly respecting the U.N.'s insistence on legality, the West supported Kasavubu, whose constitutional status as chief of state was unchallengeable, meanwhile keeping Mobutu and Tshombe on the sidelines—Mobutu because of his influence with the army, a large proportion of which is drawn from the Bangala tribe, and Tshombe because of his toughness and pro-West leanings. According to some circles Mobutu's *coup d'état* was only made possible by the American government, which provided him with the money to pay the mutinous Congolese troops.

The ONUC (Opération Nations Unités Congo), representing the U.N. in the Congo, had, however, repudiated Mobutu's regime as one "founded only on military force." The Western Powers operated largely through Mobutu. The ONUC recognized only two institutions as legal—the chief of state and parliament. But Mobutu, whose policy was "to neutralize political personalities," had suspended parliament with Kasavubu's official approval. Mobutu in fact was working hand in glove with Kasavubu, and both men were supported by the West.

Opposing the West's tactics were the Afro-Asian group headed by Ghana, Guinea, and the U.A.R. Broadly, they were working to bring Kasavubu and Lumumba together in the hope that this would induce Mobutu to cooperate later. The envoys of these three countries were later expelled by Mobutu on the ground that they were giving aid and advice to Lumumba. I met the Guinea envoy briefly, but had longer meetings with the U.A.R. envoy, Murad Ghalib, a doctor turned diplomat, and the Ghana ambassador extraordinary, Nathaniel Welbeck. Ghalib, a seasoned diplomat who had been secretary-general in the foreign affairs ministry at Cairo, was a man of considerable finesse. The maladroit Welbeck was more transparent.

"Both Kasavubu and Lumumba," said Welbeck, "have worked for freedom. In fact, after I saw Kasavubu a little while ago, he signed an agreement to work with Lumumba, but when I returned from Accra he went back on it. His explanation was that the people would not accept Lumumba. He is wrong. At least 70 percent of the people in the provinces would vote for him. Mobutu is in the hands of Kasavubu, for the young commissioners-general whom Mobutu appointed take their instructions from Kasavubu. Mobutu is slightly confused about what he is doing. His mistake has been not to maintain the balance. He has taken sides. He is haunted by his ingratitude to Lumumba."

The American ambassador, Clare Timberlake, who had served some years in India, is an old and good friend of mine. Some of his activities while in the Congo came in for criticism in India. But "Tim" was characteristically kind and helpful to me while I was there. Ian Scott, the British ambassador, also an old India hand, was once a member of the Indian civil service. He spoke frankly.

"The United Nations," he said, "is no longer an international amalgam, due to the East-West differences. Today it is under Afro-Asian pressure. That is why Hammarskjöld is swinging this way and that. But for Afro-Asian interference—I mean by the U.A.R., Ghana, and Guinea— the Congolese might have settled down. The Afro-Asian group does not exist as a consolidated group. What interest has Ghana or the U.A.R. here?"

I remarked that, like other countries, they might be interested in power politics.

The British ambassador impliedly agreed. "It's the brash new imperialism of newly independent countries," he went on. "It's like the British earlier in India. The Afro-Asians are trying to tell the Congolese what to do. It's for the Congolese to decide for themselves. I think the solution is to induce as many elements as possible to get together."

Did he include Lumumba among these elements, I inquired.

He evaded the question. "I've seen Lumumba privately and in action," he remarked. "He's a good speaker, he's intelligent, but unreliable. Kasavubu is underrated. He was a nationalist leader before Lumumba."

What did the ambassador think of Mobutu?

"Ah!" he exclaimed. "The Russians nearly pulled it off. Now the Russians, the Czechs, and the Chinese are out. It just shows that the Congolese can act firmly and drastically. It's wrong to denigrate the Congolese, to treat them as children. You don't need a university degree to run a country. The Congolese should be encouraged to send their young men abroad—for rural training in India, for military training to Europe, to France, England, elsewhere."

Clare Timberlake and Ian Scott were both to be withdrawn from the Congo by their governments not long after Rajeshwar Dayal was withdrawn by the U.N. secretary-general.

Far from simplifying the situation, Mobutu's coup complicated it further. Consolidation was what the Congo needed and what it most conspicuously lacked. What and where, one asked, were the elements which made for consolidation? Not in the U.N., which was a house divided against itself. Not in either of the two major blocs, for the withdrawal of the Russians from the Congo did not ease, but intensified the problems of the West. Not in the Afro-Asian group, which was by no means united in its attitude to the Congo. Not certainly in the Congo, already a political madhouse, which would, if left to itself, disintegrate into complete chaos. Obviously, the solution lay in the two blocs agreeing on the necessity of a neutral Congo functioning during a self-imposed political moratorium of from five to seven years, in which period a sufficient number of Congolese could be trained to man the administrative and essential services, and the U.N. could help set the Congo on its feet again. But this called for forbearance on all sides. And there was no sign of forbearance on any side. The difficulties the U.N. faced were terrifying.

Between mid-September, 1960, and mid-February, 1961, when Lumumba's murder was revealed, the differences congealed and hardened. Ileo had accepted his virtual ouster from the premiership by Mobutu, who had set up a college of commissioners-general composed almost entirely of university undergraduates, with their Belgian professors as advisers, which acted as a caretaker government, though the presidential ordinance of September 12 naming the Ileo government was not formally rescinded. Lumumba, however, refused to stand down and, though out of office, continued his political activities until he was made prisoner in his riverside villa at Léopoldville, surrounded by Mobutu's troops with an inner ring of U.N. soldiers to protect him. Stanleyville remained Lumumba's stronghold under Gizenga's charge, with the Lumumbists, centered largely in Orientale, part of Kivu, north Katanga, and north Kasai, standing for a unitary government and opposed by a loose alliance of federalists headed by Kasavubu in the lower Congo, Tshombe in south Katanga, Kalonji in south Kasai, and the provincial assembly of Equateur.

As differences congealed within the Congo, they kept hardening outside. The Russians now openly supported Lumumba and denounced the U.N. secretary-general as an "instrument of the colonialists." The Western Powers, moving more cautiously, inclined toward Kasavubu, who in November, 1960, appeared before the U.N. Credentials Committee asking to be recognized as the leader of the Congolese delegation, against Lumumba whom the Russians supported.

"Usually," Valerian Zorin, the Soviet delegate at the U.N., is reported to have remarked, "delegates come with mandates from their country as representatives here. Mr. Kasavubu wants a mandate from the U.N. to rule his country."

He got it, splitting the Afro-Asian group wide open in the process. While India, Ghana, Guinea, and Mali, with twenty-one other states, including the Communist countries, voted against Kasavubu, the West, supported by Nigeria, Tunisia, and the French Communauté states, favored Kasavubu, who was officially acknowledged the Congolese leader and representative. Kasavubu was, however, required to accept a U.N. commission charged with the job of finding a basis of conciliation between himself and Lumumba.

At this juncture Lumumba precipitated events by eluding his guards and captors two days after Kasavubu's return to Léopoldville and escaping from his villa, reportedly in an attempt to reach Stanleyville, where his close friend and supporter, Antoine Gizenga, held authority over Orientale. He never got there. On December 1 he was recaptured by Mobutu's troops in Kasai and roughed up before being imprisoned at Camp Hardy, Thysville, about ninety miles from Léopoldville.

December was a bad month for Mobutu and the Léopoldville regime. In Orientale, Gizenga proclaimed Stanleyville as the capital of the Congo and declared himself interim head of the "legal central government." On Christmas Day pro-Lumumba troops raided Bukavu, the capital of Kivu province, kidnaped the pro-Mobutu garrison commander and members of the provincial government, and set up a Lumumbist administration under the left-inclined Anicet Kashamuru, who had served as minister of information in the Lumumba government. An attempt on January 1 by a Mobutist parachutist company to invade Bukavu across the Ruzizi River, which was mounted from the then Belgian-administered trust territory of Ruanda-Urundi, was ignominiously repulsed, and the leader of this ill-conceived enterprise, with many of his soldiers, was captured. Shortly after, pro-Lumumba forces of battalion strength advanced undetected for hundreds of miles through jungle and bush in north Katanga, and, in an operation which took Tshombe's government completely by surprise, occupied the tin-mining center of Manano and set up a pro-Lumumba administration. U.N. troops had to be interposed between the two forces to prevent a further spread of civil war. Troops from neighboring Orientale had begun to infiltrate into north Equateur. Even in Léopoldville province the Bangala and the Bangongo, because of their hostility to the Bakongo, were pro-Lumumba.

On January 13 Mobutist troops guarding Lumumba in Thysville mutinied for more pay and rations, and sparked rumors that Lumumba's silver tongue had persuaded them to free him. It was then that Mobutu, with Kasavubu's connivance, decided to hand him over to Tshombe, knowing that this meant Lumumba's end. Tshombe's position was none too happy at the time, for, though Kalonji in south Kasai was opposed to Lumumba, he was for Mobutu and Kasavubu. Indeed, Kalonji said so when I met him at Léopoldville, where he had come to ask Mobutu to send troops to clean up north Kasai, failing which he would deploy his own troops. Kalonji is young,* bespectacled, light-skinned for an African, and was neatly dressed and fluent. With him were four tribal chiefs in beaded headdress, bare from the waist up, with multicolored shell necklaces, bangles, and anklets. They wore heavy flowing skirts with leopard-skin belts.

"These tribal chiefs," said Kalonji, pointing to them, "belong to many tribes, but they have transformed themselves into Balubas under the authority of a single chief—myself."

I asked Kalonji what he stood for.

* He was born in 1929.

"I stand both against a unitary and a Communist government. I am opposed to any form of dictatorship," he replied.

Why then did he accept Mobutu's military coup?

"I accept Mobutu," said Kalonji, "because he saved the Congo from civil war. I do not object to his military coup, but I object to his attempting to neutralize Kasavubu, who is the chief of the state." And Kalonji added dramatically, "To maintain the Congo we must divide the country."

It was much as Mobutu said when I saw him, a youthful thirty, also bespectacled, with full lips, tense and nervous, drumming his fingers as he spoke, ostensibly military in appearance, but with a limp handshake. His attitude to Indians, whom he dubbed "Communists," was suspicious, and I had had considerable difficulty in getting the interview.

Mobutu started by giving himself a clean bill of political health. "I am a Congolese patriot," he declared. "I am not under the influence of the Belgians. I consider the Congo as a sovereign and independent state, and until a new state of things is established no one has a right to order us about. Why did I neutralize the politicians? I did it to avoid chaos. I have seized arms from civilians sufficient to equip a battalion. Why, we have even discovered children of ten with revolvers. These arms are of Russian and Czech make, and come from Ghana, Guinea, and the U.A.R. These countries are members of the U.N. The Afro-Asian group is taking sides."

He was bitter toward the U.N., but his attitude seemed more mellow after a talk he had recently had with Brigadier Inderjit Rikhye of the Indian army, who was Hammarskjöld's military eyes and ears in the Congo.

"Until a few days ago," said Mobutu, "the U.N. treated me like a child. Now I've shown them what I am. General Rikhye took me to the Indian military hospital, and he invited me to lunch. In three months I got nothing. In two days, everything."

Mobutu was to learn that it wasn't all that easy. The only reference he made to Lumumba in a fairly long conversation was to remark that, while Lumumba was called "pro-Communist," he himself was tarred "pro-Belgian."

Standing earlier outside the barricaded gates of Mobutu's residence, which was heavily guarded, I had watched a unit of the Congolese army marching past on the eve of a military parade for which they were rehearsing. To help keep in step the soldiers sang a Congolese nationalist song which had evidently not been revised in the light of the latest developments, for one line which they chanted lustily was "Vive Kasavubu Lumumba!" Since Lumumba was by then Mobutu's prisoner, it was slightly incongruous. But the episode was typically Congolese.

Lumumba was not for long in Mobutu's hands. On January 17 he was flown with Maurice Mpolo, former minister of youth and sport, and Joseph Okito, former deputy speaker of the senate, to Elisabethville, where they were delivered over to Tshombe. At about the same time Mobutu and Kasavubu had some seven persons whom they were also holding in custody in Léopoldville, including M. Finant, a former president of the government of Lumumba's home province, Orientale, flown to Bakwanga in south Kasai and delivered over to Kalonji. Both these batches were to be butchered in cold blood.

The murder of Lumumba and his two colleagues—for it was a clear case of political murder, whatever Tshombe's Western apologists might say —took place in circumstances degrading to those who tortured and killed them. Pictures taken at Elisabethville show the three helpless prisoners being brutally beaten after alighting from the plane. Lumumba, as Godefroid Munongo, Katanga minister of the interior, declared while announcing his death, might have been a criminal "who must carry the responsibility for thousands of deaths in Katanga and tens of thousands of deaths in Kasai province." But are the hands of Munongo and Tshombe so lilywhite as not to expose them to the charge of being cold-blooded murderers of many of their own fellow countrymen with the aid of their well-paid foreign mercenaries? Two wrongs admittedly do not make a right. But if, as Munongo claimed, he was "certain that had Lumumba been brought before a court of law he would have got the death sentence," is he willing, along with his accomplice Tshombe to face a tribunal when and if retribution overtakes them both?

Nobody can authoritatively say in what circumstances Lumumba and his two comrades were done to death. The official Katanga story, lamely put out by Munongo on February 13, 1961, was that the three men were killed by villagers eager to win the $5,880 reward for their capture near Kolwezi, about 200 miles northwest of Elisabethville. This happened, according to Munongo, while they were attempting to escape from their prison or detention place near Muthshatsa, about 60 miles from the eastern frontier of Portuguese Angola. Their previous places of detention were first near Elisabethville, and next near Shinkolobwe. Munongo's story was palpably false and riddled with contradictions. If the three men were murdered by the villagers, why were they buried immediately? Munongo's explanation was that "this was not important—they were criminals in the eyes of every country in the world." The Belgian, Dr. G. E. Pieters, who signed the death certificates of the three men reluctantly admitted to a reporter, "The bodies were not fresh."

When were Lumumba and his two comrades actually done to death? It is believed that they were executed on the day after their arrival at Elisabethville on January 18. On that day they were ordered out of their Katanga prison, and told to kneel and pray in the open. An African soldier, on the orders of a Belgian officer believed to be a Captain Julian Gat, shot Mpolo and Okito, but refused to shoot Lumumba, whereupon the Belgian officer dispatched him.

Said Munongo airily at a press conference announcing the story of Lumumba's death allegedly at the hands of some irate Lunda villagers: "If people accuse us of killing Lumumba, I will reply 'Prove it.'" And he piously added: "The world has been rid of a problem."

Tshombe was even more casual. "The fuss over this evil man," he declared, "will soon die down. The people have no memories here. *C'est fini.*"

But it wasn't *fini.*

TSHOMBE AND KATANGA

NEWS OF LUMUMBA's death was received with "shock and horror" by the U.N. headquarters in Léopoldville. A frightened lull descended on the Congo as the various forces regrouped for action against one another. At the time of Lumumba's death his followers controlled nearly one-half of the Congo, including the whole of Orientale, north Katanga, north Kasai, a part of Kivu, and north Equateur, besides exercising a varied degree of influence in different parts of the country. Tshombe's hold on Katanga extended to just over a half of that province, and shortly after the announcement of Lumumba's death some 2,000 Katangese soldiers commanded by a Belgian officer, Colonel Crèvecœur, mounted an attack in two columns along the railway line between Luena and Kamina against the Baluba in north Katanga, where the pro-Lumumba tribesmen had allowed a battalion from Orientale to penetrate as far as Manono. The Katanga forces, after an orgy of arson, pillage, rape, and killing, which according to the U.N. headquarters in the Congo contained "elements of genocide," succeeded in pushing the rebel tribesmen to the Lualaba River.

Bloodletting had become a Congolese pastime. Reprisals and counter-reprisals inevitably followed the news of Lumumba's murder. In south Kasai, Kalonji summarily executed seven Lumumba supporters, while Gizenga killed fifteen anti-Lumumbists, ten of them deputies. In north Kasai and Kivu a number of Europeans were severely beaten up, and at

Bukavu, pro-Lumumba soldiers entered a convent and molested the nuns. One of them had her breasts badly burned by lighted cigarettes. A Belgian and a Portuguese who were overheard talking derisively of Lumumba in a Luluabourg café were shot by a Congolese, the Belgian being killed. At Bukavu, a Belgian priest, Father Renato Devos, was attacked on a street and his ears sliced off, after which he was beheaded. In Léopoldville, seven followers of Kasavubu were knifed in the dark by Lumumbists.

Even before Lumumba's murder was disclosed, the U.A.R., Indonesia, Morocco, and Guinea had announced their intention of pulling out their troops from the U.N. contingent as a protest against the U.N.'s inaction over Lumumba's continued detention, thereby reducing the U.N. forces from 19,000* to around 13,000. By what seemed an arrangement between the U.A.R. and the Gizenga regime, pro-Lumumba forces moved into north Equateur even before the U.A.R. troops had withdrawn. The gap in the U.N. contingent was filled after some initial hesitation by India, which was prepared to commit up to 5,000 troops† in the Congo provided they could be effectively utilized to restore peace there and not in support of Mobutu's "gangster regime."

Nehru, making this announcement in the Indian parliament shortly after the news of Lumumba's murder, declared that, despite his government's dismay at what had happened in the Congo and their disagreement with many of the policies the U.N. had pursued in the Congo in the past six months, he believed that if the U.N. withdrew it would mean disaster.

The Security Council resolution, passed a few days later on February 21, 1961, was to follow broadly the lines indicated by Nehru. By now it was clear that both the new United States government as well as the U.N. secretary-general had decided to change their Congo policy. Hammarskjöld had come round to the view that if the ONUC was to discharge its duties effectively its hands must be strengthened and its mandate redefined. A breakdown of U.N. security operations, he warned, could lead to "immediate civil war, degenerating into uninhibited tribal conflict and the complete disintegration of the remaining fabric of national unity." Endorsing Nehru's view that "if the United Nations goes out of the Congo it will be a disaster," President Kennedy warned that "any attempt by any government to intervene unilaterally in the Congo" would be resisted by the United States. He emphasized that the continued U.N. presence in the Congo was vital, since it offered the best, if not the only, possibility for the restoration of stability and order. In effect, Kennedy, unlike his predecessor, was reconciled to a neutral Congo.

The American President's warning against unilateral intervention was not specifically directed at any country, but it was plain that it was

* Of this number barely 13,000 were combat troops.
† Subsequently raised to 7,500.

intended as much for the U.A.R. as for the Soviet Union, and also included the not-so-neutral African neutralists. The U.A.R. had been the first country to follow the Soviet lead in recognizing Gizenga* as the successor of Lumumba, thereby also recognizing "the legal central government" Gizenga had set up at Stanleyville. In all, about thirteen countries had recognized Gizenga as legitimate ruler of the Congo, and the U.A.R. had supplied about six truckloads of arms and ammunition to his regime.

Neither Gizenga in Orientale nor Kashamuru in Kivu had Lumumba's popular appeal or personality. Coming from the northern part of Léopoldville province, Gizenga had no firm hold on Orientale. Kashamuru, though born on an island in Lake Kivu, found the job of being Gizenga's strong-arm man unsuited to his temperament and capacity, and the two men were soon at loggerheads following Lumumba's death. Gizenga's military commander, General Victor Lundula, who for a brief period had commanded the Congolese national army, was handicapped by lack of arms and equipment, and, though Gizenga had raised the pay of his 6,000-man army to $180 a month, which was three times what Léopoldville could then afford, his exchequer was running dry.

The Congolese national army was also divided, and the regular forces had shrunk from 25,000 to about 15,000 men under Mobutu. The rest were wandering in varied stages of disarray around the provinces, constituting, in Hammarskjöld's words, "the main threat to law and order." In south Kasai a score of Belgian officers commanded some 3,000 Baluba militiamen, who formed Kalonji's army. Tshombe had supposedly the best-trained, best-led, and best-equipped force, consisting of at least 15,000 men led by 400 Belgian officers, and supplemented by a foreign legion of another 2,000 men and officers. He had also an air force of about fifteen assorted planes, which he was to reinforce later and which he used in February, 1961, to bomb Manono and other Baluba-held centers in north Katanga. Mercenaries for Tshombe's air force were recruited from South Africa and from the two Rhodesias with the connivance of Tshombe's great and good friend, Sir Roy Welensky.

Early in February, Kasavubu, irked by the growing encroachment of the Lumumbists, decided to act. Working in close collaboration with Justin Bombako, the pro-Western head of Mobutu's army-appointed caretaker government, he nominated Joseph Ileo, a moderate who, like Mobutu and Bombako, came from Equateur, to head a new provisional broad-based government. Ileo had previously been appointed prime minister-designate in September, but before he could assume office his authority had been usurped by the student commissioners-general.

Ileo, a thin, intense man, struck me as clearheaded, though he was widely regarded in the Congo as a lightweight of no political consequence.

* He was vice-premier in Lumumba's government.

Lumumba had contemptuously described him to me as "only an individual." Ileo was of the opinion that the sole legal institutions in the Congo were parliament and Kasavubu. He agreed that parliament should be reconvened, but the difficulty, he explained, was that it might not be possible to get a sufficient number of members to Léopoldville. On one point Ileo was emphatic. The Congolese must settle their own affairs and problems without outside interference.

In the composition of the cabinet, Kasavubu, the dominating voice, turned to men from the upstream regions, including not only Equateur, but pro-Lumumbist Orientale and Kivu. A notable figure in an otherwise undistinguished cabinet was Cyrille Adoula, a trade union leader from Equateur who had once inclined toward Lumumba but now inclined to the West. He was to be prime minister shortly after the Congolese parliament reassembled at Lovanium University in July. Bombako, with his unique talent for survival, remained as foreign minister. Six ministries, including that of defense, were left vacant, and it was indicated that they would be filled when the Lumumbist faction was defeated, and the country united with the breakaway governments of Katanga and south Kasai. Significantly the posts of vice-president and vice-premier were left vacant—the former reserved for Tshombe and the latter for Kalonji.

Coincident with the announcement of the provisional government came indications of a change in the Congolese policy of the United States and the U.N. On January 1, a month before Lumumba's death was announced, Hammarskjöld, warning the Security Council that civil war in the Congo had "come closer," had asked it to authorize U.N. action to get the divided Congolese army out of the country's politics. This meant the neutralization of the army by taking "urgently appropriate measures" to reorganize it and to prevent it or its units from intervening in the prevailing conflicts in the Congo. Impliedly Hammarskjöld now recognized that it was not sufficient for the U.N. force merely to interpose itself between two contending forces and thereby become a third party to a dispute. It was necessary to disarm the Congolese army before reorganizing it. The second imperative was the withdrawal of all foreign combat troops and military mercenaries, which Hammarskjöld confessed he thought the U.N. had achieved in August, only to have foreign elements infiltrate again in various obvious and devious guises. The U.N. secretary-general emphasized that the immediate aim was to provide for the withdrawal of all Belgian combat troops.

The Belgians had come back in considerable numbers, and in their military and civilian capacities were attempting to hamper the work of the U.N. Had they refrained from political and military incitement, nobody could have reasonably objected to their presence. But the vast majority of them were obsessed with an almost paranoic hatred of the U.N., and were peculiarly obtuse in their methods and activities. The Belgians who had run away in panic returned in high hope. They were needed, but not loved, as they pretended they were.

I remember the blazing hatred in the eyes of a Lulua waiter as his Belgian employer denigrated his tribe, deriding it as inferior to the enterprising Baluba, who had formerly worked in his restaurant. The Belgian was probably right, but to me it seemed as if he were asking to be murdered in his bed.

By defying the U.N. resolution not to interfere in the internal affairs of the Congo and by infiltrating in hundreds into the country, the Belgians set a precedent for the pro-Communist elements to do likewise. Compared to the Belgians, the Russians, Czechs, and Egyptians were microscopic in number and meager in the aid they gave the Congolese. Soviet and U.A.R. attempts to drive a military supply route into the Congo via the Sudan were checkmated by the Sudan's resolute refusal to allow passage for such arms and by Khartoum's insistence that such aid should be channeled through the U.N.

Belgian, French, South African, and Rhodesian mercenaries and so-called "military advisers," apart from Belgian technicians, teachers, administrators, and civilian personnel, were returning in considerable numbers to the Congo, and had done so since the dismissal of Lumumba. Léopoldville's European population of 18,000, which had dropped to 2,000 in August, 1960, was nearly 5,000 a year later.* In July, 1961, there were over 200 Belgian officials in the central government and administration, the majority of them at a policy-making level. As early as November, 1960, Rajeshwar Dayal, the secretary-general's special representative in the Congo, had cited specific instances in his progress report of Belgian interference in U.N. work. U.N. documents and reports were frequently withheld from the Congolese officials in various ministries, and propaganda was spread that U.N. trusteeship of the Congo would emerge as a result of the U.N. mission. In the ministry of economic coordination and planning the Belgian Chef de Cabinet was responsible for delaying the submission of applications for U.N. technical aid. The ministry of public health was also strongly manned by Belgians, one of whom had publicly expressed the view that there was consequently no need for the U.N. advisory team. Dayal's report contains instances not only of Belgian interference with U.N. work, but of sabotage of equipment. However, at the lower level a good deal of useful and cooperative work was done by the Belgians. The ideal arrangement would have been for the returning *émi-*

---

* This figure may not seem considerable, but, since nearly everyone who returned left his family behind, it was in fact substantial, even allowing three members per family.

grés to work under the U.N. umbrella and be assigned technical rather than policy-making functions.

Although Belgium did not support Kasavubu as openly and aggressively as she did Tshombe, the Belgian presence became increasingly evident in the army and administration of Léopoldville. As early as January, 1961, some thirty Belgian military officers had arrived in Léopoldville, spearheading a reported total contingent of 100 then on their way to the Congo capital. France, West Germany, Italy, and the United States were also giving assistance to Kasavubu in diplomatic and technical fields, not always through U.N. channels. By that time it was estimated that 18,000 Belgians held jobs in the Congo, compared with more than 30,000 when the postindependence riots started. Of these nearly 2,000 held government administrative or technical jobs, with around 1,400 in Katanga and 600 in the remainder of the Congo. In this period over 1,000 Belgian teachers returned to their posts, thereby relieving UNESCO to some extent in its teacher recruiting task. Many judges and lawyers also returned. Had these civilians concentrated on their jobs instead of indoctrinating the Congolese against the U.N., no suspicion could have attached to them or their activities. Unfortunately, the majority of them were by no means apolitical.

The foreign mercenaries constituted the major menace, and the greatest number of them were in Katanga. Dayal's report had referred to a recruiting agency for the Congo set up in Brussels to recruit civilian personnel for Léopoldville shortly after a measure of security had been reestablished in the Congo. But there were, additionally, military recruiting agencies based in Brussels as well as Paris, the latter for the purpose of recruiting French irregulars principally drawn from the OAS then operating in Algeria. The Belgian government officially disclaimed any connection with these agencies, but it is difficult to see how they could have functioned in Brussels without official connivance or, at the least, official indifference. At the same time, Brussels stated it had no troops in the Congo apart from about ten technicians in each of the two bases at Kitona in the lower Congo and Kamina in Katanga. It admitted, however, that there were an unspecified number of Belgian officers in the Katanga gendarmerie and about fifty in the Congolese national army. Apart from these, many more mercenaries had been recruited for Tshombe by organizations such as the Mission Marissal (MM)* with offices in Brussels and Paris. According to this organization, it had recruited by April, 1962, nearly 600 European mercenaries, mostly Belgians, but also Frenchmen, Southern Rhodesians, Britons, and even South Africans, though the South Africans were later asked to leave because of their antiblack prejudices.

---

* Named after Colonel Adélin Marissal, a retired Belgian officer and war hero who headed the mercenaries.

Moreover, the MM had Katangese soldiers brought to Belgium for "moral and physical training." In the event of further fighting breaking out in Katanga, an MM spokesman declared that at least 2,000 mercenaries would "be ready to fight."

The reactions of Léopoldville and Elisabethville to the Hammarskjöld plan, which envisaged as its principal objectives the ejection of foreign military personnel, the withdrawal of Belgian political advisers, and the disarming of Congolese soldiers of any faction, were equally violent. About the time the plan was first mooted, both Kasavubu and Tshombe, threatened by the growing Lumumbist menace in the north, had been seeking ways and means of buttressing and strengthening their position by cooperation and compromise. Kasavubu, as we saw, had left six ministries vacant in the Ileo government, along with the posts of vice-president and vice-premier as bait for Tshombe, Kalonji, and Gizenga, all of whom, however, refused to bite. Instead, Tshombe and Kalonji signed political, economic, judicial, and military agreements in order, so it was claimed, to create a common front against "the puppet government in Stanleyville." Gizenga, who was then in a position of comparative strength, held aloof.

But none of the four Congolese leaders, despite their differences, was prepared to acquiesce in the Hammarskjöld plan, since all regarded the proposal to invest the ONUC with power to disarm the Congolese soldiers as an infringement of Congolese independence. Of the four Tshombe was, naturally, the most vituperative and violent, declaring that this "would lead to anarchy and slavery." It was tantamount, he said, to a declaration of war. But Kasavubu and Mobutu were no less hostile. "To disarm means war between the Congolese army and the United Nations," threatened Mobutu.

The Hammarskjöld plan signified two things. It meant the neutralization of the Congolese army, whether of the Mobutu, Tshombe, or Lumumbist faction, or comprising the hundreds then roaming the countryside, particularly in Kivu. It also meant the insulation of the Congo, with the ejection of the foreign mercenaries and Belgian political advisers. By this time the Kennedy Administration had definitely veered round to the view that a neutral Congo was preferable to a Congo caught in the coils of the Cold War, and both the United States and Britain were agreed that a return to parliamentary rule was a prerequisite to the establishment of a more stable government. Even the Brazzaville group of African states, which had stoutly backed Kasavubu, were dismayed by his ineffectualness, and eager for a solution of the Congolese problem with united African backing. This implied that other Congolese leaders besides Kasavubu would have to be taken into account. An inevitable corollary of a return to parliamentary rule would be an end to Mobutu's political usurpation. Not surprisingly, Mobutu opposed the plan and sought to consolidate himself by raising the salaries of his soldiers by 300 percent, so that they now got over $112 a month, instead of $28 as before.

Money was also sorely needed by the U.N. to implement the Hammarskjöld plan. Though still in embryonic form and awaiting U.N. approval, the plan foreshadowed a period of U.N. tutelage during which a stable central Congolese government could be set up and an effective Congolese bureaucracy created. In the interim period greater responsibilities would devolve on the U.N., calling not only for reorganizing and/or disarming the Congolese armies, but also for widening the U.N. civil administration in the Congo. This required money, and more money. The U.N. was already committed to an average annual expenditure in the Congo of around $100 million, more than the whole annual budget of the organization, the larger part of which was met by the United States and, to a lesser degree, by the United Kingdom and the Commonwealth, notably Canada. On the Congo operation *ad hoc* account for 1960 some $20 million remained unpaid, the principal culprit being Russia, which owed $6.5 million. France, which was debited with $3 million, refused "on principle" to contribute to the cost of the Congo operation, while Nationalist China was a defaulter to the extent of $1.5 million. All the Communist countries were in complete default. The Commonwealth countries, with the exception of Ghana, had paid their share. Unless some countries picked up the tab, the entire operation was in danger of foundering and the Congo of being split wide open for indiscriminate infiltration.

Shortly after the disclosure of Lumumba's death, the U.N. Security Council met on February 15 in an atmosphere of acute tension, with Russia angrily clamoring for Hammarskjöld's dismissal and demanding discontinuation of the U.N. intervention in the Congo within a month, as well as the withdrawal of all foreign troops, so as to enable the Congolese people to decide their own affairs. Hammarskjöld, in reply, made one of the most effective speeches in his career as U.N. secretary-general, conveying not only a blunt rebuke to the Russians, but also directing what could be construed as an oblique hint to the West. In effect he paraphrased his memorable retort to Khrushchev in the General Assembly the previous October, when he had suggested that the U.N. did not exist for the protection of the Soviet Union or of the other big powers, but for the protection of the smaller, uncommitted countries. Realizing that unanimity between the Big Five, which was the cornerstone of the 1945 San Francisco Charter, no longer existed, Hammarskjöld was attempting to salvage the U.N. by moving the center of gravity from the Security Council to the General Assembly. This was anathema to the Russians, for it meant that the U.N. then became greater than the sum of its parts.

In the course of the protracted proceedings of the Security Council, the Soviet wrecking resolution was defeated with eight against, two abstentions

(Ceylon and the U.A.R.), and only the Russian vote in favor. Thereafter, an Afro-Asian resolution sanctioning "the use of force if necessary in the last resort" was adopted by nine votes in favor, none against, and two abstentions. This resolution also urged the immediate withdrawal of all Belgian and other foreign military and paramilitary personnel, political advisers, and mercenaries. It called upon all states outside the Congo to prevent the departure of such personnel from their territories, and to deny transit and other facilities to them so as to interdict foreign intervention and to insulate the Congo from Cold War policies. Further it asked for an impartial investigation into the circumstances of the death of Lumumba and his colleagues, and for the punishment of the perpetrators of these crimes.

In view of subsequent developments, the caveat entered in the course of the U.N. discussions by the British delegate, Sir Patrick Dean, is interesting and significant. He thought that the main resolution was broadly acceptable, but with some reservations. Hammarskjöld's original suggestion that it was necessary to disarm the Congolese soldiers before reorgan-- izing them had been discreetly dropped in favor of a milder proposal to offer the Congolese government the full assistance of the U.N. in reorganizing and retraining the Congolese armed forces. This was acceptable to Britain, but the United Kingdom felt that the phrase sanctioning "the use of force if necessary in the last resort" should be interpreted to mean that force would only be used by the U.N. to prevent a clash between two hostile forces. Sir Patrick emphasized that there could be no question of empowering the U.N. to use force to impose a political settlement. This interpretation, or gloss, was later to influence considerably the course of Tshombe's wayward and unscrupulous conduct, and to lay the British open to the suspicion that they had a vested interest, as much commercial as political, in preserving Tshombe's authority in Katanga.

If Katanga was the Ruhr of the Congo, it was also its Ulster. By refusing to conform and reveling in the role of lone wolf, it tried to keep itself in the forefront of the Congolese and international controversy. Tshombe was in the unique position of being regarded as a "white African" by both his supporters and detractors, though for different reasons. In the eyes of radical Africans and, indeed, of the overwhelming majority of Africans outside south Katanga, he was nothing better than a Quisling prepared to mortgage the Congo's freedom to anybody willing to underwrite and guarantee his own and Katanga's economic and political independence. This, for their own good reasons, the Belgians and the British, with their economic stake in Katanga, were willing to do. It is true that Britain and Belgium, mainly through Unilever and the Fédération des Entreprises du Congo, had bigger financial holdings outside Katanga in the other five provinces, but a secessionist Katanga spelled a Katanga more amenable to

European influence, with a leader who was against communism, opposed to nationalization, and, unlike the majority of African leaders, a businessman more than a politician, with a businessman's realism and an eye on the main chance. With Tshombe buttressed by his Belgian mercenaries and advisers, Katanga also spelled security and stability.

Tshombe, who was born in November, 1919, comes of a prosperous commercial family which has ties with the royal family of the Lunda tribe. His father-in-law headed the tribe. Tshombe was educated at American Methodist mission schools, took an accountancy course by correspondence, and plunged into business, where he was reputedly declared bankrupt thrice. He has always been resilient and resourceful, and, nothing daunted, dived from commerce into politics, where before independence he organized the Conakat party, drawn mainly from the Lunda tribe. The Belgian officials and the Union Minière lent him their patronage and financial support, and Tshombe rose steadily. Few were surprised when on July 11, less than two weeks after the mutiny of the Force Publique, he declared the independence of Katanga, with the Belgians supporting him openly and vigorously. Even before independence, Tshombe had worked closely with the Belgian businessmen and *colons* in Katanga, and after the July breakdown he was to work as closely, though not as openly, with the Belgian government. Both saw in Tshombe and his declaration of Katanga's independence a chance to save Belgium's commercial interests and rehabilitate her political prestige. For his own ends Tshombe was willing to play their game so long as it suited his own purposes. It is wrong to regard him as primarily a Belgian stooge. He realized very early that if the Belgians were necessary for his continued existence, so was he to the Belgians if they wanted to continue in the Congo. Tshombe is basically pro-Tshombe.

Tshombe has charm and he is clever. What is more, he knows it. A U.N. official attempting to cajole him into entering the Léopoldville government heaped him with flattery. "People simply can't resist you," he said. Tshombe turned on him his bland round face. "I know," he murmured.

But he is also unscrupulous and disastrously unreliable. He has a streak of mulish stubbornness, and an imperviousness to truth or to inconvenient facts which would try the patience of an angel. Even the monumentally patient, mild-mannered U Thant, then the acting U.N. secretary-general, was reduced to a state of explosive exasperation by Tshombe's serpentine evolutions, and referred to his government as "a bunch of clowns."

"Me, a clown!" Tshombe exclaimed in mock innocence. "Why, only the day before the U.N. offered me the job of Congo vice-president."

It was hard to get the better of this vain, eel-like man, as even his Belgian advisers were shortly to discover. In a way Tshombe's mind is like his face, which might be that of an actor, so effectively capable is he of varying its expression to suit the situation or mood. He has been called a "black Fernandel." Tshombe's mind is at once sharp, devious, brittle, agile, and mercurial, and this complex combination finally proved his undoing.

He is not as tough as he thinks he is, or as others imagine him to be. The two strong-arm men in his government who were both consistently hostile to the Belgians were Godefroid Munongo, minister of the interior, and Jean-Baptiste Kibwe, minister of finance.* Munongo, who headed the widely feared Sûreté, was mistakenly believed by some to be more influential in Katanga than even Tshombe. Both men relied more on the French *ultras,* and on the Swiss and other technicians, than they did on the Belgians. Kibwe more than once threatened to nationalize the mines when the Belgians tried to be difficult. Munongo also made it plain that the moment the Union Minière behaved in a way contrary to the Katanga government's wishes it would be brought to heel. "The Union Minière are in our country," he once declared. "We are not in theirs." As a team Munongo and Kibwe could prove more formidable than Tshombe, whom together they often pushed into extreme positions. After Lumumba's death, Munongo made himself the mouthpiece of Tshombe, and briefed foreign correspondents on Katanga's policies and on its way of thinking. But whatever the interplay within the Katanga government, Tshombe was the key man and the propelling force.

The cumulative effect of the directives contained in the Security Council resolution of February 21 was a mandate to end the secession of Katanga. How this was to be brought about was the subject of divided interpretation of the vital clause relating to the use of force. Britain, as we have seen, had assumed the position that there could be no question of empowering the U.N. to use its force to impose a political settlement. But unless the U.N. made its force available to the Léopoldville government to bring the recalcitrant provinces, including Katanga, into line, how could the unification of the Congo be achieved and its stability ensured? By negotiations, said Britain. Which was exactly up Tshombe's street. He was prepared, with the help of his Belgian accomplices and British allies, to go on negotiating until the end of time. It is difficult to absolve Mr. Macmillan's Tory government of political chicanery and double-dealing in its Congo policy.

In the seven months between the passing of the Security Council resolution of February 21 and the resort to force in Katanga on September 12, an uneasy haze settled on the Congo. In the interval, various attempts were initiated to bring the Congolese leaders together to enable them to

---

* A third reputedly was the foreign minister, Evariste Kimba.

agree on a unification plan for the country. The idea of a central unitary government was no longer practical politics. It died with Lumumba. The point is important, since the only issue which remained was the form federation should take. Kasavubu was for federation and was in a position to neutralize Gizenga's ramshackle authority in the north, as well as Kalonji's pretentious regime in south Kasai. The only boulder which blocked the path to unity was Katanga, and behind that boulder lurked Tshombe, with his Belgian mercenaries in Elisabethville and his powerful Katanga lobby at Westminster—how powerful events were soon to disclose.

At the signing ceremony of the agreements which established a nebulous "military axis" between Kalonji and Tshombe in February, 1961, Tshombe had utilized the occasion to propound his idea of unification. Instead of trying to organize a single unified state through meetings of people with doubtful mandates, he suggested that the Congo should be organized into a congeries of smaller but viable entities of homogeneous population and interests, where order could be easily restored, following which these states in full liberty and equality could make alliances with each other. What Tshombe was proposing was not a federation but a confederation, which was something entirely different and which would result in the creation of a score or more Congolese republics, each enjoying political and economic autonomy, some converted by alliances into federations, these possibly ranged against one another, with a weak central confederate government which in effect would have no real overall authority. Tshombe was working for a *Katanga über Alles.*

This was far from Kasavubu's idea of federation, which envisaged an integrated Congo with the provinces enjoying a considerable degree of local autonomy. In order to find a federal solution to the Congo crisis, a round-table conference was held between Tshombe, Kasavubu, and Kalonji in Brazzaville. Nothing resulted. Tshombe then suggested that another conference be held at Tananarive in the Malagasy Republic. Before this took place the common military front between Katanga and south Kasai was extended to include Léopoldville. Not surprisingly, the Gizengists, who felt that the front was directed against them, though it might conceivably have signified joint action against the U.N., abstained from the Tananarive conference, which was dominated by Tshombe, who brought all the blarney and blandishment he was capable of into play. The conference agreed to his idea of establishing a loose confederation of Congolese states. It also agreed that internal and foreign policies were to be in the hands of a council of states composed of Kasavubu and the presidents of the individual states. Tshombe emerged from the Tananarive meeting with his prestige enhanced, and his capacity for intransigence and mischief reinforced.

Like almost all things attempted by the Congolese, the conference failed. Nothing came of it, and the agreement was never implemented. Gizenga, who had kept away from Tananarive, rejected the confederation plan and demanded that the Congolese parliament should be convened in a neutral country. By this time his troops were in occupation of over a third of the Congo, and his regime had the support of the Soviet Union, the U.A.R., and several Afro-Asian countries. The Russians also reacted sharply to the Tananarive conference, and Gromyko, calling for an immediate General Assembly debate on the Congo, argued that the matter was urgent, since "attempts have been undertaken of late to dismember the Congo" and the situation was "steadily deteriorating." Gromyko was right in his two statements, though Russia had contributed substantially to the outcome. The situation had deteriorated and there were indications of mushroom "states" sprouting all over the Congo, with some twenty ethnic areas reportedly seeking to establish independent states within the Tananarive constitutional framework.

Léopoldville was having second thoughts. Its hostility to what it termed "U.N. interference" now surfaced, and Mobutu's troops ejected the U.N. forces from Matadi and Banana, the supply centers on the Congo estuary, on the ground that arms were being imported through these ports, which the Congolese insisted should be controlled by them. Kasavubu followed this up by calling on the U.N. to withdraw with its arms from the Congo and "let us solve our problems in our own way." Faced by Tshombe's growing intractability and inflated sense of power, a new line-up of political forces began to evolve, with Gizenga, whose influence in Stanleyville was on the decline and whose relations with his two chief lieutenants, General Lundula, the army commander, and Manzikala, president of Orientale, had deteriorated, betraying symptoms of readiness for a *rapprochement* with Léopoldville. On his side, Kasavubu was not unwilling. Though he continued to insist for a little while on the removal of the U.N. presence from the Congo, he had come round to realizing that the practical question was not what to do with Hammarskjöld, but what to do with Tshombe.

Meanwhile, the U.N. Conciliation Commission for the Congo, composed of representatives of African and Asian countries under the chairmanship of Mr. Jaja Wachuku of Nigeria, published its report, which ignored the Tananarive confederation plan* and recommended the formation of a unitary state based on some form of federation. The commission held that a confederation of independent states would result in the breakup of the Congo into chaotic tribalism. It would create more problems than it solved. This was a shot in the arm for Kasavubu, already irked by Tshombe's slippery elusiveness and his reluctance to make any commitment on sharing Katanga's mineral wealth.

* The plan was released after the report had been largely written.

"I have five-sixths of the Congo's money," Tshombe was reported to have boasted. "The others have five-sixths of the Congo's land. I'm willing to negotiate. Let's make a deal."

The price for the deal was a loose confederation, with Tshombe controlling the purse strings. Kasavubu was moving slowly toward a showdown with Tshombe. To enable him to do this it was necessary to reach some understanding with the U.N. and, if possible, with Gizenga. Early in April he sent to Stanleyville his emissary, Cléophas Kamitatu, then president of the Léopoldville provincial government, to find out if Gizenga was willing to negotiate. Kamitatu had earlier worked with Gizenga in founding the PSA, but after Lumumba's dismissal the two men had parted politically. Gizenga appeared willing to negotiate, but Kamitatu found him still opposed to the idea of a Congo confederation and insistent that the Congolese parliament should be convened immediately in a neutral country. Mindful of Lumumba's fate, Gizenga was unwilling to jeopardize himself by returning to Léopoldville.

Alongside these overtures to the Lumumbists in Stanleyville, Kasavubu had been negotiating with Hammarskjöld for an understanding with the U.N. He announced that the Congolese government was willing to cooperate with the U.N., provided "note is taken of the sovereign rights of the Republic." He accepted the Security Council resolution of February 21, which gave the U.N. troops authority "to use force if necessary in the last resort," and to help in reorganizing and retraining the Congolese armed forces, but Kasavubu felt that the presence of U.N. troops in the Congo would "become superfluous within a few months," and he hoped that the U.N. would be able to reduce the number of its civilian technicians. He also insisted that each stage of the reorganization should be under his authority. Kasavubu was agreeable to the principle of ridding the Congo of "sinister foreign influences," evidently with an eye on Tshombe's Belgian advisers, but here again he declared that no foreign military, paramilitary, or political advisers should be asked to leave without the Congolese asking them to do so.

At this stage Kasavubu's relations with Rajeshwar Dayal, the U.N. special representative in the Congo, had slumped to the point of no return, and he indicated obliquely that he did not want Dayal, then on a visit to New York, back in Léopoldville. Nor was Kasavubu enthused by the arrival of some 5,000 Indian troops to reinforce the U.N. contingent. He had earlier protested against their coming, probably suspicious that they would favor the Gizenga regime against him. His premier, Ileo, had been even more emphatic, threatening that "blood would flow." Dayal did not return, but the Indian troops came and remained. They were to figure prominently in the successive flare-ups in Katanga.

Various Congolese politicians met at Coquilhatville, capital of Equateur, ostensibly to work out details of the Tananarive agreement in order to embody them in a new constitution. Tshombe again attempted to dominate the conference, but Kasavubu, who had developed in political cunning and finesse by his experience over the past few months, checkmated him, finally provoking Tshombe, who roundly accused Kasavubu of subservience to the U.N., into stalking out of the meeting. Tshombe did not get beyond the airport. He was arrested there, beaten up, and imprisoned. The central government then announced that Tshombe would be tried for various acts of treason, including the secession of Katanga and "counterfeiting," the latter a reference to the issuance of a separate Katanga currency.

The Coquilhatville conference adopted proposals for a republic of twenty-one states* on a tribal basis—Kasavubu was always a staunch tribalist—but organized under a supposedly strong central government. The existing chamber and senate would be replaced by a one-house congress, whose members would be elected by state legislatures, the latter comprising members returned by universal suffrage. The Congolese would have the power to veto the president's choice of a prime minister, but the president would enjoy certain overriding powers, including command of the army.

Meanwhile, Tshombe remained in Léopoldville's custody. The central government had asked the U.N. for help in disarming Tshombe's gendarmerie, and in ridding Katanga of all foreign soldiers and advisers. Almost simultaneously, the Katanga authorities, who had ostentatiously snubbed the U.N., appealed to it to secure Tshombe's release. Tshombe was released on June 24, but only after he had declared his acceptance of the Coquilhatville proposals which, as was anticipated, he repudiated once he reached the safety of Elisabethville. A showdown between Léopoldville and Katanga was now inevitable, but before embarking on this, Kasavubu set out to put his house in some semblance of order.

In July, 1961, the Congolese parliament reassembled under U.N. protection† in Lovanium University outside Léopoldville. Some sixty-four Lumumbist deputies arrived from Stanleyville to attend the session, but Gizenga abstained. Kasavubu now decided on a shrewd and imaginative maneuver. At this juncture he replaced the pliant Ileo by Cyrille Adoula, a devout Catholic and a trade unionist who was once pro-Lumumba, but who had left the MNC a year before independence and had contested the 1960 elections as an independent. Adoula, born in 1921, was a noncontroversial political figure widely respected for his moderation and independ-

---

* The 21 proposed states were: Léopoldville, Kongo Central, Kwango, Kwilu, Maidombe, Equateur, Cuvette Centrale, Ubangi, Orientale, Ucle, Kibali-Uturi, Kivu, Nord-Kivu, Manjema, Katanga, Nord-Katanga, Luluabourg, Unit Kasaienne, Sankuru, Lomani, and Sud-Kasai.

† The U.N. had exerted some pressure to reconvene it.

ence. Sensing that his own group and the Gizenga faction were about equally balanced in parliament, Kasavubu chose him as a middle-of-the-road politician who would be generally acceptable to the Congolese, to the West, and, if given Lumumbist support, to the East. Only Katanga still stubbornly stood out, but Adoula, who was favored by the West, might, with U.N. support, be able to bring Tshombe round. So Kasavubu calculated. Kalonji was a minor problem.

On August 2 Adoula and his new Congo government, with Gizenga as one of the three vice-premiers—the other two were Bolikango and Jason Sendwe—were given votes of confidence by both houses of parliament. What Kasavubu was aiming at was a national coalition government in a bid to end the Congo crisis. Of the twenty-eight ministers, five were Lumumbists, including Christophe Gbeyne, former minister of the interior at Stanleyville, who was given the same portfolio at Léopoldville.* Katanga, or rather north Katanga, was represented by Sendwe, head of the Balubakat party, but Tshombe had no place. Bombako had his usual niche as foreign minister. In his inaugural address to parliament Adoula sharply criticized Tshombe and announced that his government's major priority was to end the secession of Katanga "in the next few days."

Katanga, however, was not the only problem on Adoula's desk. The creation of a unified national army remained his special task as defense minister. There was also the job of replenishing the central treasury, which was running low. The Congolese national debt, according to Adoula, was rising at the rate of $11,990,000 a month, and expenditure exceeded income by nearly 400 percent, underlining the urgent need to end Katanga's secession. No one seemed capable of even an elementary understanding of state finance or of sufficient responsibility to end the drift and economic chaos. No investment policy existed, tax collection was mismanaged, unemployment was spreading, and wages had risen dramatically, with the army absorbing five-twelfths of the budget.

U.N. technicians, notably Dr. Sture Linner, the U.N. head of operations, and Robert Gardiner of Ghana, the U.N. political mediator in the Congo, were helpful to the new administration, which they had largely helped to father and foster. But even given such technical help, goodwill, and military aid as the U.N., with its Parkinsonian methods and machinery, was capable of extending, the task facing Adoula was formidable.

Another fifteen months were to elapse before the new national unity government of Adoula, with the help of the U.N., brought Tshombe to order. The main objective of the U.N., as of the government of Léopoldville, was to secure the expulsion of the foreign mercenaries from Katanga, end Tshombe's secessionist activities, and bring him and Adoula together. Gizenga and Kalonji posed much smaller problems, for they had not

* Gbeyne later became deputy prime minister.

Katanga's wealth or the support of the West, notably of Britain and Belgium, which continued to obstruct the U.N.'s efforts to make Tshombe see reason.

Katanga's prosperity in this period was more apparent than real, for, though the Union Minière gave Tshombe about four-fifths of his revenue in the first year of secession, much of the money was poured into armaments and expended on the mercenaries. Outwardly, the Union Minière personnel pretended to be nonpolitical, but they played a considerable role behind the scenes in the events of September and December, 1961, and to a lesser extent in those events finally leading to Tshombe's surrender in the turn of 1962–1963. During the developments of September and December, Washington's attitude, though more sympathetic to the U.N. than that of London, tended to be equivocal whenever a crisis overcame the efforts of the international organization to end Tshombe's separatist maneuvers. However, in the decisive round of 1962–1963 the U.N. owed much to the strong support of Washington, which refused to be associated or identified with London's policies.

The failure of the U.N. forces to push the September drive against Elisabethville and Jadotville to a successful conclusion was again owing to a basic uncertainty in the minds of Hammerskjöld in New York and of the U.N. personnel, military and civilian, in the Congo as to the character and extent of its brief on Katanga. Active political sniping by London and Brussels aggravated these uncertainties and difficulties, which Hammarskjöld's tragic death in an air crash near Ndola intensified and brought to a climax. The net result was an ignominious retreat by the U.N. before the barrage of verbal attacks from London and Brussels. Left to themselves, the U.N. forces, as they later demonstrated, could have reduced Tshombe to submission. As a result, Tshombe's ego, always considerable, was now inflated. So was his intransigence. Proportionately, U.N. prestige took a bad dent.

Tshombe was thereby emboldened to take the offensive against the U.N., and late in November an unprovoked attack by his trigger-happy gendarmes and paracommandos on two U.N. officials, who were brutally beaten, threatened another crisis, which erupted in sporadic fighting between the U.N. troops and Tshombe's undisciplined soldiery. London immediately came to the aid of its friend, and demanded a cease-fire, though the U.N. action was in strict conformity with the Security Council's resolution of November 24, submitted jointly by Ceylon, Liberia, and the United Arab Republic, which, while strongly deprecating Katanga's secessionist activities as well as its "armed action" against the U.N. forces, authorized the secretary-general "to take vigorous action, including the use of a requisite measure of force, if necessary, for the immediate apprehension, [and] detention pending legal action and/or deportation of all foreign mercenaries and hostile elements." The resolution was adopted, with only Britain and France abstaining. But Britain's subsequent intervention hamstrung for the second time the U.N. efforts to end Katanga's secessionist activities and gave another lease of aggressive life to Tshombe.

By then, however, Hammarskjöld's successor, U Thant, who at the time was acting secretary-general, was more fully seized of the Katanga situation and of the antics of Tshombe, supported by the British, Belgians, and French. So was the United States State Department, which at about the same time decided that the U.N. forces should be backed firmly in such action as they took to eject the foreign mercenaries and to end Tshombe's megalomaniac dreams.

U Thant made it clear that he was determined to take strong action and restore order in the Congo as early as possible. In this he was supported by Robert Gardiner, the U.N. representative in the Congo, whose encounters with the wily and elusive Tshombe had taught him that force was the only language which the Katangese leader understood and respected. So events proved.

Early in June, 1962, U Thant indicated that he would soon be seeking a new mandate from the Security Council which would permit of a satisfactory agreement on the distribution of Union Minière royalties between the central and provincial governments. If the constitutional question could also be settled, the secretary-general was confident that the Congo problem was well on the way to a solution.

Of the total Katanga revenue of $65 million in 1961–1962, some $39 million had come from Union Minière. According to U Thant, who was supported in this view by the United States, the key to the Katanga problem lay with Union Minière, for if it stopped paying its royalties, taxes, and dividends to Katanga, Tshombe would have no alternative but to come to terms with Adoula. The British, and to a lesser degree the Belgians, felt that it was wrong to expose a private company to the risks involved in such a decision. The British claimed that their financial stake in the Congo, none of which was government investment, was greater outside Katanga than in it. The share of Tanganyika concessions in Union Minière is about $39.2 million, but not all the "Tanks" shares are British-owned. In the rest of the Congo, British investments are around $28 million in Unilever, $8.4 million in Shell, and $14 million in other investments. But British holdings in Union Minière are larger than that of any other country, and British caution in the Congo could be explained by the approximately $100 million tax bill which Union Minière would in all likelihood face after reintegration, as well as by the fear of outright expropriation or nationalization. A London City plan directed at intercepting Katanga's copper tax receipts, believed to total some $67.2 million, at a point outside its territorial frontiers and diverting them to the central government was not officially approved by Whitehall. The copper buyers were mainly Belgian, but France, Italy, the United States, and Britain were also interested in the trade of selling Katanga's copper in the international market, which collectively was worth $420 million a year to them.

Tshombe argued that even if he paid over the whole of the $70-million-a-year revenue that he received from the mines, it would still be insufficient to meet the Congo's needs, since the central government's annual expenditure was nearly $378 million and its receipts, including those from Katanga, around $151.2 million. The riches of Katanga, said Tshombe, were "not for feeding the lazy Congo masses." Adoula's arguments appeared more ingenious. According to him, Katanga, whose budget for 1962 anticipated receipts of around $46 million and expenditure of $54 million, would be better off financially as a part of the Congo. Léopoldville's budget reserves for Katanga were in the neighborhood of $32 million. The central government was responsible for meeting 80 percent of provincial budgets, the remaining 20 percent being raised by the local authorities. This would give Katanga over $38 million in all, but the province would not be responsible for expenditure on such items as defense, gendarmerie, ports, telecommunications, judiciary, and customs, which would reduce its expenditure from $54 million to under $34 million.

In August U Thant outlined a program for ending, by means other than military force, the attempted secession of Katanga. The plan, which had twenty-one points, fell broadly into two parts—noncoercive and coercive—the first suggesting an immediate resumption of political negotiations between Adoula and Tshombe, the drawing up of a draft constitution for a federal system of government for completion in thirty days, a law defining division of revenue, a plan of currency unification, integration and unification of the entire Congolese army, and other correlated measures. On the division of revenue, U Thant suggested that until a new law was passed the central government and the provincial authorities of Katanga should agree to share on a fifty-fifty basis revenues from taxes, duties on imports and exports, and royalties from mining concessions. They should also agree to pay to the Congo monetary council, composed of U.N. and Congolese government officials, or to any institution designated by it, all foreign exchange earned by any part of the Congo. The monetary council would make available, for Katanga's essential needs, at least 50 percent of the foreign exchange accruing in that province. During this consultative stage, U Thant expressed the hope that no action would be taken which might jeopardize a favorable outcome.

The second half of the plan warned that, in the absence of positive results, the secretary-general would ask for economic pressures that "could justifiably go to the extent of barring all trade and financial relations." In particular, a request would be made to member nations to apply a ban on

Katangese copper and cobalt. Additionally, U Thant warned that if Katanga's secession were not ended quickly, the U.N. "both because of virtually inevitable deterioration in the Congo and its own financial limitations, may soon be confronted with the necessity of deciding whether to withdraw its military force from the Congo or to go to the other extreme of specifically authorizing ONUC to seek by all necessary measures to end Katangese efforts at secession."

Profiting by the U.N.'s unfortunate experience in the fighting of September and December, 1961, U Thant, like the elephant of his native Burma, had decided to move cautiously but firmly. Britain, however, while mildly agreeable to the noncoercive part of the plan, was implacably opposed to the imposition of sanctions of any kind, economic or military. The Americans were firmly behind U Thant, a consideration which doubtless played its part in the actions he initiated during the following critical months.

Britain continued to insist, despite Tshombe's known elusiveness, convoluted tactics, and unreliability, that a settlement between him and Adoula could be effective only if it came through negotiations. The British were of the opinion that concessions should be made by both sides, and that pressure should not be applied to the Katangese alone. In their opinion, the setting of time limits in negotiation and the brandishing of sanctions were impracticable. They counseled patience. They feared that Tshombe would resist any forceful action and would sabotage the properties of Union Minière if their revenues were denied him. They did not believe that the combined forces of the U.N. and the central Congo government could either quickly overwhelm Katangese resistance or safeguard the widely dispersed Union Minière properties. On the contrary, they held that the situation in the Congo would gravely deteriorate, and its dependence on the U.N., itself in deep financial waters, would increase. Simultaneously the British declined to accept U Thant's main argument for urgent action—that, with the U.N. operations in the Congo costing $10 million a month, a solution had to be found quickly. U Thant was also hopeful that at least $165 million worth of the U.N. bond issue* would be bought, and that this would enable him to meet the expenditure in the Congo until the end of 1962 and probably for two or three months longer. Britain instead suggested that an international consortium to aid the Congo, on the lines of the consortium assisting India and Pakistan, was the answer.

For Tshombe these were happy days. Cosseted by his foreign friends, with the central government's exchequer as well as that of the U.N. running low, while nearly $5.6 million a month of Union Minière's taxes and

* The bond issue of $200 million was launched by U Thant in December, 1961, as a short-term, stopgap measure to meet the costs of the Congo operation.

duties kept rolling into Katanga's coffers, Tshombe was comfortably placed to continue cocking a snook at the U.N., which he did. A month before U Thant announced his plan Tshombe had organized a demonstration by some 10,000 African women, who stormed Indian troops manning a U.N. roadblock outside Elisabethville. According to a government spokesman, the Katangese casualties were three dead and nineteen injured. Tshombe thrived on trouble.

Meanwhile, Adoula, who was also oppressed by his own troubles, had streamlined his cabinet, dropping in the process two deputy prime ministers—Jean Bolikango from Equateur and Christophe Gbeyne of Stanleyville—both of whom now appeared anxious to court Tshombe's favor, a not unusual procedure in the Congo, where loyalties change overnight. In south Kasai, Mobutu had failed to integrate the local troops into the central Congolese army, while chaos descended on north Kasai as the Lulua leaders fought among themselves. If Adoula's writ could not run to Kasai, how could he extend it over Katanga? So Tshombe argued.

Adoula, however, had managed to immobilize temporarily both Kalonji, the self-styled "King" of south Kasai, and Gizenga, the pro-Lumumbist leader from Orientale, by the simple Congolese expedient of taking them into custody shortly after their arrival in Léopoldville. Gizenga, who had been appointed deputy prime minister by Adoula, was detained on the island of Bulema at the mouth of the Congo River.* Kalonji was sentenced to five years' imprisonment.† for arbitrarily ordering the arrest of a political rival in south Kasai, but escaped from his Léopoldville prison and returned to Bakwanga, the south Kasai capital. A month later, in October, 1962, not long after Kalonji's regime had been overthrown by the Congolese national army, he escaped from the house arrest under which he had been placed, and made his way to Elisabethville and Tshombe. The chief secessionist, Tshombe, was, however, still at large, and Adoula, his patience strained by Tshombe's stalling tactics, decided to get tough.

Early in August, while the U Thant plan was taking final shape, Adoula ordered all firms in the Congo to shut down their branches in Katanga if they wanted to continue operating in the rest of the Congo. The central government, with a view to ending Tshombe's secessionist postures, also announced a series of measures designed to isolate Katanga. It banned all air flights into or over Katanga not authorized by Léopoldville, and demanded that all telecommunications between Katanga and the outside world, which were routed mainly through Brussels and Rhodesia,

---

* Later Gizenga was granted his parliamentary immunity and released. He was, however, again arrested but released by Tshombe when he formed a coalition government in July 1964, shortly after the withdrawal of the U.N. troops on June 30, 1964.

† The appeal court halved the sentence.

be cut off. At the same time the U.N. announced that it had stopped giving special permits for flights to Katanga to avoid creating the impression that they were under U.N. protection.

Tshombe now resorted to his familiar pantomime of prevarication and procrastination, encouraged by his foreign supporters into believing that time was on his side rather than on Adoula's. U Thant was not deceived. "They [the Katangese]," he said, "make gestures of reconciliation leading to no practical results whenever the pressure builds up, while at the same time seeking to further the aims of secession." On the last of the ten days the U.N. had allowed him to give his answer to their plan, Tshombe characteristically announced his "acceptance," but wrapped it in qualified and equivocal terms. He welcomed the plan for a federal constitution as "the basis of an acceptance settlement." He agreed that Katanga should immediately start to share on a fifty-fifty basis its revenues and foreign currency earnings with the central government, but he suggested that the U.N. financial experts should meet his own advisers in Elisabethville to "study the problem." He also agreed to the U.N.'s request for a military commission composed of Congolese, Katangese, and U.N. representatives, but he was careful to avoid committing himself to U Thant's proviso that this commission should supervise the integration of Tshombe's army into the Congolese national army within sixty days. Tshombe was back to his old tricks.

Not long after his so-called "acceptance," Tshombe declared that he had given his agreement only "in principle." Gardiner's attempts to pinpoint him to definite commitments were unsuccessful. Tshombe showed little willingness even to discuss the draft constitution for a federated Congo which the U.N. had compiled. Prolonged efforts by George McGhee, United States under-secretary of state, to presuade Tshombe to make a preliminary gesture of cooperation by sending General Moke, commander of the Katanga forces, with some senior officers, to take an oath of allegiance to President Kasavubu of the Congo also failed. Tshombe began his usual game of prevarication, punctuating it with vague promises which added up to little. He agreed to reopen the telecommunications link with Léopoldville and, with a great show of generosity, consented to put $2 million at the central government's disposal. Since Katanga received $40 million a year in taxes from Union Minière, Adoula indignantly spurned the offer. McGhee was followed by Ralph Bunche, who met with no better success. His arrival was preceded by a defiant gesture by Tshombe, whose planes attacked north Katanga, killing nine people.

By now U Thant's patience was near the snapping point. So was that of many Afro-Asian countries, who were perturbed by Katanga's growing military buildup, with more jets and fighters and foreign mercenaries.

Tshombe's bombing raids on north Katanga flamboyantly demonstrated this. Time, Tshombe calculated, was on his side, for, if he could hold out against integration until the end of 1962, he would hamstring the U.N., whose funds by then would be near the exhaustion point. Additionally, the continued impasse might bring down the Adoula government. On their side, the U.N. and Léopoldville were aware of these dangers. They had also the undefined but deep-seated feeling that, as usual, Tshombe was bluffing. With Washington supporting the U.N. without the equivocations or reservations of Britain, U Thant felt he could safely take a chance and call Tshombe's bluff.

Once the foreign mercenaries could be got out of the way and Union Minière persuaded or pushed into a more reasonable frame of mind, Tshombe's two main props would collapse beneath him. The Belgian government, under heavy pressure from Washington, was understood at this stage to favor an agreement between Katanga and Léopoldville but, less assertively than the British, it remained opposed to military and economic sanctions. Estimates of Katanga's military resources differed. Some placed the strength of Tshombe's forces at no more than 16,000 ill-disciplined, ill-officered troops, which as events proved was an exaggeration. These were strengthened by about 500 desperately fanatical white commandos whose fanaticism was likely to evaporate as Tshombe's political resistance weakened—which proved to be the case. The air strength at his command never exceeded thirty planes, reportedly led by a former Polish RAF wing commander.

Nor was Katanga's financial or political stability so unassailable. Tshombe was paying heavily for Katanga's security, the cost of his armed forces rising with the increasing precariousness of his political position. The francs rolled in less easily and they rolled out more quickly. Ordinary expenditure rated at $80 million exceeded receipts, computed at a little more than $60 million. Of its foreign exchange income, totaling about $16.8 million a month, the Union Minière and some other importers got half. Politically, Tshombe's Conakat party had secured a majority of only two seats over the Balubakat and some smaller groups in the provincial assembly in the 1960 elections, and in the Congolese parliament it had won only eight seats of 137. The greatest single ruling force in Katanga was not the Conakat, but Union Minière, which held the purse strings.

At this juncture, Adoula also faced increasing difficulties. He ostensibly had Kasavubu's support but, in one of those unpredictable moves characteristic of the Congo, Kasavubu's party, the Abako, joined the opposition in the central parliament and, though unsuccessful in securing the necessary majority to dislodge the government, defeated it in two successive rounds. Adoula was accused of being "Americanized" and of abandoning his policy of nonalignment. He denied both charges. If anything this maneuver stirred the United States to muster even stronger support for U Thant, who succeeded in persuading India not to withdraw her troops from the Congo and got Indonesia to reinforce the U.N. troops in Elisabethville with another 1,200 men. Everything pointed to a showdown.

It developed quickly, though U Thant was initially careful to restrict it to a war of nerves with a propaganda offensive which he hoped might wear down Tshombe. In this he miscalculated, for, though Britain was compelled finally by Western pressure to declare that she would not seek to prevent the application of economic sanctions, she persisted in making it clear that she was opposed to them. This naturally stiffened Tshombe in his usual dual attitude of duplicity and defiance. "I have made it quite clear time and again," declared Lord Home pontifically, "that we cannot approve of sanctions to impose a political solution. Should the United Nations decide to impose sanctions, there would be nothing we could do to stop them." This was oddly at variance with Britain's own policy vis-à-vis Egypt on Suez in October, 1956, when only the intervention of the United States and the threat of Russia deterred Britain and France. Belgium, with 18,000 nationals in the Congo, 12,000 of whom were employees of Union Minière, was also perturbed. But by then Spaak had lined up, though with some mental reservations, with Kennedy.

Tshombe reverted to his usual tactics, this time ineffectually. He professed his willingness to share with the central government the foreign exchange accruing from the operation of Union Minière provided he was allowed to retain a total of about $5,040,000 a year in addition to whatever amount Katanga would need for the purchase abroad of commodities which it would otherwise have obtained from the Congo. In effect this meant that the total foreign exchange earnings should first go to the monetary council, then be divided on the basis of 40:30:30 between Union Minière, Katanga, and the central government. The U.N. waited for Tshombe to implement his promises, but instead he characteristically threatened the United States with a scorched-earth policy in Katanga on the lines predicted by Britain and Belgium. The United States riposte was to promise military aid and equipment to the U.N. in its operations to bring Tshombe to heel. Although Washington made it clear that United States troops would not be included in the buildup of U.N. forces in the Congo, State Department officials explained that America was prepared to supply extra transport and weapons if necessary.

Not only Katanga's, but Britain's bluff was called. On the night of December 27–28, 1962, U.N. troops in Elisabethville went into action after a series of unprovoked attacks lasting over six days by the Katangese gendarmerie on U.N. patrols on the Jadotville road and on U.N. positions around the Elisabethville perimeter. This time the U.N. was both ready and determined. A considerable proportion of its 19,000-man force in the

Congo had been moved into Katanga over the previous few weeks under the overall command of General Prem Chand, assisted by Brigadier Reginald Noronha, both of the Indian army.

Tshombe, contacted at the presidential palace by the U.N. representative, Eluil Mathu of Kenya, admitted that it was the gendarmerie and not U.N. troops who had provoked the fighting, but characteristically he refused to sign an order for a cease-fire, though he agreed to issue such an order verbally. However, he accompanied the U.N. party to help accelerate the removal of the gendarmerie roadblocks. Tshombe was by now impressed by the determination of the U.N. forces, who had been instructed to take all necessary action in self-defense and to restore order. He realized that this time they meant business. Over Radio Free Katanga he had repeated his threat that if the U.N. did not stop firing within twenty-four hours he would launch a scorched-earth defense campaign, but now he faced an ultimatum from the U.N. commander that if he did not withdraw his troops within thirty minutes "general war will begin."

Tshombe decided on a getaway. Eluding the U.N. guards and roadblocks, he made his way to Salisbury, where Sir Roy Welensky and Lord Alport, the British high commissioner, were awaiting him. Within twenty-four hours the U.N. forces had secured complete control of Elisabethville, and fanned out in the direction of the copper and zinc center of Kipushi and toward Jadotville, seventy miles from Elisabethville. Welensky reportedly advised Tshombe to return, the U.N. having guaranteed that he and his ministers could reenter Elisabethville without fear of molestation "unless they should engage overtly in incitement against the U.N. personnel and operation." The U.N., however, insisted that they would regard the Katanga gendarmerie as "a hostile force" until its senior officers went to Léopoldville to take the oath of allegiance as stipulated by the U Thant plan for the unification of the Congo.

Apparently, Welensky, as well as Alport, while advising Tshombe to return, assured him that they would do everything in their power to pressure the U.N. forces into calling off their advance through Katanga. This is borne out by the action of Britain's ambassador to the U.N., Sir Patrick Dean, who stormed into U Thant's office in the U.N. to deliver a protest from Whitehall declaring that it was "impossible to impose a political solution by force." Along with the Belgian ambassador, Walter Loridan, Dean demanded an assurance from U Thant that the U.N. forces would not attempt to enter Jadotville, where Union Minière produced one-third of its copper and three-fourths of its cobalt every year. Because of a breakdown of communications, as the U.N. later explained, no instructions were conveyed to Brigadier Noronha, who was moving towards Jadotville and who took it accompanied by two jeeps and with a swagger stick under his arm. Very little damage had been done to the installations. Ralph Bunche was dispatched to sort out the tangle, but on arriving in Katanga he declared that the U.N.'s task was not completed.

By the time Tshombe, having bid farewell to Welensky and Alport, arrived in Kolwezi, 220 miles west of Elisabethville, the U.N. forces held three main Katanga towns—Elisabethville, Kipushi, and Kamina—and were preparing to march into Jadotville, which shortly after fell without a whimper. Tshombe's ragtag and bobtail army disappeared into the bush. Even the mercenaries, caught at the wrong end of the gun, ceased to be militant and scurried for safety to the Rhodesian frontier. Like Tshombe, they ran in the one safe direction they knew.

Only the western copper town of Kolwezi, where Tshombe sulked, now remained in Katanga's uncertain and precarious grip. Tshombe was still hopeful about Welensky's assurances of British intervention which would effectively immobilize the U.N.'s extending its hold over Katanga. Guaranteed his safety by the U.N., he moved back into his pink stucco palace in Elisabethville, where again the old delusions of grandeur seized him. Once again he went into the familiar Tshombe gambit, promising at first to "abstain from making any declarations against the U.N.," only to threaten the very next day a scorched-earth policy in Kolwezi if the U.N. advanced toward it. U Thant had had enough. Even before Tshombe's arrival in Elisabethville, Ralph Bunche had left, declaring that he had nothing to say to Tshombe and, in any case, was not waiting. The time for talk was past.

Slapped by the U.N. under house arrest for his threats to paralyze the dams and hydroelectric power stations in Kolwezi, Tshombe, as usual, came quickly to his senses. To save his own skin he was prepared to offer Katanga on a platter to whoever could guarantee his own existence and safety. Apart from Kolwezi, the only other vital point still in Tshombe's hands was the rail junction of Sakania on the northern Rhodesian border, which was the inlet for Elisabethville's food supplies. Tshombe agreed by his personal presence to ensure safe passage to the U.N. forces to both centers.

He realized that for the moment his devious maneuvers were checkmated. He was exposed as a paper tiger. In a black limousine he drove out of Elisabethville ahead of a column of U.N. troops and tanks heading for Sakania. Sakania was taken without a shot, as was the small border town of Mokambo en route. A humiliated Tshombe crept back into Elisabethville and retired to his palace, only to disappear again. He turned up in Ndola ostensibly to "talk to some of my ministers" but in all likelihood to ascertain from Alport and Welensky whether the U.N. forces, then some seventy miles from Kolwezi, could be deterred from entering it. By all accounts his Western allies counseled caution. Tshombe returned to Kolwezi, but not before issuing a message through Brazzaville, where his friend, Abbé Fulbert Youlou, the defrocked Catholic priest, was then president, calling on the people of Katanga to prepare "at the first signal to start a war to the finish."

At Kolwezi, Tshombe had second thoughts. Surrounded by the ragged remnants of his drunken troops, and some 200 white mercenaries who were of two minds whether they should blow up the installations or maintain the peace in order to protect the 4,000 Belgian civilians in the town, Tshombe decided to quit resistance. He announced the end of Katanga's secession and promised that Kolwezi would not be damaged. All he asked in return was a guarantee of "security and liberty." Those who saw him at the time describe him as "a dejected and frightened man." Yet even while Tshombe was at Kolwezi a Katanga spokesman in New York announced that after a cabinet meeting Tshombe had issued a statement "accusing the U.N. of blatant hypocrisy and flagrant lies."

The central government having promised Tshombe "a general and complete amnesty" for himself and his ministers, he returned to Elisabethville to work out the procedures of his capitulation with U.N. officials, who made it plain that they were there not to parley with him, but to give him his instructions. U Thant had already indicated the general line of procedure. This required the immediate presence in Léopoldville of representatives of Union Minière and of the Bank of Katanga to discuss and settle with the central government and the monetary council the details of paying into the central treasury all of Union Minière's foreign exchange and tax revenues. The senior officer of the Katanga gendarmerie must proceed to Léopoldville to take the oath of allegiance to the president of the Republic of Congo, thus registering the integration of the gendarmerie into the national army. Tshombe should assure full liberty of movement for all U.N. military personnel and equipment throughout Katanga and cooperate with the U.N. in the immediate elimination of all mercenaries from Katanga. On their side, Adoula and his government should support and press for early action in parliament on the constitution called for in the plan, which would be subject in parliament to amendments desired by any of the provinces, including Katanga.

Tshombe returned to Elisabethville to see visible testimony of his attenuated power. The blue-and-gold flag of the central government flew over Katanga's defense ministry. A corps of some 100 Léopoldville functionaries were in charge of key departments such as finance, customs, telecommunications, and immigration. Joseph Ileo was shortly to be appointed Adoula's resident minister in Katanga.*

Some fifty miles from Kolwezi, Indian infantrymen were waiting for the signal to advance. Tshombe was instructed to return to Kolwezi in order to prevent the destruction of its industrial installations and to per-

* He arrived at Elisabethville on Jan. 23, 1963.

suade his troops to surrender their arms to the U.N. By now thoroughly cowed, he had no alternative but to obey. Defiance might have meant his arrest and trial by the Adoula government for treason and sabotage. Tshombe knew what that meant. He was allowed to keep a bodyguard of Katangan gendarmerie and with these he returned to Kolwezi, which he handed over intact to U.N. troops commanded by Brigadier Noronha. During a champagne party which he threw for his conquerors, Tshombe is said to have whispered into Noronha's ear: "Never trust the whites. They're your worst enemies, too. The Belgians led me down the wrong path." It was typically Tshombe.

The new federal constitution, based broadly on the Coquilhatville proposals and initially providing for a republic of twenty-one states, immediately provoked tribal claims and counter-claims when it came before the Léopoldville parliament.* One of its first fruits was that Jason Sendwe, the Balubakat leader in north Katanga, for whose secession from south Katanga he had pressed for long, began to urge the reunification of the two areas, presumably to improve his own political position, which had declined in the north. In some ways the concept of Katangese secessionism was as authentic as most of the other Congolese tribal urges and movements, though the absurd lengths to which such postures could be pushed was highlighted by Katanga itself, where a single tribe, the Lunda, insisted that self-determination carried with it a right to appropriate to itself and to a mining company the greater part of the mineral wealth of a country some twelve times the size of Katanga and with a population twenty times as big. By whipping up local tribalism, Tshombe had hoped to make his own position secure, in the process edging out of south Katanga the talented Baluba, who are comparable to the Ewe in Ghana and Togo. On its side, Union Minière probably believed that it could exploit tribalism to forge closer the links between Katanga and the then "white bastion" of the Rhodesias. Tshombe has thrived as much on trouble as on tribalism.

The danger of inflammatory tribalism is ever-present not only in the Congo, but in all Africa. The end of Katanga's secession has not meant the end of the Congo's headaches. On the contrary, they seem likely to mount. Instead of the $16 million which the U.N. officials had hoped to find in the vaults of the National Bank of Katanga in Elisabethville after Tshombe's surrender, all they discovered was less than 15 dollars and a dead rat. Tshombe and his confederates had cleaned the cupboard bare. Later, Katanga francs to a nominal value of about $10 million were recovered from the vaults of a Ndola bank and burned at a local copper refinery under the supervision of a representative of the Congo government.

* In September, 1963, a joint statement issued by six of the opposition parties, headed by Conakat, Tshombe's party, referred to "the remarkable miniature provinces" and condemned the "Balkanization of the Congo." At the Tananarive conference Tshombe had himself suggested a loose confederation of Congolese states.

All Katanga francs were withdrawn and replaced by central Congolese currency. Some of them had trickled into Angola and South Africa. In any case, Katanga francs were of little value outside that state, because of the refusal of foreign banks to accept them ever since they were brought into circulation by Tshombe. Léopoldville faced a 1963 deficit of $100 million. The Congolese franc, officially rated at 64 to the dollar, stood in March, 1963, at 250 on the black market.* Food prices were rocketing. Strikes paralyzed the movement of goods. Foreign currency reserves were almost nonexistent. According to Adoula, the Congo could not survive without $175 million of foreign aid a year.

The West was quick to respond, but, paradoxically, its generosity has embarrassed the U.N., which had been planning to funnel aid to the Congo under a U.N. umbrella. The U.N. is now apprehensive lest the creation of an exclusively Western consortium precipitate the Cold War again into the Congo and intensify animosities within the international organization. If the United States contributed $174 million of the $382 million U.N. Congo operation, the bulk of the U.N. troops† in the Congo had been provided by the Afro-Asian nations. The task of restoring the Congo's economy, it was argued, should be a genuine U.N. effort, to which the Afro-Asian nations would also make their contributions, and possibly even the Soviet Union, though Moscow has firmly declined to do so. Russia maintains that the U.N. allowed itself to be used as an instrument for a purely Western rescue operation in the Congo of which the West took political advantage, its primary objective being to keep out the Russians. Britain, according to Moscow, was primarily responsible for obstructing the U.N. in ending the secession of Katanga in 1961. As a result $10 million a month was unnecessarily spent over an additional year. U Thant's approach to the problem of U.N. intervention is more cautious than that of Hammarskjöld, experience having taught him that unless finance is guaranteed in advance it could prove an expensive undertaking for the U.N. to project its presence. Hence his reluctance over Yemen, where he was hesitant to let the international organization intrude unless the U.A.R. and Saudi Arabia underwrote the bill, which they initially did for two months, subsequently extended another two months.

Lord Home's original proposal of an "Aid to the Congo Club," on the lines of the "Aid to India Club," was endorsed by the U.S. assistant secretary of state for international organizations, Harlan Cleveland, who visited

* Within the Congo the official rate in September, 1963, was about the same, the official "unofficial" rate was 130 francs to the dollar, and the black market rate was between 300 and 350 francs to the dollar.

† Their number was halved by the withdrawal of the Indian and Tunisian contingents in March, 1963, and due to insufficient funds it was proposed to withdraw all U. N. troops by the end of 1963. About 5,000 U.N. troops were retained in the Congo for another six months at a cost of $20 million underwritten by some of the member states. They left on June 30, 1964.

the Congo in February, 1963. On the basis of his recommendations Washington sponsored a plan to enable the United States to join with the European Common Market—which is likely to provide $80 million of aid to the Congo* over the next five years—and possibly with Britain and other European countries in the creation of the consortium. Though this would technically be done under U.N. auspices, the U.N. umbrella would be merely symbolic. Léopoldville's financial exigencies have also drawn the Congo closer to Belgium and Britain, which have been quick to respond.

All this has not been entirely to U Thant's liking. While welcoming the West's aid to the Congo, he would prefer such aid to be less exclusive. Nor does he relish the reports of United States attempts to bypass the U.N. by Washington requesting other Western countries to join in providing officers to retrain the Congolese army, since U Thant himself, as U.N. secretary-general, is engaged in a similar task. In order to reorganize the Congolese armed forces, which was necessary because of the U.N.'s desire to withdraw its troops by the end of 1963, Adoula asked for supplies and equipment from the United States, officer training by Belgium, communications training by Canada, naval training by Norway, air force training by Italy, and paratroop training by Israel. These countries have agreed to meet the cost of their assistance. But U Thant has frowned on the plan as having "definite political implications." Adoula's willingness to accept similar aid and training from African countries willing to bear the cost has brought a response, notably from Nigeria.

In December, 1963, Nkrumah, in a letter to U Thant, called for an all-African force to take over from the U.N. force in the Congo when the U.N. mandate expired. He was especially critical of the retraining program for the Congolese army which, he alleged, was carried out by a group of NATO countries. This was a strange arrangement for a nonaligned country like the Congo. Unless his proposal was adopted the Congo, which territorially constituted a buffer state between independent Africa in the north "and the territories of colonialism and white supremacy in the south," would be controlled by the West.

Adoula's headaches kept mounting. As in most other African countries, the opposition parties in the Congo were more interested in infiltrating into and undermining the government than in helping the cause of stable administration. Kasavubu's Abako party was the most challenging contender for power, and in an extensive cabinet reshuffle in April, 1963 —the third reorganization under Adoula and the sixth since independence —the representation of the Abako group was increased, as was also that of the Lumumbist Mouvement National Congolais, but the core of the government remained strongly federalist. The seemingly immovable Justin Bombako, who had been foreign minister under five governments, was

* The Congo is an associate member of the ECM.

replaced by thirty-year-old Auguste Mabika-Kalanda.* Bombako was made minister for justice. Three ministers were nominated to represent Katanga, drawn from Tshombe's Conakat.

In May, Tshombe's wings had been clipped by the creation of Luluaba province, which took in the entire western half of Katanga and sliced Tshombe's south Katanga, which contains the copper mining center of Kolwezi. Two months later, in July, yet another province, Katanga Orientale, was created, taking in all south Katanga, including Jadotville and Elisabethville, and parts of north Katanga, including the Lake Tanganyika district of Baudoinville.

It was the third division since independence in the course of which the "illegally constituted" province of south Katanga disappeared. Tshombe was ousted as head of the south Katanga government, though he could stand for the presidency of Luluaba if he so chose. The Congo was now split up into twenty-three provincettes, in many of which the undisciplined rabble of the national army posed a menace to order and security. In Katanga the local gendarmes, still waiting to be integrated into the national army, constituted another menace. To date, fewer than 1,000 of Tshombe's 20,000 gendarmes have been so integrated. Local bush Caesars, unmindful of the central authority, assumed the presidency of various provinces, most of them small areas of anarchy. The authority of Adoula's administration did not extend beyond Léopoldville and even here the national parliament, embarking on an obstructive role, seemed bent on destroying the central authority, such as it was. Kasavubu dissolved parliament on September 30, 1963, and announced that he would ask the people to vote on a draft constitution by referendum. New elections were to be held before June 30, 1964. Prime Minister Adoula was granted full legislative powers. His troubles were by no means over and were aggravated by increased inflation, the deterioration of the economy, and rebellious trade unions, which in October, 1963, on Adoula's return from Rome and Washington, staged a strike of teachers and civil servants, who demanded salary arrears which in the teachers' case totaled $16 million. Despite a vague promise by Washington of international backing for the franc, its value dropped in the free market to one-eighth of what it was in 1960. Pay arrears again provoked a mutiny by troops in Luluabourg, which Mobutu's representatives put down. The ruling cabal consisted of the Binza Group,† which included Mobutu, Bombako (then minister of justice), Victor Nendaka (head of the Sûreté), and Damien Kandolo, Secretary-General in the Ministry of the Interior. Following the strikes a

---

* Kalanda was arrested in December, 1963, on the charge of "an attempt against the security of the state."

† Binza is a suburb of Léopoldville where many of the group reside or work.

state of emergency was declared and an emergency committee set up with powers to arrest the trade unionists.

In November, 1963, Adoula announced new monetary reforms understood to include a devaluation of the Congolese franc by almost 300 percent in an attempt to reduce the inflationary effect of the deficit in public finances. This change was approved by the International Monetary Fund. In effect this will enable the Congolese government to buy foreign exchange proceeds of sales abroad from exporters at 150 francs to the dollar, and release foreign exchange to importers to buy essentials at 180 francs to the dollar. The then prevailing rate of the Congolese franc to the dollar was 65.

If the countries with the biggest political stake in the Congo are the United States and Portugal,* those with the biggest economic stake are Belgium and Britain. In the course of his European tour in July, 1963, Adoula visited both the latter countries, securing from Britain a promise of aid totaling $200,000, and from Belgium an undertaking to share in the servicing of the Congo's public debt of $900 million, and to increase its technical and military aid. Despite the extravagant postures of the Afro-Asian group, the countries of Africa continue to lean heavily on Western support and aid in many forms. Meanwhile the dissolution of the Central African Federation next door creates some menacing problems.

In November, 1963, the Adoula government, dominated by the Binza Group, ordered the entire Soviet embassy staff to leave the Congo following incidents involving two Soviet diplomats who were badly beaten up in Léopoldville by some of Mobutu's henchmen. Earlier in 1960 Mobutu had been responsible for the first ouster of Russian diplomats from the Congo, but the second time he did not escape unscathed. A week after the assault on the two Russians, Mobutu with Nendaka was badly beaten up by some Léopoldville gendarmes who questioned them on the murder of Lumumba. The following months saw a recrudescence of political unrest sparked in Stanleyville, Lumumba's old stronghold and now controlled by the followers of Gizenga, where a battalion of gendarmes mutinied but were disarmed. Trouble also broke out in Kwilu, some 350 miles east of Léopoldville, where American missionaries were attacked by the rioters.

From his exile in Europe, Tshombe stoked the flames by implicating Kasavubu and Adoula in the murder of Lumumba. The embarrassed Léopoldville government was driven to order an inquiry but by then the Lumumbists, master-minded by Pierre Mulele, former Lumumbist minister of education, were on the rampage. Mulele's followers, drawn largely

* The Adoula government has nonetheless recognized Holden Roberto's government-in-exile of Angola in Léopoldville, though it has shied away from the Algerian offer to put 10,000 Algerian troops on the sensitive Congo-Angola border.

from the Bupende and Babunde tribes in Kwilu, consisted mostly of youths between the ages of thirteen and eighteen and were known as the Jeunesse Mulele. Though evidence of direct Communist infiltration in this movement is slender, its inspiration comes from the Congolese Liberation Committee, based in Brazzaville, which now recognizes Peking. This has earned the Jeunesse the nickname of Viet-Congolese. The Congolese army, faced with incipient revolts and frontier disputes in North Katanga, Kivu, Kwilu, Kwanga and Kasai provinces, finds itself extended.

Conditions rapidly deteriorated, culminating in the murder of President Jason Sendwe of North Katanga by rebel elements late in June, 1964. The disintegration of the Adoula government accompanied the disintegration of the Congolese Army, an undisciplined rabble of about 35,000 soldiers now under the direct command of President Kasavubu. On June 30th, the fourth anniversary of independence, the last U.N. troops withdrew from the Congo, leaving the country in the throes of civil war, with a government and army incapable singly or jointly of holding it together.

Under the new constitution approved by a referendum in July, the Adoula government, which had been in power since August, 1961, resigned, and there were moves for a "government of national reconciliation" under Tshombe, who had returned to Léopoldville in June from Madrid after a little over a year's absence. Three new political blocs emerged from these maneuvers: (1) The Rassemblement des Démocrats Congolais (RADECO) under the presidency of Adoula; (2) The Comité Démocratique African (CDA), a miscellaneous moderate, pro-Western party, including Kasavubu's ABAKO; Cléophas Kamitatu's* African Socialist party; the Congolese Democratic party, headed by Jerome Anany; and the Reco from Kivu, and (3) The Front Commun National, known as the National Front, comprising 133 parties of the "legal opposition." The most important of these was the less extreme wing of Lumumba's National Congolese Movement, headed by Senator Antoine Kiwewa. The extremist wing has gone into exile in the former French Congo and in Burundi, and has joined the Communist-backed National Liberation Committee.

Tshombe had been planning for his comeback some months before he actually returned, and though the division of Katanga into three provincettes had clipped his wings somewhat, both he and mineral-rich Katanga were political factors that could not be ignored. The conveniently timed murder of his chief rival in Katanga, Jason Sendwe, who controlled North Katanga, eased Tshombe's difficulties in that area and facilitated his plan to head the "transition government" that succeeded Adoula. This government, which was provided for in the new constitution, is charged with the task of preparing for the new legislative elections within nine months.

As always, Tshombe remains unpredictable. So does the Congo, where

* Minister of Planning in the Adoula Government.

yesterday's sworn enemies are today's bosom friends. Not only did the CDA, controlled by Kasavubu, contact Tshombe, but so did the National Front and even the Lumumba extremists of the émigré National Liberation Committee. With these new-found friends Tshombe had no difficulty in replacing Adoula, who, while an able and conscientious bureaucrat, was no politician, deriving what little political influence he possessed from the Binza Group, which in turn leaned heavily on Mobutu and his rapidly disintegrating army.

Tshombe's own party, the Conakat, had meanwhile tentatively signed up with the CDA, and Tshombe set out to organize a "government of national reconciliation" that would include all the major factions from the Binza Group to the National Liberation Committee. Though he did not entirely succeed in this, he did manage to set up a small transition government composed mainly of unknown and untried men. It included one member of the National Liberation Committee. The significant and sinister feature of this setup was the concentration of power in the hands of two men—Tshombe and the baleful Godefroid Munongo, both Katangans and both actively involved in the former intrigues of secessionist Katanga and in the murder of Lumumba. In addition to the premiership, Tshombe took on the portfolios of Foreign Affairs, Foreign Trade, Information and Planning. Munongo was invested with the key ministries of the Interior and the Civil Service.

Almost exactly four years after he had declared the independence of Katanga, Tshombe found himself premier of the whole Congo. What the future holds for him and his country nobody can say. The disparate elements temporarily ranged behind Tshombe and Munongo could squabble at any moment and extend the bonfires raging in Kivu, Kwilu, and North Katanga. Even the resourceful Tshombe might find it impracticable to do much more than prepare for the national elections, which it would be difficult to hold unless law and order and communications are restored. The demoralized remnants of the Congolese Army are now under the direct control of President Kasavubu, like Tshombe, an able and ambitious man who plans to run for president again in 1965.

Such uneasy peace as the Congo in its most optimistic moments can expect depends on the cooperation of Tshombe and Kasavubu. Tshombe for the time being has the support of Anany and of Emile Zola of the Abako, but Kasavubu's cooperation is by no means wholehearted, and the Congolese president holds a watchful, wary brief. It is obviously not in Kasavubu's interest to inflate Tshombe unduly. On his part, Tshombe is attempting to secure the widest measure of support on the broadest basis. With characteristic aplomb and insensitivity he invited the family of Lumumba, who had taken refuge in Cairo, to return. He released Gizenga, self-proclaimed heir to Patrice Lumumba and the author of the bloody Stanleyville uprising in 1961, and with him and Albert Kalonji, self-appointed King of Kasai and now Minister of Agriculture, drove in a white convertible on a triumphant tour around Léopoldville. How long this improbable trio will work together is anybody's guess.

Tshombe's return to the Congo, with the support and connivance of his Western friends, must intensify the cold war in that territory. Moscow has reacted sharply, and so did the African summit conference coincidentally meeting in Cairo when Tshombe was proclaimed premier. Led by Nasser, Nkrumah, and Ben Bella, the assembled heads of state plainly indicated that Tshombe's presence was unwelcome. Tshombe and Kasavubu kept away.

"To Monsieur Ben Bella who shouts loudly," shouted back Tshombe, "I answer with equal force. Do as we do; free your political prisoners." Tshombe had earlier declared an amnesty for all political prisoners.

While the Afro-Asian countries huddled under the U.N. umbrella watch developments in the Congo uneasily, Moscow, Peking, and the West flex their muscles significantly. China's hand had been active in the Lumumbist flare-ups, and Moscow's surprise move recommending that the Security Council should provide itself with the military forces envisioned for it under the Charter is interpreted by the West, and also by some Afro-Asian countries, as a maneuver to transfer the control of peace-keeping interventions from the General Assembly and the Secretary General to the Security Council, where the Soviet Union can control them through the use of the veto. Yet with the U.N. on the verge of near bankruptcy as a result of the Congo operations, which, with economic assistance, have cost the international organization over half a billion dollars, more than five times the size of the regular budget for 1964, new ways must be found to finance subsequent peace-keeping interventions.

Tshombe meanwhile continues to indulge in his theatrical postures and promises. At a rally in Baudoin Stadium in Léopoldville shortly after assuming office, he said: "Before discovering America, Christopher Columbus said to his tired friends, 'In three days I will give you a new world.' To you who are also tired—tired of anarchy and disorder—I say, three months and I will give you a new Congo."

It is easier said than done.

11

IN RWANDA
AND BURUNDI

CHASTENED BY THEIR experience in the Congo and by the damage done to their record as colonialists, the Belgians behaved more circumspectly in the adjoining trust territory of Ruanda-Urundi, which on July 1, 1962, was to achieve independence, but as the two separate states of Rwanda and Burundi. These are their original names in the local language. Rwanda and Burundi have always been two distinct and separate kingdoms, each ruled by a *mwami*, or kinglet, of the Watusi tribe.* The Watusi, who have the distinction of counting some of the tallest members of the human race in their ranks, a few of them standing seven feet high and more, total less than 15 percent of the population. Some 85 percent of the people are Bahutu, who for long occupied a subordinate place to the ruling clan of the Watusi. Of the remaining population about 1 percent are Twa, a Pygmy people whose original blood has undergone a considerable admixture.

Of all the countries I visited in sub-Saharan Africa, none fascinated me more than the then trust territory of Ruanda-Urundi, a land of natural beauty and picturesque contrasts, with volcanic mountains and clear deep lakes, hills capped with cone tops verdant with banana groves, and corn-

* Rwanda is now a republic headed by a president.

fields undulating like a sea in waves of green, blue, and purple. Above hung an iron, steel-gray sky.

Wedged between Uganda to the north and Tanganyika to the east, Rwanda and Burundi constitute an elongated enclave which juts like a blister from the eastern flank of the former Belgian Congo. The two territories have been compared to the auricle and ventricle of a heart, and they lie almost in the heart of Africa. Burundi, which lies south of Rwanda, is territorially slightly the larger of the two, both areas together covering approximately 21,000 square miles, with a total population of nearly 5 million. They are the most densely populated in all Africa, rating nearly 250 inhabitants to the square mile, compared with less than 20 per square mile in the Congo, and at the present rate of increase the population should grow by 40 percent within ten years.

Half the population is Christian, the overwhelming majority being Catholic, but there exist nearly 350,000 Protestants with an Anglican bishop at their head. There are in all two Catholic archbishoprics and six bishoprics, five of which are administered by Africans. I met one of the African bishops, Msgr. Alois Begirunwami, the Apostolic Vicar of Nyundo, whose see extends over the northwestern districts of Rwanda. He wore a black coat over a white cassock and his sandal-encased feet were covered by purple socks. He was tall and handsome, with a warm, friendly manner, was intelligent, and had great dignity. In both Ruanda-Urundi and the Congo, I was intrigued by the arguments of a number of Belgian Protestants who claimed that they were politically more liberal than the Catholics, a claim which I am inclined to accept. Another intriguing discovery was the presence of nearly 2,000 Moslems, a microscopic island in Ruanda-Urundi's seething sea of population.

The Watusi, a pastoral people, are a handsome race. Near Nyamata in Rwanda we visited three refugee camps housing around 8,000 Watusi, who were sheltering there after the 1959 Bahutu uprising, which was encouraged and to a degree inspired by the Belgians. This culminated in January, 1961, in the overthrow of the Mwami, Kigeri V, and the proclamation of Rwanda as a republic. Under Belgian auspices, an all-Bahutu party called Parmehutu took power. Of Rwanda's nearly 2.5 million population, some 400,000 were Watusi, but their number when I visited the territory was almost halved, about 15,000 having been killed* and around 160,000 having fled to Uganda, the Congo, and Tanganyika. Thousands of Watusi were rendered homeless, their possessions burned and their cattle seized under the approving eyes of the Belgian authorities.

* In January, 1964, the Bahutu slaughtered another 35,000 Watusi while some 12,000 fled over the frontier of Rwanda. Genocide is not too strong a word to describe these massacres.

Not all the refugees were Watusi. A few were Bahutu belonging to the UNAR party, which, overwhelmingly Watusi in composition, is opposed to Parmehutu and is pro-Mwami. The capital of Rwanda is Kigali, a small, 7,000-population town perched like an eagle's nest some 6,000 feet up in the Rwanda highlands.

Burundi has more stable traditions than Rwanda. Unlike the northern territory, it decided to retain its kingship, and when independence came chose to become a constitutional monarchy with Mwami Mwambutsa IV as head of the state. Burundi's fundamental law is derived from the Belgian constitution. As a general rule, the political institutions in Burundi were less centralized than in Rwanda, where the Mwami had the right to dismiss any district chiefs. In Burundi the district chiefs belonged to the Ganwa class, descendants of the ruling clan, and could not be dismissed from office by the Mwami except in special cases. As a result, a system of finer checks and balances between ruler and ruled developed in Burundi than in Rwanda, and Mwami Mwambutsa was able to use his prestige to bring the castes together and form an all-caste party, the UPRONA (Unité et Progrès National du Burundi), which won the September, 1961, elections against the Belgian-supported PDC (Christian Democratic Party) and two other opposition parties. The capital of Burundi is Kitega, where at the Mwami's palace we met his second wife, a striking-looking woman of thirty-four with an Ethiopian cast of features. The Mwami at the time was away in Switzerland. Burundi is also fortunate in containing Usumbura, the former joint capital at the tip of Lake Tanganyika. It has a population of around 60,000, of whom well over 50,000 are Africans.

The history of Rwanda and Burundi is almost as mist-clouded as its landscape. The entity christened Ruanda-Urundi by the Belgians after the First World War had no historical existence and was a purely artificial creation.

Ptolemy was the first to ascribe the probable sources of the Nile to the land around the legendary Mountains of the Moon. This was toward the second century A.D. But not until 1858 did the first European explorers, Burton and Speke, stumble on this exotic land when they reached Nyanza-lac on the southern shore of Lake Tanganyika. They were the first white men to set foot in Urundi. At that time Rwanda and Burundi, to give them their traditional names, had existed as separate kingdoms, each under a Watusi king, or Mwami, for some centuries. The Watusi probably came in the fifteenth century, when according to some historians they arrived in this region, which sits astride the Congo-Nile Divide, and established themselves as rulers.

The original inhabitants were the Twa, who are distantly related to the Pygmies of the Congo. They number around 50,000 today, and are scorned by both the Watusi and the Bahutu, the latter of whom, a Bantu race, drove the Twa from the plains into the jungles, decimating them in the process. The Twa are a primitive people, mainly hunters and potters. I came across only two of them—between Astrida and Nyanza in a pombe bar. They were drunk and inclined to be churlish.

Following the Twa came waves of the Bahutu, who settled down as tillers of the soil, in which capacity they continued until the tall, tubular Watusi descended from the north, bringing with them an elaborate culture and an economy based on cattle. The Watusi are a pastoral people who are said to have driven innumerable herds of lyre-horned cattle before them in the course of their migrations into Rwanda and Burundi. Some say they came from the Nile Valley, while others hold that their original homeland was Ethiopia. The recently discovered Tassili Caves in the Sahara contain rock paintings of long-horned cattle like the Ankole cattle one encounters today in Rwanda and Burundi, which suggests that the Watusi might once have inhabited the grassy steppes or plains. They are of Hamitic stock.

I never came across Watusi more than seven feet tall, though I encountered a number who were nearly seven feet. There were some very tall women among them, with piled-up hair and aquiline faces, high cheekbones and foreheads, and thick but not pendulous lips. Both the men and women are slender, slim-hipped, and often of reedlike thinness. The tall, tapering Ruanda Intore dancers are celebrated, and were brought to Western notice in the 1950 movie, *King Solomon's Mines*.

Apparently the majestic appearance of the Watusi, reinforced by their droves of cattle, impressed the Bahutu sufficiently to induce them into submission as serfs or "clients" to their new masters. The so-called "client" system is based on the feudal notion of one person offering his services to another person of superior standing in return for protection. The status symbol became the cow. In return for his offer of service, the "client" received a cow, which bound him to his master, but the relationship could be terminated by the serf returning the cow and all male calves of his growing herd. That the Watusi also propagated the myth of their divine origin in order to sustain the master-serf relationship is possible. Despite the overwhelming Bahutu majority, they succeeded in being recognized and accepted as the ruling race.

This was the state of affairs when in 1892 the German explorer, the Duke of Mecklenburg, entered the two territories at the head of a scientific expedition. He was not the first European to penetrate the Mountains of the Moon after Burton and Speke. Between there had been other European explorers and missionaries, including Stanley and Livingstone, who in 1871 explored Lake Tanganyika, to be followed by Cardinal Lavigerie's "White Fathers," who did not succeed in founding a mission until 1898. The Germans, well launched on the Scramble for Africa, declared Rwanda and Burundi their domains, labeling them districts 13 and 14 in their empire of Deutsch Ost Afrika, or German East Africa. In 1899 they built the military outpost of Usumbura, which later became the capital city of Ruanda-Urundi, and set up garrisons along the frontier separating the two kingdoms from the Congo. Not until 1907 did a civilian administration take over, and its strength never exceeded ten Germans.

Two years after the outbreak of the First World War in 1914 Belgian troops entered the two territories to find them riven by civil war and palace intrigues. In 1919 the Supreme Council of Allied Powers entrusted Belgium with a mandate over the territories, which was confirmed by the League of Nations in August, 1923. In December, 1946, Ruanda-Urundi became a trust territory of the U.N., with the Belgians in charge as trustees. This arrangement was formally approved by a law dated April 25, 1949.

Until the rumblings of African freedom penetrated Ruanda-Urundi when the neighboring Congo teetered on the brink of independence, the Belgians favored the two Mwamis, along with the other chieftains, on whose support they relied and whose influence they tried to extend. As a result of this policy and partly because of their own intrinsic qualities, the Watusi were consolidated in their status as the ruling elite.

This position prevailed through almost forty years of Belgian administration, though with the opening of schools and the extension of social welfare amenities the lot of the Bahutu serfs improved, and they were quick to take advantage of the new opportunities offered. Whatever the Belgian motivations might have been, their policies resulted in releasing the Bahutu of their inferiority complex vis-à-vis the ruling Watusi, which was good, and intensified a sense of rivalry, which unfortunately the Belgians were later tempted to exploit. The Belgian policy of discounting the cow as a status symbol undermined the position of the dominant Watusi, and the recruitment of Bahutu labor for the mines of the adjoining Congo, where they came into contact with Africans like themselves, animated by new ideas and ambitions, accelerated the process. With their overwhelming numerical majority, it dawned on the Bahutu, perhaps at Belgian instigation, that under popular rule numbers meant strength.

By 1957 the Bahutu had organized a political party and began to take an active interest in the municipal councils, where their numerical majority assured them of civic domination. The Belgians actively encouraged their ambitions, hoping thereby to retain their own foothold in Ruanda-Urundi more firmly. As in the Congo, they miscalculated, forgetful of the fact that if a people are taught to shed their overlords, they are not likely to exchange them for other masters. The policy of divide and rule between the Watusi and Bahutu was extended to the two territories, which, because of their intrinsic rivalries, the Belgians were able to keep politically divided and apart. When independence came, the two territories decided to retain their separate identities with Rwanda, a republic under a president, and Burundi, a kingdom under a Mwami. But the Belgians discovered to their dismay that neither territory welcomed the continuance of the Belgian presence, and were particularly insistent on the withdrawal of the Belgian armed forces.

I visited Ruanda-Urundi, as it was then called, with a letter of introduction to the Belgian resident-general in Usumbura, who unfortunately was away on a visit to Brussels. But in his absence I was most courteously received by the Belgian authorities, who were uniformly cordial and hospitable, and helped me in many ways. It is therefore with regret that I criticize some of their administrative and political policies. There is little doubt that the Belgian hand was behind the 1959 uprising of the Bahutu against the Watusi in Rwanda, where the Twa joined the Bahutu in massacring and terrorizing the Watusi. The sympathy and support of the Belgian officials whom we encountered in Rwanda was undisguisedly with the Bahutu, who, as one Belgian remarked, "had rightly risen against the feudal regime of the Watusi." Another official at Kisenyi, a lovely resort overlooking Lake Kivu, solemnly advised us not to mention the Watusi to the local Africans, as they were unpopular in the area.

We had driven from Usumbura north into Rwanda, which is divided from Burundi by the Kanyaru River, and via Astrida to Nyanza and on to Ruhengeri and Kisenyi. The countryside of Rwanda is more beautiful than that of Burundi. It is green with hills and rolling downs, and valleys alternately swathed in mist and bathed in sunlight. A soft haze envelops the countryside. Driving early one morning from Kigali to Nyamata, we ran into a pea-soup fog through which the trees loomed out of the mist like tall plumes of smoke. It was weird and eerie, but beautiful. Late one night, driving in inky blackness, we saw as we turned a bend the glow of a volcanic mountain lighting the sky. It had a curiously Japanese-sounding name—Myamuragira.

Our driver, a nephew of the Mwami of Burundi, was an intelligent young man who was also politically minded. His name was Étienne. The Mwamis of Burundi, though Watusi, are of a less pure strain than the former Mwamis of Rwanda, but their hostility to the Belgians appeared to be no less.

"They say our Mwami is feudal," observed Étienne. "The Belgians want to make us republicans, because our kings, according to them, are feudal. Can they tell us why, in that case, they themselves are monarchists and reverence their king? Have they thereby ceased to be democrats?"

According to Étienne, the Belgians had bribed the Bahutu in Rwanda to terrorize the Watusi and to burn their huts. They had also tried to do the same with the Bahutu in Burundi.

"What did the Bahutu do in Burundi?" I asked.

"Nothing," said Étienne somberly. "They took the money and drank it up."

In Usumbura, we met Prince Louis Rwagasore, elder son of the Mwami of Burundi by his first wife. He was assassinated some months later, in October, 1961, after being prime minister of Burundi for less than a month. He received us in his house, along with his wife and sister and secretary. In appearance Prince Louis, with his protuberant eyes, reminded me of the Ethiopian crown prince. He seemed progressive and intelligent, politically wide awake, and an avowed nationalist.

"The Belgians," he remarked, "accuse us of being Communists. At the same time they accuse us of being monarchist and feudal. They must make up their minds as to what we really are."

He explained the political situation in Burundi and Rwanda in some detail. Developments in the Congo, as in other African territories, had had their impact on Ruanda-Urundi. The Belgians could not stay the march of history. They had forced Mwami Kigeri V of Rwanda into exile, and hoped through Parmehutu to delay the advent of independence until Bahutu rule was consolidated in both territories. It was easier to do this in Rwanda than in Burundi, because tribal divisions in the latter were less marked and the monarchy was strong. Prince Louis explained that his own party, UPRONA, contained both Watusi and Bahutu members. In the November, 1960, local government elections in Burundi, the Belgians had immobilized his party and himself by placing him under house arrest. As a result the United Common Front, which was Belgian-supported and led by Prince Baranyanka, had won. But in a free election the result would be different.

Prince Louis was right. In the legislative elections held under U.N. supervision in September, 1961, in Rwanda and Burundi, his UPRONA party won fifty-eight of the sixty-four seats in the Burundi legislative assembly, the remaining six being shared among the three opposition parties. In Rwanda, the Belgian-supported Parmehutu captured thirty-four of the forty-four seats, while UNAR gained seven, and APROSQMA (Association for Social Progress of the Masses) won two. A referendum on the monarchy in Rwanda confirmed the deposing of Mwami Kigeri V, and Grégoire Kayibanda, the former prime minister, was elected president, heading the government and the state.

Prince Louis, who assumed the office of prime minister of Burundi following his party's victory, was killed at a lakeside restaurant three weeks later. He was struck in the chest by a rifle bullet fired from some bushes nearby. A Greek national who admitted he had triggered the fatal shot was arrested, along with two leaders of the opposition PDC, including the minister of the interior in the former government. Later, some more suspects, including two Greeks, were taken into custody and brought for trial. The assassin, a Burundi-born Greek named Jean Kageorgis, who was sentenced to death, is believed to have been executed eighteen hours before independence. Some months later, the remaining accused, who had been sentenced to various terms of imprisonment, were publicly executed at Kitega. They included the former PDC minister and another Greek. Prince Louis was succeeded as prime minister by his brother-in-law, André Muhirwa.*

The troubled twins, though separated, continued to be restive. While conditions in Burundi remained comparatively stable in the interval until the proclamation of independence on July 1, 1962, they were disturbed in Rwanda, where another outburst of tribal fighting between the Watusi and the Bahutu led to a further exodus of refugees.

About 10,000 refugees fled into Uganda and the Congo, while 40,000, according to the estimates of African and European administrators and missionaries, went into hiding in Burundi. Some Watusi refugees regrouped in the border areas to form a terrorist organization, and their raiding parties harassed Rwanda, in the process killing some Africans and a few Europeans. This terrorist organization was known as *Inyenzi*, which means cockroach. There were still about 1,300 Belgian soldiers in the two territories, and in Rwanda they were widely accused of siding with the Bahutu. Far from ensuring stability and security, the Belgian soldiers, it was said, were spreading disorder. This had not a little to do with the subsequent insistence by both territories that the Belgian forces should withdraw. They were withdrawn on August 1, a month after independence.

By mid-June, 1962, around 5,000 of the 7,000 Europeans resident in the two areas had left, including two thirds of the 1,200 European officials. About 1,500 Europeans remained in Burundi and another 500 in Rwanda. Of these nearly 800 were Greek and Portuguese merchants and traders, while of the 1,200 Belgians a good number were priests and nuns.

The Congolese government enjoyed six days of power before the Congo achieved "nationhood," but in Rwanda and Burundi the governments were in power for ten months before independence. Nevertheless, when freedom dawned the prospects seemed almost as bleak as they had proved to be in the Congo. Following the report of a five-member commission, the

* He resigned in June, 1963, following serious differences with the majority of members of the legislative assembly, and was succeeded by M. Pierre Ngendandumwe.

U.N. General Assembly had earlier, in February, 1962, passed a resolution reaffirming its conviction that the best future for Ruanda-Urundi lay in the emergence of a single state with economic unity, common defense, and external relations without prejudice to the internal autonomy of the two parts of the territory. That, unfortunately, was not to be, for the psychosis of mutual mistrust could not be easily overcome.

When independence came there were only twenty-six graduates between the two countries and less than fifty students qualifying for the equivalent of the school certificate. Rwanda and Burundi are both poor countries with enormous economic problems. Most of their people live by subsistence farming, and the two countries have a one-crop economy based on coffee, a per capita income of less than $42 a year, one of the lowest in the world. Except for some tin mining in Rwanda, there are no signs of industry elsewhere, and lack of purchasing power discourages both industries and investment.

According to the U.N. Commission for Ruanda-Urundi, established in February, 1962, the budget deficit for the current year was approximately $3 million for each of the two territories, without counting the cost of the technical assistance then being provided by Belgium. An annual deficit of that nature could be anticipated for several years and the commission reckoned that an estimated $20 million of external aid would be required annually by the two countries.

At the General Assembly debate in June, 1962, which fixed the date of independence for both territories at July 1, Belgium's foreign minister, Paul-Henri Spaak, emphasized that some aid which would not infringe the sovereignty of either territory should be provided by joint agreement among the two countries, Belgium, and the United Nations. He said it had already been decided to spend about $300,000 in one country and $320,000 in the other to help in recruiting, equipping, and arming the national forces of Rwanda and Burundi. But in order to do this, as well as to ensure reasonable conditions of security for Belgian administrative and technical personnel to work in, the Belgian forces, numbering around 1,200 officers and men, should be allowed to stay on for three months. Though the local forces for maintaining law and order in the two territories were, according to the commission, "in an embryonic stage of development," the General Assembly, faced by the demand of both countries that the Belgian forces should withdraw, set the deadline for their withdrawal at August 1. It was explained that in so doing they viewed the problem of security not from a purely military or technical point of view, but in the larger context of the political and social situation in the country. A U.N. military mission is helping to reorganize the armed forces of both territories.

Neither Rwanda nor Burundi can be considered as a viable country on its own. Had they remained together their chances of survival would have been better, but by deciding against any form of political union each added considerably to its expenses and difficulties. Separation doubled the costs of government for both. On the basis of 200 Belgian experts and technicians remaining behind, the U.N. commission had estimated that provision would have to be made by the international bodies to finance the recruitment of another 200 foreign experts and technicians. This would entail an expenditure of about $2 million a year, which would not be noticeably reduced until 1964. For this purpose the commission appealed to member states to set up a special fund to cover at least some of the most pressing needs of the two countries, the terms and conditions of which would be settled by the General Assembly. A minimum sum of $10 million to cover a period of three years would be required for this purpose. Provision for $675,000 under the expanded program of technical assistance had already been made for 1961–1962 for Ruanda-Urundi.

A survey mission sponsored by the European Economic Community set the required total investment for the period 1962–1971 at some $280 million or about $28 million a year. From the estimates of the survey commission and other data concerning private investment, it seems likely that Rwanda and Burundi will obtain about $10 million per year from public sources to finance economic development during the next few years. The deficit to be anticipated will depend on the contributions which the two countries succeed in obtaining under the various multilateral, regional, and bilateral programs.

Overoptimistic as some of the survey team's conclusions might seem—it envisages, for instance, a doubling of national income within ten years, while allowing for a population increase by 40 percent in the same period—the prospects for the two territories could improve provided there is relative stability and security in both over the next decade. In Rwanda, the Bahutu ruling party, Parmehutu, consists of individuals who might broadly be described as social democrats, and President Kayibanda, whose wife still works in the fields, has shown himself to be no Belgian stooge, as he was suspected to be. The inclusion of two Watusi leaders, members of the opposition UNAR party, in the Rwanda government was an imaginative gesture which should make for more internal stability.

In Burundi, conditions are more stable, but the problem here is to convert a system of baronial feudalism into a more progressive order without upsetting the Watusi emblem of authority, the *mwami*. In contrast with Rwanda, there has always been a certain amount of intermarriage between the races in Burundi, coupled with a greater degree of decentralization of authority. Neither the U.N. nor Belgium wants another Congo on their hands, and both recognize their continuing responsibility as former administrators of the trusteeship. These are encouraging pointers.

In Brussels the two countries are likely to get aid from the Overseas Development Fund of the European Economic Community. Through the efforts of the U.N. Commission for Ruanda-Urundi, a high-level conference was arranged between representatives of the two territories at Addis Ababa in April, 1962, to find a formula for the closest possible political, economic, and administrative union between the territories. It resulted in an agreement to set up a council of economic union with the help of U.N. technical advisers, one of whom will serve in the dual capacity of secretary-general of the council and president of the proposed central bank. This move toward some form of economic cooperation, however skeletal, is encouraging, and, if successful, might develop into a stronger bond of economic union.

Ultimately, the stability and progress of Rwanda and Burundi will depend more on economic than political factors. If the Belgians learned a lesson from the Congo, so have the Bahutu and the Watusi. The main task is to escalate economic development and, with it, the standard of living in both countries, and this can best be done within the context of a closer economic union to improve farming, diversify crops, lift the present standards of cattle-raising and improve coffee production. U.N. officials have suggested large-scale cotton planting around Lake Tanganyika and the weaning of the Bahutu from their irresponsible husbandry, which has exhausted large areas of the soil, as well as of the Watusi from their uneconomic cattle-raising and uncontrolled grazing. This will not be easy. The Belgians set up some good research stations, but were not equally successful in carrying to the pastures and fields the results of their work in the laboratories.

The trend in Rwanda and Burundi, as in other African territories, is more toward larger economic association than toward political union. In many ways the Watusi and the Bahutu are closer to the races which inhabit Uganda and Tanganyika than to those of the Congo. This has induced a feeling in some quarters that someday Rwanda and Burundi might draw closer to neighboring Uganda and Tanganyika, though their main products are competitive rather than complementary, coffee and cotton bulking large in the output of all four countries. The setting up of monetary and customs unions, buttressed later by a strong economic union, offers the best hope for the economic development of Rwanda and Burundi. Both have manpower in plenty. The task is to train and educate this human reservoir to more purposeful and positive endeavor in the interests of each of the countries, and of both.

CHAPTER

12

EAST AFRICAN TANGLE

HOW EASILY A spark can ignite a chain of political fires in Africa was shown in January, 1964, when a sudden revolution in Zanzibar triggered a successive series of military mutinies in Tanganyika, Uganda, and Kenya.

In Africa divisiveness marches alongside an urge for closer collaboration and cooperation. No area represents this paradox more forcefully than East Africa, where the three territories of Kenya, Uganda, and Tanganyika, each a separate political entity, are striving to create a form of closer economic cooperation designed to strengthen the political ties between them.

If the East African mutinies impel the creation of a single defense force and command even before the projected politicoeconomic federation, they might hasten the general move to ensure greater stability by more cohesive association in wide areas of the Continent.

East Africa's three territories, with a collective area of around 681,000 square miles, as big as Western Europe, contain nearly 24 million people. Territorially, Tanganyika is the largest, Uganda the smallest. Their political origins differ and have influenced their constitutional growth, for while Uganda rated as a British protectorate, containing four tribal kingdoms, Tanganyika was successively under German occupation and, after

249

the First World War, a British mandated territory, which was converted after the Second World War into a trust territory. Kenya, though taken over as a protectorate in 1895, was for all administrative purposes ruled as a colony. Another factor has had an even sharper impact on their political growth. This was the presence of the white settlers, who are comparatively few in Tanganyika and virtually nonexistent in Uganda, where the 11,000 or so Europeans are mainly civil servants, business executives, technicians, teachers, and missionaries. In Kenya, however, the Europeans, though not numerically large in proportion to the population,* dominated the country's economy and, as settlers, had a stake in Kenya's best lands.

Of the three territories, Tanganyika was politically the most stable, Uganda economically the most prosperous in terms of the African people, while Kenya, the pampered darling of former British East Africa, was commercially the most advanced, but economically the poorest of the three. Tribalism and the struggle for land have proved to be the major deterrents to Kenya's political progress. At one time it was thought that Uganda, with its feudal infrastructure dominated by the Kabaka of Buganda, would be the last of the three territories to achieve independence. Not Uganda, but Kenya, which became independent on December 12, 1963, proved the main drag. Tanganyika become independent on December 9, 1961, and Uganda on October 9, 1962. Kenya had its first elections leading to self-government in May, 1963.

Even before the three territories achieved their separate independence, it was decided that following the London talks of June, 1961, the old East African High Commission, established in 1948, should be replaced by a new organization, responsible for common services in East Africa, to be known as the East African Common Services Organization (EACSO). The commission, which was an interterritorial body covering Kenya, Uganda, Tanganyika, and Zanzibar, exercised a system of colonial control over the common services of these four territories, which included currency, railways and harbors, communications, industrial coordination, and research stations. The new organization, EACSO, does not include Zanzibar, but provision is made for the island to be provided with the organization's services on an agency basis, and the way is left open for it to join EACSO later, should it so desire. But EACSO has still to be finalized. Its future depends on whether the East African federation ultimately comes into being. Here the major issues to be settled are the division of powers between the federal and state governments, the siting of the federal capital, and the formation of an East African civil service. Nairobi seems to

* They number about 70,000 in a total population of nearly 8 million.

be the obvious choice as headquarters, though Vasey,* as I recall, thought it should be Arusha. Who will be president? And what will be the position of the kingdoms within Uganda, particularly the status of the prickly Kabaka? There are also the regional susceptibilities and administrative complications of Kenya to be considered—a problem rendered more difficult of solution by KANU's reluctance to bring KADU into the picture.† Zanzibar under the sultan was hesitant, her chief difficulties then being unchecked immigration from the mainland and the status of her sultan. But the Tanzan union between Tanganyika and Zanzibar in April, 1964, has altered the picture. It must also be remembered that it took some years to produce the Nigerian federal constitution.

The significant point about EACSO is the transfer of the functions relating to the common services from colonial to political control. One of the main criticisms directed at the old high commission, based in Nairobi, was that it represented an association geared in Kenya's favor and was biased on the side of the European settlers rather than of the indigenous Africans. Kenya had a dominant voice in its deliberations and decisions. The saying, "Kenya has benefited at the expense of Uganda and Tanganyika," was common in East Africa, and though the Raisman Commission's‡ report on the East African Common Market and the high commission services did not accept the justice of this allegation, its view that the benefits conferred by the Common Market were unequal and should be redistributed through a "distributive pool of revenue" impliedly recognized its validity. About the same time a report on the high commission services prepared by Sir Richard Ramage advised a policy of more rapid Africanization.

Political advance rendered both the Raisman and Ramage reports largely obsolete. Despite the differences and rivalries of the two main Kenya political parties, KANU and KADU, Tanganyika, Uganda, and Kenya were able to present a united front on EACSO at the London talks, but unfortunately the arrangement enabling Kenya to be represented alternately by KANU and KADU proved unworkable, as neither was able to command enough support from the Kenya council of ministers to enable its representative to take decisions on Kenya's behalf. The differences between KANU and KADU over EACSO were further aggravated by KANU's Pan-African socialist approach, which did not coincide with KADU's bent toward free enterprise and moderation. As a result and also

* Sir Ernest Vasey, then finance minister in Tanganyika.
† KANU (Kenya African National Union) and KADU (Kenya African Democratic Union) are the two main parties in Kenya, though since independence KANU is paramount and Kenya functions as a virtually one-party state.
‡ Headed by Sir Jeremy Raisman, finance member of the government of India in British days. The report was released in February, 1961.

because of Uganda's hesitancy, Zanzibar's doubts, and unrest in East Africa sparked by the military revolts in January, 1964, EACSO is virtually in cold storage. Earlier, it was hoped to get it actively under way once Tanganyika had achieved its independence in December, 1961.

The failure to get EACSO going underlined the deep-seated rivalries between KANU and KADU, which, apart from slowing the pace of Kenya's advance to independence, made it difficult for the three territories to achieve closer economic collaboration as a prelude to the formation of an East African federation, which was planned at one time to embrace not only Zanzibar, but also the Central African territories of Northern Rhodesia and Nyasaland, and possibly even Ethiopia and Somalia. At least, that was the dream envisaged by the Pan-African Movement for East and Central Africa (PAFMECA) at its meeting in Addis Ababa in February, 1962. This dream threatens to be a mirage.*

The East African Common Services Organization came into being formally in December, 1961, but its active working was hampered by the political divisions inside Kenya and outside. Some semblance of an administrative apparatus was set up. EACSO took over the high commission's buildings and staff, and transacted routine business. Its policy-making body, the East African Common Services Authority (EACSA), held its first meeting in Nairobi in January, 1962, at which Kenya, Uganda, and Tanganyika were each represented by the principal elected ministers responsible to their respective legislatures. These originally were Ronald Ngala, leader of the house in the Kenya legislative council, Julius Nyerere of Tanganyika, and Benedicto Kiwanuka, chief minister of Uganda. On Uganda's achieving independence in October, 1962, Kiwanuka was replaced by the new prime minister, Milton Obote. Nyerere, who meanwhile had withdrawn from the government to put his party house† in order prior to becoming the first president of the Tanganyika Republic, made way for Rashidi Kawawa, who succeeded him as prime minister and is now vice-president. In Kenya, in March, 1961, the minority party, KADU, led by Ronald Ngala, agreed to enter the council of ministers with the support of Michael Blundell's New Kenya party. Almost exactly a year later, in April, 1962, KANU, headed by Jomo Kenyatta,‡ who had been leader of the opposition in the legislative council since January, 1962, also entered the council of ministers. However, the formation of a coalition government, far from mellowing interparty rivalries, exacerbated them, and

* Earlier, in 1961, Northern Rhodesia, Nyasaland, Somalia, Ethiopia, the Sudan, Rwanda, and Burundi had discussed federation, with Uganda, Kenya, Tanganyika, and Zanzibar, and had objected to moves by the latter four to form their own federation.
† His party is the Tanganyika African National Union (TANU).
‡ Kenyatta did not enter the ministry.

made it hard for EACSO to function effectively and for an East African Federation to come into being.

Apart from the policy-making body, a more representative legislative assembly consisting of twelve ministers—four from each territory—nine members elected by each territorial legislature, a secretary-general, and a legal secretary, was set up to replace the old assembly. This representative body was given power to legislate on certain subjects, such as civil aviation, customs and excise, research, posts and telegraphs, railways, harbors and inland water communications, and merchant shipping. Moreover, provision was made for a distributive pool of income to finance certain of its operations. This again represented a step toward "East Africanism," building up from EACSO to a federated East Africa, but unless Kenya achieved independence it was impracticable to federate two sovereign states with a dependency.

Nyerere's original idea, which he explained to me when he was leader of the house in Tanganyika, was to achieve federation before the separate territories had achieved independence. He felt that to try to achieve federation after independence would be more difficult, as the independent units might be less eager to shed some of their sovereignty to the common organization. Nyerere argued that a federation of East Africa, which might be extended to include certain Central African territories, would politically prevent the Balkanization of East Africa and adjacent countries, and economically would make it easier to develop their joint resources as larger and more compact units. It was Nyerere's idea that Kenyatta should be the first president of the East African federation.

Events compelled him to modify his plans and program. Though at one time he seemed willing to delay Tanganyika's deadline for independence, the intransigence of the Kabaka in Uganda, which slowed down the pace of that country's march to freedom, along with the stubborn persistence of party and tribal rivalries in Kenya, persuaded Nyerere that to postpone his country's independence was not politically possible or wise. He finally decided to go it alone. But even then he was willing to accommodate and adjust Tanganyika's timetable if it helped to accelerate the pace of freedom in Uganda and Kenya. Thus, he accepted the Raisman Commission's recommendations in February, 1961, for a period of two years, hoping that in the interval it might be possible to plan an East African federation. But here again Kenya's tribal obstreperousness obtruded. To overcome the difficulties presented by Kenya's inability to agree on alternate KADU and KANU representation on EACSO, the prime ministers of Tanganyika and Uganda were willing to intercede with Mr. Macmillan* to speed the coming of independence to Kenya. KADU, however, frowned on this

* Then Prime Minister of Britain.

move, Ngala describing it as "doing things behind my back." Events finally solved Nyerere's dilemma. There could be no simultaneous independence for the East African territories within a federation. The only practical alternative was independence for each territory separately, followed by federation, if it could be negotiated.

What are the chances of such a federation coming into being? In their politico-constitutional setup the three East African territories differ.

Tanganyika, as a unitary, one-party state, has enlarged the powers of the central government, deprived the chiefs of any administrative authority, circumscribed labor's right to strike, and invested the president with a wide range of authority, making him head of state and of the party, of the army and of the civil service. District councils are now required to take orders from the area commissioners, who are the political nominees of a minister. The president appoints civil servants and orders prosecutions. In Tanganyika, despite its 120 tribes, intertribal dissensions are far less than in Kenya or Uganda, and Nyerere's aim is to break down even further all intertribal barriers, resulting in one single tribe of the Tanganyikan people with one paramount chief, the president. Neither Kenya's tribalism nor regionalism, as embodied in its constitution, has any appeal to a man like Nyerere. The Tanzan union between Tanganyika and Zanzibar will not necessarily speed the coming of an East African federation, but could assist the vague ideal of African unity.

In Kenya, regionalism is tied up with tribalism and the land. KADU, representative of the smaller, principally pastoral non-Kikuyu tribes, sees in regionalism a guarantee of regionally controlled land policies providing an insurance against the thrustful, numerically larger, land-hungry Kikuyu. The constitutional model is Nigeria, divided into four regions, which in turn might be carved out into more regions. Similarly, say some in KADU, why should Kenya's contemplated seven regions not expand with administrative groupings designed more or less on a tribal basis, and in a federation where Uganda, Tanganyika, Northern Rhodesia, and Nyasaland might similarly be administratively rearranged? "We visualize," said a KADU spokesman, "a large state consisting of anything up to thirty or forty regions, and to be known as the Federated States of Africa." This is anathema not only to Nyerere, but to KANU, though it might appeal to the traditionalists and tribalists around the Kabaka of Buganda.

Uganda is a federation in itself. Besides Buganda, it has the three tribal kingdoms of Toro, Bunyoro, and Ankole which, with the chieftainship of Busoga, have been pressing for the federal status conceded to Buganda. Tribal tensions in Uganda, though not as strong as in Kenya, have their counterpart in excessive traditionalist awareness and apprehension, intensified to some extent by the aggressive rivalry between Catholic and Protestant Ugandans. The Baganda (the name for the people of Buganda) are also almost pathologically suspicious of an enlarged federation as likely to submerge the separate personality of their Kabaka in a sea of alien influences. Even so, within itself Uganda is more federal than unitary.

In effect an East African federation would imply a union between unitary Tanganyika, now linked with Zanzibar, federal Uganda, and semi-federal Kenya. While lingering doubts and suspicions of an East African federation persist in some quarters throughout the three territories, there is general recognition that some form of closer collaboration would be beneficial to all and might pave the way for an acceptable type of political federation. Tanganyika, the most loyal of the three to the federal idea, has refrained from putting through any currency or transportation reforms, and has appointed a committee which, with U.N. help, has been studying the pros and cons of federation. Uganda's prime minister, Milton Obote, at first cautiously welcomed federation, but, faced with practical difficulties, his enthusiasm seems to have waned. In Kenya, Tom Mboya expressed the hope that federation would be achieved within a year of Kenya's independence.

Since then the idea of an East African Common Market, discussed by the U.N. Economic Commission for Africa (ECA) at its sixth session in Addis Ababa in February, 1964, has come into being in East Africa. While attempts to preserve the East African Common Market (EACM) have continued after the union of Tanganyika and Zanzibar, the efforts to negotiate an East African Federation have foundered on major issues. Tanganyika (linked with Zanzibar) presses for federal control of foreign affairs and citizenship, but Uganda insists on strong states and a diluted form of federation. Obote has instead suggested the strengthening of the East African Common Services Organization.

Let's take a closer look at East Africa, peering not only into Tanganyika, Uganda, and Kenya, but also Zanzibar.

Tanganyika lies below Uganda and Kenya, and territorially is over four times the size of Uganda, being second only to Nigeria in area among the Commonwealth countries in Africa. Its capital Dar-es-Salaam, or "Haven of Peace," fronts the Indian Ocean and has an Indian look with an Arab veneer. Actually less than 1.5 percent of the country's population is non-African, but of the latter the majority are Asians who figure prominently in trade and business, and are to be found in its political and civic life, as well as in its government offices and commercial houses. Most Asians, both Indians and Pakistanis, appeared to be doing well, but underlying their talk one sensed a brooding uncertainty over their future. As generally in Africa, the Pakistanis, particularly the Ismaili followers of the

Aga Khan, seemed closer to the Africans than the Indians, realizing that their lot was with the Africans and not in between. Nevertheless, the feeling of uncertainty was shared equally by Indians and Pakistanis.

"Africanization is bound to affect us," was their general theme. "Nyerere is reasonable and farsighted. But who's below him? The extremists. Sooner or later he will have to sing to their tune."

Nyerere was equally frank. "Asians are welcome," he explained, "so long as they contribute to Tanganyika's progress. We are in no need of traders and moneylenders. But we want technicians, managerial talent, and sound investors with a stake in the country's prosperity."

Of Tanganyika's 10 million people, some 22,500 are Europeans, and another 120,000 Asians and Arabs. Because of the overwhelming African majority, which is more homogeneous than the Europeans, Asians, and Arabs, and also because the European community in Tanganyika is smaller and less cohesive than its counterpart in Kenya, it was never strictly accurate to describe Tanganyika as a multiracial country. In Kenya, the ratio of Africans to Europeans is about 100 to 1, whereas in Tanganyika it is about 425 to 1. Of the 22,500 Europeans, only about 4,000 could be rated as permanent settlers, and not all are settled on the land. A fair proportion are non-English, comprising a mixture of various nationalities. The Africans in Tanganyika are more cohesive than those in most African territories, for primarily two reasons—the fact that Swahili is almost universally understood throughout the country, and that no one tribe dominates or threatens the others, as do the Kikuyu in Kenya.

I met a few of the white settlers, including Lady Chesham, the American widow of a prominent British farmer who had worked his land in the Kilimanjaro corridor, where several thousand square miles are owned by European farmers. But the white settlements in the Kilimanjaro sector have never approached the scale of the White Highlands in Kenya, and it is doubtful if even 2 percent of the total land of Tanganyika is worked by Europeans. Large sisal plantations, owned by Europeans as also by Asians, flourish along the coast; the Karimjee clan are known locally as the "Sisal Barons."

For a territory covering some 363,000 square miles, Tanganyika is underpopulated. As Nyerere once said: "We all know it is a small country in terms of population and a poor country in terms of resources." The two big deficiencies of Tanganyika are lack of education and lack of economic development.

The territory's economy has expanded since the end of the war, but Tanganyika, like Nyasaland, is not viable on its own. Its national income per head is less than $56 a year and, though its African population has a considerable share in the output and sale of commercial crops like coffee and cotton, the total number of Africans working for wages is under 500,000. At Moshi, in the shadow of Kilimanjaro, I came across the Chagga, one of the most industrious of African peoples, and visited the headquarters of the Kilimanjaro Native Cooperative Union, which provides a superlative example of African enterprise. True, it had a European manager, but the Chagga we spoke to, including Chief Solomon Elinfoo, president of the Chagga council, appeared to be unusually intelligent and enterprising individuals. "The Chagga," observed an Indian acquaintance, "are really quite different from other Africans." I wonder.

Sisal is the most important single economic commodity of Tanganyika, which supplies two-fifths of the world's sisal, but there are very few Africans on the Sisal Growers' Association, which is the managing body. The vast majority of the people live by consuming their own products, and very few of them leave the land for commercial, governmental, or industrial employment. There was some truth in the angry observation of Ksanga Tunbo, former general-secretary of the Tanganyika African Railways' Union, later high commissioner in London, and still later Nyerere's only opponent at the polls for the presidency,* where he fared disastrously. "If you visit the railway head offices in Dar-es-Salaam," he is said to have exclaimed, "you can think you are in Bombay or London."

According to a World Bank mission report of 1961, peasant agriculture is the key to Tanganyika's main development. The problem is one of maintaining the growth of production over a long-term period. Before independence, Tanganyika received grants and loans from the British Colonial Development and Welfare Funds, which since 1959 financed some 20 percent of the government's capital budget, but even with the help of outside subsidies and grants the government was able to spend without further borrowing only about $7.50 a year for each man, woman, and child in the territory, which did not leave room for development on the scale envisaged by Tanganyika's three-year development plan. This called for an outlay of $65.2 million. Nyerere, however keen he initially was on the idea of a political East African Federation, now realizes that Tanganyika would have to pay a heavy economic price for this. Realizing it, he first talked shortly after the Tanzan union of erecting tariff barriers against Tanganyika's neighbors and introducing the territory's own currency, arguing that since it provided a market for Kenya's manufactured goods it failed to attract industrial investment as Kenya and Uganda did. Tanganyika was left shouldering the economic disadvantages. As a result,

---

* He is now resident in Mombasa, from whence he continues to attack Nyerere, and has unsuccessfully attempted to register an opposition party—the People's Convention party—in Tanganyika. Following the military mutiny he was reported to be in detention.

the three East African heads of government—Kenyatta, Obote, and Nyerere —agreed on economic measures to preserve the East African Common Market. These included a system of import quotas among the three territories and the allocation of a number of industries, inferentially to Tanganyika, to bring about more even distribution of industry throughout the whole of East Africa. Nyerere simultaneously announced a new five-year plan calling for investment of £50 million a year with the stress on industry and manufacture. Tanganyika was no longer prepared to be regarded as a reservoir of raw materials content to continue indefinitely her imbalance of trade with Kenya.

Shortly before independence, Nyerere had approached the British Colonial Office and the Treasury for more generous assistance. The plan envisaged an all-around increase in agriculture, mining, and industrial production, the government being particularly anxious to encourage industrial development and foreign investment for this purpose. Additionally, Tanganyika needed money for the compensation of expatriate civil servants after independence. The territory has considerable mineral wealth, including diamonds, gold, lead, and tin, all of which are being produced and are capable of further development. Other minerals in production are copper, silver, gypsum, lead, mica, tin, and tungsten. The basis of the territory's economy could be further expanded by oil, and in recent years the Shell B.P. Company has been prospecting around Kilwa in the southern province, though with no great success. In June, 1963, ENI, the Italian state oil company, signed a contract to build a $14 million refinery in Tanganyika which it is believed will give it exclusive refining rights in the country for some time to come. Shell, Petrofina, Socony Mobil, Texaco, Caltex, and Standard Oil, who had tried for the contract, failed to get it. ENI* draws some of its supplies from Russia, which are said to be cheaper than those from Western sources. The capacity of the Italian plant will be 600,000 tons a year, rising to 700,000. In 1962 consumption in Tanganyika was around 320,000 tons. Tanganyika is given an option to buy up to 50 percent of the shares in the new company set up to run the refinery, which is to be built before the end of 1964.

Nyerere believes that in order to deserve foreign aid a country must make every effort to pull itself up by its bootstraps. This was the argument he used when he approached the British Colonial Office and the Treasury in July–August, 1961, for larger grants and loans before Tanganyika became independent the following December. The British government's initial reaction was cool, which incensed Nyerere. "It seems," he remarked at a press conference in London, "that being moderate means that you do less well than less moderate people . . . Tanganyika's stability

* ENI also later secured a monopoly from the Adoula government in the Congo.

is being used as an argument why it should not get financial help." This was an oblique reference to turbulent Kenya, which over the previous three years had received $33.6 million in loans and $14 million in grants from Britain, while stable and orderly Tanganyika had received $7.4 million in loans and $13.1 million in grants in the same period. Tanganyika's population is around 10 million, compared with Kenya's 8 million. Whitehall relented, and Nyerere returned home with an undertaking from the British government that it would extend to Tanganyika loans, grants, and other assistance up to nearly $67.2 million. The balance was to be made up in part locally and in part by "other sources" like the Rockefeller and Ford foundations, reinforced by what the British government had earlier promised. Tanganyika would receive outright grants totaling nearly $14 million under the Colonial Development and Welfare Funds Scheme, an interest-free loan of $16.8 million to help tide over the compensation plan for expatriate civil servants, and another loan of $8.4 million carrying normal interest charges, to assist in the commutation of pensions for retiring officers. Cash assistance totaling $655,200 would be available for the Tanganyikan army, and Britain undertook to hand over to Tanganyika the assets of the Tanganyika Agricultural Corporation, valued at $2.8 million. Nyerere's moderation had paid. He also came home with promises of aid from the United States and West Germany.

Tanganyika, however, has still a long way to go before it attains economic viability. Though its national income is rising—it was about $523.6 million in the first year after independence—the territory must continue for some years to lean heavily on foreign subsidies in order to maintain and accelerate the pace of its economic development, which again is complicated by the shortage of well-educated Africans.

A year before independence there were under twenty qualified African doctors and only five African lawyers in Tanganyika, at least two of them trained in India. About 40 percent of the children go to primary school, and the number of African children attending secondary school is only around 5,000. Until 1961 there were no facilities for university education in Tanganyika, students going either to the University College of Makerere in Uganda, which specializes in medicine and teaching, or to the Royal Technical College at Nairobi. In 1961 the nucleus of a Tanganyikan university was opened in Dar-es-Salaam with a faculty of law, supplemented later by a faculty of agriculture.* Nyerere's government is giving top priority to education and economic development, and in the first year of independence nearly $14 million was earmarked for educa-

* In 1963 Makerere College in Uganda linked itself with the Royal College in Nairobi and the University College in Dar-es-Salaam to form the University of East Africa.

tion. In Tanganyika, as elsewhere in Africa, missionaries have contributed greatly to the spread of education, helped by the government and the local authorities. Until a year before independence there were three separate school systems catering, respectively, to African, European, and Asian children. These systems have now been integrated into a single system of education throughout the territory.

Why, despite these economic and educational drawbacks, was Tanganyika the first of the three territories of British East Africa to achieve independence? The answer lies mainly in the calculated moderation of one man—Nyerere. As late as 1954 there was not a single African in the nominated legislative council. Seven years later Tanganyika was free.

Julius Nyerere, who is forty-two, is the son of a chief of the small Zanaki tribe. Like many African leaders he started life as a schoolteacher, after securing his diploma in education at Makerere. In 1949, Nyerere went to Edinburgh—he was the first Tanganyikan student to go to a British university—where he took his arts degree and became interested in the problems of colonialism. He is a devout Catholic, is married, and has six children. Nyerere is a tiny man with a gentle voice, a warm manner, and a quick attractive smile. In conversation he gives the impression of sincerity. What did he consider was Tanganyika's major priority? "Raising the economic living standard of our people," he replied. He talked of his plans for stepping up agricultural productivity and developing irrigation, particularly in the Rufiji River basin, which the FAO had already surveyed. There was also room for industrial development, where he would welcome foreign investment. He thought there were great possibilities in the country's mineral wealth, especially in diamonds. He said they should be able to put up cement and plastics factories, plywood mills, and assembly plants for Land-Rovers, and to manufacture aluminum and sheet glass. Since independence, nearly 30 new small industries have been started.

"Do you plan to set up a really multiracial society in independent Tanganyika?" I asked.

Nyerere smiled. "Not a multiracial, but a nonracial society," he replied. Kenneth Kaunda had given me the same reply at Lusaka in Northern Rhodesia.

The British, Nyerere complained gently, had at one time allowed ten seats each in the legislative council to the three main races—the Africans who numbered 9 million, the Europeans who totaled 22,000, and the Asians and others who number about 120,000.

"And they called this parity and multiracialism!" he exclaimed, throwing up his small, expressive hands.

He explained how in 1954 he had founded the Tanganyika African National Union (TANU) mainly as a protest against the extraordinary notion of the Europeans that Tanganyika should be run primarily for their benefit.

"That wasn't so long ago," mused Nyerere. "If we are moving quickly toward independence, it is because of their ultimate good sense and our consistent moderation." He paused and added in his soft voice: "Africa must be governed by Africans for the benefit of Africans."

Did that mean that he would rather do without the collaboration of Asians and Europeans?

"Oh, no," he countered quickly. "But it must be understood that we are the masters of our house."

He spoke of the concept of the African Personality: "Do I believe in it? Emotionally, yes. It gives us a feeling of togetherness."

Nyerere recalled the beginnings of TANU and how African determination, helped by the cooperation of progressive Asians and enlightened Europeans, had enabled Tanganyika to move quickly and peacefully to freedom. He mentioned Amir Jamal, an Asian who at that time held the portfolio of communications, power, and works* in the council of ministers, and Sir Ernest Vasey, then finance minister, whom Nyerere had especially invited from Kenya, where Vasey had also served as finance minister.

Vasey, whom I met briefly, was courageously liberal-minded while in Kenya. He commented on Appa Pant, who had been the Indian commissioner in Nairobi and had fallen foul of the local British authorities, who had insisted on his recall. "Pant," said Vasey, "was not conspiring with the Africans. He was cooperating with them." Amir Jamal was most helpful. Of all the Asians I met in Tanganyika, he struck me as the most sincere and honest in his desire to help in building up the territory on a nonracial basis.

Jamal took me one afternoon to an open-air TANU meeting which Nyerere addressed. Nyerere arrived wearing a brightly patterned bush shirt and was greeted with ululations by the African women in the audience. His wife accompanied him. It was a different Nyerere from the Nyerere I had watched addressing the legislative council. His manner of talking to a mass of his own people was curiously like Nehru's in similar circumstances. He spoke to them as if they were one large family—gesticulating, smiling, joking, and occasionally teasing them. He is a livelier, more intimate speaker than Nehru and has a sense of humor. It was here that I heard for the first time the plaintive strains of "God Bless Africa,"†

* He is now transport minister.

† Known in Rhodesia as "Ishe Komborera Afrika." This famous South African hymn, now the national anthem of Transkei and sung fervently at African nationalist functions, was composed by a Xhosa teacher in 1897.

the anthem of the African people which, although I could not follow the words, I felt most moving.

At that time Nyerere gave no indication of envisaging a one-party state after independence, but he did refer to the fact that there was no opposition to TANU in the legislative council, the only member sitting as an independent having previously been a member of TANU who was refused its ticket in the elections. If he spoke critically of anybody, it was by way of an oblique reference to the overexuberance of certain trade unionists in TANU. I met two of them, both in their twenties—Michael Kamiliza, a forceful speaker and an influential leader of the Tanganyika Federation of Labor, and Jacob Namfua, also an ardent trade unionist. The federation, they said, was pressing for a basic minimum wage, which the government had accepted in principle but not in practice. Apparently Nyerere found it difficult to accept a basic minimum wage with his government anxious to attract foreign investors and committed to giving generous concessions to them. After independence, a new minimum wage structure was introduced on the principle of more pay for harder work, but this was opposed by the president of the Federation of Labor, Victor Mkello, who was promptly detained under the Preventive Detention Act.

In January, 1962, a month after independence, Nyerere suddenly announced his resignation as prime minister on the ground that he could better serve the country by strengthening the links, which had deteriorated, between TANU and the people. At that time this was interpreted in some quarters as denoting a decline in Nyerere's influence over the country and his party. Undoubtedly, some of the more extreme elements in TANU, spearheaded by the militant trade unionists, were beginning to irk Nyerere, whose dramatic decision to resign was, however, motivated by more long-term considerations. Nyerere's broad strategy, it would appear, was to win over the people completely to TANU, thereby paving the way for Tanganyika to be a republic, and for public opinion to accept the concept of a one-party state with overwhelming powers centralized in the president, who would simultaneously be head of state and head of the government.

Exactly a year after the declaration of independence, in December, 1962, Tanganyika was proclaimed a republic, with Nyerere as president and Rashidi Kawawa, who had succeeded Nyerere in the office of prime minister, as vice-president. A month later Nyerere announced that steps would be taken for the statutory recognition of a one-party system in Tanganyika. This, he said, had been approved by TANU's national executive, and he justified it on the ground that the overwhelming electoral support for TANU virtually ruled out the possibility of interparty contests. Electoral procedure would accordingly be revised so as to make it possible for more than one candidate to contest an election—not on an interparty basis, but on an individual basis. This seeming concession is, however, fictitious, since under the new constitution each parliamentary candidate is to be linked with a presidential candidate, the one endorsing the other, so that the pro-TANU or anti-TANU leanings of a candidate are clearly discernible to the voter.

"Inasmuch as the people recognize only one party," declared the president, "the laws of the country must recognize only one party." Nyerere's own intention in making Tanganyika a one-party state might conceivably be to keep the extremists at bay and the moderates in power. So long as Nyerere dominates the political scene, this is possible. Kawawa, a once-militant trade unionist, is close to him, and has loyally echoed and endorsed Nyerere's views on the labor extremists. In September, 1962, the Preventive Detention Act, which empowers the government to hold individuals "endangering the security of the state" in preventive custody, with no right of appeal, was passed while Kawawa was prime minister. But where is the guarantee that a future president might not be proextremist and exercise his authoritarian powers sweepingly?

The president is indeed armed with overwhelming authority. Nyerere has disclaimed any intention of dictatorship and insists that what the country needs is leadership, but the difference between the two concepts is marginal and could be invisible. Besides being head of state and head of the government, the president is commander-in-chief of the armed forces, with full executive authority over the civil services, while constitutionally he is not bound to accept the advice of his cabinet, whom he appoints and reshuffles, as he has done. "Our conception of the president's office," says Nyerere, "is incompatible with the theory that the public services are and ought to be impartial. . . . We cannot afford the luxury of administrators who are neutral." The president has no legislative powers other than under act of parliament, but he can summon, prorogue, and dissolve parliament, though its dissolution would involve presidential elections. But in a one-party state the president must necessarily owe allegiance to the party, whose head again is Nyerere. Similarly, the judiciary is constitutionally free from political pressure, but the president could, in the public interest, order or forbid prosecutions.

Is Nyerere then planning to be a dictator? I do not think so. I think he genuinely believes that with these powers he can remove all obstacles and accelerate the pace of development in the twenty or more years which he should normally enjoy in his elevated seat of authority. To some extent, judging by such measures as the rapid acceleration of Africanization, particularly his anti-Asian drive, Nyerere is pushed by the extremists. He has the moderate man's failing of dealing with criticism by adopting his critics' policies, but whether this will stave off trouble or precipitate it depends on how far the president can control and carry with him his more important colleagues, the party, and the country. Ultimately, it will depend upon whether Nyerere or the extremists are the pacemakers. A striking and significant illustration of Nyerere's inclination to follow the line of *most* resistance was his comparatively gentle attitude in January, 1964, to the military malcontents whom he quelled with British military aid which he requested, but whose demands for the replacement of British officers by Tanganyikan personnel he conceded. This is typical of Nyerere's technique of making the best of both worlds—a gambit which might ultimately land him into serious difficulties, if not disaster.

Nyerere's close colleagues, some of whom I met, struck me then as moderate and practical-minded men. Kawawa, who is thirty-six, is well informed on international trade and has traveled fairly widely, visiting India among other countries. Nsilo Swai, now minister of development planning, I have known for some years, having met him first when he was in India studying for his economics degree at Delhi University. He is warm, friendly, and knowledgeable, and a most agreeable companion. Shortly after Nyerere resigned the prime ministry, Nsilo, who was then minister for commerce and industry, was appointed Tanganyika's chief representative to the United Nations, a switch which some interpreted as virtual political exile. In March, 1963, Nyerere, as president, reshuffled the cabinet and brought him in again. Another minister close to the president is Oscar Kambona, now foreign minister, who presided very skillfully over the Afro-Asian Solidarity Conference at Moshi in February, 1963, and who acted with more decision than Nyerere did in the military mutiny. Tanganyika is one of the main bases for activities directed against South Africa and Portugal. But Nyerere is nobody's stooge abroad. Though the host country at the Moshi conference, Tanganyika separated itself from the attacks on Israel and the U.N.

Like Nyerere, Kambona was once a schoolteacher, and later studied law at the Inner Temple, London, though he did not qualify as a barrister. Like many African leaders he has a left-wing past but it is absurd to label him a Communist. Kambona is more radical than Nyerere and has differed with him on some important issues. He stands for Pan-Africanism and is skeptical of the President's efforts to build up a multiracial state in Tanganyika. Kambona was not enthusiastic about Nyerere's announcement made shortly before the military mutiny that there would be equal rights in the civil service for all Tanganyikans irrespective of race, and it may well be that the directive influenced the Tanganyikan soldiers who misunderstood it to mean the end of Africanization. Kambona's eagerness to recognize the people's republic in Zanzibar was stayed by Nyerere, who delayed recognition by over a week.

Whether the Zanzibar upheaval on January 12 directly influenced the mutiny on January 20 of the First Battalion of the Tanganyika Rifles stationed at Colito, six miles from Dar-es-Salaam, is not clear. The appearance of Okello, the self-styled "field marshal" who led the Zanzibar revolt at Dar-es-Salaam two days before the Colito mutiny provoked speculation as to whether there was a link between the two episodes. Undoubtedly the spectacle of a successful armed uprising against the sultan's government encouraged emulation elsewhere. Dissatisfaction over the economic results of independence which many Africans had believed would overnight catapult them into positions of comfort and authority provoked the flare-up. Rising unemployment intensified the frustration. On January 21 the Second Battalion of the Tanganyika Rifles mutinied at Tabora.

During these two critical days Nyerere with his Vice-President Kawawa chose to go into hiding. "I am not prepared to face an angry mob armed with rifles," Nyerere was said to have confided to a friend before slipping away. The spectacle of the head of state disappearing from the scene was hardly calculated to enhance the prestige of a civil administration faced by a military insurrection. Nyerere's default was Kambona's opportunity. Chance as well as courage made him the hero of the mutiny. Assuming charge of the situation he countermanded a request made by minister of the interior Job Lusinde for Kenya African troops and instead backed Nyerere, who had emerged from hiding, in an appeal for British troops. Royal Marine commandos were landed from the British carrier *Centaur* which was standing off Dar, and the mutiny was quickly quelled. Nyerere in turn endorsed Kambona's settlement with the rebels which promised them pay increases and the replacement of British officers by Africans. The mutineers were persuaded to return to barracks. During their brief insurrection some of the mutineers from Colito had marched into Dar-es-Salaam, and with their arrival hooligan elements in the mob started looting and pillaging Asian shops. In an adjacent village the Arabs were the principal victims.

Nyerere bemoaned "the most grievous shame" of the army mutiny but his own image was badly tarnished in the confrontation. He had run away from a crisis—a tragic reflection of his tendency to run away from solutions when these were assailed by his critics. He was also overwhelmed by the "shame" of having asked for British military aid to quell the mutiny, and at the meeting of African Unity Organization (OAU) countries which met at Dar-es-Salaam in the second week of February he tried to erase that embarrassment by calling for African troops to replace the British. The conference, which was attended by the representatives of thirty-three African nations, set up a twelve-member committee to consider the proposal. At the same time Nyerere declared that there was no evidence to suggest that the mutiny in Tanganyika was "inspired by outside forces, either Communist or imperialist, or that they spearheaded a popular revolt." He was also cautious in his reference to British military personnel who had been kept on after independence, arguing that the question had to be considered in the light of Tanganyika's geographical position which was ideally sited to be a base and a corridor for the African rebels in Mozambique and South Africa.

Is Kambona the coming strong man of Tanganyika? Will he be the rival for power or the complement in office of Nyerere? Kambona could have appropriated power during the mutiny in the absence of both Nyerere and Kawawa but he prudently refrained from doing so. This does not necessarily imply that at some future stage he may not be tempted to establish his preeminence, the more so since as the first organizing secretary of TANU in 1954 and later as its secretary-general in 1960 he knows the workings of the party machine. Nyerere and Kambona both come from chieftain families. Kambona, however, like Kaunda, is a Nyasa by ancestry, and shares the pride and ambition of the highlanders. He was suspected along with Kenya's home minister, Oginga Odinga, of a hand in the Zanzibar upheaval, and is also leftist-inclined, as indeed are most African leaders. Kambona's relations with the astute Chinese ambassador, Ho Ying, are particularly close, and he helped to set up the Tanganyika News Agency with technical assistance from the Czech News Agency. Both Kambona and Odinga have denied any association with the Zanzibar uprising.

Before the revolution the extremists were not within the inner circle but on the outer periphery of the party. It may be that they will draw nearer the center as Kambona increases in power and prestige within Tanganyika and is assisted by radical pressures from outside. Significantly Nyerere referred in his broadcast after the mutiny to the detention and arrest of some trade union leaders for conspiring with the ringleaders of the mutiny. Although this brought apologies from the Tanganyikan Federation of Labor it is an interesting pointer to the direction in which the political wind is blowing.

Like many African territories, Uganda is an artificial creation welded by the British into one loose unit which includes four kingdoms: Buganda, occupying the south with its base on the northern shore of Lake Victoria, and the three kingdoms of Bunyoro, Ankole, and Toro, covering the whole of the western province. The other two provinces are the northern and the eastern, the latter containing the paramount chieftaincy of Busoga. The Nile broadly bisects Uganda, in the process dividing the Nilotic and Hamitic people, who largely inhabit the northern and eastern provinces, from the Bantu population of Buganda and the western province.

The welding of Uganda into one unit took place roughly in three stages, beginning with the declaration of a British protectorate over Buganda in 1894. This was followed two years later by extending the protectorate to Bunyoro, Toro, Ankole, and Busoga, followed in the early years of the twentieth century by the absorption of the rest of the country. Uganda spreads like a square saucer astride the equator. The name "Uganda" is a corrupted form of Buganda, which the British devised to christen their sphere of influence in the belief that it was necessary for Britain to control the headwaters of the Nile in order to protect Egypt and safeguard the Suez Canal route to Britain's Far Eastern trading centers.

Speke had discovered the source of the Nile in 1862 in Lake Victoria, where he had earlier suspected it was sited. Lake Victoria is Africa's largest, and Speke had first reached its southern shores in 1858, parting company with Richard Burton by Lake Tanganyika. In 1862 his companion was James Grant, and, approaching Uganda from the south, he entered the kingdom of Buganda, then ruled by Kabaka Mutesa I.* Thirteen years later the American explorer, H. M. Stanley, visited Mutesa I in Buganda and was much impressed by Mutesa's interest in Christianity. Stanley's writings in the London *Daily Telegraph* encouraged Christian missionaries to go to Buganda, the first of them being the Church Missionary Society, which arrived in 1877 to be followed shortly after by the Catholic "White Fathers." The Protestants were more successful than their Catholic counterparts,† who for a while withdrew southward. From this early rivalry stems the conflict between Catholics and Protestants which was to extend into the secular field. The Moslems entered the fray later.

Mutesa's successor, Mwanga, was not as cordial as his father to the Christian missionaries and opposed the establishment of the British protectorate. He was deposed in 1897 and succeeded by the infant Kabaka Daudi Chwa, father of the present ruler, His Highness Edward William Frederick David Walugembe Luwangula Mutebi, Kabaka Mutesa II. To his British friends the present Kabaka is known as "King Freddie."

Because the British contact, secular and religious, with Uganda was first made through Buganda, that kingdom initially enjoyed a special status which it managed with fair success to preserve even with the coming of independence. The political development of Uganda revolves around the stubborn attempt of Buganda to retain its predominance not only among the four kingdoms, but in Uganda as a whole. King Freddie's efforts to

* The four kingdoms are headed respectively by the Kabaka of Buganda, the Omukamu of Bunyoro, the Omukamu of Toro, and the Omugabe of Ankole. The paramount chief of Busoga is known as the Kybazinga of Busoga.

† The Kabakas are Anglican but some say that the majority of Bagandans today are Catholic.

rock the independence boat, unless Buganda's independence were assured and safeguarded, delayed Uganda's freedom, though ultimately he was unable to prevent it.

In a way Buganda's predominance is as artificial as Uganda's unity, for both hang today on the slender thread of a coalition government within which traditionalism cannot survive without the support of the growing progressive elements in and outside Buganda, and vice versa. But in the long run it is likely that the cards will be stacked heavily against the Kabaka. Traditionalism, even within Buganda, is a wasting asset.

The British were caught in a web of their own creation, for by pampering Buganda, which appeared to them more friendly and progressive than the once preeminent Bunyoro, they elevated Buganda to a distinctive status which quite naturally the Kabakas were later unwilling to forego. Of the so-called Lacustrine kingdoms lying between the oval of lakes stretching from Lake Kyoga south to Lake Tanganyika, the northern wedge, containing Buganda, Bunyoro, Toro, and Ankole, was absorbed into Uganda. For about 300 years until the middle of the nineteenth century Bunyoro, with its center in the western region of Uganda, was predominant, but its supremacy was successfully challenged by up-and-coming Buganda. Gradually the twenty or so kingdoms of the northern Lacustrine area were merged into the four kingdoms along with the paramount chieftaincy of Busoga.

Britain's early relations with Buganda and the encouragement she gave to the latter's expansionist tendencies were to color the latter-day history of Uganda. Buganda's traditional institutions were preserved, but modified to meet the new circumstances and demands. Each of the four kingdoms was invested with a quasi-parliamentary system, but Buganda, which was more cohesive and more advanced than the other three, was endowed with a ministerial system and a parliament known as the Lukiko. The assemblies functioning in Bunyoro, Toro, and Ankole* have only the authority of the district councils operating elsewhere in the country. In 1900 Britain signed an agreement with the leading Baganda chiefs in Buganda—Kabaka Daudi Chwa was a minor—and later with the chiefs of the other three kingdoms. The agreement with Buganda placed that kingdom on a special footing.

In the so-called four Agreement Kingdoms are the Baganda, Banyoro, Batoro, and Banyankole tribes who belong to the Bantu group, and are distinct from the Nilotic and Hamitic peoples who inhabit the north and east. In the north is also a small pocket of primitive people known as the Karamojong. Roughly, while the Bantu are farmers, the tribes of the

---

* In Bunyoro and Toro the assembly is known as the Rukarato. In Ankole it is called the Eishengyero.

north and east are herdsmen, consisting mainly of a pastoral, cattle-rearing people.

Under the 1900 agreement, which was negotiated on behalf of Britain by Sir Harry Johnston, the principle of freehold tenure of land was introduced in Buganda. Johnston also agreed that half the area of Buganda should be owned by the Baganda chiefs, his idea probably being to counterbalance the influence of the Kabaka and the people by that of the chiefs, leaving Britain in a position to wield authority in both camps. The agreement additionally gave formal recognition to Buganda's annexation of a large area of land captured from Bunyoro in the course of a joint British-Baganda expedition to secure Buganda against attack. This is the genesis of the Lost Counties dispute which was to be a recurring source of contention between Buganda and Bunyoro, and still is.*

There are six Lost Counties, two of which the Molson Commission in May, 1962, recommended should be transferred to Bunyoro. The Kabaka has so far ignored the recommendation. The prime minister, Milton Obote, who heads a coalition government with the Kabaka's party, the Kabaka Yekka (Kabaka Only), as its junior partner, had indicated that a referendum would be held in the two countries in October, 1963.† This may well snap the tenuous ties between Obote's Uganda People's Congress (UPC) and the Kabaka Yekka.

If the main obstacle to Uganda's freedom in the past was the clash between the traditionalists anxious to preserve their privileges and the nationalists eager to assert their rights, the attainment of independence seems likely for some time at least to inflame rather than ease this prickly problem. For the problem has not been solved, but transferred from the lap of the British government to that of the rulers of independent Uganda. Independence became feasible only when, by a series of compromises, it was possible to attain a state of balance—which may prove to be temporary—between the conflicting claims of the traditionalists and the nationalists by inducing a coalition between Obote's fairly radical UPC and the conservative Kabaka Yekka. A more normal and logical coalition would have been one between the Kabaka Yekka and the Catholic-dominated Democratic party headed by Benedicto Kiwanuka, a barrister who comes from the Masaka district of Buganda, and is less radical than Obote. But Kiwanuka deeply offended the pride and vanity of the Kabaka by defying his order that no Baganda should register for the March, 1961, elections, where Kiwanuka emerged successful and became leader of the house. The elections were the first general elections to be held in Uganda.

* At one time British officials planned to merge all the western kingdoms in Buganda. This was stopped, but not before Buganda had absorbed large areas of Bunyoro in its territory.

† This has been postponed.

I met Kiwanuka at Kampala and thought he looked relaxed, though I had heard him described as impulsive and peppery. He gave up a lucrative legal practice to devote himself to building up his party and in that sense could be described as capable of self-sacrifice. He struck me as hard-working and not without a sense of humor. He was bitterly critical of the Kabaka, whose demand for secession made in 1960 he described as "absurd." He thought that Sir Andrew Cohen, one of the most liberal governors of Uganda, had unnecessarily inflated the Kabaka's prestige and consolidated his position by sending him into exile in 1953, when the Kabaka refused to cooperate with Whitehall in developing Uganda as a unitary state, instead demanding independence for Buganda within a stated period. Kiwanuka also dismissed as "unthinkable" the claim of the Kabaka's supporters that he should be head of an independent Uganda. Later this exotic demand was bypassed by the simple expedient of emphasizing that, so long as Uganda did not declare itself a republic within the Commonwealth, it would not be incongruous for the Kabaka to head it. In September, 1963, a constitutional amendment bill was introduced in the Ugandan parliament providing, among other things, for the replacement of the governor-general by a Ugandan head of state. The powers which the head of state will exercise will be the same as those of the outgoing governor-general. Uganda achieved its new constitutional status on October 9, 1963, when it ceased to be a dominion without becoming a republic. As an independent, sovereign state its status is somewhat similar to that of Malaya, thereby encouraging a national outlook and preserving traditionalism. The Kabaka was elected Uganda's first president. In that office his powers are as circumscribed as were those of the governor-general, thereby making the prime minister the real ruler of the country.

I asked Kiwanuka whether he stood for a unitary or a federal government.

"We have nearly thirty tribes in our country," he explained, "and in the colonial period tribal patterns have been preserved. But we are moving away from the conservative tribalism, as exemplified for instance by the Kabaka, to a new nationalism built on a closer community of interests. Personally I favor a unitary state. It would be more efficient and cheaper to run. But if the people prefer a federal system, with the component states on an equal basis, the Democratic party would accept it."

At the London conference of October, 1961, it was announced that Uganda would be granted internal self-government on March 1, 1962, and independence on October 9 of the same year. There had been a small legislative council established as far back as 1921, but it contained not a single African. This state of affairs had lasted until 1945, when three Africans were appointed as government nominees. Later a number were indirectly elected, but until 1958 there were no direct elections for African representative members. Three years later, in March, 1961, the council was virtually democratic.

At the conference in London a broad agreement was reached with the consent of Kiwanuka, Obote, and the Kabaka that Buganda should have a federal relationship with the rest of Uganda, but that the legislature should be unitary in character, with a single national assembly of elected members. It was however left to the Lukiko, or parliament, of Buganda to decide whether elections from that kingdom to the central legislature should be direct or indirect. In turn, Buganda adopted a compromise not dissimilar to the one agreed for Uganda as a whole, whose constitutional system would be both federal and unitary. Buganda's solution was that the twenty-one elected members allotted to it out of a total of eighty-two members in the national assembly should be chosen by the Lukiko sitting as an electoral college, but that sixty-eight of the Lukiko's hundred members would be elected by universal franchise, the rest consisting of twenty Saza chiefs, six ministers elected by the Lukiko, and six nominees of the Kabaka. The Saza chiefs would have no vote in choosing the Lukiko's representatives in the national assembly.

A politician opposed to the Kabaka echoed Kiwanuka's criticism but went further: "Cohen," he said, "needlessly enhanced the Kabaka's prestige. Now the British government in Whitehall have gone one step further. Under the guise of being a constitutional monarch, the Kabaka is actually armed with greater powers and will still enjoy a special relationship with an independent Uganda government."

It may or may not be so. Time will tell.

Kiwanuka, knowing that the Lukiko would never elect him to the national assembly, allowed himself, surprisingly, to be fobbed off by the soupçon of a provision for nine especially elected members, hoping probably that he might figure in the list. But he must surely have realized that unless his party won the last preindependence elections in April, 1962, his chances were slim. Kiwanuka lost.

Two contentious issues still remained to be settled after the London conference of October, 1961—the first an angry claim by the three kingdoms of Toro, Bunyoro, and Ankole to share the same federal status permitted Buganda; the second, Bunyoro's demand for the return of the Lost Counties. Whitehall decided to leave these two unsettled problems in Uganda to the new independent government. They became Uganda's headache, not Britain's.*

* Uganda's complex constitution provides for a single legislature at the Center, one fully federal kingdom (Buganda), three less federal kingdoms (Ankole, Bunyoro, and Toro), a new federal territory (Busoga), and eight administrative districts with *no* federal powers.

In March, 1962, Uganda achieved the status of a self-governing territory, with Kiwanuka as its first chief minister. Some seven weeks later Uganda went to the polls for its last preindependence elections. In the interval Milton Obote's UPC had entered into an electoral pact with the Kabaka's Kabaka Yekka, which had won an almost total victory in February's Lukiko election, thus ensuring twenty-one safe seats for the Kabaka's party in the national assembly. For the remaining sixty-one constituencies, the Democratic party put up fifty-nine candidates and the UPC fifty-eight. The elections ended in a sweeping victory for Obote, whose party captured thirty-nine seats. Many of the Democratic party leaders lost their seats and Kiwanuka, ostracized by the Kabaka in Buganda, had no hope of being elected among the nine additional members who virtually constituted a pocket borough of the ruling party. B. K. Bataringaya became the leader of the opposition Democratic party in the national assembly.

Milton Obote, who is thirty-eight—he is four years younger than Kiwanuka—comes from the northern province, which in olden days had suffered from the ravages of the Baganda. Unlike the western province, the northern province has no rigid tribal system, which might account for Obote's progressive outlook. He is said to have started life as the family goatherd until a spear wound put an end to that career. He began his schooling at the age of twelve, inevitably took to teaching, but the turning point in his career was his five-year stay in Kenya during the Mau Mau emergency, where he met Tom Mboya. For part of his stay there Obote worked as a building gang laborer. He is tough and efficient, with a rasping voice, and has a strong fiber of realism and calculation in his political makeup. This perhaps influenced his decision to join hands with the Kabaka for purposes which might ultimately prove to be temporary. His Kenya associations pointed to him as a strong advocate of an East African Federation, but Obote's attitude is now more cautious. He would welcome a federation but he is not committed to it. On the contrary, he emphasizes the need for Uganda to improve its relations with its northern and western neighbors. In October, 1963, Obote warned that federations are not made "by a stroke of the pen."

Between Obote and the Kabaka there is little in common, either temperamentally or ideologically. Though inclined at times to be volatile, Obote has none of the theatrical extravagances or extremism of "King Freddie." He has socialist leanings, but has declared himself against the nationalization of the coffee, tea, and cotton plantations on which Uganda's economy largely hinges. For the moment he can no more do without the Kabaka than the Kabaka can do without him, but theirs is a formal alliance, as both realize, and with the extension of a federal status to Bunyoro, Ankole, Toro, and Busoga, and a settlement by referendum of the problem of the Lost Counties, it is not inconceivable that Buganda's present primacy will be hedged and circumscribed by the rise of the other traditionalist kingdoms, on the one hand, and the growth of nationalist forces, on the other. Today the Baganda constitute nearly 30 percent of Uganda's African population, and Buganda produces some 90 percent of the entire territory's coffee, commanding almost half of Uganda's revenue from foreign trade. Of Uganda's 6,500,000 people the Baganda number nearly 2 million and the vast majority are fiercely loyal to the Kabaka. By far the most homogeneous and advanced of Uganda's tribes, the Baganda also occupy the central core of the country, the kingdom of Buganda covering one-fourth of the territory's total area of some 94,000 square miles. Buganda's relationship to Uganda is comparable to that of Katanga to the Congo. The necessity of keeping this kingdom, which is the country's economic hub and commercial center, within the complex of Uganda induced to a large extent Obote's formal alliance with the Kabaka. Though the Kabaka still poses a political threat, Obote's skillful handling of his own party and his cabinet has resulted in weakening the position of the Kabaka Yekka within the coalition government. By mid-1963 he had weaned away the loyalty of some members of the party and the government to the UPC, which now controls fifty-six members in the national assembly of ninety-one (consisting of eighty-two elected and nine especially elected members).

Uganda's educational and health services are remarkably widespread and, though territorially the smallest of the three former British East African mainland territories, Uganda is economically the most advanced in terms of African progress, and despite its medley of tribes has shown an unusual capacity for compromise and balance. Of its main export crops, which are cotton and coffee, the overwhelming percentage is produced by African peasant farmers. Uganda is largely self-supporting in food. Because of its dependence on cotton and coffee, the country's economy is unusually sensitive to world market conditions, and more recently attempts have been made to diversify production by the introduction of tea and cocoa. Uganda's future undoubtedly lies with argiculture, and in 1961 the International Bank for Reconstruction and Development recommended a comprehensive five-year plan involving an expenditure of $150 million, with the emphasis on the development of agriculture. The Uganda government has since then expanded the scheme to a $250-million five-year development plan covering the same period, mid-1961 to mid-1966. It includes $198.8 million for development in the public sector and $53.2 million in the private sector. This capital expenditure, it is calculated, should increase Uganda's national income by about 4 percent a year. Obote reiterated the government's intention not to nationalize privately owned plantations and industries, but warned that higher taxation might be necessary. In a foreword to the government paper, the prime minister admitted that the plan fell "pitifully short" of what was needed to secure in a reasonable period of time an adequate standard of living for the people of the country. By far the larger section of the plan, involving an expenditure of $75,040,000 by 1966, covers commodity production, commerce, and tourism. Another $42 million is earmarked for roads, railways, airports, communications, and power; $30.8 million for social services, mainly education and health; and about $22.4 million for local authority schemes, including water supplies and housing.

Envy of Buganda's prosperity and distinctive status has given an edge to competition in other areas. Obote's home district, Lango, today provides many of the country's teachers, technicians, and professional men. Two comparatively new cadres are those of the salaried worker and the scientific farmer, a product of the fairly rapid spread of education. As the non-Baganda areas progress, they will act as a curb on the independent and traditionalist spirit of Buganda, which in the developing conditions of Africa as a whole cannot long sustain its high-handedness.

"We have been free from the curse of white settlers with which Kenya is saddled," remarked a Ugandan at Kampala, now the capital instead of neighboring Entebbe. "But the Kabaka is our white settler problem."

With Makerere and Magdalene College, Cambridge, as his educational background, and an honorary captainship in the Grenadier Guards as a social cachet, forty-year-old "King Freddie" is well aware of his own personal and political importance, though the latter has to some extent been neutralized by elevating him as head of state. But time has a habit of overtaking persons and politics. It threatens to overtake both Uganda and the Kabaka. Two developments point that way, the first being an accretion of strength to the nationalist forces as against the traditionalist elements, the second the chain of military mutinies in East Africa in January, 1964.

As Obote has grown in political strength, his relations with his coalition partner, the Kabaka Yekka group, have become more tenuous, and his hint of one-party rule in the offing has not eased their mounting disquiet. Answering a question by a Kabaka Yekka member in parliament in February, 1964, Obote observed pointedly that opposition to his own advocacy of one-party rule came mainly from Buganda, where the Kabaka Yekka believed in one-party rule for Buganda but not for the rest of Uganda, so that it could select the party of its choice with which to form a coalition government for the whole country. "This," affirmed Obote while refusing to resile from his advocacy of one party rule, "is the negation of national unity and a serious source of instability." Having weaned away the loyalty of some Kabaka Yekka members to the UPC and having clipped King Freddie's wings by elevating him as president, where his powers are effectively circumscribed, Obote has shrewdly left himself more room for maneuver.

The impact of the military mutiny which was triggered by happenings in adjacent Tanganyika and roughly followed the same pattern is, however, less calculable. Insofar as it might hasten the trend toward a form of closer union, such as the East African Federation, it should whittle down some of Obote's doubts and hesitations, but simultaneously the move toward unity within Uganda should greatly circumscribe the vaulting ambitions of the Kabaka now hamstrung in a seat of nebulous authority. A joint defense command, involving the creation of a single defense force and command, even ahead of a political federation, has been mooted, but the difficulty here is how soon it would be practicable to replace British commanders by British advisers to African commanders. Even overmilitant Ghana could not logically object to this arrangement since she has set an example in welcoming a large joint services mission (for training purposes) from Britain. Kenya, also touched by the chain of mutinies, is having second thoughts.

In Uganda the army mutiny was confined to Jinja, fifty miles east of Kampala, where it broke out on January 23 when the 1st Battalion of the Uganda Rifles mutinied, demanding, like their Tanganyikan counterparts, more pay and the removal of British officers. As in Tanganyika, the Uganda minister for interior affairs, Felix Onama, first intervened but met with an unceremonious reception from the mutineers who locked him in the guardroom until he had signed certain concessions. Obote, however, called for British troops, some 450 of whom were flown from Kenya. They rapidly disarmed the mutineers; an unspecified number of the two companies involved in the mutiny were dismissed and sent to their homes.

The Uganda mutiny was not on the scale of the insurrection which shook Tanganyika for four days. Nonetheless it had its uneasy reverberations throughout East Africa, and more particularly in Uganda where the movement toward one-party rule, also visible in Kenya, has gathered strength.

In Zanzibar, which had no army, it was not a military mutiny but a political upheaval. The name Zanzibar, like Timbuktu, has a storybook flavor. Known the world over as "the island of cloves," the former British protectorate of Zanzibar consists actually of two main islands—the other is Pemba—and a cluster of tiny dots spread over the Indian Ocean, some twenty-five miles from the African mainland.

Zanzibar, as I saw it almost exactly three years before its minuscule revolution, bubbled with political uncertainty, but the atmosphere was serene. We flew there from Dar-es-Salaam in a small six-seater Dominie flying low over the palms and across the blue-green sea. Zanzibar is muggy and humid, even more so than Dar. But with its maze of crooked little streets flanked by old houses with massive wooden front doors studded with brass, its picturesque variegated population, its coffeehouses and lush countryside, Zanzibar seemed an isle of enchantment, lazy, languid, enveloped in its own *mañana*. The old Swahili saying, *Haraka haraka haina baraka* ("Great haste brings no blessing") once reflected the island's mood. Beneath this placid surface, however, simmered a new political restiveness generated from the mainland and it exploded in the overthrow of the administration of the sultan in January, 1964.

Zanzibar has an old history, and is among the last fragments of an Arab empire which in the days of the sailing ships stretched over a large area of East Africa. The Arab dhows ranging the waters between Zanzibar and Dar-es-Salaam have an air of romance and mystery. The earliest colonizers are believed to have been the Shirazis of Persia, who came to Zanzibar and Pemba nearly a thousand years ago. There are very few pure-blooded Shirazis extant, intermarriage between the indigenous Africans and them leaving small traces of the original Persian colonizers. But I did see in a street in Zanzibar a group of four lovely golden-skinned children who I was told where Shirazis.

Save Ethiopia, the two islands have a longer history than any African state. Zanzibar claims to have existed as a state when the English were engaged in the Wars of the Roses.

When the Portuguese arrived in the sixteenth century the Arabs were well established in the islands and, with the Portuguese, were soon engaged in the lucrative slave traffic, which until the eighteenth century displaced the old trade in spices with trade in "black ivory." Even today in the eyes of many local Africans the Arab carries the taint of slave trader. In 1890 Zanzibar became a British protectorate, in effect a British-protected Arab colony, with the sultan of Zanzibar enjoying certain rights and privileges, including his own red flag. Originally a colony of the Sultanate of Oman on the Persian Gulf, it was once intimately connected with India, and until recently its clove trade was largely with that country. On the death of Imam Said of Oman in 1856* his sons divided his empire, the elder son, Thawain, becoming the ruler of Oman and Majid, the younger, sultan of Zanzibar. Culturally, the island was predominantly Islamic and Arabic.

Zanzibar, in effect, was thus an Arab outpost in the Indian Ocean resentful of any attempts by the African mainland, such as were first made unsuccessfully by the Tanganyikan African National Union on behalf of the Afro-Shirazi party (ASP) in the June elections of 1961, to influence

---

* He introduced the clove tree into Zanzibar and Pemba. It is chiefly grown in Pemba.

the course of its internal politics. While the Arabs in the once much-disputed Coastal Strip in Kenya* favored its return to Zanzibar, the Africans in the Strip generally regarded themselves as Kenyans. Another Strip on the Tanganyika coast belonging to Zanzibar was bought outright for Tanganyika.

If Kampala and Dar-es-Salaam wear an Indian look, the Arab presence was unmistakable in Zanzibar. A picturesque reminder of this were the Arab coffee vendors in the street, with their tall brass pots, who announced their ware by clicking together two tiny cups as if they were castanets. Yet compared with a total African population in the two islands of some 230,000, the Arabs number only 47,000, with 24,000 Asians and 500 Europeans, most of them holding official appointments. The area of Zanzibar is 640 square miles and that of Pemba 380 square miles.

Arab political predominance stemmed from many facts. The Shirazis came to Zanzibar before them, but today count for very little. The Arabs, with a sultan who was predominantly Arab—he was said to have an admixture of African blood—regarded themselves as the ruling clan.† The Arabs generally have intermarried to such an extent with the Africans that it is difficult to distinguish one from the other. With over 90 percent of the population Moslem, Islam provides another cohesive link. Zanzibar's national language is Swahili, which is spoken from the east coast to the Congo River near Stanleyville. Though a Bantu language, about one-third of its vocabulary is Arabic. I was interested to note that it also contained some Hindusthani words: *baraf* for ice, *cha* for tea. The landowning class was predominantly Arab, while the business community was largely Asian. The Africans were mostly squatters on the clove *shambas* (farms), supplementing their meager earnings by growing subsistence crops on the bare spaces and by fishing.

Some 80 percent of Zanzibar's foreign earnings depend on one crop, cloves, cultivated on estates until recently owned either by Arabs or Asians. Zanzibar also exports large quantities of copra and other coconut-palm products. As in many other parts of Africa, attempts are being made to diversify the crops, and cocoa and citrus have been grown successfully. The seas around these islands teem with fish. Yet economically Zanzibar is in poor shape. National income is barely keeping pace with population

* Leased in 1895 by the protectorate to the Kenya government at a rental of $47,000 a year. It was under the sovereignty of the sultan but administered by Kenya. On the date of Kenya's independence it was agreed at the London conference in October, 1963, that the Strip would become part of Kenya.

† The ruler who fled during the revolution of January, 1964, was thirty-four-year-old Seyyid Jamshid bin Abdulla, who succeeded his father, Seyyid Sir Abdulla bin Khalifa, in July, 1963. He was said to be in favor of the pro-Arab Zanzibar Nationalist party.

increase. Investment is proportionately lower in Zanzibar than in any other part of East Africa. Though Zanzibar receives the services on an agency basis of the East African Common Services Organization, it seems inevitable that at some stage it will enter into an enlarged East African Federation comprising not only Tanganyika, Uganda, and Kenya, but probably Nyasaland and Northern Rhodesia. What might be construed as a first step was Zanzibar's union with Tanganyika following the January upheaval.

The constitutional history of Zanzibar follows that of most East African countries, beginning in 1926 with the establishment of a legislative council containing not a single African member. In 1956 the legislature was enlarged to include twelve unofficial members, including six elected. This was Zanzibar's first election and resulted in a victory for the ASP, led by Sheik Abeid Karume,* which routed the Arab-dominated Zanzibar Nationalist party (ZNP) under Sheik Ali Muhsin. In 1959 there emerged a new party, the Zanzibar and Pemba Peoples party (ZPPP), which is predominantly African and commands wide support in Pemba. Its leader is Mohammed Shamte Hamadi, who once belonged to the ASP but broke away from it after differences with Karume. The ASP, whose object was to unite the two main classes of Africans, the Afro-Persian Shirazis and the comparatively recent immigrants from the mainland, is also predominantly African. Karume is a "mainland African." The main beneficiary from this split was the Arab-dominated ZNP, as the outcome of the June, 1961, election proved.

This election was held following the recommendations of the constitutional adviser, Sir Hilary Blood, who suggested that twenty-one out of a total of twenty-nine members in a new legislative council should be elected on the basis of universal adult franchise. The number was later raised to twenty-two, and subsequently to twenty-three. The January, 1961, elections proved inconclusive and in a second round of elections, held in June, 1961, a curious situation resulted. The party that lost the elections formed the government by joining the opposition. Of the twenty-three elected seats, the ZNP and the ASP captured ten each, three going to the ZPPP. The election was notable for the intervention of the Tanganyika African National Union, which openly supported the Afro-Shirazi Party. Rioting followed the election, resulting in the death of nearly seventy islanders and injury to some hundreds.

A coalition government consisting of the ZNP and ZPPP emerged with the ZPPP leader, Mohammed Shamte Hamadi, as chief minister. The remaining four of the five unofficial executive council seats went to the

---

* Its co-leader was Othman Shariff Musa, now minister for education and information in the revolutionary government of the People's Republic.

ZNP, with Ali Muhsin as minister of education and welfare. Under adult franchise, which was hedged by a property and literacy qualification, some four-fifths of the electorate was African, but though the Africans won the poll by thirteen seats to ten, the Arabs held the reins.

This was due largely to the shrewdness and sagacity of the forty-five-year-old ZNP leader, Ali Muhsin, the most significant figure at that time in Zanzibar politics. While in Zanzibar I visited Muhsin at his house. He was clear-headed and precise, evidently a man who knew his mind. He spoke good English. Though he tried to dissemble the fact, it was evident from his conversation that he was basically pro-Arab and that he regarded Zanzibar as belonging more to the Arab than to the African world. After all, the Arabs were the traditional ruling class. The secretary-general of the ZNP was at that time Abdul Rahman who was suspected of leftist leanings and who bore the nickname of "Babu," which in Swahili means "father." Mohammed Babu was later the foreign minister of Karume's government. He had made frequent pilgrimages to Cairo and Peking. Before the June, 1961, elections, he resigned and formed his own UMMA Party, which had no members in the legislative council. It did not contest the elections.

"The ZNP is a truly nationalist party," observed Muhsin. "The other two are communal. The Afro-Shirazi party, for instance, had three or four years ago tried to set up cooperatives with the help of rich Indian merchants in order to take away the retail trade from the Arabs and the small Indian traders."

I asked him what the status of the sultan would be in an independent Zanzibar.

"The sultan," he replied, "is a constitutional ruler, and he will remain so in the new setup." How sadly misplaced was his optimism!

From Muhsin I heard the first criticism I encountered of Nyerere in Africa. We were discussing the prospects of an East African Federation. "Independence must come first, then federation," affirmed Muhsin. "Nyerere seems to be under British and American influence. He wanted to delay independence in order to have federation. This was contrary to the understanding we had reached at the Accra conference of 1958. We had agreed at Accra that federation should follow independence. According to Accra, it was independence first, then federation, then Pan-Africanism. Nyerere went back on that."

I could not help thinking of what Nyerere himself had said of the Accra conference: "For the first time the concept of African consciousness was brought into being." Were the worlds of Africa and Arabia so widely disparate?

Following the London constitutional tables of September, 1963, which were attended by the two government parties and the opposition, it was agreed that Zanzibar should achieve independence on December 10, as a member of the Commonwealth with the sultan as head of state and constitutional monarch. The opposition party withdrew its demand for an upper chamber, and declared its satisfaction with the safeguards covering citizenship and civil liberties. The prime minister, Sheikh Mohammed Shamte Hamadi, in his opening speech stressed the nonracial character of the state, pointing out that his ten-men cabinet comprised members of Asian, Arab, and African stock. The opposition leader, Sheikh Abeid Amani Karume, was generally cooperative, and succeeded in his demand that the new constitution should be brought into force by the convening of a special constitutional assembly which would enact the London constitution as agreed. Since the last general election was held only a few weeks previously, it was decided that the coalition government should continue, and the franchise and constituency arrangements for the next election were approved. Sheikh Mohammed Shamte accepted the principle of East African federation.

The problem of the Coastal Strip was also settled. On the date of Kenya's independence the Strip which runs from Tanganyika to the Tana River and includes the deep-water port of Mombasa was to become part of Kenya. The Strip, some 200 miles long and ten miles deep, was originally leased to the then land-locked Kenya to provide it with an outlet to the sea. Under the terms of the agreement signed between the British, Kenya, and Zanzibar governments, the annual rental was canceled and no compensation was to be paid to the sultan. Kenya gave assurances to protect the interests of the sultan's subjects after independence, to grant freedom of worship, recognize the position of the chief Kadi, respect freehold titles to land, and permit the teaching of Arabic in schools. The outlying islets of Lamu, Manda, Patta, and Siu were also ceded to Kenya.

The last preindependence elections were held in July, 1963, with internal self-government formally introduced two weeks before polling. The elections resulted in the ZNP winning twelve of the thirty-one seats in the legislative council and its ZPPP partner, six. The opposition ASP won the remaining thirteen seats, though they polled 54 percent of the votes, obtaining 85,281 votes against their opponents' 79,491. Mohammed Shamte Hamadi continued as prime minister.

It appeared to me when I visited Zanzibar that the British government inclined more toward the Arabs than the Africans. Partly, this derived from Britain's official association with the sultan, partly from the fact that the Arabs, with their stake in the land, represented a more stable economic and social element than the Africans. Arab suspicion of interference by the mainland Africans in Zanzibar's internal affairs still simmered at that time and expressed itself in a preelection appeal by the then prime minister to East and Central African countries not to try to exert their influence in favor of a particular section in Zanzibar. Shamte specifically asked the Pan-African Freedom Movement for East and Central Africa (PAFMECA) not to hold any conference until the elections in Zanzibar and Kenya were over. Such conferences, he said, were often used as propaganda platforms for one party or another. Since the Kenya Strip was first leased there has been a considerable movement of African peoples from the interior, and they now outnumber the Arab peoples on the coast. The Arabs number only 37,000, as against 300,000 Africans.

The achievement of independence by Zanzibar, as events proved, solved no problem but precipitated several more. Zanzibar faced a deficit of about $1 million in its budget, as well as a trade decline, while the prospects of East African federation, which could buttress its economy, remained bleak. At the London talks in October, 1963, the British government had generously offered to meet the budget deficit, but its attitude about funds for industrial development, particularly the diversification of agriculture, and the establishment of light and cottage industries, was more reserved. Zanzibar had drawn up a three-year development program, beginning on July 1, 1964, whose total outlay involved $14 million. The disagreement concerned the period of time over which British aid would be made available.

Muhsin seemed to me either unduly optimistic or depressingly unrealistic. "The solution," he said, "is a diversification of the economy. Today it rests almost entirely on one commodity—cloves—supplemented to a small extent by copra. We're also celebrated, as you know, for our ivory work. I realize that is not enough, but I still maintain that Zanzibar is potentially viable, and an independent Zanzibar would be viable in practice. Overseas aid could help us to develop cottage industries, fisheries, and tourism. We have the loveliest of sand beaches, but we will need help to build up proper tourist facilities." Muhsin did not, however, react enthusiastically to the idea of federation. Perhaps it was the Arab speaking with the old lurking suspicion of the African.

Events were to precipitate a drastic solution. Listening to Muhsin it seemed to me even then that the Arab hold on the island's government was artificial and precarious though I certainly did not foresee the shape of the denouement three years later. The influence of the mainland on the offshore islands of Zanzibar and Pemba was obvious with its gravitational pull represented in the makeup of their political parties. While the Afro-Shirazi party, comprising descendants of African tribes inbred with the first Persian invaders and also representative of the African descendants of mainland slaves, was the parent party pledged to press for self-government, it in time impelled the creation of a brood of other parties such as the ZNP, the ZPPP and UMMA.

There is some evidence for believing that in the immediate wake of independence certain perceptive observers saw the possibility of Zanzibar as a Cuba on the exposed flank of Africa. A few weeks before the January revolution several Israeli traders and their families left Zanzibar in a hurry for Eliath bringing stories of an imminent political upheaval on the island which seemed tailor-made for a revolution. In 1960 synthetic cloves, which had an aroma and taste better than the real product, were invented by some Swiss scientists, and by 1963 the Zanzibar Chamber of Commerce had a three-year supply of unsold stocks on its hands. Zanzibar resembles Cuba economically, the latter's trade earnings also being mainly from a single source—sugar. Cloves account for 85 percent of Zanzibar's exports. The licensed manufacture of synthetic cloves in Israel, Italy, Greece, and Spain added to Zanzibar's difficulties by further depressing the market, increasing unemployment, and affecting not only the peasants but the growers and exporters.

Compared with other offshore islands, such as Cyprus and Gabon, Zanzibar is far from rich. Cyprus, with a population of nearly 600,000, has exports and a budget of about $84 a head. Gabon, which contains a population of about 450,000, has exports of $84 a head and a budget of $42 a head. Zanzibar, smaller in area than either of these, is also smaller in population. With a population of a little over 300,000 its exports rate $56 a head and its budget $42 a head. On a budget of over $9 million there is a deficit of about $1 million.

Besides cloves, Zanzibar exports copra but its major customers, Indonesia and India, have imposed restrictions. The island was once a mercantile power but this glory vanished with the age of sail. Fortunately Zanzibar is lush with vegetation, its lagoons teem with fish, and there is an abundance of fruit and vegetable. Nevertheless Britain's shortsighted policy of discouraging local or foreign investors from building fish-canning plants or popular-priced hotels or from training fishermen in modern deep-sea fishing methods aggravated discontent.

The island's racial pattern represented an explosive mixture. African hostility to the Arabs is a hangover from slave-trading days, and dislike of the Asians is equally marked, being tied up in their case with the Asians' commercial activities. As in Tanganyika, these two races were the main targets of the mob during the Zanzibar upheaval. In Uganda and Kenya the comparative absence of Arabs made Asians the focal point of attack. In Zanzibar where the Arabs were mainly landowners, who also exercised a precarious political dominance, the Asians, traders, and the Africans, workers, the racial factor intensified social and economic discontent.

Politically the island was controlled by the descendants of the old caste of Arab slave-dealers who had used Zanzibar as the main entrepôt for the slave traffic between Africa, Arabia, and the Persian Gulf. The ZNP, led by Ali Muhsin, who in fact controlled the coalition government headed by Mohammed Shamte Hamadi, leader of the ZPPP, was predominantly Arab but had Indian middle-class support and also counted some African followers of Hamadi. It was well known that the sultan was favorably inclined toward it. The overwhelming majority of African workers and their trade unions were behind Abeid Karume's ASP from which Hamadi had seceded to form the ZPPP.

Karume, whose mother is said to have been a slave in an Arab family, once worked as a deckhand, and controls the Seamen's Union which he organized. He has also the support of the union of government servants and the clove workers' union. Though in no way sophisticated, he has managed to educate himself and is a powerful speaker in Swahili. This bluff, bull-necked forceful personality, who is about sixty, is one of the few African leaders who has had no known contact with Moscow or Peking. (Even Ali Muhsin, once suspected as a leftist, has visited Peking.) Karume also enjoys the support of the ruling parties in Kenya and Tanganyika and is said to be influenced greatly by Nyerere. He might be described as a radical with no pronounced leftist leanings but like other African leaders he has his bunch of wild men.

Inside the ASP Karume has to contend with Sheikh Ottman Sharif Musa, now minister of education and information, in the revolutionary government of the People's Republic over which Karume presides. Sheikh Ottman has a turbulent following among the younger and more dissatisfied Afro-Shirazis but some hold he is, if anything, right of Karume. The two militant Socialists with whom Karume has been forced to align are Sheikh Abdul Rahman Mohammed Babu and Sheikh Abdulla Kassim Hanga. Both are crypto-Communists, and Babu was once a member of the Communist party. Both have visited Peking and Moscow, Hanga joining Lumumba University as a student. He has a Russian-born wife* who worked in the African Institute in Moscow as an assistant to the director, Professor Potekhin, and writes occasionally for the Soviet press. In one of her articles Mrs. Hanga described Zanzibar as the "gateway into East Africa," while in another article in Trud just before the coup d'état she stressed the potentially revolutionary situation in the islands. According to her, only 25 percent of the children received a primary education, every tenth inhabitant suffered from tuberculosis, and three-quarters of the land was in the hands of alien landlords. Hanga is in his early thirties. Insofar

* She is said to be the daughter of an American Negro who settled in Russia in the 1930's.

as he is Moscow-oriented he is more moderate in the expression of his Communist views than brash Peking-oriented Babu. Hanga was vice-president in the government of the People's Republic while Babu was its foreign minister.

Babu is a more complex character than Hanga. Of mixed African and Arab blood, he was for a long time actively associated with Muhsin's ZNP and was once its general secretary and principal propagandist. Earlier he had, like Lumumba, worked as a postal clerk—in Ealing of all places! For some years he was the Zanzibar correspondent of the New China News Agency, which is believed to have paid him an excessively inflated salary. Later he was on the board of *Revolution*, a magazine published in Switzerland which supports Peking in its dispute with Moscow. Babu served a fifteen-months' sentence imposed by the then British government on a charge of sedition which he allegedly perpetrated in an inflammatory article he wrote for a left-wing journal. His Communist sympathies and affiliations grew stronger after his release, and a short while before the last preindependence election he presented a list of pro-Communist candidates for the ZNP which Muhsin rejected. Thereupon Babu left the party to form a dissident group known as the UMMA (Freedom) party which, however, did not contest the elections. At that time he complained to a foreign journalist of the ZNP's "anti-African bias."

There is an interesting parallel in the careers of Babu and Oginga Odinga, Kenya's ministers for home affairs, whose name was associated with the Zanzibar revolution, but the allegation was denied. The latter used a considerable part of his "foreign aid" to organize an underground route through Uganda and the Sudan for smuggling out scores of East African students to Communist countries where he had arranged scholarships for them. Likewise Babu used his payments from abroad totaling, some said, $28,000 a year to send activist African groups for ideological and guerilla training in Cuba. Three such groups are reported to have gone—the largest from South Africa, another from Kenya, Tanganyika, and Zanzibar, and a third from Ghana, Mali, the Congo, and Nigeria. A fourth small batch was dispatched from Spanish Guinea. Babu is known to have organized the education in Cuba of about a hundred young men, mainly of mixed Arab-African blood, through missions in Havana and Cairo. The presence of some of these activists during the Zanzibar coup and later the infiltration of some of them into Karume's government lent credence to the story of a Cuban hand in Zanzibar's upheaval. But its motivation, inspiration, and direction were entirely African.

The role of the thirty-two-year-old John Okello in this Ruritanian revolution was obscure. All that was known of him was that he was a Uganda-born tribesman who at one time had served in the Zanzibar police, had been sent to Havana University to train for a senior police post, and had allegedly been cheated out of it by the Arab-dominated ZNP government. Okello himself claimed to be a former Mau Mau fighter, and the methods he deployed in Zanzibar certainly suggested some acquaintance with that organization. At the head of some 600 men armed with pangas, bows, and arrows the "field marshal" overran two police stations and put Hamadi's government, along with the sultan, to flight. Okello then proceeded to bellow blood-curdling threats over the radio in a manner more reminiscent of a crazy witch doctor than a trained soldier. "The power behind me," he proclaimed, "is 999,999,000. I shall take severe measures, 88 times more severe than my predecessor. I can make 100 grenades in an hour. We will call all to come see how we hang people and cook them like chickens."

Russia, China, and Cuba were quick to recognize the new government. So, significantly enough, was well-informed Israel, the first non-Communist state to do so. British Intelligence did not fall down on the job. It was well aware of the rumblings beneath the surface in Zanzibar and East Africa as British troop dispositions, ready to be switched where aid was requested, proved. The 24th Infantry Brigade was already based in Kenya by agreement with the Kenya government. Number 45 Royal Marine Commando was brought by sea from Aden while Number 41 Royal Marine Commando was flown in from England. Apart from the expected trouble in Zanzibar and East Africa, there was the prospect of rebellion in Mozambique, the tribal war between the Bahutu and Watusi in Rwanda, and the troubles in Southern Sudan and in the Somali-inhabited areas of Kenya. Significantly again the government of the new People's Republic of Zanzibar invited Tanganyika to send a detachment of armed police to maintain order. This detachment, initially numbering one hundred, was the first foreign contingent to make its appearance.

Having toppled over the Karume government the revolutionaries were quick to set up their own regime. The coup had been followed by widespread looting of Arab and Asian stores and residences accompanied by indiscriminate butchery of Asians, Arabs, and Africans believed to be hostile to the new rulers. Around 800 were estimated to have been killed, while another 2,000 were put into prison, detention, and refugee camps. Of these some 400 were political prisoners. Although no political hangings took place, as Okello had threatened, his hand is believed to have been stayed only by peremptory orders from Kenya. The revolution signified the end of Arab supremacy in Zanzibar. What Odinga stigmatized as "the minority rule over the majority" was over. With it was also ended the rule of the sultan, and the accompanying ban on the former ruling parties, the ZNP and the ZPPP, came as no surprise. While Okello ruled out citizenship for Arabs, Asians, and Europeans as "unlikely," Babu declared that the islands would "quite possibly" stay within the Commonwealth. At the same time he affirmed that the Zanzibar government would be a socialist government but would not necessarily follow the Cuban pattern.

Where did Okello stand in this weird setup? According to Babu, Okello was "a revolutionary leader of equal status as President Karume and other politicians." Karume's government contains a core of Cuban-trained activists but the president himself, though a radical, is a moderate compared with most of his colleagues. Okello's strength, however temporary, derives from the fact that Zanzibar has no army, but as against this is the clear indication that neither Kenya nor Tanganyika would welcome the conversion of Zanzibar into a Communist foothold. As in many other African one-party states, the single ruling Afro-Shirazi party includes men of varying standpoints, and the thirty members of the revolutionary council range from moderates alongside Karume to extremists grouped around Babu and Hanga, though the latter two do not always see eye to eye on everything.

But Karume will still be left riding two tigers—Babu and Hanga. With his mixed parentage Babu is tarred by the Arab brush which Karume may use to further denigrate him in the eyes of a very African-conscious island. Moreover Babu's pro-Peking leanings could hardly endear him to the Kenya government which is suspicious of external, particularly Chinese, influences in the restiveness of East Africa. Pro-Russian inclined Hanga is unlikely to force the pace. If he cannot convert Zanzibar into a Cuba, he would not relish replacing it by a Congo. If not Hanga, the intellectual Mrs. Hanga should recall Lenin's castigation of communism in a hurry as "left-wing communism, an infantile disorder." She might also recall what happened in Singapore in 1948 and in Manila in 1951 as a result of overzealous and overenthusiastic Communists.

Nyerere, with Karume's cooperation, sprang a surprise by announcing the merger of Tanganyika and Zanzibar in the so-called Tanzan union in April, 1964. By absorbing this troublesome island along with Pemba into a United Republic of Tanganyika and Zanzibar, Nyerere shut for the time being at least a Communist show-window facing the Tanganyikan mainland. His trump card was probably the police contingent which Dar-es-Salaam made available to Zanzibar, as its withdrawal would leave Karume's government with no armed forces save the irregulars behind Babu. More recently these irregulars have grown in number and training. It was an African solution for an African problem. In the 23-man cabinet of the Tanzan union five Zanzibaris, including three left-wingers, Babu, Hanga, and Hassan Moyo, were absorbed in the new directorate of development planning directly under Nyerere, an assignment which also compelled their presence on the mainland. The two moderates, Karume and Aboud Jume, were left as ministers in Zanzibar to look after the islands' internal affairs. Nyerere's close friend and colleague, Kawawa, was given the defense portfolio which Kambona had previously held. Kambona was entrusted with foreign affairs. Zanzibar, however, still clings to its separate personality, and the Tanzan union has still to manifest itself as a political reality.

Simple solutions often call for complex measures, but it must be recognized that an African problem is best worked out by Africans in their own independent states, either separately or jointly.

13

KENYA CALDRON

NOT AS LARGE numerically as Nigeria nor territorially as the Sudan, Kenya nonetheless holds the key to the future of East Africa and, it may be, to the whole of the continent. Three factors make its position especially vulnerable. Opened up largely by Indian labor and serviced commercially at first by Indian traders who played a pioneering role in developing such centers as Nairobi, Nakuru, and Kisumu, its land was later cultivated and dramatically developed by an influx of hard-working, imaginative European settlers whose considerable investments enhanced the country's commercial potentialities and prestige and made it the nerve center of European enterprise in East Africa. In this process its vibrant but tribal-ridden races were economically reduced to a status not far removed from that of helots. Neither European, Asian, nor African foresaw the cyclone of change. In the second place, commercial development flowing mainly from European enterprise inflated its political prestige, making Kenya the hub of the East African Common Services Organization and generating in African minds and hearts the first faint stirrings of the political dream of an East African federation. Third, geography with history induced not only an intensification of tribal rivalries but incited frontier and regional ambitions focused today in the Somali threat to the

288

Northeastern Frontier province. These three factors, at once cohesive and divisive, combine to give Kenya a special place in the African picture.

The roots of Kenya's politics lie in land and tribalism. With the former is entwined the problem of the white settlers; with the latter the dormant regionalism which surfaced when independence drew nearer. On a wider plane, the problems of land and tribalism are enmeshed.

Capitalism, wrote Marx, provides its own gravediggers. So does colonialism. By creating a restricted affluent society, both generate an atmosphere of competition, but also of conflict, which ends either in the displacement of the possessor, the further suppression of the dispossessed, or a state of continuous turmoil. Peaceful coexistence, whether political or economic, is possible only where both sides believe that it is to their individual and mutual advantage to coexist peacefully.

Where color intrudes, the problem becomes more complicated, for when equal opportunity is denied an individual not on the basis of ability, but of color, the attitude of both sides ceases to be rational and becomes obsessively emotional. It is not in Africa or Asia alone that this was or is being demonstrated. The importance of being black has dawned on many Negroes in America, as the growing militancy in the South and the increasing strength of the Black Muslim Brotherhood testify.

Kenya should be studied and seen in this perspective. Though more advanced in terms of political consciousness than Tanganyika or Uganda, it has been beaten by both in the race for independence, and only a few weeks separated Kenya from little Zanzibar in the attainment of self-government. Zanzibar attained independence two days before Kenya. Many of the obstacles to freedom since the Lyttelton constitution of 1955, which for the first time provided for six elected African members in the legislative council, were of the Africans' own making, particularly the divisiveness which has been the curse of African politics and politicians in Kenya. But a strong delaying factor was the resistance offered by the more diehard white settler farmers, who with their families constitute or constituted a little over a quarter of the total European population of 70,000. The farmers themselves numbered some 4,000. Since 1959 the walls of European resistance have begun to crumble but the fissures in the African facade have simultaneously widened. In an unexpected way the official decision of December, 1960, to throw open the so-called White Highlands, hitherto reserved for Europeans, to Africans, far from removing a source of major tension, intensified African pressure on the landowning whites, and also created a new focus of rivalry and tension among the Africans themselves, notably between the Kikuyu and the Masai. The scramble for land was tied up with tribal loyalties and rivalries. Regionalism is only next door to tribalism.

The Mau Mau rebellion, which was led by a section of the Kikuyu laboring under a deep sense of social and political resentment at what they regarded as the treacherous European encroachment on their tribal lands, is a turning point in Kenya's modern political history. Since 1954, when the emergency was officially declared to have ended, Kenya has never been the same.

Before the rebellion, African political activity was confined almost exclusively to the Kikuyu, with Jomo Kenyatta as its leading figure. Kenyatta, who was reportedly born in 1893,* was active in politics in the early 1920's, first as a member of the Kikuyu Association under Harry Thuku, and later, in 1928, as general secretary of the Kikuyu Central Association (KCA), the name he gave to the revived Kikuyu Association. The aim of this organization, which was strongly tribalist and strongly anti-European, was to recover the Kikuyu's "lost lands." In 1931 Kenyatta left for Britain, where he stayed for fifteen years, writing during his stay there his revealing study, *Facing Mount Kenya*. Kenyatta's strong tribalism surfaces in the book.

Tribalism is the key to his political character and career. In sophisticated Britain his book gave a sort of philosophical basis to tribalism, and elevated it to an ethos. Whether while writing it Kenyatta saw the Kikuyu as the master race of Kenya is a matter on which it would be unfair to dogmatize without assured knowledge. But even if he cited the Kikuyu only as a specific and spectacular example of the manner in which the Europeans had disrupted the Africans' tribal life and moorings, without attempting to fill the social and economic vacuum, he was saying something which instinctively appealed to every African. (Just as the overwhelming majority of Indians are caste-conscious, so are the overwhelming majority of Africans tribe-conscious. Moreover, land to the African is a status symbol attaching to the tribe, not the individual. And the dispossession of the Kikuyu by the whites was as much an affront to the other African tribes of Kenya as to the Kikuyu. With the withdrawal of the European presence, it was inevitable that the tribalism Kenyatta had preached and exploited as a political weapon against the whites was to recoil on his own head and against Kenya's quick advance to freedom, for what delayed Kenya's advent to self-government was the squabble over land—not so much between Africans and whites as between Africans and Africans. The political price Kenya had to pay for independence was regionalism.)

Kenyatta returned to Kenya in 1946. In the interval the Kikuyu Central Association had been proscribed for alleged subversive activities during the war, but a new organization known as the Kenya African Union (KAU) had taken its place, with Harry Thuku as its first chairman. KAU

* The exact year of his birth is disputed. He confesses to seventy-five years.

centered among the Kikuyu. African politics, apart from being tribal, are split between moderates and extremists, with the extremists invariably coming out on top. Thuku, deemed a moderate, was ultimately to be replaced by James Gichuru, and when the Mau Mau rebellion broke out in 1952, KAU split on the familiar lines of moderates opposed to Mau Mau and extremists supporting the rebels. Kenyatta had become president of KAU in June, 1947, and though the organization was still predominantly Kikuyu in composition, Kenyatta was careful to have other tribes, notably the Luo, represented on its executive. Among the Luo recruits most prominent at that time was Oginga Odinga, widely suspected of being pro-Communist, and today a bitter antagonist of Tom Mboya, who is nearly twenty years his junior.

Shortly after the outbreak of the rebellion, Kenyatta, along with five leading members of KAU, was placed under detention on a charge of managing the Mau Mau. Kenyatta has consistently denied any complicity with Mau Mau, but there is very little reason to doubt that until his detention he was closely associated with it, though it is inconceivable that he personally took part in its grisly and gruesome rites.* Every European I spoke to while in Nairobi was convinced of Kenyatta's complicity. But, surprisingly, so were a large proportion of Africans, though they approved of Kenyatta's action. "What else could he have done?" they asked.

Kenyatta was to remain in jail and under detention for almost nine years until he was released in August, 1961. As during his earlier absence abroad, many developments had taken place during his second enforced absence. Like the old KCA, the new KAU had been banned. The Lennox-Boyd constitution, which followed the Lyttelton constitution, had met with the same fate. The Africans, though given a few more elected seats, boycotted it. A new political star, the then twenty-six-year-old Tom Mboya, soared into the firmament as general secretary of the Kenya Federation of Labor, which was assisted by American labor unions and affiliated to the right-wing ICFTU. Odinga's envy of the talented Mboya erupted into open wrath. KAU became another African party with a right and left wing.

Under the terms of the Lancaster House constitution of February, 1960, eight elected members were to fill eight ministerial seats, while the remaining four would be filled by civil servants. Of the elected ministers, four were to be African, one Indian, and three European. The elections were scheduled for February, 1961. As in many African countries, the settlement of Kenya's constitutional problem, far from easing the general situation, exacerbated it and brought into being other contentious prob-

---

* On Kenya's attaining self-government, he condemned these rites and warned against any resurrection of Mau Mau.

lems. The personal rivalries within KAU were intensified. Shortly after the Lancaster House constitution, KAU reappeared under a new name, the Kenya African National Union (KANU), composed principally of the Bantu Kikuyu and the Nilotic Luo, the most prominent among the Kikuyu being Kenyatta and Gichuru, while Mboya and Odinga spearheaded the Luo. At that time Kenyatta was still in detention, and Gichuru became *pro tem* president of KANU pending Kenyatta's release.

At the Lancaster House conference it was accepted by all parties, except the right-wing settlers' United party, that independence was Kenya's objective. On the African side this led to the emergence of new political forces based largely on tribal interests, with the minority tribes ranged against the dominant and more advanced majority tribes like the Kikuyu and Luo, whose political organization, KANU, was challenged by the establishment of another organization known as the Kenya African Democratic Union (KADU), with Ronald Ngala as president. KANU also included the Akamba tribe, though later, with the secession of Paul Ngei, one of Kenyatta's chief lieutenants, who broke away to form the African Peoples party (APP), the Akamba were largely, though only temporarily, lost to KANU. KADU is an amalgam of tribal parties comprising mainly the Masai, Kalenjin, Abaluhya, Giriama, and Taita, though members of various tribes are found in both KANU and KADU. With independence on the horizon, African politics congealed in a tribal mold, thereby reverting to the traditional form which the European intrusion had temporarily disturbed. On the European side the reaction was equally interesting. Before the Lancaster House conference there were two European parties, the extremist United party organized by the late Group Captain Briggs and Michael Blundell's New Kenya party (NKP), both formed in 1959. Blundell's NKP was designed to be a double buffer—against extreme African nationalism, on the one hand, and against the intransigence of the right-wing white settlers on the other. After Lancaster House, a new European party came into being, the Kenya Coalition founded by Sir Ferdinand Cavendish-Bentinck, who resigned the speakership of the legislative council in order to do this. While accepting the Lancaster House constitution as an established fact, the Kenya Coalition pressed for extra minority safeguards. For the February, 1961, elections, however, it forged an alliance with the extreme right-wing United party. Their common target was Blundell.

As the elections drew nearer, party and personal rivalries acquired a sharper edge. Within KANU the battle for power between Odinga and Mboya rose to a higher tempo, for KANU was confident of winning the elections, which in fact it did, though KADU was ultimately to form the government. The Kenya Coalition, backed by the United party, was train-

ing all its guns on Blundell's New Kenya party with the certainty that it
would win the primary elections confined to a purely European electorate,
but perhaps realistic enough to realize that its candidates had no chance
when it came to the common rolls, which included Africans and Asians.
The eyes of the Kenya Coalition were not focused on the governments at
Nairobi or London, but on the electorate in Britain. They were out to
prove to the British voters at home that the Kenya Coalition was more representative of the British community than any other white party in Kenya.

The Lancaster House constitution provided for a legislative council of
sixty-five members, thirty-three of whom were to be elected for the open
seats, which virtually meant thirty-three African seats. There were also
ten common-roll seats reserved for European members. In addition, the
legislative council, or Legco, after the elections, was to elect members to
occupy twelve so-called "national" seats, of which four were reserved for
Europeans. The remaining ten members comprised officials and others
nominated by the governor.

Even before the elections of February, 1961, KANU, mainly because
of the internal rivalries between the militantly leftist Odinga and the comparatively rightist Mboya, was threatening to fall apart. I was in Nairobi
shortly before the elections and met many of the KANU leaders, including
Gichuru, Mboya, and Kiano, but I did not see Kenyatta who was then in
detention, or Odinga, who was away from Nairobi. Through the good
offices of my friend Rupert Mayne, whom I had known in India and whose
family has very old associations with my country—one of his ancestors
founded the celebrated cavalry unit known as Mayne's Horse—I was able
to meet many prominent white settlers, among them Michael Blundell and
Sir Ferdinand Cavendish-Bentinck.

Mboya is intellectually head and shoulders above the rest of the Africans, and is conscious of the fact. Though he is said to be consistently
arrogant to his colleagues, he is, like many egocentrics, not without charm
of manner. He has a pleasantly persuasive speaking voice. His mind is
alert and agile and often original.

"The only African who thinks like a European," said a white settler a
little condescendingly.

Tom can be didactic in manner and, like most African leaders, has the
makings of a dictator, but it was interesting to listen to him on the occasions when he was inclined to talk seriously. He has a taste for the syba-
ritic and a liking for the fleshpots of good living. As a talker and thinker
he conveys a curiously mixed impression of flamboyance and brilliance.
He seems to be always aware of himself and is susceptible to flattery, but
he made some clever points, especially on economic themes.

"The British," he remarked, "have conditioned Kenya's economy to suit their own ends. The withdrawal of the white settlers will not seriously jeopardize the country's economy. They deliberately left untapped resources, which constituted a considerable potential capable of development by the Africans and which we shall develop on attaining independence. Nobody wants the European to go away. He is welcome to remain provided he realizes who is the master of this house."

Gichuru has none of the dazzle of Mboya and strikes one as more earnest, a political elder by African standards—he is fifty—and a man of moderation and good sense. But he has the lingering political suspicion of the European which one notices among many Indians in India, even today. He did not, for instance, trust Blundell and thought his liberalism phony. Kiano, whose wife is an African of American parentage, and was then, as he is now, minister of commerce and industry, comes to life in spasms, but is obviously intelligent and argues convincingly. "He is able, but has no staying power," was the verdict of a veteran white settler.

The weakness of Mboya is that he is a Luo anxious to be well in the center of political affairs by out-Kikuyuing the Kikuyu. As a result he has antagonized not only a fellow Luo like Odinga, but Kikuyu aspirants for power like the amateurish Dr. Munya Waiyaki, whom he trounced soundly in Nairobi East in the February, 1961, elections. Mboya's gift for survival invests him with a quality of near-indestructibility which Kenyatta, despite his long political insulation, has been quick to appreciate and which he would like to utilize without alienating Odinga, which explains why after the May, 1963, elections he allotted the portfolio of justice and constitutional affairs to Mboya and that of home affairs to Odinga. There were, of course, other considerations, such as Mboya's acutely analytical mind.

In the elections of February, 1961, KANU did not fare as well as it had expected. Instead of the twenty-two seats it had hoped to capture, it won only eighteen, KADU annexing twelve. In the European-reserved constituencies all the New Kenya party candidates except one were returned. In the Central Rural Constituency, Peter Marrian, one of the colony's leading European farmers, standing as an Independent, beat Sir Charles Markham of the Kenya Coalition.

Markham, who is a stepson of the first Lord Delamere—Markham's mother married him as her second husband—was among the white settlers I met. He struck me as a trifle overassertive and impulsive, inclined to be swayed easily, perhaps because of an inner uncertainty and conflict. But some of the views he expressed were interesting and in their way revealing.

He said the Europeans accepted the political situation and the inevitability of an African-dominated government. But the European settlers who were originally invited by the British government to come to Kenya had an economic stake in the country and now looked to the British government to buy out their holdings—in other words, to pay them compensation.

"We want an insurance cushion," said Markham. "There can be no expropriation. There must be economic safeguards not only for Europeans, but Asians."

And politically? "Politically," explained Markham, "the Africans should be invested with responsibility, but there should be no crash program. There must be an interim period. Everyone must face up to the hard financial facts of life. Kenya is a capital-importing country and in the past eighteen months there has been a considerable exodus of European capital to Britain, South Africa, and the Rhodesias. The African doesn't want our friendship. He wants our acceptance. He wants everything for nothing. He doesn't understand responsibility. He can assimilate knowledge, but where on earth is his background?"

It was the European extremist speaking. Markham also referred to the Asians. "Until 1952," he remarked, "there was a sort of Afro-Asian nationalism directed against the European, but the Mau Mau rebellion opened the Asian's eyes. Now the Asian is as much up against it as the European."

What did he think of Kenyatta? "He should be released," said Markham, "but he should renounce Mau Mau. Of course, he was involved in the rebellion, though he might have been forced into it by the strong-arm boys who overcame his resistance. He's a natural leader of both the Kikuyus and the Luos. The Kikuyus, who were up to their neck in Mau Mau, are the cleverest of the lot. The British handled Kenyatta badly. Their mistake in Kenya was that they paid no attention to the educated African who returned from abroad. They should have helped to put Kenyatta in Legco. What do I think of an East African federation? We've always supported the idea—I think as far back as 1948—because neither Kenya, Tanganyika, Uganda, nor Zanzibar is economically viable as a single unit. Economically there must be a federation."

If I talked with Markham, who was typical of the European extremist, I also talked with some African moderates, notably Musa Ambalemba, who was then minister for housing and I think among the most unpopular of African politicians in Kenya. He was a nominated member of Legco and belonged to the Idakho group of the Luhya tribe.

"I am not an enemy of my country," he said, "but I believe in practical politics, not theory. We must show the Europeans our capacity, since much will depend on how successfully the Lancaster House agreement of February, 1960, works. If we behave sensibly, independence will come quickly. If not, it will take two or three stages. It is unrealistic to deny the existence of tribal feeling, but we can and should build up from tribalism to nationalism."

Ambalemba proved a more accurate prophet than the buoyant Mboya or the optimistic Gichuru. He reminded me of an Indian liberal such as the late Sir Tej Bahadur Sapru, who was a cautious, farseeing patriot in the ebullient heyday of the Congress party.

He talked of the European settlers: "They're very uncertain and unsettled. They will play a very, very cautious game in Legco. They know they're down, but they don't mean to be out. It is true that the land restrictions in the Highlands no longer exist." Ambalemba smiled wryly. "But, then, the Ritz is open to all. There is really no difference between Cavendish-Bentinck's Kenya Coalition and Briggs's United party. Blundell's New Kenya party is different. Blundell believes in a multiracial Kenya. He wants Africans and Europeans to live together and work together. Cavendish-Bentinck wants the Europeans and the Africans to work and live separately. Of course, the economic stability of Kenya is precarious, because the settlers and investors are very largely outside this country, but I think the flight of capital has been exaggerated. On the other hand, we Africans must realize that we simply haven't yet got a sufficiency of qualified manpower or material."

I thought Ambalemba was slightly unkind to KANU and KADU about their attitude to Kenyatta, who was then in detention, though Gichuru had earlier, before the February, 1961, elections, surprised me by observing that it was not to be assumed that KANU would not take office if Kenyatta were not released. However, KANU, in contradistinction to KADU, later made Kenyatta's release a condition precedent to KANU's entering the government.

"KANU and KADU are urging Kenyatta's release," said Ambalemba, "because they know the government won't release him—at least before the elections. It will only create complications. I believe that both KANU and KADU will accept office if either has the opportunity, even without Kenyatta's release."

Ambalemba proved right so far as KADU was concerned, but KANU kept aloof until after Kenyatta's release in August, 1961. Even before the elections of February, 1961, KANU had begun to insist that it would have no part in forming a government unless Kenyatta was first released unconditionally. KADU, while demanding his immediate release, refused to acknowledge him as a national leader unless he "first proved himself." KADU clearly feared that Kenyatta, on his release, would throw in his lot with KANU, with whose political progenitors he had been closely associated. These fears, as events proved, were not without foundation, nor was this reading of the situation confined to KADU. I recall the genial, well-informed Ibrahim Nathoo, then minister for works, affirming that Kenyatta inclined toward KANU.

Instead of attempting to form a national government with KANU and KADU representatives, the then governor of Kenya, Sir Patrick Renison, ineptly tried to induce Gichuru and Mboya to form a KANU government, which they declined to do unless Kenyatta was released. Matters were not improved by a clumsy threat by Humphrey Slade, then speaker of the legislative council, that either the African leaders should form a government or the governor would impose government by decree. An attempt was made by KADU to detach Dr. Gikonyo Kiano, minister of commerce and industry in the outgoing government, from his loyalty to KANU, but this proved equally unfruitful. After seven weeks of haggling and deadlock, Ronald Ngala, president of KADU, agreed to form a government. KANU decided to stay in opposition.

As a minority party, KADU was able to sustain itself as the government only by entering into a coalition with a largely European group led by Michael Blundell, leader of the New Kenya party, who was made minister for agriculture, and Wilfred Havelock, who was given the portfolio for local government and lands. Blundell's decision to join the government led to the resignation of Bruce McKenzie from the New Kenya party. McKenzie, who had served with distinction in the war—he was a colonel at twenty-four—strongly supported KANU as a majority party.

Kenyatta was released in August, 1961. In April, while under detention in Maralal near Nairobi, he was allowed to hold a press conference, the first since his arrest some eight years before. Of his seventy-odd years Kenyatta had then been nearly twenty-five years away from his followers,* but *Mzee* (The Old Man) was by no means a spent force, and surprised the fifty or so journalists who saw him by his mental agility and political adroitness. Incarceration had deepened his suspicion of official motives and intentions, but, while condemning violence, Kenyatta refused to commit himself on specific issues. It was, however, obvious that he would like to see KANU and KADU united as a national party under his leadership, and shortly after his release he warned both parties that if they did not cooperate he would consider forming a third political party.

Meanwhile, not only was KANU riven by internal differences arising largely from the personal rivalry between Mboya and Odinga, but the attitude of KADU toward KANU and Kenyatta was hardening into a more militant tribalism, which expressed itself in assertive regionalism. Within KANU, sections of the Luo and Akamba resented what they construed as attempts at domination by the Kikuyu old guard. The Luo, incensed par-

* Fifteen years in England and almost nine in detention.

ticularly by some of Mboya's more arrogant manifestations, threatened to set up their own political group, to be known as the Luo Political Movement. Kenyatta's release brought new recruits to KANU, including some of the Old Man's close associates, such as Joseph Murumbi, Peter Koinange, and Paul Ngei, an influential Akamba leader. From KADU came a demand by certain Masai and Kalenjin tribal leaders for regional autonomy and a repudiation of Kenyatta as a national leader—a cry which was soon to be taken up officially by Ngala and Masinde Muliro, vice-president of KADU and minister of works. While KANU increasingly favored a strong unitary government, KADU leaders canvassed a blueprint for dividing Kenya into five or six regions, Ngala explaining that what was wanted was a federal state with strong reserved powers for the regions, these powers to include control of land and a degree of control over education, revenue, and administrative staff. KANU, which claimed to have won three times the number of votes gained by KADU in the February elections, protested that this was contrary to the mandate of the people. It raised the same protest after the elections of May, 1963.

The differences between the two parties were not grounded so much on policies as they were based on personal and tribal antagonisms and rivalries. Official fears that the Mau Mau was attempting to resurrect itself in the form of a Land Freedom Army (which was proscribed) did not ease matters, and intensified Kikuyu and non-Kikuyu acerbities. From the end of August a sporadic series of talks sponsored by the governor to bring the two parties together and induce the formation of a national government came to nothing, and Mboya announced at a press conference that KANU had invited Kenyatta to become its president. The rift over regionalism widened, though KANU and KADU were one in resisting autonomy for the largely Arab-inhabited Coastal Strip leased by Kenya from the Sultan of Zanzibar, as well as for the predominantly Somali-inhabited Northern Frontier District.

Kenyatta was veering closer toward KANU, and his exceptional position as an African leader was recognized by other countries of East and Central Africa, which invited him to attend a conference at Dar-es-Salaam sponsored by Tanganyika for the purpose of setting up a federation as a counterpoise to and possibly as a solvent, ultimately, of Sir Roy Welensky's Central African federation, which was even then trembling on the brink of a breakup. Kenyatta was earmarked as the head of the proposed federation.

Toward the end of October Kenyatta agreed to head KANU, Gichuru making way for him as president, as he had done earlier in 1947 when Jomo had taken over the Kenya African Union from him. Though criticized for not keeping himself above party quarrels, it is difficult to see what else Kenyatta could have done in the circumstances. KADU had spurned him as a national leader, and the minority tribes, particularly the Masai and the Kalenjin, would not easily have acquiesced in having him even as party leader.

The open identification of Kenyatta with KANU changed the political picture and greatly strengthened the position of KANU vis-à-vis KADU. Kenyatta still talked of a nation and of a multiracial society which would build up an independent Kenya, but it was noticeable that while he affirmed that land titles and property rights would be respected, his extremist lieutenants, notably Paul Ngei, who had been detained along with Kenyatta, threatened to confiscate European-owned farms after independence and parcel them out among the landless Africans. It would not be surprising if ultimately Jomo interpreted nationalism as a one-party state, with the majority on top. After all, the Kikuyu, the most advanced of Kenya's tribes, number over 2 million, which is more than a quarter of the territory's total population. The Luo count another 2 million. The pastoral Masai, who originally dominated the White Highlands, or so-called Scheduled Areas—Masailand covers an area of 15,000 square miles— and were twice moved by the administration, in 1904 and 1911, number only a little over 60,000.

Kenyatta's emergence into the center of the political stage, while it did not improve the relationship between Africans and Europeans, intensified the differences between Africans and Africans. The initiative passed, first almost imperceptibly, but later unmistakably, from KADU to Kenyatta and KANU, the latter two being the dominating factors at the London conference of November, 1961. An inevitable corollary was an increased emphasis on the tribal distinction between KANU and KADU. By a skillful show of moderation in London, Kenyatta appears to have dimmed, if not erased, the image of KADU as being the only moderate party in the mind of Whitehall. By foolishly threatening civil war at this stage, KADU fortified Whitehall in its new impression. Fear that the Somali secessionists, the coastal autonomists, and the Kalenjin federalists would break away from the party if KADU accepted merely regional guarantees increased its leaders' intransigence and insistence on unambiguous regionalism.

Mboya, preceding Kenyatta to London in October, had laid the ground for renewed negotiations between KANU and KADU with a view to establishing an interim government until the elections, which he felt might be held in February, 1962, on the basis of adult franchise and equal constituencies. The majority party emerging from the elections could function up to and past independence, for which he set the deadline at October 9, 1962. KADU's dependence on its European supporters added to its embarrassments, as Mboya knew, but Ngala refused to accept Blundell's resignation, which in any case was inevitable and came in July, 1962.

While in Nairobi shortly before the elections of February, 1961, I met Blundell and Cavendish-Bentinck, as well as other Europeans like Reggie Alexander. Their views, though outdated in the present context, are of relevance and interest, for they shed some light on the European attitude to developments which outpaced them. I thought Blundell, whose sand castles were collapsing around him, the most pathetic of them all in some ways. His was the tragedy of a well-intentioned man whose conclusions were build on premises which went sadly awry. He was to learn the hard way that there is no such thing as a moderate African. His conversation reflected some of his bitterness and frustration, for his position was equally invidious vis-à-vis the African and European. Neither really trusted him, and he seemed aware of it.

Blundell was particularly bitter toward Cavendish-Bentinck and his Coalition party. "The Coalition," he observed, "is a lineal descendant of the United party. It's only concerned in maintaining the *status quo* of the Europeans. I believe in a multiracial society and government, in a common alliance between Europeans, Africans, and Asians. Power is not around us. Power is around the people of this country. If we want to remain here, let's reconcile ourselves with Africa. Let's step out from being merely Europeans and work with, though not necessarily live like, Africans. The African is very racial. Why present him with a white pill marked 'European'? He won't swallow it."

Blundell spoke of Kenya's economy. "We're interested in developing Africa's economy," he remarked. "The Coalition means European economy when it talks of African economy. Poverty is not so acute here as in India. There's a great deal of unemployment and of land hunger. Asia lacks education. So does Africa, which has also no finance. The Africans need technical resources and finance. We've got to see the thing from the human and social aspect. It's no use calling the Africans 'apes' and 'baboons.' Blacks and whites are interlocked. Each needs the other. We have a duty to this country to transform the European scene into an African scene quietly and smoothly. We can't help Africa by running away. We must stay to help Africa. We represent a reservoir of experience."

Blundell revealed that at the Lancaster House conference the Europeans had felt that Kenya would not be free for another ten or twelve years. He had no objection to a common roll, provided it laid down a higher qualification. "MacLeod,"* he complained, "gave us a low-grade franchise. We need some sort of filter system to eliminate the stooges and Communists. With maturity of political thinking and of technical experience,

* Iain MacLeod, then British colonial secretary.

Africa can slide safely into independence. What is needed is an egalitarian approach. We cannot remain in richness side by side with poor Africans and Asians."

A sudden tiredness seemed to descend on Blundell, and he spoke wearily, like a man striving to convince himself more than me. "Events have overtaken me," he confessed. "I've been more than thirty-five years here. One needs a civilized approach to multiracialism. Africa is like that oil advertisement: 'That's Africa. That was.' C-B is a real reactionary. He's as deceptive as snow on a tree stump. Most of the Europeans are thinking of getting out. It's taking a distorted view of things to say that Whitehall has any special obligations to the Europeans. Its only obligation is to the country. The United party wants Whitehall to look after the Europeans and to underwrite their land. Why should H.M.G. do this? Why can't the Europeans look after themselves?"

And in a final burst of what seemed like near-despair, he exclaimed: "I'm fed up trying to save souls. Everything has been bitched by both sides —European and African."

Cavendish-Bentinck was more suave and smooth. Like many political extremists of the right or left, he was quiet-voiced, gentle-mannered, and friendly. His white hair gave him an air of benignity oddly at variance with the belligerence of his views.

"I was to a large extent responsible for getting the European settlers here," he explained. "The Lancaster House conference only pandered to political expediency. The Tories, who got in with an unexpectedly large majority, are worse than the Socialists. They're worried because the economy of England is balanced on a knife edge. They don't want any colonial responsibility. It's cynical. We here have a responsibility toward the people who fought Mau Mau. Everything here has been created by the minorities—European and Asian. Now by a stroke of the pen, H.M.G. are putting immature Africans into power. The Africans will have to be given political advance more quickly than either Macmillan or MacLeod pretends to think."

He spoke of the flight of European capital: "The best part of £ 1 million [$2.8 million] a month has been going abroad over a long period. I reckon that so far some £ 10 million have gone out of the country. True, some of it may come back. But our reserves are also down by £ 1 million, and on the development side of the budget we're £ 5 million down. There's a shortfall already of £ 6 million to £ 7 million. All this means a drastic curtailment of development plans, specially African social services. Where's the money to come from?"

Cavendish-Bentinck spoke of the plight of the European settlers: "I don't say it's wrong to open the Highlands. As it is, the Scheduled Areas

are surrounded by African peasant farmers. But the biggest European casualties will be the small farmers, who number around 3,000. They are the
people who are going to suffer. They have nowhere to go except to find
employment in the lower-grade services—local civil services."

What was his attitude to the United party? "I differ with them," he
replied. "Things can't remain as they were. We cannot resist the African
majority. It's stupid to think that we can. As an old man I wanted to
bring together the rightist and leftist Europeans. The United party
wouldn't support me. What could I do but form the Coalition?"

Rupert Mayne, among the kindliest of friends, arranged for me to meet
other white settlers, and through his good offices I met Reggie Alexander
and some Europeans long resident in Kenya. They were an interesting
cross section, spoke frankly, and gave me an illuminating insight into many
varied facets of the Kenya European's way of thinking. They were particularly interesting on the land problem.

For nearly forty years, from the Devonshire Declaration of 1922,
which had assured Europeans of a settled stake in Kenya and encouraged
them to develop farms, stimulate trade, and swell the revenue, until the
first Lancaster House conference of January–February, 1960, which signalized a process of political disengagement, the European settler had
enjoyed comparative security of tenure on his land. The principle of non-
European ownership of land in the Scheduled Areas was accepted in a
restricted form in the course of 1960, but was in practice confined initially
to the settlement of African smallholders on unwanted land in the former
White Highlands, though later African farmers wishing to take larger
farms of from 100 to 150 acres were helped to find and buy them.

The total area of land capable of intensive production, with an annual
rainfall of over 30 inches, covers about 41,000 square miles, of which
some 8,500 square miles lie in European areas, and the remainder, roughly
32,000 square miles, consists chiefly of African land units and some Crown
land. Thus, around one acre in five in the intensive category was available
to Europeans. By 1960 the European settlers produced 80 percent of Kenya's agricultural exports, worth $106.4 million, in the process employing
250,000 African farmers with an annual wage bill of $28 million. Accord-
ing to Margery Perham, on similar land a square mile of European farming produces annually $11,620, compared with $3,148 from African
farming. But African farming is improving and in ten years, according to
some white settlers, will overtake the Europeans. Mboya thought the
same. Most of the settlers put the collective value of European-owned
land at $364 million and estimated that of the 7.2 million acres involved in
the White Highlands, about 3 million acres were suitable for development
by African smallholders. The European mixed farming areas were, in the

reckoning of Lord Delamere, president of the Kenya National Farmers' Union, worth $84 million.

But these areas alone could not appease the Africans' growing land hunger and need for employment. Pressure of population on the African land reserves, notably in certain areas in Nyanza and Central provinces which had a density of 1,000 to the square mile, had reached bursting point. In April, 1961, some 35 percent of the White Highlands was available for purchase from European farmers anxious to leave the country, but the then Land Settlement and Development Board, with a guaranteed fund of only just over $22.4 million, had not the means to purchase the land. In any case the British government's scheme for resettlement of about 300,000 acres of the former White Highlands by 20,000 African farmers proved unacceptable to the European settlers. Save for the aid given by Britain and, in the case of the resettlement scheme, by West Germany and the World Bank, Kenya was a bankrupt country—in Mboya's words "a grant-aided one with hardly any money." Unemployment was a menace to security. In the twelve months ended June 30, 1961, some 31,500 Africans were thrown out of work, 20,000 of them agricultural workers in the Kenya Highlands, and the likelihood was that, with the European exodus, more African workers would be thrown on the scrap heap unless employment and settlement facilities were widened.

"The money-spinners," said Alexander, "are tea, coffee, and pyrethrum. The Africans are capable of developing these, given the capital and skills. But they lack both. If only they could release themselves from their thug elements! Watching them is like watching a bicycle going downhill. The leaders must beat the extremist drum in order to survive. I don't entirely blame them. On the European side it's patronage and paternalism, which looks like cooperation. On the African side there's little reciprocity to any gesture from our side. They're awfully suspicious. But, then, we haven't been overgenerous."

No European I met, including Blundell, had a good word for Kenyatta. "He's atavistic," remarked Blundell. "Prison changes a man. He's undoubtedly regarded as a charismatic leader by the Africans. In my opinion, he's a spent force."

But Kenyatta, on his release, proved to be anything but a spent force. Both KANU and KADU unrealistically set the date for Kenya's independence in 1962, KADU attempting to outvie KANU by putting the deadline earlier in February. Meanwhile, KADU stepped up its campaign for majimbo, or the division of Kenya into regional units with a federal form of government, while KANU urged a unitary government with a stronger form of local government and with vigorous economic development of the minority tribal areas. At the November, 1961, conference, the Colonial

Office made it plain that it would welcome a coalition government between KANU and KADU, which would expedite the holding of elections prior to independence. It was announced that the Colonial Secretary, Mr. Maudling, would put forward the date of his visit to Kenya. The way was also cleared for Kenyatta to be a member of Legco by withdrawing the rule which banned anyone convicted and sent to prison for more than two years from being a member. In January, 1962, Kenyatta became leader of the opposition in Legco.

The following month another constitutional conference was held in London, where, after seven weeks of unfruitful wrangling, the two main political parties agreed to sign a constitutional plan put forward by Maudling which broadly represented a compromise between the unitary form of government demanded by KANU and the federal system demanded by KADU. There was to be a coalition government, comprising the two parties, representing a strong central government with a bicameral legislature and the maximum devolution of powers to the six regions* into which Kenya would be divided. These regional governments would have certain autonomous powers derived from the constitution, not from the central government. They would administer and have power to legislate on such matters as land, education, housing, and local government, raise local revenue, and have their own legislative assemblies. Until agreement was reached on a new constitution leading to self-government, the coalition or national government, with the ministries shared equally between KANU and KADU, and in addition including some officials, would have the governor as its executive head. The central government would have powers to declare an emergency, provided such a declaration received a majority sanction of both houses of parliament soon afterward. Most changes to the constitution required a 75 percent majority in the lower chamber, while any change affecting safeguards to individual rights or entrenched rights for tribes were additionally to receive a 90 percent majority in the upper chamber. (However, this particular provision was not included in the actual interim constitution before the elections of May, 1963.) The lower chamber would be elected by universal franchise, while the upper chamber, representing each of the thirty-eight then-existing districts in Kenya, would enjoy strong powers, including a veto over proposed changes to the constitution. Early in April, 1962, the leaders of both parties agreed to take part in a coalition government. But the wrangling was by no means over.

At the root of the subsequent discord over the constitution was the question of land distribution, which intensified conflict between the two

---

* This number was later increased to seven by the creation of a seventh "Somali" region, known as the "northeast region," out of the Northern Frontier District.

parties joined in a coalition government. The Kalenjin Political Alliance, a component of KADU, favored partition, while Ngala canvassed for autonomy for the Coast Province. The Mwambo United Front, a group of parties from the Coastal Strip, advocated secession, as did also the People's Progressive party, one of the more substantial groups in Kenya's disputed Northern Frontier District. In the former White Highlands the KADU tribes, particularly the Masai, claimed that the Rift Valley should revert to them and not be allocated to the Kikuyu, who coveted the underdeveloped areas of the Masai and Kalenjin tribesmen. KADU, on its part, made a bid to wean away from KANU the Akamba tribesmen led by Paul Ngei, who was disgruntled at not being included in the coalition government. The Akamba, who number about 600,000, provide a large proportion of Kenya's soldiers and police. In the Rift Valley live some 300,000 Kikuyu who wanted to burst their boundaries and overflow into some 4,000 square miles of rich soil in Masailand, where about 60,000 Masai are engaged in purely pastoral pursuits. But KADU's intention was to neutralize the numerical power of the Kikuyu and Luo by confining these tribes to small and separate areas.

The formation of a coalition government, heralding as it did the imminence of Kenya's last preindependence elections, gave an even sharper edge to tribalism, to conflicts over land, and to regionalism. While both KADU and KANU were united in resisting secession from Kenya by the 200,000 Somali tribesmen of the Northern Frontier District in order to join Somalia,* as well as autonomy for the ten-mile-deep Coastal Strip inhabited by about 40,000 Arabs, they were strongly divided on the issue of regionalism. In July, 1962, Maudling was replaced as colonial secretary by Duncan Sandys, who also held the Commonwealth portfolio. An interesting development about this time was the end of Michael Blundell's ministerial career. He was succeeded as minister of agriculture by Wilfred Havelock in the coalition government headed by Ngala. In his valedictory speech as minister, Blundell confessed that the multiracial concept he had cherished was no longer practicable and that Kenya would emerge as an African state with no place for a separate community of European farmers. Wryly he described this as something which sprang naturally and rightly from past policy, but he feared that Kenyatta would not prove a cohesive force and that, unless plainsmen like the Kalenjin and forest dwellers like

---

* Formed on July 1, 1960, by the union of the former protectorate of British Somaliland and the U.N. Trust Territory of Somalia, formerly Italian. Somalia, also known as the Somali Republic, covers about 270,000 square miles and has a population of nearly 3 million. Its dream is to create a Greater Somalia, which would include French Somaliland and the Ethiopian Somali territories of Ogaden and Haud. Somalia has said it would consider favorably any invitation to join a future East African federation.

the Kikuyu resolved their differences, civil war seemed inevitable. The battle for a multiracial society was lost.

Though the broad principle of regional units embodied in the Maudling plan was accepted by both parties, the details remained to be settled by a regional boundaries commission headed by Sir Stafford Foster-Sutton, a former attorney-general. This commission was empowered to divide the country into six regions, subdivided into a hundred or so constituencies, for national elections. Another commission was to ascertain whether the Somali-inhabited tract in Kenya's Northern Frontier District was genuine in its demand for secession to Somalia. The latter commission, however, was not appointed until October, 1962. Besides the stipulated six regions the Foster-Sutton commission was also required to provide for a Nairobi special area. The six delimited regions were the Coast Region, the Eastern Region, the Central Region, the Rift Valley regions, the Nyanza Region, and the Western Region. On the Somali issue, while the commission felt that the people of the eastern area of the Northern Frontier District almost unanimously favored secession, the commission could make no recommendation since its terms of reference were limited to six regional units. In March, 1963, Sandys, now enjoying among Africans the sobriquet of "Solomon Sandys," ruled against secession by the Northern Frontier District, but agreed to form its eastern area as a seventh region to be known as the Northeastern Region. He also ruled that no region could surrender its powers to the center, thus allaying KADU's fears that KANU, if elected, would be in a position to undo Kenya's federal setup.

Almost the last act of Maudling as colonial secretary was to supersede the smaller settlement schemes and replace them by a more ambitious plan envisaging the purchase of around 1.3 million acres of European mixed farming land for the resettlement of African farmers under various schemes. A new Kenya Central Land Board, with General Sir Geoffrey Bourne as chairman, and consisting of a member appointed by each regional government and one by the central government, was appointed to implement the Maudling scheme, which aimed at starting a process in which those selected European mixed farmers who were bought out but wished to stay could buy land in other areas, while those not bought out could independently sell land to white or African farmers. According to Mr. Bruce McKenzie, then minister of land settlement, the scheme would cost $50.4 million,* and might be completed in four years instead of the five proposed by Maudling. As was to be expected, neither the impatient Africans nor the disgruntled Europeans were satisfied with the scheme, which the latter described as "a slum settlement." They pressed for compensa-

* Another estimate put it at $72.8 million, of which the British government would provide $56 million.

tion. The Africans feared that the British government, by cutting the money available for Kenya's immediate development plan by $4.2 million in order to extend development loans to the European farmers who were bought out, would tear a hole in the country's agricultural economy. In any case the Central Land Board would have no power to act until after the 1963 elections.

November, 1962, brought the sudden announcement of the replacement of the governor, Sir Patrick Renison, by Mr. Malcolm MacDonald, who had the reputation of being a liberal with a capacity for getting on well with the peoples of developing countries. He had been governor-general of Malaya and Singapore, was later commissioner-general in Southeast Asia, and still later U.K. high commissioner in New Delhi. In his three-year regime in Kenya, Renison, though not personally unpopular, was politically inept. He belonged to the old school of colonial administrators. MacDonald's appointment was indicative of Whitehall's anxiety to accelerate the pace of Kenya's march to independence, which would follow a period of self-government after the 1963 elections. MacDonald was expected to be the Mountbatten of Kenya.

Meanwhile, Paul Ngei, with his Akamba tribesmen, had broken away from KANU and was later to form the African Peoples party (APP), which in the elections threw in its lot with KADU. MacDonald gave first priority to the holding of the elections. During the last six months of 1962, the net European emigration was around 1,200, considerably less than half the rate in the preceding six months. MacDonald's ideal was a form of internal division through regionalism held within a united outward framework of federalism. The Regional Boundaries Commission had recommended the delimitation of Kenya into 117 constituencies.

Ngei's defection proved a blessing in disguise to KANU, inducing it to call a halt to internecine rivalries and to close its ranks. The difficulty facing KADU was that, though the two chief Luo leaders were divided in their economic approach, they were united in acknowledging Kenyatta as their leader and in recognizing that the Kikuyu were an indispensable factor in any scheme of independence.

In May, 1963, Kenya went to the polls for its last general elections before independence. Sandys, who had earlier visited Kenya, in March, 1963, rightly pinpointed the intertribal rivalries and suspicions which divided the territory. The main points of difference, he emphasized, related to the balance of power between the central government and the regional authorities, and the varied tribal aspirations and fears intermingled with them. If Kenya was to progress peacefully, its political leaders should adhere faithfully to the basic constitutional framework agreed upon by all parties at the Lancaster House conference in November, 1962, and should create a governmental machinery which would be efficient and workable. They should also provide a sufficient degree of regional autonomy to safeguard one tribal group from domination by another.

Sandys was to prove right, for the main quarrel between KANU and KADU, even after the elections of May, 1963, related to the balance between the regions and the center which precluded a regional assembly from transferring its lawmaking functions to the central legislature. Additionally, a regional assembly could not delegate its executive functions to the central government, a proviso to prevent regions with governments of the same party as the central government from handing over their powers to the center. Boundaries between regions could, according to a decision by Sandys, be amended by a two-thirds majority of the two regional assemblies concerned and a simple majority of each house of the central legislature. However, within six months of the constitution coming into force, any boundary between two regions could be amended by a simple majority of the two regional assemblies, provided that the area transferred did not comprise more than 5 percent of the population of the region from which it was being withdrawn. This arrangement was made to enable Kitale, a town assigned to the Rift Valley Region, to be transferred to the Western Region, a move which KADU was urging. Sandys also declared that the formation of a seventh region from the eastern area of the Northern Frontier District did not exclude further consideration of other solutions on the future of Somalia.

The elections of May, 1963, were boycotted by the Northern Frontier District and thus restricted to six regions. Unlike the divided ranks it presented in February, 1961, KANU fought the 1963 elections as a disciplined team and scored a more decisive victory than many had expected. Of the 117 seats in the house of representatives only 112 were contested, because of the boycott of the North Frontier District, which had five seats. Of these KANU captured sixty-six and, with the support of six independents, controlled seventy-two of the elected seats. KADU won thirty-two, while Paul Ngei's APP, working in conjunction with KADU, annexed eight seats, six from the Machakos district in the Eastern Region. Membership of the senate, which comprised forty-one seats, was reduced to thirty-eight, again due to the boycott. Here KANU captured nineteen and, with the support of one independent, had a majority of twenty. KADU gained sixteen seats and the APP two. As for the regions,* KANU gained control of the Central, Eastern, and Nyanza regions, while KADU dominated the Coast, the Rift Valley, and the Western Region. The house of representatives, sitting as an electoral college, additionally chose twelve specially elected members, of which KANU secured eleven and the opposition, comprising KADU and

* The Northern Frontier District also boycotted the regional elections.

APP, one. Thus KANU controlled eighty-three seats out of a total of 124 in the lower house.

Kenyatta had led KANU to victory, affirming that no member of any group would undergo discrimination or oppression at the hands of the majority, but at the same time he emphasized that there would be no privileges for any minority. This assurance he extended not only to all Africans, but to Europeans and Asians who wished to make Kenya their home. With the memory of similar assurances given to non-Africans in other African states, only to be flouted on the achievement of independence, European and Asian reactions were guarded. Tanganyika, which had been held up as a model of African moderation, had proved a disappointment. Apart from acts of discrimination and punitive pettiness against some non-Africans, it stressed the principles of Pan-Africanism abroad and of democratic African socialism which proved authoritarian in practice, at home.

Kenyatta, while dedicated to the same twin ideals, moved in the initial stages more cautiously. Bruce McKenzie, ironically a South African by birth, was retained in the KANU government as minister for agriculture, while Humphrey Slade was elected speaker of the house of representatives. An Asian was chosen as deputy speaker. The new KANU government also represented a careful balance between factions and tribes within the party. Odinga was appointed minister of home affairs, while his rival, Mboya, became minister of justice and constitutional affairs. Joseph Murumbi and Peter Koinange, both of whom were closely associated with Mau Mau but who, fortunately for themselves, were abroad during the emergency, were created ministers of state, the former at the prime minister's office, the latter for Pan-African affairs. Three other men who had stood in the dock with Kenyatta at Kapenguria ten years before were included in the government—Achieng Oneko as minister of information, and Fred Kubai and Bildad Kaggia as parliamentary secretaries in the ministry of labor and social services, and in the ministry of education respectively. Balancing these extremists were Mboya, James Gichuru (minister of finance), Dr. Gikonyo Kiano (minister of commerce and industry), and Lawrence Sagni (minister of lands, game, fisheries, water, and natural resources). Nor was the government restricted to Kikuyu and Luo. Murumbi is half-Goan and half-African, Sagni is a Kisii, Mwanyumba (minister for works, communications, and power) is a Taita, Mwenda (minister for labor and social services) is a Kamba, and John Konchellah (parliamentary secretary), a Masai. Kenyatta, besides being prime minister, was assigned defense, external affairs, and internal security* by MacDonald, who as governor was normally responsible for them. These portfolios were transferred without prejudice to the governor's own constitutional powers.

* Including all matters related to the police.

In his postelection statement Kenyatta urged that the cry of *Uhuru* (Freedom) should be replaced by the slogan *Harambee* (Let's work together), a variant of Nyerere's slogan *Uhuru na Kazi* (Freedom and Work). He foreshadowed the closing of the South African and Portuguese consulates in Nairobi, and the possibility of denying landing rights to the South African Airways, which has subsequently been done. Kenya also announced a trade boycott, effective from the date of independence, making it an offense to export goods to or import from South Africa and Portugal. Tanganyika and Uganda have already brought in similar regulations. Of the three African countries, Kenya's volume of trade with South Africa is the largest, totaling 40 percent of the East African Common Market's exports and 80 percent of its imports. Kenya should have little difficulty in finding alternative sources for most of her imports, which total around $8.4 million annually, the only difficulty being to find alternative markets for her export of sodium carbonate worth about $1.5 million. Kenya's trade with Portugal and its overseas territories is negligible.

The British government had earlier agreed to quit their bases in Kenya and withdraw British troops when the territory achieved independence, but asked that the orderly rundown of their forces should cover a period up to twelve months. On June 24, 1963, it was announced in London, following talks between Sandys and Mboya, who was accompanied by Murumbi and Koinange, that Kenya would be proclaimed independent on November 8. Mboya, on his return to Nairobi, said the official announcement would be put off for some time. He gave no reason for the postponement. Later the date for independence was set for December 12, 1963, partly at the request of the independent governments of Uganda and Tanganyika, which were then anxious to facilitate East African federation.

Earlier, at a meeting in Nairobi between Kenyatta, President Nyerere of Tanganyika, and Prime Minister Milton Obote of Uganda, it was decided that the three countries should form an East African Federation before the end of the year. For this purpose it was necessary to submerge a part of each country's independence in a wider unity. But the practical difficulties this posed induced second thoughts. Zanzibar's initial enthusiasm noticeably waned and Obote's caution increased. By not being a member of the East African Customs Union, Zanzibar had so far enjoyed free port status and had legislated to protect locally born workers against immigrant labor from the mainland. It was also concerned with the status of its then sultan within the federation. Uganda has all along wanted to be certain whether the objective was a political federation or an economic union, and Obote plainly prefers the latter. Assisted by Mboya, Nyerere has been the pacemaker on the federal concept, but even he admitted at a press conference in London at the end of his Scandinavian tour late in 1963 that the

December target seemed unattainable. Landlocked Uganda, with no sea-coast, and dependent for communications on Kenya, would like to see the federal capital sited in her territory. While Kenya and Tanganyika favor a strong united federation, Obote would prefer to secure substantial safe-guards for Uganda. Moreover he is faced with the Kabaka's demand, to which he is opposed, that Buganda should have separate representation in the federation. Theoretically the federal concept is attractive, but it raises some formidable problems. Economically, a federated East Africa would be in a stronger position than three or four separate states. Politi-cally, the federation would ease the problem of secessionism involved in the Northern Frontier District of Kenya.

Unfortunately, Kenya's attitude has hardened, and KANU has de-clared its intention to remain "absolutely firm." So has the attitude of the Somalis in the newly created Northeastern Region, who demand that Kenya cede the whole of the Northern Frontier District to Somalia. The breakdown of the tripartite Rome talks in August, 1963, between the Kenya government, the Somalis, and the British representatives brought renewed Somali claims for the right of self-determination and for "secession in peace." Britain's association with the Somali areas goes back to the 1880's, when the Egyptian garrisons were withdrawn from the Somali coast and the British entered into a series of treaties with the northern Somali tribes, taking them under their protection. In 1897, however, in their anxiety to keep Ethiopia neutral in the Sudan, the British made a boundary agreement with Menelik II to the disadvantage of the Somalis. This is the origin of the Somali claim to the grazing areas in Ogaden, where in 1954, by an agreement between Britain and Ethiopia, the Somali nomads were allowed restricted grazing rights on a fifteen-year basis. In July, 1960, British Somaliland and the former Italian Somaliland merged to form the independent Somali republic, whose dream is the ultimate cre-ation of a Greater Somalia by unifying the Somali areas in Kenya, Ethi-opia, and French Somaliland with the republic. The idea is by no means quixotic, as in 1945 Ernest Bevin, then British foreign minister, had can-vassed a plan for a Greater Somalian Union as a U.N. trust territory.

The Somalis, rankled by memories of alleged British bad faith in 1897, now insist that the Somali areas should be released to them and that British troops should not be used against them. They claim that ethnologically and geographically the Northeastern Region of Kenya is akin to the other Somali areas, and belongs to Somalia, whose prime minister, Dr. Sher-marke, undertook a tour of Soviet Russia, Communist China, and Egypt in August, 1963, and returned with promises of economic aid, including an interest-free loan of about $20 million from Peking. Armed Somali tribes-men threaten the borders of Kenya and Ethiopia. If Kenya's position is difficult, that of Britain is invidious, for neither Nairobi nor London would welcome the creation of a Yemen situation on the border of the Northeast Region. It is interesting to note that the Masai in Kenya make a similar charge of bad faith against Britain, to whom they allege they had by treaty relinquished their claim to the White Highlands in return for Britain's assurance that the tribe would be allocated their present area, Masailand, in perpetuity.

The federal objective is feasible only on the basis of unity within each of the three main countries. An East African federation with a divided Kenya as its keystone would hang precariously together. Even if the wrangle over regional boundaries was temporarily settled by the Foster-Sutton Commission, with Sandys's subsequent glosses, the differences on a regional, as opposed to a unitary, government persist. KADU failed in its attempt to circumscribe the Kikuyu and Luo to small disparate regions, and its dream of a sprawling Rift Valley Region stretching from Tanganyika to Ethiopia, which would keep the Highlands out of the Kikuyu sphere of influence, was unfulfilled. KADU also failed in the west to detach the Balubya and Kisii tribes from the Luo. The party stands primarily for tribal and minority rights, which KANU deprecates in the interest, ostensibly, of national unity. But can national unity be preserved and consolidated without the support of the tribal minorities?

Ngala threatened secession of the Coastal Region and warned that KADU would not tolerate any KANU attempt to undermine the constitution on the pretext of forming an East African federation. He maintained that the regions derive their authority from the constitution, not from the central government, and raised a counterslogan "Freedom and Secession." Mboya, on his part, continued to insist that the regional governments are no more than local authorities and that the central government holds that its laws are applicable throughout Kenya, irrespective of the political complexion of the respective regions.* Mboya further declared, before leaving for London in June, 1963, that any regional president trying to behave as if he controlled a regional government would be firmly and swiftly dealt with. Kenyatta's subsequent statements threatening strong action against "subversion" were a further pointer to KANU thinking. But they did not still KADU clamor. The president of the Rift Valley regional assembly, Daniel Arap Moi, demanded complete autonomy for this region, adding, "There will be bloodshed if people try to get rid of the regions." Ngala also warned that any central attempt to do away with regionalism would result in all regions becoming autonomous.

These contrary affirmations did not help to mollify feelings on either

---

* The Northeast Region is being temporarily administered by the central government because of the Somali boycott.

side, but threatened a head-on collision. KANU's declared policy was to scrap the regionalism agreed upon in the internal self-government constitution, preferably at the September conference in London, which was scheduled to sort out the final details of independence or alternatively to force these changes after independence. Its argument was that the minority safeguards provided by the interim constitution had been nullified by the majority verdict at the polls. According to the proposed amendment procedure, agreed upon by both parties, changes in the constitution would require a majority of 75 percent of each house, except that changes affecting entrenched rights of individuals, regions, tribal authorities, or districts would require in addition a senate majority of 90 percent, which KANU would find it difficult, on the prevailing figures, to obtain. With the breakaway of Paul Ngei, leader of the minority African People's party, from the opposition as a protest against Ngala's regionalism, KANU now commands ninety-two seats to KADU's thirty-one* in the lower house while in the senate it controls twenty-three seats to the opposition's sixteen, which is still far short of the required 90 percent majority. As Kenyatta observed at the preindependence conference in London—the fourth constitutional conference on Kenya in three years—the constitution bristled with massive compromises which prevented planning, obstructed the central government, and confused the civil service, thereby rendering administration ineffective. Ngala, in refuting this, emphasized that all decisions of substance regarding Kenya's future constitution were taken at the previous conference in 1962 and that the present conference could make only "technical amendments in a narrow field"—in other words, minor changes within the context of the regionalism which formed the pact of a year ago and to which the British government was a party. There could be no departing from the 75:90 formula and from the entrenched sections of the independence constitution. The British view, that the very preponderance of Kenyatta's legislative majority should make him more conciliatory to the opposition, made no impression on KANU.

The London conference of September, 1963, closed with the British government virtually resigning from its commitments to KADU and, if anything, extending the prerogatives of the central government. There was to be a reduction in the powers of the regions, particularly insofar as the police and public services were concerned, and the agreement also made easier the procedure for revising the constitution, by stipulating that, should a two-thirds parliamentary majority not be obtained, a referendum might be held to ascertain the electorate's view on revision. This in effect scrapped the 75:90 formula, which constituted a major safeguard for the minorities. On their side the Kenya government had no difficulty in promising to safe-

* Subsequent KADU defections reduced the party representation to twenty-six.

guard the rights of minorities and to respect fundamental democratic liberties. In this context Mboya's views on the one-party system, as enunciated in his book *Freedom and After*, are illuminating. "In the years immediately after independence," he observes, "a State needs to maintain unity as the basis for all development. As far as possible it needs a single, strong, and effective party. . . . The single party can best mobilise the new forces of a population ready to work with their hands and sweat to reconstruct the economy. . . . This is only possible where you have popular leadership and a strong party machine. It is impossible where you have a multi-party system with the opposition party waiting for the day it can replace the Government." This bodes ill for Kenya's future tranquility and for the position of the minority tribes.

At one stage during the conference KADU threatened to set up a Kenya republic made up of the minority regions of the Rift Valley, Western, Northeastern, and Coast regions, which would form a horseshoe round the areas controlled by KANU. Ngala, it was announced, would be president of the new breakaway state, which would have its capital at Nakura, with the party chairman, Daniel Arap Moi, as vice-president, and KADU's deputy leader, Masinde Muliro, as prime minister. This plan would leave the Central (Kikuyu), Nyanza (Luo), and Eastern (Kamba) regions to KANU. On the face of it this seems impracticable, and in any case the Somalis of the Northeastern Region, who have rejected regionalism out of hand, would probably refuse to come in. Incidentally, the Northeastern Region, which was offered special development funds by the central government—it boycotted the last elections for national assembly seats and for a regional assembly—was invited to participate in new elections to be held either before or after independence. KADU subsequently postponed its partition plan, but did not cancel it. Ngala later walked out of the London conference, accusing the British government and Sandys of having let him down. He warned that the British government might have to use armed forces in Kenya to "uphold its dishonor." KANU's reply to KADU's partition threat was a counterthreat to predate Kenya's independence to October 20, a step rendered unnecessary by Sandys's surrender to Kenyatta's demands. Sandys failed in his attempts to turn on the hose.

In November, 1963, Kenyatta's government ordered the settlement of 2,500 Kikuyu families on Highlands farms and invoked British money for the settlement of another 300,000 acres with Kikuyu families. The scheme was approved by Sandys. Simultaneously not only Kenyatta and Mboya but also Odinga sought to soothe the fears of the white settlers by mollifying assurances. The British Nationality Act was relaxed so as to enable the whites to regain British citizenship within two years should Kenya prove too oppressive. KANU had previously refused to agree to this at the September conference. If European nervousness was thereby temporarily eased, Asian disquiet persisted and expressed itself in the exodus of many hundreds of Asians from Kenya. When independence came it looked as if the only intractable problem facing Kenyatta was the demand for secession by the overwhelming majority of the 200,000 Somalis in the Northeastern Region. But there were other problems, and the short-lived mutiny on January 25, 1964, of the 11th Battalion of the Kenya Rifles* stationed at Lanet, 100 miles from Nairobi, was evidence of the rumblings close beneath the surface.

Raids by Somali *shiftas* (bandits) increased after independence, leading Kenyatta to declare a state of emergency in the Northeastern Region. Hit-and-run raids were largely concentrated in the area where the Kenya, Ethiopia, and Somali borders meet while more serious clashes occurred along the Somali-Ethiopian frontier. In December, 1963, shortly after independence, Kenya and Ethiopia finalized arrangements for a mutual defense pact initiated in November whereby either country undertook to come to the aid of the other if it were attacked by a third party. Nairobi and Addis Ababa accused Mogadishu of expansionist aims. KANU's election manifesto had promised to complete arrangements for a joint defense system with Uganda and Tanganyika. In November Somali's Prime Minister Ali Shermarke, having been stalled in his negotiations with Washington for $18.2 million worth of arms, accepted a Russian offer of large-scale military supplies, and Mogadishu concluded an agreement with Moscow for $30.8 million military aid which according to the West would enable it to create an army of 20,000. Kenya's Somali troubles combined with the Lanet mutiny will probably accelerate the move for joint defense arrangements in East Africa as also efforts to establish an East African federation. A basis for the latter exists in a common airline, railway, tax-collection system, market, and services organization which provide the functional elements of unity.

Forewarned by the Zanzibar upheaval and the successive military mutinies in Tanganyika and Uganda, Kenyatta wisely took the precautionary safeguard of soliciting British military assistance before the actual outbreak in the barracks at Lanet. The mutiny was quelled by the 3d Regiment, Royal Horse Artillery, who disarmed the mutineers within a matter of hours. Kenyatta reacted with commendable firmness, refusing to meet the mutineers who, he warned, would be dealt with by his government "most severely."

Nyerere's call for a meeting of the defense ministers and foreign ministers of the Organization of African Unity underlined the awareness of the three affected countries of East Africa of the need to act in concert. In

* Kenya's army consists of three battalions.

Kenya an interesting reaction to the mutiny was a move to place restrictions on the numbers of Chinese and other Eastern diplomatic missions operating in that country. A unification of the East African forces would entail the creation of a unified East African Transport which would require a fairly long-term agreement with Britain, extending from three to five years. Despite the more rapid advancement of an Africanized army, Kenyatta is aware of the need for reconsideration of the future of the British base in Kenya from which Britain had agreed to withdraw at the end of 1964.

Perhaps Kenyatta is also having second thoughts on the wisdom of his one-month independence amnesty to the Mau Mau "forest fighters" who have not loosened their terrorist grip on the southeastern slopes of Mount Kenya. A number of them have tried to infiltrate into the army, while others are finding it hard to adjust themselves easily to their new setting. Most of them are poorly qualified for modern jobs which at any rate have not kept pace with Kenya's growing number of unemployed. Kikuyu demand for land aggravates the problem posed by the "forest fighters" because the government has accorded the Kikuyu, Embu, and Meru tribes priority for farms under the resettlement schemes.

Growing restiveness and instability in Kenya could induce a panic exodus of white farmers and Asian traders on whom the country's economy still largely depends. Some 40 percent of Kenya's 4,000 British farmers are expected to leave by the end of 1964, though many Britons who have sold their estates to the Land Development and Settlement Board might decide to buy new farms in areas earmarked for permanent settlement, such as those on the rich slopes of Mount Elgon in northwest Kenya. Their decision to stay or go will be governed largely by the conditions of security prevailing in the country.

Even if the majority of Kenya's rulers are allergic today to communism, the countries of East Africa, including the island of Zanzibar, with growing unemployment and lower productivity are vulnerable to Moscow or China. Geographically Zanzibar and Pemba are ideally suited to serve as submarine or rocket bases since they lie off the mainland and sit astride the navigation routes of the Indian Ocean. Until the revolution the Americans had their Mercury Space Tracking Station in Zanzibar just outside the town. Within Kenya's KANU government are certain elements, who even if more exotic than revolutionary, are attracted by the teachings of Peking or Moscow.

The chain of army mutinies in East Africa demonstrates on the one hand the vulnerability of the civil administration to military adventurers and on the other the feeling entrenched in some soldiers' minds, triggered largely by Zanzibar, that the military, if they so choose, could hold the civil administration for ransom. Kenya with its dissident tribal elements and animosities could, if ignited, blaze a fire throughout East Africa. It has been called "God's own paradise but the Devil's own problem." Due to Kenyatta's foresight and firmness the Lanet mutiny flickered only for a few hours. But the tinder is there.

With its Mau Mau rebellion, its tribal flare-ups, and its fiercely emotional and independent races, Kenya is particularly vulnerable. Yet of all East African countries it is politically the most articulate and conscious. Kenya, proportionate to its population or territory, has given rise to more leaders of caliber than most African states. It has had some four disturbed years of preparation for independence. With the exception of Ghana, it has a larger number of trained youth, men and women, than any newly independent African state. It still needs the sinews of finance and technical assistance. In time it may overcome its regionalism, but in order to do this Kenya must achieve sobriety, stability, and inner strength. Their attainment calls for a major exercise in tolerance and compromise. Kenya can exist only as a unity in diversity and any attempt to stampede it into the first without recognizing the presence of the second is to court disaster inside the country and outside.

CHAPTER

14

A BASTION BREACHED

FOUR NAMES RECUR as one travels through the former British-ruled areas of Africa. They are Livingstone, Stanley, Rhodes, and Lugard, only the latter two of whom were empire builders. Stanley, who was an explorer and journalist, was rebuffed by British indifference and delivered his discovery of the Congo to Leopold II of Belgium, who was quick to size up the commercial potentialities of the river and its rich hinterland. Livingstone was an explorer and missionary, no empire builder but a gentle evangelist. His statue by William Reid Dick which overlooks Victoria Falls near Livingstone is more impressive than the squat, chunky figure of Stanley which gazes over the Congo outside Léopoldville. Near Stanley's statue is a bronze frieze of three of his faithful African porters; they look pathetic in their melancholy. Lugard had the vision of a statesman more than the brashness of an imperialist. Yet he did lay the foundations of Britain's African empire from Mombasa to Uganda, and beyond to Nigeria.

At the mammoth exhibition staged during the independence celebrations at Lagos, I came across an interesting missive dispatched by the then sultan of Sokoto to Lugard in May, 1902. Its translation reads: "In the name of God, the compassionate and merciful. The blessing of God be on the Prophet, the Exalted. . . . From us to you—I do not consent that anyone from you should dwell with us. I will never agree with you. I will have nothing ever to do with you. Between us and you there are no dealings except as between Massalmein and unbelievers [Kaffirs]—war, as God Almighty has enjoined on us. There is no power or strength save in God on high. This with salutations."

Rhodesia is a lovely land, embellished by nature, but marred by man, at least politically and socially in the white man's relations with his black fellow men. The old concept that colonialism has left the ex-Imperial peoples poorer is outmoded, as John Strachey pointed out in one of his last books, *End of Empire,* but some European colonialists, like those in Southern Rhodesia, have also to realize that imperialism is equally outmoded and out of date, and that the relationship they plan to perpetuate—one of white domination over the black—is anachronistic. The modern techniques which the European has brought to Rhodesia are there for all to see, in its cities, roads, buildings, industrial plants, and business centers, but scarring the lush commercial landscape is the ugliness of man's cruelty to man.

As countries, the Rhodesias fascinated me, and some of the natural beauty they abound in is breathtaking. Driving before dawn from Livingstone to Bulawayo, we saw the moon, a huge glowing orb, dipping like an incandescent, captive balloon behind dark clouds, and shortly after, the sun rose golden red behind the hills. The skies were angry with a blaze of vermilion. At Livingstone we stayed at the Falls Hotel, the only caravansary I've seen which contains a chapel. It was built by the Africa Company in 1914. One afternoon we visited the Victoria Falls, which presents a most majestic and awe-inspiring spectacle. A double rainbow, streaked green, red, and yellow, glimmered and glowed beneath white spumes of foam at Danger Point, and the waters of the Zambezi roared as they cascaded down the rocks, iridescent in the sunlight.

The impress of Cecil Rhodes's personality on the two Rhodesias, particularly Southern Rhodesia, is vividly evident. His rugged figure with the strong purposeful face stands in many public squares, and the breadth of Bulawayo's main streets, designed, so we were told, to enable a cart and team of eight oxen to turn around within the width of the highway, is another reminder of the empire builder's day. Rhodes's grave with the simple inscription "Rhodes" lies high on the Matapo hills crowning the Matabeleland some twenty miles outside Bulawayo. On the way there we passed rock boulders and mounds piled precariously in surrealistic formations, some shaped like Henry Moore figures, all of them nature's handiwork and reminiscent of the giant weird rocks near Zaria in North Nigeria. Bulawayo's Government House stands on the site of King Lobengula's kraal, which also houses Rhodes's conical-roofed, thatched hut and a thick-set tree with a clustering canopy of overhanging branches under which Lobengula used to hold his *indabas,* or conferences of chiefs.

The former Central African Federation, which was dissolved at the end of 1963, comprised the British territories of Northern and Southern Rhodesia and Nyasaland, and is situated south of sub-Saharan Africa's Mason-Dixon line separating the independent northern two-thirds from the white-dominated southern one-third. Flanking the federation are Portuguese Mozambique and Angola, while to the south are the trust territory of South West Africa administered by the Union of South Africa; the high commission territories of Bechuanaland, Basutoland, and Swaziland; and South Africa.

The federation's total territory covered an area roughly the size of France, Spain, and West Germany combined, with a population of over 8.5 million of whom some 305,000 were Europeans. The African population numbered around 8.3 million, with about 40,000 Asians and others. The biggest European concentration is in Southern Rhodesia (221,000), with another 75,000 in Northern Rhodesia and some 9,000 in Nyasaland. Southern Rhodesia and Nyasaland have each around 3 million Africans, and about 2.5 million live in Northern Rhodesia. The largest number of Asians reside in Southern Rhodesia (about 18,000), with another 12,500 in Nyasaland.

Until the breakup of the federation, which had functioned since 1953, Southern Rhodesia—a self-governing entity since 1923—regarded itself as a senior partner, with Northern Rhodesia, the largest of the three in terms of size, as a junior partner. Nyasaland, a British protectorate, like Northern Rhodesia, was, with its 99 percent African population, looked upon as an appendage. Economically, the three territories were complementary, with Nyasaland providing the labor; Northern Rhodesia, with its rich copper belt area, the mineral wealth; and Southern Rhodesia the secondary industries and white skills. Even if such economic association tended to keep the less developed areas static, as is sometimes argued, the diversification of the economy helped the progress of the federation as a whole and each of its three components.

European complacency and obtuseness have contributed primarily to the breakup of the federation, for entrenched in their economic privileges and in the belief that their political domination would continue indefinitely, the whites discounted the possibility of the blacks ever undermining and in the end virtually destroying their powerful, pervasive authority. It was only as late as December, 1962, that Welensky's lieutenant, Sir Edgar Whitehead, premier of Southern Rhodesia, campaigned for the first time for the abolition of the color bar in that territory and for African-majority rule in fifteen years, only to have his Rhodesia National party (RNP) beaten by the segregationist right-wing Winston Field's newly created Rhodesian Front (RF), which won thirty-five of the sixty-five legislature seats. The RNP,* which secured twenty-nine seats, returned fourteen of Welensky's African puppets, the fifteenth African seat going to a white liberal, Dr. Ahru Palley.† Rather than submit to black-majority rule, which would inevitably follow the "one-man, one-vote" cry of the Africans, Field precipitated the breakup of the federation by demanding independence for Southern Rhodesia.

Can that territory go it alone? For many years the federation has represented the most successful economic association of African states. Though Northern Rhodesia is the richest of the three units, it would be to its advantage to work more closely within a complex which includes Southern Rhodesia. Mountainous, poverty-stricken Nyasaland is not economically viable on its own, and until secession drew its economic sustenance through heavy subsidies from the two Rhodesias.

Among Nyasaland's principal exports are its laborers, a considerable proportion of whom find employment in the mines of South Africa. Dr. Banda's self-imposed isolation has also forced him to lean heavily on Lisbon, since he is now dependent on Mozambique for his import-export channels. Until independence Nyasaland's main export crop was tea, which brought in over $5.6 million a year, and it now plans to develop and intensify cooperative farming, offsetting the loss of subsidies from the Rhodesias by foreign aid, principally from America, though nothing substantial has yet materialized from that quarter. Foreign funds are urgently needed if Nyasaland's development projects, such as the approximately $6-million hydroelectric scheme at Nguia Falls, are to fructify. A British subvention would probably continue to be forthcoming unless Nyasaland chooses to secede.

Nyasaland's main cash crops are tea, cotton, tobacco, and peanuts, of which tea accounts for about 40 percent of the total agricultural income of $28 million. The idea is to encourage African smallholders to grow tea for sale in small lots to the factories. Nyasaland cannot be industrialized in the foreseeable future. It aims at developing secondary industries on a modest scale, and a survey has been made of the possibility of setting up enterprises such as a softwood industry and of producing wood pulp, plywood, and matches.

Britain's anxiety to prevent Southern Rhodesia from drifting into the arms of South Africa might also persuade Nyasaland to make tariff concessions to Southern Rhodesia, where some 130,000 Nyasas work on farms

* The RNP is an autonomous wing of Welensky's old United Federal party (UFP).

† He is a South African settled in Rhodesia.

and in the towns. Hitherto, Dr. Banda's Malawi Congress party has bitterly resented federal tariffs, which in the past have protected Southern Rhodesian industries at the expense of industrially backward Nyasaland.

The territory has also been starved of loan money for its development. Between 1953 and mid-1959, Nyasaland's share of the total of $730.8 million spent in loans was only $28 million. Nor does the Kariba Dam, which is a boon to the two Rhodesias, directly benefit Nyasaland. The economic benefit of federation to Nyasaland was assessed at around $11.2 million a year.

Northern Rhodesia has been described as the goose that lays the copper egg. In 1961 40 percent or $449.2 million of Northern Rhodesia's net domestic production came from the Copperbelt,* copper and cobalt accounting for 64 percent of the Rhodesian federation's exports in the same year. In seven years the Northern Rhodesian government contributed to the federal pool $154 million more in taxes (mainly from copper company profits and in income tax) than it received back either in federal services or as its redistributed share of the income tax. In 1961 alone, nearly $36.4 million went by way of taxes to the federal treasury from the copper mining industry. Northern Rhodesia is the world's second largest supplier of copper.

The argument that a wider economy cushions a price fall in a primary product was controverted by that territory long before internal self-government was envisaged, the then government arguing that had taxation been equitably distributed, it would have had sufficient funds in reserve to cover the losses entailed by the slump of copper prices in 1956–1958. Even in that lean period, Northern Rhodesia contributed more in income and company taxes than Southern Rhodesia—and received less benefit.

On the other hand, while the Copperbelt contains enormous ore reserves—the open pit at the Nchanga mine is likely to yield ore for at least another hundred years—Northern Rhodesia is a monoeconomy and therefore sensitive to any sudden collapse in world copper prices. In July, 1963, a government spokesman hinted at the possibility of Lusaka† imposing a tariff on imports from Salisbury.‡ It was then estimated that Northern Rhodesia bought about $58.8 million worth of manufactured goods from Southern Rhodesia every year.

Whatever Southern Rhodesia's 221,000 whites might say, that territory stands proportionately to lose more by the dismantling of the federation than the other two. Federation has extended each of their economies in a

* It consists of six modern mining towns near the Katanga border.
† Capital of Northern Rhodesia.
‡ Capital of Southern Rhodesia.

vulnerable direction, and the pace of industrialization to which Southern Rhodesia has been committed, on the assumption that the economies of the three territories would remain interlocked within an everlasting federation, must in time be impaired and slow down as capital inflow slackens its rate.

Nonetheless Southern Rhodesia, repudiating African majority rule, has decided to go it alone. Should Northern Rhodesia and Nyasaland raise their tariff walls, Southern Rhodesia's secondary industries will suffer. True, the southern territory can also twist the economic arms of the other two, since the economy of the three territories constitutes, to some extent, a complex. The Kariba Dam sits astride the frontier of the two Rhodesias, and Salisbury could stop the flow of power from the dam to the Copperbelt, but it would in turn have to build costly power installations to replace the switching station near Kitwe. Similarly, it could close its railways to the copper, which at present goes via the south to the Mozambique coast, but Salisbury would thereby lose its revenue from the copper freight. Another federal property is the Central African Airways. Kaunda's* solution is to sell all these properties to the Oppenheimer interests; the three territories could then separately buy these services from it. Britain would like the three countries to retain control in order to maintain their economic links.

African restiveness led to a drop in Southern Rhodesia in the confidence of investors, domestic and foreign. As far back as 1961, gross investment in industry sagged to $18.2 million while investment in the private sector fell from $87.9 million in 1957 to about $17 million in 1961. Unemployment in April, 1963, stood at 80,000. Two of the major copper-producing groups, the Rhodesian Selection Trust and Oppenheimer's Anglo-American Corporation of South Africa, have shifted their head offices from Salisbury to Lusaka. Increased emigration of whites will remove many taxpayers.

Southern Rhodesia hopes to develop her primary products, the chief of which is tobacco, which in 1959 produced a record crop of the value of $76.4 million. Development in the Hippo Valley has also turned Southern Rhodesia into a sugar exporter, thereby saving some $8.4 million in foreign exchange. Other revenue boosters are Mangula copper, chrome, and steel, and, though trade with both Northern Rhodesia and Nyasaland is bound to shrink, Southern Rhodesia optimistically hopes it can still keep about two-thirds of it, roughly totaling $56 million. Added to the favorable external balance of trade, this could bring a favorable balance of $112 million a year to an independent Southern Rhodesia. The Rhodesian Front government is also proposing to assist the opening of new gold mines in South-

* He is the leader of the United National Independence Party (UNIP) in Northern Rhodesia.

ern Rhodesia, thereby increasing the output from 500,000 ounces to 900,000 ounces annually. All the three territories are expected to inherit from the Bank of Rhodesia and Nyasaland a strong foreign exchange position.

Although the price index has risen, the average European income has gone up by 10 percent in seven years and the African by 42 percent. The disparity between African and European still remains glaring: about $3,181 per year per working European to $204 per year per African in cash employment. But the vast majority of Africans are outside the cash economy.

With the dissolution of the federation, Southern Rhodesia's recurrent expenditure will soar from $70 million to $126 million, necessitating a tax increase and a general belt-tightening. The maintenance of a separate army will cost an extra $14 million a year. Provided there is internal stability, Southern Rhodesia's economic future, though bound to be difficult for two or three years after the federal dissolution, need not be unduly bleak. In the long run economic truths must shape political thinking.

So much for the interlocked economic framework of the three territories which the end of federation must materially affect. At the Victoria Falls conference (June 28–July 3, 1963), which was attended by delegates from Britain, and Northern and Southern Rhodesia—Nyasaland also sent observers—and was presided over by Mr. R. A. Butler, Central African affairs minister, it was decided that the federation should dissolve on December 31, 1963, though the new form of economic association to replace this, which Mr. Butler had envisaged prior to the conference, has yet to take shape. Dissolution was inevitable once the right of secession was conceded to Nyasaland and Northern Rhodesia, for it then became illogical to refuse Mr. Winston Field's counterdemand for Southern Rhodesia's independence. Whitehall conceded this in principle in the hope that Field would agree to increase the number of African seats in the legislative assembly and repeal the Land Apportionment Act.* Field refused to do either and insisted on Southern Rhodesia's independence once the federation was dissolved.

Kaunda's United National Independence party (UNIP) was willing to consider economic links on the Kariba Dam, the railways, and Central

* The Southern Rhodesian Land Apportionment Act has since 1931 reserved 51 percent of all land for whites. It forbids Africans to live outside their townships, except as servants. It also prevents Africans from owning land in the "native locations" bordering the white towns. Africans could not buy, lease, or occupy any land in the European area. When the multiracial university was established at Salisbury, the act was amended so that nonwhites could attend. It had to be amended again to allow multiracial organizations to operate in white areas, to allow African lawyers to occupy chambers and to permit the opening of hotels to all races. But the act still stands on the statute book.

African Airways, though it still pressed for a representative African majority government in Southern Rhodesia.

In October, 1963, the Southern Rhodesian government officially announced that the $230-million Kariba hydroelectric power scheme on the Zambezi would continue to be operated and developed as a single entity under the joint ownership and control of the governments of Southern and Northern Rhodesia after the dissolution of the federation. The Kariba project, which was opened by Queen Elizabeth, the Queen Mother, in 1960, has a power station, now completed, on the south bank, producing 600 megawatts. The north bank power station, when built, will produce another 900 megawatts. This will raise the cost of the scheme to over $280 million, which is being met by loans from the World Bank (about $75.6 million), the Colonial Development Corporation, Anglo-American and the Rhodesian Selection Trust, the British South Africa Company, and Standard and Barclay's Banks. The new corporation will be known as the Central African Power Corporation.

Rhodesia Railways have presented a tougher proposition, the question being whether after the federal breakup, the two railway systems of Northern and Southern Rhodesia should split at the Zambezi border or whether they should go on as a unified system under joint control. Who will underwrite the $36.4-million pension fund? What of compensation for retrenchment? Rhodesia Railways employ 21,000 Africans and about 10,000 whites while another 1,400 workers are pensioners. The former all-white Rhodesia Railwaymen's Union, representing the higher skills, has 400 African members. Will the white railwaymen based in Northern Rhodesia be guaranteed their jobs along with the African railwaymen in Southern Rhodesia after the breakup? Rhodesia Railways have a $266-million investment of which about $109 million was provided by Southern Rhodesia, $42 million by Northern Rhodesia, and $89.6 million by the federal government. Who takes over the federal government's obligations? Disentangling these assets and liabilities calls for more than mere arithmetic.

In April, 1963, Welensky's old United Federal party was formally split into a territorial and a federal wing, the territorial autonomous wing being known as the Rhodesia National party (RNP), under Sir Edgar Whitehead, the federal wing being rechristened the Federal party, under Sir Roy Welensky. There has been a move to start a new "middle-of-the-road" party between Whitehead's "ultraliberalism" and Field's "ultrarightism," but nothing has come of it. The name of Mr. John Caldicott, former federal minister of finance, was mentioned in this connection. More recently, with Field's Rhodesian Front to the extreme right and the African nationalist parties to the extreme left, Whitehead has been attempting to make the RNP the "party of the middle," its position now approximating to that of the old Liberal Central Africa party, which was wiped out in the December, 1962, elections. Welensky's UFP is still right of the RNP, though both parties are opposed to universal franchise, or one man, one vote, and continue to insist on a qualitative franchise for the Africans. Both Welensky and Whitehead now seem prepared to liberalize the franchise within the 1961 constitution, but not to the point of entrenching an African majority in power. Welensky's attitude is more rigid than that of Whitehead. Whereas the latter is prepared to make minor changes, the former favors only nominal changes.

These moves and preparations foreshadowed an acceptance of the inevitability of the dissolution of federation. Even Field, though seemingly adamant, was prepared "to consider changes in the B-roll franchise, to simplify it so all and sundry can understand the system under which they are voting."

Under the 1961 constitution for Southern Rhodesia, the single common electoral roll was replaced by two, A and B. A included chiefs, headmen, and those already qualified to vote on a high income and education qualification, which restricted the franchise to around 20,000 of the territory's 3 million Africans. B included all persons over thirty with much lower income and educational qualifications; e.g., a man with a primary education earning $336 a year or owning property worth $700 could vote. The legislative assembly was enlarged from fifty to sixty-five members, the extra fifteen being reserved for "African" members elected by the special African electoral districts. Until then there were no African members.

Welensky had made the very word "federation" anathema to the Africans, since federation, as Welensky conceived it, implied eternal white dominance. He is not to be blamed entirely for this, for right up to the 1952–1953 conferences, during Churchill's last lap of power, he had been given to understand by the British government and particularly by three of Churchill's ministers—Swinton, Chandos, and Boyd—that Whitehall was opposed to the secession of any of the three territories. Welensky also appears to have been assured by the British government that the residual power of parliament to terminate the federation would never be used without the consent of the federal cabinet. Constitutionally, the British government enjoyed this residual power. But by treating the federal prime minister, beginning with Welensky's predecessor, Lord Malvern,* as on a par with the independent Commonwealth prime ministers and by allowing him to attend the Commonwealth conferences, it had led Welensky to

* Malvern, the former Godfrey Huggins, was premier of Southern Rhodesia from 1933 to 1953, and federal prime minister from 1953 to 1956, when Welensky succeeded him.

believe that the federation was for all practical purposes an equal member of the Commonwealth "club." Churchill, during the war, had refused to preside as British Prime Minister over "the liquidation of the Indian empire." Similarly, Welensky had thought it inconceivable that the federation would ever be allowed to dissolve. Both men had to accept the inevitable. Churchill took it with good grace, but in the circumstances Welensky's bitterness can be understood.

During my stay in the Rhodesias and Nyasaland I talked with many African leaders as well as with many European politicians of varied schools of thought. Among several prominent politicians I met at Lusaka were Kenneth Kaunda, head of UNIP, and the diehard John Gaunt, who had then just formed the Rhodesian Reform Group, which was right of Welensky. Gaunt is now minister of mines and development in Field's Rhodesian Front (RF) government in Southern Rhodesia.

Kaunda, a tall, quiet-voiced man, suggests a coiled spring, an impression heightened by his intense eyes and startling shock of upstanding hair. He was in India in 1958, has a great admiration for Gandhi, and, despite his impassioned public speeches, genuinely abhors violence. Compared with some other African politicians, including Harry Nkumbula, who leads the rival African National Congress (ANC) in Northern Rhodesia, Kaunda struck me as a moderate, though some Europeans to whom I mentioned it demurred. His father was a Nyasa who went to Northern Rhodesia as a Church of England missionary. Kaunda is forty.

"We are not opposed to federation in principle," he explained. "We ourselves hope to erase the artificial boundaries and to create large states in Africa founded on that very principle. But the Central African Federation is run on the wrong lines, for the wrong reasons, by the wrong people. We can have nothing to do with that setup. We hear a lot of high-sounding words and phrases which mean nothing. What is the use of talking about a multiracial society when there is not a single African member in the Southern Rhodesia legislative council of thirty members? [This was in November, 1960.] Now Sir Edgar Whitehead talks of having four Africans in a house of fifty. We want nonracialism, we do not want multiracialism."

Nkumbula, who leads the ANC, studied at the London School of Economics. He was sprucely turned out when I met him. He is fluent and has evasive, slightly glazed eyes. On federation he was even more emphatic than Kaunda.

"I am implacably against federation," he declared. "It must go. It was brought about to sabotage African nationalism."

I asked both Kaunda and Nkumbula whether they were prepared to accept a type of loose federation such as was then envisaged by the European Liberal party, led by Sir John Moffat in Northern Rhodesia.

They were at that time both opposed to it, though later, with the decision to break up the federation, their attitude thawed. The European Liberal party, while opposed to federation as it then existed, favored the setting up of a body analogous to the old East African Common Services Organization,* which would direct and control the railways, harbors, civil aviation, and research projects in the three territories, but not the roads, posts, and telegraphs. In the federation, defense and the armed forces were a federal responsibility, whereas internal security and the police were a territorial responsibility. To this compromise solution both Kaunda and Nkumbula, as indeed every African leader I met, were resolutely opposed. At that time it seemed to them a back-door device designed to bring in federation decked in new clothes. With the demise of federa-ation, their attitude has perceptibly changed. But in 1960 every African was allergic to Welensky and federation. Kaunda and Nkumbula were later to work together in a coalition government preparatory to the January, 1964, elections which brought in self-government.

"The basic fact," said a European liberal sadly, "is that the Africans do not want the overall white rule of Salisbury."

John Gaunt, who dined with me and with whom I had two long talks, was no liberal. He was a dyed-in-the-wool diehard, as cast-iron as they come, son of a British admiral who was once commander-in-chief of the East Indies squadron based in Bombay, and himself a product of Brasenose College, Oxford. Like many extremists of the right and left I have met, he had most charming manners and was an amusing companion, with varied conversational trivia.

"The crux of the whole problem," he observed, "is the African majority. If that comes, Northern Rhodesia and Nyasaland might as well be written off."

It came, and Gaunt, with Winston Field, is fighting a last-ditch battle to stave off an African majority in Southern Rhodesia.

"So long as secession is in the air," Gaunt remarked, "territorial parties count for more than federal. This partly explains the number of African territorial parties."

He was interesting on Welensky, about whom every African is derisive. At Blantyre in Nyasaland I had talked with Masauka Chipembere, trea-surer-general of Banda's Malawi Congress party, and Kanyama Chiume, then its publicity secretary. Both of them said they hated the very word "federation." "We want independence and secession now," they de-clared. Chipembere was a stout, pleasant individual, but Chiume struck

---

* Butler canvassed the same idea in the form of an economic association at the Victoria Falls conference of June–July, 1963, though the British White Paper was careful to avoid the term.

one as somewhat brash and self-opinionated. He kept referring to Welensky as "that ex-locomotive driver."

Gaunt was ruminative.

"It is true," he mused on Welensky, "that he was an engine driver. But he's remarkably shrewd and intelligent. His experience in the trade unions and railways has made him acutely aware of the political and economic importance of the color bar. Many poor whites have the same attitude. I think the real reason why Welensky is so extremist is that he has not a drop of British blood in his veins. His father was a Lithuanian and his mother an Afrikaner."

Coming from Gaunt, I thought his reference to Welensky as an extremist rather odd, for, though Welensky is a political and racial retrograde, his party includes Africans—undoubtedly stooges—and is at least tokenly interracial. Field's RF can by no stretch be suspected of even token liberalism, though personally he is well liked by some Africans, including Robert Mugabe, publicity secretary of the banned Zimbabwe* African Peoples' Union (ZAPU), and one of the up-and-coming ZAPU leaders, Josiah Chinamano. Field, a fifty-nine-year-old, wealthy tobacco farmer, is a soft-spoken man and is described as "self-consciously paternalist."

Another informative visitor to my hotel was a former civil servant who in his retirement had taken to farming and journalism. He was then the correspondent in Lusaka for *The Times* (London) and *The Guardian,* and was well informed. Harry Franklin was well known in the federation and had been chairman of Sir John Moffat's Liberal party in Northern Rhodesia. Like many long-time European residents he was sick of the country's politics, but he was a true liberal with an enlightened outlook, though highly critical of African leadership.

"I respect Kaunda and Nyerere," he said, "but the tragedy is that one can't rely on the African leaders delivering the goods. Sooner or later they are the victims of their own extremists."

Franklin was opposed to the principle of federation and favored some machinery like the East African Common Services Organization.

"Federation won't last," he affirmed. "It's bound to break up."

This was in 1960.

"Welensky is living in a dream world of his own," said Franklin. "His dream will end in a nightmare."

Welensky's wings have been clipped, but it would be wrong to underrate his political influence, which is still considerable. Welensky has come

---

* Zimbabwe is the African name for Southern Rhodesia, Zambia for Northern Rhodesia, and Malawi for Nyasaland. When independent, each of these three areas will be rechristened accordingly.

up the hard way. He was born in Salisbury in 1907, has had no formal education, went to work as a storekeeper at fourteen, was a fireman and an aggressive railway trade unionist, has always been as tough with his tongue as he once was with his fists—he was heavyweight boxing champion of Southern Rhodesia back in 1925–1927—and entered the Northern Rhodesia legislature in 1938. Though Malvern dominated the political scene, Welensky was soon a well-known public figure. He began campaigning for federation in 1948 and, when it came in 1953, became deputy federal prime minister, succeeding Malvern as prime minister three years later. His political career thus covers a crowded span of some twenty-five years. Welensky, though tough, can be persuasively plausible in argument and when the occasion requires can unbend sufficiently to be even pleasant to his opponents. He is hampered as much by history as by his own irascible temperament.

The early history of Southern Rhodesia is bound up with Cecil Rhodes, who was eager to extend British power north of the South African Boer republics. For nearly fifty years Southern Rhodesia was the virtual fief of the Matabele tribe, until in 1887 Rhodes tricked Lobengula, the Matabele chief, into handing over all the mineral rights of the territory for some rifles, ammunition, and $280 a month. Rhodes's British South Africa Company, which in 1889 received a royal charter, took over these rights, and the following year the company's "Pioneer Column" invaded and occupied Mashonaland. In 1893 the Matabele were provoked into a quarrel and crushed.

The two Rhodesias were administered by the BSA until 1924, when Northern Rhodesia became a protectorate under the British Crown. The Matabele were not the only tribe in this area. There were the Lozi tribe, who under their chief, Lewanika, dominated Barotseland and who in 1891 asked for British protection, which was granted to them. There are over 200 chiefs in the Rhodesias graded in a hierarchy of paramount chiefs, senior chiefs, and chiefs. Of these Barotseland, which in area is larger than Ireland, cherished secessionist ambitions when Northern Rhodesia passed from British tutelage and in this it was to some extent encouraged by Nkumbula's ANC, which in May, 1963, asked in a memorandum presented to the government committee drawing up the new constitution for Northern Rhodesia for special safeguards for the tribal chiefs. It suggested the setting up of a house of chiefs modeled on the House of Lords and empowered to delay legislation passed by the house of representatives. It also proposed that the president of the house of chiefs should be appointed deputy to the governor.

Meanwhile, Kaunda, on behalf of UNIP, carried on talks with the Litunga, or paramount chief, Sir Mwanawina Lewanika, on the future relationship between Northern Rhodesia and Barotseland, a territory which might be described as a protectorate within a protectorate, enjoying a special status. The Litunga at one time seemed inclined to have Barotseland remain under British protection, with the British guaranteeing its frontiers. If Britain had done so it would have been placed in an embarrassing, if not impossible, situation. Mr. Butler's advice to the Litunga was to recognize the realities of the situation and in return make such arrangements as he could to retain his special position. Economically and strategically, Barotseland is a pocket state flanked by Northern Rhodesia, and could not afford to alienate it. But the Litunga was stubbornly bent on preserving Barotseland's special status and, alongside it, his link with Britain, while insisting that the British should honor their undertaking, incorporated in the Rhodesian federal constitution and reiterated in 1961 by Mr. Iain MacLeod, then colonial secretary, that no constitutional change affecting Barotseland would be made without consultation with and the consent of the paramount chief. An independent Northern Rhodesian government would almost certainly not grant any special status to Barotseland, but it would probably be prepared to give the Litunga a status comparable to what Ghana has given to the Asanthena, with certain ceremonial rights but no political powers.

In Barotseland itself, a popular movement is growing, and in August, 1963, in the elections to the twenty-five elective seats on the Barotse national council, UNIP captured every one of the seats. Its local spokesman has not unnaturally interpreted this as signifying the end of the Litunga's request for secession. In September, 1963, an agreement was reached on the future association between Barotseland and Northern Rhodesia whereby the protectorate agreed to allow the new Northern Rhodesian self-governing constitution to be applied to Barotseland. This meant Barotseland's relinquishment of its claim to secession. On its part, the Northern Rhodesian government agreed to continue certain services, such as financing, and to provide career civil servants to man the senior police and administrative posts. The delegates could not agree on the question of safeguards being written into the new constitution, but the agreement overcame the major hurdle of threatened secession, and thereby removed a serious obstacle to implementation of the Northern Rhodesian self-governing constitution in January, 1964.

The January, 1964, elections in Northern Rhodesia ended in a big majority for Kaunda's UNIP, which captured fifty-one of the seventy-five seats in the legislative assembly as against nine won by Nkumbula's ANC and ten by the National Progress party, a European group which contested the ten constituencies reserved for the Europeans, winning all against the white candidates set up by UNIP. The NPP was formerly Sir Roy Welensky's United Federal party. Nkumbula's support came mainly from the southern province.

Kaunda, in announcing his cabinet of thirteen African ministers, declared his intention to abolish the reserved seats and expressed his determination to "move forward as one nation—not two." Though the Europeans did not elect any of his candidates, Kaunda got more support from them than he did in the 1962 election. The military mutinies in East Africa probably had their impact on the European voters. Among the casualties was Sir John Moffat, former leader of the disbanded Liberal party who as a UNIP candidate was beaten by a narrow margin by an NPP representative. Kaunda's cabinet replaced the old Executive Council which had consisted of six white ministers and four African ministers. The new UNIP government controlled all departments except defense, foreign affairs, public order, and the police, which remained under the British governor until full independence, which is scheduled for October 24, 1964. As an independent republic, Northern Rhodesia will be known as Zambia, with a constitution combining important features of both the British and the American constitutions. It will be an executive presidency on the American model rather than a British cabinet system in which the functions of Head of State and chief executive are separated. At the same time the President will have fewer powers than those of the President of Ghana. He will broadly enjoy the extensive powers and prerogatives of the President of Tanganyika, with a Vice-President below him, a cabinet not exceeding 14 ministers, and a National Assembly of 75 elected members, with five additional members whom the President will nominate. The present 10 reserved seats for Europeans will continue until the first dissolution of the National Assembly after independence.

What threatens to be a suppurative thorn in Northern Rhodesia's flesh is a white-dominated Southern Rhodesia stubbornly refusing to yield place to an African majority government. Southern Rhodesia ends where South Africa begins, and, as Britain realizes, without a common market to her north, the gravitational pull of South Africa might prove too strong for the southern territory. With the Copperbelt passing under the control of an independent African government, Southern Rhodesia has nightmare visions of becoming a poor white state, for now that secession is an accomplished and accepted fact, the European hoodoo is "one man, one vote." Southern Rhodesia accepted the principle of a widening franchise for the Africans in its 1961 constitution,* responsible Europeans, including Welensky, realizing that the tidal wave of an African majority must someday sweep the territory. The sheer logic of events should inexorably force this

---

* The agreement was subscribed to by all parties except the right-wing Dominion party, led by Mr. W. J. Harper.

evolution, for the same logic that made African majority rule inevitable in Northern Rhodesia, once it was conceded in Nyasaland, will make it inevitable in Southern Rhodesia. What the whites of Southern Rhodesia—except the purblind diehards—are now really fighting for is time, a transitional, closely controlled period of, say, fifteen years, within which both sides can adjust themselves to the fact of a Southern Rhodesia ultimately ruled by blacks, but also a region within which the whites can find a place.

Is this possible? One thing is certain—an African-dominated Southern Rhodesia is a matter of time, for paternalism in that territory is as much on its way out as apartheid is in South Africa. Adult franchise must follow the end of paternalism. The pattern which an African-dominated Southern Rhodesia will assume will naturally depend as much on the attitude of Northern Rhodesia as on its southern neighbor, and at the Victoria Falls conference, Kaunda, perhaps mindful of the necessity to settle about postal services, railways, airways, and electricity—all under federal control and centralized in the south—was noticeably mellow in his attitude to Field. On his side, Field,* despite his political pyrotechnics, also realizes that, if he is to preserve the high European standards of living, he must preserve the economic links with the north. Reliance on white support from South Africa and Portugal, he knows, would only precipitate Southern Rhodesia into the horrors of civil war and possibly a repetition of the ghastly bestialities of Mau Mau. The seed of representative political government in the south can best be implanted by closer economic cooperation between the two adjacent territories. Repeal of the Land Apportionment Act and other punitive penal laws such as the Law and Order (Maintenance) Act is a necessary concomitant to this exercise in *rapprochement*. "I think," Welensky is reported to have said, "that in Southern Africa the oak won't stand, but the bamboo will." They are some of the few wise words he has uttered in his long and waspish career.

Field seems to be veering round to Welensky's views, judging by his feelers in October, 1963, to the new British government headed by Lord Home. Speaking of Southern Rhodesia's intention to renew demands for independence and to request further urgent discussions on the subject, he observed: "We are prepared to negotiate on this and always have been." Field seems prepared to go a little way toward meeting the reported Butler formula of 30 percent plus one of African representation in the territorial assembly, but he is unlikely to accept it wholesale. Lord Home's government will probably stand by Butler's insistence on no independence with-

* Winston Field was replaced as Prime Minister by the more die-hard Ian Smith in May, 1964. Smith was formerly Deputy Prime Minister.

out better African representation. Alternatively, it might shelve the issue until after the British general elections, whose deadline is autumn, 1964. Nyasaland became independent in July, and Northern Rhodesia is to attain the same status in October, 1964.

African claims are based on the principle that Southern Rhodesia does not belong to one section of the people but to all of them, and any proposal for independence should therefore provide for ultimate rule by the majority. Continued uncertainty over the inflow of private investment capital combined with a fear that they will be left behind politically vis-à-vis Northern Rhodesia and Nyasaland may induce a more reasonable approach by the Europeans.

Both the British government and Sithole's Zimbabwe African National Union (ZANU) favor joint Commonwealth action to find a solution to the question of independence for Southern Rhodesia. Ndabaninge Sithole pressed for an emergency assembly of Commonwealth prime ministers before December 31, 1963, to discuss this issue. He argued that Field's Rhodesian Front government was voted to power by less than 1 percent of the population and that to grant the white minority independence would precipitate chaos and bloodshed. He rejected Sir Alec Douglas-Home's formula of majority rule with minority protection as a "subtle attempt to retain white privilege in a free Southern Rhodesia." Asked Sithole, "Against whom is such minority to be protected?" Meanwhile the extreme rightists in the Rhodesian Front declared their unwillingness to help the British government to find a solution "to suit their political ends."

Field has to contend with his wild men, who include deputy Prime Minister Ian Smith, Minister of Transport William Harper, Minister of Mines John Gaunt. In February, 1964, Field's talks in London with Duncan Sandys proved inconclusive but gave him a breathing space in which to try to negotiate independence; the moratorium can hardly extend beyond the end of 1964, when both Nyasaland and Northern Rhodesia will be fully independent.

The upheaval in Zanzibar, followed by the military mutinies in East Africa, have strengthened the diehards, and even Sir Edgar Whitehead, leader of the opposition Rhodesia National party, has his right wing to contend with, one of whose prime leaders is Dr. M. I. Hirsch. Whitehead himself has expressed his willingness to negotiate with Britain and not to make a unilateral declaration. He has also promised to abolish racial discrimination and increase the number of B-roll seats.

In this unsettled and confused situation Welensky might stage a political comeback on a platform midway between the RF extremists and Sir Edgar Whitehead. The problem, as he sees it, is a question of reconciling the legitimate interests of the most economically productive elements in

Southern Rhodesia, who happen to be in a minority, with the reasonable aspirations of the majority. However, even he could not roll back the tide of African nationalism but could only temporarily hold it in check.

With their differing background and pace of progress it is as interesting to speculate on the future development of the three territories as it is to muse on their varied past. As in every other country, history and geography have combined to condition and mold their pattern. The word "federation," in changing forms, haunts their comparatively short lives, for the land which covers the Rhodesias and Nyasaland was barely known to civilization a hundred years ago.

Livingstone reached Lake Nyasa in 1859 and the story goes that, pointing to the lake, he asked his porters what its name was. "Nyasa," said the porters, using the African term for "lake." And "Nyasa" it remained, with the territory around known as Nyasaland. Blantyre, with its twin town, Limbe, is the chief commercial center, a depressing place despite its ring of hills. It reminded me of one of our smaller Indian hill stations. The drive to Zomba, the country's capital, was more pleasant and in parts picturesque, with tall, stately blue gums and cypress lining the roadside. All around were undulating hills. Zomba stands at a higher elevation than Blantyre, is cooler and gay with green glades. It is one of the few world capitals without a railway.

We visited the local legislative council, housed in a new building, and listened to a debate on the police reserve bill, which was productive of many indifferent and some fatuous speeches from both the government and African benches. The official spokesman was ponderously sarcastic. It resembled a schoolboy debate. One of the things that struck me not only in Nyasaland, but in the Rhodesias, was the comparatively poor quality of European officials, compared with their counterparts whom one had known in India, and also the indifferent caliber (with a few exceptions) of both African and European political leaders.

Nyasaland is peopled by many tribes. There are the militant Tonga, the menial Chewa,* the Tumbuka, Achirwa, and Angoni, who are an offshoot of the Zulu. Everywhere was the Malawi Congress slogan, "Secession and independence now." We visited the party headquarters at Limbe, where we were given their cyclostyle weekly, *Malawi News*, in appearance not unlike the newssheets which were clandestinely distributed in India by the Congress party when it was proscribed or underground. In the copy we were given a quotation by Nehru caught my eye: "Freedom is dear to all, but dearest to those who do not have it."

The Nyasa women struck me as more brisk and businesslike than the men, and we attended a women's meeting addressed by a prominent

* Dr. Banda is a Chewa.

social worker, Vera Chirwa, whose husband, Orton, is vice-president of the Malawi Congress party.* The meeting was held in an African village of thatched mud huts with a most colorful assembly of women, one of whom was dressed in a brilliant red-and-green gown, and was smoking a cigar. I asked the lively African girl who took us there her name. "Margaret," she replied, "but I've changed it to Mumumba." She pointed to a hall where a protest meeting had been held recently against an African leader, Chester Kasonga, president of the then newly formed Christian Democratic party, whose house at Blantyre had been burned down the day before. "A stooge of Welensky," said Margaret contemptuously. We went that night with a British farmer who was married to an African woman to a bar Kasonga ran. He was there, but not very communicative.

The Nyasas, most of whom are the products of Scottish missionary schools, are known in the federation as the "black Scots." They are a devout, determined, ebullient, and incalculably quick-tempered people of whom their leader, Dr. Hastings Kamuzu Banda, is representative. They are also assertively independent. The Europeans were never overly concerned with the political ambitions of the Nyasas, whose territory even Malvern wrote off as "a black state." When on February 1, 1962, Nyasaland became a self-governing country, Banda, as its first prime minister, exulted, "Nyasaland is a black man's country in a black man's continent," and prophesied that when it seceded "our independence will start a chain reaction in Africa." Nyasaland's name will be changed to Malawi; Northern Rhodesia intends to rechristen itself Zambia, and the Africans in Southern Rhodesia plan to call their country, when independent, Zimbabwe.

Federation has haunted Nyasaland's footsteps, but never overtook it until 1953. One reason for this was that the largest group of Europeans in the territory comprised traders and missionaries whose racial relations with the Nyasas were generally good. Settlers were in a minority. Twice, in 1928 and again in 1939, Nyasaland opposed closer association with the Rhodesias. She did so again in 1948, when the idea of federation was first mooted, and was assured by the then British labor government that her wishes would be respected, but in 1953, when federation became a reality, Nyasaland was pushed into it by Churchill's last government. Africans were appointed to the Nyasaland legislative council for the first time in 1950, and six years later a new constitution provided for twelve official members, five Africans returned by African electoral colleges and six non-Africans elected directly by Europeans, Asians, and Colored. In 1959 two more nonofficial seats and two official seats were added. In July, 1960, a new constitution was devised, and the following year the Malawi Congress

* He is now minister of justice.

party swept the polls, winning all twenty "lower roll" seats and three of the eight "upper roll" seats. With twenty-three out of thirty-three seats in the legislature, they dominated not only the legislature, but secured all the five elected seats in the executive council, the remaining five being held by nominated senior civil servants. The Central African Federation thus had its first African government. Not only did the Africans vote almost solidly for Banda, but so did many Asians and some Europeans. The most prominent of the Asians is Sattar Sacranie, a barrister who heads the Nyasaland Asian Convention and has identified himself completely with the Nyasas. I spent many congenial and instructive hours at his home.

Along with the other Africans in the Rhodesias, the Nyasas, despite their comparatively good relations with the local Europeans, nourished a fierce hatred for federation, which Welensky had made the symbol of perpetual white domination. They used to refer to it scornfully as "the so-called federation." Exposure to the oppressive conditions in which Africans worked in the mines of Northern Rhodesia and South Africa, and in the tobacco farms of Southern Rhodesia—some 300,000 Nyasas earn their livelihood abroad in these territories—have made them acutely sensitive to all forms of racial disability and discrimination. Hence their eruptive and often inflammatory reactions.

Banda in many ways epitomizes the Nyasa character and outlook, with its charm, volatility, grit, determination, flashiness, and unpredictability. In the government formed in September, 1961, Banda was minister of natural resources and local government, while Kanyama Chiume became minister of education. Of the three Malawi ministers, one was a European, Colin Cameron, minister of works and transport, who was supported by the Malawi party at the elections.

Banda, hailed by his followers as "the Great Kamuzu"—Europeans referred to him before independence as "the Little Doctor"—is sixty-two, and worked his way through high school and college. In 1915, at the age of thirteen, he walked 1,100 miles to the gold mines of Johannesburg to get employment in order to enable him to study. He is a Bachelor of Philosophy from The University of Chicago, and studied medicine at Meharry Medical College, Tennessee, later taking an Edinburgh diploma to enable him to practice as a doctor in Britain. While there he actively organized Nyasas and Northern Rhodesians in opposing the federation idea. When federation came into being in 1953, he left for Ghana, where he set up practice at Kumasi, staying there until 1958, when he returned to Nyasaland after an absence of over forty years. He was soon embroiled in political activity and jailed. In February, 1962, Nyasaland became a self-governing country with "the Great Kamuzu" as its first prime minister, and Banda was greeted by his followers with the chant "Kamuzu Ndi Nkango"

(Kamuzu Is a Lion). Nyasaland, which had been proclaimed a British protectorate in 1891, was on the way to complete independence, which it will achieve on July 6, 1964. The legislature will then probably be increased in strength from thirty to fifty-five with five seats reserved for the racial minorities, and universal adult suffrage except for the reserved seats. The present ministerial ceiling of ten will also be removed.

Banda still expressed his determination to take Nyasaland out of the federation, but Whitehall, while raising no objection, pointed out that secession would mean the loss of economic benefits from Britain. Progress since self-government has not been on the lines along which many had envisaged it, and the creation of a Banda cult is gaining a grip in Nyasaland, as is the leader cult in other African countries. In a sense this was inevitable. The Malawi party organization originally rested on the rock of the two Chisiza brothers: Y. K. Chisiza, who was the organizational head, and the late Dr. Dunduzu Chisiza, who was secretary-general of the party and who was marked out as its first finance minister. Dunduzu Chisiza, however, was unfortunately killed in a motor accident early in September, 1962, and his death was a tragic loss to the party and the country. Alone among the Great Kamuzu's followers, Dunduzu Chisiza was nearest to him in stature and accessibility. In a pamphlet he published in 1961 called "Africa—What Lies Ahead," Chisiza foretold the dangers lying ahead for Nyasaland, and the possibility of the myth and legend growing around Banda inflating him into the position of a virtual dictator. "The deification of one leader is essential for the struggle—but it may present problems after we are free," he warned. At the same time Chisiza attempted to justify the necessity for a single leader who enjoyed the unswerving trust of his followers and the country to operate at a level above them. "When too much trust is reposed in a leader," he wrote, "the thing sometimes goes to his head and makes him believe that he is infallible. Such a man is not likely to brook criticism or to welcome alternative suggestions. It is his idea or nothing. On the other hand, when a brilliant, self-assured, well-meaning leader is begrudged trust or is dealing with a dense population, he, too, will tend to force his measures through in a dictatorial manner, believing that the masses will approve what he is doing later."

This is what has come to pass, largely as a result of the failure of the Malawi Congress party to preserve the balance between the two alternatives which Chisiza posed. To the masses, particularly to the Malawi-inspired masses, Banda appears a demi-god. He lives today in a "palace" surrounded by high walls, and guarded always by sentries and policemen. He travels in a convoy of vehicles before which all other traffic must give way on pain of the offender being penalized with a fine or worse, and he is greeted wherever he goes with resounding cries of "the Great Kamuzu,"

"Our Savior," "the Great Ngwazi, Dr. Hastings Kamuzu Banda." These manifestations have naturally gone to Banda's head, and a note of wildness appears to have crept into his old habit of sudden anger. He has been described as "a dominie whom his people heed." Today he stands head and shoulders above his lieutenants, and has been deified into a myth. He is virtually a dictator. Apart from the public adulation he receives, he is exposed to the private subservience of his chief lieutenants, whom he refers to as his "boys." He has no potential rival, though some mention Masauka Chipembere, who is the activist of the party, as a likely rival.

Although the Kamuzu has declared that he has no ill-feeling toward Europeans, since he has lived most of his life among them and "they have given me most of what I have," he has allowed various excesses to be perpetrated against the whites, some of whose reactions to self-government have admittedly been provocative. As a result racial ill-feeling, which was largely absent before independence, is now slowly surfacing.

More disquieting than the aggressive and arrogant behavior of many Nyasas in authority to their own countrymen and to the whites is the totalitarian machinery which enmeshes the government. Many Europeans in and outside Nyasaland fear that the rule of law is being seriously eroded and might soon cease to be operative. After all, the real safeguard for Europeans or for anyone who is not an African lies in the goodwill of the people of the country. Banda's recent actions have not tended to encourage his followers that way. He has threatened to deport "even on suspicion of guilt" European and Asian estate owners who deprive Africans of fair prices for tobacco and peanuts.

There are several signs that the Kamuzu looks up to Ghana as his model in his attempt to form a one-party state. One such manifestation is the setting up of the government-subsidized Malawi Young Pioneers, whom the doctor has described as "the spearhead" of the Malawi Congress party's Youth League. Nyasa youngsters joining this organization are under the instruction of Africans trained in Ghana. Indeed, Banda makes no secret of the source of his inspiration. "Ghana," he declared, "has succeeded in doing what she has done and Kwame Nkrumah has succeeded in doing what he has done simply because he has mobilized youths." Considerable uneasiness has been caused by the use of members of the Malawi Youth League as tax collectors and party canvassers, which is reminiscent of Fascist practice. The experiment is justified by Banda's followers on the ground that it is misleading to expect parliamentary democracy on the Western pattern, as this is alien to African thought, and that a one-party system, with one man as the symbol of the country, is more appropriate and is in fact essential for national unity at the present stage of development. Too often the argument is an excuse for dictatorship.

Nor are Europeans and Asians alone the object of indirect oppression and assaults. Old scores against hostile African parties and leaders are being settled in various strong-arm ways. The Malawi party police have been trained, drilled, and put into uniform, and on many occasions usurp the functions of the Nyasaland police. Membership in the party is almost indispensable, and in practice is obligatory for Africans. Cases have occurred where individuals refusing to accept Malawi Congress party membership cards have been assaulted or jailed.

On the other hand, it would be wrong to take too alarmist a view of the situation and to infer that the rule of law has completely broken down. What is happening is that a new rule of law is being substituted for the old one. Rightly or wrongly, the Malawi government believes this to be better suited to the people, despite the fact that in the process many Africans and a few Europeans and Asians suffer. While declaring that there would be no interference with the courts, Banda warned that he was watching certain judges and magistrates who were going out of their way to make his local courts look cheap. "I am not going to let them get away with it," he threatened. He also declared that when independence came residential qualifications would depend on "the individual's acceptability to the government."

Independence came on July 5, 1964, when Nyasaland was rechristened Malawi after a former Bantu empire in the area. Nyasaland has a budget deficit of about $11 million and, according to Banda, will need $14 million a year in capital investment and subsidies over five years to overcome the territory's insolvency. This cannot come from Britain alone, which has provided interest-free loans of about $7.7 million to help Nyasaland liquidate colonial rule by way of pensions and compensations to expatriate officials. International sources will also have to be tapped and more economic help and cooperation invoked from the two Rhodesias. Banda now seems to realize that without internal stability and peace external aid will not be forthcoming. Britain's Tory government is committed to "a substantial amount of aid for some years to come both in balancing Nyasaland's budget as well as for capital development." The Lourho financial company with headquarters in London has large economic interests in the country which are concerned with the development of railways and schemes to put up industries, such as a textile mill, a sugar plant, and a brewery. Agricultural development is hampered by the complicated matriarchal land tenure system, by soil erosion and the growth of irresponsible vandalism. But the Nyasas display a considerable public spirit and readiness to work. Nyasaland is poor and unlikely to strike wealth in minerals overnight, but she is rich in human resources, provided the sturdy natural independence of her people is not perverted to false political ends.

Economically, Northern Rhodesia offers a glowing picture, as compared with Nyasaland, which Lord Home once described as "an imperial slum." From the dissolution of the federation, Northern Rhodesia has emerged with the best economic prospects. Welensky shrewdly realized that if Northern Rhodesia went out of the federation, both the economic and political position of Southern Rhodesia would be endangered. He recognized that secession by an African-controlled Northern Rhodesian legislature would mean the breakup of the federation and would imperil Southern Rhodesia's political status, as well as her economic development, since the Copperbelt in Northern Rhodesia is the economic center of gravity of the whole federal structure. By standing firm, Britain was able to call the white extremists' bluff, but Welensky, who, until the report of the Monckton Commission in 1960, felt he could count on bending the British government to his will, did not give up his efforts to maintain a close association with the northern territory until the breakup of the federation. In this he was to some extent more realistic than Field, since in his heart of hearts he knew that an ultimate African majority in Southern Rhodesia's parliament was inevitable.

Until very recently apartheid functioned for all practical purposes as much in Southern Rhodesia as it does in South Africa but, as Welensky argues, the European in Rhodesia does not hate or despise the African as he does in South Africa. The white now realizes that the Africans have serious grievances and that something must be done about them. But he is determined not to be dominated by the African, although racial relations are easing somewhat in Southern Rhodesia, with white and black mixing in easier social proximity than they did. Compared with South Africa, the atmosphere in Southern Rhodesia seems almost relaxed.

Welensky knows that even if Southern Rhodesia builds a dike against African nationalism, with the 210,000-odd Europeans in that territory attempting to draw a line at the Zambezi River to mark the end of the southward advance of African nationalism, Southern Rhodesia will be the first to be exposed to African attacks. It can, of course, count on the moral and possibly even the military support of the Union, as well as the Portuguese in Mozambique and Angola. Today the Republic of South Africa is spending $28 million a year to keep the buffer state of Southern Rhodesia under possible African domination going beyond the Limpopo. On their side, the African leaders are anxious to prevent Southern Rhodesia from gaining independence under a white minority government, similar to South Africa in 1910. But with the introduction of the harsh security laws, such as the Unlawful Organizations Act and the Preservation of Constitutional Government Act, it has become extremely difficult for the Africans in Southern Rhodesia to offer any effective opposition to the government through the normal channels.

Successive bannings of their political parties have intensified their discontent and sense of frustration. Just as Welensky earlier attempted to prevent an African-dominated government in Northern Rhodesia, so now the Africans of that territory are seeking safeguards against the proclaimed independence of Southern Rhodesia. For this they rely on the British government. Even if Field's promise to simplify the electoral rolls results in giving the vote to 100,000 Africans instead of the present 20,000, the altered franchise would at most put fifteen nationalist Africans into parliament, which would hardly constitute an improvement on the present situation, since the fourteen Africans and one independent M.P. who now hold seats in the Southern Rhodesian legislative council are already all opposition members, and numerically ineffectual.

If Nyasaland is a world almost apart, there is very little in common between Northern and Southern Rhodesia, either economically, historically, geographically, or ethnically. The one common bond which unites the Africans of the three territories is the belief that Northern and Southern Rhodesia were shackled to ensure Rhodesia's white supremacy over Central Africa. The idea of amalgamating the two territories was first mooted by the British South Africa Company in 1915 on the grounds of economy, but Southern Rhodesia spurned the suggestion, looking down upon Northern Rhodesia as a poor neighbor with only 2,000 Europeans. Thirteen years later the Hilton Young Commission frowned on amalgamation because of Southern Rhodesia's harsh "native" policy. By then the idea was churning in many minds, particularly in Southern Rhodesia, which naturally viewed with favor any scheme designed to bring Northern Rhodesia and perhaps Nyasaland under its political sway. In 1939 the Bledisloe Commission favored the concept of amalgamation "in principle," but rejected it on the ground of the differing "native" policies of the Northern and Southern territories. When the Nationalists won the South African elections of 1948, the Southern Rhodesian whites, who had been toying with the idea of linking their destinies with the Union, eyed amalgamation with Northern Rhodesia, which was now a more attractive economic proposition, more favorably than they had. On their part, the Europeans of Northern Rhodesia and Nyasaland, who were uneasy over the growing wave of African nationalism, welcomed the prospect. Ironically, the idea of federation was sold by the right-wing Dominion party to Arthur Creech-Jones, then colonial secretary in a British Labor government, who agreed to let the Central African Council, an advisory body set up in 1944, be the nucleus for a closer association. Six years later, the Southern Rhodesian government threatened it would withdraw from the council, whereupon Creech-Jones's successor, James Griffiths, weakly agreed to an officials' conference to draft a federal blueprint. In 1953, with Churchill's blessing,* the Central African Federation, embracing Southern Rhodesia, Northern Rhodesia, and Nyasaland, came into being, with the federal capital at Salisbury, and Southern Rhodesia, with seventeen of thirty-five seats in the central parliament, wielding the political whip. Four years later Welensky secured from Allan Lennox-Boyd, the then Tory colonial secretary, an agreement that Britain would review the federal constitution by 1960, and meanwhile would not initiate federal legislation.

Welensky's object was obvious—to obtain Dominion status for the federation, retain Southern Rhodesia's dominating political position, and bring African agitation to heel. The Africans, whose only bulwark was Britain, were willy-nilly thrown on their own resources, and African agitation, far from being suppressed, grew more militant. Riots and disturbances broke out in Nyasaland and the two Rhodesias.

I visited the federation toward the end of 1960, shortly after the Monckton Commission† had submitted its report in October of that year. At that time segregation was nominally on its way out in Southern Rhodesia and, to a slightly more extended degree, in Northern Rhodesia. Feeling among the Africans ran high, and often expressed itself bitterly, even violently, while European opinion was guardedly on the defensive, though at times militantly aggressive. It was reminiscent of India in the five years preceding independence. Although the federal government had from the first declared its policy to be one of racial partnership, there was very little of it evident in practice. A state of interracial relationship very near apartheid existed in Southern Rhodesia, where at Salisbury only one of the top-bracket hotels was multiracial. (The then United States President's brother, Edward Kennedy, was a resident while we were there, because it was the only hotel where he could invite Africans to meet him.) At Bulawayo it was no better. In Northern Rhodesia it was more relaxed, though it amused us at the hotel at Ndola where we were staying to find separate public comfort rooms on the various floors marked "European" and "Multiracial"—this despite the hotel's racially mixed clientele. I thought our hotel at Lusaka one of the best I encountered in Africa and the service was uniformly courteous. Save for one unpleasant incident at Salisbury in

* Macmillan and Butler were members of his government.
† Headed by Lord Monckton. Its twenty-five members included five Africans. All the African nationalist parties boycotted the commission. In its report it strongly criticized racialism in the federation and recommended a substantial loosening of the federal tie, with more power to the territories. The dissolution of federation since then makes the report of academic interest.

a mixed eating house where some white Teddy boys flourished their guns at us—an American girl was among those at our table—we encountered no unpleasantness during our stay in the federation.

Both the Rhodesias wear a look of prosperity, and the standard of living even among the Africans, though markedly uneven, was higher in some of their separate townships than in many African centers I visited elsewhere. At Salisbury, Nathan Shamuyarira, whom I had met in India and who was then editing the *Central African Examiner* (he is now a university lecturer and an influential figure in the city), proved a gracious and instructive host. Nathan is one of the best-informed and most objective-minded Africans I met in the federation or, for that matter, in Africa as a whole. His tolerance, despite the indignities and hardships among which he lives, seemed to me amazing. He is one of the Africans I most admire and respect. Nathan showed us many facets of Rhodesian life, for, apart from the Africans, he has many friends and acquaintances among the Europeans, one of whom, a radical, laughingly described himself as "on the lunatic fringe of the British community." With Nathan we went to Salisbury University College and spent a couple of agreeable hours with the principal, Dr. Adams, and his wife. Adams was entertaining on the absurd complexities caused by the comedy of black and white lavatories attached to the main hall. There were thirty Africans in a total of about 160 students. We visited the African townships, including Harare, a shocking settlement with some windowless tin shanties, which was the scene of rioting in 1960, and a more recent center, Highfield, an improvement on Harare, though the townships we saw at Lusaka were among the better ones we encountered in the Rhodesias. The townships for African workers in the Copperbelt at Ndola were in an even higher bracket, but then the average income of an African miner in this area is $700 a year, while that of the European miners—many of them Afrikaners—rates annually as high as $6,048. Nathan was severely critical of the Land Apportionment Act, an unconscionably discriminatory measure, and such punitive laws as the Law and Order (Maintenance) Act,* the Preventive Detention Act, and the Vagrancy Act. He explained the irksome pass system and the indignity of so-called responsible Africans ranging from teachers, senior clerks, householders, and chiefs being required to carry identity cards in what was once their own territory. There is incidentally little tribal feeling in Southern Rhodesia, where the main tribe, the Matabele, who are established around Bulawayo, have intermarried into various tribes. Apart from Nathan and a few other Africans, I found the general

---

* Under the "hanging clause" of this Act an African was sentenced to death for participating in a petrol bomb attack, though he did not throw the bomb and no one was killed or injured.

run of African leadership in Southern Rhodesia rather low. An exception was Enos Nkala, sober and quiet-spoken, who was then secretary of Joshua Nkomo's National Democratic party (NDP).

I did not meet Nkomo, who was away from the country on one of his numerous sojourns abroad, a habit which was subsequently to contribute to his political downgrading, but I met Michael Mawema, who had preceded Nkomo as president of the National Democratic party, but who, I gather, was regarded as a moderate and dropped. He was out on bail when I encountered him and seemed reluctant to talk. Nkomo, who is about forty-eight, studied at the Jan Hofmeyer School of Social Work at Johannesburg and was at one time interested in Moral Rearmament, which misled Malvern into believing that he could use him at the 1952 London talks to support federation. Nkomo then headed the African National Congress (ANC).

The first attempt at political organization by Africans in Southern Rhodesia was made in 1915, when a moderate group known as the Rhodesian Native Association was formed. Four years later the African Industrial and Commercial Workers' Union was set up, followed in 1921 by the Bantu Voters' Association, whose membership was less than fifty. In 1938 the Bantu Congress of Southern Rhodesia was established, and after the war became the African National Congress, which was disbanded in 1959 following the arrest of its leaders. Nkomo disappointed and disconcerted Malvern by opposing federation. Since then he has disappointed and disconcerted many people, including his followers. Circumstances have also made him something of a political maverick. The banning by the Southern Rhodesian government of successive African political parties compelled the ANC to emerge as the NDP (National Democratic party), of which Nkomo was elected president in October, 1960. This party was also banned in 1961, and reemerged as the Zimbabwe African People's Union (ZAPU), which again was banned. ZAPU retaliated by forming a ZAPU-in-exile, with its headquarters in Dar-es-Salaam with Nkomo still functioning as president.

By then, however, his chief lieutenants, notably Robert Mugabe, tipped for the ultimate leadership; the fiery Leopold Takawira, Washington Malianga, Enos Nkala, and the Reverend Ndabaninge Sithole, author of *African Nationalism*, who later replaced Nkomo as national chairman of ZAPU, had tired of him. Nkomo, an indolent, easygoing, indecisive individual, is not built in the mold of leadership. Every time ZAPU was banned, Nkomo was out of the country and never showed any great inclination to hurry back. Kenyatta, Nyerere, Kaunda, and Banda are believed to have approved of his removal, though Nkomo, who has substantial support from his own Matabele people, is attempting a comeback. To forestall him, Sithole has formed a new breakaway group called the Zimbabwe African National Union (ZANU), with some of Nkomo's most prominent lieutenants on the executive. They include Takawira, Mugabe, Malianga, Nkala, and Herbert Chitepo, a Southern Rhodesian who is director of public prosecutions in Tanganyika. Among Nkomo's other critics are Nathan Shamuyarira and schools director Josiah Chinamano. Nkomo now heads the People's Caretaker Council (PCC), a temporary body which has mass support and seems to have succeeded in staging a political comeback.

Thus Southern Rhodesia, like Northern Rhodesia, has two rival African parties with two rival African leaders. In the northern territory, Kaunda and Nkumbula temporarily buried the hatchet in order to present a united front to Welensky. But with independence, the old rivalry is bound to surface and might prove a blessing in disguise, for the alternative would be a one-party state. In Southern Rhodesia, where the Africans are struggling for majority rule, a division in the ranks of the nationalists is obviously to the advantage of the European reactionaries. Sithole's demand is for universal adult franchise—one man, one vote—with "a short period" of self-government under majority rule to be followed by full independence, but this is obviously a maximum bargaining point, leaving room for compromise. He seems agreeable to discussing a timetable for African advance once the principle of majority rule is accepted and a transition period settled. But the agreement must precede the declaration of independence by Southern Rhodesia. A conference of Commonwealth prime ministers might help to induce more realism and statesmanship on all sides. However, the political spotlight is again on Nkomo.

What of the future? Will a genuine African federation replace the old so-called Central African Federation, which was dominated by the whites? It seems unlikely, for each of the three territories is looking in a different direction and the separationist tug in each of them, instinct in a desire for separate independence, separate flags, and separate presidents, threatens to be overwhelming. The big question mark is the future of Southern Rhodesia, where a white government, determined to preserve independence, might entrench itself for some years against a divided African opposition. Kaunda seems to have written off the prospect of African majority rule in the southern territory in the near future, judging by the fact that he is planning a rail link from Northern Rhodesia into Tanganyika. This would save Northern Rhodesia from being dependent on rail links through Southern Rhodesia and Portuguese Africa for the export of her copper, whose output is worth annually about $336 million and weighs 600,000 tons. At present, part of the copper is routed through Northern Rhodesia and the Congo on the Beneguela rail route, which runs to the sea at Lobita in Angola. The remainder goes through Southern Rhodesia to

A BASTION BREACHED 347

the ports of Lourenço Marques and Beira in Portuguese East Africa. The new rail line would run from the Copperbelt northeast out of Northern Rhodesia into Tanganyika, where it would link up with the East African network and reach the sea at Dar-es-Salaam. A survey team is working on the project, which is estimated to cost at least $168 million. A London-based firm, Lourho Ltd., which has already obtained a controlling interest in Nyasaland railways, is undertaking the survey on condition that, when the rail link is completed, it will receive exclusive railway copper concessions. This would entail a loss to Rhodesia Railways of $25.2 million a year in copper transport revenues.*

Superficially, this suggests that Southern Rhodesia is in a far stronger bargaining position than Northern Rhodesia. The actual ratio of respective strength is not easy to compute. If the African opposition is divided, so is European leadership, with the Rhodesian Front to the right of the Rhodesian National party. Economically, a tariff war waged by Northern Rhodesia and, to some extent, Nyasaland would embarrass Southern Rhodesia, 30 percent of whose exports normally go to the northern territory. Northern Rhodesia would not emerge unscathed, but her dependence on Salisbury and Bulawayo is less than their dependence on her. An economic, like a political, war between the two territories would be subject to various permutations and combinations, not all of which are calculable, but Northern Rhodesia has the advantage of wielding the stronger economic weapon. Nor economically does Southern Rhodesia's economy dovetail as easily into that of the Union or Portuguese Africa. Nyasaland falls into a different category, for among her principal exports is her labor, which finds employment principally in Southern Rhodesia and South Africa. Her outlet to the sea depends on Portugal.

If Southern Rhodesia faces the likelihood of economic deterioration with her northern links weakened, her position could also be threatened politically by a rebellious African majority inside her territory, the emergence of an African government-in-exile in Tanganyika, and progressive isolation within the Commonwealth coupled with the closing down of some Commonwealth and, possibly, British markets. Mboya has warned that any move by the British government to grant independence to Southern Rhodesia under its present white minority would create a grave constitutional crisis in the Commonwealth and mean the withdrawal of Kenya from Commonwealth membership. A unilateral declaration of independence by Southern Rhodesia would also lose that territory Commonwealth preferences on the sale of tobacco in the British market, which is an impor-

* An agreement signed by a minister in Kaunda's coalition government made Northern Rhodesia liable to Southern Rhodesia for its share of the loss of copper freight revenue.

tant part of its overseas earnings. Though the British government, through Butler, has conceded to Field the right of independence in principle, this is conditional on Southern Rhodesia's agreeing to extend the African franchise and to repeal the Land Apportionment Act. Theoretically, the British parliament still enjoys residual power and can veto or withhold independence for the southern territory; in practice this would be difficult. Whitehall would like to see the franchise widened so as to give the 3 million Africans enough parliamentary strength to protect their own interests and to assure them that within a reasonable period they would gain control over the country. Additionally, the existing 1961 constitution would have to be amended to accommodate further built-in safeguards which would prevent the white parties from constitutionally putting the progressive Africanization of parliament and the executive into reverse. At the London talks with Field in June, 1963, Butler is reported to have put forward a compromise formula according to which, dependent on Field accepting the formula, the present Southern Rhodesian government would be replaced by a National Front government led by Field and supported by Welensky. The terms of the formula were: (1) a territorial parliament in which one-third plus one of the members would be Africans; (2) ending of all racial discrimination; (3) widening of the B-roll franchise to give thousands more Africans the vote; and (4) repeal of the Land Apportionment Act.

Besides Kenya, Canada, Australia, and New Zealand are believed to have informed Whitehall that they would not accept an independent white-dominated Southern Rhodesia as a member of the Commonwealth. If the report is correct, this would queer Field's pitch, for the Afro-Asian members of the Commonwealth would almost certainly follow Kenya's lead. At the Victoria Falls conference, arrangements were made for a decent funeral to be accorded to the federation. The dismantling of the federation through the transfer of federal powers was entrusted to a super-liquidation committee of British, federal, and territorial officials under a British chairman, and linked with it was another committee to arrange for interterritorial collaboration on such common services as the Kariba Dam, the Central African Airways, and the Rhodesia Railways. The dissolution machinery had also to take account of the rights of and the obligations to federal civil servants and other officers, numbering about 35,000. Both the Southern and Northern Rhodesian governments expressed their willingness to take over a fair share of federal liabilities and public debt, but reserved their position as to how this could be assessed until the post-conference machinery had reported.* Britain was

* The net federal public debt of £269,432,000 was divided in the following proportion: (1) Northern Rhodesia's share £88,250,000, (2) Southern Rhodesia's

hopeful that shared economic arrangements between the two Rhodesias would include a common market in goods, labor, joint banking credit exchange, and currency facilities.

The division of the defense forces surprisingly offered no great hurdle. As it stood at the time of the Victoria Falls conference, the federal army consisted of four battalions plus an all-white territorial regiment consisting of four battalions. A battalion including armored car subunits was additionally raised in Northern Rhodesia. The Royal Rhodesian Air Force consisted of six squadrons equipped with Canberras, Vampires, Canadair Transport aircraft, Dakotas, Provost trainers, Hawker Hunter fighters and helicopters. In addition, one regular infantry battalion, a reconnaissance squadron, and a special air service squadron composed of Europeans were in process of formation. All in all, the strength of the federal forces consisted approximately of 250 regular army and 90 territorial officers, with 3,400 army regular and 3,500 territorial other ranks. According to the agreement secured by Butler, each territory, if it so desires, may take back its own infantry battalions, while the units of the air force would be divided according to the needs of the territories. This means that Southern Rhodesia would take one African battalion and the newly recruited all-white battalion, which has a majority of South Africans in its ranks. It would also take the armored car squadron and the squadron of paratroopers, consisting of 300 white troops. The air force of seven squadrons would revert to Southern Rhodesia, which, however, would take into account Northern Rhodesia's claims, which would probably be limited to transport aircraft, leaving the southern territory with eighteen Canberra bombers and twelve Hunter fighters.* Powerful as this striking force is within territorial limits, Southern Rhodesia will have to think twice before using it against her northern neighbors. It was announced later by Salisbury that the Royal Rhodesian Air Force would lose one Canberra bomber squadron, while the crack Selous Scouts armored car squadron of the federal army would be disbanded. The breakup of the federation would see the breakup of the famous King's African Rifles, one battalion being merged with the Northern Rhodesian regiment and another assigned to Nyasaland, where it will probably be known as the Malawi Rifles.

In a reference to the division of the federal forces, Field, in a broadcast in October, 1963, said that neither Southern Rhodesia's army nor its air force would be as big as the federal forces were, but "the

---

share £19,397,000. The Northern Rhodesian government accepted the apportionment under protest.

* In September, 1963, Britain was severely criticized in the Security Council for this arrangement and issued her veto against the Afro-Asian resolution—the first time since the Suez crisis. So far Britain had used her veto thrice.

units would be well balanced, highly trained, efficient, and capable of doing anything asked of them."*

Whether the gravitational pull of South Africa will ultimately prove too strong for Southern Rhodesia depends on various factors—on the attitude of Britain and the Commonwealth, and on the success or failure which attends the future policies and efforts of Northern Rhodesia and Nyasaland. Another factor which is beginning to disturb Southern Rhodesia seriously is the arms training which hundreds of African nationalists are said to be receiving in countries such as the U.A.R., Algeria, Ethiopia, and Tanganyika. Nyerere, hitherto considered among the most moderate and sober of African politicians, has thrown open Dar-es-Salaam as a base for African expatriate activities and operations, and has countenanced the use of violence. Indeed, violence is today almost second nature to the African—and who can blame him? I recall Chipembere telling me at Blantyre: "We admire Gandhi greatly. But we have no use for his nonviolence. We believe in the use of violence where necessary."

In his book *Freedom and After,* Mboya observes: "If one can draw a general rule, it is that in any colony, where there has been considerable white settlement, violence has become inevitable." Algeria, Kenya, the two Rhodesias, Angola, and South Africa reinforce this point.

Southern Rhodesia has recently begun to strengthen its watch on the border of South Africa by the establishment of new police posts with the object of sealing the frontiers to political refugees. The border with South Africa consists of about 175 miles of wild semidesert bush country. Many Africans, however, continue to trickle through Bechuanaland and make their way through Northern Rhodesia to Tanganyika from where they are filtered to various sabotage-training centers farther north. A Foreign Subversive Organizations Bill has been introduced in Southern Rhodesia to prevent Africans from Mozambique, Angola, and South Africa from organizing liberation movements in that territory. At the same time the government has recognized the growing force of African restiveness by agreeing to amend its Mandatory Death Sentence Bill, which made the death sentence mandatory in the case of users of petrol bombs and explosives as intimidatory weapons.

Will Southern Rhodesia finally fall, as a last desperate exercise in escapism, into the open, waiting arms of Dr. Verwoerd? More than

---

* In the UNIP election manifesto, Kaunda promised that the Northern Rhodesian army would be increased and an air force with modern equipment established. Since the East African army mutinies, steps have been taken to train twenty-five Africans to officer the state's two regular battalions. A $8.4 million vocational training plan was announced for the benefit of the large number of unemployed youths. An economic development plan is also being undertaken with the help of the U.N. Economic Commission for Africa.

two-thirds of the white citizens of the former federation are immigrants, and many of these come from South Africa. Some white families are African-born and are descendants of African-born great-great-grandparents, a number going even further back. The total of South African-born whites in the federation was 78,190, according to the 1956 census, which then gave them a proportion of a little over 31 percent of the white population. Since 1956 the number of South Africans entering the federation has grown, though more recently the figure shows a gradual decrease. But the reluctance of the British or Southern Rhodesian-born white to identify himself closely with the Afrikaans-speaking white is still marked. Conversely, Dr. Verwoerd would not relish the prospect of many thousands of additional British voters in the Union or the coming in of some 3 million militant Africans to add to his apartheid headaches. Even if political compulsions should one day force Southern Rhodesia to link itself with the Union, such a course would salvage neither. The intertwining of their destinies would spell the doom of both. The African upsurge can be delayed. It cannot be defeated.

15

THE LAST DITCH

"IN FIFTY YEARS South Africa will be coffee-colored."

The speaker was a British business executive in Blantyre who was married to a "Colored" woman. He spoke with disarming frankness about his social life with the local European community. "They come to my house when we invite them," he said, "but they never invite my wife and me." He did not say this bitterly but almost with a twinkle in his eye, as if he accepted it as the normal pattern of things.

I cannot say whether he will be proved right. I think not, for though I did not visit the country, having been refused a visa by the South African government, I talked with a number of Africans and Europeans in Africa —some of them South Africans—about its future and their views did not coincide with my Blantyre acquaintance's casual prognostication.

"In less than fifty years," commented an African in Nairobi, "South Africa will be ruled by Africans. She will not be white or coffee-colored. She will be black."

Statistically, on the basis of the population growth, it would seem so. The Tomlinson Report* of 1955 calculated that within the next fifty years the population of South Africa would grow to 31,248,000, of whom 21 million would be Africans, some 4 million Coloreds, 1.4 million Asians,

* Submitted by the Commission on the Socio-Economic Development of the Bantu Areas, which was headed by Dr. F. R. Tomlinson.

and less than 5 million whites. Even with attempts being presently made
to whip up the number of immigrants by bringing in 40,000 to 50,000
white settlers a year, this would not take the total of the white South African population to beyond 10 million by the turn of the century. Today,
half the immigrants are from overseas and half from the African continent.
Most of the overseas settlers are British, with the Germans next and the
Italians a distant third. Now that the Union is a republic and outside the
Commonwealth, Britons are technically aliens, and in future can become
African citizens only by naturalization after a period of five years, and
thereafter are not entitled to the privileges of British citizenship. Half the
European population of Kenya might migrate to South Africa (as Dr. Ver-
woerd claims), but at best this would be a temporary spurt. For some
years emigrants have almost balanced immigrants, the net annual gain
averaging a little over 2,000.*

To assess the South African scene accurately and fairly one must see
it as the racial complex it is, with Boer, Briton, and Bantu forming a
mosaic, though the term "Bantu," which the Boer favors to describe the
Africans collectively, is not strictly correct. The local Africans are broadly
Bantu, but they comprise different tribes—even nationalities such as the
Zulu, Xhosa, or Sotho—and linguistically there are four main groups—
Nguini, Sotho, Venda, and Tonga—each with their own traditional tribal
lands. Of the republic's 16-million-odd population, the Africans number
around 10.8 million and the whites about 4 million, with 1.4 million
Coloreds, and some 480,000 Asians. The presence of the Coloreds is a
reminder of a possible mélange of races, though as long as apartheid exists
the dream of a coffee-colored South Africa is distant.

According to the Afrikaners, as the original Boer settlers are known,
South Africa is not a Bantu territory which the whites wrested from their
original owners. They claim that while the forebears of the whites arrived
three hundred years ago and settled on what was largely no man's land,
the Bantu at about the same time came from the north and occupied
another part of the country. Their contention is based on the argument
that when Van Riebeck landed at the Cape in 1652 there were no organized or well established Bantu homelands. Van Riebeck, incidentally, did
not demarcate the people racially as blacks and whites, but religiously as
"Christians and Barbarians," and the Dutch Reformed Church for two

* More recently the unexpectedly fast increase in the African, Asian, and Colored
population, which is rising at the ratio of six to one compared with the whites, has
led Pretoria to offer special inducements by way of government grants and customs
concessions to attract white immigrants. As a result, in the first six months of 1963
South Africa showed a net gain of nearly 12,000 white settlers, which was ten times the
immigration figure for 1961. In 1963 some 32,000 white immigrants entered the
Republic.

centuries respected that line of division. Despite this, the master-servant relationship between the original Dutch settlers and the indigenous Africans was established at a very early date. (In 1685 intermarriage between whites and blacks was officially forbidden.)* The intrusion of the British, who had become permanently established in the Cape by 1806, for a while threatened this relationship, but the French Huguenots at the end of the seventeenth century and the German immigrants in the second half of the same century came to accept the relationship. Around 1830 began the Great Trek, when the frontiersmen probed into the interior to found the Orange Free State and the Transvaal, and to establish settlements in Natal and elsewhere. English-speaking South Africans are prominent in a part of Natal and in the Eastern Cape Province, but the attachment to the mother country is not as strong as in Australia or New Zealand. Since the Addis Ababa conference of May, 1963, declared open war on South Africa's racialism, Boer and Briton have come closer together, and this is exemplified in the motto *Boer en Brit moet saamstaan* (Boer and Briton must stand together). The mass withdrawal by Britain from her Southern African possessions has intensified this feeling. While the Afrikaners, who are the descendants of the original Dutch and Huguenot settlers, are essentially a rural conservative people reared in a rigid Calvinism, the British South Africans are a more sophisticated, urbanized group controlling the country's finance, business, and industry, and its gold and diamonds.

The Republic of South Africa today consists of the four provinces of the Transvaal, the Orange Free State, the Cape of Good Hope, and Natal. For all practical purposes it also comprises the trust territory of South West Africa, which occupies the Atlantic coast from the Orange River to Angola, and inland from the Atlantic to Bechuanaland and Northern Rhodesia. This territory is now virtually incorporated in the republic.

Proportionately, two of every three South Africans are black, and around 55 of every 100 whites are Afrikaner. This puts the Afrikaner ratio to the total population at one to eight, which means that one-eighth of the population dominates the country politically. As Bantustan, which signifies apartheid in operation, comes into being the Africans, who comprise two-thirds of the total population, will occupy 13 percent of South Africa, staying in the rural reserves where a good proportion of them are now confined and which are little better than rural slums. These will constitute their homelands, and here they will be allowed to exercise an attenuated form of self-government under the all-seeing eye of an all-white government. By adding the three British High Commission territories of Basutoland, Swaziland, and Bechuanaland, most of whose territory con-

* The racial demarcation was recognized and accepted by the Dutch Reformed Church in 1857.

stitutes in any case the infertile arid wastes of the Kalahari Desert, Dr. Verwoerd is attempting to create the fiction of black land covering not 13 percent, but 47 percent of South Africa. The South African premier has offered to administer these territories, adding cynically that "as the guardian of these territories the government could lead them to independence and economic prosperity far more quickly and more efficiently than Britain." This has been aptly described as Verwoerd's triple confidence trick. In reality, under the present scheme of Bantustan, twelve-thirteenths of the republic will be the white man's land.

The Verwoerd plan visualizes the creation of eight Bantustans, which will form a horseshoe straddling the Orange River as an eastern enclave of the Orange Free State abutting Natal. Apartheid is based on the principle of "segregating the most important ethnic groups and subgroups in their own areas, where every group will be enabled to develop into a self-sufficient unit." It will thus apply not only to the Africans, but to the Asians and Coloreds, who will also live their separate compartmental existence.

Apartheid was first enshrined as the policy of the Nationalist party toward the end of 1947 in a pamphlet published by its head office entitled "Race Relations: Policy of the National Party." When the Zulu power of Dingaan was finally broken at Blood River in 1868, black resistance was crushed. Henceforth white rule and domination prevailed. Following the Boer War, the Act of Union of 1910 unified the Orange Free State, the Cape Province, the Transvaal, and Natal, enfranchising not only the whites, but the Coloreds and the microscopic number of Africans who already enjoyed voting rights. The rights of the Africans were taken away in 1936, and Colored rights in 1955. Thenceforth, the Coloreds were allowed to elect a quota of white members to parliament. Four years later even the limited rights of the Africans to elect white representatives were taken away. In 1961 South Africa was declared a republic outside the Commonwealth, with an elected president enjoying a term of seven years, an assembly and senate, and equal language rights retained for English and Afrikaans.

The pamphlet on apartheid lays down, among other codes, the following principle: "We endorse the general principle of territorial segregation of the Bantu and the whites." Segregation, though ostensibly on territorial lines, is political in its working. South Africa has had four nationalist governments since 1948, when Dr. Malan was returned to power at the head of the party, but as far back as 1912 General Hertzog was enunciating the rule of white overlordship, in which the Afrikaner "should be *bass* [boss] everywhere in South Africa." Forty-six years later the idea found fulfillment under Verwoerd. The creation of Bantustan will still leave the majority of Africans, some 7 million, in the white areas, since about 4 million Africans work in the white rural areas and another 3 million in the white urban areas. Only about 4 million Africans will be settled in the eight Bantustans.

Thus apartheid signifies a political division more than a territorial cleavage, actually leaving only one-third of the total number of Africans to enjoy whatever form of limited self-government is allowed them, when the breakthrough to Bantustan is achieved. In the rural slums, which will form the Bantu homelands, where the average annual income is about $117 a head, some 4 million Africans reared on tribal traditions will eke out a precarious living in areas incapable in the foreseeable future of supporting any substantial increase in population. Another 7 million will toil in the white rural and urban areas, some 3 million of whom constitute a detribalized urban industrial labor force with an estimated average wage of $42 a month in the Johannesburg district, which is high by African standards, but insufficient to meet a minimum budget of about $70 a month for a family of five.* A detribalized, depressed, underprivileged proletariat will thus grow along with the traditionally tribal peoples vested with a semblance of self-government in the Bantu homelands. The only process which can bring about the separation of white and native is the mass withdrawal of Bantu labor from the European industries, but of this there is no sign, for the simple reason that African labor represents cheap exploited labor, with no bargaining power, since African unions are not recognized for the purposes of collective bargaining.

As Dr. Malan and the equally diehard Mr. J. G. Strijdom visualized it, the ideal of apartheid must be total separation in every sphere. Verwoerd is attempting to give this ideal a more civilized veneer by moving from the "negative aspects" of apartheid to what he calls the "positive aspects." But the disguise is too transparent to hide the crude reality.

"Verwoerd," observed the liberal South African poet and journalist, Anthony Delius, whom I met in Nigeria, "is not profound, but he is verbally clever, persuasive, and plausible."

Delius, a nephew of the famous composer, was interesting on South Africa and apartheid. He remarked that one parallel which the Nationalists had seized upon to justify apartheid was the partitioning of India into Pakistan and India. More recently, they had been citing the Naga demand for a separate homeland from India. It is a plausible parallel, but one that will not stand close scrutiny, for Pakistan, unlike the

* The average monthly wage of a white worker in industry is about $140 a month. The new South African boom has upped the minimum daily wage of some African workers to $2.80. The Nationalist government claims that Africans own around 100,000 cars, four times more than Russian citizens.

Bantustans, is as much a sovereign, independent state as India. Delius thought the Asians were disliked by both sides, as they tended to keep very much to themselves; it would be hard for them today to be a bridge between the Afrikaners and the Africans, which they might have been in the past had they played their cards shrewdly. They would now live a compartmental existence, as would the Coloreds, though both these races would not be condemned to the depressing standards of the Africans.

"Verwoerd is shrewd in his maneuvers," said Delius. "Unfortunately, the Africans outside the Union, particularly in the Congo, put a trump card in his hand.* The Cape Nationalists at one time wanted apartheid by constitutional and democratic means in preference to an imposed apartheid. But Verwoerd would have none of that. He is dead against agreement by negotiation, as it leads always to a compromise. He's a fanatic who does not bother if South Africa is isolated. The Afrikaners' chief complaint was that the British treated them as black Englishmen. Now the boot is on the other foot. The British complain of being treated as black Boers."

Delius, though critical of Verwoerd, regarded the Boer War as a heroic episode—for the Boers. "You must remember," he said, "that the Boers, with 48,000 men, held an empire at bay for two and a half years. They lost some 26,000 of their women and children in British concentration camps. This sort of thing rankles. History is being rewritten."

"Also," he went on, "you mustn't forget Verwoerd's background. He was trained in applied psychology in German universities—at Hamburg, Leipzig, and Berlin—at a time when race theories were to the fore. His sympathies were very much pro-Nazi. As a boy he was at a British school in Southern Rhodesia, where he was badly beaten by his teachers. His father was a missionary. I suppose that affected his psychology. Apartheid comes naturally to the psychological makeup of such a man. He seized on the central idea of apartheid and has clung to it. Nothing will shake him."

Delius spoke of Verwoerd's charm of manner. He can turn on his charm when he wants to: "He completely took in Montgomery, who of course is not politically profound. But he's also taken in seasoned politicians. He didn't fool Macmillan, but he certainly shook him. I saw Macmillan coming out of Verwoerd's room. He was mopping his forehead with a kerchief and murmuring 'Incredible, incredible!' "

"Of course," said Delius, "Verwoerd's got a willing audience to

* They have reinforced this by the upheaval in Zanzibar and the military mutinies in Tanganyika, Uganda, and Kenya.

listen to him. Many Afrikaners are disturbed by the rise of Africa and concerned by the growing volume of world criticism and opposition. To them Verwoerd's voice is South Africa's ringing challenge. Although I do not agree with Verwoerd, I think it is dangerous for the rest of the world, including Africa, to try to isolate South Africa. I think African countries should exchange diplomatic representatives with South Africa.* Ghana, strangely enough, had first mooted it. But the idea fizzled out."

I thought Delius's analysis frank and illuminating.

Verwoerd, who is sixty-three, has been prime minister of South Africa since 1958. He has for almost all his adult life been a racial activist, once campaigned to stop the entry of refugees from Nazi persecution into South Africa, is anti-Semitic, and was strongly influenced by National Socialist ideas during the last war, when he was openly pro-Nazi. As the architect, though not the originator, of apartheid, he has tried to sell the idea to the rest of the white world as something eminently humanitarian and farsighted.

In his view and that of his followers, the Bantu demand for national self-determination represents an irresistible force, while the white urge for continued national domination is an immovable object. Therefore the rational thing is to devise a constitution which would contain these two forces without letting them meet. This is Verwoerd's logic behind apartheid, which he clothes in persuasive language, though the reality does not accord with the image. Projecting the concept of separate development, he has proclaimed: "If Britain can establish something that the United Party† describes as a Bantustan‡ inside South Africa, and can do so with their blessing, and if their contention is that this development is inevitable and sound, why cannot the Union of South Africa, taking into account the ever-increasing desire for self-government which exists among the non-whites, say: We are also taking steps to ensure that we adopt a policy by which we, on the one hand, can retain for the white men full control in his areas, but by which we are giving the Bantu, as our wards, every opportunity in their areas to move along a road of development by which they can progress in accordance with their ability? . . . We must ensure that the outside world realizes, and that the Bantu realize, that a new period is dawning, a period in which the white man moves away from discrimination against the Bantu as far as his own areas are concerned; that the white man is leading him through the first stage towards full development."

* Kaunda has expressed his willingness to have diplomatic relations with South Africa. Northern Rhodesia is also willing to let in South African tourists.

† The main opposition party led by Sir De Villiers Graaf. It was Smuts's party.

‡ The reference is to the British protectorates of Swaziland, Bechuanaland, and Basutoland.

Brave words imbued with unexceptionable sentiments, if only they were meant to be translated into practice! But the practice differs vastly from the theory. In all spheres—educational, social, economic, and political—the Bantu is treated as a being apart from and far below the white. The so-called Bantustan which Britain envisages in the three protectorates will be multiracial in composition and pattern. But multiracialism is anathema to Verwoerd and to the basic idea underlying apartheid. The 25,000-strong Tembu tribe who, led by their paramount chief, Sabata Dalindyebo, oppose the proposed constitution for Verwoerd's Bantustan showpiece, the Transkei, have done so on the ground that the new form of limited self-government is not multiracial and that the proposed legislative body will contain a preponderance of automatically appointed chiefs, thereby denying an effective voice to the elected members.

"The freedom you are getting," the paramount chief warned his followers, "is a fowl run. A cattle kraal would be better."

The tribesmen responded with shouts of "We don't want this scarecrow!"

An additional objection to the constitution is that the change of government is being introduced while the Transkei emergency regulations of 1960 are still in force.*

What powers does the much-advertised Transkei pilot scheme actually confer on the Bantu? Of the 11 million Africans over 1,250,000 live in the Transkei,† a region of Cape province covering 15,000 square miles which sprawls southward from Natal, lying between East London and Durban and contains Pondoland, a nerve center of the terrorist Poqo‡ organization which is patterned on Mau Mau. Theoretically, the Transkei constitution introduces a new factor into South African politics insofar as the black man enjoys political rights which he exercises within his own homeland on the basis of one man, one vote. In practice, what does this glittering facade amount to? The new constitution offers the Transkei a national assembly consisting of sixty-four nominated chiefs and forty-five elected members. The control of departments of government such as defense, internal security, communications, finance, external affairs, constitutional changes, and immigration is not vested in the assembly, which represents not only the 880,000 tribesmen in the Transkei, but another 270,000 outside its borders living in multiracial areas who will

* The regulations forbid a gathering of ten or more persons without authority. One of the prominent candidates, Hemmington Majija of the Liberal party, was banned during the election campaign.

† Some 18,000 whites live there. They have no voting rights in the Transkei, but have voting rights in the republic.

‡ Poqo means more or less Sinn Fein (Ourselves Alone).

have the right to vote for a limited number of representatives in their Bantustan assembly. Every law the assembly passes goes for assent through the commissioner-general to the president of the republic, who can refer it back "for further consideration," but since there seems to be no procedure for breaking a constitutional deadlock, the legislation will in practice be shelved. Moreover, the president can dissolve the assembly. He can also make laws for the Transkei himself by proclamation. The Transkei assembly elects its own cabinet of from five to eight members, with a chief minister, but it can be dismissed by permission of the South African president. While the whites claim that the Bantustans are "in line with the old tribal system," the Africans complain that it would mortgage them to backward chieftain rule, with real powers vested in the president, the commissioner-general, and the conservative chiefs. All the laws of the Verwoerd government will continue to apply in the Transkei.

The Transkei elections for the forty-five elected seats in the 109-man legislature were held in November, 1963, and resulted in Chief Victor Poto, leader of the multiracial group, controlling thirty seats. The remaining fifteen backed Chief Kaiser Mantanzima, who supports Verwoerd's territorial apartheid policy which would make the Transkei an exclusively African state. Poto, a gentle-mannered, courteous and tolerant man who is sixty-five, is hereditary chief of the Nyandeni Pondos (West Pondos) and is closely associated with the Tembu leader, Chief Sabata Dalindyebo. Poto is a highly respected conservative elder statesman with a long record of public service. A curious twist of Bantu politics has made this conservative a protagonist of the modern policy of multiracialism while Mantanzima, a university graduate who is also a qualified lawyer, is a black racist. Mantanzima, though he agrees with Verwoerd's policy of apartheid, is no stooge. "All the whites must leave the Transkei. This is our country," he has declared. Mantanzima, who is forty-eight, was once chairman of the Transkeian Territorial Authority. He has already claimed greater powers for the Transkei, including the extension of its boundaries, a military force and control over transport, and some other matters at present reserved to the Union government. Of the sixty-four nominated chiefs who sit as ex officio members of the legislature, the bulk support Mantanzima, who with their help was elected as chief minister of Transkei against Poto, whom he beat by fifty-four votes to forty-nine.* The legislative assembly elected an ally of Chief Poto, J. Busakeve, as its chairman.

The popular votes cast in Poto's favor show that the majority of Transkei Africans support multiracialism. Poto has also the backing of at

* Two ballot papers were spoiled.

least nineteen chiefs. With the help of a personage such as Chief Botha Sigcan of Eastern Pondoland, he might at a certain stage muster sufficient support to topple over Mantanzima, whose victory is being represented as the victory of the Xhosa lords and squires over the commoners. Neither Mantanzima nor Poto, if pushed by further African pressures, particularly those of the Bantu residing outside Transkei, could avoid a collision with the South African government, which still retains real power in its own hands. Apart from controlling defense, communications, external affairs, internal security, harbors, and currency, its assent is necessary for all laws passed by the legislative assembly. The republic also retains full control over the Transkei constitution.

From all this it is evident that the scope of African self-government will be severely restricted within the leading strings of Pretoria; it will operate within the structure of a tribal organization, and not within a democratic framework. As a Johannesburg newspaper observed, "The Bantustans will be run by chiefs virtually appointed by Pretoria—instead of freely elected leaders." Albert Luthuli, the deposed Christian Zulu chief in Groutville, Nobel Peace Prize Winner in 1960 and former head of the banned African National Congress (ANC), condemned the system of Bantu authorities as "completely unacceptable, even as a form of local government." In fact the Bantu authorities of the South African reserves, whom Verwoerd describes as "home-grown democracy," are the creatures of the minister of African affairs, who retains overriding powers to depose any chief, paramount or otherwise, or any headman, and to cancel the appointment of any counselor to any of the authorities, the chief native commissioner having thereafter the right to veto the replacement. The commissioner can also veto any proposed action by the presiding chief of the territorial authority, or the secretary, or the treasurer. The Bantustans have no representation in the South African parliament.

Nearly 7 million Africans inside the republic but outside the Bantu reserves will enjoy no rights, save the right of voting for a restricted number of representatives in their own Bantustan assemblies, but this is condoned by such apologists of apartheid as Dr. Eiselen in the specious parallel that Africans in the British protectorates who go to work in South Africa have no rights there. "No one would insist in granting permanency to these foreign Bantu," argues Dr. Eiselen, "so why should Bantu from our own reserves be entitled to claim it?" The argument is as confused and contradictory as the claim that the Bantustans are self-governing and yet controlled; that the Africans in white areas are on a par with the "foreign Bantu," and simultaneously are a separate part and parcel of the republic; and that the Bantustans are to have their own flag, anthem, civil service, black cabinet and black chief minister, along with other apparent appurtenances of freedom, but must have their tribal authorities imposed from Pretoria. Incidentally, a special act makes Xhosa one of the official languages of usage in the Bantustans, along with English and Afrikaans, which were the only two official languages recognized by the South African constitution.

The reality of Bantustan is therefore far removed from the image. Socially the Bantu is treated worse than a pariah; he is regarded as a leper. Even in the field of sport, the South African government has decreed that it could not approve of multiracial teams competing as representatives of South Africa as a whole in world sport tournaments or competitions. In countries where racially mixed sport is the practice, South Africans of one race can compete against sportsmen of another race who are not South Africans. Educationally, the African is now also condemned to a separate existence. Until the passing of the Bantu Education Act in 1953, the African had educational opportunities which, though not as good as those available to the whites, were better than any prevailing for the benefit of the African elsewhere in the continent. By 1956, over a million African children were at school, and before 1959, when apartheid was enforced in the universities, there were 1,600 African undergraduates and more than 3,000 had already graduated.

As a general rule such Africans as I have encountered from the republic have been more articulate but, curiously enough, more moderate than their counterparts in other areas of the continent. Among the better known are the writers Ezekiel Mphahlele, expatriate author of *The African Image*, Blake Modisane, Lewis Nkosi, and Arthur Mainane. Yet there are only just over 1 percent of Africans in the civil service, the professions, and teaching. The annual family income of an African in the reserves is around $118, while an African laborer working for a white farmer earns $232. The annual average earnings of an African unskilled laborer in the mines is $252, though in certain districts like Johannesburg the wage levels are higher. On an overall basis, some 10 percent Africans constitute the entire body of skilled workers and 40 percent are semi-skilled. Around 85 percent Africans form the total unskilled labor strength. The Bantu Investment Corporation claims to give Africans an opportunity of establishing their own industries, but there is no provision in the act allowing Africans to hold shares, and the directors of the corporation will all be whites. Under the Extension of University Act, separate tribal colleges will be established for the Bantu. At these bush universities the African will not be allowed to rise above a certain level and the curricula, teaching methods, and staff are to be controlled by the government. In other words, African education is to be tribalized and the African developed culturally "on his own lines."

Unlike many Africans in other parts of the continent, the educated native of South Africa lays no stress on *négritude* or on his African exclusiveness. "The white man has detribalized me," writes Mphahlele. "He had better go the whole hog. In my case he must know that I'm the personification of the African paradox, detribalized, Westernized but still African—minus the conflicts." This urge to be Westernized, springing from the feeling that Western civilization is something highly desirable, and accentuated by the fact that the Afrikaner wishes to exclude and shut him away from it, distinguishes the educated South African native from most Africans elsewhere.* It is an intriguing psychological reaction and study. Apartheid stresses exclusiveness in a country where the African stress is on inclusiveness. The educated African in South Africa wants nothing more than to be like his white neighbor, enjoying the same equality and rights. Ironically apartheid has made him conscious of the importance of being white, while at the same time it has inflated his awareness of being *black* or African.

The Tomlinson Report, working on the basis of an estimated 20 million Africans by the turn of the century, with about 7 million permanently resident in European areas, calculated that over a period of ten years about $104 million would be required for soil reclamation, about $87 million for forming industries, and $84 million for the Bantu Development Corporation to build one hundred African townships. Actually the government initially voted only about $10 million for developing the reserves, though Verwoerd later declared that more money would be available if needed. More money was made available by Pretoria, and its proposed dimensions provoked a nervous outcry in some white quarters. White commercial investment in the Transkei totals over $18.2 million and local white traders resent the prospect of living even under nominal black rule and have protested to Pretoria.

The amount the South African government now proposes to lavish on the eight Bantustans far exceeds the British outlay on the three protectorates. The Transkei budget alone will total over $16.8 million, of which local sources will provide less than $5.6 million, the balance being made up by Pretoria. Against this, Basutoland's budget is about $9 million, of which about $2.8 million is raised locally and a like sum collected by South Africa from customs on behalf of Basutoland. The balance is made up from British loans and grants. Between 1945 and 1959, in the belief that the protectorates would ultimately be incorporated in South Africa, Britain spent annually on all three only about $5,040,000 in development

* Dr. Eiselen rather ridiculously dismisses the urban Africans as "an unattached mass of Bantu individuals."

aid and another $4,760,000 in subsidies. Today, the three territories are asking for $9.8 million a year for development and $15.4 million annually in grants. Can Britain afford this?

Of the three British protectorates, Basutoland, Bechuanaland, and Swaziland—which are really enclaves within South Africa and an integral part of that country's economy—Basutoland is politically the most militant and Swaziland economically the healthiest, though territorially the smallest. Bechuanaland, the largest in area (275,000 square miles), is by way of being a Cinderella among the three, but her pace of economic and political advancement is being stepped up. The combined population of the territories is 1.5 million,* with the largest number (800,000) concentrated in Basutoland, which covers about 12,000 square miles and is embedded in South Africa. Like the former Federation of the Rhodesias and Nyasaland, the three protectorates are landlocked, being without coastlines some 5,000 miles from the nearest British base. Bechuanaland has South Africa on its eastern and southern flanks, Rhodesia to the north, and South West Africa to the west. To Swaziland's east lies Portuguese Mozambique, and hedging it on the other three sides is South Africa.

The history of the protectorates goes back to the days of the Great Trek of 1830 when the Basuto and the Swazi first encountered the Boers. After various vicissitudes the Basuto were taken under British protection in 1868 and Basutoland became a Crown colony in 1884. Meanwhile, the Transvaal Boers had infiltrated into Bechuana territory which, unlike the other two protectorates, has a medley of tribes, among the largest of whom are the Bakwena and the Bangwaketse. In the Kalahari Desert are the Bushmen, who are regarded as serfs. Bechuanaland became a British protectorate in 1895. The Swazi, who at first welcomed the British and the Boers as possible allies against the Zulu, found it more difficult to gain British protection and did not achieve it until 1903. Six years later Britain granted self-government to the Boers of South Africa.

Britain's policy toward the protectorates has until recently been ambiguous and ambivalent. Until 1959 when Verwoerd was well embarked on apartheid, Britain had envisaged the protectorates as being united one day with South Africa. Hence the dual role of the British high commissioner to Pretoria, now ambassador, who is simultaneously high commissioner for the protectorates. Hence also Britain's financial niggardliness toward the three territories, and her comparative neglect of and indifference to them. When it became clear that Verwoerd's Bantustans were to be no more than glorified county councils under Pretoria's strict control, developed "in line

---

* The population of Bechuanaland is around 400,000, while Swaziland, with an area of 6,700 square miles, has a population of about 260,000, of whom at least 250,000 are Africans.

with the old tribal system," Britain set about moving the protectorates toward self-government based on "Western model" institutions and also began boosting them economically.

As a result, if the Transkei is Verwoerd's showpiece, Basutoland is Britain's political shopwindow. So, less assertively, is Swaziland. Bechuanaland is also being primed for internal self-government, but the immediate shape this will take is not clear. Verwoerd, however, has the edge on economic outlay and has declared, in accord with his more recent and calculatedly generous policy, that he is prepared to spend $159.6 million on the Bantustans between 1961 and 1966, of which $56 million is earmarked for Basutoland's neighbor, the Transkei. Britain is in no position to be so lavish.

In 1960 the Morse Commission urged the expenditure of $26.6 million over and above Colonial Development and Welfare Fund allocations on the three territories, with the caveat that this outlay would make economic viability "a near certainty in the case of Swaziland, a reasonable probability in Bechuanaland, and a possibility in Basutoland." Britain is allocating annually less than $11.2 million. Verwoerd also keeps harping —from his point of view legitimately—that Africans from the protectorates continue to pour into South Africa for work, impliedly stressing that things can't be very bad in the republic.* Britain, of necessity, must underpin the ultimate independence of the protectorates with financial support. But can the British treasury afford this?

Because of its mineral wealth, Swaziland has good prospects of becoming self-supporting. But Bechuanaland and Basutoland are nowhere near financial independence. Of the three, the most vulnerable to a change in South Africa's labor policy is Basutoland, which is ringed by republic territory. Its people derive their livelihood largely from employment in the Rand and Kimberley mines. If Verwoerd implements his threat to keep out the "foreign natives," Basutoland could be seriously affected. Britain, by enlarging her aid and subsidies to the protectorates, could help to people the vast, arid, but arable lands of Bechuanaland with the overflow of the Basutos squeezed out of South Africa, though some believe the Basutos, or Basotho, as they are known, would not resettle in Bechuanaland. Parts of the Kalahari are capable of being irrigated with waters from the Okavango Swamps. Hydrological and mineral surveys, better communications, and more organized markets, with the development of the cooperation movement, in the three territories could make them economically less dependent on South Africa.

* About 1 million Africans from other parts of Africa, officially termed "foreign natives," live and work in South Africa. It is estimated that 1,000 Africans enter clandestinely every month from across the borders of the three protectorates, Rhodesia, Angola, and Mozambique.

Will the protectorates at some time be absorbed within the oppressive, crippling framework of an aggressively white South Africa? Though Verwoerd occasionally discounts the imputation, this is almost certainly his objective.

Economically, Verwoerd is well aware that South Africa is on a strong wicket vis-à-vis the protectorates, for not only are they economically involved with the republic, but the economy of each is enmeshed in South Africa's economy. Superficially, Pretoria can also claim, as it does, that the political patterns visualized for Basutoland as a self-governing territory and the Transkei are not vastly different. The similarity, however, is superficial, for the political objective of the two governments is basically different. While the Transkei represents apartheid or complete segregation, the protectorates will all be of a multiracial pattern. According to the British, the future lies with the educated urbanized nationalists who form the detribalized elements of the people.* In the Bantustans such power as devolves will be concentrated in the chiefs, who are expected to conform to the old traditional tribal way of life. Swaziland and Bechuanaland are in the process of being put on the Basutoland road toward responsible self-government and, while a defense agreement with Britain will inevitably be of long duration, the British are inclined ultimately to accept an independent and equal status for the protectorates. Basutoland is on the way to independence, if the recommendations of a recent commission are found acceptable. If and when independent, it will be the thirty-seventh independent state in Africa, and will be called Lesotho. Basutoland should be independent in 1965, when the Paramount Chief Moshoshoe II will become Head of State with constitutional powers. There will be a National Assembly composed of 60 members elected by universal adult franchise, and a Senate consisting of the 22 principal chiefs or their nominees and 11 other persons nominated by the Head of State in his absolute discretion. The Executive will consist of a cabinet with a prime minister and not less than seven other ministers. In addition there will be a Privy Council consisting of the British Government Representative of the Prime Minister and a person nominated by the Head of State. In the pre-independence period the British Government will retain responsibility for defense, external affairs, internal security, and the terms and conditions of service of public affairs. Basutoland will thus soon confront the South African Republic as an independent multiracial African state.

* Verwoerd's efforts to woo the chieftain elements in the protectorates, such as the traditional group around the Ngwenyama in Swaziland, highlight this difference in the British and South African approach. Verwoerd's ploy seems to be to encourage the Nawenyama and other tribalist chiefs to cooperate with the white settlers, the majority of whom are still citizens of South Africa, thereby creating a Bantustan with the white population of Swaziland allied even more closely with the republic.

Despite Verwoerd's expansive protestations, an independent and equal status for the Bantustans is far from being the South African ideal. Dr. Eiselen in his booklet "Modern South Africa," published in 1959, makes the objective clear. "The utmost degree of autonomy in administrative matters which the Union Parliament is likely to be prepared to concede to those areas [the Bantustans]," he writes, "will stop short of actual surrender of sovereignty by the European trustee, and there is therefore no prospect of a federal system with eventual equality among members taking the place of the South African Commonwealth." In other words, Pretoria plans to rule the roost forever. Verwoerd operates behind a smokescreen.

Meanwhile Bechuanaland and Swaziland are being helped toward self-government, though in Swaziland Verwoerd has been trying to woo the paramount chief with hints of possible enlargement of his kingdom if he joins the Bantustan fold. Incited by the white settlers, the Ngwenyama (king) Sobhuza II has been attempting to delay the British government's plan to impose a new constitution and to hold elections in 1964 on a franchise which the traditional Swazi authorities dislike. There is an agreement between the Ngwenyama and the European Council that the Europeans would be given not less than a third of the total number of seats.

In November, 1963, one of Swaziland's most prominent white citizens, Carl Todd, suggested a plan for the protectorate, with South Africa joining Britain as one of the two "protecting powers." This meant a three-way split, with approximately equal blocks of seats for the European businessmen and farmers on the one hand and for the king's supporters in the Swazi National Council on the other. A third block of seats would be filled by unfettered vote on the common roll.

In July, 1964, the elections resulted in a sweeping victory for the "King's party" launched in June under the name Imbokodvo (grindstone) in alliance with the white farmers' party known as the United Swaziland Association. Todd, a Johannesburg lawyer, would like to lure the Swazi traditionalists headed by the seventy-five-year-old Sobhuza into Verwoerd's apartheid camp, and, like Barkis, Sobhuza is willing. With the help of his white allies and of his more obscurantist followers who revere Sobhuza as rainmaker, the "King's party" scored a resounding victory over the two young nationalist parties led by Dr. Ambrose Zwane and Dr. Allen Nxumalo.

In Bechuanaland, Seretse Khama with other leaders has been urging that their country should move forward to full African self-government on the basis of "one man, one vote" not later than October, 1964. Verwoerd, who also has his eye on Bechuanaland as a potential buffer state against the black north, is not unduly enamored of the plan which, built on the formula of self-government and African majority rule, points to ultimate independence. The breakup of the Central African Federation leaves South Africa vulnerable to an ingress from Northern Rhodesia of revolutionaries via a fifty-yard-wide strip of Bechuana territory known as the Caprivi Strip on a bank of the Chobe River. Refugees from South Africa can also cross to safety along the same route, which the Bechuanaland authorities now supervise vigilantly.

Verwoerd's trump card is the economic stranglehold which South Africa has on the British protectorates. There is some substance in his claim that though Britain might be the guide to their political freedom, "she is powerless in respect of their eventual economic freedom." The immediate cause of Pretoria's irritation is the suspicion that the three territories are the source of friction between South Africa and Britain because of the political refugees who have sought shelter there. But Verwoerd's real fear is that the rash of multiracialism might spread from the protectorates to the Bantustans, and also intensify the latter's African nationalism, which is simmering feverishly.

Verwoerd can no more contain the tide of African nationalism in South Africa than King Canute could stay the waves. Its sweeping upsurge must submerge him and his kind. Africa no longer regards herself as a limb of Asia or of Europe, for that matter, and within the continent the countries of Africa, allergic to any move which they suspect might Balkanize them, are growing increasingly interdependent and cooperative among themselves. Ultimately, the political urge for freedom must override the economic necessity of reliance on the West. Africa knows this, and Europe, along with Asia, is becoming increasingly aware of it.

One manifestation of this awareness is the South African diehard's uneasiness not so much over the immediate threat of African nationalism, as over outside interference by European countries* and by the U.N., though ostensibly South Africa continues to resist, even defy, the pressures exerted by the international organization, which has vainly called upon Pretoria to abandon its apartheid policies and to recognize U.N. trusteeship in South West Africa. South West Africa, most of which is a drought area,† though regarded as potentially rich, was seized by Germany in 1884, and became a mandated territory administered by South Africa after the First World War. Since 1933 Pretoria has been demanding its incorporation in

---

* A manifestation of this was the threat of Mr. Eric Louw, South African foreign minister, to revoke the Simonstown naval base agreement of 1955, which gives Britain use of the base at all times, even in a war where South Africa is neutral. Louw also threatened to stop gold sales to Britain, and warned Britain and the United States "not to be so sure" that South Africa would always support the West against communism.

† Its area is roughly 318,000 square miles and it has a population of a little over 500,000, some 270,000 of whom reside in Ovamboland. The chief tribe are the Hereros (50,000) with about 40,000 Hottentots. The Ovambos are numerically the largest.

the Union and after the Second World War refused to accept a U.N. trusteeship. South West Africa is the only League-mandated territory which has not become independent or been brought under the trusteeship system, though the status of the territory has been a matter of concern to the United Nations since 1946. South Africa's contention is that its original agreement regarding the administration of this territory was with the League of Nations and since the League has ceased to exist, Pretoria's international obligations in respect to this area have ended. However, South Africa initially agreed to submit reports on the territory to the U.N., but so far it has submitted only one report—in 1949, covering the year 1946. In 1950 the International Court of Justice decreed that the South African government's obligations were continuing and that the functions of supervision over the territory's administration should be exercised by the U.N., to whom reports and petitions should be submitted.

A suggestion that the territory should be partitioned was not unfavorably received by the U.N. Good Offices Committee in 1958. According to the proposal, the northern part of South West Africa, inhabited mainly by indigenous Africans, would be placed under trusteeship, while the remainder, populated also by persons of European stock, should be annexed to South Africa. Nothing came of the suggestion.

In 1961, the U.N. General Assembly proclaimed the "inalienable right of the people of South West Africa to independence and national sovereignty" and established a special committee for South West Africa which, at the invitation of Dr. Verwoerd's government, visited that territory, being represented by the chairman and vice-chairman of the committee. In their report the two representatives suggested the imperative need of continued firm action by giving the South African government a short period of time within which to comply with the General Assembly's resolutions, failing which the feasibility of revoking the mandate and assuming the administration of the territory to prepare its people for independence should be considered. Although these conclusions were endorsed by the General Assembly, Pretoria continued to be adamant. The deadlock persists.

In a report released in January, 1964, the South African government recommended that the ten nonwhite population groups in South West Africa should be granted a larger measure of self-government and judicial administration. It suggested that the authorities now functioning in most of the African homeland areas should be expanded into legislative councils headed by executive committees.

Inside South Africa, in the Transkei and other potential Bantustans, as well as in the protectorates, African nationalism grows increasingly assertive. In June, 1963, figures given by the South African prisons department revealed that there were over 67,000 South Africans—one in every 235—

in jail. The Poqo underground terrorist organization, with a strong base in the Transkei, has been responsible for the murder, accompanied by gruesome Mau Mau rites, of a number of whites whom, along with Indians,* they have sworn to drive out of the country. The banned National African Congress, whose leading figures, Walter Sisulu and Nelson Mandela, along with the leaders of the more militant Pan-African Congress, such as Potlako Leballo and Robert Sobukwe, are either in detention or hiding, are other focal points of unrest within the republic.† In a panic the government rushed through the General Laws Amendment Act, commonly known as the Sabotage Act, which invests it with draconian powers and has been denounced by the International Commission of Jurists as a "ruthless" law which "reduces the liberty of the citizen to a degree not surpassed by the most extreme dictatorships of the left or the right." Pretoria's brutality toward the Africans has led even pronounced pacifists like sixty-five-year-old ex-Chief Luthuli, the doyen of African nationalists, to despair of moderation. "Who will deny," he has said, "that thirty years of my life have been spent knocking in vain, patiently, moderately, and modestly at a closed and barred door? What have been the fruits of moderation? The past thirty years have seen the greatest number of laws restricting our rights and progress until today we have reached a stage where we have almost no rights at all."

Action induces reaction, as Verwoerd is learning, not only in the republic proper, but in the Bantustans. In the Transkei, Chief Kaiser Mantanzima, irked by the contemptuous gibes of his fellow Africans, is now talking in terms of real self-government and even independence. So too Paramount Chief Moshoeshoe of Basutoland began displaying signs of restiveness at British tutelage, prodded into doing this by the more forward-looking chiefs and by such critics as the able Ntsu Mokhele, leader of the Basutoland National Congress. Mokhele, who thinks in terms of independence, has accused Britain of looking on Basutoland as a labor reserve for South Africa—43 percent of its adult male population work in the republic—in order to safeguard the United Kingdom's $2.5 billion investment in that country. The charge is unjustified, because Britain has left Pretoria in no doubt that since the South Africa Act of 1910 she is pledged not to transfer the protectorates until their inhabitants are consulted and until the United Kingdom parliament has had an opportunity of expressing its views. This position was stated by Churchill, then Prime Minister, in the House of

* The protectorate of Swaziland has also discriminated against Asians, the chiefs being probably prompted into doing this by the South-African-oriented whites, who number nearly 9,000.

† Mandela and Sisula are among the eleven accused in the so-called treason trial which began in October, 1963. With six others they were both sentenced to imprisonment for life.

Commons in April, 1954, and reiterated by Commonwealth Relations Minister Duncan Sandys in March, 1961. While cognizant of the protectorate's economic dependence on the republic, British opinion, which is opposed to apartheid, is unwilling to allow these territories to be subjected to that system. On the other hand, it is in the cards that Britain, in order to ease tensions, might agree to negotiate a new extradition treaty with South Africa on refugees from the Union in the three protectorates. The cases of Anderson Ganyile and Kenneth Abrahams, both of whom were kidnaped by the South African authorities when they sought asylum in, respectively, Basutoland and Bechuanaland, but who were subsequently released,* disturbed white opinion generally in South Africa irrespective of party, while the cases of Arthur Goldreich and Harold Wolfe, who escaped from a Johannesburg jail and found refuge in Bechuanaland, roused Pretoria's particular ire. One reason why Verwoerd would like to absorb the protectorates is that, along with adjacent Bantu territories, he could create consolidated areas for various African groups such as the Zulus, whose Zululand is adjacent to Swaziland. This would enable him to build a solid black block to include the 2 million Zulus in Natal, taking in Zululand, which contains over 500,000 living in an area of 10,500 square miles. Natal covers an area of 33,000 square miles with a black-and-white jigsaw population of 3 million. The Zulus, however, are averse to being confined to another Bantustan, and many whites oppose it since it entails the creation of a "white corridor" running from South Africa's biggest port, Durban, into the hinterland. It would also entail the wholesale removal of tens of thousands of Africans, whites, Indians, and Coloreds, demonstrating the impossibility of implementing apartheid in practice.

South Africa, with its gold-buttressed, developing, self-sufficient economy, is Africa's richest state and its strongest military power. "We are enjoying prosperity such as we have never known before," declared Harry F. Oppenheimer, Chairman of the Anglo-American Corporation, in September, 1963. The republic's gold and currency reserves topped $700 million with an annual growth of over 5 percent. Gold production approached the $1 billion mark in 1963. Resting on these sanctions, Verwoerd calculates he can go on defying civilized world opinion. "We will not give in—ever," he keeps saying again and again. His northern buffer is Southern Rhodesia, with adjoining Mozambique, while to the north of South West Africa is Angola. But the black tide of African nationalism is creeping inexorably toward the Zambezi and some day may cross the Limpopo. Can South Africa stay it, particularly if behind African opinion

---

* Ganyile by order of the full bench of the eastern division of the South African supreme court, and Abrahams by the South African government in the interests of "neighborly relations."

is the external pressure of the United Nations? While the white South African remains contemptuous of what he derides as African incapacity and immaturity, he still retains a wholesome respect, howsoever he may disguise it, for the weight of white power and authority outside. Meanwhile, internal subversion against white domination and oppressiveness are growing inside South Africa, and caught between the pincers of internal restiveness and external righteousness, South Africa might be compelled to yield ground.

Africans outside the republic, while urging, as Haile Selassie did before the U.N. in October, 1963, "the toppling over of the ignoble and unhappy regimes that hold our brothers in Angola, in Mozambique, and in South Africa in subhuman bondage," are increasingly pinning their hopes on persuasion, on devising an effective strategy within the United Nations to help in the struggle to liberate the subjugated southern territories. Representatives of nine African countries agreed to meet the Portuguese Foreign Minister, Dr. Alberto Franco Nogueira, who came to New York in October, 1963, for that purpose, and though nothing concrete resulted, the talks were held in a friendly atmosphere though with their breakdown some African tempers changed. The initiative for the meeting came from Lisbon. Nigeria has put forward a proposal for a South African federation of racially separated and fully autonomous states. The Danes have also sponsored a plan for combining increased pressures against South Africa in the form of sanctions and declarations with guarantees to safeguard the white population after the abolition of apartheid by the establishment of "a truly democratic multiracial society" based on the acceptance of the principle of adult franchise, which means one man, one vote. Not surprisingly, Pretoria's reaction to this proposal has been chilly.

Internally the pressures are also growing. The republic's English-language press as a whole suffers from no obsessive emotion and is often coldly critical. Judge de Wet's ruling in the sabotage trial affirmed the judiciary's refusal to allow Verwoerd's government to go beyond the letter of the law. The Anglican Church's opposition to apartheid has found some unexpected allies in the hierarchy of the conservative Dutch Reformed Church as evidenced by the acceptance of the leadership of the multiracial Christian Institute of Southern Africa by the Reverend C. F. Byers Naude, Moderator of the South Transvaal. As the republic's material prosperity grows—and South Africa has never had it so good—the demand for African skilled labor must grow and with it the opposition of the white industrialists who in the main frown on apartheid. The latter believe that economic development more than political pressure will expose apartheid for the pipe dream it is, and make racial cooperation and integration inescapable. Confronted with economic realities political prejudices will wane. African

census figures taken in September, 1960, show that the African urban
population had risen by 45 percent since 1951 despite apartheid. In the
same period there was an increase of 23 percent in the white population.
As economic expansion grows, the black population in white areas is likely
to increase, and white immigration bringing new stimulus to building and
industrial activities will intensify the process. Over a million more Africans
live in towns than in 1951 and 2.3 million more Africans in South Africa
as a whole.

There are many, both white and black, who believe that the partition
of South Africa into white and black zones would prove the best solution.
Verwoerd may talk loudly about defying African and U.N. opinion, and
hold out threats of retaliation, but even he appears to be having second
thoughts. He cannot afford another Sharpeville* and the alternative is
compromise. His policy of stressing the so-called "positive aspects" of
apartheid points logically to partition, and he himself has meaningfully
remarked that he "wants a white South Africa, even if it is a small one."

This suggests that he might be seeking in the racial partition of the
country a possible solution to the impasse which apartheid threatens. If
he could incorporate the three protectorates into South Africa his position
would be easier. Partition as a solution of the South African impasse
seems to be gaining ground.

With the creation of areas of black and white liberty, there will be no
baasskap (masterhood), white or black. Else, as the Afrikaans paper, Die
Burger, warns, "the whole of South Africa will become black." Under this
plan, the Cape up to a little beyond Port Elizabeth, the Southern Transvaal,
including Johannesburg and Pretoria and the Orange Free State, will
constitute white South Africa. Black South Africa will be formed from
Natal, Zululand, the Transkei, part of the eastern Cape, and the entire
eastern, northern, and western Transvaal. The Cape Colored population
will be in the white state, though between the two states a few multicolored
areas will persist.

Various schemes of partition have been canvassed. The younger
nationalists and intellectuals, represented by the Stellenbosch group, have
put forward a scheme which would give East London and most of Natal
to the Xhosas and Zulus, while most of the Transvaal and the Cape would
be retained for the whites, with a white corridor running through to Durban.
A more or less similar horseshoe plan was suggested by the Tomlinson

* At Sharpeville in the Transvaal on March 21, 1960, a crowd of Africans unofficially estimated at 4,000 and officially estimated at 15,000 were wantonly fired
upon by some seventy African policemen. A similar episode occurred the same day at
Langa in Cape Province. Altogether, 72 Africans were killed and 180 wounded. The
crowds were protesting against the pass laws, which require every African, man or
woman, to carry a dozen or so identification documents.

Commission. Another scheme draws a line down to the Drakensberg, giving all of Natal and the eastern Cape Province to the Africans. The official partition plan seems to be based on the hope that at some stage the three British protectorates of Swaziland, Bechuanaland, and Basutoland would become the Bantu heartlands, enabling Pretoria to form with adjacent South African territories five main Bantustans—Xhosaland, Basutoland, Zululand, Swaziland, and Tswanaland. Verwoerd's supporters argue that, just as the Central African Federation collapsed because one unified integrated multiracial state was found impossible, partition on apartheid lines is the only peaceful alternative. But Verwoerd's Bantustans, according to the Africans, are not analogous to the three independent states which will follow the breakup of the federation. The Africans of the federation rebelled against Welensky's idea of all-white domination by Salisbury. Similarly, the Africans of the republic oppose the idea of perpetual all-white domination by Pretoria. Bantustan, which is apartheid in a different guise, ensures Pretoria's stranglehold on the Africans. It therefore provides no practical solution.

More drastic and ambitious is an African plan of partition sponsored by Paul Mosaka, an African businessman who founded the short-lived African Democratic party at the end of the war. According to his plan, propounded at a meeting of the Institute of Race Relations in Johannesburg in 1959, the dividing line between the black and white areas should be the 25th degree of longitude. This would place Johannesburg, Pretoria, Pietermaritzburg, Durban, East London, Port Elizabeth, and Bloemfontein in the black areas. The Karoo, and the Kalahari and Kimberley, with its diamonds, would be in the white area. Obviously a febrile dream, unrealistic in its design and planning, Verwoerd's program of "separate development" visualizes South Africa as a checkerboard of white and black areas with the riches of the country including the farms of the Transvaal, the financial wealth of Johannesburg, the gold of the Orange Free State and the industrial complexes at Durban and Port Elizabeth concentrated in the former. The Bantu tribal homelands will be no better than black ghettos.

Mosaka was trying to hoist Verwoerd with his own petard. The paradox of South Africa is the paradox of the Africans in South Africa. Here is a strange and explosive situation. For paradoxically both white and black have discovered the importance of being *white*.

Sharing the last ditch with South Africa is Portugal, whose possessions on the continent extend to Angola, Mozambique, and Guinea, along with the Cape Verde Islands and the islands of São Tomé and Principe, which lie in the Atlantic off the west coast of Africa. Portugal came to the continent as early as the fifteenth century and was the first European power to make her presence felt in Africa. She is also the last of the Western imperial powers to survive on that continent. Together, Angola and Mozambique cover some 800,000 square miles, an area roughly the size of western Europe and twenty times that of Portugal. The combined population of the two colonies, over 11 million, exceeds Portugal's by 2 million. Without her African colonies, Portugal would be a mere appendage of the Iberian peninsula, with no status in Europe. As it is, she commands the lowest literacy rate and the lowest per capita income in western Europe.*

Portugal regards herself as Greater Portugal, looking upon her possessions abroad not as colonies, but as parts of Portugal. On this basis she claims that the U.N. has no right to investigate conditions in her overseas provinces. If South Africa's racialism angers the Africans, the Portuguese notion that Lisbon's African possessions are not colonies, but elongations of Portugal abroad offends them equally. "Angola," declared Salazar in a broadcast in August, 1963, "is a Portuguese creation and does not exist without Portugal. The only national conscience rooted in the province is not Angolan but Portuguese; there are no Angolans but Portuguese of Angola." Unlike Verwoerd, to whom multiracialism is a red rag, Salazar protests that Portugal recognizes no color bar, and proclaims his belief in "the living together of races." Lisbon claims that, contrary to Pretoria, she does not oppress the African because he is black. She does so presumably because he is poor and ignorant! Portugal's double standards in Africa enable her to square her conscience by simultaneously accepting the African and exploiting him. "If he is good, we pat him on the back; if he is bad, we beat him" about sums up the Portuguese *mystique* of colonial government. These are not attitudes calculated to mollify African opinion in or outside Portuguese Africa. Even Nyerere, among the most restrained of the continent's politicians, refers to Lisbon's claim that Portugal with her overseas possessions constitutes a unitary state as "this ridiculous, not even medieval idea."

Portugal's overseas rule is governed by three main concepts, all of them based on wishful thinking, with the ideal embodied in each case contradicted by practice. Instinct in the three is a sense of historic mission. "We live in an age of renascence," declared Salazar's administrative assistant, Dr. Pedro Theotonio Pereira, minister of the presidency, "which links us with the past and which we will try to project into the future. . . . Our national values are more vigorous and rejuvenated than ever. The unity and solidarity which hold together the pieces of Portuguese territory have never been stronger, and the sentiment of all the peoples have never

* Portugal's annual per capita income is around $230 and her illiteracy rate 45 percent. It was nearly 75 percent some fifty years ago.

been more unanimous." The exact contrary represents the existing state of affairs.

The three concepts are broadly the spread of Christianity, the gospel of racial tolerance, and what the Portuguese like to call human idealism as expressed in the "unique" relationship subsisting between Portugal and her overseas territories, and the civilizing spirit which imbues it. Practice strays far from touched theory. The mission to bring to the Africans the benefits of Christian religion and culture is belied by the colonial record of their masters, who treat them as primitive children to be whipped from their squalid stupor into civilization and discipline by the *chicote,* a hide whip, and the *palmatoria,* a wooden paddle with holes. The dreaded PIDE—the secret police—are notorious for their cruelties and tortures. Officially, there is no color bar, but under the former system of contract or forced labor the blacks until very recently* were treated as little better than beasts of burden, and even with the removal of the system their labor continues to be ruthlessly exploited.

Many Indians I encountered in Rhodesia and Nyasaland who hold British passports and are freely permitted to visit the Portuguese colonies† recounted tales of Africans being flogged publicly.

"One doesn't see the color bar in evidence there," said Mrs. Sattar Sacranie, wife of the Asian political leader in Nyasaland. "The schools are interracial and intermarriage is accepted. A number of Portuguese peasant women have married Africans and there are also the normal Afro-Portuguese intermarriages or associations. There are quite a number of mulattoes in Angola. But Africans as Africans are maltreated. It is quite common to see them being flogged publicly in compounds."

Captain Henrique Galvão,‡ who in January, 1961, hit the headlines with his dramatic seizure of the Portuguese luxury liner *Santa Maria* on the high seas, has given a vivid and detailed account of Portuguese misrule in Angola, whose conditions he was officially commissioned to investigate in 1947. At that time the system of contract or forced labor, which was abolished following, among other developments, a report by a three-man commission appointed by the International Labor Organization, was very much in vogue. Galvão condemned it as worse than outright slave labor.

"Under slavery," he noted, "the bought man, acquired as a head of cattle, was regarded as an asset by his master. He was interested in keeping him healthy and strong and agile in the same way he would look after his horse or his bull. Today the native is not bought—he is simply rented from the government, though he may have the status of a free man. His

* The system was abolished in 1962.
† The Portuguese authorities refused me an entry visa. I hold an Indian passport.
‡ He is a member of the anti-Salazar Portuguese Democratic Movement or International Junta of Liberals, led by General Humberto Delgado in exile.

master could hardly care less if he falls ill or dies as long as he goes on working while he lives. . . . When he becomes unable to work or when he dies, the master can always ask to be supplied with other laborers."

For this report Galvão was imprisoned shortly afterwards, but escaped abroad in 1959.

The Portuguese colonial record is strewn with pieces of magniloquent legislation and decrees seemingly humanitarian and liberal but rarely if ever implemented. Their massive volume of laws is both prohibitive and permissive—prohibiting almost anything and permitting all manner of things. The Portuguese statute books proliferate with civil liberties which in their application, particularly to Africans, add up to very little. It is the Portuguese habit to ignore the vast corpus of laws until somebody says or does something to endanger their dictatorial regime, while the Africans, largely ignorant of the laws, are in any case in no position to appeal to them effectively. The result is that the law is for all practical purposes a dead letter, and dictatorial rule will continue in Africa so long as it continues in Portugal, where, if there had been a democratic government responsible to the people through free elections, Angola, Mozambique, and Guinea might by now have been on the way to independence. Portugal delights in a schizophrenic personality. As a correspondent of *The Economist* puts it: "Over 400 years the Portuguese have produced more extremes of behavior, good and bad, than probably any other Europeans in Africa. The two tendencies have not yet fought it out to a conclusion."

Most governmental systems bristle with contradictions, but the Portuguese dictatorial regime has more than most. Thus the Portuguese *mystique* does not recognize the existence of Portuguese and Africans in their so-called overseas territories, but only the presence of Portuguese, since wherever the Lusitanian flag flutters, all are Portuguese. Every baby, black or white, is a Portuguese citizen at birth. Yet for nearly four centuries, until August, 1961, the mass of Africans, collectively numbering some 12 million—5 million in Angola, 6.5 million in Mozambique, and 1 million in Guinea—was governed under a *regime do indigenato* which reduced the African to the position of a helot or serf, and was contrary to the much-vaunted spirit of Lusitanian identity at home and overseas. The Africans had no political rights whatsoever, were insulated in a world of ignorance and isolation, enjoying only the privilege of working under the system of contract or forced labor for their white masters, and drawing for their toil an average pittance of $6 a month. Fewer than 3 percent of the Africans are literate, and an African child is lucky if he can obtain rudimentary education for more than three years. Over 95 percent of the population of Portuguese Africa were thereby made wards of the state, enjoying no civil rights, including the right to vote. All this was perpetrated on the supposedly Christian plea of paternalism, which held that the Africans are used to dictatorial rule and "like to be told what to do and what not to do." The important thing was to make the African work for himself or his white overlords at least six months in the year.

Side by side with the nearly 400-year-old *indigenato* system to which the overwhelming bulk of Africans was subject until 1961 was the severely restricted *assimilado* system which lasted some thirty years and under which a black citizen who achieved certain standards of education and culture had the full rights of a Portuguese citizen extended to him. To qualify for this he had to demonstrate that he had given up his tribal way of life, was eighteen, had fulfilled his military obligations, was self-supporting, of good conducts and habits, and spoke Portuguese correctly. He was then allowed to lift himself from the *indigenato* element, which a statute of 1954 defines as comprising "individuals of the black race . . . who do not yet possess the enlightenment and the personal and social habits . . . of Portuguese citizens." Once assimilated, he was regarded as having climbed from the lowly rung of his primitive society to the dignity of *civilizado* or *assimilado*. To Salazar this "is one of the most daring concepts and the most sublime task of Portuguese colonization." He is a great believer in his own enlightenment.

Actually, the number assimilated has been microscopic. The process of assimilation has been rigorously selective, except in the tiny Cape Verde Islands, whose population of 190,000 (70 percent mulatto, 28 percent African, and 2 percent European) were all *civilizados* in 1962, and the islands of São Tomé and Principe, of whose 70,000 inhabitants 72 percent, the majority Africans, rated as culturally assimilated. Progress in the key territories of Angola, Mozambique, and Guinea has been noticeably slower. Of Angola's 5 million, less than 40,000 Africans were *assimilados* when the system was abolished. The figure for Mozambique, with its population of 6.5 million, was under 6,000 and for Guinea, with a population of about 1 million, less than 10,000. Of the *assimilados* a number have attained the higher echelons of the colonial and military services, and a good proportion have done well in the professions. One reason why the Portuguese pursued the system so gingerly was probably because of the fear of raising a class of African revolutionaries, which to some extent has happened, for the African leaders of opposition groups in exile are all *assimilados*.

Disturbed by the Angola rising, which exploded in March, 1961, and irked by the developing links between the black and white anti-Salazar movements abroad, the latter spearheaded by General Humberto Delgado and Captain Henrique Galvão, Lisbon decided to liberalize its repressive measures. Unrest was also on the increase inside Portugal, whose economic burdens were growing with the rising cost of operations against the Angola rebels, and the expenditure entailed by the dispatch and maintenance of more troops abroad. A Communist underground functions sporadically, and more recently a new opposition group known as the Democratic-Social Action Group has made its appearance. The principal figure in Portugal's underground Communist party is Senhor Alvaro Cunhal.

In 1961 Salazar, through the Overseas Council, proposed radical changes in the Organic Law which were shortly initiated. These, though merely laws on paper, abolished the old *indigenato* and *assimilado* systems and also removed the curse of contract labor, though not the African's liability to prove that he had work. Lisbon also proposed to decentralize authority in the overseas territories, a characteristic Portuguese contradiction in terms, for it is difficult if not impracticable to reconcile decentralization of authority abroad with the hard core of a highly centralized authority embodied in a dictatorship at home. The real reason for the change was that a considerable proportion of colonial whites, along with an increasing number of Portuguese at home, were apprehensive of another Congo being enacted in Angola. On their part the Angolan rebels are skeptical of the value of any system of decentralization which does not move authority from Lisbon to Luanda.*

Cultural assimilation was given a legislative personality after 1930 by various colonial decrees, but the policy of forced labor has existed since the late fifteenth century and has affected the lives of nearly 15 million Africans. Nothing symbolizes more brutally the exploitation of the African for the benefit of the white Portuguese. This system of near-slavery outlived the once massive slave trade, which forcibly condemned to a living death some 6 million Africans shipped abroad over the years from Angola, Mozambique, and Guinea. If slavery was justified on the ground that thereby the African's soul was saved by conversion and improved by exposure to Christianity, forced labor, which existed in various forms, was condoned on the plea that it taught the African the dignity of work and made him a productive member of society. In one way or another the African male between the ages of sixteen and sixty was compelled to work, political offenses being often punished with forced labor. Child labor was not unknown, and African women have sometimes been subjected to forced labor on road building. Penal sanctions for breach of labor laws have only recently been abolished and a minimum wage law introduced in the Portuguese colonies.

Conversion ranked higher than cultural assimilation, leading Dr. Adriano Morera, the minister for overseas provinces, to declare blandly that while the number of *assimilados* might be insignificant, the number of Catholic Africans in Angola and Mozambique totaled nearly 2 million, the

* Luanda is the capital of Angola.

implication being that Christianity, a more formative force than assimilation, leads to the development of Portuguese qualities. Assimilation, however, did not necessarily elevate the African to the top-grade Portuguese level, for Lisbon's objective was gradually to transform the Africans to a state of society akin to that enjoyed by the Portuguese peasant society, which is semiliterate and politically conservative. After all, in Lisbon's reckoning it is better to be Portuguese than to be independent.

The disappearance of the old *assimilado* system, while it has undoubtedly eased the life of the African in some respects, has so far brought him no real benefits on any considerable scale. The Angola rebellion and increasing African restiveness have recently mellowed the tone of the Portuguese administration in that its restrictive and repressive aspects are not so forcefully evident. Even PIDE, the widely feared secret police, has curbed its more extrovert brutalities. Though local censorship continues to exist, it is more restrained in its exercise, and overseas newspaper correspondents are generally permitted to send their cables uncensored. But the abolition of *assimilado* has not materially affected the daily lives of Africans. Theoretically, a black has no longer to qualify himself for full citizenship and he may now choose to live under native law, where he comes under the surveillance of his chief, or submit to Portuguese law, where he enjoys the invidious privilege of being subject to income tax. Since the chief in turn comes under the surveillance of the Portuguese authorities, neither the African's status nor that of the Portuguese is affected by the relaxation. Theoretically, again, the African has a right to vote, provided he chooses to live under Portuguese law. But to the majority of Africans who, though enjoying full citizenship, prefer to live under native law, this right is unavailable since, according to the authorities, their names are not on the voting registers. Political parties except for the official National Union (NU) are not allowed to function save for two months before the elections, and anti-Salazar candidates therefore have little chance to be returned. Some economic relaxations have accompanied the disappearance of *assimilado*. African cotton growers are no longer paid below the prevailing world price though, like their Portuguese counterparts, they must sell their cotton to Portugal, to be carried in Portuguese ships. But after January 1, 1964, all imports from the African territories to Portugal are allowed duty-free. A 20 percent duty on foreign imports into the provinces makes the purchase of foreign cotton piece goods, other than those manufactured in Portugal, prohibitive, but a cotton textile mill has been permitted in Mozambique. Education has also been liberalized, and in Angola today about 700,000 African children get some sort of schooling. The colony is now also equipped with its first university, at Luanda.

Partly in a bid to offset the abolition of the *assimilado* system and partly to ease the growing burden of economic stresses within Portugal, peasants and artisans from the mother country are being encouraged to migrate to the African colonies, where they are given freehold grants of land with an initial loan of farm equipment, cattle, and free seed. The same facilities are also extended to a few Africans. A number of Portuguese peasant girls have married Africans. Nonetheless the Africans are still far behind the whites in the matter of material benefits and amenities. Between 1940 and 1960 Angola's white population increased from 44,000 to nearly 200,000, while that of Mozambique in the same period climbed from 27,000 to around 80,000. Over 10,000 immigrants enter the two African provinces every year, the aim being to bring the white ratio up to 10 percent of the population or more. While this influx has benefited the overseas territories by stimulating their economic development, it has also brought some problems in its wake, chief among these being the growth of a racist consciousness among the poor whites, who come from one underdeveloped area to another with the color of their skin among their chief passports to advancement. A *Herrenvolk* complex has developed among them. The abrasive growth of exclusively white communities settled in the new white colonization projects such as the Cela Colonato in Angola and the Limpopo Valley settlements in Mozambique has accentuated color feeling and given it an edge which did not previously exist. As a result, a segregationist pattern of life, not unlike that prevailing in South Africa, is beginning to infect Portugal's African colonies. Economically, the pressures of the white influx are blocking the mobility of the African worker, which in any case was never high; availability at low and even the lowest levels of Portuguese skilled or semiskilled workers, apart from white clerks, maids, and taxi drivers, has increased and spreads.

Growing white immigration has changed the face of both Angola and Mozambique as new towns and ports develop, inducing a new deal which directly benefits the European and indirectly the African. Portugal is a small country with a big emigration problem. Until recently Brazil, where 30,000 Portuguese emigrated annually, was the main magnet, but currency export restrictions and the fall in the value of the cruzeiro are diverting the flow to the overseas territories. In 1960 some 32,000 Portuguese immigrants entered the African provinces. Portugal's economic plans are tied up with the belief that she will retain her African territories, developing them into richer depositories of wealth and employment, so that the home economy expands with the economy abroad. Salazar plans to make Portugal an expanding industrial nation instead of the largely rural country she is.

Within Portugal herself there are signs of increasing restiveness, particularly among the university students—there were demonstrations in 1962 at Coimbra and Lisbon universities—and rebellion in the colonies has stepped up financial imposts, with a revised income tax law, a special war levy, and rising prices. Yet Salazar steadfastly pursues his economic policies of expansion at home and abroad, though this entails leaning more heavily on foreign loans and capital from the United States, France, and West Germany. Portugal, which is a member of the European Free Trade Association (EFTA) is probing the possibilities of the European Common Market (ECM) with a view to forming a Portuguese Common Market. Her second $1.05-billion six-year development plan, dating from 1959, provides for the establishment of a chain of industries, including a steel industry on which work has begun in conjunction with Krupps. Among other projects is the Salazar Bridge across the Tagus at Lisbon, a German-backed irrigation scheme for Alentejo province, and the development of the port of Lisbon.

New towns, harbors, hydroelectric projects, colonization settlements, agricultural schemes, port installations, and expanding rail routes figure prominently in the plans for the overseas territories. While they undoubtedly benefit the Africans, they are meant primarily for the welfare of the immigrant inflow, the main beneficiaries being the Portuguese colonists and the big companies based in Lisbon. Without Angola and Mozambique, which pay their own way, though they are not as materially prosperous as South Africa or the Rhodesias, Portugal would be virtually bankrupt. A considerable proportion of Portuguese exports, notably wine and cotton goods, goes to Africa, while Portugal exports from her African colonies to the world market increasing quantities of coffee, tea, sisal, copra, and diamonds. There has recently been a slump in coffee prices. Between them, Angola and Mozambique contribute up to 25 percent of Portugal's national budget. On the other hand, trade with Africa totaled in 1962 about 1 percent of Portugal's overall foreign trade, which is why a trade embargo by African countries would not embarrass Lisbon unduly. Similarly, the closing of African airports to Portuguese or even South African airlines would inconvenience but would not seriously dislocate the air traffic of either of the two countries.*

The principal colonial beneficiaries of the six-year plans have been Angola and Mozambique, and, to a lesser extent, Guinea. Among the new projects are the Cambambe Dam in Angola, which will supply the Luanda area with power, and a settlement scheme designed to accommodate thou-

* Nairobi's ban on the Springbok service to and from London, to and from Johannesburg has deprived South African Airways of a lucrative arrangement. Other airlines affected are BOAC and Central African Airways. BOAC has since left the South African pool to which she belonged since the end of the last war. The new South African air regulations leave only one escape route—Bechuanaland—to opponents of apartheid. South African Airways has also rerouted its European flights round the western bulge via Luanda and the Canary Islands, involving an additional flight of 900 miles.

sands of Africans and Europeans in the Zambezi Valley in Mozambique. Modern ports have been constructed, notably Moçamedes in Angola and Nacala in Mozambique. Oil production has made impressive strides and Angola is self-sufficient in this commodity, with plans to export oil calculated to make a saving of some $12.6 million in foreign exchange. Due to the Angola upheaval, the pace of economic progress has slackened in the African colonies, but considerable improvements are nonetheless being registered. Port facilities at Lourenço Marques and Beira have been extended, while a number of new small harbors have sprung up along the coast. A railway to link Goba in Mozambique to the Swaziland border is under construction, and is being financed by the Anglo-American Corporation and a consortium of South African insurance companies. In the rural areas extensive government-assisted settlement schemes, mainly for the benefit of peasant immigrants from Portugal, but also indirectly benefiting the African farmer, have arisen. There has been a dramatic change in the face of Angola and Mozambique, Luanda having doubled its population within the last fifteen years, while small communities dot what was wild bush country not so long ago.

Startling as many of these economic changes have been, they have, contrariwise, generated wider political unrest among the Africans. Unemployment has increased among them, along with the growing competition between white and black for laboring jobs. The intensification of the color bar, particularly in the cities, combined with the spectacle of the economic plums being absorbed increasingly by the white immigrants; rising prices and growing depression produced by increased competition and lopsided gains in an atmosphere of growing racial discrimination and tension —these lit the fuse which set Angola on fire. Since then, trouble has spread to Guinea and threatens Mozambique.

Trouble in Angola flared up in March, 1961, when the Congo-based rebels, led by Holden Roberto's Union of Angolan Peoples (UPA), at one time controlled an area of northern Angola half the size of Portugal. Holden, whose government-in-exile is recognized by Adoula, is supported by Emmanuel Kounzika, who leads the Angolan Democratic party (PDA), which includes many Zombo émigrés and refugees now in the Congo. Holden's backing comes largely from certain ethnic groups of the Bakango tribe in northern Angola. Some 150,000 Angolans have sought refuge in the Lower Congo, though the Portuguese claim that many of these have returned and are working on the coffee plantations in the north. Holden's National Liberation Army probably numbers around 8,000 and is supported by the fugitive civil population, but they have managed to pin down a Portuguese force of about 40,000 men, though the rebel guerrilla casualties have been far higher than those of the Portuguese. Both sides are engaged in a war of attrition. At one time the rebels controlled an area from the Cuango River to the sea, but they are now confined to a 2,000-square-mile battle zone known as the Rotten Triangle, where their guerrilla units, whose training camp under Algerian-trained instructors* is at Thysville, forty miles from the Congolese border, shuttle back and forth harrying the Portuguese. Rebel losses are said to be around 400 a month. Portuguese losses are put in the proportion of one white for ten blacks, but the Portuguese admit that rebel equipment and tactics have improved in recent months. Holden's guerrillas also have better knowledge of the terrain, and their Congolese bases across the 400-mile frontier which separates Angola from the Congo and which now includes the "back door" of Katanga give them the advantage of added mobility.

Unfortunately, the African forces ranged against the Portuguese in Angola are divided. Also fighting the Portuguese is the rival Popular Movement for the Liberation of Angola (MPLA), which, unlike Holden's UPA, has multiracial backing, with mulatto leadership and ties with Portuguese opposition groups. The MPLA is led by Sorbonne-educated Mario Pinto de Andrade, a thirty-five-year-old mulatto who is believed to have Communist leanings. The more active leader, however, is Dr. Antonio Agostinho Neto, an African who was educated at the University of Coimbra and has served several terms of imprisonment, detention, and deportation. Neto is forty-one.

The rival groups are bitterly opposed to each other, and there have been attempts on the lives of both Neto and Holden. The MPLA has white support from opposition elements in and outside Portugal and has received help from the Algerians, particularly in training for guerrilla warfare, but Holden's UPA forces are larger, more mobile, better equipped, and better trained. Holden is now thinking of mounting a second front in the cotton-growing Malange area, where an abortive uprising took place in 1961.

Early in 1962 the UPA established relations with the Movement for the Liberation of Portuguese Guinea and the Cape Verde Islands (MLGC), promising to send them arms and technical assistance in the art of guerrilla warfare. The MLGC is headed by Henri Labery, and between them Roberto and Labery are trying to mobilize nationalist organizations in Mozambique and the islands of São Tomé and Principe to join them in a united front against the Portuguese. On their side, Andrade and Neto have also actively canvassed for African support and in April, 1961, convened a conference of Nationalist Organizations of Portuguese Colonies (NOPC) in Casablanca, Morocco. The conference included representatives from the African Independence party of Portuguese Guinea and the Cape Verde

* Tunisia and Morocco are also helping the UPA.

Islands, as well as delegates from Mozambique, São Tomé, and Principe.

The thirty-one African states associated with the Addis Ababa conference in May, 1963, who decided to pressure both Portugal and South
Africa, would like to see an agreement between the two rival Angolan
groups. Some of them, including the governments of Egypt, Ghana, Guinea,
and Algeria, have decided to funnel aid equally to the two parties. The
nine-nation committee set up by the Addis Ababa conference has opened
an African Bureau at Dar-es-Salaam to help in the struggle against the
Portuguese and South Africa. And an African Organization for Unity, comprising a ministerial committee, was established in Addis Ababa with the
object of unifying the various forces ranged against these two powers. It
was decided to break off diplomatic and consular relations with Pretoria
and Lisbon, and to bring international pressure to bear on both countries
to end repression against the African nationalists. Additionally, it was
decided to request the U.N. that all foreign military bases should be removed from South Africa, which should be declared a denuclearized zone.
The proposal is impracticable. The bureau established at Dar-es-Salaam is
actively supported by Nyerere, who even in colonial days took the lead in
setting up the Pan-African Freedom Movement (PAFMECA). Dar-es-
Salaam shares with Léopoldville in the Congo the task of providing an
exile headquarters for the Africans, mulattoes, and Europeans who have
fled from Angola and Mozambique. This permanent secretariat in the
Tanganyikan capital also masterminds and aids the escape of refugees
from South Africa and the Portuguese colonies.

Pan-African efforts to unify the rebel forces have resulted in more
concerted operations in north Angola with their base at the training center
of Camp Kinzu in the Congo. Supplied by war material mainly from
Algeria, Camp Kinzu is turning out rebels at the rate of 2,200 men every
eight weeks. These men undergo rigorous training in guerrilla warfare and
are equipped with mines, mortars, bazookas, and new automatic rifles. In
the closing months of 1963 the Angolan war which the Portuguese believed
they had successfully contained within the Rotten Triangle flared to life
again. Some 7,500 disciplined troops of the Angolan Liberation Army
concentrated on the Serra de Conda region where some 40,000 Portuguese
troops found great difficulty in countering the rebels' war of ambush and
attrition. Leading around 1,000 guerrillas deep in this region is thirty-two-
year-old Antonio Muandazi, who compares his wearing-down tactics with
those of the Algerian FLN who fought the French for seven years. "This is
a war of the will," says Muandazi. While the rebels control the high ground,
the Portuguese troops hold the towns and the main roads in the valleys. All
around are the jungle-sheathed mountains.

What started as a pressuring movement has developed into a holy crusade against Portuguese colonialism and racial apartheid. In secret coves strung along South Africa's 4,000-mile coastline are friendly collaborators to whom funds, equipment, and arms are distributed with the object of putting them in the hands of the rebel elements inside the republic. Volunteers are also being recruited. Both the Angolan revolt and apartheid have become international issues, and in January, 1962, the U.N. General Assembly, by a vote of 99 to 2, South Africa and Spain dissenting, called on Portugal to initiate a program leading to self-determination and ultimately to independence for the territory. African delegates have either walked out of or have forced representatives of South Africa and Portugal to withdraw from various international assemblies, including the U.N.'s International Labor Organization, the Economic Commission for Africa, and the International Conference on Education. On their side, both Portugal and South Africa have abstained from various sessions of the General Assembly and the Security Council in protest. Some African countries, such as Liberia, have turned Portuguese merchants out of their territory.

On the whole, the Africans have found little to boycott in the matter of trade with South Africa and the Portuguese colonies, since the volume of trade, particularly of Portugal, with Africa is small, and at times the embargo has not been strictly observed. For instance, when South African mining equipment arrives in Ghana the embargo is lifted for twenty-four hours. By not revealing the country of origin or camouflaging it, South Africa sells canned fish to Tanganyika and mine-blasting equipment to Northern Rhodesia. It even supplied the fireworks for Uganda's Independence Day celebrations in October, 1962.

To enlarge and intensify their boycott, the African countries have been attempting to get the U.N. Security Council to impose a worldwide trade, oil, and arms embargo on both Portugal and South Africa. To the United States and to Britain the question of sanctions poses a tricky problem, since Portugal is a NATO ally and South Africa is a major trading partner.* While the United States is willing to support an international arms embargo, which Britain is not, it rejects any attempts to expel South Africa or Portugal from the United Nations or to boycott their goods. According to the Africans, the Americans are concerned to retain their Azores base and Britain to maintain the Simonstown agreement of 1955.

Mozambique, which with Angola materially assists Portuguese economy —the latter's cotton and sugar are sold exclusively to Portugal—is also threatened with the infiltration of and subversion in its territory. At Dar-es-

* In 1962 Britain sent $426 million worth of goods to South Africa, more than 30 percent of the republic's total imports, while, excluding gold and uranium, South Africa sent to Britain nearly 28 percent of her exports. In the first six months of 1963, British exports to South Africa were 40 percent higher, while South African exports to Britain also rose. American investment in the republic totals over $600 million.

Salaam, heading the Mozambique Liberation Front, is Professor Edouard Mondalane, who gave up a lucrative job as an anthropology professor in the United States to organize the front. Mondalane believes in direct action, and is also interested in stepping up educational programs for Mozambique Africans so that they would be ready to take over the administration after independence. He plans to send his people for training abroad to the United States, western Europe, the Soviet Union, and Brazil. His activities have forced the Portuguese to mobilize troops in Mozambique, which at some stage may erupt like Angola.

Rebellion has also broken out in the southern rice-producing regions of Portuguese Guinea, which is a comparatively small colony with long frontiers with Senegal and the Republic of Guinea. Since the Addis Ababa conference, both these neighboring states are pledged to liberate Guinea; and African and Portuguese exiles from Guinea and the Cape Verde Islands are now based at Dakar, capital of Senegal, and Conakry, capital of the Guinea Republic, and have put guerrillas in the field who enjoy support within Portuguese Guinea. In July, 1963, Lisbon announced that several thousand troops were en route to put down the rebellion, the rebels having occupied over 20 percent of the territory and forced the Portuguese to the defensive. Although the insurgents have pushed northward and are concentrating their attacks in the central zone, the south is still the main sphere of military activity, the upheaval dislocating the region's commercial life severely. Several rice-buying centers have been closed down for lack of security and, though Guinea is self-supporting in that commodity and exports the balance abroad, Lisbon has recently been forced to import 3,000 tons of rice from the United States. Here again the Portuguese are helped by differences between presidents Léopold Senghor of Senegal and Sékou Touré of the Guinea Republic. While Senghor is in favor of the Portuguese African colonies moving to autonomy under pressure which might be military, but should be mainly diplomatic, Sékou Touré stands for direct action based on military insurrection. The insurgents again are divided into two parties, of which the larger and stronger is the Party for the Independence of Guinea and Cape Verde (PAIGC), led by Amilcar Cabral, which is militant and wants to fight to a finish, while the other party, the Union of the Populations of Guinea (UNGP), led by Pinto Bull, stands for peaceful evolution.

Despite his seeming intransigence, Salazar's views on the African colonies have recently thawed, and he appears prepared to give Guinea, as well as Angola, full internal autonomy which would consist of complete administrative self-government within the unitary state of Portugal. Salazar would like Senegal to use its good offices to induce Guinea to call off the guerrilla attacks, which are mainly directed from Conakry. The overpopulated Cape Verde Islands have always formed one province with Guinea, and in the rebellion the two appear to be acting jointly. In Angola, Holden stands for complete independence. He demands what he calls a "Brazilian solution."

To some extent Salazar might have been influenced by Spain's recent decision to grant autonomy to her West African island of Fernando Po and the territory of Río Muni. Like Portugal, Spain considers her African territories as provinces of the metropolitan country rather than as colonies, and this status was accorded to Río Muni and Fernando Po in 1959, and to Ifni and Spanish Sahara in 1958. The new decision means that the two equatorial territories are to be regarded as colonies, for if autonomy is intended to be a first step toward self-government, with ultimate independence in the offing, a colonial status is implied in the new decision though it is not explicitly proclaimed in the Spanish announcement. So far Spain has come off lightly in African attacks on white rule, largely because the main fire has been concentrated on Portugal and South Africa and, in a different way, on Southern Rhodesia. Ifni and Spanish Sahara were once known as Spanish West Africa.

There are signs of general rethinking on the part of the Portuguese, who for some time have realized that the colonial problem is as much political as military. Resort to the latter expedient entails heavy expenditure, loss of life, and possibly loss of the territories. The Portuguese now seem to admit that politically the colonies need a new deal. They are also faced with unrest among the white settlers who number about 250,000 in Angola and who resent being used as an economic milch cow for Portugal. While willing to concede the right of self-determination to the Africans, Lisbon refuses to entertain the idea of independence, interpreting self-determination as internal self-government under Portugal.

On the administrative side, Salazar has ordered a process of slow decentralization, with more authority given to the district governors and their staffs. The grip of Lisbon on the governor-general's office in Luanda will in time proportionately decrease. Portuguese officials on the spot demand more rapid decentralization, autonomy, and increased expenditure on education and development to be financed by taxation of the rich monopoly companies. African grievances have also been met partly by more liberal labor legislation and politically by the abolition of the *assimilado* system. Communications within the colonies are being improved and development of the land assisted. As it is, there is large-scale immigration from the overpopulated Cape Verde Islands as well as from Portugal into Angola and, to some extent, into Mozambique. Angola is the richest province of Portugal overseas, and its capital, Luanda, claims to be the third Portuguese city after Lisbon and Oporto. The economy is being diversified and deficiencies remedied. For instance, the huge hydroelectric project at Cambambe in Angola, which today only produces half its present capacity of 260,000 kilowatts, is being adjusted to produce twice that output. Salazar is also presenting a kindlier face to the African independent nations.

There are, of course, Portuguese diehards within the overseas territories who, having become increasingly skeptical of Salazar's ability to suppress the rebels, are organizing their own paramilitary volunteer corps or Vigilantes to fight the guerrillas. Some of them are even prepared to wage a campaign to preserve white supremacy in Angola on the lines of the OAS campaign in Algeria, but the more sober-minded among them recall that it took France seven years and 500,000 troops to achieve even a stalemate in her North African possession. On the other hand, an increasing number of Portuguese favor a more liberal attitude toward the overseas territories. These are to be found both within Portugal and in the African colonies. In Portugal there is a white opposition movement known as the Frente de Unidade Angola (FUA) which aims at immediate autonomy for Angola, to be followed by gradual transition to independence. This organization is willing to cooperate with the MPLA provided the latter modifies its present demand for immediate independence. The MPLA, which has a considerable mulatto membership, works in conjunction with this group and also with Portuguese political exiles abroad, notably General Delgado and Captain Henri Galvão. Andrade, leader of the MPLA, is building up a mulatto elite who might someday be the logical leaders of independent Angola. The MPLA includes the majority of Angolan intellectuals and is less militant than the UPA; though it is accused by the latter of being Communist-aligned, it would probably welcome a democratic multiracial government for Angola. At any rate neither Andrade nor Neto would allow Angola to come under the rule of the European ultras.

Believing as the MPLA does in interracial cooperation between the Angolans and Portuguese, and supported by Salazar's policy of allowing Afro-Portuguese marriages and alliances, a time may come when this process of miscegenation might produce a people so mixed in color that the cry of "Africa for the Africans" will have no meaning.

My Blantyre acquaintance talked of South Africa being coffee-colored within fifty years. It is more likely that this will happen in Portugal's African territories abroad.

16

THE CHALLENGE
OF AFRICA

AFRICA POSES A challenge largely because of its unpredictability. If it is the Dark Continent, it is also to some extent the Unknown Continent which politically has come up with a rush, the postwar fever for independence catapulting some thirty-five states into freedom within a decade. Culturally, vast tracts of Africa have leaped from the Stone Age to the twentieth century in a matter of three generations. Growing industrialization in the cities and towns between the two wars and after has led to a migration from the bush to the developing urban centers which has affected not only the economic, but the social and political values of the African, who, uprooted from his tribal moorings and exposed to a new way of life, thought, and civilization, finds himself embarked on a voyage of rediscovery which concerns not only his individual self but his people and country. Just as the sense of Africanness, however distorted, despised, and downtrodden its image, dawned on the slave transshipped abroad, so the same sense of being and not belonging infused the more assertive and articulate African of a later day. The urge to belong, to rate among the respected members of the human family, filled him with new desires and ambitions, many of them inchoate in their expression and fulfillment, but strong enough to propel him to the reality of political independence which spelled freedom and equality.

If, on the attainment of freedom and equality, the African's voice has seemed to some unnecessarily shrill and strident, who can blame him? Men who climb out of a dark void are dazzled by the light. The speed of Africa's advance and arrival took the rest of the world, unprepared for this lightning miracle, by surprise. It also surprised Africa. In their attitude to that continent and its people, both Europe and Asia are afflicted by a guilt complex—Europe as the main exploiter and Asia as its abettor—and both, recovering from the impact of the first rude shock, do not know quite where to fit in the new arrival who until yesterday was an outsider. They wonder whether all the rules of the game are applicable to him. And Africa, uncertain of its own place, tends to draw attention to itself by alternately brawling like a neglected infant or in its adult moments treading deliberately on other people's toes or, more aggressively, punching the nearest nose within reach. While Africa regards the West as being unduly complacent, the West accuses Africa of being unnecessarily truculent. Asia's heart is with Africa, though her head is often more inclined to the West.

Not all the norms common to Europe and Asia apply to Africa, which, purposeful in mind, is often willful and wayward in method. Hence the developing image of an unpredictable Africa. Like the Jews, the Africans have found their Zion, and the question arises, pertinent to the African but not to the Jew, whether the race-consciousness which now understandably permeates him may not some day explode into aggressive racialism. Vis-à-vis the rest of the world, Africa today seems to present a front which is more competitive than cooperative, again an understandable trend because of the tremendous gap the African feels he has to close up.

Pan-Africanism is an expression of race-consciousness, but *négritude* veers dangerously close to the concept of racialism, though Jean-Paul Sartre in his subtly simple way describes it as "antiracist racism . . . it is the moment of negativity as reaction to the thesis of white supremacy." Perhaps it would be more correct to say that, while Pan-Africanism poses the political face, *négritude* presents the emotional face of the same coin which is Africanness. The feeling engendered in the African by years of oppressive brutality, exploitation, and subjection that he represents "just the tail end of the human race" has naturally created in him an obsession to lord it over others from the top. The African is both dual and ambivalent— the duality seen in the strangeness felt and expressed by many sensitive American Negroes when transplanted to the Africa of their forefathers, the ambivalence surfacing in the educated African's love for and questioning of his own culture along with his simultaneous rejection and acceptance of Western culture. This duality and ambivalence, induced partly by environment and partly by history, account for much of the African's unpredictability. A prominent Nigerian has tersely expressed the average African feeling: "Blackism is the answer to our problems."

Thus, Africa presents a challenge to the rest of the world with a sort of inverted *Herrenvolk* cult. It stresses the importance of being black in its most exuberant and uninhibited form. Yet the attitude bristles with contradictions, for, whereas *négritude* owes much to the French-speaking African who also admires French culture and lays great store by the French association, it is looked at askance by most English-speaking Africans who at the same time are often aggressively assertive in denouncing British political institutions and ideas. To the South African writer, Ezekiel Mphahlele, *négritude* is "just so much airy intellectual talk. . . . Imagine a Chinese waking up one morning and shouting in the streets that he has discovered something Chinese in his sculpture or painting or music."

Chauvinism, in its many manifestations, is common to the human race. But in the emancipated Africa of today it takes shapes which often puzzle and sometimes repel the European and Asian, stressing color as the dividing line, with the minatory promise that the oppressed will soon inherit the earth. Over sixty years ago, at the first Pan-African Congress in London in 1900, Dr. William E. Burghardt Du Bois, who died in Ghana in September, 1963, at the age of ninety-five, prophetically proclaimed the nature of the battle facing the human race. "The problem of the twentieth century," he declared, "is the problem of the color line—the relation of the darker to the lighter races of men in Asia and Africa, in America, and the islands of the sea." Whether Du Bois is proved right depends as much on the darker as on the lighter races of men in the world of today.

While some older historians, anthropologists, and sociologists pooh-pooh the African as a savage whose history begins only with his exposure to European civilization, more modern and sympathetic observers of the African scene, notably Basil Davidson and Harold Isaacs, recognize that his cultural roots are longer and deeper, and not necessarily derivative, as the "Hamite hypothesis" suggests. The seaboard cities of Kilwa and Malindi cannot be written off as Arab contributions in which Africans had no share and which they merely appropriated as part of a civilized veneer. Else, how explain the mysteries of the pillared splendors of Husuni Kubwa, that medieval palace poised on the edge of the Indian Ocean, or the scattered ruins of the city of Engaruka in the recesses of Tanganyika? Like Hinduism, Africanism has a strong assimilative pull, evidenced by its adaptation of Arab cultural influences in the Swahili tongue and civilization. Granted that Africans are often juvenile to the point of being infantile in their reactions and manifestations. But is this surprising against their background of slavery, ostracism, and oppression, which has intensified their inferiority complex, leading them to regard as naturally inherent what has in fact been artificially imposed?

The brand of slavery survives like the mark of Cain. Because of his appearance and color, which he has been taught to regard as attributes of the helot, the African's race-consciousness has its roots in color-consciousness, once furtive and ashamed, but now often proudly arrogant. Even a light-skinned Negro like the poet Langston Hughes, who is of mixed descent, flaunts "blackism" like a banner:

> I am a Negro
> Black like the night is black,
> Black like the depths of my Africa.

The sense of differentness assails a European and, frankly, even an Asian in the presence of an African. As Africans become more and more part of the social and political landscape this sense of differentness will dim and must in time disappear. But to deny its presence is to be deviously evasive. An English observer* remarks on the sudden turnabout in African attitudes which bewilder, confuse, and exasperate the stranger. "Mr. Mboya," he writes, "can within the space of a few weeks deliver a challenge to Europeans in Nairobi, a revolutionary call in Cairo, a reasoned analysis of Kenya's constitutional difficulties in London, and a human appeal for help in New York. ... President Nkrumah attacked the United Kingdom last year for sending a warship to Angola, yet the British Government received private assurances from Ghana which seemed to render the attack harmless. ... One is left holding the broken pieces which somehow have to be fitted into an intelligible pattern."

The same observer suggests that the explanation for this pattern of peculiar behavior is that, while all utterances in all parts of the world are conditioned by the circumstances in which they are made, in Africa the conditioning is not controlled. It stems from a habit of mental indiscipline born of the colonial hangover, of uncontrolled personal ambitions, and of the triple continental curse—poverty, ignorance, and disease. Africa is afflicted by its own special type of behavior common to all cloistered communities, such as Communist China and Soviet Russia, which have their own yardsticks of behavior applicable to an insulated society. As *The Times* correspondent comments: "The conference table in Lancaster House and the African political scene are as far removed from each other as Bernard Shaw and a No play."

The African's extrovert exuberance fortifies the foreign belief that a certain untamed wildness characterizes him. Yet among themselves African politicians differ as sharply as their counterparts elsewhere, nourish-

---

* In an article in *The Times,* London, of June 25, 1962.

ing their own moderates and militants, Nigeria's Prime Minister Balewa having, for instance, little or nothing in common with Kenya's Oginga Odinga and differing even from a moderate like President Senghor in not sharing his belief in the African Personality. In his modes of thinking Balewa intrinsically is no different from any European politician of similar stature, save that his emphasis is naturally on his Africanness, though not on *négritude*, whereas the European's interests are primarily European. The vital question however is: Does Africa possess a sufficiency of Balewas to hold her together within a sober framework? A South African has sourly observed: "The layer of cream at the top of the bottle is too thin." The remark unfortunately has some justification.

What is culture no one can really say. I recall an occasion while driving through the night from Dar-es-Salaam to Arusha with some friends who included a woman M.P. from Tanganyika when our car had its gasoline tank dented badly by a wayside stone and sprang a leak. We got back to a gas pump in a small isolated village called Msata, which was inhabited by some Africans, but unfortunately they had not the wherewithal to repair the tank. Some four miles down the road was a missionary station where the Africans suggested we might get help and possibly be put up for the night. Two of our members, including the woman M.P., who spoke Swahili, hitchhiked their way to the center and asked for help from the European missionaries there. Not only were they rudely refused any assistance, but they were bawled out by a missionary who shut and padlocked the gates in their faces. It was early morning by the time our friends returned, having trudged most of the way. Meanwhile those of us at the gas pump were most hospitably treated by the Africans, who had no place to shelter us but who made us as comfortable as they could in our car for the night. One of our group drove back some 120 miles to Dar-es-Salaam in a truck that morning to get the gasoline tank repaired, and it was night before he returned. During our stay, the Africans provided us with food and tea, and were most solicitous in their attention. They refused to accept any money when we left. We kept asking ourselves: "Who really were the more cultured and civilized—the raucous European missionaries or the courteous and friendly Africans?"

Political systems, like individuals, are conditioned by circumstances. A question often posed by the constitutional pundits is whether democracy as practiced in the West has a future in Africa or for that matter in Asia. Most of the postwar independent governments in both continents, while protesting their allegiance to democratic principles, have veered far from democratic practice. The latter expresses itself constitutionally in elected legislatures, the two-party system, a cabinet, and an independent judiciary. Both in Asia and Africa the trend toward a one-party single-leader state is developing, the second following consequentially from the first, for with the emergence of a one-party state the legislature is at a discount and with the weakening of the legislature power tends to pass, not to the executive, but to the individual who dominates the executive. Hence, a single-leader state seems a natural corollary to a one-party state. This is happening conspicuously in Africa, but it is also developing in Asia.

There are many reasons for this, some of them applicable to both continents. In Africa, as in Asia, colonial governments have generally yielded power under the pressure of a single nationalist party which on the attainment of freedom carries with it the aura of national fervor, sacrifice, and suffering. Contrariwise, those parties who oppose it are labeled "ingrates," "antinationalists," and "reactionaries." In a small minority of independent states in Africa multiparty systems exist but, with the possible exception of Nigeria, the opposition is nowhere else evident in any strength, and even in Nigeria the strength of the coalition government tends to coalesce and grow at the expense of the parties or groups ranged against it. The presence of more than one party in Nigeria derives largely from its federal structure, which is demonstrated in the highly regional character of the various parties.

The same state of affairs prevails to a considerable extent in Asia, where virtual dictatorships masquerade as "guided" or "controlled" democracies. Indonesia and Pakistan fall in this category, while Burma and Thailand are for all practical purposes military dictatorships. In Ceylon the parliamentary system exists on paper, with the island really under the control of an oligarchy of the left. India enjoys democracy poised on a razor's edge, dependent as it has been for many years on one party and a single leader faced by a nominal and divided opposition. But the force of institutional democracy is stronger in India than in other Asian countries, as evidenced by the loosening grip of the party in power and the growing militancy of the opposition. This is because the tradition of learning and knowledge of representative government go back in India to ancient days which not only knew the village *panchayat* or committee but the *sabha* or council of Elders, and the *samiti* or house of the people. For centuries sayings such as *Janata Janardana* (the people are God) have been current throughout the country. India has also enjoyed the advantage of being exposed to English education for over a hundred years.

A striking parallel which suggests itself to an Indian is that between the old village *panchayat* and the old African tribal council, both of which have subconsciously molded constitutional concepts in the two territories. Common to these two systems is the idea that decisions should be arrived at by discussion and not through force, by a consensus rather than by the numerical measuring of strength between the majority opinion and minority. In this context, a formal opposition becomes unnecessary. A feature of the tribal council, as of the village *panchayat,* to adapt the words of the late Prime Minister Sylvanus Olympio of Togoland, is that minority opinion should be allowed to express itself within the party without intimidation—in other words, opinion may be freely expressed within the party, group, or council, the ultimate decision representing a consensus. Like the Indian village headman, the African tribal chief rarely enjoyed or exercised the sanction of force behind him. The only force he had was the passive weapon of social ostracism. What counted was the moral voice of the community as a whole, as expressed collectively by the *panchayat* or tribal council.

In my journeyings through Africa I was often faced with this challenge by African acquaintances who defended the one-party system. The parallel between the *panchayat* and the tribal council then struck me forcefully. Was it possible, I wondered, that the way of political thinking of many Asians and Africans was conditioned by their separate but in some ways similar backgrounds? Why should they slavishly copy and adopt Western institutions when the rule of law, which is the core of democracy, could be equally respected and safeguarded in other forms? As the Africans also argued, the West had itself given different shapes to democratic institutions, pointing to the familiar example of the difference in the division of powers between the judiciary, legislature, and executive in the United States and Britain. Women do not have the right to vote in certain democratic countries, and the right is often circumscribed in various ways by property and educational qualifications in others. Some elections to legislatures were direct, others indirect. "Why," they demanded, "should Africans be expected to accept Western institutional forms of democracy? We believe in democracy, but in democracy which suits our conditions and background. So long as we lay store by the values of democracy, how do the forms matter?"

Judging from the utterances and writings of various African intellectuals these values theoretically conform to Western norms, for they postulate: first, respect for the rule of law; second, respect for fundamental freedoms; and third, the presence of a representative body. "An organized opposition is not an essential element," writes President Nyerere of Tanganyika in defending one-party democracy, and his opinion is supported by an Asian, no less a man than U Thant, secretary-general of the U.N. "The notion that democracy requires the existence of an organized opposition to the government of the day is not valid," he affirms. "Democracy requires only freedom for opposition, not necessarily its organized existence."

Happily, not all Africans or Asians subscribe to these views, which are based on a series of assumptions collectively expressed by Nyerere in the

omnibus phrase, "Democracy is a declaration of faith in human nature"—
a large assumption which begs the question, "Faith in whose human nature
—an omnipotent individual's or a responsible, responsive, representative
body's?" The Africans who are opposed to the one-party system come
significantly from the more forward-looking southern regions of Nigeria and
include the former governor-general and present president, Dr. Nnamadi
Azikiwe, and his political opponent, now languishing in jail, Chief Obafemi
Awolowo, once leader of the opposition Action Group.

Democracy, as many Africans and Asians insist, can exist without a
party system. They forget that, without the existence of an opposition or of
alternative parties, the average citizen is left to the perpetual rule of one
party, which in practice usually spells one dominating leader, for the
tendency hinging on the personality and experience of a leader—even in a
village *panchayat* or a tribal council—is for decisive power to gravitate to
the hands of one man.

Here, Welensky has a point when he argues that in Africa the gift of
freedom has been to the politician in power, not to the people, who could
not now easily change the governments they have. Change could only
come with the death of the dictator or by assassination.* Another perceptive point he makes is that socialism in the newly independent African
countries invariably goes with national socialism, or dictatorship. According to him the prime necessity is to speed the economic and social development of Africa and, if at all possible, to slow down the political development.
There he is unrealistic. As Nyerere once said in a reference to the discriminatory liquor laws: "We decided we are not going to waste our time
talking about whiskey." Freedom is what the African desires.

The dictator's disappearance from the scene usually leads, in a comparatively orderly community, to group rule or, in a disorganized community, to disorder, which might culminate in chaos ending in the emergence
again of a dominating man at the helm. The French Revolution produced
Napoleon, industrial strife gave Mussolini his opportunity, the futilities of
the Weimar Republic brought Hitler to power. If the rule of law has a
purpose, it is the avoidance of personal power, and the canalizing of power
through institutions which provide for curbs or limits on the executive.
Power without limitations is autocracy, not democracy.

To a country fighting for its freedom, multiple parties are a luxury,
since they divide and dissipate nationalist strength. Apologists for the one-
party, one-leader state carry the argument further by contending that this
system is necessary for a decade or so after independence if a united nation
is to be welded out of freedom. Africans often argue that a multiplicity

* An exception is Fulbert Youlou of the Congo (Brazzaville), who resigned when
faced by a workers' demonstration.

of parties intensifies and consolidates tribal divisions. Similarly, many Asians affirm that a single party makes for national cohesiveness. The argument is plausible and would be justifiable if within a single-party state the values of democracy, quite apart from its institutional forms, would thrive. But Asian and African experience proves the contrary. Democracy under such a system tends to wither and wilt. Despotisms are built and survive only through one sanction—force. And force, visible or invisible, is the negation of democracy.

The rule of law, emanating from a single person, can, despite the veneer of a general consensus, make nonsense of fundamental freedoms and representative assemblies. While the latter in such circumstances represent no more than the will of an individual, the former depend for their scope and magnitude on his whims. Respect for the human personality, which is the essence of democracy, is thereby transmogrified into reverence for an individual. The difference between the Indian village *panchayat* and the African tribal council, on the one hand, and a modern legislature or senate, on the other, is more than a difference in form, for it affects the substance and spirit of democracy as that term is commonly understood. The African argument that separate parties tend to intensify tribal divisions is based on the assumption that a party must necessarily be organized on strictly tribal lines. The argument loses its validity in the context of the tribal council which, if anything, offers greater encouragement to fissiparous divisions than the party system. Nor is it easy to reconcile this attitude with the cry for one man, one vote, which most Africans identify with democracy. The tribal council, like the village panchayat, has its place and use in an essentially rural society. It is incongruous and anomalous in the developing urban social structure of today. Yet even astute, forward-looking African leaders like Mboya base their conception of African socialism on the concept of tribalism seen as a cohesive community with property owned by the individual and still belonging to the tribe.

Margery Perham makes a shrewd point when she stresses that African nationalism, compared with Western nationalism, has an extra ingredient which is a major ingredient—the sense of racial feeling which derives from a consciousness of color. To a lesser, but nonetheless discernible degree it is also evident in Asian nationalism. From this sense of derogation and repression of his race arises the inverted complex of superiority toward the nonblack which the African, from a compulsive urge, brings himself to feel. With independence the Asian has largely climbed out of this. But with the African it still lingers and rankles, though time is bound to efface it, for, as the African achieves political freedom and an acknowledged status in the comity of peoples, the world's color consciousness will fade. Miss

Perham also makes a perceptive point when she observes that "it is not so much the principle of democracy for which Africans have struggled as the end of the rule of white over black." Theirs has been as much a revolution as the French Revolution, with its slogan of "liberty, equality, and fraternity," but the motive force has differed, for, whereas the European revolutionary was reaching out for a form of democracy, however tinsel, the African revolutionary was primarily interested in ending race rule and white domination. Color, not creed, provided the stimulus. Hence *négritude*, which arose from the African's long isolation and the loneliness which he sought to sublimate in a feeling of togetherness with his own kind. The gulf which once separated the sensitive educated African from his European counterpart was almost as wide as that which divided him from the passive ignorant masses of his own country. The layer of cream at the top of the bottle was too thin. What the South African writer, Lewis Nkosi, terms the African's "quest for identity and selfhood" might, following the encounter with Europe, "produce a new man altogether in Africa." Nkosi sees the perpetual quest for self ending in the achievement of a synthesis. But obviously this calls for a greater two-way traffic between Europe and Africa than exists today. Both Europe and Africa must lose their color-consciousness.

Is authoritarian government essential for rapid economic growth in a society with precarious political moorings? If one applies the Rostow formula,* which envisages economic growth in five stages, a large part of backward Africa is still in the first stage of being a traditional rural society. There are, however, some African territories, such as Nigeria, Ghana, and the Ivory Coast, which are in the second formative stage preparatory to the "takeoff." Africa has still to attain the takeoff stage which Britain reached with the Industrial Revolution at the end of the eighteenth century. India and China achieved it to some extent in the late 1950's, which saw a rise in investment and savings as compared with the national income. Rostow's fourth stage is the ordered advance toward maturity. In his reckoning this occurs some sixty years after the takeoff, to be followed by the fifth stage when consumption exceeds basic needs, a stage attained by the United States forty years ago and by western Europe and Japan a decade back. Russia is trembling on the brink.

Africa stands betwixt and between the traditional and the takeoff stage, the latter following the march of modern science and technological advance. The takeoff stage is generally reached by the modernization of industry, which calls for considerable capital formation, and Africa is in no position to achieve this without drastically stepping up her agricultural output. In a backward, developing society such as exists in most parts of the continent,

* Walt Whitman Rostow, *The Stages of Economic Growth,* 1960.

this cannot be done on a basis of private enterprise, but needs government support and intervention supplemented by foreign aid, investment and technical know-how. It does not, however, demand detailed, centralized planning on the Soviet model, but can be achieved as effectively, if not better, on the Japanese model, which is a sound guide for Africa, since Japan, like Africa, lacked at one time the necessary capital formation for the takeoff, and set about creating it with intensified agricultural output and increased returns from business enterprise. During the Meiji era, which lasted from 1868 to 1912, Japan built herself into a modern state by adopting the industrial and commercial techniques of the West, and adjusting them to suit her particular needs and resources. Agricultural development, which was based on better small-scale farming, improved irrigation, fertilizers, seeds, and pesticides, represented a fruitful marriage between Western and Eastern techniques, between imitation and improvisation, and resulted in a more fecund output. In the period of the Meiji restoration, production per person in agriculture doubled. This was done largely by piecemeal planning, with improvisations as one progressed, and not by wholesale collectivization.

As a Japanese businessman remarked to me in Osaka: "We chose wisely and well. We went to England for our naval and mercantile services. We took our law from France, our business and banking methods from America, our science and medicine from Germany, on whom we also modeled our army. We improved our agriculture on our own lines, borrowing what suited us from other countries. Within twenty-five years we were independent of Europe. Within another twenty-five we ranked as a great power." He paused and turned to me: "Japan took fifty years to industrialize herself. You must do it in twenty-five."

India, however, by laying too great stress on governmental intervention and planning—though theoretically her economy is mixed—has retarded the pace of her economic growth and progress. Africa can benefit from Japan's example and India's mistakes, chief among which is overnationalization. It is wrong to believe that collectivization on the Soviet or Chinese models accelerates agricultural output. Both provide dismal examples of failure, for, if there is one field where the two countries have displayed their inadequacy and inefficiency, it is that of agricultural production. Collectivized farming means mechanized farming, since the primary object of collectivization is to coalesce small peasant holdings under communal ownership, and to develop the integrated areas by mechanical means and methods. But mechanization in overpopulated areas leads to unemployment or underemployment, and is suitable only to areas rich in land and short in labor, such as the American prairies, not Russia, China, or India. It can, of course, be argued that in relation to her size Africa is underpopulated, but on the other hand her economy is largely rural, and pressure on the land is considerable. Under such conditions agricultural output is better promoted by the use of more fertilizers, better seed, planting, and irrigation—as Japan has done—than by the use of tractors and other labor-saving equipment.

Development on these lines does not call for an authoritarian government, which becomes necessary only in a collectivized society, for the first to rebel against collectivization are the peasant holders, as the *kulak* revolt in Russia proved. Africa is nowhere near the developed Western-type societies or Russia. Lack of agricultural resources spells misery to the African masses, as it does to the 2 billion people in underdeveloped countries, and the answer is to be found not in collectivization, but in increased productivity, which Africa can achieve, as Japan did, by mixed methods work, by piecemeal planning concentrated on priorities rather than by detailed centralized planning. Given political stability and more cohesiveness in inter-African cooperation, there is every reason to hope, as the more enlightened of that continent's leaders do, that Africa can move toward a fruitful system of group consultation and cooperation in trade and commerce which might in time lead to a variety of political or other functional alliances through regional federations. Unhappily, divisiveness both within the states and along interstate frontiers, the latter of which have been artificially demarcated by the old colonizers, afflicts the continent as a whole. The practical difficulties are many, but not insuperable.

Africa must evolve an economic and political pattern suited to her environment, and enriched by the example and experience of other civilizations. Being the latest arrival, she can benefit from the mistakes of others. The road to progress and fulfillment does not lie either along chauvinism or communism. "African unity," writes Nyerere, "is not, to us, a chauvinistic racialism but an essential step towards our full participation in the main stream of human development." What Nyerere and other sober-minded Africans visualize is not a single Africa, but a united Africa, which is what Pan-Africanism signifies to them—an Africa which has its own contribution to make to the pool of human progress and cooperation from which she has for so many years been excluded by the majority of mankind. From this sense of grievance and of cruel isolation comes the chauvinism which characterizes many Africans in their speech and patterns of behavior. In the African, chauvinism is a racial holdover which will evaporate as the continent moves toward maturity. Islands of white reaction, such as South Africa and the Portuguese possessions, polarize black hostility and ignite racial venom.

There is, however, a strong adventurist streak in the African's makeup which, arising from his comparatively adolescent background and sense of being deliberately retarded, elevates the demagogue above the democrat. Asian leaders are more sophisticated in their political approach, their dynamism at times being imbued with a dedicated resolve. African leadership is emotional, obsessive, often explosive, and though capable of being volcanic in energy, is not seldom misdirected, erratic, and even purposeless.

Today around thirty-five independent states exist in Africa compared with three—Ethiopia, Liberia, and Egypt*—before World War II. All of Africa north of the Zambezi, which separates the two Rhodesias, is now ruled by African governments. Yet the brief record of most of these independent governments is far from reassuring, and the coming decade bristles with the menace of more bloodshed and upheaval. Apart from the continuing violence and disorder in the Congo there have in the past eighteen months been successful coups in Zanzibar, Dahomey, Togoland, and Brazzaville with attempted coups in Senegal, the Ivory Coast, and Gabon. Ghana exists in a state of tension, with intermittent attempts to assassinate Nkrumah. In Nigeria Awolowo and other Action Group leaders are in prison on a charge of treasonable felony. Thousands of Watusi have been slaughtered in a tribal outburst of genocide by the Bahutu in Rwanda, and the Zanzibar coup triggered a chain of military mutinies there and in Tanganyika and Uganda. Having achieved independence, Africa's independent countries find themselves in a ferment of revolution generated by frustration and discord.

To the mass of unsophisticated Africans independence was an end in itself, signifying the replacement of the white man by the black man. When this naïve expectation failed to materialize and when the average African's inflated hopes were not fulfilled, his wrath turned on his new rulers and on the remnants of the old white regime symbolized by the Europeans, Asians, and Arabs who had stayed behind. This largely explains the frustration of the urbanized Africans who had flocked to the cities and towns in search of employment, and were confronted by the higher living standards of the Europeans and of some Asians. Disappointment and resentment were also focused in organized groups of Africans like the trade unions and military forces, and these feelings intensified black racialism.

The problem which faces African governments is how to protect their countries and peoples against the disintegrating inroads and influences of the continental revolution. Nothing was more shame-making from the exuberantly nationalist point of view than the compulsive necessity which impelled the governments of Tanganyika, Uganda, and Kenya to solicit British military aid to put down the army mutinies. An immediate reaction once the danger was passed was to rehabilitate national self-respect by an

---

* A fourth was the Union of South Africa, which cannot be rated an independent African-ruled state.

appeal to the Organization of African Unity to help the three countries to accelerate the replacement of British officers by Africans.

The protracted Congo operation brought the U.N. to the verge of bankruptcy and dented its image not only in Western but in African eyes. One manifestation is African acquiescence in the scheduled withdrawal of U.N. troops from the Congo by June 30, 1964, although the African governments are well aware that the Adoula administration will be in no position to deal militarily with the law and order situation by that deadline. It may also be that certain African governments feel that the U.N. withdrawal will facilitate their own plans to assist armed uprisings in South Africa and the Portuguese territories by creating a situation where the U.N. cannot intervene and use its forces except in self-defense or with the authority of the international organization which could be prevented from being active by the Afro-Asian vote. While the Africans are not averse to utilizing the U.N. to bring pressure on South Africa and on the Portuguese colonial administrations on the continent they are opposed to its interference in intra-African disputes which they would prefer to refer to the OAU.

These pressures, political, economic, and military, seem likely to hasten the African trend to turn away from free democracy and resort increasingly to so-called African solutions. The African Personality, African individuality, and African democracy are some of the more prestigious terms in the African's advanced vocabulary. Reduced to simple equations they emerge as the one-party state, economic authoritarianism, mass and individual indiscipline, and a general descent into tyranny. The major menace facing Africa, as the chain of coups, successful and unsuccessful, the insistent pressures from organized groups like the armed forces and the trade unions, and increasingly militant racialism demonstrate, is the comparative ease with which a handful of determined fanatics can overthrow a government or dislocate the social and economic order. Such a process, unless the African is prepared to abide by and uphold certain standards of public conduct, can only end in disruption and disaster.

So far communism has played a very small part in these disorders and upheavals even if Chou En-lai in the course of his African tour which coincided with the Zanzibar coup and the East African mutinies congratulated the Africans on seeing the revolutionary light. As yet communism has attracted no significant numbers in any part of the continent.

Many, including not a few Marxists, hold that African economic and social conditions are not favorable to communism, and that the African, being acutely aware of himself and lacking a class consciousness because of the absence of compradors, entrepreneurs, or large property owners, is not easily vulnerable to Marxist dogmas or doctrines. Even according to Sékou Touré, who is generally but mistakenly regarded as an African extremist, a social revolution is possible in Africa without a class struggle. Sékou Touré rejects the Marxist theory of class struggle as inapplicable to Africa, where, according to him, class differences do not exist. This is also Senghor's view. "Our socialism," he has declared, "cannot be exactly that of Marx or Engels which was worked out about a hundred years ago according to scientific methods and circumstances of the nineteenth century in western Europe."

The single-party system, as it exists in the continent, is not impregnated with Communist ideas, but regarded as being representative of the mass of people as a whole. Moreover, land does not normally attach to the individual but to the tribe, and Africa, it is argued, can therefore skip the stage of proletarian dictatorship and move from the communal ownership of property to a socialist system, which is Mboya's argument.

Plausible as the African hypothesis is, it does not stand up to close examination. In West Africa, particularly in Nigeria and Ghana, a class of African businessmen, along with successful lawyers, doctors, and other professional men, has grown in recent years, especially since the war. A leaven of African "master farmers," helped by loans from the marketing boards and other kindred public bodies, has also come into being. African-owned estates, worked by paid labor, are on the increase, and the creation of farmers' unions testifies to the emergence of a rural bourgeosie. African labor shows an increasing tendency to migrate across the open frontiers of underpopulated territories, thereby making inroads into the old social cohesiveness. Yet African socialism, whether in the guise of nationalization, a planned economy, or the building of cooperatives, clings stubbornly to its African character. Mali and Guinea, for instance, have banned the Marxist-Leninist group known as the Partie Africane de l'Indépendence. In Ghana Communist aid has produced only disillusionment. Collective ownership of the land and of the means of production, where it exists in Africa under a planned economy, is still on a restricted scale.

Yet the question arises whether, with the end of colonialism and with the political withdrawal of the White Presence, certain countries of the continent might not be tempted to resort to the Communist solution. There are several reasons against this: the weakness of the Communist party within Africa; the reluctance of the leaders of the newly independent countries to exchange one form of foreign domination for another; the open rift between Moscow and Peking; and the realization, particularly by African students and leaders, that the Russians and Chinese are as color-conscious as the Western democracies. Informed observers place the number of Communists in the continent at only around 50,000, and, despite the suspicion once attaching to Sékou Touré, the Communists include none of the top-ranking leaders. What Lumumba remarked to me is typical of the attitude of militant Africans. "I am not a Communist. I am an African."

Only seven full-fledged Communist parties operate in Africa south of the Sahara. The oldest of these is the Communist party of South Africa, founded in 1921 and operating underground since 1950. The other six are in Nigeria, where the party is small, inactive, and China-oriented; in Basutoland and Swaziland, where the Communist party (formed in Basutoland in 1961) is mainly the work of South African exiles; and in Malagasy, Senegal, and Réunion, where the parties are tiny. North of the Sahara the former Communist parties in Tunisia, Algeria, and Morocco are in exile. In the Sudan the Communists are banned.

In addition to the full-fledged parties are crypto-Communist groups such as the UMMA party in Zanzibar; the so-called nucleus of about thirty professional men in Nigeria; and the Swaba party in the Niger. The Senegal Partie Africane de l'Indépendence was once a crypto-Communist group but is now allied closely with the French Communist party, with whom it has published some joint declarations.

Communist powers work mainly in Africa through the trade unions, various Pan-African organizations and certain nationalist parties susceptible to leftist pressures. The Red-dominated World Federation of Trade Unions has financed the building of a workers' university near Conakry which trains "African anti-imperialist and anti-colonialist cadres."

Quite apart from their rift on the international plane, Sino-Soviet ideological differences are projected into Africa, Peking being in favor of direct action by provoking armed uprisings, while Moscow inclines to the slower and cautious approach of helping the more militant African governments, such as those represented in the Casablanca group, to range themselves more aggressively against the moderates. Here again it would be misleading to define the differences in terms of Red and not-so-Red, for, while countries like Ghana, Guinea, and Mali are more socialist-inclined than others, they have no intention of being tied to the chariot wheels of either China or Russia.

"We stand for a Ghanaian way of socialism," said Krobo Edusei, then flying high in Accra. He was echoing Nkrumah, who has often emphasized the necessity of "projecting the African Personality." At a function in connection with the Black Star Line, I heard Nkrumah refer to "the need of giving shipping a truly African outlook." Neither Nasser nor Nkrumah would welcome the Communists stepping into their shoes.

Peking, in line with its policy, aims at being the pace setter in Africa, as Chou En-lai's African odyssey in January, 1964, revealed. Earlier Peking had promised military assistance to Nasser during the Suez crisis and has offered to give military training to black South Africans who manage to smuggle themselves out of the country. Moscow's approach is more wary, though it has encouraged Africans, among others, to the special "schools for partisans" which it runs at Houstka, twenty miles from Prague on the Elbe River, and at Bernau, near Dresden. It has helped to train Ghanaian cadets, and has offered similar facilities to Mali and Somalia. On the other hand, while there has been a dramatic fall in arms supplies to South Africa by many Western countries, the Communist states of eastern Europe, notably Czechoslovakia and East Germany, have not hesitated to fill the breach. Poland sells the Union its vodka, Russia its caviar, while cameras come from East Germany, jewelry and musical instruments from Czechoslovakia, and cigars from Cuba. Countries such as Sweden and Austria continue to circumvent their own arms embargos by employing intermediaries. Switzerland has permitted the sale of military equipment to South Africa, but explains this on the ground that the equipment is of a purely defensive nature. China has no arms traffic with South Africa, but Peking has placed no embargo on general trade with that country and is known to have imported large quantities of corn from there.

Russia's incursions into Africa are fairly long-established, going back to Czarist days, when it sought to block the extension of Italian, British, and French interests in Ethiopia.* When the Communists came into power, they approached the problem of Africa from the rigid, doctrinaire Marxist-Leninist standpoint, though Lenin's works contain no specific reference to Africa, which does not seem to have entered seriously into his political calculations. But as far back as 1920, some three years before he died, Lenin laid out a blueprint for Communist strategy in the colonial field which included "the more backward states and nations in which feudal or patriarchal and patriarchal-tribal relations predominate." Here he recommended initial support of the bourgeois-democratic national movements, with the ultimate aim of training and ranging the future proletarian parties against them. This strategy was embodied in the "Theses of the Revolutionary Movement in the Colonies" adopted at the Sixth World Congress of the Comintern in 1928, and the so-called 1928 Theses served as a blueprint for the Stalin era. As late as 1950, judged by the writings and utterances of I. I. Potekhin, director of the African Institute at Moscow, the Kremlin clung to the belief that colonialism could not be abolished without "the liquidation of capitalism and the establishment of a Soviet system." The Russian attack was accordingly concentrated on *petit bourgeois* national reformers, which in the Soviet vocabulary included Gandhi in India, and Nkrumah and Azikiwe in Africa. This attitude implied the acceptance of a class- and tribal-ridden society in Africa.

The political awakening of Africa after the war brought about a change in the Soviet approach. Hitherto the Stalinist theory that colonial revolu-

* Haile Selassie visited the Soviet Union in 1959.

tions everywhere must inevitably be dominated by the proletariat—which meant the Communists—had held the field. About 1957, four years after Stalin's death, the Leninist-Stalinist thesis was amended. Facts, such as the achievement of Indian independence, in which the Communists played a very small part, Nasser's revolution spearheaded by the army, and the comparatively peaceful transition of some African countries to independence with the help of the U.N., impelled this change. Colonialism had disappeared without the liquidation of capitalism or the establishment of communism. Khrushchev began preaching "peaceful coexistence." In December, 1958, Potekhin was an interested observer at the Accra Conference of African Peoples, and from Accra he returned a convert. Though Pan-Africanism was not to his liking, he saw the gleam of incipient communism in the new nationalism. The time had come to change from absolutes to a more pragmatic approach. Tribalism and "religious separatism" constituted the two main barriers to a united national front, but, in keeping with Marxist ideology, which has no use for any brotherhood but its own, Potekhin also frowned on *négritude* and Pan-Africanism as "not too felicitous." What political affinity was there between the African Negroes and their descendants in the United States? On the same basis Potekhin rejected the idea of African socialism, since it "underestimates the degree of class differentiation in African society." The question of political and ethnic borders in Africa, he urged, could not be lightly dismissed and should be a special subject of Communist study and research. At some stage the class struggle between the national bourgeoisie and the proletariat was inevitable. Communal land ownership, on which the theory of African socialism is partly built, was there, but its disappearance was not necessary for the transition to communism. The village community could be used as an instrument of revolution, provided power was maneuvered into the right hands, and this could be effected through the national-democratic state, which would enable the proletariat to liberate the nation by waging a ceaseless war against imperialism, feudalism, and medievalism. The Communist task, according to B. Ponomarev, the noted Soviet theoretician on international communism, was therefore to "combine national independence with democracy," and thus proceed to "socialism" along the Soviet path. In the process the "treacherous national bourgeoisie" must be crushed.

This theory runs counter to the prevailing Peking thesis, which makes Mao censorious of Khrushchev's habit of backing non-Communist nationalist leaders in the uncommitted countries and of inveigling them into taking a neutralist or nonaligned line toward the Soviet Union. It has happened in India and may well infect Africa. Mao has no use for peaceful coexistence, and he insists that the proper course is to stir up revolutions headed by local Communist parties. Potekhin ruefully admits in a pamphlet that,

while socialist ideas are widely disseminated in Africa, a considerable proportion of the African intelligentsia does not accept the Soviet-type
socialism, preferring the Yugoslav variant, Israeli socialism, Nasser's cooperative socialism, or even the cloudy socialism of the British Labour Party.
Such thinking, says Mao scornfully, proceeds from the idea of peaceful
coexistence, and in opposing the Russians the Chinese have not hesitated
to stress the nonwhite racial angle in areas such as Asia, Africa and Latin
America. China has made consistent efforts to stage a tricontinental conference of the countries of these three areas where the Soviets would only
have observer status. This was the main purpose of Chou En-lai's African
trip, on which he vigorously canvassed the idea of a second Bandung conference of Afro-Asians, a team extended by Sukarno to include Cuba and
nongovernment delegations from Latin America. Indonesia and Pakistan
supported China's plea. Thereby the Chinese probably hope to persuade the
Afro-Asian countries that a non-European Communist state could give
them more genuine moral and material assistance than the Russians.

Chou En-lai skillfully if obliquely struck this chord during his African
journey, which carried him from Cairo to Ethiopia, Algeria, and Morocco
and after an interlude in Albania to Ghana, Guinea, Mali, and Somalia.
The Zanzibar coup followed by the military mutinies in East Africa took
Tanganyika off his planned circuit, but in Mogadishu, on the last leg of his
tour, Chou, in a reference to these episodes, blithely observed that China
was undeservedly getting the credit for revolutions abroad! He sought to
sell "Afro-Asian solidarity" in his role as a nonwhite Communist representative; to plug Mao's interpretation of the Bandung spirit; and to carry
on China's propaganda war with the Russians, following the Chinese line
of representing themselves as part of the world's colored population in
contrast to the "white Soviet imperialists." Here he was helped by the
coincidental storm raised in Moscow by some Ghanaian students who
accused the Russians of doing away with a fellow-Ghanaian.* The game
of *le rouge et le noir* was being played two ways. In the course of his
journey, Chou also held out the bait of economic aid which, being restricted,
had no spectacular impact.

That Peking laid great store by the African odyssey was testified by
the organized press barrage that preceded it. An editorial in the *People's
Daily* recalled the ancient ties between China and Africa, which "knew each
other more than one thousand years ago," and cited the seven expeditions
of Cheng Ho, the emperor's representative in the early part of the Ming
dynasty who had visited Mogadishu, Malindi, and Kenya. These friendly

---

* The Russian explanation was that the student had died as a result of "exposure
to cold in a state of alcoholic intoxication." The incident took place in December,
1963.

contacts "were not broken off until after the sixteenth century as Western colonialists forced their way into Africa and China." Historically, however, Cheng Ho's real mission was to "pacify" the "outer barbarians" of Southeast Asia and to open the route leading through the seven seas to Africa with its "devil slaves," ivory, and "magic animals." Much later in the nineteenth century Kang Yu-wei in his book *Great Unity* derided the Africans for their "extreme ugliness and stupidity" and described them as "the hardest to change." Chou's journey was in line with the old "civilizing mission," the emperor's edicts being replaced by the doctrines of Mao Tse-tung.

In Cairo,* Chou echoed the sentiments of the *People's Daily* by describing the friendship between the peoples of the U.A.R. and China as "eternal, like the Yellow and Nile rivers" and drew a graceful analogy between the Great Pyramids and the Great Wall. The Egyptian reception to Chou, while correct and cordial, was far from delirious. Algeria, though a special target, also failed to register any great enthusiasm. The message of Chou's speech to the cadres of the Algerian National Liberation Front was underlined by the *Kwangming Daily* which pointed out that "in our present era all oppressed nations and peoples eventually attain great victories in their evolutionary struggle so long as they persevere in unity and a correct revolutionary line and dare to take up arms and engage the enemy in a tit-for-tat struggle, no matter how hard and tortuous their path may be. The Algerian people have set the African people a brilliant example of daring to wage armed struggle and seize victory and have designated a correct path for the oppressed nations of the world." The loaded rebuke to Russia was obvious.

With a brief break for the Albanian interlude, where Chou again had a thrust at Moscow by acclaiming the Albanians "for their heroic spirit and principled stand in the struggle against imperialism and modern revisionism," the peripatetic Chinese leader moved on to the Ghana-Guinea-Mali group who have been China's friends for some time and the recipients of such aid as China is in a position to offer. These were also countries disappointed by the Soviet aid they had received. The Yugoslav report that Chou offered a triangular deal to Africans in the franc zone whereby the Africans would buy Chinese products to enable China to buy French machinery was probably correct. Chou wound up his African trip in Somalia, where at Mogadishu he was welcomed by the Prime Minister, Dr. Ali Shermarke, who was the recipient of a Chinese loan of $20,160,000 when he had visited Peking in August, 1963. China had also made an outright gift of over $2.8 million to Somalia, but this had not prevented Shermarke from taking aid from the Russians. Somalia is an area which China must tread carefully because of its abrasive relations with Kenya

* Egypt established diplomatic relations with China in 1956.

and Ethiopia. The Chinese Foreign Minister, Marshal Chen Yi, had earlier visited Kenya for the Independence celebrations. In East Africa as a whole, Peking's key man is Ho Ying, the Chinese ambassador to Tanganyika and Uganda.

The prime motivation of Chou's tour was political, though it also had its economic undertones. China is making a determined bid to extend its influence in Africa where it is also out to drive a diplomatic wedge against Russia. The majority of African Communist parties are more pro-Chinese than pro-Russian but that does not reflect the overall African outlook which remains basically pro-African. Africa is also not unaware of China's expansionism and of Peking's need to find *Lebensraum* for her surplus population in the underpopulated areas of the world.

China's interest in Africa began after the Korean War, and in 1955 at the Bandung conference she attempted to prise the door into Africa. She did this through trade agreements, facilities for students, cultural delegations, exchange visits, exhibitions, and radio and press propaganda. The fact of the two territories sharing a common background of foreign occupation, military oppression, and poverty was stressed. Particular attention was lavished in Guinea, Mali, Ghana, the Cameroons, and Morocco. China, however, was in no position to rival Russia in material aid. And her student program, with its crude attempts at indoctrination, its restrictive measures, the difficulties of language and interracial communication, has met with no great success. With Russia, China has been accused by many African students of racial discrimination. Perhaps nothing has boomeranged so forcefully on the two countries as the critical and hostile reactions of African students who have stayed there. In both Russia and China the authorities have disapproved of the Africans forming their own independent student unions, have tried to prevent them from following courses of their own choice, and have subjected them to "shocking humiliation" through various forms of racial discrimination. They were often asked to make public comments on controversial issues along Communist lines. African students in Sofia complained of race prejudice, of being dubbed "black monkeys," and being advised to "go back to the trees" and "stick to your bananas." In China racialism did not take such openly insulting forms, but the Africans were nonetheless made to feel their inferiority. The uninhibited behavior of the Chinese delegates to the Afro-Asian solidarity conference at Nicosia, Cyprus, in September, 1963, angered the Africans, who openly rebuked them. Highly suspicious, the Africans invariably resent being muscled into doing something.

Their attitude to Asians, whom they regard with some justice as abettors of white imperialism during the period of Western domination in the continent, has not visibly thawed. If anything, it has hardened. I recall a white settler in Northern Rhodesia remarking angrily: "Once we are gone, the Africans think they can step into a 20-a-week [$56-a-week] job and ride in American cars. They are nowhere as good as European employees, but demand the same salaries." He agreed, however, when I said that the Asians and not the Europeans would be the first economic casualties, which is what has happened.

In Kenya, Uganda, and Tanganyika, Asian employees in government offices and commercial concerns are being replaced more quickly than Europeans, and there has been a considerable Asian exodus from Kenya since the 1963 London conference. This is natural, since big Asian-owned commercial establishments and industries are few and far between, and the Indian serving as a bank assistant, a store salesman, or a government clerk signifies to the African a competitor who can now be easily dislodged and replaced. The European's economic presence operated institutionally through large corporations such as shipping units, insurance companies, and banks. As many Asians, both Indians and Pakistanis, explained, their primary concern was trade, and because of this they had kept for the most part away from the politics of the continent. It was obvious, though they did not say so, that in the process they were interested in preserving the political *status quo*.

A truth which suddenly dawned on me in Africa was the realization that the Asian, particularly with his caste and community consciousness, found it comparatively easy to accept the compartmental way of social life common to the African and was not excessively embarrassed by it, for the average Indian is habituated to living within his caste and community, whether in his own country or abroad. He has accepted segregation with less resentment than the African, for within his own caste and community the Indian lives a fairly full life. True, he resented the European's attitude of social superiority, but curiously his own attitude to the average African was not very different from that of the European. And the African was acutely aware of it. To a cosmopolitan Indian, the spectacle of Sindhis, Gujarathis, and Sikhs, each with their own separate housing colonies and schools, living separately among themselves and within the larger African society, appeared anomalous and contradictory. At the same time there was a common, composite Indian awareness among them. In all this it very largely reflected Indian society at home.

On the other hand I noticed that Israel occupies in some ways a special position as a friend of Africa and is intensifying her own Asian personality. Most Africans are philosophers and fundamentalists, curious to see problems not as mere solutions and techniques, but to probe the underlying principles beneath them. The West is equated with colonialism, and Africans view America's economic imperialism with suspicion. They regard with caution the Communist way of life as expressed by the Russians and the Chinese. The Israelis, however, have no colonialist fancies. They are not in the pocket of the West and are distinctly socialist in their approach without being Communist. A selling point in Africa on which the Israelis have shrewdly capitalized is that Israel was once part of Palestine and under the same old British heel. They were also, like the Africans in non-African societies, subjected to persecution in anti-Semitic communities. In Israel, Africans see the "bootstrap miracle" taking place on a small scale, with fruit trees flowering in the desert, new crops, new industries, new ways and means, roads, bridges, dams, airports, and even nuclear power stations all reared by indigenous ingenuity. They see the Israelis as a defiantly rational people, but with a rationality that generates its own "magic," and the Africans would like to share in it. That is why they welcome Israeli cooperation.

By and large, Africans have obtained their independence with less violence than Asian countries, and largely in agreement with the colonizing powers. Their chief rallying cry today is against neocolonialism, which belongs to the postindependence phase of liberated colonies and poses a conflict between the world of haves and have-nots. Africa, moreover, is not afflicted by the appalling population problem which weighs on many Asian countries. The Congo and the Sudan, each about two-thirds the size of India, have each a population of around 15 million in comparison to India's 450 million. When technical training and capital become generally available, the per capita incomes of the two African countries may increase at a faster rate than in India. Africa's main economic problem is that the countries of the continent are too often reliant upon a single crop in a single area, which puts the local economy at the mercy of world raw material price fluctuations. For the most part, Africa is devoid of those apparently insoluble problems that make countries like India an economic nightmare. Nor is Africa unduly oppressed by the necessity of belonging to one bloc or another. As Nyerere has picturesquely put it, African states have no intention of becoming "jumping jackasses," siding automatically with West or East. They want to live their own way of life in peace and cooperation.

Slowly but surely they are climbing out of the sense of not belonging which for so many years has burdened them and which the American Negro poet Claud McKay expressed so forcefully in his poem "Outcast":

> Something in me is lost, forever lost,
> Some vital thing has gone out of my heart,
> And I must walk the way of life a ghost
> Among the sons of earth, a thing apart.

> For I was born, far from my native clime,
> Under the white man's menace, out of time.

Africa is no longer a thing apart, a continent of faceless millions. A vital force animates her being, and with the lifting of the white man's menace she seeks a place among the sons of earth.

BIBLIOGRAPHY
of Indian Publications on Africa

1. *The African Personality,* by Suniti Kumar Chatterji. Bengal Publishers, Calcutta, 1960.

2. *Africanism—The African Personality,* by Suniti Kumar Chatterji. Bankim Chatterji Street, Calcutta.

3. *The Afro-Asian States and Their Problems,* by Madhu K. Panikkar. George Allen & Unwin, London, 1959.

4. *Against the Cold War: A Study of Asian-African Policies Since World War II,* by Chanakya Sen. Asian Publishing House, Bombay, 1962.

5. *Angola in Flames,* by Madhu K. Panikkar. Asian Publishing House, Bombay, 1962.

6. *Apartheid in South Africa,* by P. S. Joshi. Kimberley, 1950.

7. *Colonialism in Africa,* by T. Ganesh. People's Publishing House, Bombay, 1952.

8. *Colonialism in Africa,* by B. S. Krishnamurthy. Dewan House, New Delhi, 1959.

9. *Contemporary Africa,* by Bisheshwar Prasad. Asia Publishing House, Bombay, 1960.

10. *Contemporary Africa,* by Visvesarprasad. Asia Publishing House, Bombay, 1960.

11. *The Indian Problem in South Africa,* by P. Subramania Aiyar.

12. *The Indians in South Africa,* by Shafat Ahmed Khan. Kitabistan, Allahabad, 1946.

13. *Indians of South Africa,* by Bhaskar Appasamy. Padma Publications, Bombay, 1943.

14. *Indo-Ethiopian Relations for Centuries,* by I. M. Muthanna. Artistic Printing Press, Addis Ababa, 1961.

15. *Jomo the Great: A Short Pictorial Story,* by Ambu H. Patel. New Kenya Publishers, Nairobi, 1961.

16. *Multi-Racial Society,* by S. N. Varma. 1960.

17. *The Problem of Uganda: A Study in Acculturation,* by Ramakrishna Mukherjee. Akademic-Verlag, Berlin, 1956.

18. *Revolution in Africa,* by Madhu K. Panikkar. Asia Publishing House, Bombay, 1961.

19. *Tanganyika: A Background Study,* by S. N. Varma. Africa Publishers, New Delhi, 1961.

20. *Tanganyika: A Government in a Plural Society,* by Ansu Kumar Datta, Delhi.

21. *True Facts About the Congo: A Study of the Congo Crisis.* Tejnarayan. Central Press Syndicate, Delhi, 1961.

22. *Unrest in South Africa: The Tyranny of Colour,* by P. S. Joshi. Hind Kitab, Bombay, 1958.

Africa Diary, Weekly, Africa Publications, Bhagat Singh, Market, New Delhi.

Africa Quarterly, Indian Council for Africa, New Delhi.

African Recorder, Fortnightly, Dr. Rajendra Prasad Road, New Delhi.

Al-Arab, Fortnightly, League of Arab States to India, New Delhi.

INDEX

Abbas, Ferhat, 79n.

Abboud, General Ferik Ibrahim, 62, 63

Abdulla, Seyyid Jamshid bin, 277n.

Abidjan, education in, 15

Abrahams, Kenneth, South Africa, 371

Aburi, 9

Accra, capital of Ghana, 9; conference of April, 1958, 33-34, 182, 407; Legon University College at, 15

Adamafio, Tawia, Ghana, 111, 115, 118, 120, 121

Addis Ababa, Ethiopa, 41, 58; conference of 1963, 80, 84, 106n., 142n., 145n., 354, 385; education in, 43; highways from, 50; University College of, 43

Adegbenro, Alhajii, Nigeria, 101, 102

Adjei, Ako, Ghana, 120, 121

Adoula, Cyrille, 206, 218, 383; and Katanga crisis, 218-236 *passim*

Aflak, Michael, 67; and Nasser, 83

Africa, animism in, 12; arable land in, 17; and Asia, 411; Asians in, 35-36; blindness in, 27; challenge of, 390-412; and China, 21, 407-411; Christianity in, 12, 47; and cold war, 20; colonialism in, 33; Communism in, 403, 404-408; declining influence of Christianity in, 11; deterrents to economic development in, 19; disease in, 27-28, 34; divisiveness of, 25; economy of, 17-19; European scramble for, 41; gap between the urban and rural areas in, 9; geographic conditions in, 32; in history, 4-8; impact of different European civilizations on, 134-135; impact of Industrial Revolution on, 5-6; impact of West on, 34; impediments to economic progress, 18; and Industrial Revolution, 13; and Islam, 11, 47, 62-85; and Israel, 411; need for education in, 14-17; the new, 1-38; new alignments in, 38; paganism in, 11-12; and Pan-Africanism, 24; population increase, 353; population of, 17-18; problems of, 30; racial stocks, 25-27; religion in, 10-11; resources

Kassem General, 66, 67, 70, 82; overthrow of, 81, 84

Katanga Province, and Congo crisis, 177, 186, 203-237 *passim;* economic interests in, 190, 219-222; secession of, 84. *See also* Congo, Republic of the

Katsina, Emir of, Nigeria, 88, 95

Kaunda, Kenneth, Northern Rhodesia, 323, 324-325, 327, 330-331, 346, 358

Kawawa, Rashidi, vice president of Tanganyika, 252, 262, 265, 266

Kayibanda, Grégoire, president of Rwanda, 244, 247

Kebede, Lij Haile Mariam, 53

Keita, Modibo, Mali, 142, 151, 152, 153, 157; and democratic centralism, 156; and Senghor, 79, 157

Kennedy, Edward, in Southern Rhodesia, 343

Kennedy, John F., and Congo crisis, 204, 209, 266; and development plan for Africa, 15

Kenya, 1, 5, 35, 38, 47; African Democratic Union (KADU), 252-255, 292-317 *passim;* African National Union (Kanu), 252-255, 291-317 *passim;* African People's Party, 292, 307, 313; African Union (Kau), 290-317 *passim;* background, ethnography, and size of, 249-250; blindness in, 27; coalition, 292, 293; constitutional plan for, 304-305; and Devonshire Declaration, 302; and EACSO, 250; and East African Federation, 310-311; economy of, 18, 303; and Ethiopia, 315; ethnography, geography, history, and politics of, 288-317; Federation of Labor, 291; government in, 305-312; and Great Britain, 313-315; independence of, 289; Kikuyu Central Association in, 290-317, *passim;* and Lancaster House Constitution, 292, 300, 302; and Lennox-Boyd Constitution, 291; and London Conference of 1963, 312-316; Mau Mau rebellion in, 35, 290, 291, 316, 317; mutiny in,

138n., 249, 315, 357, 402; New Kenya party, 252, 292, 293, 296; northern Europeans in, 38; Northern Frontier District, 306; productive land in, 302-303; regionalism and tribalism in, 254, 289; southern Europeans in, 38; strip, 281; United party, 292, 296

Kenyatta, Jomo, Kenya, 31, 252, 253; and Kikuyu Association in Kenya, 290-317 *passim*

Kergaravot, General, Gabon, 138n.

Khalifa, Sir Abdulla bin, 277n.

Khama, Seretse, of Bechuanaland, 367

Khalil, Sayed Abdalla Bey, 63

Khan, Sir Syed Ahmed, 77

Khartoum, 63-64

Khatima sect, 14

Khedda, Ben, Algiers, 81

Khrushchev, Nikita, 210; and Mao Tse-Tung, 407

Kiano, Gikongo, Kenya, 293, 309

Kibwe, Jean-Baptiste, 213

Kiger V, Mwami of Rwanda, 244, 299

Kilimanjaro, Mount, 9

Kilwa, 8

Kimba, Evariste, 213n.

I Kings, quoted, 40

Kiswahili, as lingua franca, 25

Kiwanuka, Benedicto, Uganda, 252, 269

Kiwewa, Antoine, Congo, 235

Koinange, Peter, Kenya, 298, 309, 310

Konate, Mamadou, Mali, 157

Konchellah, John, Kenya, 309

Korsah, Sir Arku, 117, 121

Kottmann, Mathilde, 165

Kounzika, Emmanuel, Angola, 383

Krim, Belkasem, 79n.

Kubai, Fred, Kenya, 309

Kuwait, and Iraq, 82; and Lebanon, 67; petroleum production of, 71; and U.A.R., 66

Kuwatly, Shukry, 67

Kwangming Daily, 409

Labery, Henri, 384

Lagos, Nigeria, 8, 91, 98